TYBURN'S MARTYRS
Execution in England, 1675–1775

At Newgate: Oh let not that Word fright you, because so many have gone to the Gallows from thence! martyr'd Innocence does often dye where Thieves and Robbers do; a Gallows may be sanctify'd, why not a Prison? Come Sir John your hand.

Thomas Betterton, *The Revenge; or, a Match in Newgate* (1680)

This illustration depicts the pressing of a 'mute' defendant, or the practice of *peine forte et dure*, the punishment inflicted on prisoners who refused to plead to their indictments.

Tyburn's Martyrs
Execution in England, 1675–1775

Andrea McKenzie

hambledon
continuum

Hambledon Continuum is an imprint of Continuum Books
Continuum UK, The Tower Building, 11 York Road, London SE1 7NX
Continuum US, 80 Maiden Lane, Suite 704, New York, NY 10038

www.continuumbooks.com

First published 2007

British Library Cataloguing-in-Publication Data
A catalogue record for this book is available from the British Library.

ISBN 978 1 8725 171 8

Typeset by Egan Reid, Auckland, New Zealand
Printed and bound by Cromwell Press Ltd, Trowbridge, Wiltshire, Great Britain

Contents

Illustrations   vii

Acknowledgements   ix

Note on Sources   xi

Abbreviations of Frequently Cited Works   xii

Preface   xv

1 From Newgate to Tyburn: Setting the Stage   1
   Execution, discretion and the 'Bloody Code'   3
   The Tyburn procession and execution ritual   7
   Tyburn Fair: mythology and historiography   21

2 From the Gallows to Grub Street: Last Dying Speeches and
   Criminal 'Lives'   31
   Origins of printed last dying speeches   33
   Literacy in early modern England   41
   The market for criminal 'lives' and confessions   45

3 Everyman and the gallows: contemporary explanations
   for criminality   55
   The slippery slope   59
   'Guilt is the offspring of the heart': nurture versus nature 68
   Excuses: mental incapacity, necessity, gender, youth   72
   The decline of the criminal as 'everyman'   87

4 Highwaymen Lives: Social Critique and the Criminal   93
   The criminal as a vehicle for social satire   99
   Criminal celebrities   105
   The decline of the highwayman tradition   115

5 The Ordinary's *Account*: Confession and the Criminal   121
   The Ordinary: question-monger or plain dealer?   126
   The uses of a 'free, full and ingenuous confession'   140
   The decline of the *Account*   152

6 Dying Well: Martyrs and Penitents 157

Dying in charity with all the world 165
Religion in Newgate 170
Methodism and the decline of the *Account* 182

7 Dying Game: Bridegrooms and Highwaymen 191

Dying like a man 195
False courage and Christian courage: changing sensibilities 205
Weddings and hangings 219

8 God's Tribunal: Providential Discoveries and Ordeals 225

Man's justice and God's justice 227
Calling God to witness: sacred oaths and signs 233
The meaning of suffering 238

9 Conclusion: The Adjournment of God's Tribunal? 251

Appendix A: The Ordinary's *Account* 261

Appendix B: Ordinaries of Newgate, 1676–1799 267

Notes 269
Index 303

Illustrations

1   A woodcut from *The Lives of the Most Remarkable Criminals* 1735.

2   The eleventh plate in William Hogarth's *Industry and Idleness* series 1747, entitled *The idle 'prentice executed at Tyburn.*

3   A late seventeenth-century depiction of an execution at Tyburn, from John Seller, *A Booke of the Punishments of the Common Laws of England* 1678.

4 and 5 These are images of the title pages of *Ordinary's Account* from 27 January 1717/8; the other from 14 March 1721/2.

6   A satirical sheet entitled *The Several Degrees taken by Jonathan Wild's Pupils from their Comencement under his Tutorship to their final Promotion at Tybourn*, depicting the progress of Wild's 'pupils'.

To my mother and father

Acknowledgements

Any original contribution to the crowded historiography of seventeenth- and eighteenth-century English execution will be indebted to the pioneering work of other scholars – Peter Linebaugh, J.A. Sharpe, Douglas Hay and V.A.C. Gatrell, in particular. This work is no exception; and the debt is perhaps most apparent where I differ from them. I am profoundly thankful for the tremendously important work of all those involved in the microfilm and online versions of the Early English Books, the Eighteenth-Century Collections and the Old Bailey Proceedings. I am grateful to the publishers of the following academic journals for permitting me to reproduce material from my previously published work. Chapter 4 is a reworked version of 'The Real Macheath: Social Satire, Appropriation, and Eighteenth-Century Criminal Biography', published in *Huntington Library Quarterly* 69, 4 (2006), pp. 581–605, © 2006 by the Regents of the University of California. Sections of Chapters 1 and 7 are from 'Martyrs in Low Life? Dying "Game" in Augustan England', published in *Journal of British Studies* 42, 2 (April 2003), pp. 167–205, © 2003 by The North American Conference on British Studies; parts of Chapters 8 and 9, from 'God's Tribunal: Guilt, Innocence and Execution in England, 1675–1775', in *Cultural and Social History* 3 (2006), pp. 121–144; sections of Chapter 8, from '"This Death Some Strong and Stout Hearted Man Doth Choose": The Practice of *Peine Forte et Dure* in Seventeenth- and Eighteenth-Century England', in *Law and History Review* 23, 2 (Summer 2005), pp. 279–313, © by the Board of Trustees of the University of Illinois; and some passages of Chapters 3, 6 and 9, from 'From True Confessions to True Reporting? The Decline and Fall of the Ordinary's *Account*', in *The London Journal* 30, 1 (2005), pp. 56–70. I am grateful also to the John Rylands Library, the Guildhall Library, the British Library and the Henry E. Huntington Library for permission to reproduce images from their collections.

I am thankful for financial assistance from the Government of Ontario, the University of Toronto, the William Goodenough Foundation of Canada and an Andrew Mellon fellowship which allowed me to spend a very enjoyable few months at the Huntington Library and benefit from its convivial atmosphere and intellectually stimulating discussions with many visiting scholars. I have benefited greatly over the years from the kind assistance and insights of various mentors, employers, staff, friends, instructors, colleagues and students at York

University, the University of Toronto (both in the History Department and in the Centre of Criminology), the University of Queensland and the University of Victoria. I am grateful as well to the members of various seminar and discussion groups and academic conferences in Canada, the USA, Australia and Great Britain who have given me feedback over the years. It is a great pleasure finally to be able to acknowledge the kind assistance of many knowledgeable and helpful staff members at various research institutions, particularly the British Library, the John Rylands Library, the Henry E. Huntington Library, the Bodleian Library, the Bishopsgate Reference Library, the Corporation of London Record Office, the Guildhall Library, the London Metropolitan Archives, the City of Westminster Archives, the King's Inn Library in Dublin and, finally, the Osgoode Law Library, Robarts Library and the Fisher Rare Book Room in Toronto.

I owe special thanks to a number of people who have commented on earlier drafts or who have been otherwise instrumental in the completion of this project: Jenny Anderson, Sara Beam, Andrew Bonnell, Penny Bryden, Phil Coogan, Paul Crook, Mark Cryle, Peter Cryle, Marion Diamond, Faith Eiboff, Sarah Ferber, Mariel Grant, Margaret Higgs, Tim Hitchcock, Allyson May, Linda Middleton, John Money, Clive Moore, Elaine Naylor, Ed Pechter, Dana Rabin, Robert Shoemaker, Bruce Smith, Greg Smith, Dan White and Eileen Zapshala. I am grateful, too, to the ever-patient and kind Tony Morris at Hambledon and to the incredibly efficient editors at Continuum Books: Ben Hayes, Barbara Ball, Clifford Willis and Slav Todorov. Last but not least, I owe particular thanks to several people, without whom I would have long since fallen through the cracks of my profession: my parents, who have offered unconditional support (and refrained from asking when I would finally be finished); Donna Andrew, whose insights and suggestions have been invaluable; Nick Rogers, who first encouraged my interest in eighteenth-century crime when I was a master's student at York University and who has generously continued to act as a mentor; and to my former doctoral supervisor, John Beattie, who has been, from beginning to end, a wonderfully kind and supportive advisor and friend. I owe greatest thanks of all to my husband and fellow scholar of the eighteenth-century criminal law, Simon Devereaux, who has supported and encouraged me for the last ten years. His insights and suggestions, not to mention access to his unpublished database, have been invaluable, although of course neither he nor anyone else but myself is responsible for any of the shortcomings of this work.

Note on sources

Unless otherwise indicated, all printed primary sources are published in London. Scriptural quotations are from the King James Bible. I have retained original capitalizations and spellings, except in cases of obvious typographical error or where confusion might be generated – as in the common seventeenth-century tendency to spell gaol 'goal', for instance. In some cases, I have in the interests of clarity, replaced italicization with quotation marks, and have retained italics only where they were clearly intended for emphasis, rather than for all proper nouns, as was common contemporary practice. When there are alternate spellings of names, I have chosen the most common usage: e.g., Jack Sheppard instead of Shepherd; Captain Vratz instead of Vrats; James Maclaine instead of Maclean; John Gavan instead of Gawan. Authors have been omitted in citations of serial publications, such as the Ordinary's *Account*, as well as works whose authors are identified by pseudonyms or initials, except in cases where the identity of the author is reasonably established (I have attributed to Daniel Defoe only those works recognized by Furbank and Owen). Most titles of seventeenth- and eighteenth-century works have been abbreviated: full citations are available through Early English Books and the Eighteenth Century online projects and microfilm collections. Dates before 1752 are in Old Style, but I have taken the year to begin 1 January; citations of sources, however, follow the contemporary convention of including both Old and New Style years between 1 January and 25 March (i.e., 17 February 1717/8).

Abbreviations of frequently cited works

Less frequently cited sources, not included here, will be cited in full or slightly abbreviated form at their first occurrence in each chapter and by a shortened version thereafter.

SERIALS

OA (followed by date of execution): *The Ordinary of Newgate His Account of the Behaviour, Confessions and Dying Words … of the Malefactors Executed at Tyburn … [date]*. This title did not become standardized until 1701; before then, the account was published under a number of different titles (e.g., *The Behaviour, Last Dying Speeches and Execution* or *A True Account of the Behaviour … of the Malefactors Executed at Tyburn*). Accounts published before 1701 will be cited by abbreviated forms of their long title, followed by the date of execution.

OBP (followed by date of sessions): *The Proceedings of the King's Commission of the Peace and Oyer and Terminer, and Gaol-delivery of Newgate, held for the City of London and County of Middlesex, at Justice-Hall, in the Old-Bailey … [date]*. The *Proceedings* did not assume its standardized title until after 1684; before then, the 'Sessions Paper' (as it was called by contemporaries) was published under a number of different titles. Earlier publications will be cited by abbreviated forms of their long title, followed by the date of the sessions.

GM: *The Gentleman's Magazine.*

LM: *The London Magazine.*

COLLECTIONS OF CRIMINAL LIVES AND TRIALS

Compleat Collection of Remarkable Tryals: N. B., *A Compleat Collection of Remarkable Tryals of the most Notorious Malefactors, at the Sessions-House in the Old Baily, for near Fifty Years past … Together with A particular Account of their Behaviour under Sentence of Death, and Dying-Speeches … 4 vols (1718–1720).*

Johnson, General History of the Pyrates: Captain Charles Johnson, *A General*

History of the Robberies and Murders of the most notorious Pyrates, 2 vols, repr. in Manuel Schonhorn ed., Daniel Defoe, *A General History of the Pyrates*, 2 vols in 1 (Mineola, 1999; reprint of 4th ed., vol. 1 published in 1726; vol. 2 in 1728. First edition published in 1724).

Johnson, *General History of the Highwaymen*: Captain Charles Johnson, *A General History of the Lives and Adventures of the Most Famous Highwaymen, Murderers, Street Robbers &c.* (1734).

LMRC: *The Lives of the Most Remarkable Criminals who have been condemn'd and Executed; for Murder, Highway, House-Breakers, Street Robberies, Coining, or other Offences; From the Year 1720, to the Present Time … Collected from Original Papers and Authentick Memoirs*, 3 vols (1735).

Mather, *Wonders of Free-Grace*: Increase Mather, *The Wonders of Free-Grace: or a Compleat History of all the Remarkable Penitents that have been Executed at Tyburn …* (1690).

***Remarkable Trials* (1765)**: *Remarkable Trials and Interesting Memoirs, of the Most noted Criminals, Who have been convicted at the Assizes from Year 1740 to 1764. With an Account of their most memorable Exploits, Adventures, Confessions, and Dying Behaviour …* 2 vols (1765).

***Select and Impartial Account of the Most Remarkable Convicts* (1745)**: *A Select and Impartial Account of the Lives, Behaviour, and Dying Words, of the most Remarkable Convicts, from the Year 1700, down to the present Time*, 3 vols, 2nd ed. (1745).

***Select Trials* (1742)**: *Select Trials at the Sessions-House in the Old Bailey, for Murder, Robberies, Rapes, Sodomy, Coining, Frauds, Bigamy, and other Offences. To which are added, Genuine Accounts of the Lives, Behaviour, Confessions, and Dying Speeches of the most eminent Convicts … From the Year 1720, to this Time*, 4 vols. (1742).

***Select Trials* (1764)**: *Select Trials for Murder, Robbery, Burglary, Rapes, Sodomy, Coining, Forgery, Pyracy, and other Offences and Misdemeanours at the Sessions-House in the Old Bailey, to which are added Genuine Accounts of the Lives, Exploits, Behaviour, Confessions, and Dying-Speeches, of the most notorious Convicts, from the Year 1741, to the present Year 1764, inclusive. Which completes the Trials from the Year 1720*, 4 vols (1764).

Smith, *Lives of the Highwaymen*: Captain Alexander Smith, *The History of the Lives of the most Noted Highway-men, Foot-pads, House-breakers, Shop-lifts and Cheats, Of both Sexes, in and about London, and other Places of Great-Britain, for above fifty Years last past …* 2 vols. 2nd ed. (1714).

State Trials: *Cobbett's Complete Collection of State Trials and Proceedings for High Treason and other Crimes and Misdemeanours From the Earliest Period to the Present Time* (1809).

OTHER PRIMARY SOURCES

Burnet, *History of his own Time*: *Bishop Burnet's History of his own Time: with Notes by the Earls of Dartmouth and Hardwicke, Speaker Onslow, and Dean Swift*, ed. Martin Joseph Routh, 2nd ed., 6 vols. (Oxford, 1833; repr. Georg Olms, 1969).

CLRO: Corporation of London Record Office.

CSPD: Calendar of State Papers Domestic.

Life of Silas Told: Silas Told, *The Life of Mr Silas Told Written by Himself* (1786; repr. London, 1954).

Walpole's Correspondence: *The Yale Edition of Horace Walpole's Correspondence*, ed. W. S. Lewis (London, 1960), 48 vols.

SELECT SECONDARY SOURCES

Beattie, *Crime and the Courts*: J. M. Beattie, *Crime and the Courts in England, 1660–1800* (Princeton, 1986).

Faller, *Turned to Account*: Lincoln B. Faller, *Turned to Account: the Forms and Functions of Criminal Biography in Late Seventeenth- and Early Eighteenth-Century England* (Cambridge, 1987).

Gatrell, *Hanging Tree*: V. A. C. Gatrell, *The Hanging Tree: Execution and the English People, 1770–1868* (Oxford, 1994).

Harris, 'Trials and Criminal Biographies': Michael Harris, 'Trials and Criminal Biographies: A Case Study in Distribution', in Michael Harris and Robin Myers, eds., *Sale and Distribution of Books from 1700* (Oxford, 1982).

Hay *et al.*, *Albion's Fatal Tree*: Douglas Hay *et al.*, *Albion's Fatal Tree: Crime and Society in Eighteenth-Century England* (London, 1975).

King, *Crime, Justice and Discretion*: Peter King, *Crime, Justice, and Discretion in England, 1740–1820* (Oxford, 2000).

Linebaugh, 'Tyburn Riot': Peter Linebaugh, 'The Tyburn Riot Against the Surgeons', in Hay, *Albion's Fatal Tree*.

Linebaugh, 'Ordinary of Newgate': Peter Linebaugh, 'The Ordinary of Newgate and His *Account*', in J. S. Cockburn, ed., *Crime in England, 1550–1800* (Princeton, 1977).

Linebaugh, *London Hanged*: Peter Linebaugh, *The London Hanged: Crime and Civil Society in the Eighteenth Century* (London, 1993).

Sharpe, 'Last Dying Speeches': J. A. Sharpe, 'Last Dying Speeches: Religion, Ideology and Public Execution in Seventeenth-Century England', in *Past & Present*, 107 (1984).

Preface

The public execution at Tyburn is perhaps the most familiar and evocative of all eighteenth-century images. Whether it elicits horror or prurient fascination – or both – the early modern hanging day has become synonymous with the brutality of a bygone age and a legal and political system which valued property over human life. Countless London pubs and tourist attractions regale visitors with dramatic, if often dubious, tales about the various gruesome punishments of 'olden times'. But however good for business, the lurid mythology surrounding seventeenth- and eighteenth-century English execution poses something of a problem for the historian. The image of the eighteenth-century public hanging as a kind of debased spectator sport has become so familiar – it is, after all, almost certain to figure largely in any novel or film set in the period – as to raise the question of why we should revisit it. Horror and disgust seem the only appropriate humanitarian responses to the excesses of the unreformed early modern criminal law; further investigation into the mechanics or the aesthetics of execution appears gratuitous, not to mention tasteless. 'What's a nice young lady like you doing, studying an awful subject like this?' numerous well-meaning people have asked me. A gentleman I met in the Guildhall Library kindly suggested that I turn my attention to 'something pleasant, like great battles'.

Perhaps inevitably, respectable interest in public execution tends to be confined to expressions of sympathy for those who lost their lives on the gallows as well as, perhaps, condemnation for the architects and administrators of the 'Bloody Code' which hanged them. Equally inevitably, academic discussion of the seventeenth- and eighteenth-century gallows has been shaped and informed by a larger modern preoccupation with capital punishment as a current political issue. However, my aim is not to judge the past, but rather to understand the early modern English execution on its own terms and within its own particular social and cultural context. While public executions may not have been 'pleasant', the gallows were nonetheless a stage on which the condemned fought what contemporaries would have viewed as the greatest battle of all, publicly confronting the so-called 'King of Terrors': death. The title of this work should not, however, be taken to imply that the men and women executed at Tyburn were 'martyrs' either to capitalism, or even to an unjust criminal code (although both, to be sure, claimed their share of victims). Rather, I hope to demonstrate the degree to which the language of martyrology, legitimation and resistance were intertwined in this period, and that traitors, martyrs, murderers and robbers alike drew from a common eschatology in which the 'good death' was not only an ultimate goal, but a powerful political and metaphysical statement.

One example may suffice to illustrate not only the political significance of early modern public executions, but their semiotic instability; that is, to the degree to which the behaviour of the central actors could work against the intentions of the authorities whose business it was, presumably, to stage-manage such events. In 1679, at the height of popular hysteria over an alleged 'Popish Plot' to overthrow the government, five Jesuits were hanged at Tyburn for supposedly committing treason. While few people had doubted their guilt during their trial, the execution of these men marked a critical turning point: although others would follow them to the scaffold, popular belief in the existence of the Plot had begun to waver. To a large extent, this can be attributed to the five Jesuits themselves, whose solemn protestations of innocence and, above all, whose bravery, charity and apparent cheerfulness at the place of execution, literally 'stagger'd' spectators, sowing seeds of doubt in even the most rabid of anti-Catholics.[1] This was an age in which courage and composure communicated not just strength of character, but innocence: according to popular belief, God granted to those who died in a just cause, such as martyrs, a 'divine assistance' and 'encouragement' that carried them above sorrow, passion or fear. The last dying words of even ordinary criminals were invested with particular weight and meaning, as it was believed that only an idiot, a lunatic or an atheist would risk appearing before God with a lie in his or her mouth.

Much ink was spilt in publishing various 'animadversions' on the last dying speeches of the five Jesuits: more than a dozen such publications are still extant, many of them boasting titles like *Lying Allowable with Papists to Deceive Protestants*. Some pamphlets claimed to explain how 'according to their Principles, they not only might, but also ought to die ... with solemn Protestations of their Innocency'; others, supposedly offered 'Confutation[s] of their Appeals, Courage, and Cheerfulness, at Execution'.[2] But it is significant that in all these attempts to place the five men outside the pale of truth-telling, there was no attempt to undermine or to refute the sanctity of the gallows as a kind of supernatural forum – a literal preview of 'God's Tribunal' itself. Rather, such accounts strove to demonstrate that the Pope routinely granted dispensations and absolutions to those Catholics who died for their faith, even those who died in the commission of a mortal sin – that is, swearing a false oath. It would subsequently become almost de rigueur for condemned Catholics at the place of execution to solemnly renounce, as did the five Jesuits, 'all manner of pardons, absolutions, dispensations for swearing [falsely]'. But, ultimately the gallows afforded the five Jesuits the forum they had been denied at their trial, and one which they successfully appropriated: there, in the words of the Anglican divine Gilbert Burnet (no great friend to Catholics), their 'behaviour and last words ... made impressions which no books could carry off'.[3]

The notion that the early modern gallows was a forum of truth is so obvious as to verge on truism; however, despite or perhaps because of this, this concept, and the presumptions underpinning it, have gone relatively unexplored. We are most of us familiar with Michel Foucault's characterization of execution as a 'moment of truth', a 'spectacle of sufferings truly endured' wherein 'one could decipher crime and innocence, the past and the future, the here below and the eternal'.[4] Indeed, many of Foucault's critics have joined with his adherents in viewing the body of the condemned not only as both 'language and spectacle' but, more particularly, as a spectacle upon which the authorities who had stage-managed the execution attempted to inscribe a normative message. After all, execution was theatre (and this, too, has become something of a truism), 'dramatized in order to serve as a sort of morality play' reflecting the magistrates' (i.e., the stagers') 'view of the world'.[5] There is no doubt that the ideal execution from the point of view of officials featured a penitent malefactor whose words and demeanour legitimated his or her sentence of death, and acquiescence therein. However, the extent to which authorities in early modern England, at any rate, could successfully command such displays of 'internalised obedience' is open to debate.[6] Many English social historians have viewed the gallows not as a site of social control but of class conflict, where the normative message intended by authorities was all too liable to be reappropriated and inverted by an irreverent crowd.[7]

More recently, scholars have argued for a 'far more complex dialectic' than that implied by any simple consensus–conflict dichotomy – one which emphasizes the degree to which early modern English executions were inherently 'unstable' events (and thus not easily stage-managed), on the one hand, while taking into account the shared, largely religious, language and beliefs that made sense of the behaviour and words of the condemned, on the other.[8] For even if, as the historian of crime J. A. Sharpe has argued, early modern men and women 'clearly read the theatre of punishment in religious terms', it does not necessarily follow from this that the gallows functioned as a mechanism of social control.[9] Rather, expressions of faith and adherence to religious forms and agency – even resistance – were not mutually exclusive. Indeed, recent scholarship has emphasized the degree to which 'religion could serve both as a language of legitimation for established hierarchies *and* as a revolutionary idiom' which could 'be used tactically' by the 'weak' as well as the 'powerful'.[10]

Nor were accounts reporting the last dying words and behaviour of the condemned particularly amenable to stage-management, even before the final lapse of the Licensing Act in 1695 put an end to pre-publication censorship. The promulgation of last dying speeches was popularly viewed as one of the inalienable rights of the 'free-born Englishman', and was closely identified with the triumphalist narrative of English Protestantism disseminated by John Foxe and subsequent Protestant hagiographers: the image of the Marian martyrs, who had been forbidden to make dying speeches on pain of having their tongues cut out, came to represent embattled righteousness pitted against an unjust and tyrannical regime.[11] Certainly by the late seventeenth century, the gallows constituted a forum so open, and generated a trade so brisk – not to mention competitive – that overt forgeries were unlikely to go undetected or unchallenged.

The last dying speech came into its own as a print genre in the wake of the politically charged treason trials and executions of the second half of the seventeenth century, and the market soon extended to common criminals. By the mid-1670s the Sessions Paper and the Ordinary of Newgate's *Account* had emerged as regular and even 'semi-official' accounts of the proceedings at the Old Bailey courthouse and the last dying speeches and behaviour of malefactors executed at Tyburn, respectively.[12] While such publications and their numerous competitors were formulaic documents, scripted both by convention and the demands of their audience, these conventions and formulae are nonetheless significant and instructive – not least because they address the preoccupations and concerns inherent to the execution genre, as well as the larger eschatological discourse within which they were situated.[13] Even a source so mediated as the Ordinary's *Account* of the biographies and last dying confessions of condemned malefactors is useful in that it highlights discursive fault-lines and flashpoints, as the Ordinary (the chaplain of Newgate) testified at length to his own diligence and travails, the bad behaviour of his charges, and his refutations of and (almost) inevitable triumphs over their wrong opinions. As we shall see, such contests centred not merely on the convict's penitence or obstinacy, guilt or innocence, but on competing providential interpretations and strategies: against the Ordinary's disapproval and protests, many of the condemned solemnly swore to their innocence of the crime of which they had been convicted, yet were equally ostentatious (if perhaps often disingenuous) in their claims that they were willing to accept their condemnation as part of a larger divine plan for their souls' salvation.

The dates of this study correspond roughly with those of the Ordinary's serial publication, *The Ordinary of Newgate His Account of the Behaviour, Confessions and Last Dying Speeches of the Malefactors Executed at Tyburn*, which proliferated in the late seventeenth and early eighteenth century and then disappeared with surprising suddenness by the early 1770s, considerably predating the 1783 abolition of the Tyburn procession. While the Ordinary's *Account* (and its rival publications and forgeries) constitutes one of the principal sources for this work and explains, if not wholly excuses, the emphasis on London, I have drawn extensively from criminal literature generally – trials, criminal biographies, highwaymen 'lives', collections of last dying speeches – as well as newspaper accounts, diaries, journals, plays, novels, sermons and devotional literature, and other print and manuscript sources. The Ordinary's *Account*, traditionally dismissed by disapproving nineteenth- and early twentieth-century commentators as a vulgar catchpenny sheet, has until recently been largely overlooked by historians, many seeing it as too mediated to be reliable – despite the fact that the *Account*, along with the printed accounts of the proceedings at the Old Bailey, was the principal and often the only source for the Newgate Calendars and other later compilations assumed to be fairly dependable (as well as a source frequently plagiarized verbatim by such publications). In large part, then, this book is a story of the rise and fall of the Ordinary's *Account* and related literature featuring the last dying words of criminals, aimed at a broad general audience. In the early nineteenth century, the aging Francis Place would recollect with horror and disgust the kinds of criminal ballads and catchpenny sheets which had survived into his own youth among the blackguards of the streets; he deplored and marvelled still more at the 'grossness' and debased reading tastes of the middling and respectable working-class men and women of his father's and grandfather's generation, who routinely purchased and read last dying confessions and other criminal pamphlets and broadsides.[14] How and why did public tastes change after about the middle of the eighteenth century?

Not least, what can the stories of the lives, gallows behaviour and last words of such condemned men and women, the vast majority of whom were hanged for property offences, tell us about late seventeenth- and early eighteenth-century English culture? These malefactors were not significant simply because, being relegated to the social and moral margins, they provided a kind of negative normative blueprint. Indeed, most of the malefactors hanged at Tyburn were from the respectable labouring and artisan classes rather than the upper or very lowest ranks of society. Nor were even the poorest malefactors entirely excluded from a larger mental universe in which criminality was conceived of, not as a pathology or even solely a socio-economic problem, but as a point on a moral continuum. In an age in which all men and women were sinners and hypocrites, the common criminal functioned as both a moral and satirical trope: an Everyman (or Everywoman) qualified to preach to spectators on the dangers of sin on the one hand, and a social critic who could expose the hypocrisy of more respectable but equally dishonest citizens on the other.

In the following chapter, I will return in more depth to a discussion of the mythology and historiography of Tyburn, but only after first setting the stage; that is, providing a description of how executions were conducted, and placing them within a larger legal and social context. Chapter 2 expands on the subject of last dying confessions and criminal literature generally – its audience, origins, authorship and marketing. Chapter 3 explores contemporary beliefs about the root causes and nature of criminality, and examines the degree to which the moralist paradigm explaining early modern criminality was inherently ambiguous, with its emphasis on the 'slippery slope' not only allowing those criminals asked to enumerate their past sins the opportunity to introduce extenuating personal and economic circumstances, but reinforcing contemporary notions about the universality and relativity of guilt and sin. Chapter 4 examines the satirical tradition within criminal reportage, particularly highwayman literature, and the ways in which malefactors not only served as vehicles for social commentary, but could themselves appropriate satirical messages. In Chapter 5, I discuss the second major stream of criminal literature, the confessional tradition; in particular, the Ordinary's *Account*. Chapters 6 and 7 deal with the various strategies for dying well – whether as a penitent, a martyr or a 'game' criminal – and how both popular and elite religious practices and ideas, especially those relating to grace and the metaphysical significance of gallows courage, were expressed, contested and transformed over the course of the eighteenth century. Chapter 8 explores contemporary notions of human and divine justice and the extent to which the gallows were seen as a forum of truth – a stage upon which spectators could discern in the words and gestures of the condemned divine dispensations and providential designs. In the conclusion, I discuss how and why the sacramentality of the gallows – specifically, the notion of Tyburn as 'God's Tribunal'– gradually eroded during the second half of the eighteenth century, a period which witnessed a concomitant decline of the notion of the criminal as 'Everyman', and that of last dying speeches and confessional literature generally.

From Newgate to Tyburn: Setting the Stage

> All you that in the condemn'd Holds do lie,
> Prepare you, for to Morrow you shall die;
> Watch and pray, the Hour's drawing near,
> That you before th'Almighty must appear:
> Examine well your selves, in time repent,
> That you may not t'eternal Flames be sent;
> And when St. 'Pulcher's Bell, to Morrow, tolls,
> The Lord above have Mercy on your Souls.

Sometime around midnight on 4 May 1722 these words, or ones much like them, would have been pronounced in an appropriately 'dismal Voice' by the Bellman of St Sepulchre's (and accompanied by 'twelve solemn tolls') as he stood outside the condemned hold in Newgate, London's largest and most famous prison. The Bellman would also ring his handbell and deliver one last pious exhortation to the malefactors as they passed by St Sepulchre's church on their way to be executed at Tyburn the following morning.[1] But for those four men, all convicted street robbers, the reality of their situation would have sunk in several days earlier, when the 'Dead Warrant' – the list of the condemned who had been denied pardons and were thus scheduled to be executed – had been brought down to Newgate. It was then, according to the Ordinary (or prison chaplain), that they finally left off 'their vicious Practice of leud Talking and Swearing … and grew more serious, lamenting with Tears their mistake' in having presumed that they would be reprieved as part of a general act of clemency to mark the convention of a new parliament.

John Thompson, 33, a former weaver's apprentice and sailor, claimed that 'he had fully and amply repented, and was well prepared to Suffer, as the Law directed', although he expressed grief at leaving his wife and young child, and complained of the neglect of his brother and other 'Friends' – an early modern term referring primarily to family connections – who 'refus'd to come to see him in his Distress'. James Tims, 26, a drover, was 'most observant of his Duty', claiming to have been 'much disturb'd' by the 'swearing and cursing' of his fellow inmates, and seemingly eager to follow the advice of his wife and relatives to be 'serious and attentive'. In contrast, John Hartly, alias 'Pokey', 'spent most of the time … bewailing his miserable Fate in being condemn'd (as he would always affirm) wrongfully'. At under twenty years of age the youngest of the four and the only bachelor, Hartly's attempts to obtain a reprieve were strenuous, if unavailing – going as far as to solicit 'six Maidens' all dressed in white to petition the king to 'grant him a Pardon upon condition that one of them Wedded him'.

Finally, there was Thomas Reeves, 28, a quintessentially 'game' criminal: ostentatiously bold and – in the Ordinary's view, if not his own – indecently cheerful and impenitent. He boasted alike of his superior 'Share of Boldness' as a criminal (he was 'always the Captain of his Gang, and the Purse-Bearer after every Robbery'), and of 'how Manfully' he intended to go to his execution. Reeves 'peremptorily always affirm'd that he doubted not of going to Heaven', a 'Happiness', he claimed, which could as readily be 'receiv'd from the Gallows, as from the Bed'.[2] These assertions – not to mention his unorthodox views on such vexed theological 'Points' as the existence of an 'intermediate State' between 'Bliss' and 'Torment' – were cited as evidence that Reeves was a 'free-thinker' (essentially, a deist).[3] While his fellow prisoners were supposed to have complained of his levity during devotions – 'Jesting and Laughing one Moment and Reading the next, and sometimes mixing Prayers and obscene Talk together' – Reeves was by his own account far from irreligious. Despite 'his Laughing way', he claimed, he 'was no whit the less serious and attentive at his Heart'; he was, moreover, he said, 'so far from fearing Death, that he rather chose to die than to live'.[4]

On their way to Tyburn, Thompson and Tims 'were full of Tears and with wringing Hands implor'd God's Pardon'. According to one account, Hartly also 'wept and lamented exceedingly his miserable Condition', a fact that, combined with his youth and avowals of innocence, excited pity from onlookers. (The Ordinary of Newgate, sceptical alike of Hartly's truthfulness and penitence, claimed to have detected in him 'a settled and deaden'd Look' denoting reprobation.) At the place of execution, all four men 'took their Leaves of each other', asked spectators to pray for them, and claimed to be reconciled to their fate. 'They all said, they were even glad at going out of this careful World.' Thomas Reeves gave a short speech in which he exonerated his wife from any blame for his crimes, and asked that no one 'Reflect upon her for his ignominious Death'. Reeves not only acknowledged the 'Fact for which he suffer'd', but others besides. He was 'extreamly desirous to tell the Spectators' that his alleged accomplice, Hartly, was innocent of the crime for which he was to hang – although the latter, he added ingenuously, 'in other Robberies had assisted him'. Here the Ordinary saw fit to remind Reeves that 'his Friend had been found Guilty by 12 impartial Men' and 'that they ought both to submit to the Hand of Providence, and to think more of another World and less of this'. Moments later the signal was given for the cart on which the condemned stood under the gallows to be drawn away, leaving them to die of asphyxiation. Suddenly the 'Mob, for want of Regulation', pressing against this moveable scaffold, knocked down one of the horses, leaving the cart 'leaning side-ways' and the malefactors 'half hanged'. Reeves seized the opportunity both to 'ease himself of his Misery' and to demonstrate that the 'Resolution' on which he so prided himself had indeed 'continued with him to the last Moment'. He 'threw himself over the Side of the Cart to his Death' – and, as it were, to another world.[5]

EXECUTION, DISCRETION AND THE 'BLOODY CODE'

This last rather dramatic hitch aside, it was a typical early eighteenth-century execution. Excepting only that three out of the four condemned were married, they otherwise conformed to the standard profile of the Tyburn hanged: male, single, working-class, mid- to late twenties. Thompson, Tims, Hartly and Reeves were also typical in that they were all robbers who had used or threatened violence in the course of their crimes: the sort of offence, second only to premeditated murder (a relatively uncommon crime), most likely to be prosecuted and punished to its utmost rigour. They were typical, too, in that they were all four perceived as career criminals or 'Old Offenders'.[6] This was something usually emphasized by contemporary chroniclers – in combination with the usual progress in vice (Sabbath-breaking, drunkenness, lewdness and so on), and an idle or 'roving' disposition generally. John Hartly, we are told, had never been bound apprentice to a trade, only working casually as a butcher's boy; John Thompson had failed to complete his apprenticeship, and confessed to having had difficulty readjusting to civilian life after developing the 'Custom of bloodshed' and 'Plunder' at sea. Although Thomas Reeves claimed to have been apprenticed to his father, a tinsmith, it seems unlikely he served out his time; he had at any rate been tried several years earlier at the Old Bailey courthouse for housebreaking, although acquitted for lack of evidence. James Tims had a prior conviction for theft: he claimed in his defence that this was only 'thro' the Instigation of an Acquaintance, who over perswaded him when he had drank after a very sultry Day, and was almost disguised in Liquor'.[7]

The eighteenth-century English criminal code was notoriously harsh, with approximately two hundred capital statutes, most of them property offences, on the books. Later commentators have emphasized the degree to which this 'Bloody Code' privileged property over human life – citing such famous anomalies as the fact that, while under eighteenth-century law kidnapping a child was only a misdemeanour, stealing the shoes from that same child (if they were valued at over a shilling) was a capital offence. Victorian and Edwardian writers delighted in pathetic descriptions of young female shoplifters executed for stealing to put bread in the mouths of their starving babies.[8] Yet one of the most striking features of the so-called 'Bloody Code' was that relatively few of those who fell under its purview were actually executed: the majority of men and women accused of capital crimes, even if prosecuted and found guilty, could expect to be pardoned and/or sentenced to a punishment less than death. This paradox was often cited by contemporary apologists for the English criminal law as evidence of its flexibility and lenity: only the most violent or hardened repeat offenders (they claimed) would suffer, and by their example strike terror in the hearts of would-be criminals. However, a growing number of eighteenth-century critics argued that far from deterring crime, the severity of the law made it unenforceable: the fact that prosecutors and juries were reluctant to send men and women to the gallows for property crimes meant (*they* claimed) that criminals believed they could rob with impunity. But, as modern social historians have argued, the unreformed capital code had weapons other than terror: the very mercy and discretion that ameliorated the severity of the criminal law also performed an ideological function, cementing and legitimating the bonds of deference and patronage, obedience and authority between the poor and the propertied classes. And whatever the degree of social control exercised by employers, officials and administrators, there is no doubt that discretion was at the heart of the early modern English legal system – a fact plainly illustrated by a summary of the sessions preceding the 4 May 1722 execution described above.[9]

Thompson, Tims, Hartly and Reeves had been among sixty-seven men and women tried four weeks earlier at the Old Bailey, the central criminal court for the City of London and the county of Middlesex. Forty-one (61%) of the defendants were male; twenty-six (39%) female. Almost all of them were charged with capital felonies and thus were at least ostensibly on trial for their lives. The overwhelming proportion of trials (91%) were for property offences: shoplifting, pickpocketing, horse-theft, burglary and robbery. Only seventeen (25%) of the defendants were acquitted; one woman, accused of bigamy, was discharged without penalty. Most (60%) were found guilty, but of a reduced, non-capital charge, a common practice known as a 'partial verdict' or 'pious perjury', in which the jury downgraded the value of the item stolen so that the offence fell below the capital threshold. (This amount varied according to the particular crime; for example, one shilling for stealing from the person, five from a shop, forty from a house, although property crimes including violence or the threat of violence, 'putting in fear', were by definition capital regardless of the amount stolen.) Thirty-two men and women (48%) were sentenced to transportation (i.e., a term of penal servitude in the American colonies); eight (12%) to lesser punishments: the pillory, fines, imprisonment, branding. And of the seven men and two women sentenced to death, three of the men, two horse-thieves and a burglar, were subsequently granted pardons on condition of transportation. The two women, both accused of stealing from men in taverns (contemporaries would have immediately inferred that they were prostitutes) were also reprieved:

the first received a transportation pardon; the second successfully 'pleaded the belly'; in other words, was respited because she was pregnant. In theory, this meant that she would be executed after giving birth; in practice, it almost always translated into either a full or conditional pardon.[10] In the end, as we have seen, only four men – Thompson, Tims, Hartly and Reeves, all street robbers or 'footpads' – were hanged.[11]

This was also a fairly typical early eighteenth-century execution in terms of its scale. Estimates of executions in the Tudor and early Stuart period were high, if impressionistic: both a late Elizabethan and an early Jacobean travel account put the average number hanged per execution day in London, regularly held eight times a year, at about twenty-five. These figures are conservative, however, in comparison to William Harrison's famous claim that in the reign of Henry VIII, 72,000 'rogues' and thieves, or just under 2,000 a year, were hanged in England as a whole. Execution rates appear to have declined markedly after the Restoration, despite the fact that the metropolis continued to grow, from an estimated population of 70,000 in 1550 to 200,000 in 1600, 400,000 in 1650, 575,000 in 1700, and 675,000 in 1750 (the population of England as a whole grew from about three million to just under six million in the same period).[12] Narcissus Luttrell records 455 London executions reported in the newspapers from 1693 to 1700, giving an average of 7.1 malefactors per execution. According to the statistics compiled by Paul Lorrain during his eighteen-year tenure as Ordinary of Newgate, 494 malefactors condemned at the Old Bailey had been executed between 1701 and 1718, an average of 27.4 annually or 3.4 per hanging day.[13] From December 1729 to October 1749, a twenty-year period for which we have complete data, 622 of the Old Bailey condemned were executed – an average of 31.1 annually, or 3.8 per execution. Of these 11% were executed for violent crimes; 89% for property offences (including robbery).[14]

These of course were only averages: conviction and hanging rates fluctuated, tending for instance to be higher in peacetime than in war, when large numbers of the unemployed poor were enlisted in the army or navy and when many condemned men, moreover, were offered pardons conditional on military service. While there were a few 'maiden sessions' in which no one was even condemned, some executions were very large: on 29 June 1649, twenty-four malefactors were hanged at Tyburn; twenty-three were executed on 6 May 1685; twenty on 18 March 1741. The 1649 figure constituted a practical maximum in the sense that only eight people could be hanged on each cross-beam on the triangular gallows at Tyburn (or the 'Triple Tree'). While a large minority – in some periods almost half or more – of those brought before the Old Bailey on capital charges were women,[15] they were much more likely to receive reduced sentences or to be pardoned than were men, and constituted a small proportion of those hanged, generally less than 10%. From December 1729 to October 1749,

45 women were executed, compared to 577 men: thus women comprised 7% of those executed. This percentage could be higher, however, in periods in which the government was cracking down on crimes more likely to be committed by women, such as coining or clipping (filing the edges from coins) in the 1690s, or shoplifting in the early eighteenth century: in March 1741, for instance, six out of the twenty malefactors hanged were female. Convicted murderesses, like their male counterparts, were almost always executed, but their numbers were comparatively small, if disproportionately publicized – only ten in the twenty-year period from December 1729 to October 1749.

Tyburn, the main place of execution for the City of London and the county of Middlesex, was located at what was, in the early modern period, the north-west edge of the metropolitan area, at the junction of Oxford Street with Edgware and Bayswater Road, near the present-day site of Marble Arch (marked today by a small plaque in a traffic island). The 'Elms' at the crossroads that had served as the medieval gallows had probably been replaced by a beam placed across the branches of two trees sometime in the fifteenth century. The first mention of the distinctive 'Triple Tree' design dates from a 1571 account of the execution of the Catholic cleric John Story, in which it was claimed that 'a new payre of Gallowes made in triangle maner ... was prepared for him'. This structure seems to have been replaced from time to time: in the late 1670s, the Court of Aldermen ordered 'the setting up of a new Gallowes at Tyburne the old Gallowes there having for a good while past been altogether useless', while a 1678 execution sheet makes specific reference to 'the new Gallows'. A newspaper report of a June 1759 execution noted that 'all the Cross-Beams [had been] pulled down', possibly as a result of vandalism; in October of the same year, the permanent structure was replaced by a 'new Moving Gallows'.[16] From this time until the last execution at Tyburn in November 1783, a temporary scaffold was erected and dismantled for each execution. After the abolition of the Tyburn procession, malefactors were hanged outside the Debtor's Door at Newgate, the first execution taking place there in December 1783.

While the vast majority of the hangings of common criminals took place at Tyburn, there were other execution sites in London: traitors of noble blood were beheaded on Tower Hill, or sometimes at other locations (Lord William Russell was executed at Lincoln's Inn Fields, for instance). Execution of commoners for high or petty treason – the former including coining offences; the latter, women convicted of murdering their husbands or masters – could take place at Smithfield or at other locations, including Tyburn. Pirates and others condemned at the Admiralty Sessions at the Old Bailey, dealing with offences at sea, were hanged at Execution Dock in Wapping. There, malefactors would be hanged at low tide under a gallows consisting of two posts and a cross-beam where, until the late eighteenth century, the body was left until three tides had washed over it.[17] In the seventeenth century, many malefactors deemed guilty of particularly heinous acts, such as murder, were hanged at or near the site of their crimes, or some other appropriately 'Exemplary' location. The coiner Elizabeth Hare was executed at Bunhill Fields in October 1683 apparently because she had confessed to having buried alive a bastard child there several years earlier. In 1680, John Marketman, an Essex man who had murdered his wife, was supposed to have been hanged at 'the common place of Execution' in Chelmsford but was 'at his own Request' executed outside his own house at Westham where the crime had been committed. This practice of hanging malefactors at the site of their crimes had largely fallen into desuetude by the early eighteenth century, but was revived in the 1770s.[18]

In the metropolis, the place of execution was determined by the sheriffs of London and Middlesex, two city officials elected annually by the Court of Aldermen, and who had considerable discretionary power. The sheriffs were supposed to supervise the Tyburn procession in person although, especially in the early eighteenth century, it was common for them to nominate deputies to attend in their stead. (Technically the hangman himself was a deputy hired by the City to execute the function of the sheriffs.)[19] Executions in London and in England as a whole shared many similar features and rituals, such as a public progress from the prison to the place of hanging, but Tyburn, with its procession and associated traditions, was the most famous: in fact, provincial towns such as York adopted Tyburn as a generic name for their place of execution (Newgate was similarly applied to prisons outside of London, such as in Bristol). By the time that Thompson, Tims, Hartly and Reeves were hanged at Tyburn, these rituals were both well established and elaborate, and warrant a brief outline here – not least because such a description will help set the stage for the discussion of criminal accounts, contemporary notions of criminality, human and divine justice and eschatology that will follow.

THE TYBURN PROCESSION AND EXECUTION RITUAL

The Sunday before every execution, the Ordinary preached a condemned sermon in the Newgate chapel to what was almost invariably a 'full Auditory', swelled by numerous 'Strangers' who had paid admission fees to the gaolers, and were almost certainly drawn more by curiosity than 'Christian compassion'.[20] Several days before the execution, the Dead Warrant came down, an event which generally marked a dramatic change in the piety and seriousness of those whose names were included therein.[21] Around midnight on the night before the execution, the Bellman or sexton of St Sepulchre's, the church adjacent to Newgate, recited his verses outside of the wall of the condemned hold or 'Hole'. This too was expected to have a salutary effect, eliciting 'dismal Cries and Lamentations' on the part of those about to die. Some were apparently less concerned: in March 1733, when the Bellman came to give the condemned 'Notice', the notorious murderess Sarah Malcolm was told to 'Mind what he said'. Malcolm supposedly waited until 'he had done', upon which she cried out: 'd'ye hear Mr Bellman, call for a Pint of Wine, and I'll throw you a Shilling to pay for it'.[22]

The morning of the execution itself – which in the seventeenth century generally fell on Wednesdays or Fridays but by the eighteenth century could take place on any day apart from a Sunday – the condemned heard prayers in chapel, where the sacrament was administered to those wishing to receive it, and deemed fit by the Ordinary. The procession from Newgate to Tyburn, a distance of about two and a half miles or four kilometres, could take an hour or more and usually started between nine and ten in the morning – or, as our more matutinal forebears would have said, in the 'forenoon'. The condemned were first led out towards the Stone Hall, near the gateway of the prison, where their irons were struck off (by the second half of the eighteenth century, this ritual seems to have taken place in the Press Yard, a narrow but open passage on the south-east side of Newgate). Their hands were then tied in front of them with rope, presumably to allow them sufficient mobility to clasp them in prayer and to read on the way to the gallows, although many availed themselves of this privilege to remove their hats and to '[salute] the bystanders' and make other gestures at the place of execution. This custom was evidently firmly established at Tyburn and elsewhere: one pirate executed in Africa in 1722 with his hands pinioned behind his back indignantly 'observed, that he had seen many a Man hang'd, but this Way of the Hands being ty'd behind them, he was a Stranger to, and never saw before in his Life'. While many state criminals (traitors) were trusted to go to their executions unbound, some common malefactors considered high security risks were fitted with 'Iron Hand-cuffs' or even leg-irons. The celebrated escape artist Jack Sheppard – petty housebreaker turned prison-breaker extraordinaire, escaping twice from Newgate – was also handcuffed on his way to be executed at Tyburn in November 1724, thus dashing 'his last Hopes of Escape'. (Sheppard had secreted a penknife in his clothes, hoping to cut his bonds and seize an opportune moment to jump out of the cart and disappear into a crowd only too likely to abet his escape).[23]

In May 1733 the convicted highway robber John Davis so successfully feigned illness that 'out of Compassion they did not tie his hands fast together, as is usually done'. Lying 'like a dead Lump', Davis was drawn to the place of execution where, just as the unsuspecting Ordinary had begun the 7th verse of the 16th Psalm, he 'put his Foot to the Side of the Cart' and 'jumpt over among the crowd in the twinkling of an Eye'. With both 'Officers and Spectators … surprised and astonish'd' and some of the latter 'favouring his Escape', Davis managed to reach a nearby field before he was apprehended and, in a dishevelled and 'dismal

Condition ... hurried into the Cart'. Over the vehement protests of the Ordinary – who 'desir'd they would allow me to sing and conclude, with recommendary Prayers to God in their last Moment' – officials 'caus'd the Cart to drive off in a hurry, as soon as the Executioner could do his Duty'. Escape attempts at Tyburn and elsewhere were rare and almost invariably doomed to failure: in Bedford in 1697 a horse-thief 'called Honest John (though abusively)' jumped off the ladder that served as a scaffold and 'leapt down amongst the people' before being 'knockt down' and forced to reascend the fatal tree. Such attempts tended to be opportunistic and not particularly well thought out: in April 1725 Bryan Smith, 'an Irishman of parts so mean', as one chronicler drily noted, that he could hardly '[pass] for a rational Creature', went to Tyburn very penitent, dressed in a shroud. However 'there being many Persons to suffer' (seven men and one woman), Smith, 'observing the hurry slipp'd the Rope over his Head, and jump'd at once over the Copse of the Cart amongst the Mob'. He might have escaped 'had he been wise enough to come in his Cloaths', but his 'white dress rendering him conspicuous even at a distance', he was easily retaken by the sheriffs' officers. The Tyburn procession was flanked by a cavalcade of city officials – sheriffs, undersheriffs, sergeants, high constables and/or their deputies and assistants – many armed with pikes and not averse to using force. When, in 1726, the highwayman John Map, 23 ('a young audacious Fellow' who boasted to the Ordinary of committing 'above 200 Robberies'), succeeded in extricating himself from his halter and 'Hand-strings', vaulting from the cart 'upon the Heads of the numerous Crowd of People', he was immediately 'seiz'd again by an Officer, who wounded him with his Halbert' and delivered him still bleeding to the executioner.[24]

The halters or nooses were traditionally placed around the necks of the condemned while they were still in the Press Yard. Malefactors were loaded three to a cart; traitors, however, had to endure the added indignity of being dragged to the place of execution in sledges. Those common felons who could pay for the privilege were allowed to ride to Tyburn in a closed mourning coach. In 1750 this custom came under attack as part of a larger effort to reform execution practice, with one newspaper reporting that such invidious 'Distinction[s]' would 'not be suffer'd for the future'. This 'Favour' remained, however, 'in the Sheriffs breast': the middle-class forgers William Baker (in 1750) and Samuel Orton (1767) were permitted coaches; one was in 1763 denied to John Rice, another gentleman forger, although he was permitted to travel to Tyburn in a cart separate from the rest of the malefactors. Captain James Lowrey, hanged for murder in 1752, was obliged to go to Execution Dock in an open cart and not in the coach he had requested 'upon account he had laid so long upon a sick Bed'. Another murderer, Francis David Stirn, was told in 1760 that as his offence called for 'a more exemplary punishment than other crimes' his petition for a coach was 'not proper to be recommended to the Sheriffs'. In 1760 Earl Ferrers, convicted for the murder of his steward, rode to execution in his own landau; much was made, however, of the 'Impartiality and Justice' demonstrated by the fact that he was hanged 'at the Place appointed for the Execution of common Felons' – Tyburn – rather than beheaded on Tower Hill (the usual prerogative of peers). Ferrers was, moreover, anatomized in accordance with the Murder Act, a 1752 statute which decreed that the corpses of executed murderers be either gibbeted (hanged in chains) or delivered to the surgeons for public dissection.[25]

While visiting ministers sometimes accompanied the condemned in the cart, the Ordinary of Newgate either rode in the mourning coach of one of the more distinguished malefactors or travelled to the place of execution in a coach that was, from at least the early eighteenth century, 'appointed for [him]' by the City. Probably the most memorable image of the eighteenth-century execution, the eleventh plate in William Hogarth's 1747 *Industry and Idleness* series, in which the idle apprentice is hanged at Tyburn, paints a stark contrast between the apparently indifferent Ordinary peering out of his coach window in the distance and the Methodist minister (often assumed to be Silas Told) in the cart with the condemned Thomas Idle, earnestly exhorting him to repentance. Those whose 'Friends' could bear the expense, hired hearses or other vehicles to carry coffins to the place of execution; coffins could also be carried on the cart itself to Tyburn (another image popularized by Hogarth), although it is likely that this practice, like that of hanging the cart with mourning, or draping it with black cloth, was a relatively recent innovation, part of a larger campaign by early and mid-eighteenth-century officials to invest the Tyburn procession with more solemnity and decorum.[26]

The condemned halted briefly at St Sepulchre's, where the Bellman delivered another 'Exhortation' from the churchyard wall:

> All good People, pray heartily to God for these poor Sinners, who now are going to their Deaths; for whom this great Bell doth toll. You that are condemn'd to die, repent with lamentable Tears. Ask Mercy of the Lord for the Salvation of your own souls, thro' the Merits, Death, and Passion of Jesus Christ, who now sits at the Right-hand of God, to make Intercession for as many of you as penitently return unto him. Lord have Mercy upon you! Christ have Mercy upon you!

The last lines were repeated three times for added dramatic effect although, according to Samuel Richardson, such was the 'silly Curiosity' and 'Noise of the Officers, and the Mob' that these edifying verses were lost on the malefactors.[27] (In June 1698 the press of people was so great that part of the churchyard wall collapsed, killing one person and wounding dozens.) However, at least some of the condemned were reported as being 'dreadfully affected with the horror of their situation' upon the pronouncement of the 'admonitory Words', weeping and bowing their heads; all were obliged to take off their hats, or the executioner would do so for them. (In October 1778, one of the condemned, a Jew, refused to implicitly abandon his confession by removing his.) The great bell of St Sepulchre's would toll for the malefactors from the beginning of the procession until the time it was estimated that the awful proceedings were concluded. Significantly, the bell tolled only for 'Felons' and not for 'wicked Traytors'; at the execution of state criminals, spectators were supposed to shout and cheer triumphantly – rather than lament, as for common malefactors – as the condemned were launched into the next world.[28]

Other church bells would join the dolorous chorus as the procession made its way up Snow Hill and High Holborn towards St Giles. It was supposed to have been customary since the Middle Ages for the condemned to drink a bowl of ale at the leper hospital established by Matilda, Henry I's queen, in St Giles in the Fields. By the late seventeenth century, the condemned would stop at the Crown Inn in St Giles' Pound, near the present-day intersection of Shaftesbury and High Street, 'to enliven their drooping Hearts' with wine or spirits before continuing on to Tyburn (or elsewhere: in 1684, John Wise, condemned for burglary and murder, 'called for half a pint of Canary', a sweet white wine, while passing through St Giles on his way to be hanged near the site of his crime in Piccadilly). In 1724 Jack Sheppard's accomplice, Joseph 'Blueskin' Blake, is supposed to have 'call'd at the Griffin Tavern in Holborn, where he drank and shew'd much Insolence and ill Behaviour'. Such practices were reinforced by various gallows legends like that of the abstemious sadler of Bawtry, hanged at York 'for want of a drink'; had he stopped for one, the story goes, he would have been spared, as a reprieve arrived only minutes after he had been turned off.[29] And, indeed, reprieves for criminals who had already embarked on the execution procession were a fairly routine occurrence in the late seventeenth century, although less common thereafter.

No Tyburn custom elicited as much criticism from contemporaries – and horror from later commentators – as that of drinking on the way to execution. The Swiss traveller de Saussure, writing in 1726, was struck by the numbers of condemned who were 'so impenitent that they fill themselves full of liquor and mock at those who are repentant'. In 1725 Bernard de Mandeville complained of malefactors drinking to 'stifle their Fear' before setting off for Tyburn, only to stop 'a half a dozen times, or more' along the way to re-fortify their 'Courage'. Many of the condemned were inebriated even by the liberal standards of the eighteenth century (according to a witness in a 1733 trial, 'if a Man is capable of sitting upon his Horse, I can't think he can be said to be drunk'). Joseph Blake was, by all accounts, at the place of execution so 'disguised in Liquor' as to 'Reel and Faulter in his Speech'; in 1729 the 'Foot-Pad' Thomas Neeves 'stagger'd and was scarce able to stand' at Tyburn. When 'reprimanded' by the Ordinary for having drunk too much, 'Neeves answered, "no indeed Sir, I only took a Dram"'.

Drunkenness, an index of impenitence, hardihood and reprobation, tended to be emphasized by hostile commentators – and correspondingly downplayed or refuted by partisan accounts, not to mention the condemned themselves. Nor did all robbers drink even in the 1720s, the bacchanalian heyday of the Tyburn procession. In 1722, for instance, John Hawkins and George Simpson, two notorious highwaymen, 'appear'd in the Carts with uncommon Tokens of Repentance, scarce ever raising their Eyes from their Books ... nor tarrying to drink Quantities of Liquor as is usually done'.[30]

In 1735 the Court of Aldermen ruled that henceforth 'the Sheriffs Officers [were] not to permit the Prisoners, in their Passage from Newgate to the Place of Execution, to drink any Wine, or any other strong Liquors, on any Pretence whatsoever'. Subsequent newspaper reports emphasized that the new regulations were 'strictly observ'd', despite 'Endeavours ... to get the carts to stop, in order for the criminals to drink'. While Richardson claimed in 1741 that this 'late good Order' was ignored by officials, with malefactors 'greedily' quaffing wine, the fact that observances in the breach continued to attract disapproving notice – in July 1750, the *Gentleman's Magazine* reporting that the malefactors 'were drunk, contrary to an express order of the Court of Aldermen, against serving them with strong liquors' – may actually suggest a diminishing tolerance for such behaviour. But, as always, rules could be suspended: when in 1737 the attorney-cum-condemned robber Thomas Carr was 'offer'd a Glass of Wine in his Passage thro' Holbourn', he was told by one of the sheriff's officers that, while it was 'contrary to their Rule and Orders', as 'he was a Person of Discretion' he would 'suffer him to drink'. (Carr demonstrated his entitlement to this 'Indulgence' by refusing 'it with the calmest submission'.) In 1776 the *Public Advertiser* reported that the horses drawing the cart to Tyburn 'turned into the Swan Inn Gateway' and were only 'turned back again' with 'difficulty'. They must have been ancient horses with extraordinarily retentive memories, however: by 1763, the Ordinary of Newgate was asserting that the 'unseasonable indulgence' of drinking on the way to the gallows had 'long since [been] disused and abolished', a claim substantiated by other newspapers.[31]

The execution procession travelled from St Giles up High Street, following Oxford Street until it became Tyburn Road. Typically the streets were 'thronged with Spectators', most largely sympathetic or merely curious, although certain offenders – informers, rapists and some murderers – ran the risk of being pelted with 'Brickbats', 'Dirt, and other Things'. Such was the fate of the criminal mastermind and self-styled 'Thief-Taker General' Jonathan Wild, the model for *The Beggar's Opera*'s Peachum. Wild had for years passed as a respectable and useful citizen, earning favourable notices (and the prefix of 'Mr') from newspapers impressed with his ability to locate 'lost' and stolen items and to apprehend robbers and burglars. However, by the early 1720s, rumours were rife that the thief-taker was in fact a 'Thief-Maker' – an unscrupulous receiver who 'had [bred] up' numerous 'foster Children' (among them, 'Blueskin' Blake) 'to be thieves' and, after they had outlived their usefulness, delivered them to the gallows for the reward money. In May 1725 Wild, who had once 'rode triumphantly, with pistols before the criminals, whilst conveying to the place of execution', was a condemned felon seated in the cart with the other malefactors: enraged spectators marked his passage with 'violent Huzzas' and jeers of 'Blewskin', pelting him with stones and dirt: in Holborn his 'Head [was] broke' by a stone thrown from a window.[32]

The execution procession, passing the turnpike where Tyburn Road intersected with Tyburn Lane, would finally arrive at the fatal crossroads where the Triple Tree stood. Here, according to Saussure, 'the noise and confusion' was 'unbelievable' and, of course, the crowd thickest: in July 1669, 'there were such numbers that the Carts could not come up to the place of Execution' and the malefactors had to be 'led thither on foot'. In the late seventeenth and early eighteenth century, these numbers were typically characterized in vague terms; such as, a 'vast Multitude of Spectators'. Reports of the executions of state criminals, celebrated highwaymen, notorious murderers or genteel forgers routinely claimed, as did one account of the Jacobite lords Balmerino and Kilmarnock in 1746, that there were 'present the greatest Number of Spectators ever seen together in the Memory of Man'. Newspapers began to hazard figures in the later eighteenth century, a trend which may in itself reflect a growing public disapproval of and discomfort with the noisome excesses of the Tyburn procession: 'not less than 17,000' were supposed to have attended the hanging of the highwayman Jack Rann in 1774, the 'melancholy Proceedings' capped by an unseemly scramble on the part of 'at least 1000 People' to apprehend a pickpocket caught plying his trade (the frequency of such scenes was often invoked by reformers as evidence that public executions tended rather to brutalize and corrupt spectators than to deter criminals). In 1773, 20,000 were said to have watched Elizabeth Herring strangled and burnt for the murder of her husband, 'many of whom were much hurt, and some trodden to death in gratifying a barbarous curiosity'. In 1762, an estimated 50,000 witnessed the execution of Sarah Metyard and her daughter for the murder of a poor female apprentice, while in 1767 80,000 people, 'the major part of whom were women', were supposed to have watched that of John Williamson, for starving his wife to death.[33]

Nearby houses were rented out and stands and other impromptu structures erected to afford spectators a better view: at Execution Dock in Wapping, ships and scaffolds were on occasion so crowded that they were 'overset' or collapsed. In 1746 the deputy-lieutenant of the Tower of London granted permission to the gaolers to build 'Shedds or Scaffolding from which to see the Lords [Balmerino and Kilmarnock] beheaded'. A 'Gentlewoman that keeps the House near

Tyburn' was said to charge admission for standing room in the 1720s; various entrepreneurs rented out platforms or carts for people to stand on near the gallows. In 1750, several people were injured when such a cart was overturned; in 1752 a Tyburn carman was killed in a 'Skirmish' over his vehicle, which the perpetrators appropriated to carry off the corpses of two of the condemned. As at any other public spectacle, seating arrangements replicated social distinctions, with places on crates and carts hawked for a few pence, and good berths in the 'sort of amphitheatre' or stands erected near the Triple Tree going for as much as two shillings and sixpence in the mid-eighteenth century. 'Tyburn Gallery' or 'Mother Proctor's Pews' (supposedly named after the widow of a cow-keeper who rented out the land) had burned down at least once (in 1741). At the May 1726 execution of the notorious murderess Catherine Hayes three separate sections of the scaffolding were reported to have collapsed at different times, injuring many but failing to deter spectators who quickly 'gathered upon it again in numbers'; in August 1763, the 'loud cracking of the timber in the nearest galleries … alarmed and terrified the numerous crouds that were on and near them', and momentarily distracted the condemned from their prayers. More serious accidents were reported in December 1770, January 1776 and January 1777.[34]

Once at the place of execution, the condemned set about the serious business of preparing for death. Here the resolution of game criminals like Reeves was tested; here the most apparently indifferent or hardened criminal could suddenly succumb to terror. James White, hanged in 1723 for returning from transportation before expiry of his sentence, had behaved so badly in Newgate that the Ordinary had pronounced him 'Unqualify'd for the Reception of the Holy Sacrament'. At Tyburn, 'he seemed to be surprized and astonished, looked wildly round upon the People, and then asking the Minister who attended him, what he must now do?' (He was instructed to 'shut his Hands close' and 'cried out with great Vehemence, Lord receive my Soul'.) While state criminals and certain eminent sufferers were often allowed an hour or more for their 'private Devotions', the customary time allotted to Tyburn condemned was about fifteen minutes. The Ordinary would stand in the cart with the criminals, 'giving them Ghostly Admonitions and exhortations, praying and singing some Penitential Psalms with them and making them rehearse the Apostles Creed'.[35]

Here too, the dying malefactors were supposed to ask for pardon and in turn forgive (as they themselves hoped to be forgiven) 'all the world': fellow condemned, 'Friends', prosecutors, even former associates who had 'turned King's evidence'; in other words, testified against them in order to gain immunity for themselves. Friends, family members and other interested parties, including relatives of murder victims or of individuals previously hanged on the evidence of the condemned, crowded into the cart to say their farewells or to conduct final interviews with those malefactors who had persisted in their innocence. In April

1730, a woman 'was allow'd to come into the Cart' to tax the highwaymen Robert Drummond and Ferdinando Shrimpton ('two of the most unconcern'd and obdurate' malefactors the Ordinary had ever seen) with a robbery for which her husband had been hanged. 'They were offended and a little Surly at this Question', simply saying, when 'press'd': 'Would you have us to take upon ourselves all the Robberies that are committed in the Country?' and going off 'the Stage ... adding nothing to their former Confessions'. The street robber Thomas Neeves was more forthcoming, despite (or perhaps because of) his drunkenness: at his February 1729 execution, the father and wife of Richard Nichols, one of three men who had been hanged for robbery the previous spring on his evidence, climbed into the cart and 'earnestly enquir'd' whether Neeves' 'Deposition' against Nichols 'were the truth or not'. While Neeves had been hitherto 'inflexible' in asserting Nichols' guilt, he now burst into tears and, falling into 'a greater agony than ... ever', he 'own'd that it was not': he had never met, let alone robbed with Nichols, and had sworn against him in hopes of collecting reward money.[36]

For the most part, last interviews between friends and family members provided a satisfactory degree of what modern popular culture would term 'closure': in August 1729 the wives of Joseph Kemp and Benjamin Wileman 'went up to the Cart just before they were ty'd up, and very Lovingly and with many Tears embrac'd and took leave of [them]'. Messages were relayed and debts paid: in October 1687, John Lovewell, after failing to find his wife in the crowd, 'desired a Friend to remember his Love' to her, enjoining her also to 'take care of his Child'. Of the six men hanged for robbery on 8 August 1750 one, Thomas Crawford, 'talked some Time with a Friend' who climbed into the cart 'and took what Money he had out of his Pocket by his Direction'. Another, Benjamin Chamberlain, 'desir'd a Friend that stood by to give his Love to Betty, and to let her see him after he was dead. The rest said nothing, only [Ely] Smith called to a Man in the Crowd, and bid him adieu'. Sometimes these performances of public reconciliation were inhibited by the sheer size of the audience: at his execution in December 1729, the highwayman James Drummond (brother to Robert, mentioned above) 'was very desirous to speak to his Sister, whom he spy'd at the Place of Execution, but the Crow'd being so great that she could not come to him'.[37]

As a rule, last dying speeches were brief and generic. Some execution accounts reported that the voices of the condemned were too faint to be heard above the noise of the crowd; others claimed that certain malefactors, at least, were perfectly audible at a distance. A few, 'what with Sickness' – particularly 'gaol fever' or typhus – and 'the Apprehension of Death ... were so terrified' as to be unable 'to stand up, or speak at the Place of Execution'. In February 1740, officers were 'oblig'd to carry' the burglar Thomas Motte 'on their Backs to the Cart'. In March 1752, the robber William Girdler 'was so weak' at Tyburn 'that he could not stand, and almost hanged himself, by his Legs sinking under him, before the Cart drew away'; Anne Baker, a 19-year-old prostitute condemned for pickpocketing, 'fainted, and was only supported by the cord' at her March 1764 execution. More wretched still was Mary Harris, alias Murphey, who 'was but 27 Years, though so disguised by Dress and Constitution, she look'd rather to be near 50'. Harris and her common-law husband (with whom she had committed the robbery for which both were hanged) were both 'miserably Poor' and 'very much addicted to drink': Mary 'was almost dead before she turn'd off, trembling and shaking to a great Degree, very naked, and in a most miserable condition'.[38]

Some of the condemned confessed their crimes; a significant minority, like John Hartly, persisted in their innocence. Most remained silent or simply acquiesced in stock statements warning spectators to beware of Sabbath-breaking and the company of loose women as the first steps down the slippery slope to the gallows. A few, like Sir John Johnston, hanged in 1690 for abducting an heiress, were suspected to have 'prolonged' their 'Speech and Devotions at the place of Execution, in hopes of a Reprieve'. At his 1724 execution, the highwayman Lumley Davis 'endeavour'd as much as he could to linger away the Time, spoke to the Ordinary to spin out the Prayers, and to the Executioner to forbear doing his Office as long as it was possible'.[39] But there was a small but conspicuous proportion of the condemned – both common and state criminals – who seemed genuinely eager to seize the forum provided by the gallows. Such malefactors were, like Thomas Reeves, whose execution was described in the opening pages, typically willing or even eager to assume responsibility for their misdeeds, to exonerate spouses and parents of blame, and to maintain the innocence of associates and fellow sufferers. It was, as we shall see, characteristic of many bold and cheerful – or 'game'– criminals to assert their refusal to impeach comrades and their willingness, even eagerness, to die (however disingenuous such claims may have been). It was also common for such malefactors to maintain their innocence as to the 'Fact' for which they were condemned, yet to freely acknowledge a catalogue of other misdeeds for which (they declared) they richly deserved to suffer.

At Tyburn, the condemned died of strangulation after the cart upon which they stood was drawn away. The 'drop' – in which the malefactor ideally died from a broken neck – was not introduced until the gallows were moved to the Debtor's Door at Newgate after the abolition of the Tyburn procession in 1783. (Earl Ferrers was an exception: at his 1760 execution a special scaffold was set up with a drop which, however, failed to sink 'so low as was designed' and had to be pressed down by officials.) In other parts of the country, malefactors were 'turned off' by means of a ladder or other platform kicked away from underneath them. It was customary for the hangman to pull a handkerchief or a cap over the eyes of the condemned: in March 1735 a novice executioner botched the job, leaving several of the faces of the condemned exposed to the view of spectators. As we shall see, it was characteristic of many game highwaymen and street robbers, as well as various state criminals who died maintaining the justice of the cause for which they suffered, to pull down their own handkerchiefs or caps, as well as to ostentatiously arrange the noose around their necks. The Duke of Monmouth made an even stronger statement by declaring that he 'would make use of no cap, or other circumstance'. And we are told that 'it is certain that never man died with more resolution and less signs of fear, or the least disorder' than Captain Christopher Vratz, hanged in 1682 for murder: he 'would not cover his face as the rest did', continuing 'undaunted' to the end, 'often looking up to Heaven, with a cheerfulness in his countenance'. When Vratz and his fellow sufferers 'were asked when they would give the signal for their being turned off, they answered that they were ready, and that the Cart might be driven away when it pleased the Sheriff to order it'.[40]

It was customary for traitors or other eminent offenders to give a signal for the cart to be drawn away, the ladder to be turned off, or for the axe to fall. (The executions of common criminals tended to be less elaborate; at any rate a signal was impracticable when many people were hanged at the same time.) Most famous in the later lore of Tyburn was the dropping of a handkerchief: the late eighteenth-century wit and avid execution-goer George Selwyn was supposed to have dropped his own to communicate to his dentist his readiness to have 'a tooth drawn'. Pious ejaculations (typically some variant of 'Lord Jesus receive my Spirit') generally served as 'Watch-words' in the seventeenth and early eighteenth century, and usually constituted the last words – and thus, the effective signal – of common criminals hanged at Tyburn. Some state criminals, like Sir William Parkins and Sir John Friend, nervously arranged elaborate signals, such as knocking; others made a point of 'refusing to give any Sign', communicating their unshakeable composure (and hence, spiritual fitness) by telling the hangman to 'Draw away when you please'. Lord Russell's famously botched 1683 execution, in which it took two or even '3 butcherly strokes' to dispatch him, was attributed to his resolution to die with 'more Gallantry than Discretion': Russell could not 'be perswaded to give any signa[l] or pull his Cap over his eyes' and thus, it was claimed, instinctively flinched as the axe descended.[41]

It was customary not only to forgive the hangman before he performed his office but to tip him. As the clothes of the deceased were traditionally the perquisite of the executioner, malefactors like the highwayman Colonel James Turner, whose 'Friends were desirous of all his Clothes', compensated the hangman by giving him '20s. and 6d. to drink; and about 15s. to the Searjeants and Yeomen ... to see his Body and Clothes delivered to one Mrs. Smith'. The Marquess of Pallioti, executed in 1718 for the murder of his servant, 'bought his Cloaths from the Hangman for three Guineas, and gave him a Guinea more to execute his Office well'. Spectators were treated to a 'very undecent Spectacle' in May 1731 when Francis Woodmarsh, a former army officer who had always insisted on dressing like a 'Gentleman', was 'stript naked to the Skin' (even if 'naked' in eighteenth-century parlance probably did not exclude a shift or undergarment). Those of modest means occasionally begged the Ordinary's 'Offices' to ensure they would not be thus 'stripp'd after an indecent and savage Manner at the tree', asking that their clothes be delivered to the hangman after their corpses had been cut down. In July 1750, when three women were hanged at Tyburn (an unusual circumstance which itself excited remark), their bodies 'were delivered to their friends ... after a promise made to return their clothes to the executioner, as being his perquisite'.

One account of the execution of the Fifth Monarchist John James in 1661 for delivering a treasonable sermon claimed that the 'Hangman, came to demand Money, that he might be favourable to him at his Death'; that is, mitigate the severity of the sentence of hanging, drawing, quartering and disembowelling. The executioner initially asked for twenty pounds and finally compounded for five, threatening that if he were not paid 'he would torture [James] exceedingly'. Although James refused, crying poverty, in the end 'the Sheriff and Hangman were so civil ... as to suffer him to be dead before he was cut down'. According to the letter of the law, male traitors were supposed to be cut down still living from the gallows, upon which they were disembowelled, their privies cut off, and finally they were quartered and decapitated. By the late seventeenth century, however, it had become customary for the executioner to wait until condemned traitors were dead or unconscious before dismembering them; by the eighteenth century, the additional penalty of quartering was often waived.[42]

Female traitors were burned at the stake (generally after being garrotted or hanged) rather than drawn and quartered; a dubious privilege accorded them, Blackstone explains, because 'the decency due to their sex forbids the exposing and publicly mangling their bodies'. At her 1684 execution for coining, Alice Pattison left nothing to chance, 'intreating the Executioner, who took a Crown out of her Pocket, to strangle her before the Fire came at her'. Although women convicted of high or petty treason (the murder of a husband or master) were by the later seventeenth century almost always strangled so as to be unconscious before being burned, there were, however, some exceptions: the German traveller William Schellinks reported seeing a woman 'who had stabbed her husband to death with a tobacco pipe' burned alive in 1662. Another woman executed in Leicester in 1684 for the murder of her mother, husband and two others was not permitted to 'be hanged first', but was reportedly 'soon choaked' with smoke and the rope that fastened her. There was also the famous case of Catherine Hayes, burned alive in 1726 for the murder of her husband.[43]

Malefactors could petition the hangman to 'tye [them] up as to Die easie'; for instance, positioning the knot under the left ear (in 1750, Benjamin Chamberlain called out to the executioner to halt proceedings after the cart had drawn away because he had not yet moved 'the Noose from behind his Neck under the left Ear'). The highwayman Jack Rann is supposed to have given 'Jack Ketch' (a generic name for the hangman) 'half a guinea to do his business well' and a servant 'a quarter of a guinea to pull him by the legs while hanging'. Foreign observers noted with fascination the English custom of 'Friends or Relations' pulling at the legs of the condemned (or sometimes striking the chest) 'to dispatch [them] as soon as possible'. At his 1695 execution, the highwayman William Hancock addressed the spectators: 'If there be any one here that knows me, let me desire them to pull me by the Legs when I am turn'd off … Pray God bless you all I hope you'll pray for me'. Sometimes well-meaning bystanders would pull so hard on the legs of the condemned as to break the rope; at the execution of the highwayman John Everett in 1730, the hangman himself broke the cord when 'to put him the sooner out of his pain [he] jumped upon the Shoulders'. Mishaps involving the cart were occasionally reported – in 1698, for instance, the wheels of the cart stuck in a rut, stretching the rope so that 'two of the [nine] Prisoners were hang'd, the rest having sav'd themselves by their hands till the Cart was drawn forwards and placed right'. (None volunteered, as did Thomas Reeves in 1722, to leap off the side.) Particular attention was drawn to the 'Struggles and Convulsions' of those sufferers who died with more difficulty than their fellows – explained either by their being insufficiently 'compos'd' or by the fact that they were 'slender and light-built', like the 23-year-old Jack Sheppard, who at Tyburn 'behav'd very gravely' and 'spoke very little' but was supposed to have died 'with much Difficulty, and with uncommon Pity from all the Spectators'. One newspaper reported it as 'remarkable' that Abraham Ward, executed for murder in 1752, 'was full ten minutes in visible agitation, after being turned off, which is four times more than is ordinary'.[44]

Although the condemned were supposed to hang for an hour, they were often cut down sooner – in the case of Jack Sheppard, after only fifteen minutes. Sheppard had apparently 'desired some of his Acquaintance' to deliver him down from the gallows 'as soon as possible, put it into a warm Bed, and try to let [his] Blood' in hopes that thus 'they might bring him to Life again'. While Sheppard was rumoured to still show signs of life as he was hurried into a waiting coach, he was however 'kill'd with Kindness' when the crowd, suspecting he was being taken to the surgeons to be dissected, 'bruised his Body in a most shameful Manner at Tyburn, in pulling it to and fro, in endeavouring to rescue it'. A handful of malefactors had in fact survived hanging: Anne Greene, hanged in Oxford in 1650 for infanticide, was found breathing in her coffin (despite the fact that at her execution friends had pulled at her legs and thumped at her breast 'insomuch that the Under-Sheriffe fearing lest they should break the rope, forbad them to doe so any longer'). Greene was subsequently pardoned by officials who 'readily apprehended the hand of God in her preservation'; similarly, William Duell, 17, condemned for participating in a horrific gang-rape and murder, was granted a transportation pardon after surviving his 1740 hanging, reviving just as he was about to be anatomized in Surgeon's Hall. Such pardons were not automatic: Thomas Savage, an apprentice who had robbed his master and murdered a maidservant, survived his 1668 hanging and was put 'in a warm bed' on the advice of an apothecary; however, Savage was soon apprehended by the sheriffs' officers and hanged again, this time 'till he was quite dead'. In 1736, after 'a woman desired a Sight of [the] Body' of the turnpike rioter Thomas Reynolds, the coffin was opened to reveal the latter breathing and stirring. Reynolds 'vomited about three Pints of Blood', was bled and given brandy 'but by reason of cold and other mismanagements' – he had been carried in a wet coffin – 'he at last expired'. That same year, two malefactors executed in Bristol survived their hanging, although one died shortly afterwards. But the most famous example was that Tyburn legend, John 'Half-Hanged Smith', who, when a very last-minute reprieve came down for him, was cut down still living seven minutes into his December 1704 hanging for burglary. But 'as he had been but half-hanged, so it appeared he was but half [reformed]': Smith was on numerous subsequent occasions apprehended and charged with burglary, reputedly dying in Newgate in 1722.[45]

The bodies of those of the condemned who had made funeral arrangements (hiring hearses, buying coffins) were delivered to 'Friends' after they were cut down. Charity provided for some: in 1758, 'a Subscription was made at the Gallows of 27s. 6d. to interr' the body of Jeremiah Bailey, a condemned robber who 'declared his Innocence to the last moment of his life'; in 1778, the Ordinary and fellow malefactors contributed £3 towards a coffin for a poor soldier. Unclaimed bodies were buried in an anonymous grave (a 'Hole near the Gallows' 'against Hide-Park Gate'); or, as was increasingly common from the early eighteenth century, carried away by surgeons to be anatomized. The College of Physicians was often provided with warrants signed by the Sheriffs promising them one or more cadavers: this was the fate of Thomas Neeves, upon whose perjured testimony the innocent Nichols had been hanged – proof, apparently, that 'Divine Vengeance pursued him'. Such was the popular antipathy to dissection that Vincent Davis, hanged in 1725 for murdering his wife, reportedly attempted to 'provoke [the court] to hang him in Chains'; that is, to gibbet his body after execution – 'by which means' he hoped to 'escape the Mangling of the Surgeons Knives, which to him seemed ten Thousand times worse than Death itself'.[46]

The crowd, many of whom shared this fear and loathing of dissection – there was a popular notion that post-mortem dismemberment could interfere with the resurrection of the body on Judgement Day – frequently clashed with the surgeons, sometimes '[tearing] away ... Bodies' and carrying them 'off in Triumph'.

Riots were not uncommon, particularly when celebrated criminals were hanged: following Jack Sheppard's execution, the Riot Act had to be read to disperse the crowd. After the execution of the famous highwayman Richard (Dick) Turpin at York in 1739, 'the Mob having got Scent that his Body was stole away to be anatomiz'd', themselves 'brought it away almost naked', buried it, and filled the grave with lime. Relatives even held graveyard vigils in order to ensure that the recently interred condemned would not be taken from their coffins and delivered to the surgeons. The crowd did not, however, always behave in the fashion that social historians would prefer: newspapers delighted in reporting instances in which the 'giddy ... Mobile' (i.e., *mobile vulgus*, or 'mob') snatched the condemned from the hands of the surgeons, only to '[drag] their naked Bodies about' and even to 'hawk' them for sale: rescuing 'the Body from being anatomis'd one Hour, and the next [selling] it themselves for the same Purpose'. After the 1752 Murder Act guaranteed surgeons the bodies of executed murderers, riots became less frequent although, as we shall see, as late as the 1760s, execution crowds still occasionally carried off the bodies of those whom they believed had been unjustly condemned in order to lay them on the doorsteps of prosecutors.[47]

TYBURN FAIR: MYTHOLOGY AND HISTORIOGRAPHY

The noisome scene immortalized by Hogarth – complete with last-dying speech sellers and hawkers of gin, drunk and indifferent spectators, a remote and ineffectual Ordinary, with the figure of the condemned eclipsed and all but forgotten by the bestial crowd – has come to be accepted as 'a faithful picture of one of the customs of the past age'. Indeed, whether it elicits self-congratulatory scorn or prurient fascination (or both), the image of the early modern hanging day as a kind of debased spectator sport has become a byword for the brutality and 'grossness' of the eighteenth century: virtually any novel or movie set in this period is bound to feature a raucous execution scene. Historians and literary critics have also been fascinated by execution: not as a mob scene, however, but as a theatre of punishment in which the actions and words of spectators and participants can be read as a dramaturgical exposition and reproduction of power relations. While scholars influenced by the work of Michel Foucault have viewed the execution as a site in which social control is maintained and legitimated, others read the public hanging as a 'carnivalesque' occasion, or at least a contested and unstable one, in which the normative message intended by the authorities is reappropriated and inverted by an irreverent crowd.[48] For Marxist historians, Tyburn is the locus of class conflict: in the words of Peter Linebaugh, the 'conflict of the Powerful and Propertied against the Weak and the Poor'.[49]

The tendency on the part of scholars to characterize execution as either a normative and scripted performance on the one hand, or a potentially subversive and unstable one on the other, has translated into a disproportionate emphasis on either penitent offenders or game and seemingly defiant ones. Those who have focused on the former have generally assumed that the condemned expressed a kind of 'internalized obedience' that legitimated the values of the society whose norms they had transgressed: by dying penitently, the malefactor was ritually reintegrated into the body politic.[50] In contrast, the game street robber or highwayman has often been seen as representative of a larger plebeian resistance to normative religious doctrine and even nascent class consciousness. Certainly, contemporary critics devoted inordinate attention to what they viewed as the vulgar ideal of dying game (i.e., with the 'pluck' of the gamecock; failure to do so was supposed to have been characterized as 'dying dunghill').[51] Foreign observers often expressed their admiration of the 'extraordinary Courage' of 'the English', who 'laugh at the Delicacy of other Nations, who make it such a mighty matter to be hang'd'. Many of those, however, who marvelled at the 'sang froid' and 'the indifference verging on heroism' of the English were in fact making oblique criticisms of their own culture (for instance, the Catholic Church and its supposed tendency to '[sap] courage'). And even foreign commentators acknowledged that if some malefactors dressed 'gayly' and went with 'an Air of Indifference' to execution, 'many others [went] slovenly enough, and with very dismal Phizzes' (expressions).[52]

A range of behaviour was in fact typical of most executions and presumably it was, at least in part, such variety that drew spectators. The earliest execution sheets routinely distinguished between those who died 'very penitent, confessing their sins, and begged of the Lord for pardon' and those who 'seemed not at all concerned, though they had not many minutes to live'. At one December 1694 execution of seventeen men and one woman at Tyburn (the woman and seven of the men for coining offences, two men for burglary and eight for highway robbery), the condemned were at the gallows 'all exhorted by the Ordinary, to consider of the great Work they were now about, being upon the Brink of Death and Eternity', and reminded that 'there were many Persons in great Expectations to see the Signs of their Penitency'. We are told that they 'unanimously' expressed their sorrow for having embarked on a course of sin which, by 'provoking Almighty God, had brought them to so shameful a Death, otherwise they mightt [sic] have dy'd in their Beds like other Men, desiring all the Spectators to take Warning by their untimely end'. Several of the coiners bemoaned their fate: 'there is no Mercy to be found. The King is resolv'd to hang all the Clippers'. 'Never fear Boys,' interjected one of their fellows, 'we are not hang'd for breaking Houses, but for clipping the King's Coin, I do not question but we shall have Mercy'. While one of his fellows reproached him, saying now was the time to 'call upon God' for

'Mercy in Heaven', another expressed his confidence that 'God will forgive us'. Still another coiner, holding a Bible in his hands, lectured spectators on the dangers of Sabbath-breaking, drunkenness and company-keeping. As for the highwaymen, the one who had first seemed most 'undaunted' now broke down upon realizing that the reprieve he had expected was not forthcoming, trembling and piteously imploring mercy from God. One of his stauncher comrades reproved him: 'What are you afraid of? Ne'er fear, God will have Mercy upon us ... let us have some Prayers, and a merry Psalm; I don't fear Death at all. Gentlemen, I have been a great Highway man, but hope God will have Mercy upon me.' This sentiment was echoed by another robber who 'smil'd often' and requested, as did most of the others, the 'Prayers' of all 'good Folks'.[53]

As this last brief example suggests, there was a considerable range even within the conventionally penitent speech, in which confidence of salvation and cheerfulness could easily shade into the kind of presumption and levity condemned by contemporary moralists. Dying well – the script, as it were – was both a common point of reference and bone of contention: just as whether regicides or Jacobites died martyrs or traitors depended on the account, the same criminal might be characterized as 'decent' by the clergyman who had attended him, and 'hardened' by the prison chaplain whom he had rebuffed. But, as the example of Thomas Reeves suggests, few even of the most ostentatiously bold and cheerful street robbers or highwaymen were as irreverent or irreligious as either contemporary caricature or later antiquarian stereotype would have us believe.

Much of this stereotype of the game criminal owes its expression to the radical tailor Francis Place (1771–1854) who, drawing freely from contemporary attacks on the execution procession by Henry Fielding and Bernard de Mandeville, has to a large extent supplied a text to Hogarth's visual representation of Tyburn. Antiquarians and subsequent historians of eighteenth-century execution have relied heavily on Place's disapproving but salacious recollections of late eighteenth-century street ballads and 'bawdy songs ... commemorating the acts and deeds of highwaymen, and other thieves', as well as his clippings and scathing commentary on earlier criminal literature. Place was scandalized by the 'grossness' and 'debauchery' of the eighteenth century generally and the Tyburn procession in particular: the promiscuous mixing of the sexes in Newgate, drinking on the way to the gallows, visiting on the cart, the stripping of and riots over the corpses of the condemned, and the 'mummery and barbarism' of execution rituals ranging from the Bellman's exhortations to popular superstitions regarding the supposed curative properties of the hangman's noose and of the bodies of the condemned (i.e., 'credulous women' 'touching' afflicted parts of their bodies with the hands of hanged malefactors). Spectators crowded to 'Tyburn Fair' or the 'Hanging Match', Place claimed, 'not to take a lesson of morality' but 'to enjoy the prospect of a fellow dying game'; while 'the criminal knowing how the vile mob felt, endeavoured to put on a false bravery to meet their expectations', and thus 'set an example' which acted as an 'excitement' rather than a deterrent to crime. In short, 'Tyburn fair was no solemn procession' (a shot at Boswell, who shared Johnson's nostalgia for the Tyburn procession): 'it was just the contrary, it was a low lived, blackguard merry-making'.[54]

There is much about early modern English sensibilities – or what we would see as the lack thereof – to horrify the modern reader. Notices in late seventeenth-century newspapers routinely advertised such performances as the 'Monstrous Cock Eater' who, for 'but 2d.' admission, 'Any Person' could witness eating a live rooster at a Southwark tavern, complete 'with the Feathers, Bones and Garbage'. Bloodsports such as cockfighting, bull, badger and bear-baiting were openly frequented by all classes of people, while one of London's regular tourist attractions was visiting mentally ill inmates at Bedlam (Bethlehem Hospital). The curious could also obtain admission to view the condemned in Newgate or even the corpses of the malefactors dissected at Surgeon's Hall. The rotting cadavers of gibbeted highwaymen – 'hanging in chains' was an aggravated penalty reserved for offences viewed as particularly dangerous, such as robbery accompanied with murder – were a common sight on the roads leading out of London, while the heads and quarters of executed traitors were posted on London Bridge, the Tower and other prominent locations in the City. After the execution of two Jacobites in 1746, Horace Walpole reported passing under 'the new heads at Temple Bar, where people make a trade of letting spying-glasses at a halfpenny a look'. Such heads were still mouldering on pikes in the late eighteenth century when, as Place noted with disgust, one was blown down into the street by the wind and picked up by a passer-by.[55]

While, as I have noted, the full punishment for treason was generally mitigated (offenders hanged until they were dead before being mutilated, and their remains often returned to family members), there was clearly a different sensibility about dead bodies in the late seventeenth and early eighteenth centuries. In 1660, when Cromwell, Bradshaw and Ireton were exhumed for posthumous execution as traitors, 'the people crowded very much', paying 'sixpence a peece' to see Cromwell in his vault. One late seventeenth-century murder sheet described – in graphic detail – a heavily pregnant woman being terribly mauled and killed by five mastiffs, reporting that 'the Deplorable Spectacle' (her remains) were 'Expos'd to the sight of hundreds that came to see it'. In 1728, the corpses of three street robbers executed three days earlier at Tyburn lay 'in State at an Alehouse all the Day, where vast Numbers of People resorted to see them'. In 1761, the mother of a woman apparently murdered by being thrown out of a window was reported to have exhibited the body to passers-by 'for penny gratuities'. When in 1718, the body of a woman executed for murder was brought by the crowd to her father's house, 'he at first refused to take her in, but at length consenting;

and letting People come to see her at a Penny apiece, got near 8*l*. thereby, part of which was apply'd toward burying her'. Such gruesome exhibitions could serve practical purposes: the bodies of murder victims and other anonymous dead were routinely advertised in the papers and exhibited at public houses in order to be identified. In 1719 the body of a man believed to have been drowned in the Thames 'was put into Lambeth Church-Yard, for his Friends to own him'. In March 1726, after Catherine Hayes and her two male accomplices murdered and dismembered her husband, John Hayes, the latter's head was found bobbing in the Thames near Westminster. Parish officers 'caus'd the Head to be cleaned ... and the Hair to be combed, and then the Head to be set upon a Post in public View in St Margaret's-Church-Yard'. The head 'drew a prodigious Number of People', including a woman whose husband had gone missing the day before its discovery, before being placed in a 'Glass of Spirits' for its better preservation. Catherine Hayes eventually fell under suspicion after one observer identified the head as her husband's.[56]

It might be more accurate to describe early modern sensibilities as different rather than deficient, or better still to say that the different conditions of their lives desensitized them to some things to which we are today sensitive (and perhaps vice versa). Thus, the seventeenth-century diarist John Evelyn, who had refused to 'be a Spectator' at the baiting of 'a very gallant horse' tortured 'under pretence that the horse had killed a man, which was false', clearly felt remorse and shame in admitting that he had later been 'forc'd to accompanie some friends to a Bear-garden' and to witness various 'butcherly Sports, or rather barbarous cruelties'. (He nonetheless could not resist recording which animals 'did exceedingly well' and which 'beat' others.) Certainly, the sight of death, the so-called 'King of Terrors', had the power to inspire fear, shock, pity and disgust in early modern spectators. According to an early seventeenth-century Italian visitor, execution at Tyburn was 'really barbarous and strikes those who witness it with horror'. Narcissus Luttrell describes one execution in which one of the spectators, a friend of the condemned man, 'just as the cap was pulling over his eyes, and the cart drawing away, fell down dead therein at the sight of it and by no means could be brought to life again'. And even the staunch royalist Samuel Pepys was dismayed at the news that Cromwell's body would be hanged, drawn and quartered: 'Which (methinks) doth trouble me, that a man of so great courage as he was should have that dishonour, though otherwise he might deserve it enough'.[57]

It is, however, important to bear in mind that seventeenth- and early eighteenth-century men and women shared neither the modern liberal abhorrence of the death penalty or the more generalized post-Enlightenment conviction that human life is precious. For while some contemporaries, such as Quakers, objected to capital punishment as an abrogation of God's prerogative and a violation of biblical law, it was not until the later eighteenth century that a sustained humanitarian opposition to the capital code began to emerge. According to early modern religious orthodoxy, life was not sacred, but forfeit: death was the debt that all men and women owed to nature as a result of original sin. Our own modern discomfort with execution and our preoccupation with capital punishment as a current political issue has not only tended to lead scholars into presentist arguments and assumptions, but has also obscured the centrality of the gallows in early modern political culture. The late seventeenth- and early eighteenth-century execution should not be viewed as a somehow pathological event, of interest only to a debased urban mob and a few crank devotees of the macabre: rather, it was at the very heart of everyday contemporary eschatological discourse.

This book, then, aims to provide a cultural history of the seventeenth- and eighteenth-century gallows and the larger belief system underpinning it. This study is not intended merely as a corrective to older triumphalist 'Whig' narratives condemning the barbarism of the unreformed English capital code, however. Nor is it my aim to pursue a relativist agenda, avoiding moral judgements. On the contrary, history should not only constitute a dialogue between the present and the past (or why would it be of any relevance?) but also one in which larger questions about morality and social justice are addressed. But good history begins with an attempt to understand the past on its own terms and within its own frame of reference. To this end, the religious discourse which framed gallows accounts must be viewed not merely as 'superstructure' or 'false consciousness', normative ideology or a societal coping mechanism, but as a common language within which values were situated, legitimated and even contested.

While people from all walks of life attended executions – including such 'amateurs' as James Boswell and George Selwyn, the Duke of Montague and other 'distinguished members' of his 'coterie' – the composition of the Tyburn crowd was largely plebeian, and almost undoubtedly more so in the later eighteenth than in the late seventeenth century.[58] The audience for printed accounts of the behaviour and last dying words of condemned malefactors was, on the other hand, primarily (if not exclusively) composed of those from the middle ranks of society. Such accounts were, by definition, partisan and scripted documents, mediated by the conventions of the genre and the expectations of their audience. Yet the gallows constituted a forum so public that goings-on there were unlikely to be grossly misrepresented, while the market for last dying speeches was so brisk that obvious forgeries would not pass unchallenged. Indeed, as we have seen in the case of the five Jesuits, the condemned could on occasion successfully appropriate the scaffold as his or her own forum, and by his or her behaviour make a strong impression even upon the most hostile of audiences.

Early modern men and women were clearly willing to read into the carriage of the individual sufferer the righteousness or iniquity of the cause writ large. While

John Bunyan was languishing in a Bedford prison in 1660 – his only reading material reputedly the Bible and Foxe's *Book of Martyrs* – he was tormented, not by the fear that he would be obliged to suffer for his faith, but that he should, while making 'a scrabling shift to clamber up the Ladder ... either with quaking or other symptoms of faintings, give occasion to the enemy to reproach the way of God and his People'. (Not unlike the game criminal, who famously leapt from the scaffold before being turned off, Bunyan finally resolved to 'leap off the Ladder even Blindfold into Eternity', confident that Christ would 'catch' him.) According to royal martyrologists, Charles I had on the morning of his execution (a cold January day) requested an extra shirt, to avoid any 'Imputation' that he shook from 'Fear' rather than the 'sharp[ness] of the Season'. And at his execution, the regicide Thomas Harrison was said to have defended himself against the 'scoffing' of spectators by assuring them that his legs shook not because he was afraid – God had 'carryed [him] above the fear of death' – but 'by reason of much blood' he had 'lost in the Wars'.[59]

The countenance of the accused was widely believed to constitute a sacred sign, given the popular belief that God 'assisted' the righteous under physical or mental duress with divine 'encouragement' and 'support'. This conviction helps makes sense of the early modern English trial, where the defendant was neither entitled to defence counsel nor informed as to the exact nature of the charges or the evidence against him or her. But what we would view as grave legal disabilities, contemporaries would have seen as 'truth-promoting', in that it was believed that the countenance of someone who had either had no time to dissemble, or whose predicament was solemn and so shocking as to preclude any attempt at artifice, was in itself the best index of guilt or innocence. In her spiritual autobiography, Agnes Beaumont wrote of how she was acquitted by a coroner's jury of murdering her father in 1674 on the basis of her 'Chearful Countenance as I stood before them all. They said I did not look like one that was guilty'. Contemporaries made similar judgements about the condemned, especially in those moments – the reading of the verdict or sentence and execution itself – so awesome as to expose any artificially assumed composure or cheerfulness as 'false courage'.[60]

At his 1729 execution for the murder of a fellow servant, James Cluff stubbornly persisted in his innocence, despite overwhelming evidence to the contrary. Nonetheless, contemporary observers were swayed by the fact that he had 'behaved with a Calmness very rare to be met with' while awaiting execution, and 'did not change Countenance ... when he was told the Day was fix'd for his Execution, as it is ordinarily observed the other Malefactors do'. Nor did Cluff 'lose any thing of that chearful Sedateness' on his way to Tyburn, where he stopped in a public house to speak to his former master, the principal prosecution witness, vowing, 'with a great deal of Composure' that 'I am not Guilty of [the murder], as I am to appear before my Great Judge in a few Moments, to answer for all my past Sins'. It was noted as particularly significant that 'his Countenance in no ways chang'd, not even to the very last; when the Executioner came to pull the Cap over his Face'.[61]

Needless to say, observers did not always agree on how to read the signs: according to one account, the fact that the condemned murderess Mary Edmondson, hanged in 1759, seemed not 'in the least affected' at her trial was attributed to her being 'harden'd' rather than innocent. Moreover it was noted that after the verdict was read, Edmondson 'turn'd hastily for the Bar, in a seeming Passion and Confusion'. When she came 'to the fatal tree' – the gallows – 'her Countenance seemed to change a little', until, with a visible effort, she 'recovered herself'. In contrast, a more sympathetic account reported that 'It is remarkable, that during the whole Time of her Trial she never changed her Countenance, or seem'd in the least affected before that awful Court of Justice.' The Methodist Silas Told, who attended Edmondson at her execution, was for his part convinced by her solemn declarations of being 'as ignorant of the crime for which she was going to suffer, as at the day of her birth'. Edmondson, like many others who were executed for crimes of which they claimed to be innocent, expressed both a nominal willingness to die and implied that by doing so she had expiated all of her sins: 'I do not lay anything to the charge of my Maker ... although I am clear of this murder, yet I have sinned against Him in many grievous instances; but I bless God, He hath forgiven me all my sins'.[62]

For someone who was habitually timid, dying bravely was counted as more definitive proof of innocence than for those who were 'naturally' hardy. Gilbert Burnet described Sir Henry Vane as 'naturally a very fearful man', yet noted that he met death with 'a resolution that surprised all who knew how little of that was natural to him'. Indeed, 'some instances' of his good spirits 'were very extraordinary, though they cannot be mentioned with decency'. (Vane had, the night before his execution, fathered a child with 'his lady'.) And even one of the Marquis of Argyle's worst enemies supposedly admitted that he was sure the former had gone to heaven, as Argyle, whom 'he knew ... was naturally a very great coward ... had died with great resolution' – clear evidence that he had been the recipient of 'supernatural assistance'.[63]

The involuntary evidence of the body was valued perhaps above all. At his execution the Duke of Monmouth attempted to convince the sheriff's assistant that he was able to die 'like a Lamb', not because of any 'natural Courage' of his own (for he was 'as fearful as other men') but because of 'something within [him]' which convinced him he was going 'to God'. The fact that such noted preachers as John Donne and John Bunyan inveighed against this 'opinion of the ignorant' – that is, that the elect died peacefully, without apparent pain or struggle (Bunyan has his reprobate Mr Badman die 'as quietly as a Lamb') – only testifies to its popular currency and prevalence. Sometimes spectators were obliged to rely on the claims of the condemned as to whether or not they had been granted divine dispensation from the pain of the 'first death' as well as the 'second' (eternal damnation). When the convicted murderer Gill Smith's irons were knocked off preliminary to execution, 'he undauntedly said to the Keeper, 'That the Pain was the worst of all he should feel': and upon a Reply from one present, that he believ'd he was mistaken, he answer'd, 'he was sure he was not', with an unbecoming Warmth'. On other occasions, the signs were there for any that chose to see them: Silas Told reported that immediately after 'being turned off', Mary Edmondson's 'body dropped against my right shoulder, nor did she once struggle or move, but she was as still as if she had hung three hours'. As for Sir Henry Vane, according to one seasoned execution-goer, 'his Countenance did not in the least change' even after he was decapitated; 'whereas the Heads of all he had before seen, did some way or other move after severing, which argued some Reluctancy and Unwillingness to that Parting-blow; the Head of this Sufferer lay perfectly still, immediately upon the Separation'.[64]

No less than those traitors or heretics (or martyrs) who went bravely to the block on Tower Hill or to the fires of Smithfield, men and women who went to Tyburn exuding both courage and cheerfulness made a statement that was profoundly political, regardless of whether they spoke, or tried to speak, against the government or the courts that had sentenced them. In an early modern context, to speak to one's spiritual state was to make a statement about guilt or innocence – a statement that could, if accompanied with the right signs, convincingly testify to the justice of the cause in which an individual died. I will discuss these signs of guilt or innocence at more length in the following chapters, as well as the extent to which this cultural shorthand of righteousness, as it were, could and did resonate in the words and gestures of ordinary malefactors. But first we will turn to the question of audience and authority: specifically, how seventeenth- and early eighteenth-century men and women read and rendered comprehensible the last dying speeches and execution performances of both state and common criminals.

2

From the Gallows to Grub Street: Last Dying Speeches and Criminal 'Lives'

Blessed be his Name who hath made me not only willing, but thankful for his honouring me to lay down the Life he gave for his Name, in which were every Hair in this Head and Beard of mine a Life, I could joyfully sacrifice them for it, as I do this … It was therefore in Defence of this Party, and their just Rights and Privileges, that I took Arms – *But here the Officers told him that anything relating to his Civil Affairs, or Religious Preparations, he might be allow'd to speak but they could not allow him to talk Treason; and thereupon order'd the Drums to beat: But on his promising to say no more on that Point, they were ordered again to stop.*

Speech of Richard Rumbold, Rye House plotter (1685)[1]

[it is customary for those] who are Condemn'd by the Laws of their Country … to give some Account of the course of Life that they have led, and make a relation of the Crimes they have been Guilty of. I have further observed that when some have departed Silent, and willing that the World should take no Notice of them, there are those who have made it their Business for the sake of filling a sheet of Paper to say something either True or False concerning those Persons of whom they have had no knowledge, and of whose Affairs they have been altogether Ignorant. [Therefore] I have thought it proper to spare an hour or two in letting the World know the most material Circumstances and Accidents of my Life from my own Pen.

Confession of condemned forger John Alexander Emerton (1733)[2]

In *Colonel Jack*, Daniel Defoe's 1722 pseudo-autobiography of a pickpocket and soldier of fortune turned prosperous plantation-owner, the narrator expresses his surprise that the 'Stories' of 'private mean Person[s]' like himself had become 'so much the Fashion in England'.[3] For while sensational tales of murder, monstrous births and the deeds and misdeeds of eminent citizens had long captivated the reading public, the late seventeenth and early eighteenth century witnessed a dramatic and unprecedented proliferation of the last dying speeches and 'lives', not only of traitors and other notable malefactors, but of property offenders whose crimes were as episodic and petty as their social origins were humble or obscure. Just as the perception that crime is dangerously on the rise is common to most societies in most periods, an interest in and a preoccupation with criminals seems universal. Yet in late seventeenth- and early eighteenth-century England, criminal accounts occupied a more central place in popular consciousness, and were produced on a scale which beggars comparison with any period before or since. Beginning in the mid-1670s, there was a veritable explosion of printed matter addressed to a wide audience devoted to the lives, trials and executions of criminals of all types and degrees.

This seemingly insatiable public appetite for last dying confessions and criminal biographies was fed both by regular serial publications reporting on the trials at the Old Bailey and the behaviour and last dying speeches of the malefactors executed at Tyburn and elsewhere, and by other pamphlets and collections of criminal trials, confessions and 'lives'. The appeal of such literature can be explained, at least in part, in terms of its role as a purveyor of news to a public eager for reasonably factual, up-to-date information: the newspaper, although beginning to emerge in an early form in the mid-seventeenth century, did not come into its own until the 1690s in London (and considerably later elsewhere). Criminal accounts could also function as a forum in which anxieties about crime, punishment, sin, salvation, the workings of providence and social and moral transgression generally could be expressed and negotiated.[4] According to Lincoln Faller, criminal biographies constituted a 'kind of cultural practice', a way to '[gloss] or to make sense of' the 'real': that is, to 'palliate' contemporary fears about the incidence of violent crimes and to assuage or to displace societal guilt in regard to the execution of property offenders.[5] Others have focused on the seventeenth- and eighteenth-century criminal pamphlet as a precursor to realist fiction and the novel and, by extension, evidence of a burgeoning 'public sphere', the rise of the middle class, a new preoccupation with individualism and the origins of modern subjectivity.[6] On a more prosaic level, this fascination can be explained simply in terms of a natural human curiosity for all things strange or titillating. Yet in the early modern period it was widely believed that all men and women were inherently sinful, and thus at least potentially criminal as well. The late seventeenth- and early eighteenth-century robber served as a metaphor for the frailty and inherent depravity of human nature – in essence, a sort of 'Everyman' (or 'Everywoman'), whose offences were different not in kind but only in degree from those of the rest of mankind.

Once dismissed as ephemera 'catering to the vulgar instincts of the vulgar many' and thus 'fall[ing] below the dignified historian's line', late seventeenth- and early eighteenth-century execution literature has only recently attracted serious and sustained academic interest.[7] Increasingly, too, it has become apparent that such publications had a much wider audience than originally believed.[8] For despite the complaints of contemporaries and the tendency of later, more fastidious, commentators to characterize seventeenth- and eighteenth-century criminal accounts as 'catchpenny sheets' whose 'crudity and grotesqueness ... limited their sale to the most vulgar', the principal (if not the sole) audience for such literature appears to have been middling or even genteel, rather than working-class.[9] Such is certainly suggested by the condemned murderer John Mausgridge's refusal to give an account of his life to the Ordinary, or chaplain, of Newgate: 'he had not a Mind to be the Sport and Ridicule of vain, idle Fellows in Coffee-Houses'.[10] Criminal pamphlets and broadsides were advertised in, as well as published in, the same format (and sold for about the same price) as newspapers, sermons, serial instalments of novels and other mainstream publications, and by the same printers and booksellers. When the Thames froze over during the cold winter of 1683–4 and a printing press was set up in the market or 'Continual faire' held on the river ice, George Croom, one of the principal publishers of last dying speeches, cornered the market on printing out tickets for 'People & Ladys' who took a 'fansy to have their names Printed & the day & yeare set down, when printed on the Thames'.[11] John Applebee published the Ordinary's *Account* for almost twenty-five years (from 1720 to 1744, after the mid-1730s assuming a very active editorial role) as well as numerous other criminal pamphlets – many of them attributed to Defoe – but is perhaps best known for his eponymous periodical, *Applebee's Original Weekly Journal*.[12] Another prominent printer, Charles Rivington, published both Captain Charles Johnson's picaresque and irreverent *General History of the Pyrates* in 1724 and Samuel Richardson's *Pamela* in 1740. Criminal literature, then, was 'popular' only insofar as its readership was socially inclusive – although, over the course of the second half of the eighteenth century, elite and middling demand for such material would fall off rapidly, for reasons which will be explored in later chapters.

ORIGINS OF PRINTED LAST DYING SPEECHES

While it had long been customary for condemned persons to declare their guilt or innocence at the gallows and to issue a short statement warning young men and women to beware of embarking on the slippery slope to crime, the regular practice of publishing confessions and last dying speeches became common only in the second half of the seventeenth century. This coincided not only with the rise of the newspaper but with a wave of political executions, beginning with the execution of the regicides (those who had signed the death warrant of Charles I) in 1660 and continuing with those implicated in the various treason trials and plots of the 1670s and 1680s. According to an account of the behaviour and dying speech of one of the first of the innocent men executed for the Popish Plot: 'although at other times bare Curiosity, and the Itch which is Epidemical to Humane Nature of hearing News, be sufficient to justifie Accounts ... of the last and dying exits of Malefactors', in this 'Particular the considerations thereof are of so Publick and Universal a concern, that there is no person whose Interest is not concerned therein'. While authorities from Tudor times had staged such executions as propaganda and ideological exercises, they could backfire badly, with popular execration turning to sympathy, as we have seen in the case of the five Jesuits who had died bravely and cheerfully attesting to their innocence. As one pamphleteer complained in 1679, at the height of the Popish Plot hysteria, ''tis the nature of the *many-headed-beast* [i.e., the crowd] to be suspitious, calumnious, querulous mad to have folks hanged, and as mad to pitty them when they hear them lying at the Gallows'.[13]

The right both to speak and to hear the truth in the form of public confessions of innocence or guilt was, by the late seventeenth century, popularly (if not entirely accurately) viewed as one of the inalienable privileges of the free-born Englishman. When the regicide Thomas Scot was repeatedly interrupted by the sheriff in the midst of a speech attacking 'Popery', he supposedly retorted that ''tis hard that an English man hath not liberty to speak'; adding, 'That it is a very mean and bad Cause that wilt not bear the words of a dying-man: it is not ordinarily denied to people in this condition'. When his fellow regicide, John Cooke, loudly testified to dying in the 'Cause of God and Christ', he too was silenced, but not before complaining that 'It hath not been the Manner of English men to insult over a dying man'. Indeed, any attempt to silence scaffold speeches inevitably conjured up images of the Marian martyrs – and, by extension, the illegitimacy of the regime under which they suffered. According to Protestant hagiography, officials guaranteed the silence of the martyrs by threatening to cut out their tongues if they attempted to make speeches. Although the latter acquiesced, anxious to preserve their tongues to praise God, speeches were of course unnecessary: their joyous prayers and their saintly carriage provided more than sufficient testimony of their innocence.[14]

Gallows censorship persisted into the late seventeenth century. Political prisoners were warned, as was the regicide Colonel Barkstead in 1662, that they could 'say any thing between God and [themselves], but nothing in justification of the Act'. In 1684, Thomas Armstrong was told at Tyburn that he had 'leave to say what you please, and shall not be interrupted unless you upbraid the Government'. Such malefactors were instructed to 'confine themselves to speak to God' rather than to make 'excuses for the crime'. And while late seventeenth-century traitors, unlike the Marian martyrs, did not have tipstaffs thrust into their mouths if they spoke out of turn, the words of those who persisted in seditious expressions were liable to be drowned out by trumpets or drums ('a new and very indecent practice', according to Gilbert Burnet). At his 1662 execution, Sir Henry Vane was repeatedly interrupted by the Lieutenant of the Tower, who 'said that he rail'd against the Judges, and that it was a Lye'. Vane retorted: 'God will judge between me and you in this Matter. I speak but Matter of Fact, and cannot you bear that?' When Vane continued to question the legality of his sentence, 'trumpets were order'd to sound or murre in his Face ... to hinder his being heard'. Although we are told that 'the Prisoner was very patient and composed under all these Injuries', Vane was by no means shy about advertising his Christian forbearance: 'my Usage from Man is no harder than [Christ's] ... and all that will live his Life this Day, must expect hard dealings from the worldly Spirit'. All the while the sheriff was attempting 'to snatch the Paper out of Sir Henry's Hand'; Vane 'now and then reading part of it' before finally tearing the speech into pieces and handing the shreds 'to a Friend behind him' who in turn was 'forc'd to deliver it to the Sheriff'. Not content with this, officials rifled Vane's pockets for copies.[15]

Such overt attempts at censorship 'bred great Confusion and Dissatisfaction to the Spectators, seeing a Prisoner so strangely handled in his dying Words', and it is no accident that authorities, at least in London, soon thereafter abandoned the use of trumpets or drums.[16] Such measures were deeply resented and viewed as a violation of the much-vaunted English freedom of speech. Not only did the English enjoy a degree of liberty unheard of in continental Europe (frequently remarked upon with admiration by foreign visitors), but such gallows censorship was in any case ineffectual. For as far as last dying speeches were concerned, the medium – that is, the bearing and countenance of the condemned – *was* the message. Vane demonstrated such 'undaunted couradge together with that meeke and Christian frame of spirit ... on the scaffold' as to '[astonish] all the spectatours'. Even less partisan accounts conceded that Vane 'died with so much composedness, that it was generally thought that the government lost more than it had gained by his death'.[17]

Not only traitors but common criminals who made 'bitter Reflections' about courts or prosecutors were sometimes reprimanded or silenced at the gallows by officials or attending ministers. When, in 1713, two of the condemned 'were going to speak to the People in their own Vindication', the Ordinary intervened, telling them it was 'more proper for them to apply themselves to GOD, for the Pardon of their Sins, and Salvation of their Souls'. These men were typical of most malefactors thus upbraided in that they supposedly 'comply'd' willingly enough with 'this Advice ... earnestly praying to God'. For the majority of even those criminals who claimed to be wrongly condemned were also keen to demonstrate their spiritual fitness to die – like the highwayman Joseph Leath, whose gallows 'Reflections, which are not worth repeating' were prefaced by his insistence that 'he was a true Penitent, and died in Peace with all the World'. Nor indeed should we underestimate the degree to which prayers and expressions of piety could in themselves be subversive. Sometimes this was overt, as in the case of the regicide Thomas Scot: he was, as we have seen, repeatedly interrupted and silenced during his dying speech, but nonetheless able to pray loudly to God praising Him for allowing him to die 'in a Cause not to be repented of. I say, in a Cause not to be repented of'. But for common criminals as well as for traitors – and this is a theme to which I will return in subsequent chapters – the most effective critique of justice was simply dying well: calmly, bravely, and without passion or rancour.[18]

The publication of printed last dying speeches was considered necessary to ensure that the public was informed of the true spiritual state and political testament of the condemned: to some degree, as I have suggested, the two were synonymous. Moreover, the mere act of writing such papers could undermine the moral credibility of authorities by advertising the possibility that they might attempt to silence malefactors at the gallows. Richard Langhorn, executed for the Popish Plot in 1679, claimed to have composed a written speech attesting to his 'innocence and loyalty' because he was 'under some doubt' whether he would be permitted to speak, or whether his voice would be heard over the 'noise of the people'. He was, however, forced to deliver this paper to the sheriff before embarking for Tyburn, 'repeat[ing] there only so much of it as he could remember'. When he was, at the gallows, told to 'shorten' his 'business', Langhorn responded by referring the spectators to his paper and requesting the sheriff to have it printed. The sheriff claimed that Langhorn had already published a confession (this Langhorn denied); then, that such a speech was 'not fit to be printed'; but in the end went so far as to promise to 'do [Langhorn] no wrong'. There were rare periods – for instance, during or shortly after the Jacobite rebellions – in which strict censorship was maintained: in 1746, a group of condemned Jacobites simply flung a number of papers 'containing treasonable Expressions ... among the Mob'. At other times, officials themselves requested that the condemned read out their papers 'publiquely', in order that false speeches could not be published in their stead.[19]

Many of the condemned claimed that they preferred delivering a written speech to speaking publicly at the gallows. Lord Russell told the sheriff that he had left behind a 'Paper' because he 'expected the Noise would be such, that I could not be very well heard: I was never fond of much speaking, much less now' (he nonetheless proceeded to deliver a short speech). Others, like the condemned murderer Robert Haynes, hanged in 1727, 'intended to have spoke to the People, but finding himself too weak, he referred' instead to a 'Paper' he had delivered to John Applebee, attesting both to his innocence and his forgiveness of prosecutors. According to the robber Thomas Taverner, executed in 1734, he had left a paper not only because it was 'customary' but because he had been 'disabled' by illness 'from speaking so audibly as is necessary'; finally, he thought it best to 'have the last Moments of my Life the more at Liberty, to recommend my immortal Part to the Hands of a blessed Redeemer'. This last reason was politically as well as personally compelling in the context of a world in which a good death could testify to the truth of the cause for which one died. In the words of John Friend, a non-juror executed for treason in 1696, upon presenting his written speech to the sheriff: 'Sir, Here is a Paper, I desire it to be Printed: For I came here to Dye, and not to make a Speech: but to dye, and resign my self to God ...' Nor should we underestimate the popular conviction that agitation or discomfiture in one's final moments could jeopardize one's immortal soul: John Salmon, hanged in Surrey in 1739 for robbery, supposedly delivered a written speech to a printer so that he would not 'spend' his 'last Minutes' at the place of execution 'in fruitless Declarations to a confused Multitude, when the Neglect or Misapplication of one Moment might endanger my Soul's Happiness to all Eternity'.[20]

Reading out a speech at the place of execution could also function as a means of authenticating a written paper that would later be published. As one attack on Russell's dying speech noted sarcastically, it was divided 'into Two Parts; the Speech & the Paper, & every body knows the Substance of the Speech to be Right. And then the Speech Vouches for the Truth, and Authority, of the Paper'. At the 1696 execution of three Jacobites, the executioner took a 'Paper' from the 'Bosom' of Charles Cranburne; the latter, however 'coming forward, desir'd it again' and, after it was returned, read from it to the spectators, although he was frequently interrupted by the sheriff, with whom he entered into arguments which the crowd could not hear. Similarly, in 1689, the condemned murderer Greenway Feild 'produced' a 'Paper, publickly reading it with an audible Voice, then gave it to Mr Ordinary, and desired it might be printed and published'. Even illiterate malefactors could adopt such tactics: at his 1725 execution for robbery in the course of a riot, Charles Towers, 'in a very loud and exclaiming Voice ... asserted his Innocence to the Spectators'. He admitted to having attempted to rescue a friend from a bailiff, but denied that he or any of his accomplices had either committed robbery or blackened their faces in disguise – an offence made capital under the Waltham Black Act of 1723 targeting traditionally anonymous 'social crimes' such as rioting or poaching – 'unless the dirty Condition he was commonly in, could be so term'd'. He then asked for permission to have a speech which he had dictated to an 'Acquaintance, for he could not write himself ... now read before all these People, for 'tis not against any Court'. This request was granted although, as the Ordinary noted disapprovingly, the speech, far from containing any 'Discovery' or 'Confession', only reiterated Towers' innocence. The speech claimed 'That as he was in other matters a great Sinner (and had for other things Deserved Death) he underwent the Punishment with Patience' and in hopes of obtaining mercy from God. 'He also inveigh'd against the Bailiffs, but declared that he died in charity with all Mankind.' The paper was later offered for publication to the printer of the Ordinary's *Account*, John Applebee, who declined it on the grounds that it had already been made public; however, this did not prevent the publication by a rival printer of a paper signed by Towers and witnessed by two condemned malefactors, an account condemned by Applebee as 'an Imposition on the Town'.[21]

It was not only customary for state criminals to hand over at the gallows any papers to the sheriffs, who were then supposed to make them public (many common criminals delivered speeches to the Ordinary or other ministers or printers), but to take precautions against having their speeches suppressed or forgeries published in their place. Lord Russell gave a copy of his last dying speech to the sheriffs to publish, but consigned the original and three more copies to his wife's safekeeping. Algernon Sidney, another Rye House plotter beheaded the same year, told the sheriffs that 'he intended not to make any Speech', but handed them a paper containing 'what he thought fit to leave behind him', and delivered what appeared to be a copy to a 'Gentleman' standing by. The Jacobite Christopher Layer arranged for several copies of his speech to be made before his 1723 execution, taking elaborate precautions not to implicate the friends to whom he had entrusted the sealed (and unread) copies. With common criminals, rituals tended to be less elaborate: in 1698, John Johnson, alias Denny, 'call'd for Pen and Ink' at Tyburn, and 'writ about four Lines on his Knee' as he was 'sitting in the Cart', delivering the paper to a friend before tearing 'another Paper to pieces with his Teeth'. And, in 1681, the minister who attended Edward Fitz-Harys asked permission to keep one of the latter's letters to his wife 'to compare hands with his Confession, if there should be occasion'.[22]

It is unclear how audible such speeches may have been, particularly when large numbers were hanged. The Ordinary frequently acknowledged that individual words or prayers were faint or indistinct or, as in one 1709 execution, 'utter'd so fast, that they were not all of them intelligible ... but, I hope God heard them'. However, there are many reports of malefactors speaking 'sufficiently loud' to be heard by spectators, while the latter were on numerous occasions clearly attentive: at the execution of Sir John Johnston in 1690 for abducting an heiress, 'hee made a strenuose speech at the Galows' which 'proved so insinuating to the foolish Mob as to draw teares from their eyes insomuch ... that a little prompting would almost have prevayled with them for a rescue'. Increase Mather's 1690 collection of the dying words of 'Remarkable Penitents' executed 'at Tyburn and elsewhere, for these last Thirty Years' assumed that these were 'such as are fresh in the minds of a great number of People, of the greater part of which we have been Eye and Ear witnesses'. In any case, the gestures and bearing of the condemned could be discerned even if his or her words were lost (we will examine the importance of this kind of gallows theatre in more detail in later chapters). And for those who did not attend executions, details of the dying speeches and behaviour of malefactors were not far to hand: 20,000 copies of Russell's 1683 speech were supposedly printed, presumably reaching a far wider audience.[23]

Such accounts were in fact rarely suppressed, even before the lapse of the

Licensing Act in 1695 put an end to pre-publication censorship. Not only were there so many printing presses and booksellers in London (not to mention street-sellers and ballad-singers) that prosecuting every objectionable speech was impracticable, but there were other constraints: authorities could not press too hard against what was widely considered to be a sacred national prerogative. This was especially the case when their own moral credibility was shaky – as in London from 1682 to 1688, when the City's charter was revoked, and officials were appointed by the Crown rather than elected by civic bodies such as the Court of Aldermen and Common Council. But there were periods, even after the so-called Glorious Revolution of 1688/9, when printing seditious material could be a matter of life and death: the printer William Anderton was executed in 1693, for instance, for publishing Jacobite propaganda. Significantly, however, while Anderton was repeatedly silenced by the Ordinary of Newgate during a bitter gallows diatribe against the government, not only was a partisan account of his trial and execution printed shortly thereafter, but also a paper which Anderton had intended to read out at Tyburn 'but being frequently interrupted by the Ordinary' had delivered to the sheriffs 'to publish or dispose of it as they should think fit, seeing a dying Man was not suffered to speak'.[24]

In 1725, Dryden Leach, after printing an account of a convicted murderer which called the justice of his sentence into question, was called to the Old Bailey 'to answer for this Offence' but, upon making a 'most humble submission', escaped 'only with a Reprimand'. By the eighteenth century, it was enough for most editors and printers of criminal lives and speeches to take the simple precaution of deleting libellous, seditious or otherwise actionable material, striking out all but the first and last letters of names, or replacing offending words or letters in words with asterisks (Lord Lovat's seditious but heavily edited speech was a famous case in point). Comparatively little was left to the imagination: in a last dying speech prepared by the convicted robber William Wreathcocke, the latter affirmed his innocence and prayed that God would give the prosecutor, judge and jury 'a due Sense of their Sins' and that they would live long to repent. Several other phrases apparently even less 'proper to be inserted' were replaced with asterisks. In his 1738 dying speech, Gill Smith claimed to be as 'innocent … as the new born Babe' of the murder of his wife, but consoled himself with the thought that he was 'going before a more just Judge than I was before here' and, while we are told that 'the remaining Part of the Sentence contains too gross a Reflection on the Justice of the Court' to be published, there was nothing subtle about Smith's assurance that he at least would 'enjoy eternal Happiness'. And while the Ordinary often suppressed or briefly glossed over those speeches or confessions that he considered uncharitable, or which complained overly of injustices or other 'Hardships', criminals of sufficient notoriety seldom had difficulty finding other publishers, as we shall see. Those of sufficient means could also have speeches or other accounts printed at their own expense. In 1719 Edward Bird, an officer executed for killing a man in a brothel dispute, showed the disapproving Ordinary a 'Draught of a Paper which he said he had prepar'd by the help of a Friend, and which he intended to publish', which 'insinuate[d] he had not Justice done him at his Trial'. Bird ignored the Ordinary's protests and sent the paper to the press.[25]

Not only was the market for such accounts so brisk that forgeries were unlikely to pass unchallenged, but there was a surprising degree of consistency even between hostile and sympathetic descriptions of last dying words and behaviour. This has also been noted by a recent scholar of martyrdom in early modern Europe, who has gone so far as to claim that – post-structuralist rejections of objective truth notwithstanding – execution accounts can be used 'with a high degree of confidence'.[26] This is not to say that last dying speeches and confessions were unique or original personal expressions. Not only did such statements typically conform to one of several familiar scripts, but most contemporaries, wary after the Civil War and Interregnum of anything smacking of enthusiasm or personal revelation, would have regarded any departure from the formula with suspicion. After all, given that the confession of sins was like any other 'set solemn constant Prayers unto God', it was 'very impudent, and too presumptuous to trust to your own *extempore* expressions, and boldly say only what at present comes into your mind; for this is to be *as one of them that tempt the Lord*'. Yet it does not follow that because last dying speeches were formulaic, they were meaningless. When Lord Russell was awaiting execution, he solicited the advice of his friend and spiritual advisor Gilbert Burnet in composing his speech, as he had 'not been accustomed to draw such papers'. Burnet obliged, writing up 'a scheme of the heads fit to be spoken to, and of the order in which they should be laid', much as he would have written the outline for a sermon. Russell supposedly laboured for three days fleshing out a larger speech from this template. This example seems to suggest that the condemned could, within the boundaries of convention, exercise some choice in terms of expression – much in the same way we may choose one of a variety of standardized greeting cards to express a range of sentiments.[27]

Most contemporaries agreed that overt forgeries were rare, as the condemned 'seldom or never gives a Paper, at the Place of Execution, to the Sheriff, but he leaves other Copies in the Hands of Friends, to be compar'd with what shall be publish'd', and who should 'soon give publick Notice' of 'any Interpolations, Additions, or Abridgment in the Prints'. However, accusations that speeches had been dictated or written by other hands persisted, especially in those politically volatile instances in which state criminals had died with visible cheerfulness, composure and charity – this last was critical, as forgiving one's enemies was the touchstone or *sine qua non* of the good Christian death – while leaving papers solemnly asserting their innocence. Those who attempted to discredit those involved in the Rye House or so-called 'Protestant Plot' could not, however, resort to the conventional, if dubious, attacks on Catholic truth claims (mental reservations, papal dispensations, absolutions for taking false oaths, etc.). Thus, it was necessary to demonstrate that someone other than Russell had masterminded both 'the Speech he made & Paper he gave the Sherif, declaring his Innocence … [which] wrought effects of much pitty, & various discourses on the plot &c'. Suspicion naturally fell on Burnet, who, although later released, was questioned by the King on the grounds that he was the true author of 'that wicked paper that bears the title of Lord Russell's speech'.[28]

But now let us move away from traitors (or Catholic and Whig martyrs), from Lord William Russell and Dr Burnet, the future Bishop of Salisbury, into a less elevated sphere of life, for interest in the 'lives' and confessions of common criminals – murderers, robbers and other property offenders – overlapped with, and seemed to have followed from, a demand for the last dying speeches of traitors and other eminent seventeenth-century offenders. Both were published by the same printers in similar formats and presumably for similar audiences, with publications such as the Ordinary of Newgate's *Account* explicitly bridging the gap, in that they reported on last dying words and confessions of Jesuits, Whigs and Jacobites executed at Tyburn, as well as those of the more obscure malefactors who suffered there. How much editorial control, then, did common criminals exercise over their own last dying words – which were, in theory, supposed to be printed after they were dead? How many malefactors were sufficiently literate to write or even to effectively dictate their own 'lives'?

LITERACY IN EARLY MODERN ENGLAND

In his 1749 novel *Tom Jones*, Henry Fielding told the following story to 'illustrate' the 'pretty deep … observation' that 'very artful men sometimes miscarry by fancying others wiser, or in other words, greater knaves than they really are':

> Three countrymen were pursuing a Wiltshire thief through Brentford. The simplest of them seeing the Wiltshire House written under a sign, advised his companions to enter it, for there most probably they would find their countryman. The second, who was wiser, laughed at this simplicity; but the third, who was wiser still, answered, 'Let us go in, however, for he may think we should not suspect him of going amongst his own countrymen'. They accordingly went in and searched the house, and by that means missed overtaking the thief, who was, at that time, but a little way before them; and who, as they all knew, but had never once reflected, could not read.[29]

Literacy rates in early modern England have proved nearly as elusive a quarry as Fielding's Wiltshire thief. This is owing partly to the paucity of concrete evidence and the difficulty of interpreting the data that do exist – mainly, signatures on marriage registers. Some scholars ('optimists') have assumed that more people could read than could, or would, sign their names; others ('pessimists'), have argued that signatures accurately represent or even overstate the proportion of those who can be considered literate.[30] It is, however, generally accepted that more men were literate than women; that more people in towns, particularly in London, could read than in rural areas; and that there was a positive correlation between literacy and wealth and social rank. A recent study of literate and oral culture in early modern England has estimated that 'by 1700 it may reasonably be assumed that … at least half the adult population could read print'.[31]

The Ordinary of Newgate's *Account* suggests that most condemned malefactors had received some schooling, however rudimentary and brief in duration, many from the charity schools established in the late seventeenth century by the Society for Promoting Christian Knowledge. A 1735 newspaper report claimed that 21,399 poor children had been educated in the 132 charity schools within the Bills of Mortality (the inner-city parishes).[32] However, contemporary estimates of literacy tended not only to be impressionistic, but shaped by different criteria than those of modern scholars. The Swiss visitor Henri Misson claimed in 1698 that 'at present there is hardly the meanest Peasant in England but what can read'. Yet he was referring to the reading test to qualify for benefit of clergy, a means by which capital punishments had traditionally been mitigated to branding on the thumb (this loophole had by the eighteenth century closed for most serious crimes, although manslaughter, bigamy and some property offences remained clergyable). The reading test (abolished in 1706) consisted only of reciting – or memorizing – the so-called 'Neck Verse', Psalm 51:1: 'Have mercy upon me, O God, according to thy lovingkindness: according unto the multitude of thy tender mercies blot out my transgressions'. Moreover, as Misson himself added, the Ordinary of Newgate, who administered the test, simply prompted those malefactors who had paid him a fee.[33] In fact, most contemporaries – the Ordinary not least – complained of the endemic illiteracy of prisoners. As late as the early nineteenth century, Elizabeth Fry estimated that of the female criminals in Newgate, 'about one third are unable to read at all – and another third can read a very little'.[34]

The Ordinary of Newgate frequently remarked with dismay upon those of the condemned who, like the housebreaker Thomas Hunter hanged in 1704 ('a young Man, but an old Offender'), were 'most ignorant' and 'could neither read, nor write' nor knew 'any thing in Religion; no, not so much as the Creed, or the Lord's Prayer, or any Prayer at all'. This was a common refrain, and illustrates the degree to which literacy was defined by the Ordinary and other ministers, not as the capacity to read books or broadsides, but rather as the ability to follow along and to make responses in prayer time. In this context, 'reading' meant praying. In

May 1721, the Ordinary Thomas Purney was clearly sceptical of the condemned malefactors' insistence that, with the exception of one 'young Man come lately from the Country', 'they could all read'. Purney 'requir'd them to repeat the Psalms and the Responses over frequently to themselves ... That they might be able to read them tolerably true and right in the chappel' and exhorted them to 'recover at least so much of what they once were taught, as to be able to read the Holy Scriptures when alone'.[35]

The 1742 *Prisoner's Director* reminded those of the condemned who 'read best' that they 'ought in Duty to your Fellow-Prisoners' – that is 'such of them as are grosly [sic] ignorant and cannot read' – 'to read often to them ... Psalms and Chapters from the Bible' and 'other good Books of Devotion'. And, indeed, there is frequent mention in the Ordinary's *Account* and similar publications of literate prisoners (including debtors) who 'proved very useful' to the condemned, spending 'whole Nights in reading &c.' to them. In 1720 the highwayman Robert Jackson, after expressing a pious (or politic) interest in one of the Ordinary's own draft publications on the sacrament, was 'very diligent in reading and explaining it to those who could not read, in the Condemn'd Hold'. In August 1725, the burglar Thomas Woolridge 'happened to be the only one amongst the Criminals that could read' and 'with great diligence applied himself, to supply that Deficiency in his Fellow-Prisoners'. One of these, the housebreaker John Price, 'endeavoured to make up for ... his incapacity of Reading' by 'attending constantly at Chappel and ... listening attentively at Sermon', and 'lost very little out of his Memory of what he heard there'. The traditional eighteenth-century working-class education, after all, consisted of learning the Bible 'by rote'. And in the tradition of some of Foxe's more humble martyrs, there was the occasional malefactor with a 'Gift' for memorization who managed, like Samuel Badham, hanged in 1740 for the murder of his common-law wife, to pass himself off as a 'rare Scholar', able to 'talk Scripture ... at every Word', despite the fact he 'could not read a Chapter'.[36]

To a large degree, literacy was defined in terms of an active and public participation in a larger religious culture. Conversely, illiteracy was seen both as a function of an irreligious life and an idle or obstinate temper, specifically as an inability or unwillingness to submit to the discipline of the chapel or the charity school. James Baker, alias 'Stick in the Mud', executed in 1733 for robbery and burglary, was born of 'mean Parents, who could not give him Education, and who himself was of such bad inclinations, that he would not go to publick Schools'. The parents of John Stephens, a robber executed in 1746, however, 'would have given him some education, but he hated the sight of a school, went only one quarter of a year to it, and could never attain the knowledge of his letters so as to be able to read'. The poacher William Gates, alias Vulcan, was both illiterate and 'grossly ignorant of Religion ... not for any neglect of his Parents or Relations, but because of his own wicked and obstinate Temper when a Boy' and 'unwillingness to be instructed'. Similarly, the shoplifter William Bourn or Burn, had 'honest Parents' and was in 'his younger Years ... put to school, but was obstinate and would not learn'. The robber William Newman, hanged in 1751, 'was put to School, and never would attend to learn his Book; so that by his own Fault he was illiterate'. Literacy, then – like crime itself – was a choice. It was, moreover, a moral faculty that must be exercised or it would be lost: James Campbell, hanged in 1725 for robbery, claimed that he had 'by his own Care and Industry' learned a little 'of God and Jesus Christ' but 'by Drinking and idle Diversions, had almost worn out the Remembrance of it'. As for Mary White (or 'Mary Cut and Come Again'), executed for robbery in 1745, what 'little learning' she had received from her stint at a charity school was 'forgot ... almost as soon as she had learned it'. Interestingly however, White worked as a 'ballad singer ... when she had nothing worse to do'.[37]

Some of the condemned were patently unable to write, or even to effectively dictate, their own 'lives' or confessions. When the accused murderer Daniel Blake was brought before the magistrate John Fielding (half-brother to the novelist) in 1763, he offered to write a confession. The court clerk, William Marsden, recounted giving Blake pen and paper. 'He put the Letter *I*, and, addressing himself to me, said, how do you spell *Murder?*' While Marsden was 'shocked', feeling 'it was an improper Thing for me to Dictate', the Earl of Sandwich, standing nearby, had no such scruples, and 'told him how to spell it; then he wrote the rest ... [i.e.,] *I murder'd the Man*. Sir John Fielding said, "this is not enough; *I murder'd the Man*; what Man?"' Yet other condemned malefactors were literate or even learned: genteel murderers, forgers and the occasional gentleman highwayman. Some robbers made very practical use of print media, sending letters to victims offering to return stolen items of sentimental value (for a fee), and reading the newspapers to see if anyone they had robbed had, in turn, put notices in newspapers offering to buy back stolen goods with no questions asked. Horace Walpole, after being robbed at gunpoint (and indeed, shot at) by the so-called 'gentleman highwayman' James Maclaine in November 1749, advertised a reward of twenty guineas for the return of his watch and seals. Maclaine sent him a long letter 'compounded of threats and apologies', offering to sell back the items at double the cost, and naming the Tyburn gallows as a meeting place (a rather macabre touch, especially as Maclaine would be hanged there in less than a year's time). Upon Walpole declining both the 'rendezvous' and the terms, Maclaine eventually returned the items for the original asking price. Henry Cook, a highwayman hanged in 1741, claimed to have made 'a fixed Rule' of dining in post-houses 'for the Benefit of the News-Papers', which he regularly scanned to see if the stolen horse he was riding had been advertised as missing: if so, he would make haste 'to robb, and exchange my Nagg with the first Man I mett, and should like his'.[38]

Recent scholarship has warned us against making hard and fast distinctions, not only between popular or elite culture, but between 'the different media' of 'speech, script and print'. Oral and literate traditions were not overlapping, but symbiotic, with print borrowing from, and reinforcing, the spoken word and vice versa. Not only did those who could read share their knowledge with those who could not, but many printed accounts were read and sung aloud in the streets (even, apparently, by illiterate ballad singers like 'Mary Cut and Come Again').[39] One early Ordinary's *Account* was prefaced with the notice that 'this Sheet is make publick, as a Seamark to all that read or hear it, that they may avoid those fatal Rocks of sin, on which these unhappy persons lamentably Shipwrackt'.[40] In short, not only was literacy contingent, a question of degree rather than an absolute advantage (or handicap), but even those who were wholly illiterate could find other entries into the world of print. For, as we shall see, the market for last dying confessions and criminal 'lives', particularly at its height in the first third of the eighteenth century, was so competitive – and relatively undiscriminating – as to permit and even to facilitate a certain freedom of expression on the part of the criminal about to be hanged.

THE MARKET FOR CRIMINAL 'LIVES' AND CONFESSIONS

The public interest in criminal lives could be a double-edged sword, as the robber and burglar Martin Bellamy would discover. In February 1728, while Bellamy was in Clerkenwell New Prison awaiting trial, he was approached by a 'certain understraping News Monger' pretending to be 'employ'd' by the Prime Minister Robert Walpole 'for the detection of Street-Robbers', who claimed to offer him immunity from prosecution and a handsome reward in exchange for a 'Particular Confession' of his crimes and the names of his accomplices. Bellamy, taken in by the reporter's 'natural Front of Assurance', delivered a fulsome confession of 'about twenty Burglaries and Street Robberies', along with the names of ten accomplices. It was not an implausible story, as there had been a recent royal proclamation advertising rewards of £100 for the successful prosecution of robbers (in addition to an existing parliamentary reward of £40 per offender). Indeed Bellamy had several days earlier 'entered … into a Treaty with a certain Justice of the Peace' to exchange a 'full Discovery' for a pardon, and evidently word of these negotiations had reached 'the Ears' of the said 'News Monger'. But Bellamy was rudely disabused of any hopes of either reward or pardon (or acquittal, for that matter) when, the following morning, 'the Publick were entertain'd in the Daily Journal' with an 'imperfect Recital of several Robberies and Burglaries' committed by Bellamy and his accomplices – by which means the latter, named in the paper, 'had timely Notice to make their Escapes'. Authorities claimed to believe that Bellamy had in fact operated in concert with the reporter, deliberately leaking the names of his accomplices to the press 'as a Warning for them' to abscond. Thus, 'instead of being admitted as an Evidence against them' the hapless Bellamy 'was order'd to take his Tryal, for some of those very Facts he had Confess'd'. The issue of the trial was hardly in doubt: Bellamy was convicted, condemned to death and hanged at Tyburn on 27 March 1728. What is perhaps more interesting is the fact that he dictated an account of his crimes – and of his being duped by the 'worthless Wretch' of a reporter who, he claimed, was 'the immediate Cause of my Death' – to the printer John Applebee. Bellamy was also reported as delivering a conventionally penitent speech to spectators at the place of execution.[41]

Among the various writers and publishers of criminal lives, confessions and dying speeches, it seems to have been not merely commonplace, but common practice, to characterize rival publications as 'catch-penny accounts ... calculated for, and compiled by, the sons of Grubstreet, who daily palm their spurious works upon the public for authentic'. Grub Street (now Milton Street, near the Barbican), located near the disreputable neighbourhood of Moorfields, was a traditional haunt of professional or 'hack' writers (from 'hackney', meaning anything – usually a carriage, however – let for hire). By the eighteenth century, 'Grub Street' had become a generic term of opprobrium applied to anonymous reporters and pamphleteers of sensational news, scandal and crime. As Smollett's Mr Melopoyn explained, 'I have made many a good meal upon a monster; a rape has often afforded me great satisfaction; but murder well-timed, was my never-failing resource'. Grub Street opportunism was proverbial: as one late seventeenth-century 'dying Penitent' lamented, 'it is hard that for the Lucre of a Penny, a Man dares write so many Lies; but God forgive them that did it, for he would have writ the same upon his own Brother on the like Occasion'. Just as pickpockets were notorious for their trade on hanging days, so in a sense did art imitate life: the writer of criminal biographies and last dying speeches had 'no other View than that of filling his own Pockets, by picking those of other People.'[42]

While awaiting his 1726 trial for killing a man in a duel, Major John Oneby 'entertained spectators with Vollies of Oaths and Curses, which he plentifully poured out upon the Printers of some Grub-Street Papers'. Oneby was incensed at the temerity of the author of an unflattering account of his life who, he believed, had come to visit him at Newgate under the guise of a well-wisher, offering to help suppress a negative 'Paper ... in the Press by some other Hand'. Oneby immediately suspected that his visitor was, in fact, the author of the pamphlet in question, and that he only 'wanted Matter to fill up his Paper, and came with this Pretence, in hopes of hearing or seeing something that might answer his Purpose'. The Major had to be restrained by the gaolers from assaulting his visitor, who made a hasty escape. Oneby, who was convicted of murder and sentenced to hang, committed suicide shortly before his scheduled execution. He spent his last days on earth reading the offending pamphlet, 'bestow[ing] many horrible Curses on the Author' and devising 'diverse Stratagems to decoy the Fellow to the Prison, that he might give him the Discipline of the Gaol' – that is, 'take his Leave of this Person with a Bull's Pizzle' (a whip).[43]

Publications like the Ordinary of Newgate's *Account* were quick to distinguish themselves from such 'Grubstreet papers, as daily sacrifice truth for a farthing'. According to a 1752 paper delivered to the Ordinary John Taylor, the condemned murderer Captain James Lowrey not only refused a visit from a printer who later published a 'crude and spurious' account of his life, but informed his would-be interviewer that 'had he not been in the situation he was, his reproachful and insolent Behaviour would have obliged him to kick him down Stairs'. Not that the Ordinaries were above suspicion. In March 1764, the condemned forger John Prince suspected that the then Ordinary, John Roe, was the author of a 'Grub-street half-penny speech ... much to his disadvantage'. After Roe indignantly denied such a charge, Prince transferred his hostility to a printer on his way to the Newgate chapel, 'seizing him by the collar' and 'using the bitterest imprecations against him, for having published his life', as well as threatening to 'tumble him down stairs'. Prince later apologized to both Roe and the printer, perhaps realizing that it was impolitic to antagonize the press while he was actively campaigning for a pardon.[44]

The Ordinary of Newgate's *Account* was published, ostensibly, 'to reclaim vicious Youth and admonish other ill Livers' as well as to prevent the spiritual 'inconveniency ... consequent upon ... false Accounts': a distorted or exaggerated account of the penitence of malefactors could, it was claimed, lead readers to 'delay their Repentance to a Dying Hour, and to imagine that so serious a Work may soon be Effected'. In a 1712 petition, the early eighteenth-century Ordinary Paul Lorrain argued (unsuccessfully) that his paper, published 'for the general Satisfaction of the Publick' and 'the necessary Information of Honest People', should be exempt from a new tax on single sheets as it contained 'nothing but Divinity, Devotion, and what may be most useful to the World'. As various Ordinaries would reiterate, a 'free, full and ingenuous Confession' constituted the necessary 'first step to a sincere and hearty Repentance'. It did not escape the critical notice of contemporaries, however, that the money from the sale of the confessions and biographies of the *Account* constituted a lucrative perquisite of the Ordinary's office.[45] In 1707 the disgruntled former printer of the Ordinary's *Account*, Dryden Leach, complained of his having been jettisoned in favour of a rival who offered Lorrain more money for his paper: 'whether this is a Practice becoming a Clergyman or a Tradesman', Leach left to the readers' 'own just Reflections'. Nor were the Ordinary's brother clergymen exempt from such charges. As late as 1751, the rector of St George the Martyr in Southwark, Leonard Howard, was accused by the printer J. Gaylord of 'shuffling' between himself and other competitors bidding for an account of a Kennington Common execution, which included a graphic description of the violent gang rape and murder for which two of the condemned were executed (a case doubly notorious because an innocent man had been hanged for the crime two years previously). The printer in this case was, however, aggrieved that, although Howard had claimed that he would give the account to 'those who would give the most Money for it', he later delivered it to the dying-speech seller John Nicholson, who had offered a guinea less than Gaylord.[46]

A number of the condemned loudly questioned the motives of the Ordinary and other ministers who solicited their confessions. The highwayman Charles Speckman, alias Brown, hanged in 1763, complained that the Ordinary refused to administer the sacrament to him 'under pretence of [my] not being prepared, but in reality, to get from me an account of my life and transactions'. In 1724 Jack Sheppard supposedly complained that 'the several Divines who visited him' were 'all Ginger-bread Fellows' who 'came rather out of Curiosity, than Charity; and to form Papers and Ballads out of his Behaviour'. In 1682 Captain Vratz threatened the attending ministers, Anthony Horneck and Gilbert Burnet, to 'Print his own story ... set[ting] forth the behaviour and manners of the English Clergy, and the strange ways and methods they take with poor prisoners to extort confessions from them'. The condemned murderer John Mausgridge, hanged in 1708, claimed that 'he had given no Account of himself to the Ordinary of Newgate ... 'tho often opportun'd by him' because 'he had not a Mind to be the Sport and Ridicule of vain, idle Fellows in Coffee-Houses, who only laugh at unfortunate dying Men, who are frighted into a Confession of their private sins ...' Indeed, Sheppard, Speckman, Mausgridge and many other malefactors apparently exercised the option of giving 'authorized' accounts to rival publishers. In one such account, supposedly dictated by the highwayman James Carrick, readers are explicitly instructed to disregard 'whatever the Ordinary may take upon him to set forth after my Death ... if it shall be in contradiction to what I have here related'.[47]

Many, if not most, complaints about the forgeries and lies supposedly palmed off by the Ordinary or professional 'Dying-speech-makers' emanated from the authors or editors of rival criminal accounts or longer compilations. The writer of a 1735 collection of criminal lives speculated that fellow inmates or visiting divines 'drew up' the 'Paper[s]' of some of the more illiterate prisoners, while the editors of the Select Trials frequently questioned 'the Chaplain's Veracity', claiming to recognize as 'inimitable' that 'incomprehensible Stile by which the Chaplain so wisely distinguishes himself from all other Writers' (the collection nonetheless appended verbatim the biographies of criminals published by the

'Reverend Author'). Late seventeenth- and early eighteenth-century critics made much of the fact that the Ordinary's *Account* was published *before* the malefactors were actually hanged; and, although by 1704 the *Account* was not sold until shortly afterwards, in the late morning or afternoon of the day of the execution, complaints that the paper had gone to press earlier persisted. It is impossible to know how much control, if any, the condemned exerted over the copy of such accounts, although it is likely that authors and editors erred on the side of comprehensiveness (or exaggeration) rather than expurgation or abridgement: Charles Brown or Speckman apparently 'owned' to the Ordinary that 'he had put in some things, particularly about horses, that were not true' into the 'copy of his life and discoveries' he had sold to another publisher, but 'the rest he said was pretty right'. It seems more likely that material would be added than altered or withheld, especially in the early and mid-eighteenth century, when demand for details of robberies and criminals' lives was at its height. Under John Applebee's editorial direction from the mid-1730s to 1740s, the Ordinary's *Account* routinely included a picaresque 'Appendix' containing accounts of robberies, letters and other material supposedly written by, or relating to, the condemned.[48]

It was a common practice for criminal accounts to be witnessed by officials, ministers, the condemned and fellow prisoners.[49] From the late 1670s, the Ordinary of Newgate subscribed his name and declaration of authenticity to the authorized account of the malefactors executed at Tyburn. An account of the 1692 trial and execution of the condemned murderer Henry Harrison was signed and authenticated by the Mayor of London, Thomas Stamp, who warned that nobody but the two printers specified by him should 'Presume to Print the Same'. Other accounts referred the public to reliable witnesses who could testify to the accuracy of the contents; some invited readers to examine 'the original Manuscript' or other 'original and incontestable Papers and Evidences' in the 'Hands' of authors or publishers. Printers likewise prefaced accounts with claims that their 'Narrative' was 'Printed from the Genuine Copy' written by the criminal's 'own Hand' (such claims to exact accuracy could also insulate publishers from criticism about the questionable language and content of accounts). An account of the life of the notorious street robber James Dalton, executed in 1730, was introduced with this notice 'to the Reader': since 'Things of this Nature being generally pyrated, or false and spurious Ones impos'd upon the Publick, I thought it proper to let the World know, that this is the true and exact Account of my Life' – for, despite the best efforts of 'several Persons ... endeavouring to obtain it from me ... I have deliver'd it to none, nor any part of it, except to Mr Robert Walker, and for which I have received full Satisfaction'.[50]

It was also common for famous criminals in particular to publicly endorse their true confessions at the gallows and to warn spectators against being imposed upon by false accounts. At her 1733 execution Sarah Malcolm 'delivered her confession sealed up, requesting it might be opened before the lord mayor and the sheriffs, and that Mr Pedlington might publish it'. At his 1724 execution, Jack Sheppard invited the ubiquitous John Applebee 'into the Cart, and in the View of several thousands of People, deliver'd to him a printed pamphlet, entitled, A Narrative of all the Robberies and Escapes of John Sheppard ... which he desired might be forwith printed and publish'd'. According to the Ordinary's *Account*, the robber John Dyer made a short speech at the gallows, asking for the prayers of spectators and warning them to 'avoid lewd Women', adding 'I have given a particular Account of all the Robberies by me Committed, to the printer of this Paper [Applebee], which I desir'd might be made Publick for the satisfaction of my Self; and all those I have Robb'd; which was Yesterday Publish'd'. So fierce was the competition for such accounts that the Ordinary James Guthrie pointedly noted that when 'a Friend of George Richardson's came up to the Cart' shortly before his 1733 execution, urging 'him to take notice to the People, that no body had any Confessions, but what he had given him', Richardson refused: 'perhaps conscious that he had told me [Guthrie] several things before, and therefore he was in the right not to tell a Lye'.[51]

It was, of course, conventional to justify the utility of accounts either as cautionary tales or a public service 'to forewarn innocent people of the subtile practices of Villains'. But as far as the condemned themselves were concerned, perhaps the most compelling reason to have their confessions or 'lives' published was to prevent 'false Reports of them when they are Dead'. The robber Daniel Tipping, hanged in 1732, left a written account not merely in deference to 'Custom', but so 'That no fictitious Account ... may at once impose upon the Publick and add to the number of those real Offences I have committed a Catalogue of imaginary Crimes'. According to the highwayman John Everett, executed in 1730, 'I thought it proper to write my own life, lest the publick should be imposed upon by narratives that might be altogether untrue, and the idle imaginations only of some members of the Grub-street society'. When in 1758 the condemned forger Richard William Vaughan 'requested that no account of him or his dying words, &c. might be published, that his family might not suffer; he was answered, it was as impossible as to stop the mouth of common fame'. Since accounts were inevitable, many reasoned along with John Alexander Emerton that it was better to pen your own 'Life' than to leave it to those who were 'altogether ignorant' of your 'Affairs', and whose 'Business' it was to '[fill] a Sheet of Paper' whether 'True or False'.[52] Many of the condemned seemed genuinely eager to set the record straight. James Dalton doubtless spoke for many when he said 'he would not be displeas'd at his being blam'd for what he did, but could not endure to bear the Blame for what he had not done'. Others, like the murderer James Hall, hanged in 1741, felt compelled to give their accounts not merely to 'undeceive the Town' but to 'confute the Scoundrel-like Author[s]' of defamatory accounts. A 1722 account published by Ralph Wilson, a street robber who had turned King's evidence against his former associates, was vehemently refuted by the brother of one of the men whom he had helped send to Tyburn, as an 'erroneous, false and reflecting' 'Libel … defaming those unhappy Persons, whose Bravery was always superior to him in all Respects whatever' (a significant part of the account was devoted to demonstrating how 'Cowardly [Wilson] behav'd himself' in all of his robberies).[53]

Financial considerations clearly played a large part in determining whether condemned criminals would sell their accounts, and to whom, for if accommodations at Newgate were among the most insalubrious in London, they were equally among the most expensive: prisoners were not only obliged to pay for their own food, drink and bedding – the indigent were forced to subsist on charity or the proceeds of begging – but were liable to various fees, such as 'garnish', an admission fee exacted both by gaolers and other inmates.[54] The condemned would also need money to defray funeral expenses, as well as to contribute to the maintenance of their families. Much of Charles Speckman's animus towards the Ordinary seemed to stem not only from the fact that he had refused to offer Speckman 'one farthing' for 'an account of my life and transactions', but that his 'charity' did not '[extend] … so far … as to furnish me with a little food to keep soul and body together till the time of my death'. James Maclaine is supposed to have requested a friend to 'Have my Life done as soon as you can, to prevent any body else doing it after I am no more', and to donate a share of 'any Profits arising from it' to his 'poor Orphan'. Certainly, few of the more famous criminals would have any doubt about the value of their 'free, full and ingenuous Confessions' to the Ordinary or other ministers on the one hand, or to enterprising Grub Street reporters on the other. The condemned housebreaker Stephen Harding 'often promised that in case his life was spared he would write a particular account of it … for the warning of others and the public safety', and was described as thunderstruck when he nonetheless found his name included in the Dead Warrant. In 1763, the highwayman Paul Lewis attempted to string along the Ordinary and other ministers with the promise of a penitent account – 'such as would deter others from following his steps, and not allure them' – and the discovery of his accomplices, in exchange for receiving communion (from which he had been excluded on account of his bad behaviour). In the end, Lewis was admitted to the sacrament but the Ordinary and other ministers were forced to 'be content with general expressions of repentance': the highwayman flatly refused to name former comrades whom, he explained, he had sworn a solemn oath not to betray.[55]

But we should not dismiss out of hand the importance many contemporaries genuinely placed on the value of confession – which, for the condemned, served as a means of making peace with God and reparations to society. Jack Sheppard was supposed to have dictated his 'life' in part because "'tis necessary that I should say something for my self' to 'set' things 'in a true light; every Subject, how unfortunate or unworthy soever, having the Liberty of Publishing his Case'. He was also supposed to have claimed, however, that 'it will be no small Satisfaction to me to think that I have thoroughly purg'd my Conscience before I leave the World, and made Reparation to the many Persons Injur'd by me, as far as is in my poor Power'. In 1734 the burglar William Howard allegedly delivered up an account of his robberies 'not out of any Pride he took in the Repetition thereof; but on the contrary, that innocent Persons might not lye under the Imputation of having committed them'.[56] While such expressions were conventional and formulaic, it does not necessarily follow that they were insincere. Most, if not all criminals, subscribed to, or at least paid lip service to, the accepted formula for dying well: forgiving others as one hoped to be forgiven, repaying debts and making reparations, admitting and assuming responsibility for one's own wrongdoings – a formula, moreover, which applied not only to 'public' sinners, or criminals, but to 'private' ones as well. Certainly, as we shall see, a large proportion of criminals seemed to be sincerely motivated by a desire to absolve spouses and other family members of any guilt in connection with the crimes for which they were to suffer.

And there was a small but conspicuous number of the condemned who were not only willing to recount past crimes but who seemed to revel in their notoriety. The author of a 1735 collection of criminal lives complained of the 'ridiculous Spirit of vain Glory' and the 'vain Inclination' on the part of 'especially the younger Criminals ... to be much talked of'. Some malefactors were apparently both willing and able to impress accounts with their own imprimatur. In an account attributed to the street robber Joseph Shaw, hanged in 1738, the latter complained vociferously about his former companion James Harrison, who had turned evidence against him: 'a meer Drone' whom, Shaw claimed, he had only consented to go robbing with out of charity, after Harrison had been released from Newgate penniless, 'almost naked, and swarming with lice'. Shaw went on to boast of his prowess as a boxer ('I could beat most Men of my Inches in 2 Minutes', he claimed), and of having a 'great many Wives ... too many for one Man' (although 'I never supported any of them, on the contrary, have had many Pounds from them'). Shaw concluded his account with a less than subtle message to a 'Gentleman' who had 'lost' a valuable watch: 'the Owner of it may have it again for 5 Guineas – 'tis in pawn at present for 4, and if he thinks fit to have his Watch again, this Notice will be a Hint to him who to apply to hear of it'.[57]

The degree to which common criminals were capable of exploiting the media of the last dying speech and criminal 'life' – and even appropriating the moral and satirical critiques inherent in confessional and rogue genres – will constitute one of the central themes of this study. For even if suspiciously picaresque, accounts like that of Joseph Shaw are nonetheless so self-serving as to have the ring of verisimilitude. And some criminals may have been relatively successful in dictating the terms with which their accounts would be reported, capitalizing perhaps on publishers' promises to reproduce criminals' lives in 'their own Words'. In 1749 the condemned coiner Usher Gahagan was supposed to have delivered his signed and witnessed confession to 'the Printers of the Dying Speeches, with a strict Charge, neither to add to it or diminish from it'. But it was at the gallows that malefactors could make their most dramatic statements. At his 1722 execution, the street robber Thomas Wilson not only 'delivered with much Ceremony' a 'Paper' he claimed to have written, but accompanied his printed account with a clear visual text. At Tyburn 'he seem'd less daunted than any of the Malefactors who suffered with him' and 'shew'd himself several times by standing up to the Spectators', warning them 'to give no Credit to any spurious Accounts which might be published of him' and referring them to his 'Paper'. He concluded by telling the crowd that he had just been informed that 'one Phelps had been committed to Newgate for a Robbery mention'd by him in his Paper'. However he solemnly asserted, 'as he was a dying Man', that he had never met or robbed with Phelps, who was innocent of any involvement in the said robbery. Wilson 'then put the Rope about his Neck, and submitted to his death with great Resolution'.[58]

Even if late seventeenth- and early eighteenth-century criminal confessions and last dying speeches can be seen as the inventions of partisan party politics, unscrupulous Grub Street writers or even of a larger society which sought to represent the 'real' in palatable ways, they were stories in the same way that all life histories are stories – stories shaped and appropriated by clergymen and pamphleteers, readers and listeners and even, sometimes, by the malefactors themselves. Some accounts borrowed freely from fiction; others, perhaps, were bald-faced forgeries; yet nonetheless they still have much to tell us about the world in which late seventeenth- and eighteenth-century men and women lived and died. Not least, the forms and formulae employed by the condemned to justify their actions and to testify to their spiritual state are in themselves instructive and bear further examination. As Defoe wrote in his preface to the life of *Colonel Jack*, 'It is [not] of the least Moment to enquire whether the Colonel hath told his own Story true or not; If he has made it a *History* or a *Parable*, it will be equally useful, and capable of doing Good, and in that it recommends it self without any other Introduction'.[59]

3

Everyman and the Gallows: Contemporary Explanations for Criminality

Why should art answer for the infirmities of manners? Hee had his faultes, and thou thy follyes/ Debt and deadly sinne who is not subiect to?

Thomas Nashe, *Strange Newes* (1592)

… how naturally, as it were Step by Step, Swearing, Cursing, Profaneness, Drunkenness, Whoredom, Theft, Murder, and the Gallows, succeed one another!

Samuel Richardson, *The Apprentice's Vade Mecum* (1734)

… it might be said of us all, that if God should give us poverty, we should steal … Let the man who can say otherwise of himself, begin to cast Stones

Daniel Defoe, *Applebee's Journal*, 16 June 1722

In what was an otherwise unremarkable robbery case tried at the Old Bailey courthouse in January 1740, a witness called by the defence attempted to discredit the prosecutor's testimony by implying that the latter had been in the company of prostitutes at the time the crime was alleged to have taken place. While the prosecutor claimed that he had been returning from a visit to his brother's when a strange man knocked him down in an alley and stole his watch, the defence witness, Robert Harrison, testified that when *he* had come home for the evening, he had seen 'a Tumult about my Door in the same Alley'. Upon his asking 'what was the Matter', the prosecutor told him (or so Harrison claimed), that 'the Bitches had robbed him of his Watch'. To this the defence witness supposedly replied: 'what Business had you in Bitches Company? If you have been in Bitches Company, you must take Bitches doings.' While the defendant was in the end found guilty and sentenced to death, it is significant that even the constable who had made the arrest had instructed the prosecutor to 'be cautious in what he was about', asking him repeatedly if he were sure that 'no Women had been in his Company'. Clearly, the constable as well as the defence realized that, stolen watch or no, the court would have seen any prosecutor who kept ill company as the sole author of his own misfortune.[1]

This example illustrates not only the colourful language routinely employed by witnesses in trials of this nature (and regularly recorded and published in the

Sessions Paper, the printed account of the proceedings at the Old Bailey), but one of the assumptions central to early eighteenth-century thought: that people of known ill-life had no one but themselves to blame for any misfortune that befell them. This was an age in which sin and crime were seen as ontologically connected: crime was a choice, or rather, the inevitable product of a series of previous bad moral choices or lapses. This moralist discourse, although more familiar in its application to criminals than to prosecutors, could nonetheless prove a double-edged sword. The author of a 1735 collection of criminal lives complained of the longstanding practice of prostitutes accused of picking their clients' pockets regaling the court with their prosecutors' alleged unsavoury or embarrassing sexual predilections, 'hoping by this Reverberation of Ignominy to blacken each other, that the Jury may believe neither'. He added that 'in late years', a similar 'Excuse' had 'grown as common with the Men', with a number of defendants accused of robbery claiming that their prosecutors were 'mollies' or 'sodomites' who had propositioned or sexually assaulted them. (Such accusations were treated with increasing scepticism by the late 1720s, after a rash of successful prosecutions of young men for robbing and extorting money from victims they had met in parks and other areas frequented by gay men.)[2]

Thus, somewhat paradoxically, both moralists seeking to explain the irreclaimability of criminals, and defendants attempting to extenuate their own behaviour and discredit their accusers tapped into a larger universalist conception of guilt – one in which criminality was not an absolute, but rather a point on a continuum; and culpability relative, a matter of degree. In a famous (if apocryphal) attribution, the Marian martyr John Bradford was supposed to have exclaimed, when seeing malefactors taken to the place of execution: 'But for the grace of God there goes John Bradford'.[3] This was intended not as a prescient reference to his own ultimate fate, but as a simple statement of universal human depravity. All men and women were potentially criminals, and only by vigilantly guarding against the blandishments of Satan and their own wicked and corrupt hearts could they hope to escape a sad and shameful death at Tyburn. This notion that the criminal, or 'public sinner', was different from the 'private sinner' only in degree, and not in kind, was regularly illustrated in seventeenth-century criminal literature by relevant passages of Scripture: 'Wherefore him that thinketh he standeth take heed lest he fall'; 'there is none that doeth good, no, not one'. In the words of one 1673 pamphlet, 'neither Birth, Wit, Education, Industry, nor a habit of well-living, can, without the especial Grace of God, free us from the Snares of Satan'. Even 'the best of men' was deep 'amidst Death-Threatning Dangers', warned one late seventeenth-century Ordinary's Account; even the 'true Penitent' was 'vile' in the sight of 'God's Holiness', intoned another.[4]

The seventeenth-century Ordinary's Account regularly billed itself 'as a Seamark to all that read or hear it, that they may avoid [being] Shipwrackt' on the 'fatal rocks of sin'. The image of the criminal as a 'Seamark' was common to confessional literature, as was the insistence that such warnings 'may be aptly applied' to all readers. Late seventeenth-century criminal accounts frequently touted themselves as a mirror, or 'Looking-glass' for 'young Gentlemen' and 'Gentlewomen'; indeed, 'for all degrees of people, but especially of Christians'. As one 1692 account of the trial and execution of a woman for infanticide lamented, 'how many's Curiosity will tempt them to buy this Paper', but 'how few's Consideration will lead them to make useful Application of it to themselves'. Readers were warned that they could not be certain that they 'shall not commit the Crimes, or worse than those for which she dy'd; til you get your Hearts renew'd and chang'd'. Moreover, God was no respecter of persons: not only (in the words of an early eighteenth-century Ordinary's *Account*) were 'all Men, whether Rich or Poor, High or Low ... bound to appear at the great Assizes' (i.e., 'God's Tribunal'), but there many repentant criminals would have the advantage of their less spiritually prepared social betters. According to Bunyan, 'a repenting Penitent, tho' formerly as bad as the worst of Men, may by Grace become as good as the best'. Many seventeenth-century penitents were held up as glorious monuments to the power of God's 'Free-Grace', by which they were to attain 'a higher degree of true Christianity ... than many Professors of long standing ... could ever reach'.[5]

This Calvinist rhetoric was toned down in later accounts, as the notion of the condemned as a monument of free grace was increasingly equated with an 'enthusiasm' that jarred with the more restrained latitudinarian Anglicanism of the early and mid-eighteenth century. Significantly, while eighteenth-century Ordinaries of Newgate continued to preach on 'the Sin of our Nature, commonly called Original Sin', the spotlight had shifted subtly but markedly to the particular iniquity of the condemned rather than that of the *Account*'s audience. By the middle of the eighteenth century, Enlightenment ideas had made significant inroads into the older, more pessimistic Calvinist view of human nature and its emphasis on predestination over free will, grace over works, divine omnipotence over human frailty. Methodists and later evangelicals would react both against rational religion's implicit rejection of the principle of universal depravity and the concomitant denigration of miraculous last-minute gallows redemption narratives (a subject to which I will return). Significantly, an emphasis on a universal human propensity to sin persisted not merely in evangelical literature, but in popular crime ballads and broadsides; in 1777, one of the *Gentleman's Magazine*'s correspondents reported hearing a street-ballad sung on the occasion of the execution of the Anglican divine, Dr William Dodd, for forgery, in which listeners were reminded 'How frail we are, both great and small,/ And so let him who thinks he standeth,/ Always take heed lest he fall'.[6]

Scholars have tended to distinguish between a seventeenth-century moral paradigm in which crime was explained as an adjunct of sin and the 'social

determinism' or environmental explanations gaining currency in the eighteenth century, along with emerging notions of modern individualism and
subjectivity.[7]

The rise of insanity defences is a case in point. Although the special verdict of
'not guilty by reason of insanity' did not come into existence until the nineteenth
century, the defence of being 'lunatic' nonetheless constituted a regular, if
relatively infrequent, feature of trial before the eighteenth century (translating,
if successful, in the Tudor period into a pardon, and, in the seventeenth and
eighteenth centuries, acquittal). The incidence of insanity defences would rise
dramatically after about 1750, however.[8] Yet for all this, moralist explanations
of criminality proved remarkably persistent, and have continued to explain
criminality well into the modern period – and, in the wake of victims' rights
movements, seem to have carried the day in many parts of the West. The story
in regard to late seventeenth- and early eighteenth-century criminal literature is
similarly complex: while it is generally assumed that criminal biographies and last
dying confessions can be situated within the earlier moral discursive framework,
moral and environmental arguments often existed within a dialectic. Not least,
the rhetoric of the 'slippery slope' – in which the sinner was encouraged to
deliver a detailed enumeration of his or her sins to demonstrate the addictive and
progressive nature of vice – itself provided the condemned with an opportunity
to deploy environmental and congenital excuses within an ostensibly moralist
framework of personal responsibility.

Certainly, a large proportion of the condemned, including those who claimed
to be innocent of the offence for which they were to die, were willing enough to
portray themselves as sinners whose shameful example should serve as a warning
to others. This was in part because malefactors were expected to 'die in peace
with all the world', something best accomplished by delivering a speech exonerating spouses and family members of blame and accepting full responsibility
for their own actions. But even if such men and women conceded that they
had been egregious Sabbath-breakers, oath-takers and company-keepers (and
so on), most were also careful to recount details of their lives which at least
implicitly extenuated the gravity of their crimes. Some criminals cited unhappy
childhoods, cruel step-parents and abusive masters, alcohol or various forms
of mental disorder – ranging from romantic disappointments to head injuries
– as excuses for their actions; others invoked that most powerful, if problematic,
of justifications: 'Necessity'. And the very vehemence with which criminal
biographies denied that environmental factors could be seen as justifying criminal
behaviour would seem to testify to the popular currency, and perhaps even utility,
of such explanations. The idle apprentice's progress from Sabbath-breaking to
a felon's death at Tyburn, so famously depicted by Hogarth, may have been in
theory a journey as inevitable, and hence (on more levels than one) as inviting

as the road to hell. However, the path mapped out by contemporary chroniclers of criminal lives was often far from straightforward, and the normative messages they intended to convey, often distorted or undercut not only by the voices of the condemned, but by what seems to have been ambivalence on the part of those who interviewed them.[9]

THE SLIPPERY SLOPE

It was a commonplace of seventeenth- and eighteenth-century thought (if by no means new or unique to the period) that sin was both addictive and progressive. Contemporary moralists warned that from such little acorns as childhood raids on orchards and the pilfering of 'Farthings and Marbles' grew great oaks of iniquity – much as some modern commentators claim that smoking marijuana leads inevitably to the abuse of harder drugs. While the doctrine of original sin was as old as St Augustine (himself a youthful robber of orchards), the notion that small transgressions inevitably hardened the offender and emboldened him or her to venture further down a slippery slope of sin is most famously associated with the eighteenth century – and dramatically illustrated by William Hogarth's 1747 *Industry and Idleness* (a series of plates depicting the divergent careers of two apprentices, Francis Goodchild and Thomas Idle, one to the mayoralty, the other to the gallows), and George Lillo's 1731 play, *The London Merchant* (the story of an honest apprentice seduced by a lewd woman into robbery and murder). And while seventeenth-century criminal accounts placed much more emphasis on supernatural agency, they too portrayed crime as essentially a choice. Men and women were exhorted to pray constantly and fervently to God to deliver them from the snares of the Devil, who, according to one early Ordinary's *Account*, 'always watches his advantage over such as misspend their precious hours in Sin and Vanity'.[10] (Idleness as the first step down the slippery slope was another common thread running through both seventeenth- and eighteenth-century criminal literature.)

Late seventeenth-century criminals – sometimes at the prompting of officiating clergymen and other witnesses, sometimes (apparently) voluntarily – frequently attributed their ruin to the fact that they had committed small, 'secret Sins, not repented of', which had caused God to withdraw His grace from them, 'suffer[ing] the Tempter to prevail more and more against' them, until 'in the end' they were 'brought to misery'. When, in 1678, the convicted murderer Nathaniel Russell maintained his innocence, claiming the killing had been accidental, the Ordinary retorted that he surely must have 'been guilty of many grievous sins, that God should so give him up to such a Fact without any provocation'; to this Russel was made to admit that 'all his life' he had, indeed, 'run on in a course of wickedness and rebellion against God'; he 'particularly bewailled with tears, his continual breach and neglect of the Sabbath and Religious Duties'. Similarly, Margaret Palmer 'did not deny the Crime for which she is Condemned [burglary], but wept, saying, that she was prevailed upon to commit it, because she did not pray against it'. Nor was the occasional or half-hearted prayer sufficient to thwart the subtle designs of the 'Enemy of Mankind': Thomas Benson attributed his rape of the 8-year-old daughter of his master to the fact that he 'seldom Prayed to God to keep him from Temptation'; the robber Thomas Reeves, executed in 1695, claimed that 'God let him fall justly into this Crime, because tho he pray'd often to him to keep him from Sinning, yet he did it with little Devotion, and not with Fervency'.[11]

In contrast to God, who earns mention most often simply by withdrawing His grace and abandoning the criminal to his or her own depravity, Satan, the great 'Tempter', plays an active role in seventeenth-century accounts. Frequent reference is made 'to the power, malice, and sedulity of the devil, to enter and possess Mankind, and to stir up both Men and Women to horrid and evil Actions and Murthers'. Francis Nicholson, condemned for murder in 1680, claimed that he 'had made a Vow to kill a man before I went from Hampton-Court and the Devil appeared to me and told me, I was damn'd if I did not perform my Vow'. Edmund Kirk claimed he had murdered his wife because 'the Devil told me, no less than her Innocent Blood could give me a proper Satisfaction'; William Gilbert, hanged in 1705, insisted that 'the Enemy of Mankind … never let me rest Night nor Day till I had Murthered my Wife and Child'. Such supernatural encounters are recorded without apparent scepticism by the late seventeenth-century Newgate chaplain Samuel Smith. In 1691 the horse-thief Francis Black told the Ordinary that 'since his Condemnation, he dream'd that an Evil Spirit came to him, and would have haled [sic] him out of his Bed: But upon praying that God would preserve him, he grew more quiet in his Mind'. When, in 1693, the midwife Mary Compton, condemned for the murder of four children, reported that 'she was assured of her Salvation' because 'the Night before, an Angel appeared to her and told her she should be saved', Smith did not dispute that she had had such a vision, only that she may have been deceived: 'he should be glad if it were the true heavenly Angel, and not Satan the Great Enemy of Mankind, who oftentimes does transform himself into an Angel of light'.[12]

But, by the early eighteenth century, references to active divine or demonic intervention in the lives of criminals had all but disappeared. The anonymous author of a 1735 collection of criminal lives included an appendix of several cases demonstrating various miraculous and providential discoveries of heinous crimes, although aware that such 'Relations' would 'Expose me to the Raillery and the Ridicule of a very numerous Tribe of Wits in this Age, who value themselves extreamly on their Contempt of supernatural Stories'. Although murder indictments would continue well into the modern period to employ the traditional wording – that the accused had committed the crime 'not having the fear of God before his eyes, but being moved by the instigation of the devil' – by mid-century, criminals who invoked demonic agency to justify their actions tended to be perceived as liars or madmen. In 1743, John Riggleton, who 'was really at intervals quite a lunatic', stabbed his wife to death while 'he was in one of the worst of his fits'. When asked 'why he did it, he only told them an incoherent story about the devil'. In 1752 the Ordinary's reaction to John Salisbury's claim that 'the Devil put it into his Head (it is his own words)' to commit a robbery verged on incredulity: 'And he gave no other Reason for such his Behaviour, than it came into his Head of a sudden, and he was in Liquor at that Time'.[13]

In the eighteenth century, crime was still seen as the result of hardening one's heart against God's grace (thus 'deaden[ing] the Force of Natural Conscience'), but this process was generally described in more secular terms as the product and symptom of a long course of private vices. If the idle apprentice's ignominious death at Tyburn had obtained the status of a proverb, so too had his passage through various and progressive stages of venial sin: idleness, Sabbath-breaking, company-keeping, disobedience to parents and masters, not to mention lewdness. In *The London Merchant* we are told that 'one vice as naturally begets another, as a father a son'; and, according to one mid-century collection of criminal lives, such was 'the Force of ill Habits', that even the smallest sin, 'if wilfully committed, easily draws on another, and *that* more; and a Man cannot tell when or where to stop, till it end at last in a sad and shameful death'.[14] The fact that Matthew Clark had slit the throat of a fellow servant (while pretending to give her a kiss) was attributed not only to his naturally vicious 'Disposition', but his habit of 'sitting in the Church-yard with other idle Fellows, during the Time of Divine-Service'. It was a commonplace that 'Idleness, lewd Women, and ill Company' were 'the sum Total of Excuses … urg'd by criminals' (as well as chroniclers) 'when they come to be punish'd'. Not only did time spent in prison – whether as a felon or a debtor – bring individuals into dangerous 'Conversation' with 'wicked Persons', but it was also believed that stints in the army ('that Sink of Vice and Laziness') or at sea ('another odd Academy to learn Honesty at') tended to harden young men and inure them to 'Blood and Plunder'. Similarly, some pastimes, or even occupations, were viewed as demoralizing: boxing, for instance, contributed to 'an inhumanity of temper'; the trade of a butcher, 'a bloody and barbarous Disposition'. Nevertheless, no 'Excuses' could serve as justifications for crime. If even the most promising youth could be drawn, like Lillo's George Barnwell, down the proverbial slippery slope, he alone could be held responsible for taking that initial and fatal first step. When, in 1690, William Bristow bemoaned 'his Hard Fortune to fall into bad Company', the Ordinary reminded him 'that it was his own corrupt Heart which led him aside to commit the crime' and, 'had he resolved in God's strength to have departed from Iniquity, sinning would not so easily, upon Inticement, prevailed with him'.[15]

The argument that all those who embarked on a course of crime would eventually end their lives on the gallows seemed – simultaneously, if paradoxically – to justify both the excessive rigour of the Bloody Code in principle as well as the too-tender way in which it was often seen to be administered in practice. The belief that a habitual course of vice hardened the criminal and inured him or her 'to Crimes the most heinous and most shocking to human nature' not only laid the onus for the crime on the shoulders of the individual ill-liver, but justified both the execution of first-time or young offenders – those who, by being 'nip'd in the Bud ... by their being suddenly apprehended much Wickedness was prevented' – and of those 'Old Offenders' who were convicted on flimsy evidence, or for crimes of a relatively trivial nature. The author of a 1735 collection of criminal lives includes several accounts of people executed for crimes of which they were almost certainly innocent, concluding philosophically that 'that is the Danger a Man runs, from being known to be of ill Life and Fame, of having himself accused from his Character, only, of Crimes [he is] guiltless of ...' After all, according to Roger Wykes, Ordinary of Newgate in 1700, 'if what the Apostle affirms to be true ... he who is guilty of one sin is guilty of all'.[16]

Sometimes the Ordinary's attempts to detect the 'secret sins' of criminals seem almost comically strained. Duke Cooke, while 'chast' and 'free from Acts of Uncleanness', nonetheless 'sometimes ... did Drink to Excess, and Walkt abroad on the Sabbath'. Joseph Shrewsbury, executed in 1726, although 'not at all inclined to, or guilty of Robbery or Thieving', was so 'addicted to Dancing, that he could by no Means abstain from it'. A 'Person of no Vicious Principles', such as John Austin, executed in December 1725 for robbing a man of his coat, clearly posed something of a problem for chroniclers. It was noted with some bemusement that he 'had been guilty of very few enormous Crimes, except drinking to Excess sometimes, and that but seldom. The sin which most troubled him', apparently, was his habit of 'spending the Lord's Day mostly in hard Work'. Criminal biographers, notoriously insistent that serious crimes were invariably preceded by Sabbath-breaking, were clearly perplexed when confronted with offenders who had left behind them no discernible trail of private sins. After all, 'it is an old Saying', wrote the editor of a 1745 collection of criminal lives, 'that nobody becomes profligately wicked at once'. The case of the servant Matthew Henderson, who murdered his mistress in 1746 for no apparent reason and who had no known history of vice, caused no little consternation not only in the Ordinary's *Account*, but also in such periodicals as the *London Magazine* and the *Gentleman's Magazine*, which followed the story closely. Henderson 'declared solemnly, before two reverend clergymen', that he had never been 'vicious' or drunk in his life ('saving one time when he was a child he was made to drink too much for the sport of a company'). Henderson himself cited an aunt who was 'disordered' in her 'mind', believing 'he might partake of some of her distemper', being 'at times in ... excess of mirth', and at others 'melancholic and gloomy'. Contemporaries were apparently reluctant to accept what we would today diagnose as a bipolar disorder as a sufficient cause of the crime, and, with evident relief, discovered that Henderson had been reprimanded and threatened with dismissal several weeks before the murder, after he had 'accidentally trod upon his lady's toes'.[17]

One of the central themes of criminal literature was that, after having once taken to illegal courses, the criminal was both so abandoned to God and so hardened as to be irreclaimable. According to one 1725 newspaper editorial:

> The oftner a young Rogue steals with Impunity, the sooner he'll be a thorough-paced Villain, that will venture on more hazardous Undertakings ... He may baffle his Prosecutor, find a Flaw in an Indictment, elude the Force of an Evidence, come off once or twice, be repriev'd, break Gaol, or be pardoned, the Gallows will be his Portion at last. The Wretch that is train'd up to stealing is the Property of the Hangman: He can never entirely leave off his trade: Many, after Transportation, have, with great Hazard of their Lives, found the Way back again to Newgate. A Thief bred must be hang'd if he lives.[18]

Criminal accounts routinely described a large proportion of the condemned as 'Old Offenders', or 'old notorious and incorrigible Thieves'. One newspaper, reporting the apprehension of Nathaniel Hawes in 1721 for robbery, added that he had 'been once burnt in the Hand, and been twice an Evidence and hanged some of his Comrades', as well as having 'about a Fortnight ago broke out of [Clerkenwell] New Prison': evidence that 'Once a Thief and always so, till Jack Ketch [the hangman] comes with his Anodyne Necklace' – a reference to a cure-all remedy (largely for venereal complaints) frequently advertised in early eighteenth-century newspapers. Ordinaries of Newgate, particularly the long-serving and active court officer Paul Lorrain, regularly took note of those malefactors who had previously pleaded full or conditional pardons, or who had been acquitted of or received lesser punishments for prior felonies. Particular energy was invested in portraying female property offenders as hardened recidivists, beyond hope of rehabilitation. In 1704 Lorrain claimed that the 48-year-old Sarah Smith (who claimed to be a street seller, but 'could not deny that her chief Trade was stealing'), had 'receiv'd the Law about 30 times', having been 'whip'd and burnt [i.e., claimed benefit of clergy] diverse times' and 'three times at least under Sentence of Death'. In 1712 Lorrain brushed aside the 37-year-old Elizabeth Price's protestations of innocence, whom he remembered as having at least five previous convictions for housebreaking, the details of which he painstakingly enumerated ('the true, though not fully-compleat History of her sad Life'). Several years later, Lorrain taxed another veteran female burglar, the 38-year-old Ann Wright, with no fewer than twelve prior convictions, all of which 'sad Particulars' were again duly recorded. Young offenders too elicited shock and notice and, perhaps, defensiveness: one late seventeenth-century newspaper reported that 'a young Boy' had been committed to Newgate 'for felony, who has been in 6 times within the compass of 8 months for the same Crime'.[19]

Such was 'the corrupt nature of man', contemporaries lamented, that 'no Exhortation, no Examples' could 'reclaim' offenders, even the sight of the gallows itself. It was axiomatic that pickpockets plied their trade on hanging days – that 'those that were crowding Spectators at one Execution, come themselves to suffer at the next'. The notorious John ('Half-hanged') Smith's heart did for a moment 'misgive him and fail him' when, on the way to commit a robbery, he walked past the gallows at Tyburn; his companions, however, 'egg'd him on; telling him, "What matters it, Jack? 'Tis but hanging, if thou shouldst come to that"'. When the street robber William Blewitt was caught picking a gentleman's pocket, the latter released him, moved by his youth, but 'with a kind of prophetic kindness' warned him lest he 'come to be hanged'. When the burglar Stephen Gardiner was in his youth briefly detained in St Sepulchre's Watchhouse for 'some trivial Thing or other', the Bellman happened by before he could be discharged, leading the constable to remark, 'be careful, I am very much afraid this Belman will say his Verses over you'. Gardiner was momentarily 'so much struck, he could scarce speak', but did not in the end profit from the warning. Criminals were only emboldened by such narrow escapes to greater crimes, until their luck at last ran out: 'as the Pitcher seldom goes so often to the Well, but it comes Home broke at last'; or, to invoke several popular scriptural images, returning like a dog 'to his vomit', or a sow to her 'wallowing in the mire' (Proverbs 26:11, 2 Peter 2:22). In the spring of 1724, Blewitt's former companion in crime, the street robber Joseph ('Blueskin') Blake was released from Newgate after two witnesses (in the pay of Blake's then patron, Jonathan Wild) appeared in court to vouch for his good behaviour, leading a 'Gentleman … then present' in the courtroom to speculate 'how many Sessions might be given Blake before he was to be seen again at the Old Bailey'; another answered him, 'thrice'. Blueskin was indeed a defendant at the same bar three sessions later; and, that time, hanged.[20]

If we are take criminal chroniclers at their word, rehabilitation was unlikely even in the case of very young or first-time offenders. When, in 1742, the 19-year-old John Jennings 'wept and lamented grievously, promising amendment, and made strong Resolutions if he was spared, the Ordinary of Newgate reflected that 'he was acquainted with too many of the gangs, so that it would have been a hard Matter to reclaim him', and 'in all Probability if he had lived longer, he would have committed a great deal of more Wickedness, but he was cut off in due Time, and cropt in the Bud'. After all, a 'wicked Way of Life, which once engaged in, is not easily to leave off' – not simply because morals are corrupted and habits of self-indulgence take root, but because 'having once enter'd into a Gang, if any one breaks off, they have another's Life in their Power, giving Informations against their wicked Companions, and then they become Evidences for the King, and hang one another'. Many criminals would themselves lament that, after falling in with a gang, they 'were made a Property of, by every Villain that knows or guess at [their] Circumstance', and thus, even if they had chosen to do so, found it impossible to leave off their former course of life. This rationale could salve the consciences of those who might be moved to pity youths such as John Johnson, 17, who was 'in the preceding Part of his life ... honest, did not steal nor thieve, and kept in his Master's Service, till taken up for this Robbery, which was the first and last he ever committed, which he freely confessed'. Yet 'Justice', in 'instantly overt[aking]' Johnson and his accomplice, 'prevented much Mischief, which in all Probability they might have done, if suffered to go on in such a hellish Course as they had engaged in'. Occasionally, condemned criminals obliged by echoing such sentiments: the 22-year-old Robert Hickson (also executed for his 'first Fact', a robbery committed while he was drunk), 'expressed his Joy that he had been concern'd in no more [robberies]; if he had escap'd now, he said, he might have committed more'; moreover, the fact that 'it had pleased God to suffer him to be taken so early ... prevented a further Reckoning, which might have render'd the making Peace with his God a more difficult task'.[21]

Criminal biographers expressed their horror, not that adolescents – what a later age would term 'juvenile delinquents' – were hanged for what often amounted to rather paltry crimes, but at 'the present Depravity of human nature, that we have sometimes Instances of Infant criminals, and Children meriting Death by their Crimes, before they know or can be expected to know how to do any thing to Live'. Typically, chroniclers such as the Ordinary of Newgate stressed the necessity of 'nipping' such precocious offenders 'in the bud'. In 1744, James Guthrie (chaplain of Newgate from 1725 to 1746) expressed less dismay over the youth of the condemned robber Henry Gadd ('about 14 Years of Age') than his utter ignorance 'in point of Religion'. When the Ordinary attempted to catechize him, he was shocked when Gadd could not answer the question 'Who made him'; and, 'astonish'd and grieved' when, upon asking 'Who redeem'd him', Gadd replied: 'the D—l'. Guthrie 'sharply reprimanded him' for this 'improper and wicked Answer' but, he feared, 'to little Purpose, for he was the most obstinate inconsiderate little Villain that I ever saw, since I have had the honour to serve the City [almost twenty years]'. In 1731, Guthrie characterized another 14-year-old robber, Bernard Fink, as 'irreclaimable', with 'a natural Inclination to Villainy'; he was reputed to have 'said in the Cells, "If he were let out he would go straight to his old Trade"'. As though to emphasize Fink's precocity, Guthrie added that 'he drank and swore very much' and 'he said he was very much addicted to Women'. In short, 'This Boy was a sad Instance of the depravity of humane Nature, destitute of the Grace of God, and left to itself'. Evidently less moved by pity for Fink's youth than for his unfitness to die (itself a product of youthful heedlessness and ignorance), Guthrie noted disapprovingly that Fink, in their private interviews as well as 'in Chappel', frequently 'wept like a Child', in sorrow for his own misfortunes, rather than for his sins, like a true penitent.[22]

Like many of their contemporaries, mid-eighteenth-century Ordinaries were clearly critical of a penal code that was too severe to be effectively or consistently enforced, and was thus, in practice, too indulgent to serve as either a deterrent or as a means of reforming petty offenders. In 1758 the Ordinary Stephen Roe, shocked by an execution in which three out of five malefactors were under the age of twenty, urged that the 'civil Magistrates … lop these early Shoots of Impiety and Immorality in the Bud, by a diligent inforcing of the lesser penal Laws [e.g., whipping], in due Time'. Yet it was often claimed that most secondary punishments – with the possible exception of transportation – were insufficient to deter such 'Young and Ignorant … thoughtless and unwary Offenders' from the commission of further crimes. Moreover, it was well known that most people were reluctant to prosecute young offenders for capital crimes (it was no accident that prosecutions of juveniles skyrocketed after the early nineteenth-century decapitalization of those crimes most commonly committed by such offenders: shoplifting and pickpocketing). In 1752 John Taylor complained of the way in which such 'unhappy' adolescents 'boldly violate the Laws of Society … fondly presuming that the Plea of Youth, and the Pretence of its being the first Fact will, whenever they are taken, save them from the Gallows, tho', he added cynically, if they 'meet with Mercy, 'tis ten to one if they reform'. Taylor bemoaned the precocious 'Wickedness' of the 15-year-old burglar Anthony Westley, who displayed 'scarce any Signs of Remorse or Contrition'; and, although 'his tender Years and Ignorance may with us be pleaded an Excuse … how hereafter [i.e., on Judgement Day] this may be respected, we must leave to the Disposer of all Things'. Like Guthrie, Taylor's main concern was for such youthful offenders' insensibility to the spiritual enormity of their predicament: ''Twas Pity such a little Wretch should come to a Halter' (here Taylor could not refrain from adding, ''tho he richly deserved it'); 'he was much fitter for a Rod, which held over him would have made him tremble. His Want of Sense entitled him to no Fears of Danger at a Distance, nor was the Gallows a Terror to him, till he had it before his Eyes'.[23]

But if a belief in the inevitable forward progress of vicious habits could still leave room for pity, or at least ambivalence, it was also possible to conceive of exceptions to the rule. The notion that some delinquents could in fact turn their lives around constituted one of the main themes of Defoe's novels *Moll Flanders* and *Colonel Jack*; moreover it was, with the passage of the 1718 Transportation Act, a principle enshrined in the criminal code itself. The author of the 1735 *The Lives of the Most Remarkable Criminals* included several examples of malefactors voluntarily transporting themselves to America in order to live honestly, far removed from their former haunts and vicious companions. While such success stories were clearly viewed as extraordinary, the fact that they were accorded mention at all is in itself significant. And indeed, in practice if not in theory, those who administered the English criminal law routinely distinguished between those criminals who were most and least likely either to re-offend or to pose a danger or nuisance to the community. Age and gender, as well as character, were critical factors in such decisions (a point to which we will return). Not only were youthful offenders unlikely to be hanged, but so too were men who were older, married with children, and gainfully employed. Women of any age were much less likely than their male counterparts to be executed for property crimes, as I have mentioned: from December 1729 to October 1749, 70% of women condemned to death at the Old Bailey for property crimes were reprieved, compared to only 32% of male property offenders.[24]

And even if most commentators agreed that 'we are all born into the world' with 'a natural Propensity ... to Evil', it was also generally acknowledged that vicious tendencies could, if arrested early enough and with sufficient vigour, be nipped in the bud. According to Daniel Defoe's *Family Instructor*, 'this Bent or Inclination must be rectified, or driven out either by Instruction, or if that proves insufficient, by Correction; and it is to be done while the Person is young, while he is a Child, and then IT MAY be done'. For 'Nature like some Vegetables, is malleable when taken green and early; but hard and brittle when condens'd by Time and Age; at first it bows and bends to Instruction and Reproof, but afterwards obstinately refuses both.' And while most criminal chroniclers were quick to stress that young criminals were, like the 23-year-old Jack Sheppard, youths only 'in Age and Person', but 'old [Men] in Sin', it goes without saying that such writers would have had a vested interest in seeing their subjects as beyond all hope of rehabilitation. On one very obvious level – as literary scholars such as Lincoln Faller and Paula Backscheider have pointed out – such accounts certainly functioned as a means of relieving social guilt or anxiety in regard to the execution of criminals and of 'reinforcing the moral values and conventional choices of their readers'. Even so, it is occasionally acknowledged, however tacitly, that justice was not infallible, and that the human beings who administered it were not all-seeing or all-knowing. Not that this meant that the criminal's excuses or protestations of innocence could be credited. As the Ordinary of Newgate told one of the condemned in 1723, a convicted murderer who insisted on his innocence: 'should human Courts of Judicature (where the Mind of men can not otherwise appear, but by their Actions) allow Excuses, every Criminal would find such Pleas as would put an End to Justice'. At least they could both console themselves with the fact that there was a higher court.[25]

'GUILT IS THE OFFSPRING OF THE HEART': NURTURE VERSUS NATURE

In 1733, the condemned murderess Sarah Malcolm reputedly comforted her fellow-prisoners with the following words: 'As to the ignominy of your Fate, let not that trouble you, none but the Vulgar will reflect either on you or your Relations; good Fathers may have unhappy Children; and pious Children may have unworthy Parents, neither are answerable for the other'. However suspiciously eloquent such a speech may have seemed coming from the mouth of a 22-year-old laundress, the sentiment itself is well-documented; indeed, it is a constant refrain of early eighteenth-century criminal lives that parents could not be held responsible for the actions of their children. The author of a biography of William Cranstoun (rendered notorious for his involvement with the parricide Mary Blandy), reminded 'the Reader' that 'no Reflections are intended to be thrown on the noble Family to which he belongs'; after all, 'How many a Hero has had the Misfortune to be the Father of a Coward! How many an honest Man ... has produced an Heir of Shame! ... Guilt is the Offspring of the Heart, and cannot be communicated to us by that of others.' In the words of one late seventeenth-century murder sheet, 'every days Experience demonstrates this as Truth: A good Father may have a bad son, Virtue and Vice rarely running in the Channels of Nature.' Moreover, those criminals 'descended of an Honourable Family' and 'possess of a considerable Estate' had even less excuse for turning to crime than those of humbler origins: 'certainly their Crimes are greater, who are the Offspring of such Parents, and run Counter, not only to their Examples and Instructions, but also, the benefits of that Education they generally bring them up under'. Conversely, the parents of working-class criminals are typically characterized as poor but honest and industrious – or, to borrow several verses penned in honour of Jonathan Wild: 'Born of honest Friends he was/ (But many an honest Parent has/ An ugly froward Knavish Child,/ And one of these was Mr Wild)'. Indeed, it is a stock claim of criminal lives that even parents like those of the street robber Joseph Shrewsbury, hanged in 1726, who were 'in so mean Circumstances, that they were not able to give him any Education at all', were nonetheless 'careful in carrying him constantly to Church with them ... and did every Thing their narrow Capacity would give them Leave, in order to enable him to get his Bread in some honest Employment'.[26]

A claim commonly made by the Ordinary and other criminal biographers was that malefactors were wicked from the 'Cradle', being born with 'vicious Inclinations'. This was often, if not usually, despite all attempts on the parts of masters and parents to curb such evil tendencies: John Barnet, hanged in 1730, was 'from his Cradle of the most wicked, dogged, perverse Disposition in the World, would not go to school, nor do any thing that was Virtuous and Good, in

Obedience to his Parents or Relations, but went about the Streets and acted the Blackguard, when there was not any Occasion to do so, from his very Infancy'. Criminal lives abound with errant and incorrigible children who thwart all efforts on the part of parents to keep them within bounds. John Lowden, hanged in 1742, 'a wicked Youth' (he was 22) who would never '[mind] any Business at all', and on whom 'all Advice or Reproof was thrown away', would 'immediately run away and be gone for Weeks ... if his Father offered to beat him'. Similarly, the 23-year-old highway robber William Dawson, hanged in 1750,

> was such an untoward, unlucky Lad, that it was with the utmost Difficulty his Parents kept him within any Bounds of Decency at all; he frequently making Elopements from them, occasioned their giving him proper Chastisement, in Hopes to reclaim him by Severity, being heartily tired of trying every good-natured Method they could invent; but this had the contrary Effect on William, for being of a wandering, roving Disposition, and finding his Parents were determined to keep a more strict Hand over him than usual, he was resolved to prevent them, by taking himself from them for good and all.

Parents were seldom criticized for disciplining their children; rather, severe methods were seen as both justifiable and necessary, if not always effective. The author of *The Lives of the Most Remarkable Criminals* claimed to be 'far from ... an Advocate for great severities towards young People', but nonetheless maintained that there were 'Cases' where 'they are as necessary as Amputations, where the Distemper has spread so far, that no Cure is to be hoped for by any other means'.[27]

Indeed, seventeenth- and eighteenth-century parents were far less likely to be castigated for their essays at what modern popular culture would term 'tough love' than for their 'too great tenderness and Compassion'. The formula of the overly-indulgent parent and the wayward child was such a standard trope that it lent itself to parody, as in the 1708 pamphlet supposedly 'penn'd from the Mouth' of the street robber John Hall (the erstwhile 'Joy and Darling' of 'Good and Honest' but 'Doating Parents'), whose confession, or 'catalogue of sins' is diligently solicited by the Ordinary, and duly repeated by the 'poor shivering Malefactor' at the place of execution. This theme was frequently taken up by more earnest pens, and, at the end of the eighteenth century, immortalized in one of Hannah More's Cheap Repository Tracts, *The Execution of Wild Robert: a Warning to All Parents* – in which the malefactor's overindulgent mother is 'by conscience struck' down dead at the foot of the gallows after her son dramatically denounces her for not only having 'doom'd' him to death by her negligent fondness, but 'to hell'. Such 'notable Warning[s] to all Parents' were a staple of seventeenth- and eighteenth-century last dying speeches. A malefactor hanged in 1680 supposedly confessed to having 'followed the Trade of a Thief ... ever since he was Five Years of Age' and, at the place of execution, 'with many tears, accused his Parents, for promoting his ruine, by encouraging or at least winking at his petty Childish thefts, and not sufficiently Correcting him for the same; whereby he became emboldened to go on, and attempt greater Rogueries, which now brought him to this untimely End'. According to *The Lives of the Most Remarkable Criminals*, 'the ordinary kind of People in England' were all too liable 'to wink at' such early 'Essays in Dishonesty' on the part of their children as 'cheating at Chuck, and filching at Marbles', only to severely chastise these same 'smart Boys' when they graduated to the 'stealing of Handkerchiefs and the picking of Pockets'. Parents of all social classes were warned against 'over lenity', or a 'tender-hearted' reluctance to 'suppress ... Youthful Follies with too much Rigour'. In the words of one crime pamphlet, 'Parents should be very cautious, and act very delicately in the bringing up their children, not to grant them too much Indulgence, seeing such conduct often produces fatal Consequences'. In fact, 'the truest Way for a parent to demonstrate his or her love to Children, is not to let them know [i.e., that their parents love them]'.[28]

Indeed, despite the fact that criminal accounts continue to portray crime as a failure of a moral order for which the individual alone could be held responsible, this does not mean that contemporaries did not, in practice (as Sarah Malcolm's speech implies), reflect on a criminal's relations. According to *The Lives of the Most Remarkable Criminals*, 'the Misfortune of not having early a virtuous Education, is very often so great a one, as never to be retrieved', so much so that those who 'prove remarkably wicked and profligate for want of it ... if they had been so happy as to have received it, would probably have led an honest and industrious Life'. Nor did the prevalent belief in a universal human propensity to sin entirely exclude a notion of *tabula rasa*; that is, that 'the Minds of young Persons are generally compared to Paper, on which we may write whatever we think fit'. And however much 'spare the rod and spoil the child' sentiments may have enjoyed the ascendancy, parents and other 'Friends' were supposed to strive for a happy medium: 'As indulgence is a very common Parent of Wickedness and Disobedience, so immoderate Correction and treating Children as if they were Stocks, is as likely a Method as the other to make them stubborn and obstinate, and perhaps even force them upon taking ill Methods to avoid Usage which they cannot bear'. Indeed, sometimes the parents of the condemned were called on to defend themselves. The 'sorrowful father' of the 15-year-old John Swift, hanged for robbery in 1763, when asked by the Ordinary 'why he did not train him better, and keep him within bounds', replied 'that he had done the best he could for him, and blamed the boy's unruly temper and behaviour' – not his own efforts to reclaim him, which were, he maintained, strenuous (if unavailing). Other parents complained of the difficulty of striking a balance between severity and indulgence: in 1735 one exasperated father claimed to 'have taken what Care I could in giving my Boy good Instructions, but my Care had but little Effect on him. He was always very perverse, and a notorious Lyar, for which I have often corrected him' – although here he was careful to add, 'though not with Severity, for fear of hardening him'.[29]

Some parents were singled out as having set a bad example for their children or neglected their education: the father of Captain John Stanley, a soldier, was supposed to have hardened his young son by regularly 'prick[ing] him with a Sword', plying him 'with Wine, or other strong Liquors', and allowing him to indulge in such dubious pastimes as 'when a Battle was ended', walking 'about the Field and trampl[ing] upon the dead Bodies'. (Stanley was hanged for murder in 1723.) Elizabeth Branch's daughter was said to have 'inculcated such barbarous Notions' from her mother – 'a great Reader' whose 'favourite Pieces were said to be those that treated of tyranny and Inhumanity; particularly that of Nero, who ript up his Mother's Belly to see how he was born' – that 'she would often cut open Mice and Birds, torturing them for three Hours together before they expir'd'. (Both mother and daughter were executed in 1740 for beating a servant maid to death.) Anticipating the insight of later criminologists and animal rights activists, John Locke warned his pupil, the third Earl of Shaftesbury, that tormenting 'very young birds, butterflies and such other poor things' tended 'by degrees' to 'harden [one's mind] towards men'.[30]

Sometimes, criminal tendencies were attributed to heredity: the highwayman William Barton 'inherited a sort of hereditary Wildness and Inconstancy' from a father who had 'been always of a restless Temper, and addicted to every species of wickedness'. Despite having the opportunity to 'have done well' in an 'easy condition' (serving out an apprenticeship to a 'tender' grandfather) Barton instead indulged his 'roving' inclinations by going to sea – the fatal first step on the road to ruin. The notorious street robber James Dalton's mother and sister had been transported and his father executed for robbery (the young James was reputed to have ridden 'between his Father's Legs in the Cart' on the way to Tyburn): 'being the Son of such a Notable Family', the Ordinary remarked, 'one may easily conjecture what sort of a Tree grows from such a Stock'. James Dalton saved his life in 1728 by turning King's evidence against three of his comrades, but was hanged in 1730 for a robbery that he maintained he had not committed, despite freely admitting to having been 'one of the most impudent irreclaimable Thieves that ever was in England'. This family tragedy was complete when Edward Dalton followed his brother to the gallows in 1732 for his part in pelting to death in the pillory the man upon whose perjured evidence James had been hanged.[31]

Many readers may have agreed with the sentiment expressed by one early eighteenth-century pamphleteer; that is, 'that Rapine and Theft often run in the Blood and become Hereditary' (even if they would have balked at the author's suggestion that thieves and robbers be castrated to prevent them from 'leaving any of their pernicious Brood behind them'). But few would have conceded that heredity constituted an excuse. When the condemned murderer Lewis Rantzau claimed that 'his education had been Mean, as his Father's Example had been evil, who committed an Unnatural murder on his own Brother', the Ordinary informed him that, as 'it is Observable, that Cruelty of Nature ... may descend upon Posterity', Rantzau should have been 'forewarned' and all 'the more circumspect to avoid those Inclinations ...' Similarly, even when criminal accounts conceded that cruel or abusive parents and masters did exist, this was in no way a sufficient justification for embarking on a life of crime. According to *The Lives of the Most Remarkable Criminals*, 'those who are so unhappy as to suffer from the ill-usage of their parents' should 'try every honest Method to subsist' rather 'than by committing dishonest Acts, thereby justify all the ill treatment they have received, and by their own follies, blot out the Remembrance of their cruel Parents Crimes'.[32]

Clearly, the task of assigning moral responsibility for crime could not be reduced to any one simple explanatory formula. Even contemporary folk-sayings reflected this tendency to attribute criminality to a variety of different, and often contradictory, causes: 'an ill cow may have a good Calf'; 'he that brings up his Son to nothing, breeds a Thief'; 'spare the Rod, and spoil the Child'; 'that, which is bred in the Bone, will never be out of the flesh'; and even, 'he that has no Fools, Knaves, nor Beggars in his Family, was begot by a Flash of Lightening'. Criminality, according to the author of *The Lives of the Most Remarkable Criminals*, was as difficult to predict as it was to prevent: 'such is the frailty of humane Nature, that neither the best Examples, nor the most Liberal Education, can warrant an honest Life, or secure to the most careful Parents the certainty of their Children's not becoming a disgrace to them'. Thus it would seem that, even if crime was not solely the fault of the individual, it was his or her own responsibility and not that of parents, or of society at large. To what degree this assertion can be qualified, however, will form the subject of the following discussion.[33]

EXCUSES: MENTAL INCAPACITY, NECESSITY, GENDER, YOUTH

On the surface, at least, the principal thrust of late seventeenth- and early eighteenth-century criminal lives was that crime was a choice, and that men and women took to illegal courses because 'work did not agree' with them and they 'lov'd an idle life best'. Over and over we hear of the 'unhappy Tempers', 'rambling Notions' and 'inconstant and vagrant Dispositions' which prevented such ill livers from 'settling to any Business' – despite all the efforts of well-meaning and long-suffering 'Friends', and many opportunities 'to have done well' from their own labour, if they had so chosen.[34] Nathaniel Jackson, hanged in 1722 for highway robbery, confessed to often having been 'at Variance' with his master, 'an honest industrious Man', who frowned on his apprentice's 'Delight ... in Idleness, Extravagance and keeping loose Company'. When Jackson finally ran away from his master, his 'Friends' tried to convince him to purchase an annuity or to set himself up in business with money he had inherited from his father. 'But', Jackson supposedly admitted, 'their Advice was thrown away, for a Settlement was not what I wanted, I thought a loose rambling Life was much more preferable'. Similarly, John Jones, executed the previous year for robbery, while 'put to several Trades on liking ... could not fix or settle to any of them, having an idle Inclination to remain at Home and Subsist upon the Labour and Industry of his Parents'. As for the burglar James Stansbury, hanged in 1746, 'his coming to poverty and disgrace was not owing to want of Business', for he had been 'in a good Way of getting his Bread ... by a very good Trade', but rather 'to his own brutish and hellish Inclinations averse to Virtue and prone to Vice. He followed his Trade very little, loving to loiter and idle away his Time, in a silly insignificant manner, especially in the Company of vile, lewd Women'. Clearly, 'the only way to reform him was the Gallows'.[35]

Like Moll Flanders, who traced her undoing to her early aspirations to becoming a 'Gentlewoman', the foundation of many a poor youth's ruin was his desire to 'make the appearance of a Gentleman', and a corresponding distaste 'to be made ... a Drudge of'. Many young men and women claimed to have been seduced by what they 'fancy'd' to be 'genteel Accomplishments'; that is, idleness, drinking and gaming. However, by thus imitating the leisure pursuits of their social betters, working people not only impoverished themselves, but developed an 'Aversion' for honest employment, seeing it as degrading as well as onerous. The highwayman William Page, in a letter supposedly written to his wife, exhorted her to 'banish' from the 'tender Minds' of their children 'all Notions of Gentility and the Affectation of appearing in an Rank of Life to which they have no Pretensions, the fatal Rock on which their unhappy Father unfortunately split'. The robber Thomas Butledge claimed that 'he might have lived happily enough, if I could but have apply'd myself to Trade, and been contented with a moderate Station of Life: but I was impatient to make a gay Figure in the World, and that hastened my Destruction'.[36]

But if most malefactors seemed willing enough to confess to those weaknesses to which all men and women were prone – and those which their social betters were even more guilty of than they, if with less fatal results – many went on to cite various extenuating circumstances which, in the words of one condemned criminal, even if they did not 'excuse ... the Mischiefs that are inseparable from our Course of Life ... ought to make us pitied'. One of the most common excuses was that of being 'in liquor', even if criminals who suggested that they could not be held fully responsible for their actions because they had been 'fuddled' are typically given short shrift. This, according to the Ordinary of Newgate Samuel Smith, was 'only adding Sin to Sin'. As Mary Hanson, who had been drunk when she stabbed a family member to death in 1724, was obliged to admit, 'she did not think her Drunkenness and Passion an Excuse but an Aggravation of the Crime she had Committed'. Many criminals nonetheless claimed to have been demoralized by a habit of drinking, particularly gin – that scourge of the London poor in the second quarter of the eighteenth century. According to an account supposedly given by one prostitute, 'Drunkenness' began as a 'relief': a means to forget 'all Thoughts of Sin', only later to become 'an incurable Disease'. Robbers would claim that they drank alcohol to embolden themselves to commit crimes: in 1743, the 16-year-old Elizabeth Cannon claimed to have only been able to break into houses after having 'made herself drunk with Gin'; in 1745, the 'constant Street-walker' Martha Tracey, alias Stracey, claimed that she did not remember the robbery for which she died or, for that matter, any other, 'for she was always dead Drunk when they were committed'. The Ordinary claimed that only copious infusions of gin gave three 'little Urchins' hanged in May 1750 for robbery – 'scarce any of them, one would think … fit to rob a Hen-roost' – the 'Courage to be so audacious'. In August 1740, the beggar and casual labourer Samuel Badham, one of two men hanged for murdering their common-law wives in the course of drunken quarrels, complained that 'the Deceased' was 'excessively given to drinking Geneva … that she was continually fuddled, and constantly out of her Senses, and that she had sold or pawn'd all her Cloaths, and had (about a Year ago) in one of her drunken Fits, over-laid [smothered to death] a Child he had with her'. The other man, John Foster, similarly blamed his victim, citing provocation and the fact that both were 'too much addicted to drink Geneva, and other strong liquors'.[37]

Some criminals cited some kind of mental disorder: in 1744, the 50-year-old William Clark was condemned for a burglary he explained as having resulted from his having been 'bitten by a mad Dog, which sometimes put him out of his Senses'. At his 1721 trial for stealing £4 from a house (a capital offence), William Shaw 'in Excuse said that he had received a Kick in his Head by a Horse, since which he oftentimes knew not what he did. The Jury considering the matter found him Guilty to the value of 10d.' – thus undervaluing the goods stolen, or committing 'pious perjury', so that he could be sentenced to transportation rather than death. (Mental incapacity arguments were of course most commonly invoked during the trial phase, when they could result in acquittal or a partial verdict, even though this did not preclude the incarceration of those considered to be dangerously insane.) Some criminals had unusual, even whimsical excuses at their disposal: Thomas Rice, hanged in 1722 for shoplifting, claimed that he had had 'his Senses in some Measure taken away, on Account of a Young Woman he was in Love with, who died the Day before he was to have marry'd her, and upon whose Grave he laid every Night, for half a Year together'. The robber Thomas Wilson, executed later the same year, blamed the break-up of his marriage (by his wife's 'Friends') for driving him to crime. 'Till this (he said), he never Thiev'd; but being greatly fond of her, after this he was scarcely in his Senses, could not go to Bed for several Nights thro' Grief for her Absence, nor car'd what became of himself'. He then, 'to divert his Melancholly', got 'into leud Company', who enticed him to take up highway robbery. Another robber, John Ward, hanged in 1765, claimed to have taken to 'drinking' and 'defrauding' to 'drown his sorrows' when, his wife not receiving from her parents the settlement he had expected and being unable to provide for his young family, he was obliged to consign his child to a workhouse.[38]

The reason most frequently cited by criminals for turning to crime was poverty, or 'Necessity'. While perhaps the most powerful excuse of all – even Blackstone conceded that 'theft, in case of hunger' deserved, if not clemency, at least 'compassion', while Defoe's oft-repeated dictum, 'Give me not Poverty [lest] I steal', derived from no less an authority than the Bible (Proverbs 30:8–9) – it was probably also the most problematic. Early eighteenth-century writers such as Mandeville and Fielding, who tended to view crime as the result of the 'luxurious' and 'extravagant' habits of the 'loose and indigent vulgar' seen to make up the bulk of malefactors executed at Tyburn, characterized poverty less as a justification or a mitigation of crime than as a product of idleness and intemperance. In 1745 the Ordinary of Newgate told the condemned 'that all the evils now attending their unhappy state were entirely owing to idleness … had they applied themselves to honest labour, they would have acquired more with safety and reputation, than could possibly be got by robbery'. According to a collection of criminal lives published the same year:

> We find no Cause either so frequent or so fatal in Respect to Malefactors as an Aversion to Work. The Law given by God to Man is in the Sweat of thy Brow, shalt thou eat Bread. It is vain therefore to struggle against it, for if we will avoid honest Labour, we must sit down either with grievous Want or afflicting Shame, nay very often both fall in one Lot … therefore they who are lazy, are the Authors of their own ill Fortunes, and talk idly when they would lay the Fault on Fate.[39]

And while ultimately, in the interests of dying well, most criminals were willing to assume nominal responsibility for their actions, many nonetheless seemed intent on divulging details of their past lives which tended to extenuate their guilt – and which present a very depressing picture of the eighteenth-century working-class life-cycle. James Appleton, hanged in 1722 for burglary, went to sea at the age of 12, 'where he said he met with an infinite deal of Barbarity and Cruelty, from those who should have been his Masters, but were really his Tyrants and Butchers, being scourged and lashed and salted &c. which hard'ned his

Mind, and made him hate and defy almost all Mankind'. Samuel Ellard, executed in 1744 for returning from transportation before the expiry of his sentence, claimed to have run away from his American master because of the latter's 'Savage Disposition' (he had, reputedly, 'whipp'd seven of his Men to Death'). More pathetically still, Ellard claimed to have been transported for his first offence, a robbery committed while 'he was in Liquor' (and 'at the Instigation of ... a Sailor'), and to have lived honestly for two years after his return to England.[40] Some criminals claimed to have been orphaned young, or to have been turned out of doors by cruel step-parents. Robert Perkin, hanged in 1721 for returning from transportation (he too claimed to have run away from a cruel master and to have worked honestly in the two years before his apprehension), told of being, along with his sister, forced onto the street by his 'Mother-in-Law' (stepmother) and, after his father's death, cut out of his share of his inheritance. While this was much more rare, the occasional malefactor complained of mistreatment by his or her biological family: the 19-year-old robber William Meers, hanged in 1740, 'blam'd' all of his 'Misfortunes' on 'his Brother, Sister and all his Friends, who always complain'd on him to his Father, who often Horse-whipped him, and beat him most unmercifully, banishing him from the House, and forcing him to take up with the worst of Company', the 'Cause of his Ruin'.[41]

Other malefactors claimed to have served as apprentices to abusive or negligent masters. Henry Abbot, 19, hanged in 1718 for burglary, claimed to have been apprenticed to a carpenter with whom he had not served out his time 'on account of his great Severity to him and Hastiness in giving him Blows on the Head, and any where else he could hit'. (The Ordinary was careful to add that Abbot had subsequently left a second master without completing his apprenticeship.) James Putris, another young burglar, claimed that he had been orphaned young and apprenticed to a shoemaker who was so 'severe and cruel to him' that he ran away and fell into bad company (the Ordinary noting, however, that Putris freely acknowledged the 'heinousness of his past Sins', and of being irreparably 'harden'd'). William Miller, hanged for highway robbery in 1727, complained of 'the Churlishness of his Master's Temper, who was continually picking Quarrels with him, and thereupon beating him inhumanly'. After running away from his master before serving out his time, and thus having neither a trade nor a character reference, Miller was unable to find employment, and was 'by Degrees ... reduced to the greatest Necessity', and 'tho' he was willing to work, yet he could not tell which way to turn his hand'. John Cooper, hanged in 1742, claimed to have been born to poor parents who could not give him 'any tolerable Education' (the Ordinary interjecting that whatever 'he got, he was sure to make no good Improvement of, being of a very wicked, perverse and dogged Temper'). Cooper was apprenticed to a fisherman, who 'treated him most barbarously, beating him in a most cruel Manner with Ropes, Sticks, and whatever came to Hand' to the point, he claimed, of endangering his life; after this master died, however, Cooper was 'put to his shifts', not being able to find another. The Ordinary, however, scandalized by his bad behaviour and numerous 'Disorders in Chappel' (including an attempt 'to spit on the Pulpit and Desk'), maintained that Cooper's 'natural Disposition' was 'very wicked and perverse', and that he had been 'nothing but a professed Thief and Robber from his Cradle'.[42]

Many criminals related a series of mishaps which owed more to the unkindness of fate than to any particular individual. Thomas Jones' first master died half-way through his apprenticeship; his second was 'one of those unhappy Persons, that suffered at Kennington Common' (i.e., a Jacobite). After the execution of the latter, Jones set up shop in London, but was obliged to enlist as a sailor after his business failed. When his ship was, soon afterwards, put out of commission, Jones made his way back to London and contracted a debt of £14, for which he was put in the Marshalsea. Jones finally forged a banknote (the crime for which he was condemned) after being 'under Confinement for upwards of three Months there, without ... a farthing in [his] pocket' or 'the least Support imaginable, from any person'. Other malefactors complained of illnesses or injuries, trade depressions and hard winters. Robert Legrose, whose father had died when he was young, leaving his mother in great poverty, had not been put 'Apprentice to any Trade', but scraped by, sometimes as a sailor, sometimes as a casual labourer. But, as he told the Ordinary, several years earlier, 'as he was carrying up a [load] of Mortar to the Bricklayers ... he fell from the Top of St Thomas's Hospital, into the Street, since which he has been almost unable to do any Work'. Henry Neal, hanged in 1733 for burglary, also claimed that his father's death had left his mother too poor to give him an education or apprentice him to a trade; he had eked out a living serving 'Carters and Scavingers' – those who carted refuse from the city streets – until his leg was injured when he was run over by a cart. Neal insisted that 'what he did was merely for poverty and want, he having been disabled for Work, having fasted for three Days, and everybody refusing him Charity'. (Or at least, the Ordinary interjected sceptically, 'This is the Account he gave of himself'.) The Irishman Richard Quail, hanged in 1740 for theft, had 'according to his own Account, served his Time honestly' as a weaver's apprentice but, following a trade depression in Ireland, came to London, where he worked sometimes as a weaver, but 'when his Business was dead' made ends meet by selling 'Butter, Eggs, Roots, Greens, or any small Things he was capable'. After marrying and having children, he 'endeavoured to provide for them by his Trade, and other Times by Marketing, but having little to do, and brought into great Straits by the hard Weather last Year, and not knowing how to live, he took to bad Company, who led one another into fatal Scrapes ...' (The Ordinary added that 'he was much addicted to drinking, and to vicious Conversation, and filtched and stole what he could lay his hands on'.)[43]

The Ordinaries of Newgate routinely expressed their scepticism of the excuses of the condemned by interjecting editorial remarks or parenthetical comments. We are told that the burglar James Hacket, hanged in 1707, being 'low in the World, and finding no present Employment (such as he desir'd) ... he was therefore soon brought to Poverty, and (as he pretended) to the necessity of committing those ill things, which he otherwise' – here the sarcasm is merely implicit – 'would have not done'. When, in 1687, Thomas Jervas claimed that he had been unable to support himself honestly, because 'he was not put forth to be an Apprentice' and because his father had 'spent his Estate, [he] had not wherewith to provide for his Family', Samuel Smith retorted that 'the pretence of his Father's Poverty, however contracted, did not necessitate him to Commit any unlawful Act, but his own evil disposition', and that 'he ought rather to submit to the meanest Employment', or, failing that, to depend 'on Divine Providence for a subsistence'. Criminals who pleaded poverty were constantly reminded that 'this was a very bad Excuse', and that if they had been 'honest and diligent', they 'might have supply'd [their] Wants otherwise than by such unlawful Means' or that, at the very least, they should have 'pray'd to God ... trusting on the Divine Providence for Relief in [their] Necessity'. In 1691 the shoplifter Jane Williams cited 'Poverty', claiming that her husband, a sailor, had not 'provided ... for her' and that 'she was forced to work hard for a Livelihood'. The Ordinary, however, soon brought Williams to an acknowledgement that she had succumbed to temptation because she was 'not ... content with moderate gain' and had become 'by degrees, negligent of her Duty to God, and followed not her Employment as formerly'. When Mary Skip, 24, a casual nursemaid and washerwoman hanged in 1715 for robbing several children of their clothes, similarly claimed she had committed the crime ('which she said she was very sorry, and beg'd Pardon for') from 'meer poverty', the Ordinary retorted parenthetically that 'it was more the want of Grace'.[44]

Not infrequently, the voices of the condemned and the disapproving Ordinary are interwoven without particular effort at coherence: in 1711 Lorrain simultaneously ascribed the theft for which Edward Paine 'deservedly' suffered to the 'great Crosses and Losses' he endured in his trade as a 'Carrier' and 'his vicious Inclinations and habits of Sin' to 'his great Necessities, and want of Grace'. On rare occasions, the plaintive voice of the condemned had full sway: in 1724 the deputy Ordinary James Wagstaff (perhaps less cynical than other, more experienced, Newgate chaplains) wrote that John Horn had been 'reduc'd to a very low Ebb of Poverty' and, 'hurried by mere Necessity' had committed a robbery which, 'he solemnly declar'd ... 'twas his first, and hop'd that God would show him Mercy, tho' he had none from Men'. For the most part, however, even the most poignant misfortunes cited by the condemned tended to be interpreted by the Ordinary as either the product of vice or as providential warnings which the criminal had chosen not to heed. In 1686 Elizabeth Churchill, condemned (but later reprieved) for a theft committed after her husband, a soldier, had fallen into poverty, told of being 'grieved … almost to distraction' after losing three children within a short period (two from smallpox; a third drowned while playing in 'the Town ditch'). Samuel Smith attributed her crime to her not having 'improve[d] that afflicting providence of God [the death of her children] as she ought, to bring her to a sincere repentance for her sins' – which, he implied, would have made her proof against both temptation and want.[45]

Clearly the Ordinary, and the authors of criminal lives generally, preferred to view those executed at Tyburn as hardened characters who, by wilfully disregarding all warnings (both human and divine) and neglecting countless opportunities to live honestly, had not only brought misfortune down on themselves but demonstrated themselves to be eminently incapable of rehabilitation. Yet, paradoxically, it was also acknowledged that, having once lost one's good character, the criminal had little chance of turning his or her life around. In an account of the street-robber and burglar Richard Sheppard, hanged in 1720, we are told that after he had married before serving out his time as an apprentice ('an error in Conduct, which in low Life is seldom retrieved'), he was soon 'Ruin'd' by having to repay his former master a bond for £30; nor was his situation improved by 'his Wife bringing every Year a Child'. As though to discourage the sympathy of the reader, we are informed that 'Dick rubb'd on mostly by Thieving and as little by working as it was possible to avoid'. Sheppard had, moreover, persisted in a life of crime even after having turned King's evidence against companions to save his life and, on a separate occasion, having been condemned to death but subsequently pardoned: 'This proximity to Death made little impression on his Heart, which is too often the fault in Persons, who like him receive Mercy, and have not withstanding too little Grace to make use of it.' The account nonetheless concludes on something of an equivocal note: 'Dick partly driven by necessity, for few People cared after his Release, to employ him; partly through the instigation of his own wicked Heart went again upon the old Trade [i.e., robbing]'.[46]

Not only did such accounts frequently betray ambivalence but, on occasion, the Ordinary conceded, if only in a backhanded way, that poverty, accident, or the burden of supporting a family could mitigate an offender's guilt. Edward Tudor, hanged in 1734 for burglary, could have 'liv'd by his Trade' – he was a blacksmith – and 'kept his Family, like one of his Station, but was too much addicted to Idleness, and lov'd wicked Company'. The highwayman Charles Oglesbay apparently admitted that he 'got sufficiently' making the heels of shoes 'whereby to Maintain himself' in an appropriately 'industrious and sober way'; John Barton, a 'noted House-breaker', acknowledged that 'he had very good Business' as a butcher, 'by which he might have liv'd and maintain'd his Family very well' without resorting to crime. Some claims were more of a stretch: Henry

Norris, hanged in 1710 for theft, supposedly asserted that he had been able to make an adequate 'Livelihood by mending old Shoes' and other odd jobs, 'his Wife getting her own by begging about the Streets'. The Ordinary was on surer ground in regard to malefactors in better circumstances: the fact that Daniel Jackson had enjoyed 'a tollerable Education' and was well provided for by his parents was considered 'no small Aggravation of his Barbarity'; the fact that Ann Clark 'by her industry lived well and wanted for nothing ... made her the more inexcusable in taking to bad Courses'. Daniel Tipping had no reason to prefer the 'Company' of 'black guards, thieves and pick-pockets ... to any settled Business or Imployment', since 'he need not have wanted for any Thing, having had his Mothers House to go to, who was concern'd for and took a special Care of him'. As for Joseph Leath, 'as he was a single Man, there was no Pretence for his turning Thief or Robber'.[47]

Indeed, men frequently claimed they had been driven to crime in order to support their families. John Harold, hanged for burglary in 1700, insisted 'it was mere necessity drove him to it, having married an honest Woman whom he was unwilling shou'd starve before his Face'. James Attaway claimed to have been unable to 'earn a sufficiency' for his 'wife and young babes' even when 'most assiduous and industrious' at his trade as a watch movement maker and, 'when out of employ, his only recourse was pilfering and stealing'. Henry Woodford, hanged in 1721 for returning from transportation before serving out his full sentence – something malefactors were seldom willing to admit as a serious offence – claimed that 'returning to this Wife and young Children, in order to keep them from Starving in his Absence, was so far from being a crime, that it was his Duty so to act'. William Bond, executed the same year for the same crime, claimed to have been unable to honestly 'procure a Maintenance' from his trade as a barber and wigmaker, citing as a reason for his precipitate return to England, 'the dismal Uneasiness and Distraction of Mind, that tortures a Man, who has a Wife and Children he loves like himself' and was unable to supply with 'the common Necessaries of Life'. The highwayman William Barton claimed to have returned four times from maritime service or transportation, 'tho' he knew it must be his Ruin', because 'he could not bear the Thoughts of ... his Wife and Child being reduc'd to extream Necessity', 'Starving, and calling for Bread, and blaming his Absence and Neglect'. William Sperry claimed that he had taken to the road when his wife was 'nigh the Time of her Travail [labour], and destitute of almost all the Necessaries of Life'; in 1744 Thomas Bonney claimed to have succumbed to the same temptation 'when his Wife lay in', 'in a poor languishing weak Condition', and he was 'entirely out of Work' and without 'a Penny'.[48]

While many such stories were undoubtedly true, others were fabrications: in 1721 the receiver John Thompson admitted to having claimed in his pardon petitions 'that he had 2 small Children which must inevitably Perish if he was not reprieved', later admitting that he had 'no Child of his own'. George Stacey, hanged in 1741, claimed 'for an Excuse' that he 'took Care of his Mother' – a claim which the latter herself refuted, telling the Ordinary that her son only 'wasted her Substance' and 'was rough and rude to her in his Carriage and Words' ('for which', Guthrie assured the reader, 'I sharply reproved him'). Yet other stories were so pathetic as to disarm reproof. John Moore was hanged in 1746 for robbery, in a 'desperate Attempt ... to relieve his poor Wife and children, who had been ill nine Weeks of a raging Fever', and his 'Goods were seized for Rent'; Moore himself claimed to have been 'so weak and giddy, that he could scarcely sit a Horse' when he committed the robbery. In a similar story, Richard Arnold was hanged in 1742 for what he swore 'was the first and last Robbery he ever committed'. He 'solemnly declared upon the Word of a Dying Man, that it was absolutely Necessity, his Wife being lame and sick, and he himself sick and distressed, and having nothing to supply their wants, but both ready to perish, knowing no Remedy, which drove him to this desperate and unhappy Course'. Given the fact that up until the commission of the crime, 'no Man was reckoned honester' than Arnold, and that the latter was described as looking 'more dead than alive' at the time of his arrest, the Ordinary's pronouncement that Arnold had 'received his deserved Doom' seems a little forced. In a sad postscript to this story, we are told that at the place of execution, Arnold vehemently denied the rumour 'that he sold his Body for seven Shillings, or any Money whatsoever to any Surgeon'.[49]

If male property offenders claimed to have turned to crime to support their families, many of their female counterparts cited negligent or abusive husbands. Mary Haycock, executed in 1735 for coining, 'complain'd very much of her Husband ... a vile, naughty Person' who 'left her for three Years and a half, taking no Care of the Children which she was obliged to keep, without the least Help from him', leaving her with 'no other way to live but by wicked and unlawful Practices'. Anne Hazzard, executed in 1743 as accessory in the death of a man thrown out the window of a brothel, claimed to have been seduced and abandoned at the age of 14; she then lived as a 'common Prostitute' before marrying a man whom she later discovered already had a wife and children, and who 'began to use her ill, and frequently beat her very barbarously'. She absconded from her lover and resumed 'her old Course of Life' ('as she said much against her Inclination') after being reduced to 'a wretched State of Poverty and Rags'. Typically, the Ordinary urged such women to acknowledge that their sentences had been preceded by a descent into idleness and vice and a hardening of their hearts towards God – that crime, essentially, was a choice. Elizabeth Wann, hanged in 1694 for theft, was induced to confess 'that not Poverty, but only her wicked Heart, inclined her to commit the Crime'. When Mary Knight claimed to have been 'driven to follow an ill Course of Life to keep herself from Starving', after having married 'a Seaman who prov'd a bad Husband' and who 'brought' her 'to great Poverty', the Ordinary sternly reminded her that 'the best and safest way for her to have ... been comfortably reliev'd in her Necessity, was to have kept herself honest, and to have look'd out for some Place [as a servant] in a good Family, or for some other lawful employment'. We are told that Knight meekly assented: 'All this she own'd was very true'. Yet with women as with men, such lip service to the notion of moral responsibility clearly did not preclude the recital of various pathetic details or extenuating factors. Indeed, the opportunity to tell such stories may have been the tradeoff for the criminal's acquiescence in this normative script.[50]

Like the convicted shoplifter Elenor Gavenor, hanged in 1712, countless women – many of them single, widowed, or abandoned by their husbands – 'pleaded great poverty and inability to get Bread for herself and four small Children'. Deborah Hardcastle claimed to have stolen only after the death of her husband, a sailor, had 'reduced [her] (with an old Mother and 2 small Children), to great Poverty and Want'. Mary Nichols, alias 'Trolly Lolly', similarly claimed to have been 'driven to stealing' by 'extream Poverty', not to mention 'her Husband's Unkindness' and the expense of 'providing for her small Children as well as for her self'. Even if such excuses were not always effectual (especially in the case of women who, like 'Trolly Lolly', were perceived as old offenders), they nonetheless had resonance in a patriarchal society in which women were viewed as dependants entitled to protection and support. Up to half of all property offenders brought before the Old Bailey in the eighteenth century were women, a percentage that could rise even higher in the case of crimes such as shoplifting and 'stealing from the person' – this last often, if not always, involving the robbery of men by women from whom they were soliciting sex. The frequency and volume of such offences reflected both the stark economic realities of life in early modern London, where single women abounded and wages for (respectable) female occupations almost invariably fell below the subsistence line, as well as the degree to which casual prostitution often shaded into opportunistic theft.[51]

There is little doubt that female offenders who were perceived as hardened and of easy virtue – women, like Lillo's villainess Millwood, who corrupted young men and perpetuated the cycle of vice – commanded less sympathy than those who traded on their feminine frailty and vulnerability. Yet, even before the sentimentalization of 'fallen women' became fashionable in the second half of the eighteenth century, many contemporaries acknowledged – as Lillo has Millwood herself proclaim at the gallows – that every whore traced her original seduction to a man; some, according to John Bunyan, were 'plunged into this sin at first even by promises of Marriage'. Juries and judges were nonetheless much more likely to exercise mercy towards women who appeared to be respectable or 'decent'. Contrition, tears and deference did not hurt, either. In 1720 Katherine Compton 'wept bitterly, and produced four Children at the Bar, when Sentence was passed upon her' for shoplifting; although condemned, Compton was later reprieved. The attempts of others to elicit sympathy were less successful: at her 1751 trial Mary Gillfoy claimed in her defence that she committed the theft with which she was charged 'in Company of her Husband, and under his Influence; yet when she saw it went hard against her, she thought to move the Compassion of the Court by saying, she had six fatherless Children'. Whether owing to the inconsistency of her logic, or her 'rough and masculine Temper', Gillfoy was sentenced to death and subsequently hanged.[52]

Indeed, perhaps particularly after about 1740, when idealized notions of feminine sensibility were fast gaining currency, female criminals were frequently characterized as masculine. Mary Edmondson, executed in 1759 for the murder of her aunt, was described as not only 'headstrong and hardy', but 'somewhat passionate, resolute, and of a masculine Spirit'. In 1741, the Ordinary of Newgate expressed his shock at the 'Brutallity and Savageness of Mind, contrary to the Nature of the tender Sex', evidenced by Elizabeth Bennet, condemned (but later reprieved) for infanticide. Conversely, most condemned women seemed anxious to demonstrate, as did the prostitute turned pickpocket Mary Dymar, hanged in 1749, that they were 'of too tender a Nature to have been Conversant in these wicked Practices'. Certainly nearly all women were eager to 'plead the belly'; that is, to obtain a respite (which in practice usually translated into a full or conditional pardon) on the grounds of pregnancy. Nor were such pleas restricted to women of childbearing age: if we are to credit the report of one newspaper, 'an Old Woman of near 60 years of Age ... pleaded her belly' and was 'found quick with Child' in 1696; in 1716, the condemned shoplifter Mary Williams, alias Spencer, over fifty years old, was reprimanded by the Ordinary for attempting to bribe the jury of matrons, whose task it was to determine whether or not a woman was 'quick' (that is, whether pregnancy was sufficiently advanced for movements of the foetus to be felt, generally after about four months).[53]

Female violent offenders were no less eager than thieves to play upon stereotypes of female dependence and vulnerability. Some, tapping perhaps into the legal assumption that a woman who committed a crime in the company of her husband was not responsible for her actions, blamed male accomplices. In a particularly famous example, Sarah Malcolm, a charwoman executed in 1733 for robbing and murdering two elderly gentlewomen and their maidservant, maintained that she had only kept watch outside the door, while one female and two male accomplices broke into the apartment and, without her knowledge or consent, committed the murders. (Her story was not credited, nor were any accomplices ever apprehended.) Similarly, many women charged with the murder of their husbands tended to claim that they had been battered wives (to borrow the modern phrase), even if such excuses were often given short shrift by contemporaries. Mary Hobry, a French midwife executed in 1688 for murdering her husband, claimed that the latter had regularly subjected her to such 'Beatings and Revilings' that she was 'every day in danger of her Life', as well as forcing her to 'submit to a compliance with him in Villanies contrary to Nature' (presumably sodomy). Hobry's defence proved ineffectual, perhaps because neighbours were convincing in their testimony that Mary herself was physically abusive towards her husband, as well as sexually promiscuous.[54]

A particularly notorious case involved the murder of John Hayes by his wife, Catherine, and his apprentice and lodger, Thomas Billings and Thomas Wood, respectively; the first reputed to be Catherine's illegitimate son and, by many accounts, her lover as well. Such lurid stories circulated in part because the crime was sensationally gruesome: John Hayes had been murdered while sleeping off the effects of a drinking contest premeditated between the three accomplices, his body dismembered and identified only after his head was found bobbing in the Thames and later displayed at the end of a pole in a Westminster churchyard. Catherine Hayes claimed that her husband had 'abus'd' her (to the point of 'breaking her Ribs and Bones') and 'almost starv'd' her; had 'murdered two new-born Children of hers'; and, on another occasion, caused her to miscarry through his 'ill Usages'. According to Catherine, her male accomplices had been 'prompted ... to kill him' after he had beaten her 'one day in their Presence', claiming that it was no more 'Sin to Kill him than a Dog or Cat', because he had been so 'cruel to that poor industrious Woman' and was 'so atheistical and wicked'. Although Thomas Billings supposedly corroborated her claims of spousal abuse (and it seems that John Hayes was indeed a 'Free-Thinker' or deist, if not an outright atheist), contemporaries clearly preferred to view Catherine as a promiscuous and grasping woman who wanted to have unlimited access to her husband's fortune, estimated at £1,500. Neither Catherine Hayes's claims during her trial of being pregnant (and fears that she 'should miscarry'), nor even the fact of her giving birth after her conviction, earned her sympathy: in May 1726 she was burned alive for petty treason, denied the customary mitigation of being strangled before being consigned to the flames.[55]

Another murderess demonized by the press was Elizabeth Jeffryes, hanged in 1752, along with her accomplice and lover John Swan, for the murder of her uncle and guardian. Jeffryes was widely believed to have plotted her uncle's death because she feared the latter was about to cut her out of his will. Elizabeth herself claimed that her uncle had sexually abused her from the time she was fifteen, and that she had twice become pregnant by him – miscarrying once and the second time losing the baby after her uncle 'gave her Things to cause an Abortion'. Despite Jeffryes's allegations of incest, and her many public displays of feminine frailty – she swooned and clutched a bottle of smelling salts at her trial (where, 'to draw Compassion from the Spectators', she gave her age as 23, instead of 25), and fainted and fell into 'strong Fit[s]' at her arraignment, sentencing and at her execution, where an unsympathetic 'Mob' was 'very rude and hooted at her' – contemporary pamphleteers represented Elizabeth as promiscuous and duplicitous. Jeffryes, like Hayes, was cast as a scheming and sexually predatory woman, who gambled, drank and swore 'excessively', and was 'prodigiously profuse in spending on clothes'; her male accomplice (who carried out the actual murder), was seen as her unfortunate dupe.[56]

Another woman executed later the same year for poisoning her father, Mary Blandy (or the 'Fair Parricide') attracted considerably more sympathy. Blandy admitted to having laced her father's gruel with arsenic, but claimed to be innocent of any attempt to commit murder; rather, she was acting on the instructions of her suitor, the (already married) Scottish adventurer Captain William Cranstoun, who had told her that she was administering an innocuous 'love potion' that would induce her father to look favourably upon their union. Although Blandy had her detractors (Horace Walpole was among the sceptics), many contemporaries credited this story, seeing Blandy as a 'poor lovesick girl' misled by the true villain of the piece, 'that damn'd villain Cranstoun'. At her execution, where many spectators 'were observed to shed Tears', Blandy's last words before ascending the ladder were, 'Gentlemen, don't hang me high for the sake of decency'; and then a tremulous, 'I am afraid I shall fall'. Although widespread sympathy for Mary Blandy did not translate into a pardon, largely because there was little doubt of her having poisoned her father, she clearly conformed more closely to contemporary ideals of female passivity and vulnerability than did Jeffryes or Hayes, women who were seen as sexually aggressive and acting independently of male control – and worse still, directing the actions of male accomplices.[57]

Criminal accounts betrayed perhaps the most ambivalence and discomfort in regard to youthful offenders. Despite the arguments of some scholars that, until after the eighteenth century, childhood and adolescence were not recognized as a unique or different phase of life, the apprehension and execution of young offenders was frequently reported with shock, disbelief and disapproval (if often more on account of the precocious wickedness of humanity than the severity of the capital code).[58]

Boys and young men in their late teens, or even in their early twenties, are routinely referred to as 'Lads'. One 1732 newspaper reported with interest the arrest of 'two Lilliputian Street-Robbers', one 'a boy about 16 Years of Age'. The prosecution witness who had turned state's evidence, and three more of the Lilliputian Gang, in their mid- to late teens, were also described as 'Boys'. The 14-year-old Henry Gadd, characterized disapprovingly as a hardened 'little villain' by Guthrie, was nonetheless referred to several times in the Ordinary's *Account* as 'the little Boy'. Far from being viewed as miniature adults fit to be judged on the same moral scale as their elders, adolescents clearly attracted particular attention and sympathy. There are countless examples of execution crowds who 'expressed great pity towards' young offenders such as John Parkin, 19, and Charles Cane, 20, hanged in 1756, 'on account of their youth'. Also typical was a May 1763 execution of a 15-year-old boy for shoplifting which 'excited great compassion in the spectators'.[59]

Youth was a compelling excuse, judging at least from the lies many defendants apparently told about their age. Joseph Redmond, hanged in 1764 for robbery, 'declared himself to be but 17 years old, though by his appearance he seemed above 20, but that is common with many malefactors, who would be thought younger than they really are, to excite compassion'. James Rockett, another youth hanged the same year for robbery, 'pretended he was but 16 years of age, but it was proved afterwards he could not be less than 22 or 23 years old', and an 'old offender'. Even men in their early twenties apparently still qualified as youths in the eyes of many; in 1754, the Ordinary remarked sourly that the condemned robber Charles Fleming 'said he was 22 years of age, not only to me, but to several others; he might have added about eight years more, and then he might have been near the mark'. The plea of being of 'tender Years' was, of course, most relevant before, rather than after, the Dead Warrant had come down, and of most weight in the courtroom itself: at his 1756 trial for theft, the jury recommended George Langley for mercy after questioning several witnesses 'upon [their] Oath', as to the age of the defendant, and determining that he was 'really ... between Sixteen and Seventeen'.[60]

Chroniclers such as the Ordinary were, as we have seen, very careful to characterize juvenile offenders as 'old in Sin' (though 'young in years') and 'bred' thieves 'from the Cradle'. A 1683 execution account reported that three of the seven condemned had 'scarce ... seen 20 Years', but that all three youths 'confessed they had followed this way of living [theft], ever since they were seven years old, & that they had deserved death several years ago'. We are told that the condemned burglar George Peters, 17, refused to learn his father's trade (that of a carpenter): 'the only Business he ply'd, almost from his Cradle, was Thieving, Stealing, Robbing and Company-Keeping, with the vilest Miscreants, both of Men and Women, that could be found in the World'. Randolph Branch ('almost seventeen Years of Age'), thwarted all the efforts of his tender and 'reputable Parents' to keep him on the straight and narrow: he fell 'into bad Company both of Men and Women, and there was no Scene of Iniquity and Debauchery, but he was ripe for it at about fourteen Years of Age, if not sooner'. Similarly, the parents of William Hatton, 17, 'could have no Influence on him': he 'would pilfer and steal, tho' it were but an Apple or a Nut'. Edward Perkins, 17, 'was a Thief from his very Infancy, so that he could not remember the Time he began to Pick Pockets, and take every Thing he could lay his Hands on'; William West, '16 Years and 6 Months old', had begun 'to pick pockets and steal as soon as he was able to go about or do any Thing, when he was but 10 or 11 Years old; nay, he scarce remember'd at what Age he commenc'd Thief'. Yet such accounts often betray what, to the modern reader at least, seems like uneasiness or ambivalence. Paul Lorrain described the 15-year-old Roderick Awdry, executed for burglary in 1714, as 'little acquainted with any thing that was good', and

> Tho' he was so Young, yet he had been a great Offender, having committed several Robberies ... he acknowledg'd he had, by his own Folly, brought [condemnation] upon himself, and justly deserved [it]: That the causes of his betaking himself to such ill Courses, as he had done, were his Father's dying when he was very Young, and his being brought up to no Trade, and turn'd out of Door, unprovided for by a Father-in-law [stepfather], as soon as his Mother had marry'd again, which was not very long after his own Father dy'd; That being thus turn'd into the wide World, he was then to seek what Course to take, and what shift to make to get a Livelihood; and that which seem'd to him the readiest, was to steal and pilfer. Which wicked Trade he began with robbing of Orchards ...[61]

Late seventeenth- and early eighteenth-century criminal lives were ambiguous texts, reflecting the various and often conflicting intentions and preoccupations of both author and subject and even what often seems to have been a contest between two versions of the truth. Far from being rigidly normative, such literature frequently reproduced the dilemma of Henry Fielding's hypothetical prosecutor of 'good Mind', who finds himself torn between the demands of justice on the one hand, and a tacit acknowledgement of the 'violent Temptations, Necessity, Youth and Inadvertency' that has 'hurried' the criminal to 'the Commission of a Crime' on the other. As the author of the 1735 collection *The Lives of the Most Remarkable Criminals* conceded, there was 'no Plea so often urged in excuse of taking base measures to procure money, as Necessity, and the Desire of Providing for a Family, otherwise in danger of Want. The reason of this is pretty evident, because nothing could be a great[er] Alleviation of such a Crime'. However, he added, 'the Word *Necessity* is so equivocal, that it is hard to fix its true Meaning', and 'as hard to judge of the Reasonableness of such an Excuse'.[62] Such authors could simultaneously concede that poverty could, under certain circumstances, qualify as an excuse, while continuing to maintain that the root causes of both poverty and crime were idleness and vice (or, by extension, universal human depravity).

THE DECLINE OF THE CRIMINAL AS 'EVERYMAN'

As the eighteenth century progressed, the notion of the criminal as 'Everyman' would become increasingly problematic. In part, this may have reflected a larger epistemological shift in the way that execution itself was viewed, as educated people began to abandon the notion that gallows behaviour had metaphysical correlations (a subject to which I will return). But there was also a growing tendency, both in the Ordinary's *Account* and in criminal literature generally, to make an explicit distinction between the 'meaner sort' to whom the moral was directly pertinent and, in the words of a June 1745 Ordinary's *Account*, 'the better kind of readers ... in whose power it is to put a stop to the growing evil': that is, the proliferation of those 'poor wretches' who were 'born thieves'. Significantly, this particular *Account* was published just a few months after the Ordinary, James Guthrie, had fired John Applebee, the long-serving printer (since 1720) and editor (from 1735) of the Ordinary's *Account* – ostensibly on the grounds that the content and tone of the paper had deteriorated, 'being published in a stile and language a little too gross and indelicate for the better kind of readers'. Not least, Guthrie complained that Applebee's Appendix was, 'a Silly Paper ... stuff'd with a Number of incredible Stories and robberies, of which no body knew but himself'. The first *Account* clearly under the direction of '*a new editor*' (not named, but referred to as male, and thus unlikely to have been the new printer, Mary Cooper), advertised the intention to 'henceforth to 'set out ... on a right principle', providing an account 'wherein the lives and manners of those who are enemies of society, are fairly and honestly delineated'.[63]

Paradoxically, then, the confessions of the condemned were viewed with increasing distaste and detachment at the same time that greater claims were being made for a verisimilitude which would, supposedly, shock or disgust the polite readers the *Account* wished to address. Such tensions were at least superficially resolved by an explicit commitment on the part of Guthrie and his successors to unvarnished and strictly factual verbatim reporting. Samuel Rossell (Ordinary from 1746 to 1747) informed the reader that, although 'some of the following relations may appear dry and insipid', yet they were true, both because 'dying men could have no interest in declaring falsehoods [sic]' and because accounts of crimes would be given 'as near as possible in the manner they were related, and in the order of time they were committed'. However, claims that the 'Life and Conversation' of the condemned would be 'faithfully and ingenuously' given in 'almost their own words' were almost invariably accompanied with apologies that exact verbatim reporting was necessarily compromised to make 'a better dress' of the 'Ideas and Thoughts' of malefactors 'altogether illiterate and ignorant'. As John Taylor (Ordinary from 1747 to 1757) explained in 1749, because 'these Poor Creatures were quite illiterate, and could hardly deliver their accounts intelligibly, I have only endeavoured to make it fit to read, keeping to their own Words as near as Possible'.[64]

By the 1760s it had become increasingly common for the Ordinary's *Account* to include badly spelled letters and other documents supposedly penned by the condemned. One such account, by a man who claimed to be innocent of the robbery for which he died, stating that he had worshipped with the 'people called methadis [Methodists] but wose ... neever joyned to ... their sociatey', was prefaced with an editorial 'N.B.' informing the reader that 'the spelling was as false as some of the assertions'. Such an emphasis on the grammatical and orthographic shortcomings of the condemned tended to undermine the fundamental principle of confessional literature – the universality of its message – suggesting as it did that common criminals lacked the moral as well as the intellectual faculties of those 'readers of taste, who may look into this account'; and who, it was 'hoped', would 'not be offended at its plain narrative stile'. From the mid-eighteenth century, it became routine for criminal pamphlets to apologize for having as their 'subject[s]' such 'mean' individuals, explaining that 'the vulgar mind', incapable of benefiting from 'precept', could only 'be struck into a little sense by the terror of example.'[65]

Far from being a 'Glass' or a 'Seamark' for all readers – let alone 'readers of taste' – the condemned was by the middle of the eighteenth century increasingly relegated to his or her proper social sphere. In 1757, for instance, the 60-year-old housebreaker William Hadley was invoked as a warning to 'his brother tradesmen in the smith's way, and his brother soldiers ... [to] learn lessons of honesty and industry, and to be content with their wages'. Similarly, the coachman-cum-horse-thief Peter Hopgood inspired a homily on the dangerous practice of 'servants in general, and coachmen in particular ... purloining and pilfering their masters hay [and] oats ...' Coachmen (and cooks, for good measure) were likewise warned against 'tending their charge' on Sundays, leading to a 'fatal neglect' of 'divine service'. The 'Young and the Ignorant' were frequently targeted, but servants most of all: 'This, we hope, will be a Warning to Servants to be honest and faithful in their different Stations', concluded one 1774 pamphlet published by the Ordinary of Newgate John Villette. Another late Ordinary's *Account* was prefaced with the announcement that 'It is humbly hoped, that all of the lower class, who may happen to read [this], will profit by [it] ... SERVANTS in particular'. One 1758 Ordinary's *Account* called 'aloud on all Parents, and Masters of Families, especially the labouring Class, no less than those of higher Stations' to educate and to 'promote true Religion and Virtue among their Children, Servants and Dependants'. Laments that 'parents, masters and guardians' were 'not only careless in the instruction and management' of youth, 'but even by their own bad examples encourage and lead them on in the ways of vice and wickedness' became something of a chorus in the later Ordinary's *Accounts*.[66]

To some extent, of course, these were age-old themes: Sabbath-breaking, the reciprocal obligations and duties of both masters and servants, parents and children, not to mention the dangerous temptations to which apprentices – young George Barnwells or Thomas Idles – were subject. Yet despite obvious continuities, there does appear to be a gradual shift from an older, universalist conception of crime to one more concerned with, or at least more apt to cite, environmental and class-specific causes of criminality. Indeed, Samuel Rossell viewed the *Account* quite explicitly as an 'attempt to describe low-life in affliction'. According to one 1745 Ordinary's *Account*, when 'the great are so unhappy as to forget themselves', they were 'preserv[ed] from absolute deviation' by 'the bias of education, and bright examples constantly before them'. As for 'lower sort of people', lacking 'advantages of both education and example', once they strayed 'from the road of virtue, they are, generally speaking, lost past redemption'. But there was a 'third rank' – who, having 'never any opportunity of knowing the good things of either heaven or earth, [were] lost from the moment of their birth, and immersed from their cradles in ignorance, stupidity and misery'. It was 'no wonder', then, that those trained 'from the cradle in swearing, lying, thieving, and all other immoralities … should come to a shameful and miserable end'.[67]

However tempting it may be to anticipate the creation of the kind of modern 'criminal class' popularized by Henry Mayhew, this would be not only premature, but would neglect the fact that belief in the existence of a coherent (and often hereditary) criminal underworld dates from at least the Tudor period. Equally, moral explanations of crime persisted and even remained ascendant well into the nineteenth century – and continue to persist today. The later eighteenth-century Ordinary's *Account* nonetheless reveals a distinct, if subtle, shift from an emphasis on the criminal as wilfully ignorant and impious and hardened in vicious courses – in other words, a sinner – to someone who was dangerously deficient in intellectual and moral capacity. 'Want of a proper Education' (that is, religious instruction) had always been cited as a principal cause of criminality, but from the late seventeenth century, a gradual reconfiguration of morality itself, as 'rational religion' – in which man was the rational creature of a reasonable, benevolent, and increasingly distant creator – came to replace the older, pessimistic Calvinist conception of mankind as frail and degenerate, and God as a vengeful and frequently interventionist judge. Increasingly, morality was internalized in the conscience of the rational individual. From the 1690s various Ordinaries – like their latitudinarian Anglican brethren – castigated their Newgate congregations for violating 'the rules of right Reason, and that natural light infus'd into the breast of reasonable Creatures'.[68]

The early eighteenth-century Ordinaries Paul Lorrain and James Guthrie may have conceded to their auditories the enjoyment of a 'Rational Soul … which is no less than the Breath of God', and the possession of an 'internal Magistrate' or moral 'principle … implanted' by 'the wise Creator of our Beings'. But such men not only complained of the difficulty of inducing the condemned to act as penitently and feelingly 'as would have become Reasonable Creatures under such Melancholy Circumstances' but, increasingly, of their very incapacity to do so. The author of a 1735 collection of criminal lives blamed 'that Degeneracy we observe amongst the lower Part of the Human Species' on the fact that their children were never taught to 'mak[e] a due Use of their Reason' in regard to their eternal 'Happiness or Misery'. Such men and women were not only irrational, but scarcely human: the author of a 1773 account of the execution of the highwayman William Cox expressed his amazement that human nature should be capable of such enormities, especially 'if we ... consider man as a rational being, furnished with powers and faculties that enable him to distinguish right from wrong, good from evil ... that he has a monitor in his breast, which frequently admonishes him of the heinousness of his crimes ... and of the sad consequences that will inevitably follow'. Indeed, 'a man can hardly forbear wishing himself of another speicies [sic], and sorry he is connected, in nature with such a profligate race of mortals'. Mid- and late eighteenth-century Ordinaries often complained, not merely that the condemned were hardened, but 'void of any thoughts of religion, and ignorant of its first principles', if nonetheless obliged to hope that their missionary efforts were 'not bestowed in vain, even on such as these'. The Newgate chaplains' exhortations that their flock 'reflect and consider' that they are 'better than the beasts that parish [sic]' seemed only to underscore the psychological gap between the prison chapel pulpit and pews. Many of 'those poor unhappy wretches' were, seemingly, unable to make the leap: the prostitute and thief Judith Tilley, hanged in 1746, was characterized as 'like the beast[s] that perish, as if they were no part of the human specie'.[69]

Rational religion had after the first third of the eighteenth century lost much of its dynamism as a coherent system of thought (like deism, which many religious conservatives believed it abetted), even if many of its precepts were generally absorbed and percolated down the social spectrum. After about 1740, the emphasis was increasingly on sensibility, a capacity for feeling, as not only the mark of refinement, but as an index of one's moral faculties. As a category, however, sensibility lacked even the nominal inclusiveness of reason, supposedly a part of the divine essence imparted to all men.[70] Certainly the ostensibly charitable, and frequently reiterated, claims on the part of mid- and late- eighteenth-century Ordinary's Accounts that the condemned were 'fellow creatures' deserving of pity (and the attentions of moral reformers) betray a certain ambivalence. Although the language is superficially inclusive, the Ordinary's (or the editor's) condescension only serves to emphasize the distance between 'these unhappy people' and the author and reader capable of sympathizing with them. In a newspaper-style essay (a format increasingly common in the post-Applebee era) included in a 1746 Account, featuring the edifying tale of Dick Whittington, the editor confesses that 'I for my part have a great deal of love and tenderness for my fellow creatures, and while humanity reigns supreme in my breast, I cannot help being pleased with such stories, as contribute by example, to make them better and happier'. And, when a 1758 Account attempted to tackle the thorny question of how readers could derive 'rational entertainment, or profitable improvement', from 'the calamities inflicted on our fellow creatures', it was suggested that 'every dispensation of Providence have their various beauties and peculiar uses'. For, 'though the attentive reader be here led through the valley of the shadow of death, yet need he fear no evil; the rod inflicted on others may be turned into a staff and a stay to save, or recover his steps, and comfort him because he is saved'. The notion of the criminal as Everyman, morally no different from his audience – still less that of a monument of grace fitted to preach to the execution crowd – had eroded to the point that the reader was invited to console himself with the knowledge that he at least was 'saved'.[71]

While I will return in subsequent chapters to the decline of confessional literature and the concomitant erosion of the notion of the criminal as 'Everyman', it is worth reiterating here that early and mid-eighteenth-century men and women clung with surprising persistence to a definition of crime as a failure of a moral order. Criminal biographers, for reasons which are not difficult to understand, clearly preferred to view crime as a function of individual choice and a product of a long course of vice rather than as an act of desperation. More surprising, at least at first glance, is the degree to which this was a preference exercised not merely by the authors of criminal lives and confessions, but even by condemned criminals themselves. For as we shall see, while many men and women who suffered at Tyburn were in their last dying speeches eager to extenuate the gravity of their crimes or even to proclaim their innocence, most nonetheless – by assuming sole responsibility for their actions and for their fate – seemed willing enough to acquiesce to what appeared to be a normative moral script. But this script, and the role of Everyman or Everywoman which it conferred, allowed many to make implicit relative moral comparisons between themselves and their audience, messages that were reinforced when the malefactor in question visibly died well, and which could, moreover, be readily appropriated as social commentary, as we shall see in the following chapter.

4

Highwaymen Lives: Social Critique and the Criminal

[the Old Bailey,] Where angry Justice shews her awful Face;
Where little Villains must submit to Fate,
That great Ones may enjoy the World in State.

Samuel Garth, The Dispensary (1699)

Such is the unaccountable Impudence intail'd by a ROGUE making his exit at the tree, [or] a ROGUE that's surviving, that if you examine him concerning the Infamous Life he leads, he'll tell you, every Man robs in his own Way; and will not believe you (though ever so honest) an honester Man than himself.

Captain Alexander Smith, Lives of the Most Noted Highway-men (1714)

Since laws were made for every degree,
To curb vice in others, as well as me,
I wonder we han't better company,
Upon Tyburn Tree!
But gold from the law can take out the sting;
And if rich men like us were to swing,
'Twould thin the land, such numbers to string
Upon Tyburn Tree!

John Gay, The Beggar's Opera (1728)

In the spring of 1763 the highwayman Paul Lewis awaited trial, and subsequently execution, in Newgate – a place where, as one newspaper reported sarcastically, 'this *gentleman* … was well known'. Here he scandalized the Ordinary by 'strutting and rattling his irons' in chapel, 'boasting of his heroic spirit and genius for the highway', and loudly invoking that 'common excuse for all thefts and robberies' – that is, that he 'only robbed the rich to give to the poor'. The 23-year-old Lewis 'affected to be a real McHeath [*sic*]', literally, claiming that 'he could, like that hero, buy off the Old Baily', and 'merrily [singing] *if gold from the law can take out the sting*', one of the most famous, and satirically charged, of all the airs of *The Beggar's Opera*. But, despite the Ordinary's insistence that 'his behaviour and conversation was such as shocked every one who were witnesses of it', Lewis was clearly performing to an appreciative (and not entirely captive) audience. For the 'prophane ribaldry' that so dismayed the prison chaplain seems to have diverted the 'croud of curious spectators' that flocked to see him, as well as the turnkeys and fellow prisoners who, the Ordinary complained, 'daily tickled [his ears] with the title of captain', and 'soothed and bolstered [him] up' with assurances that 'you have always behaved like a gentleman, as you are'.[1]

The original Captain Macheath was the hero of *The Beggar's Opera*, first performed in 1728, and arguably the most popular play of the eighteenth century. Contemporary audiences loved it and moralists condemned it – not so much for its satire of the Walpole administration, perhaps, as for its seeming glorification of its rakish highwayman hero. The eighteenth century abounds with apocryphal but persistent reports of robbers who confessed to having 'raised their courage at the playhouse, by the songs of their hero Macheath, before they sallied forth on their desperate nocturnal exploits', of youthful highwaymen arrested with copies of *The Beggar's Opera* in their pockets; or of the 17-year-old who, 'on quitting the theatre' where the play was performed, 'laid out his last guinea in purchase of a pair of pistols, and stopped a gentleman on the highway'. James Boswell, too, fancied himself something of a 'Captain Macheath', noting in a journal entry dated 19 May 1763 an encounter with 'two pretty little girls' with whom he drank and 'toyed' while regaling them with 'Youth's the Season', an appropriately amorous air from *The Beggar's Opera*. Only a fortnight earlier Boswell had witnessed Paul Lewis's execution, an event which had 'thrown [him] into a very deep melancholy' – not least because he clearly identified with the young highwayman, whom he described admiringly as 'a genteel, spirited young fellow'; in short, 'just a Macheath'.[2]

The choice of a game and unrepentant highwayman as the hero of *The Beggar's Opera* reflected not just a burgeoning interest in modern individualism and subjectivity, or what one recent scholar has termed the 'charismatic, deviant, *individualist*', but rather that the practice of drawing satiric parallels between high life and low had a long pedigree.[3] Elizabethan and Jacobean beggar and cony-catching pamphlets had long capitalized on the old theme that, while all men (and women) were rogues (and whores), great villains not only committed – with impunity – the same offences for which little rogues routinely hanged, but on a far greater scale. By the early eighteenth century, however, the stock figures of earlier rogue literature, the sturdy beggar and the card-sharper or confidence man, had been replaced by the highwayman as the 'social critic' par excellence. Moreover, the highwayman delivered a more specific and hence potentially more powerful social critique than that of his predecessors. The underworld fraternities of sturdy beggars and cony-catchers (and their female equivalents, 'cross-biting' prostitutes) were often represented as an inverted mirror image of respectable society, positing a largely universalist critique of the frailty and hypocrisy of human nature. In contrast, the highwayman was discriminating in his choice of victims, collecting 'contributions' only from the rich, or those who travelled by coach. Moreover, the fact that the highwayman robbed on horseback and dressed like a beau seemed to suggest the possibility that the 'Knight of the Road' was not the only thief disguised as a gentleman.[4]

The highwayman is one of the most evocative and indelibly familiar of all eighteenth-century images, not least, perhaps, because of his social ambiguity. Was the 'Knight of the Road' a gentleman or a popular hero, the product and satirical vehicle of the Augustan literati or the common property of a larger culture? Some scholars have read late seventeenth- and eighteenth-century highwaymen accounts as plebeian fantasies of freedom, leisure and empowerment, or expressions of an alternate morality and resistance to the 'new discipline' of early industrial capitalism. Others have characterized highwaymen 'lives' as a genre whose escapist content and picaresque form served to 'palliate' the guilt of its (primarily middle-class) audience in regard to the execution of property offenders.[5] Here I will explore the degree to which such literature constituted not merely an index of respectable anxieties or popular wish-fulfilment or class conflict, but formed part of a larger dialectic between oral and literate traditions, representation and practice. For early and mid-eighteenth-century demand for highwaymen lives not only reflected and facilitated a dynamic interchange between patrician and plebeian culture, but cast certain real-life property offenders – burglars and street robbers as well as highwaymen – as media personalities whose currency transcended class lines. However ironically these criminals' claims to gentility may have been treated by pamphleteers, such Newgate celebrities were nonetheless both willing and increasingly able to capitalize on both the opportunities and the anxieties generated by the burgeoning eighteenth-century 'public sphere' and its relative social fluidity and ambiguity.

From the middle of the seventeenth century there was a great proliferation of pamphlets, ballads and broadsheets celebrating the exploits of famous highwaymen. Many, like the former Cavalier officer turned 'Knight of the Road' Captain James Hind, were invested with a distinctively counter-cultural allure, although such accounts clearly tapped into older cultural traditions about the heroic English outlaw/robber, such as Robin Hood.[6] The late seventeenth-century popularity of highwaymen lives can also be linked to more prosaic developments, not least of which was the rise of the highwayman himself on the heels of such technological advances as the flintlock pistol, not to mention increasing traffic on the roads leading in and out of the metropolis. Even the myth of the gallant highwayman had, to some extent, a basis in fact. Many 'real-life' mounted robbers were reported as behaving chivalrously, anxious not to frighten ladies, refraining from pointing their guns or searching their victims – sometimes returning items of sentimental value, such as wedding rings, or even a small sum to bear return travelling expenses. The relative civility of such encounters can be explained, in part, by the fact that, unlike the 'footpad' or street robber, the highwayman was mounted and armed, and thus had little need to resort to physical violence or to bind his victims in order to facilitate his escape. Many highway robbers, as we shall see, seemed to have been only too willing to subscribe to such a code of civility, if only because victims who had been courteously treated would be less likely to prosecute their assailants or to positively identify them if called to testify in court.[7]

The early eighteenth-century reading public eagerly devoured collections of the lives of highwaymen, pirates and other robbers. Captain Alexander Smith's *History of the Lives of the most Noted Highway-men* expanded to two volumes and ran to three editions within a year of its first printing in 1713. Smith's rival, Captain Charles Johnson, published *A General History of the Robberies and Murders of the most Notorious Pyrates* in 1724 (a work sometimes attributed to Defoe)[8]: by 1726, it had run to a fourth edition, and by 1728, a two-volume fifth edition had been issued. In 1734 Johnson followed up with *A General History of the Lives and Adventures of the Most Famous Highwaymen, Murderers, Street Robbers &c.* In 1726, Smith published *Memoirs of the Life and Times of the Famous Jonathan Wild*, which included other 'Lives of Modern [i.e., eighteenth-century] Rogues'. Over the course of the eighteenth century, Smith and Johnson's work would spawn many imitators – or plagiarists – some of equal pseudonymous rank, such as Captain Mackelcan and Captain Mackdonald.

These semi-fictionalized seventeenth-century highwaymen typically robbed lawyers, quack doctors, moneylenders and crooked tradesmen, declaiming at length against their perfidy and hypocrisy, and forcing them to deliver up their ill-gotten gains. Such accounts clearly functioned on one level simply as a means through which the most timeless and universal of social grievances could be identified and resolved, however momentarily. Episodes featuring highwaymen robbing their landlords are legion; also common are stories in which robbers succeed in forcing those travellers who most loudly plead poverty to deliver up what invariably amounts to considerable wealth. The implication is that those who are most adept at avoiding paying their fair share are often the same people (certainly in the popular imagination) who have managed to hoard or secrete the most riches. One of the most popular, and frequently reproduced, of such stories involved Captain James Hind and a 'Committee-man' – an official during the Interregnum – on his way to London 'to buy many commodities', riding on a decrepit old mare and dressed in rags. Hind stops the official but, instead of robbing him, takes pity on his apparent poverty – giving him a piece of gold with which to 'drink his health & be merry at his Inn'. Once at the inn, however, the 'old Miser' boasts of his narrow escape and, vowing that he would rather see the 'Rogue' (Hind) 'hang'd before i'le spend one penny for his sake', retires to bed after an early and abstemious meal. Hind, following the committee man to the inn, soon gathered that the latter had, far from drinking his health, 'called him Rogue thousand times'. The highwayman exacts his vengeance the following morning, overtaking the committee man for the second time on the road. Hind, after denouncing as 'lyes' the official's protests that he had drunk Hind's health (and that of the royal family) until he was 'never so drunk in all my life', announced that 'I will now make you call me Rogue for something': he then forced the man to 'untye his greatte knap-sack, where he found fifty pound in gold, and his own peice [sic] besides'.[9]

Hind not only righted social wrongs by robbing various types of villains (thus exposing them for the misers, hypocrites or parasites that they were); he also styled himself as a kind of Robin Hood who would neither shed 'blood unjustly' nor 'wrong any poor man of the worth of the penny', but make 'bold' with 'rich Bomkin[s]' and 'lying Lawyer[s]'. In a typical episode, Hind rescues an honest innkeeper from the clutches of 'two Bailies and a Usurer' by paying his debt of £200 – a sum promptly recouped when, shortly afterwards, he met with the bill collectors on the highway. Smith and Johnson not only recycle these, and others of Hind's exploits, but include accounts of other highwaymen who free poor debtors and rob grasping moneylenders and bailiffs. Smith's Captain Dudley, 'when ever he had got any considerable Booty from Great People' would give 'to such whom he really knew to be poor'; thus, he claimed, he kept 'pretty close to the Text, Feed the Hungry and send the Rich Empty away'.[10]

Much of the highwayman's effectiveness as a social critic stemmed from the fact that he could so convincingly ape the mannerisms of his social betters. Such literature abounds with stories of highwaymen who, under the guise of honest fellow-travellers or lodgers, not only fraternize with their victims before they rob them, but blithely commiserate with them afterwards. Ironically, the 'Knight of the Road' has only to remove his mask to pass as a gentleman, and to replace it when he is again reduced to raising contributions on the highway. ''Tis Impudence and Money makes a P[ee]r', Daniel Defoe observed; he could well have added that, in a world that judged on appearances, a good horse and fine clothes also went a long way. The highwayman not only called social distinctions into question by passing himself off as something he was not (and thus insinuating that in this, too, he was only imitating his betters), but by suggesting that his counterfeit gentility was not necessarily inferior to the genuine article. Even at his most dissipated, the highwayman was no worse than the aristocrat in terms of 'his profuse Living, in keeping right Quality's Hours ... by dining when others sup, supping when others breakfast, going to Bed when others get up, and getting up when others go to Bed', and, perhaps inevitably, 'by being soon left Moneyless'. In contrast to their grasping and miserly but law-abiding victims, highwaymen are often characterized as 'liberal' in their 'Entertainments' and 'free' with their 'Money'. It is their very 'Generosity', in fact, that is frequently cited as the reason they have been obliged to take to the road in the first place. Many real-life robbers were invested with the reputation of being heavy tippers and scrupulous about repaying their debts. One newspaper reported that the famous highwayman Dick Turpin and an accomplice, after fleeing a public house in Whitechapel upon the approach of a constable, paid their reckoning by Penny Post – a bill they were so 'punctual' to honour, hinted the author, because 'their land-lord was as honest as themselves' (that is, a confederate of thieves).[11]

Smith and Johnson's heroes not only caricatured aristocratic vice and bourgeois respectability but could, by inverting the natural order, deliver a more pointed critique of legal morality and institutions. According to the pirate Captain Bellamy, 'Laws' are made by the rich 'for their own Security, for the cowardly Whelps have not the Courage otherwise to defend what they get by their Knavery': 'they rob the Poor under Cover of Law … and we plunder the Rich under the Protection of our own Courage'. Johnson juxtaposes the rough-and-ready 'Form of Justice' meted out by pirates with the 'bribing of Witnesses', 'packing of Juries' and 'torturing and wresting the Sense of the law' characteristic of more 'lawful Commissions'. One of the central themes of such literature is that the robber is the only honest man in a world of rogues; his victims, his superiors not only in roguery but in criminal culpability. When Johnson's highwayman Old Mob robbed Sir George Jeffreys, the notorious hanging judge of the Bloody Assizes, it is the criminal who threatens to charge a constable with the magistrate, claiming that Jeffreys had put him 'in Bodily Fear' several months earlier at the Hertford assizes.[12]

The image of the law as a spider's web which caught only the smallest flies but which let larger ones break through was as old as the third-century BC Greek philologist Aristarchus. Nonetheless, early eighteenth-century collections of highwayman and pirate lives placed an unprecedented emphasis on the large-scale depredations of great, or 'State' villains, making frequent and specific reference to the notion that great rogues grow rich from engaging in activities no less scurrilous or injurious to society than those petty offences for which little wretches routinely hanged. After all, Johnson asks, 'Who was Nimrod, but a successful Free-booter? And what were all the Founders of Monarchies, but Incroachers on the Properties of their Brethren and Neighbours?' Alexander the Great was 'a Plunderer of the first Magnitude', and 'all his extraordinary Exploits … were only Robberies committed upon every one better than himself'. If the lives of such illustrious brigands were omitted from Johnson's collection, this is, he explains in characteristically tongue-in-cheek fashion, only for want of space. The 'Memoirs' of 'Great Villains' would 'swell to a very large bulk': 'were we to give our Readers an Universal History of ROBBERS, of all Ranks and Degrees, from the Beginning of the World to this Time, our Scheme would be almost as extensive, as if we proposed to write a General History of all Nations'.[13]

In addition to more traditional villains, Smith and Johnson's highwaymen also robbed various officials, courtiers and other expensive parasites. The Royalist highwayman James Hind was supposed to have confined his depredations primarily to 'the Republican Party', frequently robbing regicides and other enemies of his 'Royal Master' – who, it would seem, frequently travelled by coach. In one of Smith's more improbable episodes, the highwayman Zachary Howard robs Oliver Cromwell in his own bedchamber, striking 'the Republican Hero with such a Pannick Fear' that he meekly submits to being robbed, bound hand and foot, and even having a 'Close Stool ... clapt ... on his Head'. (Such scatological humour was characteristic of rogue literature, and acted at least in part as a social leveller.) Nor did Smith and Johnson spare Royalist favourites such as Charles II's mistresses. 'Honest Nell' Gwynn proves herself to be not only a Protestant, but a 'sharitable W—re', when she cheerfully bestows ten guineas on the Irish highwayman Patrick O'Bryan. When, however, the Duchess of Portsmouth is less forthcoming, Old Mob is quick to remind her that 'I am King here, Madam, and I have a Whore to keep on the Publick Contributions, as well as King Charles'.[14]

Even if such social commentary was, by the early eighteenth century, displaced onto an increasingly distant past, readers would have had little difficulty drawing parallels between the various bêtes noires of the Interregnum and the Restoration, and the South Sea Directors, stock-jobbers and placemen of the Robinocracy. Indeed, as we shall see, the notion of the criminal as social critic formed part of popular discourse, and could be appropriated in various ways by various readers or listeners – even by 'real' criminals themselves. And it was this fluidity that opened up a space in which self-styled Macheaths such as Paul Lewis could, by their last dying words and behaviour in that most public of theatres – Tyburn – vividly illustrate Samuel Garth's oft-quoted adage: 'little *villains* must submit to fate,/ that great ones may enjoy the world in state'[15] – an epigram which also adorned the title pages of Smith's 1726 collection of criminal lives and Johnson's 1734 *General History of the Highwaymen*. Such robbers-cum-real-life social critics could, moreover, raise the potentially troubling suggestion that the little rogue was not only no worse than many of his betters, but more honest, in that he at least was willing to risk his neck for his pleasures, and to pay for them with his life.

THE CRIMINAL AS A VEHICLE FOR SOCIAL SATIRE

Moralists found *The Beggar's Opera* objectionable largely in that it was so accessible – and, indeed, so amenable to appropriation – by the lower orders.

As one late eighteenth-century commentator complained, 'The agreeableness of the entertainment, and its being adapted to the taste of the vulgar, and set to easy tunes (which almost every body can remember) makes the contagion spread wider'. The play was 'the Thief's Creed and Common Prayer book', offering the robber the consolation that 'he is no worse than his betters', and 'very ill calculated to mend the morals of the common people', as it brought 'the highest and most respectable characters ... down to a level with themselves'. Contemporaries viewed the representation and reception of the play as evidence of a dangerously promiscuous – if to some, titillating – social fluidity, or ambiguity, in and outside the theatre. Random encounters between 'real' criminals and respectable citizens would seem to illustrate this two-way traffic. In April 1728, Anne Pearson's purse was snatched by two women while she was 'in the Passage going into the new Playhouse' on her way to see *The Beggar's Opera*. In December of the same year, the forger Paul Kerney, an 'idle person' posing as a substantial Spanish merchant, was apprehended while attending a performance of the play at Tunbridge where, like a gentleman, he had 'gone ... to take his Pleasure'. The famous highwayman William Cox was supposed to have confessed that 'the Beggars Opera was the first and principal cause of his ruin, and that he had frequently robbed in order to obtain money to see that pernicious piece'. Indeed, in one of his very first thefts, Cox stopped at a stationer's shop to ask for a copy of *The Beggar's Opera*, 'which he said was for his sister'; and, while the mistress of the shop went to fetch the play, 'filched a silver spoon'. Criminals themselves may have been most sensitive to this kind of irony. In the account supposedly 'taken from his own Mouth' in Newgate, the street robber James Dalton claimed that 'in the height of all our Robberies' he and his companions 'used to go to the Playhouse, dressed like Gentlemen', and that once, while watching *The Beggar's Opera*, 'Captain Macheath's Fetters happening to be loose', one of them 'call'd out, *Captain, Captain, your Bazzel is undone*'. The real thieves, having shown up the actors with their superior knowledge of both irons and cant, then retired in style to an alehouse, 'in four Chairs, with six Lights before each Chair'.[16]

Perhaps no one criminal better exemplifies this dialectic between practice, representation and print than the celebrated petty thief and prison-breaker, Jack Sheppard, believed by some to have been the model for Gay's Macheath.[17] Sheppard's second escape from Newgate and his subsequent recapture 'made such a noise in the town, that it was thought the common people would have gone mad about him, there being not a porter to be had for love nor money, nor getting into an ale-house, for butchers, shoemakers and barbers, all engaged in controversies and wagers about Sheppard'. Street-singers were said to have 'subsisted many days very comfortably upon ballads and letters about [him]'; and, in the account of his life which he himself endorsed at the gallows, Sheppard was supposed to have claimed that after his escape from Newgate, he disguised himself as a beggar, overhearing (and sometimes participating in) numerous conversations about himself, and even 'mix[ing] with a Crowd about two Ballad-Singers' who were very 'merry' on the 'Matter' of his own adventures. The young housebreaker also inspired, according to one contemporary, at least 'six or seven Histories of his Life', as well as many prints, both of his exploits and of his portrait (after the original painted by Sir James Thornhill, Hogarth's father-in-law). One newspaper even reported that George I 'was pleased to send' for two of the copper-plates detailing Sheppard's escape from the condemned hold. In a persistent if improbable report, it was claimed that a contemporary minister preached a sermon exhorting parishioners to emulate Sheppard's famous escape, albeit 'not in a carnal, but in a spiritual Sense': that is, to 'open the Locks of your Hearts with the Nail of Repentance ... break through the Stone-Wall of Despair', and so escape both 'the Prison of Iniquity' and 'the Clutches of that old Executioner the Devil'.[18]

Sheppard was also good newspaper copy. Shortly after his execution, *The British Journal* published a 'Dialogue between Julius Caesar and Jack Sheppard', in which the latter argued that he had 'only infringed the Laws, not overturned them' and 'did not grow too big a Villain for them to punish me, as [Caesar] did'. Not surprisingly, Sheppard emerged the victor of the debate, demonstrating that his 'Actions' were not only 'as wonderful, and somewhat honester' than those of his opponent, but that they 'were enterprized upon a justifiable Score, the Maintenance of Life'. Many contemporary accounts of Sheppard's life, while less overtly satirical, invoked similar themes. Newgate during Sheppard's (intermittent) residence there is described as an 'Assembly Room' 'crouded with *Gentlemen* and *Ladies* of the strictest Honour and Reputation', all of whom had paid 'Lusty Fee[s]' to the gaolers to attend the 'Levee' of the famous prison-breaker. The notion of Sheppard presiding over an assembly 'of Persons of Figure and Distinction' was intended to be ludicrous, but also conveyed the impression that the burglar's proximity to his guests was as much moral as physical.[19] And the fact that one of Sheppard's visitors was the Lord Chancellor, the Earl of Macclesfield, who was the following year convicted for embezzling public funds, was an irony not lost on Grub-Street wits, as we shall see.

Nor did contemporary biographers shy away from the question of who had profited more from Sheppard's depredations on the public – the thief or his publicists. Sheppard was described as the 'Benefactor' to many 'Lyrick as well as Prose Pamphleteers', particularly the printer John Applebee, whose account of Sheppard's life was publicly endorsed by the latter at the gallows, and who was said to have 'crackt several Bottles of good Old Port ... on [the prison-breaker's] Account'. In one of several plays based on his exploits, Sheppard breaks into the house of a Welsh lawyer and, while rifling through his effects, finds an account of his own life, which it seems, 'the old Rogue' (that is, the lawyer), had 'design[ed] to send into the Country' or, in other words, to sell to a provincial publisher.[20] The scene ends predictably enough, with a watchman and constable mistaking the homeowner for the housebreaker and hauling him off to the roundhouse, while Sheppard, passing himself off as the lawyer, makes a leisurely escape. Sheppard's robbery of the lawyer is, moreover, justified by recourse to the old rogue adage that 'No Mortal can deride us If we a Biter bite'; in other words, it is no crime to plunder those who live by despoiling others. Sheppard's escapes from Newgate are also described as a species of 'Rob-Thief' – that is, snatching back his liberty from those who had deprived him of it in the first place. One pamphleteer, after first noting that 'Liberty and Property are the two Darlings of an English Subject', ironically condemned Sheppard's 'unruly Desires after other Mens Goods', which had led him to break out of prison with his shackles still attached to his ankles.[21]

Sheppard was not the first thief to be used as a mouthpiece to denounce the hypocrisy and corruption of a society of which he was merely the mirror image. As the author of a 1708 'Elegy' on the execution of the street robber John Hall reminded the reader, 'If ev'ry Rogue throughout the Nation/ Should die, like HALL, by Suffocation,/ Some, now in Coaches, would in Carts/ At Triple Tree receive Deserts'. Not only would 'Lawyers, Physicians, Courtiers, Jaylors ... march in Troops [to Tyburn], and all the Taylors', but even 'a L[or]d' or two.[22] However, it was not until the 1720s that the robber or housebreaker as social critic really came into his own. The satirical juxtaposition of roguery in high life and low seemed especially apropos in the wake of the South Sea Bubble, the first stock market crash in English history, and the meteoric rise to power of Robert Walpole, the first English prime minister. In a fictional 1721 letter from 'John Ketch' to the 'South-Sea Directors', the executioner complained that 'it really affects me with Pity to be obliged to strangle so many ... poor harmless Offenders, that only commit Murders and [robberies]' each sessions, 'while Whole-sale Plunderers ... the known Promoters of Villany, and the merciless Authors of Misery, Want and General Ruin' – the brokers, directors and others in high places who escaped the Bubble unscathed, when so many investors were bankrupted – 'go on to ride in Coaches and Six'. Johnson's pirates are represented as 'dividing the Spoil and Plunder of their Fellow-Creatures among themselves ... satisfying their Consciences with this Salvo, that other People would have done the same Things, if they had had equal Courage, and the like Opportunities'. Yet, the narrator adds, if they 'had known what was doing in England, at the same Time, by the South-Sea Directors, and their Directors' (that is, politicians like Robert Walpole, whose deft management of the disaster served to advance his own career), the pirates would have had the additional consolation of knowing 'That whatever Robberies they had committed, they were not the greatest Villains then living in the World'.[23]

Shortly after the South Sea Bubble debacle, a satirical account of 'the Last Dying Speech and Confession' of the outgoing parliament was published, boasting that 'neither the great Robber Cartouch abroad, nor any of the Fraternities of our Thieves at Home … can equal our Atchievements, or so much as light a Candle to us their Superiors'. According to the epigram on the title page, 'Should Vulgar Criminals like These offend,/ Their Lives at T[ybur]n they would justly End'. The parliament is equated with the infamous thief-taker and criminal mastermind Jonathan Wild: a man who simultaneously made a lucrative trade in receiving and in reward money, maintaining both his control over a large network of thieves, and for some years even the appearance of respectability, by periodically apprehending and informing against the most expendable or problematic of his 'Pensioners'. The parliament was made to admit that 'we have follow'd in [Wild's] Steps in every Thing but the bringing to Justice of our Brother Malefactors … but in all other Respects, the World will confess we are very much Superiour to this Honorable Person'.[24]

Wild – as *The Beggar's Opera*'s Peachum (i.e., 'impeach 'em'), or *The Prison-Breaker*'s Jonathan Wile – played both the villainous foil to Macheath or to Sheppard, respectively, and the underworld analogue for Robert Walpole. The analogy could extend to any crooked minister, as is illustrated by a 1725 'Epistle' from Jack Sheppard to the disgraced former Lord Chancellor, the Earl of Macclesfield, describing 'your Lordship in short' as 'no more than the Jonathan Wilde of the Court'. Sheppard not only complains that Macclesfield 'broke through all Laws, while I only broke Jail', but asks why it is that 'We who rob for our Living, if taken must die' unlike 'Those who plunder poor Orphans' and who surely 'deserve … a Rope more than Blueskin and I'. Joseph 'Blueskin' Blake, Sheppard's former accomplice, was one of the many unfortunate 'foster children' whom Wild had 'bred … up in the Art of Thieving' only to abandon to the gallows. In October 1724, when Blueskin was outside the Old Bailey courthouse waiting to be arraigned on charges of burglary, he asked Wild (who was, as usual, appearing at the sessions to give evidence) 'to put in a word for him' at his trial. Wild, however, demurred, saying that while he would provide him a coffin and 'a good Book or Two', he 'believe[d Blake] must die'. Enraged, Blake fell on Wild and slit his throat – an attempt promptly celebrated by street-singers announcing the 'Good News' that, since 'Blueskin's sharp Penknife hath set you at ease … Ye honester poor Rogues' could, like those 'Sharpers so rich [they can] buy off the Noose' (i.e., more 'Learned Rogues' such as lawyers, 'Courtiers', 'Peers' and 'some Parliament Men') now also rob with impunity. Such celebrations proved slightly premature, as Wild survived the wound; his reputation, however, was not so easily salvaged and, as we have seen, the famous thief-taker followed his former pupil to the gallows in May 1725.[25]

Newspapers (especially opposition newspapers such as *The Craftsman*) continued to invoke such themes in the 1730s and 1740s, characterizing Walpole as 'a *Publick Highwayman*' guilty of crimes 'seldom pardon'd in *petty Malefactors*', and bemoaning the fact that 'of all Delinquents, none can do so much Mischief as Ministers and Magistrates', who were authors not of 'Common Rogueries', but of 'Public Calamities'. Ostensible discussions of 'real' highwaymen such as Dick Turpin often degenerated into covert assaults on more eminent robbers, by innocently asking how 'a Fellow … known to be a Thief by the whole Kingdom, shall for a long Time' not only 'continue to rob us … but to make a Jest of us for being robbed; shall defy the Laws, and laugh at Justice'. Moreover, 'none of the *great Robbers* of the *Publick* ever made a full Confession of their Crimes … as 'tis customary for *low Felons* to do at Tyburn'. Nor did 'these purpled Robbers', unlike the 'petty Rogue', expiate their sins at the gallows, as the recently executed highwayman Henry Simms, or 'Gentleman Harry' was made to complain in one satirical pamphlet.[26] It is, the latter argues, 'a gross Affront upon your worshipful Fraternity [t]o rank such petty Fellows' as pickpockets and thieves 'with such eminent Personages as merit the high Title of Villain'. Nonetheless, Harry comforts himself with the conviction 'that I am in a much better state … with regard to Futurity … than many eminent Villains whose Stations screen them from the Gallows', for 'if I robbed the Publick, I did it openly, and risked my Life for every Trifle I became Master of'. Harry was like Macheath or Sheppard's stage incarnations in that they not only (unlike their betters) 'had Courage enough' to 'pick a Pocket, or take a Purse on the Road', but professed their willingness to pay for their 'Follies' with their lives: in the words of Macheath, 'death is a debt,/ A debt on demand. So take what I owe'. Harry concludes by assuring the reader that 'I am contented, now that I am going to die, to gain the Character of a little sneaking Sinner, and confess myself by many Degrees honester than most of you'.[27]

While the little-rogue-versus-great-villain trope was less common after the 1740s, it was occasionally revived in the later eighteenth century. The highwayman Jack Rann, who had at his 1774 Bow Street preliminary examination delighted some onlookers and scandalized others by wearing ribbons and flowers in his irons – in short, 'exhibit[ing] the Character of Mackheath highly improved and exaggerated' – was posthumously recruited to play the low-life foil first, to 'Lord Nabob' (an exchange identical to that of Sheppard and Caesar fifty years before); and second, to the newly elected mayor, the former radical and notorious libertine John Wilkes. The debate between 'Sixteen-string Jack' (so-called for Rann's famous fashion statement, that of tying his knee-breeches with strings rather than buttons) and 'Gold-collared Jack' (Wilkes) effectively demonstrated, among other things, that 'Sixteen-string Jack's attempts upon women were all of the most gallant kind', while 'Gold-collared Jack's Essay on Woman was the most infamous and unmanly'. If Rann, 'to answer the necessaries of life, occasionally collected from a public he knew nothing of, at hazard of his neck', not so the 'burner of capital bonds' and author of 'the blackest catalogue of private and public frauds', the Lord Mayor elect, who 'to pander to the extravagancies of ungovernable passions, robbed the fatherless infant, whom he was confided in to protect'.[28]

CRIMINAL CELEBRITIES

The 1720s marked the apogee of the highwayman or street robber, not only as a social critic, but also as a celebrity in his own right. Crowds of people of all walks of life thronged to Newgate to visit such famous criminals as Sheppard, Blueskin, Edward Burnworth and his gang of street robbers (hanged in Kingston in 1726), and the dashing Irish highwayman James Carrick (hanged at Tyburn in 1722). Indeed, the latter was an even more likely candidate for the original Macheath than Sheppard: described by one newspaper as 'Major Kerrick the Chief of the Street Robbers', Carrick was the quintessential game highwayman, spending his last minutes smiling, cracking jokes, taking snuff, and assuming 'genteel Airs in fixing the Rope aright about his Neck'.[29] Public fascination with certain eminent offenders persisted into the second half of the eighteenth century. Horace Walpole complained in 1750 of 'the ridiculous rage there is of going to Newgate', noting that three thousand people visited the so-called 'gentleman highwayman' James Maclaine in his cell the Sunday following his condemnation. Walpole had himself been robbed in Hyde Park at gunpoint by Maclaine several months earlier, but had declined to prosecute – even though, in the course of this robbery, Maclaine had accidentally discharged his gun near Walpole's cheek, 'scorching his face'. Walpole described himself as 'almost single' in not visiting his 'friend' in Newgate, claiming not to want Maclaine's 'idea' – mental image – although whether from distaste or sympathy is not clear. (The son of the prime minister parodied in *The Beggar's Opera* was not reticent, however, about comparing Maclaine's genteel female visitors, ladies of his acquaintance, to Macheath's 'doxies' Polly and Lucy). As late as 1774, the highwayman William Cox was supposed to have 'exclaimed with an oath' that the turnkey who admitted spectators to his cell 'gets more money by making a show of me, than ever I did by thieving'.[30]

Interest in, as well as anxiety about, robbers and robbery was roughly correlated with the incidence of such crime itself, peaking in the 'crime waves' of the 1690s, 1720s and 1740s, periods following peace treaties and military demobilization. At such times, large numbers of young unemployed men would converge on the metropolis, principally former soldiers and sailors familiar with firearms, many of them demoralized by military service and accustomed to rapine and plunder. The housebreaker John Appleton, hanged in 1721, claimed to have been so 'scourged and lashed and salted &c' at sea that it had 'hard'ned his Mind' and 'made him hate and defy almost all Mankind': 'he was no sooner set on Shore' than he began 'spoiling and preying on all whom he thought he could with security'. One newspaper remarked on the fact that, of the eight robbers sentenced to death at the Old Bailey in July 1746, all but two were soldiers.[31]

The late seventeenth-century diarist John Evelyn wrote in 1699 of 'Horrible roberys, high-way men, & murders committed such as never was known in this Nation since Christian reformed'. During 'an extraordinary Fog' earlier the same year, no fewer than fourteen people in and around London were 'stript', 'Robbed and Knockt down' and 'Robbed, Bound, Gag'd and thrown into a Ditch' on a single day. Complaints rose to a fever pitch again in the 1720s, when one criminal chronicler wrote that 'possibly in future Times 'twill be thought an Exaggeration of Truth to say that even at Noon-day, and in the most open Places in London, Persons were stopped and robbed, the Offenders for many Months escaping with Impunity'. In 1726, Edward Burnworth and his gang of street robbers shot a thief-taker dead at his home in Clerkenwell; later, while the victim's wife and others were 'shrieking', they fired a pistol to disperse a gathering crowd. For several weeks after this bold murder, Burnworth's gang 'continued to carry out their rapacious Plunderings, in almost all Parts of town', often in broad daylight. Burnworth himself continued to frequent his local alehouse in Holborn, 'laying a Pistol down on the Table', calling for and drinking off pints of ale, 'defying any Body to touch him'. (The gang was finally broken when one of its members turned evidence against the others; Burnworth was apprehended and brought to justice only after he had been betrayed by the woman with whom he was then living.) Anxieties about crime were again on the ascendant in the late 1740s, when one newspaper claimed that 'not only pickpockets, but street robbers and highwaymen were grown to a great pitch of insolence … robbing in gangs, defying authority, and often rescuing their companions, and carrying them off in triumph'.[32]

Early eighteenth-century clergymen and enterprising pamphleteers vied for the exclusive possession of the 'lives' and confessions of the most notorious robbers. Such publications ranged in price from roughly twopence to sixpence and, while longer, more elaborately illustrated pamphlets sometimes cost as much as a shilling, broadsides and cheaper pamphlets would not have been beyond the reach of artisans, or even labourers or servants – especially when we consider how this literature would have been recycled, passing through the hands of the purchaser, then to a coffee-house or to a tavern, finally making its way, perhaps, to grace the workshop wall of some real-life Tom Idle. 'In this land of liberty, of general wealth, curiosity, and idleness', wrote one commentator in 1765, 'there is scarce a human creature so poor that it cannot afford to buy or hire a Paper or a Pamphlet, or so busy that it cannot find leisure to read it.' This was seen as less a testimony to progress than to the increasing luxury and indolence of the lower orders. According to one 1729 newspaper, 'Authors have one sure Comfort'; that is, 'none can write so low' as to be unable to 'find Readers': while their masters and mistresses diverted themselves with 'dull Plays and long romances,/ Down in the Kitchen, honest Dick and Doll,/Are studying Collonel Jack and Flanders Moll'.[33]

Although the audience for such literature was less popular and more 'middling' than such complaints would imply, this did not exclude the active participation of famous criminals themselves, as I have suggested. Certainly many malefactors, even – or sometimes especially – those who withheld their confessions from the Ordinary of Newgate or other clergymen, seemed willing enough to take an active part in their own self-mythologization. Robert Rhodes, hanged in 1742, 'was always very merry amongst his Fellow Sufferers, and took delight in telling of [his] Rogueries'. The author of one 1722 pamphlet supposedly sought out the company of the street robber John Hawkins 'because I took much pleasure in hearing him speak of his merry Pranks and many Robberies'. The street robber Edward Reynolds, hanged in 1726, claimed that 'between' liberal infusions of 'Liquor' and tall 'Tales' of 'Gentlemen highwaymen', he had allowed himself to be persuaded by his drinking companion Stephen Barnham that robbery was 'a gallant Action' preferable to 'the Drudgery of hard Labour'. In 1700 John Simpson (later one of Smith and Johnson's highwayman heroes), claimed that he had killed '4 or 5 Men upon Quarrels' and that, while a soldier in Flanders, he had robbed various officers' tents (including, he claimed, that of the King) as well as numerous 'Papists', even stealing £1,200 worth of plate from St Peter's in Ghent. The Ordinary 'told him ... it was impossible that all this should be true, that he only spoke of it to be talk'd of'.[34]

Thomas Cross, hanged in 1721, 'seemed to glory in the Robberies he had committed', boasting to the Ordinary that he and his accomplice, William Spiggot, had once robbed 'one Hundred Passengers' in a single night. Such men seemed to delight in large metric units. Spiggot told the chaplain that 'it was vain to mention his numerous Robberies on the High-Way, being perhaps a Hundred'. (A witness at his trial testified that Spiggot had 'swore he would kill a Thousand before he would be taken'.) In 1741 Henry Cooke supposedly confessed to having 'committed an innumerable Sight of Robberies, more than an hundred'. At their execution in Kingston in 1726, Edward Burnworth and his accomplices 'all acknowledged that to have given a particular detail of their several Robberies (a Work mightily sought for by some poor Printers that hung about them) would be an endless Task; Burnworth saying, that for his part alone, an hundred Sheets of Paper wrote as close as could be, could not contain them'.[35]

It is interesting that Cross, Spiggot, Burnworth and Cooke also distinguished themselves by standing 'mute' at their trials, and were all accordingly threatened with the terrible punishment meted out to accused felons who would not plead to their indictments: *peine forte et dure*, or being slowly pressed to death under heavy weights. Spiggot and Burnworth persisted in their resolution, enduring the horrific torture of the press for about thirty minutes and an hour, respectively, before finally consenting to enter pleas of not guilty. Although there had been instances of men of substance subjecting themselves to the *peine* in order to escape criminal conviction and forfeiture of their estates which, in the event of their being pressed to death, could be transmitted entire to their heirs, this rationale hardly extended to working-class criminals of little or no property. Such bravura displays are perhaps better interpreted as a kind of rejection of the tribunal and of legal morality generally.[36] Not surprisingly, contemporaries tended to explain such behaviour as a function of 'the ridiculous Spirit of vain Glory' of young robbers, and their 'vain Inclination to be much talked of'. In 1721, Nathaniel Hawes, another young street robber ('not 20 Years old') and would-be 'hero in low-life', refused to enter a plea, 'affecting' unconcern as to the consequences, until a 'handsome Suit of Cloaths' was returned to him. He was then subjected to the press, labouring under a weight of 350 pounds for seven minutes before relenting and consenting to plead. Hawes supposedly explained that 'his Behaviour at the Sessions House was as became a Man of Courage and bold Spirit': thus, he claimed, he would 'Merit a greater Reputation by the bold-ness of his Behaviour, than any Highwayman that had died these seven Years.'[37]

Criminal celebrities were often active in their own mythologization. Burnworth 'diverted himself' while in Newgate (when not occupied by visits from 'People of Distinction') 'in sketching his own Picture in several Forms', including a picture of himself as 'he lay under the Press', later the frontispiece of 'a six Penny Book which was published of his Life'. Some three months before he was executed, the street robber Stephen Barnham is reported to have publicly exhibited a stolen spoon and other silver goods in Little Britain (the neighbourhood where he grew up), boasting that they were 'the produce of the Day's Work'. Upon this, Barnham supposedly climbed up a lamp post and put his head through the iron ring at the top, swearing 'loudly' that 'before four Months were expir'd', he would 'be Hang'd in that Place' – to which the Ordinary added drily, 'as to Time, he has been as good as his Word, tho' by the Lenity of our Laws, he suffer'd at the usual Place with the other Malefactors'. Several days before his execution, Barnham was said to have 'employed his Time in his Cell, in composing a Song to celebrate the glorious Actions of himself and his Companions' – a 'Work he very much valued himself upon'. However, the printer John Applebee refused to publish it on the grounds that 'it contain[ed] excitements to their Companions to go on in the same Trade'.[38]

In general, however, John Applebee, who published and sold the Ordinary's *Account* from 1720 to 1744 (a period, interestingly, almost coterminous with that of Walpole's political ascendancy) seemed to have welcomed, rather than suppressed, even the most picaresque of criminal confessions. From the early 1730s, when Applebee assumed editorial control of the *Account*, until 1744, when the disgruntled Ordinary finally sacked him as printer, the short biographies and confessions of the condemned malefactors were followed by lengthy appendices containing letters and supposed autobiographies of some of the most famous criminals.[39] Applebee's appendices abounded in highwayman 'Pranks' and 'frolicks' of every description: lawyers and quack doctors were forced to deliver up their ill-gotten gains, misers obliged to disclose the location of their hoards, and foolish countrymen cozened out of their savings. Many of these stories sound suspiciously familiar, recycled as they often were from contemporary jest-books, which drew in their turn from such older sources as Chaucer and Boccaccio, while at the same time forming part of an oral tradition with which criminals themselves were clearly conversant. (In a 1722 pamphlet attributed to the robber William Hawkins, explicit reference is made to Smith's *Lives of the Highwaymen*, as well as to Richard Head and Francis Kirkman's picaresque Restoration work *The English Rogue*.)[40] Often, it is difficult to distinguish where art is imitating life, or vice versa. Nonetheless, many of these accounts have the ring, if not exactly of verisimilitude, at least of popular appropriation, if only because they so obviously strove to place the narrator in the best possible light. Many highwaymen touted themselves as Robin Hoods who robbed only those 'within the coach', and frequently spared those who pled poverty.

The street robber Joseph Shaw, hanged in 1738, was supposed to have claimed that whenever he and his companions 'had got a good Booty', they 'bestow'd a small Part of it in Charity, and often relieved poor People, but we generally told them how we came by the Money; charging them not to spoil our Sport, for then 'twould be out of our Power ever to give them any more'. Similarly, a 1742 account supposedly dictated by the highwayman Jesse Waldon describes the latter not only returning money to a victim who claimed to be a 'poor Man' with a 'large Family', but giving him an extra shilling to 'drink' his 'Health'. Waldon also related another incident in which he robbed a gentleman, while his accomplice, Tom Easter, stood guard some distance away. The hapless gentleman, not realizing the two men were in cahoots, rode up to Easter and exclaimed, 'Sir, I am likely to be robbed; for that Man is a Highwayman! Sir, (said Easter) I am afraid that you are, and taking hold of his Horse's Reins, pulled out a Pistol, and demanded his Money. Why (said the Gentleman) I took you for an honest Man!' To which Easter replied, 'So I am ... because I rob from the Rich to give to the Poor'.[41]

In the appendix to a 1737 Ordinary's *Account*, we are told that the robber John Purdy 'would fain have appear'd – tho' a Thief – a conscientious one,' claiming that 'he never robb'd any Poor Person, but only such as were able to bear it ...' Purdy apparently maintained that he had not 'committed any great Crime in robbing the Rich ... for to let you know Sir, said he, *all the People I used to rob had too much Money, and I had too little.'* (Suspiciously similar words had been attributed to the burglar James Gardner, hanged in 1706, a fact that suggests that some speeches may have been recycled from older material, especially during the period that the *Account* was under Applebee's direction.) It was, at any rate, a frequent refrain: some criminals claiming that it was hardly a 'Sin' to rob 'those who would have spent the Money ... in Gaiety and Luxury, or those who perhaps had unjustly acquired it by Gaming'; others even invoking the Winstanleyian principle that, since 'the Air, the Earth, and all the Elements were given for the Enjoyment of all alike', it was not just that 'a few worthless Fellows should roll in Heaps of gold', while other 'free-born Souls ... pine[d] with Want'. Jack Sheppard himself, when asked 'how he could use poor People [those he robbed] so', supposedly retorted that 'I wish you and I were as Rich ... making it no Crime in him to steal from those in better Circumstances than himself'.[42]

Far from being exclusive to Applebee's appendices, such themes cropped up regularly in other Ordinary's *Accounts* and in late seventeenth and early-eighteenth century criminal literature generally. In 1679 George Rawlins informed the Ordinary not only that he had 'never used violence to any person's life', but that he had once reimbursed a poor man whom he had robbed of twenty shillings on his way to market with double the sum, to compensate him for what he 'might otherwise have gain'd by his Market'. The highwayman Charles Lee, who died 'very resolute' at Tyburn in 1689, clearly fancied himself a second James Hind, throwing a handful of coins among the crowd and announcing that he had 'followed the Road these Seven Years and more' and that 'the late King [James II] had £1500 of my Gettings'. He concluded by asserting 'That he never committed Murder, nor never Robbed any poor Man in his Life'. At his 1721 execution, Thomas Butledge reportedly told spectators that 'he never committed Murder: nor ever robb'd any poor Man; but relieved them, whenever in his Power, even on the High-Way'. We are told that John Turner, or 'Civil John', a highwayman executed in 1727, would hold out his hat, only requesting whatever money his victims 'thought fit to give him', and returning all or part to those whose 'Aspect' or 'Dress ... gave him room to suspect, that their Wants were as great as his'. Another highwayman, James Wright, hanged in 1721, was supposed to have claimed that he only robbed those coaches 'whose Equipage and Appearance show'd them best able to sustain a loss: That he never would rob a poor Man, but pittied him, as much as himself', and that as 'he fancied that as the Rich could better spare it than the Poor, there was less Crime in taking it from them'.[43]

As I have suggested, such literature reflected the degree to which highwaymen, and even street robbers, aspired to a certain chivalric code, or at least sought to represent their actions in such a light. Like the legendary seventeenth-century highwayman Claude Duval, Henry Simms ('Gentleman Harry') was famous for his gallantry to the 'Fair Sex'. On one occasion he robbed a coach in which a 'beautiful young Lady' was travelling, supposedly asking nothing of her but 'a kind Salute' (a kiss): a request with which she 'readily complied'. Even the street robbers John Levee and Joseph 'Blueskin' Blake apparently prided themselves on their forbearance towards a 'Gentlewoman' who, during the course of a robbery 'struck them ... on the Face, and us'd them very roughly', but 'as she was a Woman, they let her go, and got nothing of her'. Levee also claimed that on another occasion, he and Blueskin robbed a man of two shillings and some copper coins but, upon his pleading illness as well as poverty, they 'helped him again on Horseback, because he was unable to get up himself, and returned him his Money, and led his Horse safe into the Road again'. The street robber Thomas Pinks, hanged in 1742, claimed that he had attempted in vain to dissuade his comrades from robbing a man who had 'cry'd very much, and said he was Poor' and that 'his Wife was sick', finally giving him the contents of his own pocket 'to compensate his Loss'. Joseph Cole claimed that after stealing a parcel from a shop and discovering it contained bridal clothes, a gift from a young man to his betrothed, he arranged (for the fee of a crown) 'to return the young Woman her Things again' so that 'she should not be disappointed' on her upcoming wedding day.[44]

A central component of the highwayman mystique was his reluctance to resort to violence. In 1693 James Whitney (another of Smith and Johnson's highwayman heroes) 'solemnly protested' to the Ordinary 'that he always declin'd any cruel dealing toward those whom he robb'd'. While he freely 'confessed that he had been guilty of many Robberies', he insisted that 'he never killed any Person; and that he did refrain from wounding any Man, lest he should die of his Wounds'. In 1705 the highwayman Joseph Johnson assured the prison chaplain that he had been 'so far from designing Murther at any time, that he always resolved rather to be killed than Kill'. Many street robbers, as well, were quick to represent themselves as having scruples about gratuitous violence, whatever the reality of their own actions or those they attributed to their companions. Stephen Phillips claimed that his former accomplice's rape of a maidservant in the course of a home invasion 'gave him more uneasiness than all his Robberies', and expressed his remorse 'for letting the young Woman be us'd after so barbarous a Manner'. The two men subsequently parted ways after 'having some Words ... about the young Woman'. Humphrey Angier, hanged in 1723, renounced the 'Cruelty and Barbarity' of his two former associates Mead and Butler, claiming that he 'refus'd to sit down or drink with' Mead after the latter had boasted of the murder of one of his victims, telling Butler 'that Cruelty was no Courage'. An overwhelming majority of robbers, footpads as well as highwaymen, expressed their abhorrence of murder. The highwayman John Winship, hanged in 1721, expressed the conviction – far too common for the Ordinary's liking – that 'tho' he had been guilty of all other Sins', because 'he had never committed Murther ... God would graciously pardon him'. All six men hanged at Tyburn in December 1707 'expressed great Satisfaction' that 'not one of them had ever kill'd any Person', although the Ordinary was quick to 'put them in mind, that the very attempt or design to kill [i.e., robbery], was murther before God'.[45]

The 15-year-old street robber Bernard Fink, hanged in 1731, insisted that when on one occasion he and fellow gang members overheard a murder being committed, they responded by giving chase to the perpetrators 'for being so barbarous to commit Murder; (for that I always did abhor)'. Fink also claimed that when one of his own confederates threatened to shoot a robbery victim 'for having nothing', he (Fink) 'stepp'd up to him, and said if you hurt the Gentleman, I will shoot you thro' the Head; the Gentleman reply'd, "God bless you, you are all young Men, I wish you better Success"'. Highway civility was often represented as a two-way street. Early and mid-century newspapers regularly reported not only instances of robbers returning money to their victims, 'lest [they] meet with an Accident on the Road', but also polite exchanges in which gentlemen who did not carry money or watches on their person extended invitations of 'a Glass of Wine' if their would-be robbers chose to call on them at home, and in which all parties 'took Leave very genteelly'. Henry Simms ('Gentleman Harry') was conforming to a familiar script when, upon robbing a coach and seeing one of his victims burst into tears over the loss of a valued keepsake, he 'presented my Hat, wherein I had taken my Booty, and said for God's sake take that or any thing else you please'. The gentleman responded by telling Simms 'he was sorry I had not a better Way of Living' and 'bid me make what Haste I could off, for he saw a good many People coming up. I thank'd him, and took my Leave'.[46]

In a curiously picaresque story attributed to the street robber Edward Burnworth, he and one of his confederates were travelling with a gentleman they intended to rob but who, after hearing them complain of 'a Shortness of Money', freely offered to make them a loan. 'This generous Offer made them decline all Thoughts of robbing him'; later Burnworth 'was so ingenious [sic] as to acquaint him with his Course of Life, and with what a narrow Escape he had met with by falling into the Hands of *Men of Honour*'. This gentleman supposedly later served as a juror at the Old Bailey, 'where he related the whole Story, and sent his Fellow-Traveller Mr Burnworth several Books of Devotion to the Condemn'd Hold of Newgate'. Such highway civility not only reduced the likelihood that a robbery would end in violence or that the victim would prosecute his or her robbers, but could in rare cases result in a pardon for the perpetrator. We are told that, in 1761, the highwayman David Morgan received a last-minute reprieve from the gallows because, in the course of one of his robberies, he had refrained from returning fire after one of his victims had attempted to shoot him. When the gentleman in question then 'begged his Life; Morgan replied, "God forbid I should take your Life"', claiming 'Necessity' for his actions. Another gentleman in the coach then addressed the highwayman: 'All you can desire of a Gentleman is to ask Pardon', to which Morgan humbly replied, 'I do not desire even that'.[47]

If such stories featured moments of social détente, others were more pointed in identifying the larger socio-economic causes of robbery and theft. The highwayman William Selwood, alias Jenkins, hanged in 1691, refused to name any of his accomplices or give 'any account of his wicked life', saying only 'he wisht he had never been born, but every one must live and not starve'. In 1736 the condemned horse-thief John Tarlton was reported to have written verses on the wall of his cell, asking 'Poverty God D[am]n you, what makes you haunt me so', and lamenting the fact that he had been reduced to pawning all his clothes and 'Forc'd to Eat dry crusts, instead of butter'd Buns'. Many phrases commonly attributed to property criminals tapped into a discourse of social levelling: for instance, the robber James Lamb was supposed to have 'd[amne]d' one of his victims 'because his Shoes were best, and swore he must exchange with him, telling him, Exchange was no Robbery'. Michael Bewley supposedly claimed that he had intended to return the money he had robbed from one of his victims, but upon hearing that he was a stockbroker, was overruled by his accomplice, who insisted it was 'no Sin to rob a Broker, for it is only playing at Rob Thief'. Some condemned criminals were clearly both willing and able to make connections between their personal predicament and larger satirical discourse. In his dying speech, Thomas Bean, executed in 1716 for rioting, declared that 'I shall not Inlarg, upon the hardship of my Trial, to which I was hurryed without a Moments Notice', and to which he was not able to summon defence witnesses, 'nor upon the Wickedness, Falshood, and Malice of the evidence that swore against me, &c'. Rather, he contented himself with 'put[ting]' the reader 'in mind' of 'the Fable of the Crows and the Pigeons' by Roger L'Estrange, citing fable and page numbers, as well as the moral; that is, 'one Criminal upon the Bench, will be sure to bring of [sic] another at the Barr', concluding, 'one might easily guess who ... the Crows ... and who the poor harmless uppress'd Pigeons are'.[48]

Just as many seventeenth- and eighteenth-century criminals appropriated political causes such as Jacobitism as 'idioms of defiance',[49] so too did some street robbers draw implicit parallels between their own petty rogueries and the larger crimes committed by their betters. In an account supposedly written by the robber Ralph Wilson, the latter describes robbing a coach in Chancery Lane, and committing two other robberies on 'one Night in August 1720, when all Mankind were turn'd Thieves' – a tacit reference to the South Sea Bubble. Wilson later claims to have been visited in prison by 'a Man of very odd Aspect' (probably the then respectable Jonathan Wild) who attempted to bribe him to swear falsely against another prisoner whom he had never met, a 'Relation' illustrating 'that sometimes the Men of Reputation are the greatest Villains'. A similar point seems to have been made by the street robber Edward Burnworth, who boasted of robbing the house of Lord Chief Justice Eyre and stealing 'his Lordship's Hat ... an excellent Beaver'. Later, while being visited in Newgate by 'several Persons of Quality', including 'a noble Duke' and 'several Earls', Burnworth 'entertain'd' his guests with 'Stories of his many Robberies, and shew'd them the Trick of *pricking the Girdle*, &c'. 'His Grace' was then supposed to have remarked that 'it was a pity he did not discover [testify against] his Gang, and get the favour of being transported', to which Burnworth 'reply'd ... that *He thought himself FUR enough already*'. 'Fur' was Latin for thief, and while perhaps also a play on being transported far ('*FUR*') away, the main point seems to have been that while Burnworth was thief enough to steal the beaver hat of a chief justice, he was not rogue enough to betray his companions – or even, perhaps, rogue enough to assume the role of judge. Significantly, the contemporary cant word for aldermen (and, by extension, magistrates) was 'fur-men,' in reference to their fur-lined gowns.[50]

It may, of course, be objected that such accounts are too mediated to be taken as genuine plebeian indictments of the criminal law. However, in the case of the 'game' criminal – that is, the dashing highwayman or street robber who, like Swift's Clever Tom Clinch, dressed 'like a beau', and 'hung like a 'hero', without tears or 'flinch[ing]' – the condemned could at the place of execution provide a visual text to accompany or reinforce the most picaresque of biographies.[51] It may not even be too far-fetched to suggest that the game criminal's flamboyant dress could communicate to spectators that, while he resembled the dissipated aristocrat or courtier in exteriors, he differed from him, first in that he was neither a hypocrite nor a coward; and second, in that he was both willing and able to discharge his debts. And, in the context of a culture in which it was an article of belief that death was a debt all men and women owed to their maker as a result of original sin, the game criminal's ostentatious display of courage was potentially subversive. For the criminal who met death boldly – rejecting the passive role by fixing the noose around his own neck and by jumping off the cart before it was drawn away (or the ladder before it was 'turned') – not only advertised his prefer- ence for a quick death over a slow one by strangulation, but implicitly conveyed Macheath's message 'that death is a debt ... so take what I owe'. Such a bold leap into futurity could, possibly, also serve to remind spectators that while *he* had settled accounts, many more respectable but less 'honest' rogues had not.

Some criminals made this connection more explicit than others. In May 1741, the highwayman Francis Piggot 'behaved with great boldness' at his preliminary hearing, 'and went out snapping his Fingers, singing, *At the Tree I shall suffer with Pleasure*' (one of Macheath's most famous lines), and announcing that 'he should have a short Life and a merry one' (a quote attributed to the pirate Captain

Roberts). Another highwayman, Isaac Darkin, not only 'frequently diverted himself with reading *The Beggar's Opera*' while awaiting execution, but loudly broadcast his 'Determination ... to suffer without discovering the least Dread of Death; never to betray his Connections, but to die like a Hero'. Moreover, such self-styled Macheaths were in a position to make a more powerful statement than that of their fictional role model, whose resolution to 'die as brave as the best', was never actually put to 'the test' (Macheath was reprieved at the foot of the gallows). At his execution, Isaac Darkin boldly threw himself from the cart before it was drawn away; similarly, Paul Lewis to the last 'still affected the McHeath', fixing the noose about his own neck and, also without waiting, throwing himself off the cart so 'violently' that he broke his neck.[52]

THE DECLINE OF THE HIGHWAYMAN TRADITION

After the middle of the eighteenth century, as Lincoln Faller has pointed out, the highwayman's earlier role as a social critic exposing 'the pretensions of the rich and privileged' had largely fallen into desuetude; instead, 'it is the pretensions of the highwayman himself', a diminished and 'pathetic parvenu', 'that comes under fire'.[53] While seventeenth- and early eighteenth-century criminal literature had tended to focus almost exclusively on universal human depravity as the root cause of crime, there was after the first third of the eighteenth century an increasing emphasis on the 'Train of ill Consequences' following from that 'dangerous Passion' so common to the young: the 'mean and foolish Ambition of ... imposing themselves upon the World, for Persons of much higher rank than they really are'. Countless pert servants and idle apprentices, it was believed, followed the example of the highwayman John Turner, alias 'Civil John', whose 'Vices arose ... from the Imitation of those fine Gentlemen, on whom he had waited while a Lad'. Joseph Leath, another highwayman who claimed never to have robbed 'any Person without the Coach', was supposed to have cited 'Pleasure' as 'the Bait' which had drawn him to a life of crime. 'We see Gentlemen in their idle Hours, and are tempted to imitate their Courses' which, 'though it does not excuse it ought to make us pitied'.[54]

The so-called 'gentleman highwayman' James Maclaine, hanged in 1750, provides a good example of both a growing preoccupation with, and an anxiety about, robbers who attempted to 'pass' as gentlemen. According to Horace Walpole, the 'fashionable highwayman' had generated 'as many prints and pamphlets' as the recent London earthquake. Several of these accounts still contained elements of social satire: according to one pamphlet, Maclaine's accomplice, Plunket, 'used to brag in Company, that he was a free Man of the World, tho' he could not boast as some of the Great did, of borrowing Thousands'.

In one robbery, Plunket and Maclaine were supposed to have declared, when a 'Roman Catholick Priest ... expostulated with [them]' for taking from him his 'Linnen', 'that it was Necessity forced them upon those hazardous Enterprizes: that they did not rob thro' Wantonness, as the great ones did, who daily rob'd 'em of Millions, for the Support of Luxury and Corruption, but that they were forced to it for their immediate Subsistence'. Yet this same pamphlet describes how Maclaine was foiled in his plans to marry an heiress through the interference of a certain 'Captain M', who 'very justly acquainted [her family] with Mac's Character', and who subsequently refused Maclaine's challenge of a duel, 'answering very properly, that he was not obliged to fight every Scoundrel, and that he [Maclaine] was no Gentleman'. Stung, Maclaine applied to an officer of his acquaintance for a letter '[testifying to] his being born a Gentleman'; however, when confronted with this document, Captain M declared it a forgery, loudly and publicly reiterating his refusal to fight, even when Maclaine threatened him with a horsewhip. (While in prison Maclaine expressed his indignation when a curious visitor claimed to recognize him as a footpad who had robbed him: he 'stiffly deny'd it, and insisted that he never robbed on Foot in his Life.')[55]

While Maclaine's genteel appearance initially garnered him considerable sympathy, particularly from the ladies – who, when Maclaine delivered a tearful confession at his preliminary hearing, responded with 'simpathetic Tears, and opened [their] Purses' – (male) commentators were ultimately less impressed, dismissing his tears as 'Pusillanimity' rather than sensibility. As one writer claimed, even when Maclaine had taken grand lodgings and moved in fashionable circles, 'he was always slighted by People of Sense and Discernment; who can always discover in the most dazling Dress, Assurance and Insolence from good Breeding'. The Ordinary of Newgate concurred: 'tho' ... in his Dress and Equipage [he] very much affected the fine Gentleman, yet to a Man acquainted with good Breeding, that can distinguish it from Impudence and Affectation, there was very little in his Address or Behaviour, that could entitle him to that Character'.[56] Even the account written by the clergyman who had attended Maclaine, and 'drawn up and published at the earnest Desire of Mr Maclaine himself', exhorted the reader to 'let the fall of this Man to be a Lesson to young People of moderate or low Circumstances, to be content in the humbler Stations they were designed to fill', and 'a Warning to them not to affect a Taste and Appearance above themselves'. Maclaine, according to this author, 'told me more than once, that he dated his Guilt and Ruin from the first moment he stept into a MASQUERADE'. Certainly this was a period of mounting concern and debate about 'those Marts of Lewdness and Gaming ... called by the softer Name of Publick Diversions, especially those where all Distinctions of Quality, Fortune, and Sex, are confounded; and where so much as Shame, the thinnest Defence and Guard of Virtue, is dropt'. Stories about highwaymen dressing as gentlemen and 'frequent[ing] Masquerades, Balls,

Assemblies, Installations, and Places resorted to by Ladies of Quality' in order to rob them of their purses – and worse – clearly played to such anxieties. Not merely masquerades, in which one could disguise one's identity, but also gaming halls were viewed not only as dens of vice, but dangerously liminal social spaces: in the words of Samuel Foote's popular 1760 play *The Minor*, 'death and the dice level all distinctions'.[57]

Interestingly, it was the highwayman's resemblance to the gentleman in those very externals which had, in the early eighteenth century, ideally qualified him as a social critic – his dress, his dissipation and his reputation for gallantry – that increasingly opened him up to scorn after about mid-century. In a 1754 essay in *The World*, highwayman pretensions to gentility are used as a means to illustrate the ridiculous extremes to which contemporary 'refinements' inevitably tended. 'A highwayman would be reckoned a BRUTE, a MONSTER, if he had not all manner of attention not *to frighten the ladies*, and none of the great Mr Nash's laws are more sacred than that of restoring any favourite bauble to which a robbed lady has a particular partiality'. Horace Walpole is ironically chastised for having declined James Maclaine's offer of a midnight rendezvous at Tyburn in order that he might '*purchase again* any trifles he had lost' – which refusal 'seemed liable by ill-natured people into a doubt of the *honour* of a man [Maclaine], who had given him [Walpole] all the satisfaction in his power, for having *unluckily* been near shooting him through the head'. English highwaymen (unlike their French counterparts) were above all '*good company*', but none 'carried TRUE POLITENESS so far as ... the VISITING HIGHWAYMAN'. 'This refined person made it a rule to rob none but people *he visited*' – politely requesting of his hostess 'some favourite ring or snuff-box that he had seen her wear and which he had a mind to wear for her sake', after which he would 'take his leave with a cool bow, and without scampering away, as other men of fashion do from a visit with really the appearance of having stolen something'. The author concludes: 'as I do not doubt but some of my fair readers, as propose being *at home* this winter, will be impatient to send this charming smuggler (Charles Fleming by name) a card for their assemblies, I am sorry to tell them he was hanged last week'.[58] While, of course, still in part an attack on vice and corruption in high life, the highwayman is not portrayed here as a social critic, but rather as no less an imposter than the beau or courtier he so successfully emulated. His ignominious death is reported with a casual abruptness which serves as much to mortify the pretensions of the 'visiting highwayman' as to call into question the conduct of fashionable ladies.

Similarly, in a 1764 'History' of the Robin Hood debating society, the gentleman highwayman Scamper delivers a pious speech on 'the Doctrine of Repentance'; however, while 'this great Advocate for Religion and Morality was speaking', one of his auditors 'recollected that it was on Hounslow-Heath he had had the Misfortune to have seen him'. Scamper was hauled before a justice, committed, and later tried and condemned for highway robbery. However, although he 'had very little Hopes of gaining a Reprieve' he 'did not prepare for Death in the Manner he ought', scarcely thinking of 'his favourite Doctrine, Repentance'. Rather, he died very ill indeed: 'he drank to such Excess, that when the Hour came that he was to suffer ... he seem'd quite insensible of his Fate'. Again, the criticism of the highwayman extends to more respectable citizens, the author expressing his wish that Scamper's hypocrisy and immorality 'were not a common Case in the World'; however, it is significant that Scamper is portrayed as deficient in the one particular that was central to the game criminal's self-representation – his courage at the place of execution.[59]

Such courage seems to have always been problematic, judging by the extent to which contemporaries took pains to dismiss or refute it. Macheath himself, after boasting that at the gallows he would 'scorn to wince or whine', 'raises' his spirits by drinking wine and spirits in quick succession, announcing that 'a man can die/ Much bolder with brandy'. Real-life game criminals, too, had long been accused of resorting to 'artificial' courage – or 'cordial-Spirits'. But even if Macheath's courage was Dutch courage, and his vow to 'stand the test' and 'die as brave as the best' never in fact was put to the test, the association of the game criminal with the brave death was perhaps the aspect of the play most troubling to moralists (a theme to which I will return). Charles Duncombe, writing in 1728, complained of 'how shocking' it was to see 'upon the stage ... a gang of highwaymen and pickpockets ... braving the ignominious death they so justly deserve, with the undaunted resolution of a Stoic philosopher'. For 'the courage expressed in the following lines ['death is a debt ... so take what I owe'] would have become a Seneca or a Raleigh, but seems not so suitable to the character of a criminal'. Nor would it be too far-fetched to argue – especially in the light of moralists' longstanding conviction that 'the Beggar's Opera ... never was represented on the stage without creating an additional number of real thieves' – that this association was particularly problematic, in that it was one that was all too readily appropriated by 'real thieves' themselves, many of whom, at least until the middle of the eighteenth century, commanded a considerable audience.[60]

After mid-century, certain 'gentlemen highwaymen' such as Jack Rann, William Page (hanged in 1758), William Cox (hanged in 1773) and William Hawke (hanged in 1774), continued to attract the attention of the press, but increasingly such attention was confined to the almost invariably facetious question of whether such men indeed qualified as gentlemen. Commentators such as the Ordinary were quick to point out that 'gaudy dress' was not a sufficient claim 'to this denomination'. Later eighteenth-century reporters and pamphleteers generally alternated between a tone of detached pity at such 'melancholy' examples of young men 'split' on that 'fatal Rock' – 'the Affectation of appearing in a Rank of Life to which they have no Pretensions' – and a contemptuous amazement at the audacity of highwaymen like Page, who 'was so infatuated with the Notion of his being a Gentleman, that he carried the Quixotism of Gentility to the Gallows', signalling his readiness to die by 'the dropping of a Cambrick Handkerchief'. And it would seem, too, that real-life criminals such as Paul Lewis revelled no less in his fellow-prisoners' assurances of his having 'always behaved like a gentleman, as you are', than in the title of 'Captain' which they also bestowed upon him. Perhaps the ultimate arbiter of such questions, *The Gentleman's Magazine*, also conferred the epithet of '*gentleman*' upon Lewis, but sarcastically – heartily abusing this 'wretch' who fancied himself 'a man of honour'.[61]

In 1773, in response to resurgent criticisms of the performance of *The Beggar's Opera* – this time by the Bow Street magistrate Sir John Fielding – a letter was published defending the play on the grounds that

> the heroism ... of Macheath is not contagious, and the advice of his companions to *die brave* does not proceed from a contempt of the laws they have violated, but meant merely as a consolation, which in their poor capacities they think will give him spirits to bear the terrors and melancholy apprehensions of death with fortitude. It is their method of philosophizing – they have no abstract ideas, and I suppose never argued whether death in itself is good or evil.

This suggestion that those who lacked the sensibility, and by implication, the education of true gentlemen were congenitally incapable of true moral courage may perhaps explain the Ordinary of Newgate's rather curious characterization of the 20-year-old street robber William Signal in 1752. The latter, who 'made ... Brags of several robberies' he and his companions 'had committed', and broadcast his resolve 'to die game' was, according to the Ordinary, 'a poor, unhappy, ignorant youth, [who] yet had the Vanity to set up for the Macheath of the Day, tho' he was no way equal to the Character, and nothing but Ignorance and Audaciousness, those two despicable, ill Qualities, could give him any Pretence to it'. We can only assume that it was this same 'Ignorance' and 'Audaciousness' – and probably poverty as well – that rendered Signal apparently unsuitable for the role of the stage hero.[62]

Paul Lewis, the 'real Macheath' with whom we began this chapter, is significant not only in that he provides a vivid example of a 'real' highwayman self-consciously performing to, and adapting, a satirical script, but also because he was one of the last game criminals whose words and dying behaviour received extensive, if largely disapproving, notice in the newspaper and pamphlet press. Ballads celebrating the exploits of highwaymen who 'served the poor and robbed the great' – not only 'lords and ladies' in St James's Park, but even Lord Chief Justice Mansfield himself – survived and indeed flourished well into the nineteenth century, long after the age of highway robbery itself had passed into memory.[63] But no new editions of Smith or Johnson were issued in the second half of the eighteenth century, and highwaymen literature featuring recently executed criminals died out as a species of current social satire. While several new highwaymen collections were published in the later eighteenth century – and a third edition of Johnson's *Lives* in 1839 – these were bowdlerized and abridged versions of the older stories, clearly intended for a juvenile audience, and concerned with robbers who hailed from an increasingly mythical past (or who were overtly fictional, like Robin Hood and Falstaff), and whose satirical messages, diluted as they were, were aimed at regimes long since defunct. Thus, long before the introduction of the drop in 1783, the criminal celebrity had lost a platform upon which he could regale the world with his exploits. The speed with which this relatively open forum closed in the second half of the eighteenth century may well testify to the degree to which many of the condemned had not only embraced the role of social critic, but had been able to appropriate this satirical discourse as their own. And, as we will see in the next chapter, last dying speeches and confessions, although an entirely different genre in both form and conception, followed a similar trajectory over the course of the eighteenth century.

This is not to say that the last dying speeches of condemned criminals ceased to invoke the older rogue critiques of the law after the middle of the eighteenth century. Such speeches, however, tended to take the form of street ballads and ephemeral execution sheets aimed at a plebeian audience, without a date or a publisher's imprint, rather than the pamphlets and broadsides once printed for, and sold to, a broader, more middling readership.[64] In some cases, late eighteenth- and early nineteenth-century authorities even took steps to suppress printed criminal confessions containing overt social satire. In an April 1805 letter James March, the Mayor of Norwich, asked the Home Secretary Lord Liverpool what measures should be taken in regard to a printed last dying speech containing 'sentiments' that March, 'as a magistrate', felt 'it is my Duty not to overlook'. March enclosed a copy of the paper (which, he added, was an 'unjustifiable fabrication'), including these lines:

> Am I more criminal now than he who every where affects to be what he really is not; and for no other reason but that he may the more easily possess what is not his own? … The laws that condemned me were made by the great, and have no other object than to keep the wealth of the world in their own power, and entail on others the keenest poverty and the vilest subjection.

The speech went on to claim that 'many an honest fellow has been hanged before me', and concluded with a declaration the Mayor of Norwich would probably have found still more objectionable: that is, the writer's claim to 'see a better fate awaiting me in another [world], and a better state of being'.[65]

5

The Ordinary's Account: *Confession and the Criminal*

> By this may be seen the Necessity of able and experienced Divines, for Posts
> of such Importance as the Preservation of the Souls of dying Men … the
> Characters of the Persons employed to induce them [to a confession of their
> crimes] are as low, as their Salaries, and under the Pretence of Benefiting
> others by the Terrors of Offenders Punishments, and the Odiousness of
> their Example, they only consult their own Interest, by committing these
> Confessions to the Press, for the Lucre that is obtain'd for so doing.
>
> *History of the Press-Yard* (1717)

> There was at that time, a morbid desire for confessions – which continued
> until within a few years – and still exists with a few fanatics. The Ordinary
> used to torture the persons under sentence of death for confessions, the
> purpose being publications by which he obtained money, his pretences,
> relieving the conscience and saving the soul of the criminal.
>
> Francis Place Papers, Vol II: Manners. Morals (1824)

After having been 'Twelve Year a Thief', that most famous of fictional shoplifters, Moll Flanders, is at last apprehended and committed to Newgate. Here she is 'harrass'd' not only by 'the dreadful Apprehensions of Death' and the 'Terror' of a conscience reproaching her for a life ill-spent, but by the unwelcome ministrations of the prison chaplain:

> The Ordinary of Newgate came to me, and talk'd a little in his way, but all his Divinity run
> upon Confessing my Crime, as he call'd it, (tho' he knew not what I was in for) making
> a full Discovery, and the like, without which he told me God would never forgive me;
> and he said so little to the purpose, that I had no Manner of Consolation from him; and
> then to observe the poor Creature preaching Confession and Repentance to me in the
> Morning, and find him drunk with Brandy and Spirits by Noon; this had something in
> it so shocking, that I began to Nauseate the Man more than his Work, and his Work too
> by degrees for the sake of the Man; so that I desir'd him to trouble me no more.

Some fifty years after Moll is reprieved and transported to Virginia – ultimately (if no thanks to the Ordinary) living 'Honest' and dying a 'Penitent' – another famous, but real-life female criminal, the murderess Sarah Malcolm, awaited sentence at Newgate. Here she received a letter from one Morgan Maccay commiserating with her misfortune in being 'daily persecuted by that ignorant Heretick and most *ordinary of all ordinaries*, whose godliness is gain and filthy lucre … who, under pretence of giving saving knowledge, is endeavouring to extort false confession, &c.'[1]

There was no love lost between Moll Flanders' creator and Paul Lorrain, Ordinary of Newgate during Defoe's own incarceration there (and the object of the latter's 1703 verse attack, *A Hymn to the Funeral Sermon*); as for Morgan Maccay, 'he seems to have been a Popish priest'.[2] Yet however partisan, such accounts are nonetheless representative of the kinds of criticisms routinely directed towards the Newgate prison chaplain during the late seventeenth and eighteenth centuries. In his memoirs, Peter Drake describes how Paul Lorrain initially made a good impression when visiting the condemned Jacobite Captain Smith in his cell in 1708, delivering 'a pretty long and moving Exhortation suitable to the Occasion'. Undeterred by Smith's admission that he was a Catholic, Lorrain promised to have 'any Speech or Confession' he wished to make 'truly and carefully publish'd'. When Smith demurred, explaining that he had promised his account in lieu of wages 'to satisfie a poor Man that had attended him since the Beginning of his Confinement', Lorrain vehemently objected: 'it was giving away his Perquisites'. The captain, now 'put … in an Humour unbecoming to a Man appointed to die', seized the Ordinary 'by the Arm, and bidding him begone, asking him if it was a proper Time to talk of Perquisites, when he came to exhort him for the good of his Soul'. Perhaps concluding discretion the better part of valour, Lorrain 'replyed not a Word' but 'went away quietly'.[3]

Common felons cherished even fewer illusions about the Ordinary's motives. 'Instead of his presence being agreeable to them as a Christian pastor should be', the highwayman Charles Speckman and his fellow prisoners 'looked upon [the Ordinary] as come for nothing but his own advantage; and rather to disturb them with insignificant and impertinent questions, than to take care of their poor souls'. Such complaints emanated not only from the condemned, but also more official channels. In 1730 Dr Bedford, minister of Hoxton, complained of the 'scandalous practice of the Ordinaries of Newgate and other prisons in obliging the prisoners to auricular confession, or declaring them damned if they refuse', so that they could 'extort from them an account of their lives … to fill their printed papers and get a penny'.[4]

Like the Ordinary himself, the Ordinary's *Account* has laboured under an almost universally bad press. It was, in the words of one 1737 pamphlet, an 'incoherent Magazine of Trash and Scandal'; a paper so 'slovenly' and 'wretched', another complained in 1763, that it was 'confounded hard to pay six pence' for it. For Francis Place, writing in 1824, the Ordinary's *Account* epitomized the 'Grossness' of the eighteenth century and its 'morbid desire for confessions': its 'bad taste, bad stile, and bad grammar … would disgrace any decent tradesman's son' – let alone clergyman – 'of the present day'. Most nineteenth- and early twentieth-century commentators have shared Place's distaste both for the Ordinary's paper and the Ordinary himself – characterized as morally lax, if not outright 'drunken and dissolute'. And if morally upright Victorian and Edwardian writers had an investment in conflating the Ordinary and his *Account*, respectively, with the corruption and depravity of the eighteenth-century Church and the debased reading tastes of 'those bloodthirsty times', modern scholars have tended to read into the Ordinary's office and his paper alike their own preoccupations with social control and class conflict.[5] The Ordinary has been seen by late twentieth-century literary critics and historians as an officious and intrusive 'public servant' whose 'function was to 'break' the criminal': to 'extort' confessions, prevent a 'bravura performance' at the gallows and enforce conformity to a normative penitential script intended to legitimate his or her sentence of death and, by extension, the socio-economic status quo. Peter Linebaugh's work would suggest that the Ordinary's ministrations were met with almost universal indifference, if not concerted resistance, on the part of the condemned. Linebaugh's Ordinary, with his unceasing efforts to squelch the prisoners' 'infractions of chapel-time solemnities' and 'disorders and petty acts of individual rebelliousness', is an agent of modern alienation and repression, evoking Blake: 'And Priests in black gowns/ Were walking their rounds/ And binding with briars my joys and desires'.[6]

Until very recently, most scholars have tended to view the *Account* as too sensational and scripted – and perhaps too tainted by its religious agenda – to constitute an accurate or reliable source.[7] Indeed, as we are all too aware of in this postmodern era, all historical documents are in fact 'representations'; that is, mediated by the perceptions and various subjectivities of their authors and readers. The *Account* was certainly shaped both by the preconceptions and preoccupations of the Ordinary and that of his audience. It was also – like most periodicals, including newspapers – undeniably formulaic. Its core format varied little from the late seventeenth to the mid-eighteenth century: a brief summary of the sessions at which the criminals were condemned, often including a list of those subsequently reprieved, a recapitulation of the Ordinary's sermons and a report on the behaviour of the condemned in Newgate, followed by short biographies and finally a section detailing the behaviour of the malefactors at the place of execution. The language of the *Account* was also, inevitably, dictated by the conventions of the confessional genre: both the Ordinary's discourses and malefactors' speeches and meditations borrowed heavily from Scripture, *The Book of Common Prayer* and other devotional works.

The Ordinary's *Account* nonetheless constitutes a particularly rich source, in part because of its sheer volume: it was published up to eight times a year for almost a century (and, from the early 1730s to mid-1740s, often including appendices and sometimes in two parts). It is also, as Peter Linebaugh's pioneering work has demonstrated, probably unique as a window into the everyday lives of otherwise ordinary and obscure late seventeenth- and eighteenth-century condemned men and women. Even if their stories and words were contradicted by the prison chaplain, or occasionally punctuated by cynical parenthetical asides, the Ordinary's exchanges and interviews with the condemned generally constituted a dialogue, rather than a normative and univocal or baldly catechetical text. Indeed, as we shall see, far from striving to gloss the accounts of the behaviour and speeches of the condemned as uniformly penitential, the Ordinary tended, if anything, to play up and exaggerate the rigours of his position and the recalcitrance and bad behaviour of his charges. This served both to underscore his own diligence and dauntless missionary efforts and the subsequent, and hard-won, improvement on the part of most (but by no means all) of the condemned. In fact, the Ordinary frequently expressed doubts as to the sincerity and sufficiency of the repentance of the condemned even at the gallows, a place where most malefactors – including many of the hardest cases – took the business of penitence seriously enough. In part this was because false reports of penitent gallows performances would have been quickly refuted in the press, but also because the Ordinary was eager to emphasize not only the rigours of his office but also his very exacting standards.

And however quick Augustan literati were to dismiss it as a Grub Street paper, the Ordinary's *Account* was far from an ephemeral or marginal publication. In the late seventeenth and early eighteenth centuries the market for last dying confessions was so brisk that the *Account* frequently ran regular notices warning against being imposed on by 'false reports' and 'Sham-Papers', or even illicit copies of the Ordinary's sermons to the condemned. Forgeries of the *Account* persisted into the 1720s, with the name of the Ordinary, and sometimes the printer, judiciously misspelled. It is also worth reiterating here that the Ordinary's *Account* was the principal source of later compilations generally assumed to be reliable, such as the *Newgate Calendar*: large sections from the *Account* were cut and pasted verbatim for use in such collections, as well as appended to the end of accounts of trial in various editions of the *Select Trials ... at the Old Bailey* and similar works.[8] The Ordinary's *Account* was also a more mainstream publication than has been traditionally acknowledged, selling for a comparable price and published in a similar format, and by the same publishers, as more respectable pamphlets, newspapers and other serials – most notably the Old Bailey *Proceedings*, widely accepted as an accurate record of trial. Indeed, the Sessions Paper (as contemporaries termed it) and the Ordinary's *Account* began as sister publications. They both emerged as regular serials in the mid-1670s, and became semi-official – that is, published by authority of the City of London – after 1679 in the case of the *Proceedings*, and 1684 in that of the *Account*. In the late seventeenth century the two papers were generally published by the same printers, and in a similar format: both changed from folio broadsides to six-octavo-page pamphlets to evade the 1712 Stamp Tax. Both the *Proceedings* and the *Account* grew dramatically in length in the 1730s, when they also began to be numbered and, later, paginated consecutively according to the mayoral year (i.e., beginning and ending in November). Until the middle of the eighteenth century, the two publications routinely sold for about the same price and were advertised as companion volumes designed to be bound together by the 'gentlemen' who bought 'setts' of both.[9]

And just as we should take nineteenth- and twentieth-century antiquarian and scholarly distaste for the Ordinary's *Account* with a grain of salt, so too should we be careful not to equate contemporary criticisms of the *Account* with an indifference to, or a blanket condemnation of, last dying speeches or confessional literature generally. As I have suggested, the gallows was a central political forum in the late seventeenth and even (if to a lesser degree) the early eighteenth century, with interest in the words of traitors and other eminent offenders spilling over into a demand for information on the lives and confessions of common felons. Last dying speeches were published not only by the Ordinary and various enterprising Grub Street writers but by other ministers, including several luminaries of the Anglican Church: Edward Stillingfleet, Anthony Horneck and, particularly, Gilbert Burnet were frequent visitors to Newgate in the late seventeenth century. The latter's zeal in soliciting last dying confessions was satirized in a 1682 Tory pamphlet in which 'the Reverend Scot, Dr B—', harangues a hapless wooden kitchen counter-top ('the True Protestant Elm-Board') which had unwittingly been scalded – and hence, tainted – by a 'Popishly-affected Cook-Maid'. Burnet would also later publish several sermons he had delivered in the Newgate chapel while Lord William Russell was awaiting execution. And as late as 1708, the Bishop of Oxford permitted his 'Transactions' with several condemned murderers executed in Worcester to be published in a rather sensational criminal pamphlet.[10]

Moreover, even the most scathing contemporary attacks on the Ordinary were predicated on the belief that his office was both important and necessary, if seldom executed as it ought to be. This at any rate is one of the clear messages of the eleventh print in Hogarth's *Industry and Idleness* (1747), which unfavourably contrasts the Newgate chaplain cowering in his closed carriage with the Methodist preacher accompanying Thomas Idle to Tyburn, piously exhorting him to repentance. *The History of the Press-Yard* (1717) lambastes the former Ordinary, Samuel Smith, as a fatuous and blustering 'Question-monger' more concerned with prying into the venial sins of the condemned than bringing them to a sincere and effectual repentance. Yet it is the *Account*, rather than the office of the Ordinary itself, that is called into question: the author appeals to the City magistracy to 'stiffle' the paper 'by putting the Ordinary, who ought to

be chosen out of the most Learned and Brightest Ornaments of the Church …
into a Capacity of living handsomly upon his Salary, without having Recourse
to such mean and unjustifiable Shifts'.[11]

Finally, far from being objectionable in itself, a fulsome confession of sins,
both private and public, was widely considered to be both a necessary condition
and a proof of true repentance. In the end, after all, it is the 'good minister' who
acts as a foil to Defoe's Ordinary, 'whose business it is to extort Confessions
from Prisoners, for Private Ends, or for the farther detecting of other Offenders'.
In what are probably the most powerful passages of the novel (and Defoe
clearly intended them to be such) the good minister 'reviv[es]' Moll Flanders'
'Heart', converting the picaresque heroine into a 'true Penitent'. But first, in
order 'to qualifie him to apply proper Advice and Assistance', he exhorts Moll
to 'disburthen' her 'Mind' to him – promising, however, to keep her confession
confidential. It was 'this honest friendly way of treating me', Moll is made to say,
that 'unlock'd all the Sluices of my Passions: He broke into my very Soul by it;
and I unravell'd all the Wickedness of my Life to him'.[12]

THE ORDINARY: QUESTION-MONGER OR PLAIN DEALER?

The term 'Ordinary' simply means a diocesan officer – in this case a prison
chaplain – appointed to a regular post, rather than a clergyman awarded a living,
or a minister deputed for a particular occasion. The Ordinary of Newgate was
a city official as well as an Anglican clergyman: although his name would have
probably been put forward by an influential church patron and his appointment
ratified by his ecclesiastical superior, the Bishop of London, he was first and
foremost a servant of the City of London, elected (often in a race against several
competitors) by the Lord Mayor and the Court of Aldermen.[13] The Ordinary's
duties included visiting the condemned, preaching and conducting morning
and afternoon services on Sundays and reading morning and evening prayers
at least three times a week; by the middle of the eighteenth century, a bi-weekly
sermon was added to the 'Conditions' of the post, as was the stipulation that the
Ordinary administer the sacrament at least once a month. Unlike many other
London officials, the Ordinary was not permitted to appoint a deputy in his
stead without permission from the City, which was only likely to be granted on
the grounds of serious ill heath. In the late seventeenth century, the City ordered
that the chaplains of other London prisons, such as Ludgate and the Woodstreet
and Poultry Compters, take turns spelling the Ordinary in his attendance on the
condemned. The Ordinary also cheerfully accepted the assistance of numerous
'charitable [Anglican] Divines' who visited on a more voluntary basis, and
tolerated – on a roughly ascending scale of disgruntlement – Dissenters, non-

jurors, Catholic priests and, later, Methodists and even a few Jewish rabbis.[14]

The salary was modest but comparable to many small livings: in 1663 the total annual stipend from various sources was £75, in line with that of other London prison ministers. By 1733, this had risen to £91: a figure including the right to sell two 'Freedoms' of the City annually, valued at about £25 apiece, and moreover supplemented not only by 'a House to live in' on Newgate Street, but the income generated by the *Account*, estimated at as much as £200 per annum in the early eighteenth century. (Paul Lorrain, whose estate was valued at £5,000 at his death in 1719, almost certainly owed a considerable share of his wealth to what he styled his 'melancholly Paper'.) By 1746, the post paid about £100 a year (excluding profits from the *Account*); by 1799, this figure had doubled, in part reflecting the steep inflation of the late eighteenth century, but also, presumably, the fact that the Ordinary's *Account* was now defunct.[15]

Comparatively little is known, outside of contemporary caricature and the Ordinary's paper itself, of the various individuals who officiated as chaplains of Newgate from the beginnings of the *Account* in the mid-1670s until its disappearance almost a century later.[16] But as difficult as it may be to resist the temptation to rehabilitate the reputation of the Ordinary in the face of such nearly universal disapprobation, it must be conceded at the outset that some of the seventeenth-century Ordinaries, at any rate, were certainly corrupt. In 1697, the Secretary of State, James Vernon, complained to the Bishop of London that Samuel Smith (Ordinary from 1676 to 1698) was 'a weak man and very unfit for administering the dutys incumbent on him'. Smith was accused of having 'behaved himself corruptly'– among other things, of having 'taken Mony of the Prisoners for the bringing them of[f] when they should be put to read'. The charge that Smith corruptly administered the reading test for benefit of clergy was a general one: a satirical 'Epitaph of that profound and learned Casuist, the late Ordinary of Newgate' published in a newspaper shortly after his death claimed that, 'In case he were fee'd/ He'd teach one to read/ ... But if no Money came,/ You might hang for old Sam'. His paper, according to contemporary critics, was also for sale: anyone who greased the Ordinary's palm was daubed 'with Church-paint' and made 'a Saint'; on the other hand, if 'any dy'd hard, / And left no Reward', Smith would 'kill them again,/ With his murdering Pen'.[17]

By all accounts, the next Ordinary, John Allen (1698–9), surpassed his predecessor in venality, and was in fact discharged by the Court of Aldermen scarcely six months after his appointment for 'undue practices', including the 'frequent prevariccons in ye printing and Publishing the pretended Confessions of the respective Criminalls That are executed at Tybourne'. Allen went so far as to fabricate false confessions and dying speeches in order to prosecute a feud with his new wife's former brother-in-law, Captain Charles Newey. Allen was, moreover, reported to have pocketed charitable donations and money sent to prisoners by relations, and to have solicited bribes from condemned malefactors under the (false) pretext of obtaining reprieves for them, as well as from illiterate defendants wishing to claim benefit of clergy. As one complainant testified, 'Dr Allen did Cheat me of Five Shillings, under pretence of being my Friend, when I was Try'd at the Old-Baily, to say I could Read my Neck Verse [Psalm 51:1] when I could not read at all, but the said Allen kept my Mony and did me no service'.[18]

It is unlikely that subsequent Ordinaries would have dared to abuse their office so flagrantly; at any rate, the elimination of the reading test for clergy in 1706, during the tenure of Paul Lorrain (1700–1719) removed one important source of temptation. It seems unlikely that Lorrain himself, a Huguenot emigré and former secretary to Samuel Pepys, was corrupt. He was, however, an astute businessman, under whom the *Account* assumed its familiar title and became both a high-profile and profitable publication – as Lorrain was supposed to have explained to Dryden Leach, after rejecting him in favour of another printer who offered him better terms: 'truly he must take him that would pay him best'. Under Lorrain, the *Account* often boasted several columns of advertisements; certainly, his claim in one 1714 *Account* that 'I have nothing to do with whatever comes in after my name' (i.e., his concluding subscription) seemed rather disingenuous in the light of the fact that this particular issue advertised – alongside notices for chocolate, Captain Alexander Smith's *Lives of the Highwaymen*, and water purported to cure 'the itch'– a list of a half a dozen of Lorrain's own publications 'set forth … before he was, and since he is Ordinary of Newgate'. Nor did Lorrain scruple to use the *Account* to defend himself against a variety of charges. To the accusation that he accepted money to administer the sacrament, Lorrain claimed that 'so far from having sought any Temporal Advantage that way … ever since his being Ordinary of Newgate, he has provided Bread and Wine … there … at his own Charge'; 'nor was he ever Brib'd for obtaining, or endeavouring to obtain Reprieves for any'. Lorrain claimed in 1712 that 'in the Twelve Years (almost) I have been in this unpleasant and ingrateful office', he had only recommended three condemned felons for reprieves. (For despite the denials of Lorrain and subsequent Ordinaries, their good opinion clearly carried at least some weight in this regard.) Lorrain also defended himself against the charge that he had ever accepted any 'Gratuity for his representing the Case of Malefactors, better or worse, than it really appear'd to his judgement'. As for an unnamed woman who supposedly claimed 'that by Bribes one might have any thing put into the Dying Speech', he had this ominous rejoinder: 'If ever that Gentlewoman comes under my Hand (which God Forbid) she will find, that I am not a man capable of being bribed.'[19]

Nor were accusations of venality the most frequent, or even perhaps the most damning, of those levelled against the Ordinary. Contemporary critics typically dismissed the Ordinary as a laughably incompetent minister, whose threats of hellfire and brimstone were more likely to be met with scorn and indifference than with tears and trembling. According to one 1698 'Elegy' to the recently deceased Samuel Smith: 'Heav'n at last has hear'd the Pris'ners Pray'rs/ And took Thee from this Worlds attending Cares;/ Aged in Years, and Worn with Greif to see,/ Thy Counsel lough'd [sic] at, as they laugh'd at Thee./ And let the silent Grave thy Body take/ Offenseless now, Because it cannot speak'. Nearly twenty years after his death, Samuel Smith's hectoring yet ineffectual pastoral style still set a low benchmark; in the anonymous *History of the Press-Yard* (1717) a tongue-in-cheek story is told of Smith's 'Examination' of a condemned thief, in which the Ordinary is increasingly incensed at the latter's refusal to admit he had been a 'Sabbath-Breaker' (rather, 'it was his Business to frequent [church] for the better carrying on of his Trade, which was that of Picking Pockets'); 'an abominable Drunkard' (he had always, he claimed, had an 'Aversion to strong Liquor'); or, finally, a 'flagrant Whore-master' (never having 'known what a Woman is, carnally, to this Day'). Thus baffled in regard to 'the only three Topicks' he could 'in any ways enlarge upon', Smith is 'at a loss to say any thing' of the condemned in his 'Paper'. When the pickpocket had the temerity to point out 'then it's nothing with you to be a Thief ... I am sure I find it otherwise, for I am justly Condemn'd for so being', he is ordered out by the irate Ordinary: '"such Case-harden'd Rogues, as you, would Ruin the Sale of my Paper, I'll e'en write you down OBSTINATE"; and so he did; But others afterwards came in, and made him amends by more ample Confessions.'[20]

Although the same author described the current chaplain, Paul Lorrain, as 'a very Tertullian in respect to some of his Predecessors', distinguished (if, again, comparatively) for his 'Sincerity and Plain-dealing', the condemned had apparently 'conceived such an indifferent opinion of him from common Report' that all of his discourse went 'in at one Ear and out at the other'. Fairly or not, Newgate chaplains were almost universally described as weak and ineffectual, unequal to the demands of their office. In 1725 Mandeville noted with disgust the inability of the Ordinary to exert any control over the condemned at Tyburn, where they were described as 'either drinking madly, or uttering the vilest Ribaldry, and jeering others, that are less impenitent; whilst the Ordinary bustles among them ... distribut[ing] Scraps of good Counsel to unattentive Hearers'. And just as late seventeenth-century critics ridiculed the literary pretensions of the 'Reverend Drone', Samuel Smith, the Augustan literati inevitably characterized the Ordinaries of Newgate as Grub Street hacks and minions of Dulness (the goddess of dunces, or literary mediocrities, in Pope's *Dunciad*). Thomas Purney (Ordinary from 1719 to 1727), was a favourite butt of satirists – possibly because, in addition to the more conventional religious works expected of an early modern clergyman, he had published several pastoral odes; or, perhaps simply because he was Ordinary during the execution of some of the most famous criminals of the eighteenth century, such as Jack Sheppard, Blueskin and Jonathan Wild.[21] In the 1725 pamphlet, *News from the Dead: or a Dialogue between Blueskin, Sheppard and Jonathan Wild*, the disgraced thief-taker, his neck still crooked from being hanged, is scarcely reunited with his former cronies in hell when he is asked what had 'become of that fellow, who used to Murder the dying Speeches of Malefactors, and put his Readers to more pain in finding out his meaning, than the Criminals suffered in getting rid of his Non-Sence?' Wild replied that 'he [Purney] was the very same numerical [i.e., rhyming] Blockhead' as ever: 'From Paths of Dullness never vary/ But still be N–g–te's Ordinary'. Sheppard then puts an end to the subject, so as not to 'trifle away Time, and talk about a *Thing* that is not worth regarding'.[22]

The Ordinary was thus frequently represented as an abstruse pedant, incapable of the plain speech necessary for the cure of hardened criminals. The condemned attorney-cum-robber Thomas Carr supposedly rejected the Newgate chaplain's ministrations in favour of a more 'worthy Gentleman', telling the former that he should instead 'assist the Rest of my Fellow Sufferers, if you can make them understand you, which I fear; for they have all declared to me, they could not receive any Benefit from you'. Fielding's Ordinary (historically Purney, but probably intended as a more general caricature) is a fatuous epicure who refuses to drink wine with such an 'atheist' as Wild, but nonetheless condescends to join him in a bowl of punch: 'a liquor ... nowhere spoken against in Scripture'. The chaplain promptly puts Wild to sleep by discoursing very 'learnedly' on several 'grave matters' (the dullness of which is suggested by the fact that much of the text, supposedly too 'blotted' to be legible, is replaced by ellipses), finally delivering a particularly nonsensical sermon on the 'FOOLISHNESS' of Greek philosophy.[23]

Other accusations routinely levelled against Newgate chaplains included not only that of gin-tippling and – perhaps inevitably, given the anti-popery of the age and the Ordinary's association with auricular confession – crypto-Catholicism, but even dubious sexual practices. Lorrain's French name and ancestry made him an obvious target. In a May 1719 *Account*, the ailing Lorrain (he died several months later) vehemently repudiated the report of a 'Scandalous Lying Paper' that he had 'taken too large a dose of Jenevre [gin] at a Brandy-shop in Newgate Street' and then gone to chapel, where he 'spued upon his Cushion, and presently dy'd', as well as apparently related charges that he had been a 'French Dancing-Master' and that 'he was try'd at the Old-Bailey, &c.' Unfortunately the offending 'Paper' which might have elaborated on the nature of these allegations does not appear to have survived. 'Frenchness', of course, suggested a host of undesirable attributes to the early modern English mind: not only Catholicism and all of the supposed associations with popish corruption and Jesuitical duplicity, but also sexual immorality and venereal disease (one of the definitions of 'Frenchified' given by a late seventeenth-century canting dictionary was 'Clapt or Pox't'). The charge of being a 'French Dancing-Master' in particular implied worldliness, vice and over-refinement or possibly even effeminacy: a veiled accusation of sodomy could perhaps explain both the reference to a trial at the Old Bailey and the Ordinary's indignation.[24]

Apparently equally inflammatory, if still more mysterious, was a 'Paragraph inserted by Way of Derision' in *Parker's Weekly Journal* in 1732 (evidence of which, again, seems to exist only in the form of a rebuttal in the Ordinary's *Account*) 'calling the Chaplain of Newgate [James Guthrie] great B——p of the Cells; and that on a Day about that Time, there was a great Stir and Confusion in the Chappel'. The word struck out was probably 'Bishop', intended both as an ironic jab at the Ordinary's low ecclesiastical status and a reference to the surname of a man tried for attempted sodomy at Hicks' Hall on 6 September – and who would have probably been imprisoned in Newgate at the time of the newspaper report, dated by Guthrie at six weeks earlier than his *Account* of 9 October. (The full name was probably omitted for fear of a libel prosecution; indeed, as it turned out, the said William Bishop was not only acquitted but seems to have been the victim of a malicious prosecution.) This interpretation would certainly explain the heat with which Guthrie refuted 'the said Account' as 'a scandalous malicious Lie, and a false Reflection, without the least Foundation of Truth' – not to mention the otherwise inexplicable 'Stir and Confusion in the Chappel'.[25]

The *Account* served not only as a vehicle through which the Ordinary could refute personal slights, but also as a showcase for his diligence and exertions. The earliest *Accounts* chronicled, under the modest cover of the third person, the 'abundance of Christian pains both by Preaching, Praying and private Exhortations' taken by 'Mr Ordinary', who was 'deputed, to deal with [the condemned] in their last conflict with the King of Terrors; and whose wholesome advice is to be to them as ... the last help of their shipwrack'd lives'. Samuel Smith is regularly reported to have visited 'the condemned Prisoners every day'; in July 1689, dividing twenty-one hardened malefactors awaiting execution into three tutorials 'of 7 at a time, renewing Counsel and Prayer with each Company'. In what was only his second *Account*, in December 1700, Paul Lorrain claimed that he had visited the prisoners twice daily, 'notwithstanding the apparent Danger of my Health ... because they desir'd me to see them, and pray with, and for them, as often as I could, and seem'd to take good notice of what I said to them, with relation to their Spiritual State ...' While experience would temper Lorrain's initial optimism, he never ceased to remind the reader of his 'constant' visits to the condemned, and the many other rigours of his 'arduous and melancholy Office' – including preaching two Sunday condemned sermons in the Newgate chapel both to the prisoners and the 'Strangers' who flocked there 'in great (and indeed too great) Numbers'. Lorrain frequently signed his paper complaining of the 'great Fatigue' and 'Hurry' occasioned by his having to complete the *Account* with so many 'other Religious Services ... coming so close upon me'.[26]

Certainly there is much in the Ordinary's officious and intrusive pastoral style which offends modern sensibilities. Peter Linebaugh has written disapprovingly of the way in which the Ordinary of Newgate 'harried and worried, sometimes unconscionably, the men and women waiting to be hanged'; Lincoln Faller has evinced similar distaste for the 'performance' the prison chaplain 'invariably ... tried to extort (the word is not too strong) from the ... criminals who, in their last miserable moments, had been left in his care'. According to Robert Singleton, 'nothing in the Ordinary's conception of his duty was calculated to endear him to his clients', and 'such questioning, under such conditions, was simply intolerable to many prisoners'. However, in an age which took a decidedly dim view of human nature, condemned criminals were not so much 'clients' as delinquent souls teetering on the brink of eternal perdition. Indeed, seventeenth- and eighteenth-century critics of the Ordinary took him to task not so much because the office was unsavoury in itself as for his perceived slackness and negligence in carrying out its duties – objecting not so much to the Ordinary's persistence in obtaining confessions per se, as to the way in which he pressed criminals to own a series of secret private sins in addition to the crimes with which they were charged. As one group of sufferers was supposed to have complained, 'the Chaplain urged the confession of sins they were never guilty of, to such a degree, as put them out of temper, and hindered them from that great work which they had but so small a time to perform'. Such questioning was seen not only as prurient and self-interested (i.e., 'to fill up their printed papers and get a penny'), but superficial and peremptory, suggesting that the Ordinary had little time or inclination to conduct in-depth personal interviews with the condemned.[27]

Mindful perhaps of such criticisms, Newgate chaplains often stressed their disinterested missionary exertions. Smith, despite finding many of his flock 'lamentably ignorant of the Principles of Religion, as if they had been born in Africk, and bred up amongst the Savages of America', nonetheless 'endeavoured with his utmost pains, both to inform their Understandings of the mysteries of Salvation, and perswade their stubborn Wills to submit to the Yoak of Christ ...' Lorrain, too, broadcast his heroics in 'informing' the 'dull Understandings' of the malefactors, 'awakening their drouzy Consciences, enlightening their dark Minds, changing the Affections of their wicked Hearts, and turning them unto the Lord ...' In December 1707, Lorrain reported having baptized two of the condemned – one a Jew who had converted to Christianity – concluding his paper asking the 'Reader' to 'excuse' him for any shortcomings in the *Account*; he had, he explained, been distracted by 'what a great deal of Work I have had to dispatch in a few Days: In which the Thoughts and endeavours of making Converts and Proselytes to the Christian Religion, had, above all others, the prevalence with me'. (In 1770, the Ordinary John Wood expressed his amazement that one of the condemned had never been baptized and performed the office himself.) Not only Lorrain, but subsequent Ordinaries boasted of venturing into the prisoners' cells even when 'it was not very safe to do it, because of the Heat and confin'd Air'. This was no small matter in light of the infectious diseases rampant in Newgate: after the April 1750 sessions at the Old Bailey (the so-called 'Black Assizes'), over forty people – including the Lord Mayor and several judges, jurymen and other court officers – succumbed to 'gaol fever', or typhus.[28]

The confrontational format and sanctimonious tone of the *Account* strikes many modern readers disagreeably, as does the apparent lack of compassion or charity on the part of the Ordinary towards the malefactors condemned to death. James Guthrie (Newgate chaplain from 1725 to 1746) has been seen by modern scholars as a 'notably unsuccessful chaplain' who 'completely lost control of the prisoners for whom he was responsible'. It is admittedly difficult to appreciate the way in which Guthrie felt himself 'oblig'd often to threaten' the 'extravagantly wicked, obstinate and impudent young Fellows' under his care 'with Hell and Damnation, and to tell them, that all the Misfortunes they met with, were a Punishment too little for their villainies'; or, that 'because of their abominable, wicked and scandalous lives, now God's judgement had most justly over taken them and therefore they ought to "bear the rod, and him who hath appointed it"'. By modern pastoral standards, Guthrie comes across as hard and cynical. In April 1742, he dismissed the condemned 19-year-old robber Christopher Jordan's protestations of innocence, in light of Jordan's prior record and the fact that he was reported to have fallen 'upon his Knees, and begged [his victim] not to prosecute him, which an innocent Man would hardly have done'. When Jordan later attempted to hang himself in his cell, he was 'sharply reproved by all the rest of his Fellow Sufferers' as well as the chaplain, who 'endeavoured to convince him how great a Sin that of Self-Murther was, that he had already been but too great a Sinner that this was heaping Crime upon Crime …' Guthrie appeared to have been little moved even when Jordan 'wept bitterly', noting sceptically that he 'promised not to attempt the like any more (though this was his 2d attempt)'.[29]

The degree of cynicism with which the Ordinary approached his duties depended on the temperament of the individual and, perhaps especially, the length of time he had spent in office. Often an Ordinary began his tenure with high hopes: in his third *Account*, Lorrain 'truly perceiv'd, that God's Holy Spirit had wrought a good Work upon every Soul of [the condemned], even a Throu [sic] Change of their Hearts'. In general, however, appropriately 'decent and quiet Behaviour' – manifested in 'weeping … most plentifully' and in the condemned 'declaring themselves such Sinners, that they neither deserv'd, nor desired to live'

– was cited as exceptional or even unprecedented. Typically, Newgate chaplains stressed their high standards and made, if anything, a parade of their doubts. In March 1734, Guthrie remarked that the condemned were 'apparently devout and serious, and attentive' to his ministrations, while most of them 'wept pretty often'; however, he nonetheless expressed his suspicions that their tears were 'more for fear of Death, than an Effect of true Repentance'. This was a constant refrain, Guthrie frequently conceding that the condemned 'appear'd to be devout, serious and very grave' yet lacking 'that deep Concern requisite in Men upon the brink of Eternity'. Guthrie continually chastised inmates for laughing or even smiling in chapel. Even those criminals who, like Elizabeth Powell (a thief who received a transportation pardon), 'in the General behaved well', were 'sometimes obliged to have a little sharp Reproof for indecent Carriage'. Samuel Smith routinely tagged onto the accounts of the most penitent malefactors such qualifications as 'I hope he was penitent'. In 1708 Lorrain cautiously characterized William Gregg as 'if not a true Penitent', then 'one of the great Hypocrites in the World'; John Taylor (Ordinary from 1747 to 1757), remarked that John Rogers 'always pretended to be penitent, and appeared so to the last; Christian Charity obliges us to hope, and wish, that he might really have been in earnest'.[30]

Indeed, contemporaries were far more likely to take Newgate chaplains to task for being too lax than too rigorous or insensitive. In 1696 a pamphlet war erupted after Jeremy Collier and several other non-juring ministers publicly absolved two unrepentant Jacobites at Tyburn: critics objected, simultaneously, to the fact that the ceremony was conducted 'like a Popish Absolution', and that it had been administered at all to two such unworthy objects. After all, 'if the Ordinary of Newgate, should presume to Absolve Notorious Fellons or Highwaymen at the place of Execution, without a public declaration of their sorrow for their Crimes, all men would say that he did thereby encourage Felony and Robbery'. The debate was brought home to Paul Lorrain in 1703, after he had published a funeral sermon for Thomas Cook, a prize-fighter who had been executed for killing a constable in a brawl, comparing the deceased malefactor with Enoch, who had, albeit in an 'imperfect State', nonetheless succeeded in 'walking with God' (significantly, too, Cook obstinately maintained his innocence of the intent to commit murder). Despite Lorrain's disclaimer that even 'if now and then God is pleased to single out some one or other great Sinner for the Object of his special Mercy … such an extraordinary Mercy shown to a few' should not be taken as 'the least encouragement to Sinners', the sermon nonetheless elicited a verse attack attributed to Daniel Defoe, *The Hymn to the Funeral Sermon*, accusing the Ordinary of accepting bribes to transform 'Men of infamy' into saints by means of the 'Priest-craft Paint' of the *Account*, and asking 'What need we Mortifie and Pray/ If Gibbets are the *Shortest Way?*'

Lorrain had, if not his opponent's literary gifts, Scripture on his side – citing 'the Thief upon the Cross' whom 'Our Saviour Christ receiv'd' as evidence that 'the Manner of Death your Case wont alter/ Be it on your Bed or in a Halter'. Several years later, after the condemned malefactor Thomas Smith was reprieved, at least in part upon Lorrain's recommendation, the latter defended himself from anonymous critics who 'do whatever they can to render the Ministers of Christ contemptible; and to call Thieves their Disciples, as if instead of Preaching the Doctrine of the Gospel to Men, they taught them to rob and steal, or do any other wicked thing'. Clearly, even in the early eighteenth century, the presumption of free grace – that is, the notion that even the greatest sinner could be saved if truly penitent, regardless of his or her personal merits – was at once an indispensable justification for the Ordinary's office and a source of tension and controversy.[31]

Newgate chaplains were vociferous in their condemnation of the spiritually deleterious effects of reprieves. On the one hand, those criminals who 'are spared, forget the Vows made to God in their Distress, and their good Resolutions of Reformation vanish when their fears of Death are blown over'; on the other, as Lorrain complained in 1711, 'the more time is allow'd' the condemned 'to prepare for Death, the more their Thoughts are intent upon … contriving Ways and Means to save their Lives here' in this world, instead of 'obtaining of a better Life elsewhere'. However, in the words of a 1742 prayer book for prisoners penned by the future Ordinary Samuel Rossell (1746–7), when death was truly imminent, even 'the most obdurate Sinners' would at least claim to wish to repent. The Ordinary routinely reported 'a sensible Alteration' for the better in the behaviour of the condemned after the Dead Warrant came down to Newgate. Typically, malefactors would behave with 'much greater Decency and Submission' and appear 'to be much more concern'd'; many who had previously been 'obstinate' would then also confess to their crimes. The transformation was perhaps most dramatic in the case of the most hardened offenders: in 1728, Martin Bellamy had at first, although 'outwardly comply[ing] with Prayers … behav'd himself with Audacity' and an 'air of Indifference and Boldness', taking 'Delight in recounting his Villainies'. But 'some time after the Dead Warrant came out' his 'Conscience' began 'to Awake' and (thanks largely to the Ordinary's 'frequently and sharply reprov[ing] him') finally 'acknowledg'd himself one of the greatest of Sinners, begg'd God and Man Pardon for the many Offences of his Life'.[32]

The Ordinaries were anxious to discriminate, or to be seen to discriminate, between true repentance, based on an abhorrence of sin and a turning towards God, and a too superficial and transitory eleventh-hour 'Deathbed Repentance'. As Defoe's reprobate heroine Roxana confessed after her own incomplete 'Storm-Repentance' (i.e., abating after the dangers of the tempest were past): 'I had no thorow effectual Repentance; no Sight of my Sins in their proper Shape; no View of a Redeemer, or Hope in him: I had only such a Repentance as a Criminal has at the Place of execution, who is sorry, not that he has committed the Crime' but '*that he is to be Hang'd for it.*' After one 1690 execution, Samuel Smith noted that 'in Charity, I think several of them were Penitent', but added, 'the Truth of Repentance requires some time of Tryal, in bringing forth meer Fruits thereof', for 'a late Repentance is most what is slight and false, as being more for fear of Death, than out of any true Love to God, or Hatred of Sin'. Smith and subsequent Ordinaries were careful to emphasize their awareness that 'an over-hasty, undue applying of the Promises of Pardoning Mercy to an impenitent Sinner, is to flatter him to his eternal Ruin'. Rather, the ideal minister was a 'plain dealer' unafraid to tax the sinner with unpleasant truths. As Samuel Rossell wrote in his *Prisoner's Director*, ministers were 'spiritual Watchmen, whose Duty it is, to warn the Wicked to turn from their Way' and 'to speak the Words of God unto them, whether they will hear, or whether they will forbear'.[33]

Like a surgeon, a good minister had to be cruel to be kind, and probe the very wound he sought to heal. In *The Christian-man's Calling* (1662), ministers are exhorted not 'to provide meat toothsom for polluted pallats, to the feeding of their distempers' but rather 'to distribute food' more 'wholesome and sutable', if less palatable. 'Though my patients may be angry at present, when I search their festered wounds to the bottom, and thereby put them to pain, yet when upon my faithful dealing they recover, they will give me hearty thanks … if I be fearful to tell men of their sins, I murder their souls'. In his *Holy Dying*, Jeremy Taylor stresses that if a 'sick man be backward' and unresponsive to more gentle methods, the minister must 'take care that some way or other the work of God be secured'; if necessary, 'he must be halloed to, and asked in plain interrogatives concerning the crimes of his life'. Such advice applied to sinners both private and public (i.e., criminals), and should be followed 'without partiality, or fear or interest … having no other consideration, but that the … man's Soul be preserved …' Paul Lorrain was keen to represent himself as no respecter of persons: in 1715, he 'advis'd' the condemned murderer Nathanael Parkhurst, 'Esq.' 'impartially and without Flattery to examin [sic] himself' not only as to his internal spiritual 'Disposition' but also 'the several Passages and lamentable Miscarriages of his former Life'. Several years later Lorrain, however 'unwilling to offering any thing to a Gentleman that might grate upon his Spirit', nonetheless declared it his 'Duty' to bring another genteel murderer, Edward Bird, 'to a just Abhorrence and Detestation of … his Sins', to this end asking him to recount 'the vicious Steps that had led him to this barbarous Crime'. (Disappointingly, Bird replied 'but little, and so I left him for that time.') The Ordinary on several occasions represented himself as a plain dealer even with his employers: in 1678, Smith chided the City in his paper for the crowded conditions in the condemned hold; after John Davis's abortive gallows escape attempt in 1733, Guthrie complained of having his prayers with the condemned cut short by officials – who, in addition to having 'no regard for the Souls of Men', also spoke rudely to him. Both Lorrain and Purney petitioned the City about the 'Inconveniences and Disturbances' occasioned by malefactors 'Tipling' in the Press Yard during chapel time on the one hand, as well as the numerous curious spectators who attended the condemned sermons on the other, distracting inmates by staring at them and whispering – not to mention the 'continued Noise & Swearing & rattling of money' caused by either the 'Strangers … refusing to pay' various admission fees or the turnkeys attempting to withhold 'ye full Change'.[34]

Needless to say, it was the common convicts who came in for the lion's share of 'plain dealing'. And most contemporaries would have agreed that, when it came to reclaiming the souls of hardened sinners, tough measures were not only justified but necessary. As Lorrain wrote in his *Dying Man's Assistant*, 'a Person of Quality' should not 'be addressed to in the same Stile, as those that are ignorant, rude, and of a morose Nature'; for the former, 'a few Words' sufficed, but for the latter, more plain (and extensive) speaking was necessary. Moreover, as Samuel Rossell explained, 'Men of ill Lives, as too many of them are, may many Times have more Comfort administered to them, than they are fit for, or than is fit for them': in the case of such 'miserable Wretches', 'I have thought Corrosives to be more proper for the Patients than Applications of a milder Nature'. In 1711, Lorrain recorded that the condemned burglar William Maw found his 'plain (and indeed Charitable) Dealing' – namely, his insistence that Maw confess to 'Faults' he claimed to 'know nothing of' – to be 'very unpleasant and grievous to his Temper'. Although Lorrain tells us that Maw thanked him for the 'great Comfort and Instruction' he had received from his ministrations, he nonetheless refused to deliver the 'ingenuous and sincere Confession' that the Ordinary considered 'Proof of his Repentance'. The indefatigable Lorrain, however, 'would not give over pressing him', informing him that 'I would deal with him as a good Physician or Chirugeon, who does not so much mind the Cries of the Patient, as his Cure … Though you exclaim never so much against what I offer you, I am fully resolved to endeavour the Salvation of your Soul'. (Maw, however, persisted in withholding the 'Particulars' the Ordinary sought so strenuously: 'All I could get out of him, was this Answer only, "I am a great Offender, and what can I say more?"') When Lorrain similarly pressed several condemned Jacobites for their confessions in 1715, they protested that 'They wou'd not hear me if I harp'd any longer upon this String; and what they only desir'd of me was, my reading to them the Prayers and the Lessons appointed for the Day, and no more'. Lorrain, resuming the medical metaphor, retorted, 'That as I found them under a spiritual Disease, so I would not give over trying what spiritual Medicine I cou'd administer to them while they were under my Cure'.[35]

Perhaps not surprisingly, in the light of what seem to be the aspersions cast on their masculinity, Ordinaries such as Paul Lorrain stressed not only their diligence but their manly fortitude and the firm – yet charitable – manner in which they confronted the most hardened malefactors. In 1707 Lorrain visited seven career criminals 'in the Condemned Hold, (where some People told me was not safe for me; but I was not of their Opinion)', reporting that, 'far from offering Rudeness, or doing any Mischief to me', they behaved with great 'Decency' and 'showed' him all due 'Attention' and 'Respect'. In March 1714, Lorrain reported that, after he had refused to administer the sacrament to the highwayman Thomas Grey on the grounds that he was 'very stubborn' and 'very unwilling either to be ask'd, or to resolve any Question', the latter 'cursed me to the Pit of Hill [sic], and said That he would certainly kill me, if ever I durst venture to come to pray with him and the rest in the Cart at Tyburn'. Lorrain assured him that he would 'nevertheless do my Duty to his Soul to the very last; and tho' he curs'd, yet I pray'd God to Bless both Him and Me, and lay not this additional Sin to his charge'; 'that I heartily pray'd for his Conversion and Salvation; and, That I much pitied him, but fear'd him not in the least'. Another 'wicked Person' in the same group, the robber Charles Weymouth, issued similar threats, and was answered much in the same vein. Lorrain reported with satisfaction that he not only prayed with Grey, Weymouth and the other malefactors in the cart to Tyburn, but that there 'those that had been rude to me, and threaten'd my life, begg'd my Pardon, and thank'd me for the Pains I took with their Souls'. (Although, to Lorrain's obvious disappointment, none of them offered to make 'a further Confession').[36]

In a still more dramatic confrontation in 1715, the pirate Alexander Dolzell told Lorrain that 'He hated to see my Face, and wou'd not attend in the Chapel … nor receive any publick or private Admonition from me, but with his Dying Breath declare that I was the Cause of his Death' (Lorrain had acted as a translator for several of the prosecution witnesses at his trial), 'and he would do me some Mischief or other before he dy'd, or haunt me afterwards.' Lorrain told him, 'I fear'd him not, nor his Ghost, but was sorry to see him in that furious Passion (very unfit for a Dying Person).' After being forced to attend chapel, Dolzell threatened to 'kick' Lorrain 'down Stairs', and 'threaten'd also to tear the Bible … saying; He would see none of my books'. To this Lorrain thundered, '*that* was not my Book, but the BOOK OF GOD, and let him tear it if he durst'. Lorrain is careful to report that at the place of execution, Dolzell 'was somewhat affected' with the Ordinary's 'Admonitions', saying that 'he repented', asking for Lorrain's prayers, and begging his 'Pardon … for his rude and unjust Behaviour toward me'.[37]

James Guthrie similarly emphasized the manly courage and resolution with which he met challenges to his authority. In 1731, when Guthrie exhorted the 18-year-old robber Thomas Beck ('the most Audacious, and Impudent young Fellow that I ever saw') to 'think of Death, Judgement and Eternity', the latter responded flippantly that 'he had been judg'd already, and that the next thing they were to do was to make a button of his Head'. Guthrie reported that when he reproved Beck for talking and laughing in chapel, the young man told him that 'he should be very glad of an Opportunity to shoot me', but noted with some satisfaction that Beck later apologized to him for his behaviour. For although the tendency of most Ordinaries, particularly James Guthrie, to play up the (initial) resistance of prisoners to their ministrations has led many scholars to view them as less successful than they may have actually been, such reportage was clearly intended to emphasize both the Ordinaries' own diligence and travails and the subsequent improvement of the malefactors under their care. For Guthrie, the point is surely not that, in November 1730, Hugh Morris 'laugh'd, and provoked some of the rest to do so once in Chappel', but that upon being 'reproved sharply', 'he behaved afterwards with great Respect'. Such incidents were regularly reported by Guthrie; for instance, Joseph Parker, a 'very obdurate, obstinate, negligent, and (it's to be fear'd) impenitent young Man' talked during sermon and, when 'gently' upbraided, 'had the Assurance to speak against, and insult me in the Pulpit', but later 'begg'd Pardon and promised to mind his Soul'. Benjamin Branch, another audacious Sinner 'reprov'd sharply' by Guthrie, explained 'that his sometimes laughing and speaking proceeded not from any Contempt of God's Words and Ordinances, but from his Youth and want of Consideration'. The young highwayman William Udal, 'reprov'd' for 'speaking sometimes and smiling', told the Ordinary 'he had a smiling Countenance, and did not speak out of any Disrespect, but could not help it'. The irrepressible 'Cockey Wager' apologized several times to Guthrie for smiling or laughing in chapel, promising 'not to be guilty of any such frolick again', eventually maintaining 'an apparent decency' and acknowledging himself 'a very atrocious Sinner' whose 'Sufferings were most justly inflicted on him'.[38]

While the modern reader of the *Account* is unlikely to sympathize with the Ordinary's campaign against the smiles, laughter and 'frolicks' of the 'miserable Wretches' under his care, it is important to bear in mind that anything resembling levity on the part of the condemned would have signified to contemporaries that their repentance was incomplete, and their prospects of salvation bleak. According to Samuel Rossell's *Prisoner's Director*, 'True Repentance is ever accompanied with a deep and afflicting Sorrow; a Sorrow that will break the Heart in Pieces, and make us so irreconcilable to sin, as that we shall chuse rather to die than to live in it.' Moreover, 'to be sorry for our Sins ... does not consist in a little Trivial Concern, a superficial Sigh or Tear, or calling ourselves Sinners, &c. but in a real ingenious and afflicting Sorrow'. Such sorrow was not only proof of penitence, but the surest means of obtaining salvation, being 'the proper Satisfaction for Sin which God expects, and hath promised to accept'; i.e., Psalm 51: 'The sacrifices of God are a broken spirit: A broken and contrite Heart, O God, thou wilt not despise.'[39]

THE USES OF A 'FREE, FULL AND INGENUOUS CONFESSION'

While many contemporaries objected to the Ordinary's person, methods or questionable motives in soliciting 'particular', or detailed, confessions from the condemned, most believed that some sort of confession was necessary, both as a proof of the sincerity of one's repentance and a means of becoming penitent, by mortifying pride and sin. There also was a conviction, roughly analogous to that of modern psychoanalysis, that a rigorous self-examination was a necessary precondition for spiritual regeneration, or saving penitence. One of the ministers who attended the condemned Jacobite Lord Kilmarnock told the latter he hoped he 'did not expect to be flattered, nor to have the malignity of his Crimes disguised or softened', for 'the Wound of his Mind occasioned by his publick and private Vices, must be probed and searched to the Bottom, before it could be capable of receiving any Remedy'. Protestant clergymen who published confessions were of course anxious to distinguish themselves from any association with popery and auricular confession. While Catholic tenets prohibited confession (a sacrament) from being made public, 'our ayme of the Church of England', explained one early seventeenth-century criminal pamphlet, 'is not such, as that of Rome, to creep into mens secrets [sic] hearts, to hold them in awe, but discover [i.e., make public] their sinnes, to save that way their soules'. Thus the author was no father-confessor but a 'chyrugion' treating the 'noysome foul ulcerated body' of the sinner'.[40]

Scriptural quotations illustrating the necessity of confession were regularly invoked by the Ordinaries of Newgate, both in their sermons and in their private exhortations to the condemned: 'He that covereth his sins shall not prosper: But whoso confesseth them shall have mercy' (Proverbs 28:13); or, 'Examine yourselves, whether ye be in the faith; prove your own selves' (II Corinthians 13:5). Favourite biblical examples included II Samuel 12–13, where Nathan taxes David with adultery and murder ('Thou art the man'), and the latter admits his guilt (also in II Samuel 24:10), as well as David's penitential psalms, particularly Psalms 32 and 51. (The last had an obvious resonance with malefactors, as Psalm 51:1 was the so-called 'Neck Verse', or reading test for benefit of clergy.) The Prodigal Son's lament to his father in Luke 15:21 ('I have sinned against heaven, and in thy sight'), as well as the penitent thief's general expression of guilt in Luke 23:41 were also popular – if sometimes problematic, in that they could be cited by the condemned themselves as evidence of the sufficiency of general, rather than particular, confessions. The Ordinaries had a special fondness for texts illustrating the need for evil-doers to confess to man, as well as to God: 'Confess your faults one to another, and pray one for another, that ye may be healed' (James 5:16); as well as Joshua's exhortation to Achan, 'give, I pray thee, glory to the Lord God of Israel, and make confession unto him; and tell me now what thou hast done; hide it not from me' (Joshua 7:19).

THE

Ordinary *of* NEWGATE *his* ACCOUNT

Of the Behaviour, Confeſſions, *and* Laſt Dying Words *of the* Malefactors *that were* Executed *at* Tyburn, *on* Wedneſday *the* 14th *of* March, 1722.

AT the Seſſions held at *Juſtice-Hall* in the *Old-Bayly*, and which began *Feb.* 28th, were Convicted of Capital Crimes, 13 Perſons; *viz.* W. *Burridge*; *J.* Roberts; *J. James*; T. *Picket*; *J. Applebie*; R. *Winter*, E. *Claxton*; G. *Biſhop*; *J. Lanman*; S. *Armſtong*; *W. Edwards*; R. *Drumman*; T. *Plowman*. Three of theſe being young Boys, and Four others being found proper Objects of *His Majeſty's* Clemency, the ſix Firſt were order'd for Execution, agreeable to the Sentence pronounc'd upon them by Law.

Some of them during the Time that they lay unde Sentence of Death, frequently complain'd of the great Interruption and Diſturbance, occaſioned by thoſe who had an aſſur'd Expectation of a Reprieve, which prevented the hearing *William Burridge* when he read the Scriptures and Prayers to thoſe who deſir'd him ; adding, that they could not but regret their great Misfortune in having no Place or Corner to retire unto, or to be private in, from the fooliſh and idle Clamor of ſome of their Companions. But ſome of thoſe who were certain of a Reprieve, found themſelves diſmally diceived, when the Warrant was carried to the *Priſon* ; yet ſo ſtrongly had their Friends flatter'd them with the Hopes of Life, and ſo deeply was the Aſſurance ſettled in their Minds, that they could not credit the Account, or make themſelves immagine they ſhould ſuffer Death, tho' they were not without thoſe among them, whoſe filthy Diſtempers occaſion'd by their Vices and Lewdneſs, made this Life as Uneaſy to them, as the next muſt be fearful and terrible.

They were adviſed not to trouble their Minds with difficult Queſtions, tho' of ſome Importance, but conſidering the great Work they had to perform, and the time they had to compleat it in, to ſet erneſtly about the main and neſeſſary Duties of Repentance and turning to God. This they

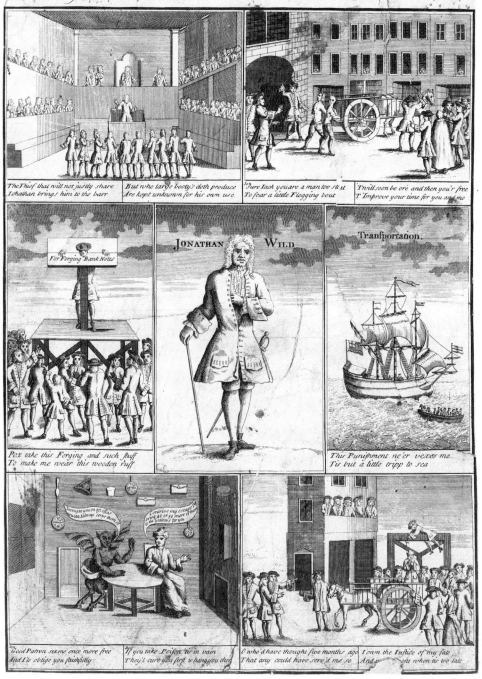

6. A satirical sheet entitled *The Several Degrees taken by Jonathan Wild's Pupils from their Comencement under his Tutorship to their final Promotion at Tybourn*, depicting the progress of Wild's 'pupils' from trial at the Old Bailey, and from lesser to greater punishments, culminating in execution at Tyburn (bottom right). Reproduced by permission of the Henry E. Huntington Library

There had long been tensions within the Church of England between more Calvinist and 'sacramental' (essentially, high church) traditions regarding confession. Puritan writers were particularly anxious to renounce anything smacking of 'Popish shrift', emphasizing that confession was 'a thing meet & convention' but not, as with 'the Papists … a thing necessary to the remission of sins'. Protestant teaching, moreover, 'requires onely a confession of that or those sins which lye upon a mans conscience', as opposed to 'Popish doctrin', which called for 'a particular enumeration of all a mans sins'. In the *Book of Common Prayer*, however, ministers were told that the ill or dying person whose 'conscience [was] troubled with any weighty matter' should be encouraged 'to make a special Confession of his sins' before being absolved. This seemed to suggest that 'public sinners', or criminals, were indeed obliged to publicly acknowledge their transgressions. According to the Anglican divine Jeremy Taylor, confession was not only a 'necessary … duty', but 'Penitents' should make 'Confessions proportionate to their Repentance, that is, public or private, general or particular'.[41]

The Ordinaries of Newgate constantly urged condemned men and women to deliver 'a free, full, and ingenuous confession' as both 'a necessary Duty' and 'first step to a sincere and hearty Repentance'. There was, they stressed,

> great difference betwixt a Person lying on a sick Bed whose Sins are more secret, and who may recover to a longer Space of Repentance. Such, are not so strictly obliged, to confess their particular Enormities. But for those, who by Notorious Crimes have given Publick Scandal to the Christian Religion, and brought themselves under the Sentence of Death; such ought to make Publick Acknowledgement of their Excesses in Sinning, that their Repentance may be as Exemplary, as their Conversation hath been Vicious.

Late seventeenth- and early eighteenth-century Newgate chaplains reminded condemned malefactors that they were in good company, citing not only Mary Magdalene, the prodigal son and the penitent thief crucified alongside Jesus, but the anointed king David as 'an excellent Pattern for their Imitation'. When, in 1700, the burglar John Harold refused to deliver a confession 'because he would have as little as possible to reflect upon his Wife and Family', he was told by the then Ordinary Roger Wykes that 'the manner of his Death was not the consideration, all his business was with *the Thief upon the Cross* to make a Penitent and Holy end'. Harold, whose crimes, like David's, were 'left on public Record', was obliged to make a public confession. For 'should not we who have David's Failings do all we are able to have David's Repentance?' (This, apparently, 'melted' the hitherto obstinate criminal both 'into Tears' and a fulsome confession.) By the mid-eighteenth century this distinction between the kind, rather than the degree of the offence – that is, between moral and criminal offences – was increasingly overt. According to Rossell's *Prisoner's Director*, 'where the sin against God is complicated with Injustice towards Men (as in condemned Malefactors it always is), there it is requisite that the Sinner confess to Man'.[42]

Confession was above all 'a Token of the Sincerity of our Repentance': the true penitent, far from extenuating 'his Sins … rather aggravates them … thinking and speaking worse of himself, than any One else can do'. As Samuel Smith frequently reiterated, it was 'impudent Atheism … to seek the hiding of any Sin'. Those who falsely denied their guilt called down the wrath of God, while 'secret Sinners' fell fast captive to 'the Prince of Darkness'. In one of his prayer books, Paul Lorrain explained that 'obstinacy' on the part of a 'Sick Person' of known ill life could be explained either by his being an atheist, having entered into a demonic pact, 'Laziness' in 'Examining the Conscience', despair from having committed and persisted in so 'many enormous Crimes and Immoralities', or being 'so tied to some beloved Sin, that he knows not how to bid Farewell to it'.[43]

Late seventeenth- and early eighteenth-century Ordinaries proudly chronicled the 'great Pains and unwearied Industry' with which they urged malefactors to 'a free and ingenious Confession', placing considerable dramatic weight on their heroics in extracting eleventh-hour gallows confessions/conversions. At his execution in 1684, the condemned murderer John Gower initially refused to deliver a confession although, upon being pressed by the Ordinary, finally acknowledged that 'he had been the Contriver' of his wife's death, but 'would not explain it further'. Over the protests of the impatient sheriffs' officers, the Ordinary and another minister continued to pray with him for an hour and a half in the hopes that 'God … would work in him a Confession of his bloody Crime'. When Gower appeared to be weakening under a barrage of questions from spectators, the Ordinary redoubled his efforts and 'the poor Penitent' finally 'melted into Tears' – delivering an 'Ingenious' (i.e., ingenuous) confession not only of having shot his wife with a pistol, but of the sinful courses that had brought him to the gallows, beginning with an indulgent master and Sabbath-breaking and ending in bigamy and murder. Such triumphs were, however, rare; over ten years later, Smith was still invoking what appeared to have been Gower's example to illustrate to another condemned wife-murderer, Edmund Allen, the necessity and efficacy of last-minute confession. Smith claimed that this model penitent had addressed spectators, praising God 'for the Ordinary's Plain-dealing and Patience with me, for had I dyed denying [the murder], I had been damn'd'. (Allen, for his part, persisted in his 'obstinate Humour and Impenitency'.)[44]

Late seventeenth- and early eighteenth-century Newgate chaplains readily discerned in the semiotics of gallows behaviour a larger providential design. A notable example was the execution of Captain Kidd in 1701. The hardened and recalcitrant pirate not only rebuffed the Ordinary's ministrations but, to the latter's 'unspeakable Grief', arrived at the gallows 'inflamed with Drink'. Although at Execution Dock Kidd declared 'his Confidence in God's Mercys' and 'that he dy'd in Charity with all the World', Lorrain 'suspected his Sincerity', both because he continued to 'excuse and justify himself' and 'lay his Faults upon his Crew and others', and because he refused to deliver a full confession. However, in what Lorrain characterized as 'a remarkable (and I hope most lucky) accident', the rope on which Kidd was hanged broke, 'mercifully' granting him a 'farther Respite'. The Ordinary seized this opportunity to renew his exhortations and, indeed, now found Kidd 'in a much better temper than before'; however, given the constraints of time and his own 'very incommodious' position (perched precariously halfway up the ladder), Lorrain was forced to be content with Kidd's general expressions of penitence rather than a more detailed confession. While some scholars have viewed such gallows exertions on the part of the Ordinary as excessive or intrusive, it is unlikely many contemporaries would have concurred. Not only did many spectators, especially relatives of murder victims, attend executions in the hopes of hearing last-minute confessions, but most believed that those who died without acknowledging their crimes – or worse, persisting in a lie – were damned.[45]

Modern scholars have tended to view confession as a means of social control, of 'linking the interior conscience with the exterior public order'. Undoubtedly Newgate chaplains had a vested interest in inducing condemned malefactors, especially traitors, to deliver penitent speeches at the place of execution and, on at least several occasions, Ordinaries (as well as other clergymen) passed along information obtained from prison confessions to authorities. Moreover, before the abolition of the reading test for clergy in 1706, the Ordinary was not only a City official, but a court officer. Late seventeenth- and early eighteenth-century Newgate chaplains regularly attended the sessions at the Old Bailey, and thus were often able to distinguish between first-time and repeat offenders. In November 1715, Lorrain (who, as we have seen, on occasion acted as courtroom translator) recognized no fewer than five of the condemned as old offenders. When the housebreaker Edward Shaw insisted he 'never did an ill thing in his life', the Ordinary reminded him that he had been convicted of a clergyable offence a year and a half earlier; three other burglars maintained their innocence of the 'Facts' for which they were condemned, but were finally brought to acknowledge that they had been 'under the Lash of the Law' before. The fifth, a pickpocket, initially claimed 'he had never robb'd any Person of any thing in his Life, only his own Mother, when he was a Boy', but confessed upon Lorrain's reminding him of his prior convictions.[46]

Newgate chaplains stressed that reparation was part of the necessary business of repentance and occasionally even took an active role in arranging the return of stolen goods to robbery victims. In April 1713, the robber George Smith returned some papers to their owner 'upon [Lorrain's] perswading him to make what Reparation he could to the Persons he wrong'd'; in 1708, Lorrain informed readers of his *Account* that a malefactor had 'left a Direction' with him where to find some stolen 'Goods' (providing his address for 'the Persons who lost them' to make further inquiries). Several Ordinaries promised confidentiality to those who revealed the names of former associates: in 1700, Roger Wykes urged one of the condemned to name his accomplices with the promise to 'make no other use of it, than either personally, or by Letter, to beg them to be Reform'd'. In 1723, Thomas Purney claimed to have acceded to the robber William Duce's request to conceal the names of his accomplices on the grounds that they had amended their lives and 'should he make them Publick … it would tend to the Ruin of them, and their Innocent Families'. It was more common, however, for the Ordinary to tell malefactors, as did James Guthrie in 1746, that 'it was better for their comrades to be hanged and repent, than to go on in their wicked ways', and that 'the discovering of them would be doing justice to their fellow creatures'. Not least, gallows confessions and speeches served an obvious exemplary purpose. At one 1678 execution, an unnamed 'Minister' told the condemned 'that the onely service they could now do Godward, would be to warn others at the place of Execution to avoid Passion, Uncleanness, and all other sins … which hath brought them to this untimely end'. Such confessions were, moreover, 'commonly the only Satisfaction [that] can be given to the injur'd Party'. A reason cited more frequently as the eighteenth century progressed was the 'Duty to confess to the World the Robberies they had committed, lest innocent Persons might be suspected'.[47]

To many, a detailed and particular enumeration of private sins smacked uncomfortably of Catholic auricular confession. Captain Vratz complained to Gilbert Burnet that he 'thought it was a piece of Popery to press him to confess'; the robber John Ives 'said that particular confessions were too much like Popery, and asked, Can words make restitution?' John Kello, a Dissenter hanged for forgery in 1762, 'denied there was any Command in Scripture … to confess his Sins; adding, these were no Protestant Doctrines, and no better than that of auricular Confession'. John Perrot, executed for bankruptcy fraud in 1761, 'challenged' the Ordinary Stephen Roe (1757–64) 'to shew, where the Bible or Church of England required any such Thing', subsiding when Roe indicated relevant passages in *The Book of Common Prayer*. Many criminals, like the highwayman Paul Lewis, seemed to object most to being closeted with the Ordinary in his office, a small room that resembled a 'confession-box'.[48]

Some challenged the Ordinary's authority to absolve them of their sins. The highwayman John Bennet alias Freeman ('the Golden Farmer'), refused to 'make a more thorow Discovery of his wicked Life … saying I could not pardon him'. While conceding that this was 'God's sole Prerogative', Smith claimed that 'as a Gospel Minister', he 'might furnish him with a good Grounds of a Lively Hope of Pardon and Salvation, if he did not hide obstinately his Sin'. At his 1684 execution

Francis Robinson refused to 'say something to the People to warn others to take heed of the like Crimes, &c.', claiming 'that the Confession he had to make was to God Almighty'. This was a common refrain: the highwayman James Phillips said 'he needed not to make any Acknowledgement of any publick Miscarriages; secret Repentance would obtain their Pardon'; William Marslin 'did not deny the crime for which he was to dye, but refused to make any particular Confession; which he said, he had done to God Almighty'. John Mausgridge refused to be 'frighted into a Confession' of his 'private Sins' and made into the 'Sport and Ridicule of vain, idle Fellows in Coffee-Houses', being 'satisfy'd in his conscience' that 'he was oblig'd to confess to none but his Heavenly Father, who knew the Secrets of his Heart'.[49]

The street robber Thomas Neeves broadcast his refusal to deliver confessions more simply because 'he would give no Occasion to *Books or Ballads* to be made about him'. Others wished to spare their families: the housebreaker Mary Green refused to divulge even her birthplace, 'saying that she would not shame her Kindred, and that she had a good old Father alive there, as gray as my self [Lorrain], and she was unwilling he should hear of her shameful Death, least it should bring his *Gray Hairs with sorrow to his Grave*' (Genesis 44:31). Others resisted naming confederates because, like Robert Congden, executed in 1691, they 'would not be a means of bringing any Man to a sentence of Death, if taken'; or, like the highwayman John Winship, hanged in 1721 (and described 'in other respects' as 'Penitent and Devout') because they did not think they were 'obliged to make any Discoveries, which might affect the Lives of others'. Indeed, what the Ordinary characterized as 'wicked obstinacy' often reflected similar scruples on the part of otherwise penitent men and women. In 1707, the street robbers Charles Moor and William Elby refused to name their accomplices, Moor objecting that 'what good would it do with me to hang three or four men, and ruine their Families as well as Mine?' As for Elby, 'he intended to die in Charity with the World; which he could not do, if he brought any into trouble'.[50]

However, some malefactors clearly felt compelled to confess to those sins – including some unrelated to the crime for which they suffered – which lay most heavily on their consciences. At his 1690 execution, Christopher Tremane admitted not only to committing several robberies, but of having falsely accused Anne Moor, a goldsmith, of melting down stolen plate. In 1714 the highwayman Andrew Harper told the spectators at Tyburn that he had been 'a very great Offender' but that 'nothing ... grieved him more, than his taking four men's Lives away, by the Evidence he gave against them at the Old Baily' six months earlier. In 1722 the robber Thomas Milsop delivered a conventional gallows speech, asking that 'none would reflect on his Innocent Parents', adding that he 'hop'd God would pardon his great Sin' in shooting his pistol into a coach 'before ever he spoke' (i.e., by asking passengers to stand and deliver), and in 'abusing [sexually assaulting] a single Woman … whom he first robb'd of an Apron, Necklace, &c.' In 1697, the 17-year-old robber John Shorter was tormented by the fact that he had kept silent about a murder committed two and a half years earlier at Newgate. Shorter was 'put into a great Consternation' after seeing the ghost of the murdered man while praying in chapel, and finally confessed to being an accessory after the fact. Three days before his September 1720 execution, the burglar John Norridge requested a private audience with the Ordinary, confessing to him that he had stolen two silver candlesticks from a church, a 'Sin … that had lain at his Heart and made him very Uneasy, so that when he went to Pray or to Read, he could not do either with Attention'. In June 1719, the robber John Wood and his accomplice, Richard Williams, shamefacedly confessed to 'using some undecent Gestures, to induce Men to Sodomy, whom [they] fancy'd might be inclinable that way', accepting money for sexual favours only to tell their hapless victims that they were 'not for their Sort', and extorting 'more of their Money' with threats that they 'would accuse them, and defame them'. A few malefactors themselves confessed to having committed 'that monstrous Iniquity of Sodomitical Practices', often characterized by contemporaries as a 'crying sin' – a sin so grave that it cried out to God for vengeance.[51]

Most of the condemned, however, confined themselves to more general admissions of guilt and sinfulness. The eighteen malefactors hanged in July 1689 were all fairly penitent but, despite Samuel Smith's attempts to persuade them that, unless exposed, 'Wounds in the Conscience will fester and prove desperately mortal', they remained 'very unwilling to give any account of their particular Offences against God or Man' – although acknowledging 'that they had been great Sinners' in general. Contemporary clergymen, however, emphasized that such general confessions were almost as bad as none at all. 'General knowledge never worketh any reformation', claimed the early seventeenth-century divine Samuel Smith (not the Ordinary), in his much reprinted tract, *David's Repentance*. After all, 'the vilest Atheist in the world, a Reprobate, and one that shall never be saved, may confess this in a general and confused way, We are all sinners, but if we will truly repent indeed, we must look to confess our particular sins, to find them out one by one, and to acknowledge them unto the Lord with grief, sorrow and hatred of them'. According to Rossell's prayerbook for prisoners, confession must be 'as minute and particular as it can', both as 'the best Test' of one's 'Humility, Sincerity, and Conversion' and because 'by confessing our Sins in this Manner, we effectually kill the Root of Pride, and acknowledge the Justice of God, in Punishing us'. As always, however, there was room for ambiguity. Jeremy Taylor stressed that the more 'particular and enumerative' the sick or dying person was of his sins, the more 'pungent and afflictive, and therefore more salutary and medicinal' his repentance. However, the minister 'must not be inquisitive into all the circumstances of the particular sins, but be content with those that are direct parts of the crime, and aggravation of the sorrow', and avoid any 'questions springing from curiosity, and producing scruple'.[52]

The majority of the condemned appeared willing enough to declare themselves penitent, if only to qualify for the reception of the sacrament. Communion was customarily celebrated on the morning of execution, although early eighteenth-century Ordinaries periodically urged malefactors to partake of it several days before they were hanged so that they would have time 'to put into Practice [the] good Resolutions inspir'd by the Sacrament'. Newgate chaplains characteristically advertised their high standards for admitting malefactors to the 'Holy Table', stressing the necessity of being in charity with 'all the world' (forgiving others as one hoped to be forgiven by God), and having an 'Entire Hatred of every Sin'. In October 1708, Lorrain indignantly refuted a newspaper report that he had administered the sacrament to three of the condemned whom he did 'not judge … fit for it': two of them 'appearing stubborn and unwilling to confess their Guilt' and the third 'being so ignorant of that Ordinance, as not to be able to discern the Lord's Body'.[53]

But eighteenth-century malefactors who, like the badly-behaved James White, were deemed 'Unqualify'd' to be administered the sacrament 'as is usually done to Malefactors on the Day of their Death', generated notice and, presumably, controversy. At their 1718 execution, the robbers John Stone and Henry Chickley 'exclaimed against me [Lorrain], for not administering the Holy Sacrament … to them', and the Ordinary was obliged to defend himself publicly, 'telling the People that were about the Cart, of their wicked and unheard-of Behaviour'. (These two 'prophane and impious Wretches', Lorrain explained, were not only impenitent, but drunk and disorderly in chapel; on the very morning of their execution, 'when I was at Prayer, Stone took out of his Bosom one of those creeping Creatures [lice], with which I suppose he abounded' and, putting it on Chickley's prayerbook said, 'See how he is galloping over the Prayers'.) Newgate chaplains were, needless to say, vulnerable to accusations such as that made by the highwayman Charles Speckman, alias Brown; that is, that the Ordinary withheld the sacrament 'under pretence of my not being prepared, but in reality, to get from me an account of my life and transactions'. And indeed, despite the conventional Anglican position that communion should be administered 'to any Christian that desires it and professes Repentance of his sin' – and that, as 'the Minister is only the Judge of outward act', such professions should be taken at face value – it seems that many Ordinaries did on occasion use the sacrament as leverage to extort confessions or simply to enforce better behaviour on the part of malefactors.[54]

In April 1760 Stephen Roe (who appears to have clashed with malefactors more frequently on this issue than other Ordinaries) refused to administer the sacrament to the burglar William Beckwith 'without a full and true confession of his guilt'. Beckwith had written a nominally penitent but – in Roe's opinion – insufficiently charitable paper (in which he claimed to have been 'condemned falsely by false people'); and, when admonished by the Ordinary, 'affected rather to instruct his teacher, than to hearken and obey'. Roe also denied the sacrament to the forger John Kello, less because of the latter's reservations, eventually overcome, about kneeling during the ceremony (Kello was raised a Dissenter), than his refusal to give 'satisfaction to the questions put to him' – not to mention his repeated assurances that 'he was prepared to die; that he should meet death like a man; that he had no sin to repent of'. In November 1762, the condemned forger James Farr persisted in what Roe considered blasphemous avowals of his innocence (the Ordinary viewing such 'repeated appeals to God' as evidence of 'enthusiastic phrensy and misrule'). On the morning of his execution, Farr 'began to lament and cry, what a cruel thing it was to refuse him the sacrament'. Farr unbent enough to acknowledge that he was 'a very great sinner, and repent of all my sins', but balked when the Ordinary 'required him to add, – and "of that in particular for which I am to die"'. In the end Roe prevailed and Farr confessed – and received the sacrament. The sailor Archibald Nelson, hanged in 1764 for fraud, was similarly induced to tell the Ordinary 'I suffer justly' before he could join the other communicants although, because 'time pressed', Roe did not question him further as to specifics.[55]

Like Nelson, most malefactors were eager to qualify for the sacrament and, to that end, took what was essentially a middle course: acknowledging a catalogue of general misdeeds, from Sabbath-breaking on, but typically stopping short of admitting to more serious sins and (especially before the Dead Warrant came down, when their sentence of death was apparently final), the crime for which they had been condemned. Many such confessions were nominal and apparently grudging, like that of John Collet, alias Cole, who, when the Ordinary insisted that he could not 'get the pardon of his sin … till it be confest in all its Aggravations', volunteered that 'he had prophaned the Sabbath, had been excessive in drinking, and assisting others in carrying on their wicked Practices'. Even those who delivered more fulsomely self-accusing confessions often remained vague in regard to particulars. Edward Paine, hanged in 1711 for theft, was initially 'very unwilling to be undeceived in this his great mistake' – that is, that 'his private Confession to God alone was sufficient for his Repentance'. However, as his execution drew nearer, 'then was he (or at least he seem'd to be) less sullen and reserved', admitting to being 'highly guilty of Prophaning the Lord's Day, of Swearing, of excessive Drinking, or Whoredom, and all manner of Lewdness, and all Crimes, the Sin of Murther only excepted', if still less forthcoming than the Ordinary would have liked 'relating to private Persons Concerns'. (At the place of execution, Paine covered his bases by praying to God for forgiveness for 'the Sin for which I die, and all other the Sins of my Life, both known and unknown'.)[56]

Such confessions were inevitably shaped by the Ordinary's tendentious questions. It seems to have been Samuel Smith's regular practice to ask the condemned 'One by One, of the Employment they were bred up into, and how they fell into a vicious course of Life'. In July 1685, the 18-year-old William Vanderhurst, after confessing to have begun gaming and drinking on the Sabbath at the age of 14 and 16, respectively, was asked by the Ordinary 'what he thought might be the occasion of his early growth in sin'. He replied 'that he neglected Prayer every Morning, and at Night, if he Prayed, he did it very coldly'. One of his fellow condemned, the horse-thief George Atwell, 'told the Ordinary that he did Drink to Excess, and Swear sometimes. That he Prayed sometimes in the Evening, but not in the Mornings'. Many of the 'private sins' of such individuals are depressingly mundane. John Austin, who in 1725 was hanged for what appeared to be his first offence – robbing a man of a coat – 'would not acknowledge himself guilty of any heinous Sins', but did admit to sometimes 'Drinking too much' and working on Sundays readying produce (he was a gardener) for sale on Mondays. One 20-year-old 'Cloath-worker' condemned (but subsequently reprieved) for his part in a fatal bar-room brawl 'confess'd that he had been guilty of breaking the Sabbath, and did walk in the Fields, when he should have been at Church, or otherwise well employ'd. That he drank sometimes to excess, was apt to Swear and some other vain courses he had not refrained from'. Frequently, the confessions of criminals resembled something of a checklist: William Marple, hanged in 1729 for robbery, 'claimed that lewd Women were his Ruin', and 'own'd that his Parents (particularly his Mother) were very indulgent to him, but that he never took her advice, which might have prevented his misfortune'. He 'believ'd he had been Drunk seven times, for he had no pleasure in Drinking, but he was very much addicted to Whoring, Covetousness, and Idleness, not much to Swearing'.[57]

But the Ordinary's *Account* was not so scripted but that many – often a majority – of the condemned were recorded as maintaining their innocence of the crime for which they were condemned. Some of the more hardened cases, such as Jane ('alias Elizabeth') Wells ('alias White, alias Dyer, &c.'), simply refused to confess to anything 'saving what was most plain and universally known'. But many other malefactors who otherwise conformed to a penitential script stopped short of admitting to the 'Fact' for which they were convicted, presumably for fear of jeopardizing their chances of a reprieve. Mary Raby, hanged in 1703 for robbery, 'owned that she had been a very great Sinner indeed', guilty of 'Sabbath-breaking, Swearing, Drinking, Lewdness, Buying, Receiving, and disposing of Stoln Goods' and 'Harbouring of ill People', but – despite many professions of charity and gratitude to the Ordinary for his attentions – 'still deny'd her being in the Robbery'. And while some malefactors were clearly willing enough to be cast in the role of an Everyman preaching to the crowd, many even of these confessions and last dying speeches left something to be desired. At his 1724 execution for robbery, Thomas Burden addressed the spectators 'begging that all by his Example would learn to stifle the first Motions of Wickedness and Sin, since such was the Depravity of Human Nature, that no Man knew how soon he might fall'. He then delivered the Ordinary 'a Large Paper ... containing chiefly of Hardships done him' and extenuations of the crime'.[58]

And some of the most ostentatious penitents seized the gallows as a forum to claim their innocence. At his 1690 execution, Sir John Johnston, although making what spectators viewed as an 'exemplary' end, praying, reciting psalms, and warning spectators to 'remember' their 'latter end', nonetheless broadcast his innocence and imprecated against some of the witnesses at his trial (although adamant that he did not intend to 'find any Fault, or any ways arraign the Constitution of the Law or Justice of the Nation'). Edward Jackson, at his 1684 execution for coining, solemnly swore that as 'he believed in God, and as he expected Relief and Comfort from Jesus Christ, he was as clear [of the crime] as that Child', pointing to a 'little Child' in the crowd (his printed speech also claimed he was 'as Innocent as the Child in the Mother's Womb'). Despite being repeatedly 'reproved' for reflecting on the evidence of the prosecution witnesses, Jackson went on to declare 'That he had deserved this Death for his Sins, and he desired to take Publick Shame to Himself' and that 'he forgave all the World', including 'those who swore falsely against him'. 'Hundreds of Spectators' were reported to have 'melted ... into Tears' at the 'Passion, Loudness, and earnestness' of Jackson's prayers just before the cart was drawn away.[59]

Many of the condemned who claimed to die for crimes of which they were innocent paid lip-service to the penitential script by embracing their sentences as providential judgements from God for the other sins of their lives. As the robber Isaac Ford told the Ordinary in 1689, 'he was falsely accused, yet he had committed many sins for which God might permit such a sentence to fall upon him'. In 1684, the solicitor John Hutchins owned up to a series of 'inormities', from Sabbath-breaking to adultery, for which 'God had suffered him to be Accused and Condemned for a Murther, he said he was innocent of'. This was a frequent refrain: John Moore, executed in 1695 for coining, solemnly swore to his innocence, yet acknowledged 'God is very just in my Condemnation' – he 'sometimes in Trading did drink to excess, and was not so Circumspect' in his 'Conversation' as he should have been. As late as 1741, one newspaper reported a condemned burglar delivering a dying speech in which he solemnly attested to his innocence of the crime but admitted that 'Providence had overtaken him for his Wickedness, and punish'd him with so ignominious a Death' because he had deserted his wife and six children and taken up with a 'wicked Woman'. Such claims easily shaded into a kind of 'general and indefinite Confession' with which, as Jeremy Taylor complained, sinners were but too 'apt to excuse themselves'; that is, that 'They are Sinners, as every man hath his infirmity, and he as well as any man: But God be thanked, they bear no ill will to any man, or are no Adulterers, or no Rebels, or they fought on the right side', etc.[60]

At one level such statements also served as a reminder of the inherent and universal depravity of human nature, and the degree to which all guilt was relative. George Duffus, when apprehended by a constable and his prosecutor for committing sodomy, 'cry'd for Mercy, and begg'd that we would not expose him to public Shame; adding, that we were all Sinners, and it was hard for a Man to suffer for the first fault'. Not all of his contemporaries would have classified sodomy as a venial sin: Usher Gahagan, executed in 1749 for coining offences, consoled himself that, although 'guilty of the Frailties of the Children of Men', yet no one could 'charge' his 'Memory' with robbery, murder or sodomy, 'or any such crying and enormous Crimes'. In 1727 the 56-year-old thief John Fox refused to make any particular confessions (he had been tried four times, and had three prior convictions, on capital charges), saying only that while he 'own'd himself to have been a great Sinner', he was 'not so notoriously wicked as many others'. Even an offender as reprehensible as the former hangman John Price, who was in 1718 himself hanged for the brutal robbery and rape of an elderly street-seller who later died of her wounds, apparently took solace in the fact that 'if he had many Sins, they were such as were common to other Men as well as himself', and that 'whatever his Condition might then be, it would be no worse than theirs'.[61]

But even many of the condemned who otherwise qualified as penitent frequently clashed with the Ordinary and other clergymen about what constituted a sufficient confession. The convicted burglar George Gosse asked for the Ordinary's prayers and instructions, and acknowledged to having been once before in Newgate for what he characterized as 'a malitious Prosecution in Man, tho' a just Judgement from God'. But he maintained, over the Ordinary's objections, that he was guilty of 'no other than common Crimes, which the Almighty knew', and for which a 'general Confession' was 'sufficient'. Such expressions of nominal resignation to providential judgements often doubled as criticisms of the secular courts. The robber John Wilkes, hanged in 1752, professed amazement that, after committing numerous 'actions worthy of Death' he should now be 'hanged for a crime of which he knew himself to be innocent'. In many cases, such men were embittered towards former confederates who turned evidence against them. These fallings-out among thieves were often convoluted affairs: in 1729, Benjamin Wileman 'own'd that the Judgement of God has justly overtaken him, for such a notorious wicked Course of Life', but 'reflected on Doyle the Evidence', claiming that the latter had falsely accused him 'out of Spite, because he threaten'd to take up a third Person for a capital Crime, against whom he had Proof'. Many were far from subtle in invoking a court higher than the one that had convicted them. Charles Towers, hanged in 1725 for a theft supposedly committed during a riot, 'in a very loud and exclaiming Voice ... asserted his

Innocence to the Spectators' at Tyburn, denying that he had ever been 'guilty of any notorious Offence' (except for 'unfaithfulness to his Wife's Bed; for which', he conceded, 'he deserved Death'). Towers claimed to be 'easy and contented' with his sentence, rejoicing that he was 'going from a Life of Trouble and Noise and Confusion, to a World of Quiet'. Those executed for treason in particular frequently cited their willingness to bow to a higher authority, invoking similar providentialist, but scarcely normative, language. As three Jacobites executed in 1715 told the Ordinary: they would 'resolve no Questions, nor confess any Sin, but to God only, saving this, That in general they had been grievous Sinners … therefore God in his Justice had brought this Calamity upon them for their former Sins, and they submitted to his Providence'.[62]

THE DECLINE OF THE *ACCOUNT*

In late 1744 the Ordinary James Guthrie dismissed his printer John Applebee, who had published the *Account* for almost twenty-five years, and who had exercised editorial control of the paper since 1735 (when Guthrie had apparently agreed to cede the profits and management of the paper in return for an annual payment). Guthrie claimed to have fallen out with Applebee over the fact that the latter, in his picaresque 'Appendix', had on several recent occasions 'expressed himself in a most undecent manner against our Superiors and the grandeur of this kingdom', making 'sarcastic Expressions against the honourable Magistrates of this most noble City'. Whatever the truth of the disagreement between the two (it is significant that the Court of Aldermen dismissed the Ordinary's petition seeking redress against the printer), Guthrie's scruples had not prevented him from working with Applebee for nearly twenty years, including the more than ten-year period in which the Appendix was regularly attached to the Ordinary's own account. If Applebee was identified in the 1730s and 40s by his journalistic colleagues as a criminal biographer of the 'Curlean', or Grub Street, order (after Edmund Curll, one of Pope's most egregious 'dunces'), Guthrie was linked with his printer in satirical publications of the day as a fellow 'Son' of Grub Street.[63]

Guthrie himself was dismissed only a little over a year after the falling-out with Applebee, ostensibly because he had been 'rendred incapable of performing the Duty' of his office because of 'Age and other Infirmities'. It may be significant that although Guthrie had officiated as Newgate chaplain from September 1725, during and after Thomas Purney's final illness, he had not been officially appointed as Ordinary, but had only acted under two special orders of the Court of Aldermen. In October 1733, the City decided to review 'the terms and conditions under which the … Office [of Ordinary] shall in future be held', advertising in a number of London newspapers its 'Resolution to appoint a new Ordinary of Newgate'; and that, in order 'to encourage some able Divine to execute that important Office as it ought', an additional freedom, valued at £25, would be added to the regular salary and perquisites. Both Guthrie and Samuel Rossell petitioned for the office, but the decision was repeatedly put off until 19 February 1733/4, when 'It was resolved ... That Mr James Guthrie shall continue to Officiate as Ordinary of Newgate during the pleasure of this Court'. It is not clear whether the Court of Aldermen had seriously considered replacing Guthrie with someone more suitable, or whether the review of the office was simply part of a larger constellation of City reforms in the early 1730s. In October of 1732, a house on Newgate Street (and thus a mandatory residence requirement) was added to the terms of the Ordinary's post, while the Court of Aldermen had conducted a review of the office of the keeper of Newgate the previous July. Guthrie's rival, Samuel Rossell, continued to covet the office of Ordinary – in 1740 petitioning the Court of Aldermen for 'proper' 'Encouragement' for his recently published prayerbook for prisoners, which he had dedicated to the Mayor, the Court of Aldermen and sheriffs. While Rossell succeeded Guthrie in June 1746, he did not long enjoy the fruits of office, such as they were, dying in March 1747.[64]

Under Rossell and his successors, John Taylor (1747–57) and Stephen Roe (1757–64), the *Account* continued as a regular serial publication, but in a much more staid and scaled-down form. Regular reportage of sermons had disappeared by the later 1740s, their place often supplied by newspaper-style editorials about various moral and social problems of the day. Not only was the *Account* markedly shorter in length after 1745 but a series of editorial and format changes seem to suggest that the paper was unable to find a new niche. Although the publishers of the Ordinary's *Accounts* of the 1750s continued to bill themselves as the only 'authorised' printers of the 'dying speeches', competition for the lives and confessions of ordinary criminals seemed to be in steep decline. Forgeries of the Ordinary's *Account* after the 1740s tended to take the form of satire rather than any attempt to encroach on the Newgate chaplain's privileges. In 1747, for instance, a mock Ordinary's *Account* of the last dying speeches of the outgoing Pelham administration was published; the following year saw the publication of another such account pillorying the libertine Earl of Chesterfield for ravishing a young girl. (The Earl was portrayed as the very 'surly' object of the Ordinary's ministrations; fortunately, the latter, 'used to those kind of sulky Fits in lower Life', was 'not deterr'd from doing [his] Duty'.) Oliver Goldsmith wrote a satirical account of Theophilus Cibber that the Ordinary was supposedly unable to publish after Cibber died from drowning in 1758 – a cruel play on the proverb that 'he that is born to be hanged, will never be drowned'. Such satires drew from older themes from rogue literature but also suggested the ridiculousness and incongruity of anyone who cut any figure in society being included in the Ordinary's calendar.[65]

The later *Account* was also subject to pressures from the City itself: in 1763 Stephen Roe was reprimanded for making a critical statement in his paper about Newgate conditions. Henceforth, one of the stipulations of the post was that Ordinaries 'be very cautious' in their 'Publications relating to the condemned Prisoners' – a warning reiterated by the Court of Aldermen upon the appointments of Joseph Moore (1764–69), John Wood (1769–74) and John Villette (1774–99). The *Account* seems to have been periodically discontinued in the later 1760s, but briefly revived under Wood in 1770 – who took the opportunity to reassure his readers that 'future Publications' should 'be true and authentic, and as free as possible from all particular *Censures and Animadversions improperly pointed*'. John Villette published several pamphlets of the execution of such notable criminals as Dr William Dodd (although not under the title of the Ordinary's *Account*), as well as *The Annals of Newgate* (1776), a compilation of earlier criminal lives and confessions. Tellingly, at his successor Brownlow Forde's appointment, there was no mention of publications, which had long since fallen into desuetude.[66]

It is difficult to chart the popularity or marketability of the *Account*, or even the frequency of its publication, quantitatively: for instance, the fact that there seems to be no extant copy of the Ordinary's *Account* of Jack Sheppard's execution certainly does not mean that none was published (indeed, the Ordinary's biography of Sheppard was extensively cited and plagiarized in other crime publications). Anecdotal evidence is also problematic: early eighteenth-century criticisms of the Ordinary's *Account* as a Grub Street paper may well reflect its currency and ubiquity, but then what is to be made of similar characterizations of the last *Accounts* in the early 1770s as 'slight' and 'superficial', 'little better than the Grub-street accounts cried about in the streets'?[67] This last passage reminds us, however, that while last dying speeches continued as an ephemeral genre – that is, generally printed without date or imprint – regular printers and booksellers stopped publishing and carrying accounts of the speeches of ordinary malefactors in the later eighteenth century. And, while the publication of various notable trials (for 'criminal conversation' as well as for felonies) would continue into the late eighteenth and early nineteenth centuries, they no longer routinely appended biographies, confessions or last dying speeches, as early and mid-eighteenth-century *Select Trials* and similar publications had done. Moreover, no new editions of the *Select Trials* were published after 1765, and the various Newgate Calendars of the late eighteenth and early nineteenth centuries were almost exclusively confined to criminals hanged long before (drawing from earlier *Accounts* and Sessions Papers, although increasingly bowdlerizing and editing these sources). And while newspapers and pamphlets continued to cover the execution of eminent or particularly notorious criminals, experiments with reporting the speeches of the ordinary malefactors hanged at Tyburn were shortlived, presumably reflecting a decline in public interest in the lives and executions of unremarkable property offenders.[68]

But this was not the last word on gallows conversions and Newgate penitence. The second half of the eighteenth century would see the revival of the older notion of the criminal as Everyman – in a form, moreover, particularly obnoxious to the Ordinary, not to mention the polite audience he was so intent on cultivating. For after about 1740, John Wesley and his followers began to preach a radical and peculiarly optimistic brand of free grace, one divorced from its older Calvinist predestinarian underpinnings: free not so much insofar that it was in God's gift and did not depend on the merits of the recipient, but in that it was free for the taking by all men and women who truly believed in Christ as their redeemer – those who, in short, felt themselves to be 'born again'. This doctrine would raise troubling, even antinomian implications, undermining the foundations of the confessional genre, as we shall see in the following chapter on prison penitence and dying well.

6

Dying Well: Martyrs and Penitents

Bene mori est libenter mori. To dye well is to dye gladlye & wilfully.

The Boke of the Craft of Dying (*c.* 1500)

In Shore Ditch there I did Dwell
Where many People knows me well;
In Brandy Shops I did use,
And lewd Women I did choose,
A wicked Sinner I have been,
In Whoring and in other things;
Two Wives I have been Married to,
Which now alas! does make me rue.
I freely forgive every Body,
And hope they will forgive me.

Thomas Past, (Ordinary's *Account* 5 March 1731/2)

A 1697 prayer book provided condemned felons with the following penitential template:

when you are brought from Prison to Execution, own the justice of your Sentence: Profess your abhorrence and true Repentance of the Crime which you Dye for, and all your other Sins. Declare the Satisfaction you have made, or would make, were you able, to all you have wronged. Beg all Persons to forgive you, who have suffered by you in any kind, and all who have ever learnt any ill from your Acquaintance and Example. Declare that you do from your Heart, forgive all Persons, and that you bear not the least ill will against any of your Prosecutors, or the Judges and Juries who were concerned in bringing you to Justice. And … be sure nothing fall[s] from you, that may bring the Sincerity thereof into Question. And therefore take Diligent Care, not to shew uneasie Remembrance and Resentment, of the Evils or Injuries which you have suffer'd, but only of those which you your Self have done.

The condemned was exhorted to submit to his or her sentence 'meekly' and 'as a Lamb … as your Blessed Saviour did', who (although 'he had no real Guilt but was perfectly Innocent') 'suffered the worst things without aggravating them or being angry at them, and on the Cross spake nothing of his bitter Enemies, but to Excuse them, and Pray for them'. The malefactor was likewise instructed to warn spectators of the dangers of embarking upon the slippery slope of sin; to clear those wrongly blamed for his or her own misdeeds; to testify to his or her communion and to repeat the Apostle's Creed; to 'humbly profess your lowly Hope in Gods free Mercy'; to 'beg the Prayers of all the Beholders' and to bid friends farewell; and finally, to continue to pray until the 'Executioner … stops your Breath'. The author conceded that 'to remember all these Points at the Place of Execution, may be thought hard for the Poor Prisoner'. But fortunately, 'he may have this little Book in his Eye, for his Remembrancer'.[1]

This *ars moriendi* for felons (as it were) reflected contemporary execution practice as well as simply prescription, as we shall see. It is also suggestive of the beginnings of a shift away from an older ('Puritan') seventeenth-century emphasis on crime as a 'public sin' – that is, predominately an offence against God – towards an eighteenth-century ('Anglican') emphasis on crime as an offence against the community.[2] In an early Ordinary's *Account*, Samuel Smith defined the 'Seven Signs' of true 'godly sorrow' in progressive stages: 'carefulness' (consciousness of sin); 'clearing of yourselves' (confession); 'indignation' (remorse); 'fear' (of God's judgement); 'vehement desire' (for forgiveness); 'zeal' (hope for salvation) and 'revenge' (hatred of sin). By the 1730s, James Guthrie routinely characterized saving penitence as an effectual 'turning' from 'Sin and Impurity, to Holiness and Virtue', effecting 'a Change in the whole Man, so that he becomes a New Creature, willing and desirous to please God …' Here can be discerned a subtle shift from an emphasis on divine wrath and grace (or, as Smith put it, 'the Effect of God's Power') to man's voluntary conversion and reformation – a point to which I will return.[3]

One theme that remained constant throughout the period was the need for penitents to strive for that 'happy mean between presumption and despair'. Lillo's tragic hero George Barnwell exhibits the 'genuine signs of true repentance' at the foot of the gallows: 'I hope in doubt, and trembling I rejoice. I feel my grief increase, even as my fears give way. Joy and gratitude now supply more tears than the horror and anguish of despair before'. Weeping, as well as trembling, was a necessary part of true repentance: 'a broken and a contrite heart, O God, thou wilt not despise' (Psalm 51:17). Godly sorrow often manifested itself in 'Floods of Tears' – as with the highwayman John Young, hanged in 1730, who spent his time in Newgate 'in continual Prayer, Meditation, and reading of godly Books[,] … appeared to be in raptures of Devotion' and appeared even 'to the nicest judgement' as 'a true Penitent'. Tears, especially in seventeenth-century accounts, were often characterized as 'melting' even the most 'obdurate' criminals and bringing them to a humble confession of their sins. Yet, as Samuel Smith wrote in 1690, 'Salvation' was a weighty thing, to be 'work[ed] out with a cautious Fear and Trembling'; it was 'not so cheap and easy a performance' as to be effected by 'a few Tears, Sighs and Lord have Mercy on me'. The true penitent must evince 'an hatred and Detestation of Sin, as well as a Sorrow for it' – that is, a hatred of sin for its own sake, as an offence against God, rather than because it had brought him or her to 'condign temporal Punishment'.[4]

On the other hand, the Ordinary was supposed to guard his flock against despair. In May 1721, Thomas Purney attempted to relieve John Thompson's fears that God 'would not have any regard to his Repentance, because it was forc'd and not voluntary', referring him to several texts, including that of the penitent thief (Luke:23). Paul Lorrain, in his *Dying Man's Assistant*, comforted despairing malefactors with the reminder that 'God knows whereof we are made: He is not ignorant of our Natural Frailty and Propensity to Sin'; moreover, 'were all the Sins both of Men and Devils, joyn'd together in one and the very same Person' they all 'might be wholly done away by one single Drop of Christ's Blood'. The mere prospect of public execution was in itself dreadful. As Mary Carleton, the so-called German Princess (the daughter of a Canterbury fiddler-turned confidence artist) was supposed to have confessed before her 1673 hanging for shoplifting, 'it was a great thing to dye, a harder matter than she had thought it'. A small proportion of the condemned were regularly described as being at the gallows 'quite stupid, either with Fear or Sickness', or by virtue of their being 'quite ignorant of their unhappy Condition'. Some malefactors were indeed almost incapacitated with terror: at his April 1735 execution at Kingston, Philip Wilkinson 'was taken with such a Trembling, that he could not hold one Joint of him still for some Time. All the Time that his Fetters was Knocking off, and likewise while the Executioner was a Haltering of him, he cry'd out, Oh! Lord what Have I brought myself too [sic]. Lord have Mercy on me, Christ have Mercy on me'.[5]

There were some whose penitence was merely 'a Sort of Mask' assumed in hopes of obtaining a reprieve: in 1752 John Taylor complained that Robert Lake, after regular and apparently devout attendance at prayers, resumed 'his own Face, audacious and impudent', after finding out that 'all Hopes of saving [his] Life were over'. Some few, however, met even the Ordinary's rigorous penitential standards. In March 1677, Samuel Smith reported that 'no man could be more penitent' than the condemned highwayman William Johnson, who supposedly spent 'almost all these few remaining moments of his life in Prayers and Tears', and even writing pious verses on the wall of his prison cell ('My precious Lord, from all Transgressions free,/ Was pleas'd, in tender pity unto me,/ To undergo the Ignominious Tree./ I suffer justly; but his Sacrifice,/ I trust, shall make my grovelling Spirits rise,/ And from the Gibbet mount the glorious Skies'). The housebreaker Stephen Gardiner, hanged in February 1724, was not only 'remarkably observant of his Duty', and 'never easy, nor would let the others be so, but when they were reading or praying', but insisted (despite the 'extream Cold') on wearing a thin shroud to Tyburn, 'for he was of Opinion, that he could not too much punish and afflict his Body for the Crimes he had committed'.

Even some of the most hardened old offenders could qualify as true penitents: in February 1723, Purney noted that the condemned murderer Charles Weaver 'endeavour'd to settle his Thoughts every Hour and Minute upon Heaven', rising every morning at three, and often joined by his three fellow sufferers – notorious street robbers all – who 'delighted to get up three or four times in the Night' to pray and to sing psalms. Even the more cynical Guthrie occasionally noted that some of the condemned behaved 'christianly and devoutly' – such as the condemned highwayman Charles Oglesbay, hanged in 1731, who attended chapel 'constantly', 'often shed Tears', and whenever 'the Cell Door was open'd ... was always found upon his Knees praying very devoutly and seriously'.[6]

However scripted last dying confessions may have been, many of the condemned were clearly willing enough to use the scaffold as a pulpit, readily conflating their own sins with that of their audience. The last dying confession of Edmund Kirk, hanged in 1684 for the murder of his wife, is typical of the genre: 'Time was when I had as great a delight in vanity, as the most Debauched amongst you. The Day was lost in my apprehension, in which I met no Jovial Companion to Drink or Carouse away the Hours; the Nights misspent, that was not improved in the Embraces and Dalliances of some Dalilah' (and so on). Before her 1679 execution, Margaret Clark supposedly proclaimed, 'Oh! this is my Wedding day, I shall surely be married to my Saviour: O Lord, that ever I should offend so good and gracious a God as thou art; O the Joys! I long to be at the place'. On the morning of his 1682 execution for murder, Lieutenant John Stern 'appeared in a rapture of joy', weeping (as he explained, not from 'Sorrow' but 'from excess of Joy'), and expressing his eagerness to 'exchange a Prison for a Paradise; a Prison that had been to him better than any Palace; for that God had touched him and drawn him, and quickned him ...' Such ostentatious displays of public penitence were more characteristic of condemned murderers (who figure largely in Increase Mather's *Wonders of Free-Grace*) than property offenders, and were moreover on the wane in the early eighteenth century, as respectable contemporaries were increasingly uncomfortable with viewing converted rapists, robbers and murderers as suitable exemplars of the good death.[7]

Death by hanging had, of course, always been viewed as ignominious – even the Methodist Silas Told admitted that when in 1748 he first rode in the cart with malefactors to Tyburn, it was 'not without much shame, because I perceived the greater part of the populace considered me as one of the sufferers'. However, these shameful associations coexisted with older traditions in which execution was viewed as a variant of the '"good death" ... the single occasion when a Christian could know the exact moment of his or her death, and thus prepare for grace up until the final blow'. In a traditional spiritual context, what was most to be dreaded was the sudden, unprepared death, *mors improvisa*.[8] The ultimate exemplar of the good death was of course Christ; and while no human being could hope to emulate Christ in his sinlessness, the penitent thief crucified along with him provided a popular – if, as we shall see, an increasingly problematic – model of effectual late repentance. For, by the Evangelical Revival of the late 1730s and early 1740s, most educated contemporaries had become distinctly uncomfortable with the older Calvinist trope of the penitent murderer or robber as a monument of God's free grace.

This is not to say that seventeenth-century execution accounts did not make social distinctions. One of the earliest Ordinary's *Accounts*, from 1679, wondered aloud how such 'untimely Wretches' as the condemned, 'most of them men of leud Conversations', could be 'our Fellow-creatures, cast in Nature's Mould, the same by Heaven made'. But this suspension of disbelief – the charitable concession that even apparent reprobates were potentially regenerate – was central to the doctrine of free grace, whereby 'the Almighty's goodness is as boundless as his power, and he can save unto the utmost all that come unto him'. After all, the glory and the omnipotence of God was illustrated best by such criminal brands plucked from the burning, for much the same reason that women, children and the disabled figured largely in the works of John Foxe and other Protestant martyrologists: God's potency was all the more apparent for its being manifested in a weak vessel. (Indeed, those who were arrogant or blasphemous enough to think themselves worthy of such distinction were by definition suspect, as lacking the requisite humility for true holiness.) God's grace was 'free', as John Wesley claimed in his famous, and controversial, 1740 sermon on the subject: it did 'not depend on any Power or Merit in Man', nor on 'the good Works or Righteousness of the Receiver'.[9]

And many ordinary malefactors (some, but by no means all, Methodist converts) continued well into the eighteenth century to express their assurance of salvation and their eagerness to die. In 1742 the Irish robber Matthew Mooney 'was so far from repining at the manner of his Death, that he said, were it not for the Shame, it was the best exit a Man cou'd make, because being in Health he was the better able to prepare for Eternity'. Similarly the highwayman Richard James, hanged in 1721, 'thank'd God for taking him off so soon from Sin; and for letting him die a death that gave him time and space for Repentance: Nor could it at all affect his Soul, whatever the World said of the shame of such an End'. A number of the condemned claimed that they would prefer to die on the gallows than to risk the chance of backsliding, and 'add[ing] to the number' of their 'Sins'. Robert Hickson, hanged in 1750 for two robberies (which, he claimed, he had committed while 'warm with Liquor'), 'express'd his Joy' that 'it had pleased God to suffer him to be taken so early' as 'it prevented a further Reckoning, which might have rendered the making Peace with his God a more difficult task'.[10] Both earlier Calvinist and later evangelical literature agreed in their characterization of true (i.e., 'saving') penitence as being evidenced by a melting and a breaking of the heart ('truly broken for sin'), followed by 'powerful motions of the Holy Ghost', or a 'strange warmth' denoting regeneration, or being born again – that is, as a creature more like Christ. True penitents then not only felt a loathing for sin, but were free of temptation, finding joy only in holy things – evidence of their spiritual 'weaning from this world'. Methodist converts sometimes spoke of feeling a lightness of heart, much as though the shackles of sins had (like Christian's burden) suddenly fallen from them. But while mid-eighteenth-century Methodist descriptions of the 'new birth' were in many respects consistent with their earlier Calvinist antecedents, from the late seventeenth century, the Ordinaries of Newgate were increasingly sceptical of the spiritual self-diagnoses of malefactors. As Samuel Smith cautioned one over-confident penitent in 1693, 'the Heart of Man is very deceitful in Judging its Spiritual State Godward, especially when Persons have contracted a Custom in Sinning, and thereby hardned their Hearts.'[11]

More problematic still were those malefactors who not only advertised their confidence in their salvation and their willingness to die, but who also maintained their innocence of the crime for which they were condemned. In 1750 Thomas Reynolds 'declared in the Press-yard, while his Irons were knocking off' – a place where curious spectators often converged – 'that he went to be hanged with as much Satisfaction as if he was going to be married; for that he was innocent of the Crime for which he suffer'd [recruiting for the French army], and freely forgave his Prosecutor'. Many cited providential signs which, it seemed, implied that they were 'saved': the condemned horse-thief William Simpson, hanged in 1729, claimed 'he was very willing to leave the World, it being full of Sin and Sorrow, altho' he was in a years time to Possess an Estate of 300*l.* per Annum', noting that the day of his execution was the fourth anniversary of his mother's death. At his 1746 execution, the condemned robber George Thomas 'said this was his birth-day' – literally, but also with a clear connotation of his faith in a life to come – 'and a blessed day to him'. At her June 1728 execution, in which 'it rain'd and thunder'd violently', Eleanor Benson 'said, that it is a good Rain … I hope the Dew of Heaven will rain down Grace upon our Souls'. When in 1763 the highwayman Charles Speckman, alias Brown, and his fellow sufferers were loaded on the carts that would take them to Tyburn, they all 'seemed greatly supported', with Speckman remarking that 'it was the finest morning he ever saw'. The condemned were duly 'warned against presumption and to be humble'.[12]

While an appropriately humble hope of salvation was the hallmark of the true penitent, too much assurance – in contrast to the continual doubt and self-examination that were widely held as evidence of a regenerate heart – was often seen as a sign of reprobation (as in the case of Bunyan's complacent 'Ignorance' who is bound hand and foot and cast into hell after presumptuously knocking at the gates of the Celestial City). According to a 1695 sermon preached at Newgate by a visiting London minister: "'tis better for Notorious Criminals to go out of the world with much Anguish and Dejection ... rather than with the least Air of Pride and Confidence'; after all, 'God the Searcher of Hearts will never condemn any one (if really Penitent) for an Excess of Humility, or an Holy Diffidence, when 'tis so truly agreeable to his present Circumstances'. Assurance could all too easily shade into the forms and conventions of martyrological literature, with ordinary criminals borrowing the words and gestures of sixteenth- and seventeenth-century martyrs and political prisoners, who in turn borrowed from older scriptural models. Nor should we neglect the degree to which the works of Foxe and other Protestant hagiographers enjoyed a wide readership, with many early modern men and women engaging in a kind of 'postfiguration' – that is, measuring themselves against righteous scriptural figures and seeing their own lives as literal re-enactments of biblical events.[13]

While in prison, John Lilburne, 'by reading the Book of Martyrs ... rais'd in himself a marvellous Inclination and Appetite to suffer in the Defence, or for the Vindication of any oppress'd Truth'. During his imprisonment, John Bunyan also read Foxe's *Acts and Monuments* and, while in no real danger of execution, compulsively rehearsed in his mind his conduct on the gallows. Many of those who actually suffered for their religious or political beliefs made overt connections between their lives and those of biblical heroes: the regicide Colonel John Jones, 'speaking of the sled in which he was to be carried to Execution; it is (said he) like Elija's Fiery Charriot, only it goes through Fleetstreet'. At his 1655 execution, Colonel John Penruddock, 'as he was ascending the Scaffold ... said, This, I hope, will prove to be like Jacob's Ladder; tho' the Feet of it rest on Earth, yet I doubt not but the Top of it reacheth to Heaven'.[14]

While the expressions of charity and forgiveness of enemies on the part of Christ and other martyrs, from Saint Stephen on, were held up as exemplary, such words were obviously problematic for authorities when cited by felons or political prisoners asserting their innocence. If Jesus's last words, 'Father, into thy hands I commend my spirit' (Luke 23:46) constituted a traditional final pious ejaculation for dying penitents, many would-be martyrs also appropriated Christ's words on the cross, 'Forgive them; for they know not what they do' (Luke 23:34), or Stephen's 'Lord, lay not this sin to their charge' (Acts 7:60). Many early modern state criminals advertised their assurance of salvation by referring to the day of their execution as their wedding day to Christ – like Shakespeare's King Lear, broadcasting their determination to 'die bravely, like a smug bridegroom'. A partisan account of the execution of the five Jesuits in 1679 represented them as going to their deaths 'seriously and cheerfully', with the youngest sufferer, John Gavan, described as having 'smug'd himself up as if he had been going to a Wedding'. The regicide Thomas Harrison, in a letter to his wife, described his forthcoming execution as 'his wedding day'; the Fifth

Monarchist John James, executed in 1661 for delivering a treasonable sermon, referred to his friends accompanying him to Tyburn as his 'Bride-men'. On the night before his execution – during his 'last supper' – Nicholas Ridley cheerfully invited his hostess and fellow guests 'to his marriage; "for", said he, "to-morrow I must be married"'.[15]

Martyrs typically comforted grieving friends and family: at his 1680 execution, the Catholic Lord Stafford 'sweetly saluted his Friends, bidding them not grieve for him; for this was the happiest day of all his Life'. In a famous example, Sir Thomas More 'said merrily' to an officer helping him onto the scaffold: 'I pray you, Master Lieutenant, see me safe up; and as to my coming down, let me shift for myself'. The regicide John Barkstead advertised his good cheer on the eve of his execution by telling his wife, upon being asked to wash his hands for supper, that there was no need, as 'to morrow they would be put upon the City Gates on spikes, and the rain would save him that labour'. Richard Rumbold, executed in Edinburgh for treason in 1685, after being asked if he thought his sentence – that is, drawing and quartering – 'dreadful', was reported to have said that 'he wished he had a limb for every town in Christendom' (officials seemed to have responded to this piece of bravado by issuing a special order for Rumbold's quarters to be taken from Scotland to be exposed in London and other parts of England). Typically, such individuals advertised their non-resistance as further evidence of their willingness to die. At his 1685 execution, Henry Cornish supposedly told an officer about to tie his hands that 'a brown Thred might have served the turn, you need not tye me at all, I shall not stir from you, for I thank God I am not afraid to die'. Thomas Harrison reportedly insisted to spectators, 'I do not lay down my life by constraint but willingly', as he had had 'many opportunities' to 'have run away' if he had so chosen; later, as though to reinforce the impression of his execution as an event of his own staging, Harrison 'thrust up again' the cap that the hangman had just pulled down over his head, to add 'one word more to the Lords people' – which was that, 'though we may suffer hard things, yet … God will make hard and bitter things sweet and easie to all those that trust in him'.[16]

Numerous seventeenth-century state criminals imitated the example of Marian martyrs, who were reported as kissing the stake at which they were burnt: Sir Henry Hyde kissed the executioner's axe before being beheaded in 1651; two Catholic priests executed in 1679 'kissed the Post of the Gallows'; at his execution the same year, Richard Langhorn 'when the hangman was putting the rope round his neck … took it and kissed it'; when the noose was put around the neck of the royalist John Sares in 1652, the latter 'with expressions of joy said; what a Gallant morning [sic] Ribbon is this which I weare for the sake of my King'. Most subversive of all was the implicit claim on the part of such individuals to a courage and a composure that was of divine issue; after all – according to the much reprinted collection, *The Mirror of Martyrs* – 'the constancy of Martyrs is not to be ascribed to any natural Power of their own, but unto the power of God's holy Spirit, who comforteth and encourageth them in all their sufferings'. In the words of Christopher Love, executed in 1651 for treason: 'tho' I come to die a violent Death, yet that Death is not a Terror to me ... God is not a Terror to me, therefore Death is not dreadful to me; I bless my God, I speak it without Vanity, I have formerly had more Fear in the drawing of a Tooth, than now I have at the cutting off my Head'.[17]

DYING IN CHARITY WITH ALL THE WORLD

Needless to say, the majority of ordinary malefactors fell somewhere in between the two extremes of abject despair and confident assurance (with the important exception of the game criminal, treated in the following chapter). Moreover, most condemned men and women (including game criminals) appeared to be, at least ostensibly, willing to conform to most of the articles of dying well as outlined in the opening section. Central among these was the notion that anyone wishing to make a good end must assume responsibility for his or her own mistakes and misfortunes. In marked contrast with modern popular culture, seventeenth- and eighteenth-century men and women generally began their last dying speeches by exonerating long-suffering and tender mothers and fathers of blame. Many refused even to identify their parents. Thomas Jones, alias 'Toothless Tom' ('so called by reason of his having had his Teeth knocked out by a Man whose Pocket he attempted to pick'), asked the Ordinary to keep his real name confidential, 'because he would not bring a Reproach upon the honest and pious Family he belong'd to'; the highwayman Joseph Johnson confided to the Ordinary that Johnson was 'not his right name ... which he desir'd should be here conceal'd, lest it should come to his Old Father's Ears, and so bring his Gray-hair with Sorrow to the Grave'.[18]

Deborah Churchill, executed in 1703 as an accessory to murder, acknowledged that she had been well educated by worthy parents, and had 'none to reflect on for my Misfortunes but my own giddy and ungovernable Inclinations'. The shoplifter Jane Dyer, alias Brown, hanged in 1705, claimed that she had been 'virtuously and religiously brought up by her Parents; to whom she had been very undutiful and disobedient; and that she had broke their Hearts by her Wickedness; which was now a great grief to her'. In 1726 Samuel Sells lamented 'his Disobedience and disrespectful Carriage to a good indulgent Mother, so that he spit in her Face, beat her, and curs'd her, which bad Usage with his other Miscarriages broke her Heart, and prov'd the occasion of her Death'.[19] It was in fact customary for malefactors at the place of execution to ask spectators not to 'reflect on their Friends and Relations'. In 1733 the robber Joseph Fretwell 'commended his

Father, and Mother in Law [stepmother] as good, kind Parents, and imputed the whole of his Misfortunes to his own unaccountably wicked Dispositions'. At his 1715 execution for burglary, John Smith, alias Mackintosh, 'desir'd that his poor Mother (an honest and virtuous Woman) might not be reflected on for this his shameful End, which (had he follow'd her good Advice and wholsom Admonitions, he might have avoided)'. [20]

And indeed it is clear that some spectators *did* reflect on the parents of malefactors, especially those of young offenders. The 15-year-old Charles Patrick, hanged in 1732 for robbery, supposedly requested a letter 'to be inserted in the Dying Speech' in which he refuted the rumour that his mother was to blame for his predicament, insisting that 'if I had taken her Council I had never come to this untimely End. So all People I desire that you would never reflect upon my dear Mother, nor any that belongs to me, for it was my own Doings that brought me to this shameful End'. And in 1716 the condemned rioter William Price, 21, 'was much concerned to hear that his poor Mother had been misrepresented by some Persons, who had reported, that she us'd no Endeavours to save his Life [i.e., procure a pardon]; for he was fully satisfied she did that to her utmost'.[21]

Many malefactors attempted to clear their wives of any involvement, or even knowledge, of their crimes. In 1733 the condemned burglar William Brown was supposed to have requested the readers of the *Account* 'not [to] Reflect on my Unfortunate Wife and four small Children, for she was unsensible of my way of Life; for I always told her several different Stories how I got my Money; and if I had taken her Advice, I had never brought myself to this untimely End'. Katherine Fitzpatrick (alias Green, alias Boswell) hanged in 1726 for theft, ingenuously (and depressingly) 'vindicated' her husband from involvement in any of her crimes, claiming 'that upon Suspicion of her applying her self to such hellish Courses, as Thieving and Shop-lifting, he had given her many desperate Blows, and Beaten her severely'. The highwayman William Barton, executed in 1721, claimed that he had returned from sea (at least once from penal transportation before expiry of his sentence) no fewer than four times, because he could not bear the thought of his wife and child suffering from want in his absence, insisting that 'his Wife … never knew of one of his Ill Actions'. The editor of the *Select Trials*, in which Barton's biography was included, added drily, 'how his Wife could be entirely ignorant of his Practices, when he had no visible Methods of living honestly, but followed a continual Course of Rapine and Plunder and had been transported for an Offence of that Kind, is a little extraordinary'.[22]

Not all condemned malefactors were as uxorious as William Barton. The street robber James Shaw, hanged in 1722, although freely exonerating his parents of blame, 'endeavoured to cast the whole of his Vices and calamities upon his Wife', whom he accused of spending all of his money, all the while keeping their home 'in a melancholly Confusion'. To the consternation of the Ordinary, Thomas

Purney, 'no Threats of Hell fire, no Assurances of being Forgiven, if he heartily forgave Others, could abate this settled Eternity [sic]; nor could the Sight or Speech of her be supportable; [Shaw] saying also, that the Child which she had was nothing related to him'. Purney's successor James Guthrie had better success with John Mattocks, who claimed that 'the immediate cause of his Ruin was … he had the Misfortune to marry a naughty Woman' who 'heed[ed] nothing but Drinking and Idleness' and ate 'and drank it [their money] all up' until he was 'put to his Shifts'. Although Mattocks refused to reconcile with her – 'she had turn'd a common Street Walker (as he was informed)' – he nonetheless heeded the Ordinary's advice to 'be at peace with her, before he left the World', acknowledging that, since 'she was once his Wife, it was not proper that any one of 'em should die, having the least grudge at the other'. On the eve of his execution Edward Reynolds 'turned into a little passion' at his wife (another 'naughty Woman') for not 'doing more for him', and Guthrie 'reproved him sharply, and told him the necessity of being reconciled to all Men, especially, his Wife'. Reynolds, seemingly affected by this advice, 'went to her and was heartily reconcil'd, falling out into a flood of Tears and an hearty Sorrow for Sin, as in Charity we are bound to think'.[23]

Sometimes such reconciliations were delayed until literally the eleventh hour. Katherine and Elizabeth Tracey, two sisters condemned in 1734 for coining, had made a 'daily Practice' of 'Jangling', each blaming the other for her fate: 'Katherine frequently telling her Sister, that if it had not been for [her], she should not have been brought to that miserable End, and accusing her of being a vile Woman, a Shop-lifter, a Stealer of Pewter Pots, and such like Discourse'. Yet the Ordinary noted that at the place of execution, 'the two Sisters, who had been at Variance, most kindly kiss'd and embraced one another several times'. That same year, two former companions in crime, William Sweet and Philip Wilkinson, hanged for stealing from a church, fell out after Sweet (according to Wilkinson) did 'things under-handed, in getting a Petition sign'd for a Reprieve, and not acquaint[ing] him with it, which caused some Uneasiness between them'. Yet we are told that at the place of execution the two men quickly reconciled, kissing each other just before the cart drew away.[24]

The condemned were subjected to pressures not only from the Ordinary and other clergymen, but also from spectators at Tyburn and numerous curious visitors to Newgate. Matthias Brinsden, condemned in 1722 for murdering his wife, refused to forgive his 16-year-old daughter for testifying against him in court; and, when she 'appear'd in the Chapel, to beg he'd forgive her, he turn'd away and would not see her'. Not only the girl – who knelt before her father, weeping and holding up her hands beseechingly – but 'near 20 other Persons, some of them kneeling to him beg'd with Tears, he would pardon his Daughter, &c'. It took 'about half an Hour before he could be perswaded to say he forgave;

and it was next Day, before he could be induc'd to kiss her'. It was only after the spirited intercession of 'two Clergy-men, and others' that Brinsden 'at last … seem'd really to be in Charity with her', and began 'crying very lamentably', and begging his daughter to forgive him and pray for him.[25]

While Brinsden was a particularly hard case, some malefactors – while less difficult to crack – were at least as grudging and probably not so sincere in their professions of charity. After all, in the words of a 1742 prayer book for felons, 'It is an easy matter to say, we forgive all men, and are in charity with all the world; but these words are sometimes said hypocritically, and for form's sake only'. Charles Drew, hanged in 1740 for the murder of his father, claimed in a letter supposedly written to his mistress that 'I die in Charity with all the World; I forgive my Enemies from the bottom of my heart, and may those who have given me evil Counsel … live to repent. I don't reflect on them, but on myself, who might easily have seen where to such evil Counsels tended. But I forgive'. Many confessions, especially where they impinged on witnesses and prosecutors, were similarly passive-aggressive. William Rowland, a smuggler hanged in 1748, strenuously maintained his innocence and reflected on the evidence against him, saying, 'though he wrongfully accused me, I forgive him, and wish he may be found to receive the same at the hands of God'. The coiner Ralph Cook, executed in 1680, was like many in that while 'in words he did forgive', he was at times 'transported with passion at his wife', upon whose information he was apprehended. Thomas Williams, condemned in 1722 for theft, told the Ordinary that if he were to see the man who had turned evidence against him, 'He would stab him to the Heart', although, as the Ordinary noted, he had 'Conceal'd' this 'Malice' while hoping for a reprieve, often claiming that 'he bore no Man any Grudge, but could freely dye without Resentment'. (Williams, despite his uncharitable behaviour, nonetheless did obtain a transportation pardon.)[26]

On the Saturday before his 1736 execution, George Ward supposedly announced that 'he only wanted to do one Thing more before he dyed, and then he should be easy'; when asked what that was, he explained: 'he wished that the Person who was the Cause of his being Apprehended would come to see him, [then] *he would stabb* him to the Heart'. In 1725 the condemned robber James Campbell, thinking he had spotted his prosecutor in chapel, 'express'd his want of a proper Instrument to dispatch him immediately, nor could the Prisoner rest til the said person was put out of the Chapel'. (The Ordinary was careful to add that 'before he dy'd he was instructed more fully in the Nature of Christianity, and the chief Requisites of Repentance' – particularly the notion of forgiving others, as one hoped for 'Forgiveness from God'.) In 1747 the burglar John Exelby, while pretending to shake the hand of his common-law wife (and principal evidence against him at his trial) through his cell door, 'drew a Knife, and in a Butcherly Manner Hack'd' at her hand'. (When reproved for this 'barbarous' action, 'very unbecoming to any Man, more especially one who … might expect to die soon', Exelby claimed she had 'used provoking Words to him' and that he was 'concern'd in Liquor … otherwise he believes he had not been so wicked'.) Similarly, when the robber Thomas Talbot enticed a former accomplice who had impeached him to the prison gate to shake hands in token of forgiveness, Talbot 'stabbed him under the right Breast which had near depriv'd him of Life'.[27]

Yet most condemned men and women seemed to take the business of 'dying in peace with all the world' rather more to heart. In 1739 the coiner David Roberts was visited in Newgate by his first wife, whom he had abandoned to bigamously marry another woman. The two embraced and drank 'a Pot of Beer together', the first wife agreeing 'to receive the Sacrament with him before he died … in Token of perfect Reconcilement with him'. On the Friday before his hanging, the highwayman John Young was visited in chapel by the constable who had arrested him; Young 'wept at the Sight of him, took him by the Hand, and heartily forgave him; and when they went down Stairs, in Token of Friendship drank with him'. On the day before his 1742 execution, Christopher Jordan wept publicly and 'freely forgave' a 'Man' who 'happen'd to be in Chapel who had done him a very great Injury'. At his 1750 hanging the 'gentleman highwayman' James Maclaine made a point of shaking the hand of the constable 'who first took him up' and of assuring him of his forgiveness. Another highwayman, Henry Simms, or 'Gentleman Harry', at his 1747 execution 'happening to see in the Crowd' a person he had wrongly accused of a crime, 'most heartily ask'd his Pardon', to which the 'Person' replied, 'he forgave him with all his Heart'. Simms then 'owned the Robbery' for which he died, 'saluted' (kissed) his fellow sufferer Mary Allen (with whom he had been conducting a turbulent and sometimes physically violent affair); and finally 'joyning Hands, [they] went off, taking hold of each other'.[28]

Many spent their final moments clearing others suspected of crimes they had themselves committed. Alexander Afflack, hanged in 1742 for burglary, claimed 'he could not be easy' until he had 'sent Word' of his having committed a crime for which a 'poor innocent Woman' was suspected. On the morning of his 1731 execution for robbery, John Davis 'desir'd … that the World might be acquainted, that he committed the Highway Robbery, for which one Walker was blamed, and that he is altogether innocent thereof'. In 1720 Richard Cecil confessed at Tyburn to a robbery, as 'he could not be easy till this was divulg'd, because a Person was suspected, and (I think) taken up for that Fact'. At his 1706 execution the housebreaker Thomas Betts announced that in all the 'Robberies he committed, none of the Servants belonging to these respective Houses were in the least concern'd, so as to be in any wise assisting or privy thereto.' Occasionally, a dying malefactor attempted to exonerate one of his fellow sufferers: at his 1726 execution, William Swift solemnly swore that he was 'as innocent of the Crime for which I suffer as the Child unborn', which another of the condemned, John

Barton, 'confirmed with a loud Voice', claiming that he and several others had in fact committed the robbery for which Swift was to die.[29]

RELIGION IN NEWGATE

POPULAR RELIGIOUS BELIEFS

Despite alarmist contemporary discourse about the encroaches and pernicious tendencies of deism or natural religion (most clergymen viewed 'free thought', as it was often called, as a slippery slope to atheism), self-professed religious sceptics seem to have been thin on the ground in early modern England. Even the dissipated Earl of Rochester was supposed to have denied ever having met 'an entire Atheist'; and, at the end of his long life, John Wesley claimed that he had encountered only two in the whole of the British Isles. Samuel Johnson, citing Dr Brocklesby, put the figure higher (two hundred in England), but agreed that in spite of 'a great cry about infidelity', there were 'in reality, very few infidels'. The evidence of the Ordinary's *Account* and other confessional literature would seem to support such impressionistic statements – not to mention the adage about there being no atheists in foxholes. To be sure, some of the condemned were characterized as lamentably ignorant of religion, like the 20-year-old horse-thief Thomas Pickard, who could not tell the Ordinary whether he was an Anglican or a Catholic and, when instructed about 'the Damnation of Hell … startled, and seem'd to be very much concern'd and afraid'. A handful of others, like the street robber Thomas Wilson, 'pretended to question the Being of a God, and would talk as if there was no Futurity, believing he should dye like the Bruits'. However, 'when the Prospect of Death was immediately before him', Wilson was also like many others in that he appeared regularly at prayers, 'preparing himself with much care for the Reception of the holy sacrament' and acting 'very desirous of making his Peace with God'.[30]

The accusation of atheism was a blunt but apparently potent means of blackening one's character. Thomas Billings, reputedly the illegitimate son of Catherine Hayes and an accomplice in the murder of her husband, supposedly rationalized that 'it was no more a Sin to kill [John Hayes] than a Dog' as he 'was an avow'd Atheist' who denied the immortality of the soul. It was assumed that the genteel murderer Nathanael Parkhurst's crime could be attributed to his keeping company with 'Men of Erroneous and Dangerous Principles' who denied Christ's divinity and dismissed the Bible 'as an idle Romance'. But while Newgate Ordinaries and other clergymen tended to apply the term 'atheist' loosely to those with unorthodox or overly liberal religious notions, many malefactors thus characterized would have resented the imputation. In 1682 Captain Vratz told Anthony Horneck that 'he feared no Hell … He was not such a fool as to believe, that souls could fry in material fire; or be roasted as meat on a great hearth, or in a Kitchin'; rather, the punishment of the damned consisted in being deprived of 'the gracious and beatifick presence of God'. Yet, Vratz insisted, he was 'far from [being] an Atheist'. This was a heterodoxy increasingly fashionable in the early eighteenth century, when many Enlightenment thinkers were openly questioning the notion that a benevolent and reasonable God would sentence His creatures to eternal torment. Echoing Vratz, another educated malefactor, Edward Jefferis, declared in 1705 'that there was only a Heaven, and no Place of Torment for bad Livers, but to be put out of the Presence of the Lord'.[31]

Impiety and sacrilege were often linked to insanity; or perhaps, insanity tended to manifest itself in religious terms. In April 1721 Mary North, who was 'at certain times Lunatick', disturbed the other prisoners by crying out, 'That she should go to Hell, that she cared not if she was damned, that she could not say the Lord's Prayer she had so much Enmity in her Heart', and threatening to hang herself or 'dash out her Brains against the Stones'. However 'at other Times, when she was right in her Mind, she appear'd to be very Devout, and earnest in her Addresses to Heaven for the Pardon of her Sins'. Opposition to the Ordinary often took place within a religious frame of reference: even his sermons – dull as they may have been – were not always merely background noise. In September 1712, two condemned murderers, William Holloway and Jane Housden, interrupted Lorrain's sermon, claiming that his 'Discourse' (Numbers 35:31) 'did not belong to them, nor was that Doctrine I preached proper for them; for they were not guilty of Murther'; in February 1744, when Guthrie was preaching on 2 Samuel 12:7, 'describing the Sin of Murder', the sailor Andrew Miller 'with a loud Voice said, he was not guilty of direct Murder'. Guthrie, perhaps intimidated by Miller, 'a Man of undaunted Courage and Resolution' who 'could not bear an affront', assured him that 'no Reflection was intended against him', but he was 'speaking … only of Murder in General'. (Newgate chaplains viewed robbery, too, as tantamount to the intent to commit murder, as it involved the threat of violence.) The obstreperous highway robber Paul Lewis began to argue with the Ordinary Stephen Roe in the middle of a service about 'a supposed contradiction between St Matt. 27.44 and St Luke 23. 39–42. A stale exploded objection', Roe sniffed, 'that has been often answered'. (Matthew has both thieves executed with Christ unrepentant; Luke characterizes one as penitent.)[32]

Popular religious notions tended to be more lax and optimistic than those of the Ordinary and other clergymen. Indeed, as the historian Ralph Houlbrooke has pointed out, the Protestant abolition of purgatory did not create the widespread anxiety and despair that might have been anticipated; rather, 'popular expectation widened the entrance to heaven to accommodate those who might previously have gone to purgatory' – this despite the regular warnings of ministers that 'God was not as merciful as people liked to imagine'. The street robber Thomas

Reeves 'always affirm'd, that he doubted not of going to Heaven, and seem'd to think it next to impossible, that he could in that cheat himself, and impose upon his own Soul'. As his execution drew nearer, he began to question the Ordinary as to 'how Christians were to fare immediately after Death, supposing that they did not immediately enter upon Happiness or upon Torture'. (He was 'prest to lay aside that Curiosity' and to 'look upon it as an extream favour at the Hand of God if his Soul was rescued from any Degree of Torture'.) The burglar William Parkinson was similarly sanguine as to his spiritual prospects, despite the fact that 'he privately made Scoff at the word of God, and especially the Prayer for His Majesty', and spent his time in Newgate conspiring to escape. While admitting he had been 'remiss and negligent of his Duty', he 'alledged' in his defence 'the Frailty and Infirmity of Human Nature', claiming that 'the sight of death made even the Son of God cry out, "If it be possible let this Cup pass from me!"' Moreover, 'as the Thief on the Cross was accepted at the Moment of his Death, why (he said) might not he?' (The Ordinary retorted that, unlike Parkinson, 'the Thief on the Cross never heard of Christ before'.) Similarly, many of the more educated malefactors were too liberal in their religious views for the tastes of the Ordinary and other attending ministers. In 1682 Gilbert Burnet complained that Lieutenant John Stern (who had conformed to Catholicism while abroad) was 'much corrupted with that principle which is too common in the world'; that is, 'That if a man was honest, and good, he might be saved in any Religion; and that it was fit to be of the Religion of the Country where one Lived'.[33]

Many of the condemned took a very functional approach to religion. In 1679 Samuel Smith recounted how a woman condemned for coining was 'perverted' by a Catholic priest who had told her 'that if she died in the Protestant Religion, she was sure to be damned'. She seemed 'attentive' to Smith's remonstrations and 'somewhat sensible of her being deceived', but hedged, saying 'She was willing to be saved betwixt us both'. One can imagine the indignation with which Smith retorted that 'she must not halt 'twixt two Religions so opposite to each other; and that it was very dangerous to dye in the Roman perswasion'. The line between religion and magic was a fine one for many malefactors: John Holliday, executed in 1720 for returning from transportation before the expiry of his sentence, 'could neither Write nor Read, nor even say the Lord's Prayer', and initially 'was very fully determined not to receive the Sacrament; But afterwards dreamed a certain Dream, which had disposed him he said thereto'. Anne Senior, condemned (but later reprieved) for theft in 1727, described as penitent but lacking a 'due Concern'(and reproved by Guthrie for smiling in chapel), 'told a Romantick Story of an Angel appearing to her'. In 1682, John Stern decided to confess to the murder of Thomas Thynn after having a dream in which he heard the ninth verse of Psalm 32 ('Be ye not as the horse and the mule which have no understanding, whose mouth must be held in with bit and bridle'); as for his accomplice, George Boronsky, he was 'wonderfully changed' after a vision 'was sent from God to him'.[34]

Certainly, posturing at penitence could serve practical aims, and not only where reprieves were concerned. In 1689 eight of the condemned malefactors digging under the condemned hold in an attempt 'to find out the Common Shoar' (sewer) and make their escape underground, busied themselves 'singing of Psalms all the while they were at work, pleasing themselves with the Conceit of being upon their Duty towards God, as they were condemned'; that is, they hoped to live longer to repent. They were, however, most likely trying to muffle the sound of their burrowing, like the convicts in a 1725 escape attempt in which 'to conceal their Purpose from the Keepers, while part of them were Working, the rest sung Psalms, so that the Noise might not be heard'. They, too, attempted to explain to James Guthrie that they had wished to escape 'only out of a desire of Self-Preservation, and because so little time was allowed 'em to repent'. (Guthrie also reported that they denied having any 'Quarrel' with him personally: 'no Sir, God bless you, for you have been very careful of us'.) These malefactors ended up by barricading themselves in the condemned hold, finally giving themselves up when officials promised that their demand to be respited a few more days 'should be taken into Consideration'; this was denied them, but they were at least humoured in their 'great desire to receive the Sacrament' and 'allowed to attend service in the Chapel'. However cynical one may be about the psalm-singing, the request for prayers seems to have been more than just a stalling tactic.[35]

Truly impenitent malefactors appear to have been in a minority in the condemned hold, judging at least by the complaints of their fellow prisoners: in April 1721 the condemned malefactors told the Ordinary that 'they should have been more prepared for Death, had they not been disturbed by two Boys, Jasper Andrews and James Dalton, who interrupted their devotions, and even as they slept play'd vile Tricks, burning their Feet, and pouring Water, &c'. In 1721, the street robber William Spiggot 'complain'd' that his former accomplice Thomas Cross 'not only refus'd to joyn with' Spiggot and the others 'in Prayer, but would beat at the Candles, and rattle his Irons, so that they could not perform their Duty'. After the Dead Warrant came down and 'the rest of the Prisoners grew more Devout he became more wicked ... Till at length the others all requested ... that he might be remov'd from among them'. (At the place of execution, Cross 'continued very Stubborn and Obstinate', yet claimed 'he did not fear to dye, nor doubt his going to Heaven'.) Several years later, his fellow condemned complained about James White's 'bad Behaviour, desiring he might be hinder'd from Laughing and foolishly Talking, and from Vices of a very gross Nature' – 'threatening' and 'terrifying' several 'Women who came into the [condemned] Hole to visit modestly' in order to induce them 'to comply with his wicked Commands and Resolutions'.[36]

To be sure, not all of the condemned were enthusiastic about attending services. In November 1742, two young street robbers, John Squire and John Cooper, 'slipt' out of chapel and 'skult about some of the Rooms' until apprehended and 'confined to their Cells ... for their ill Behaviour'. In 1693, Samuel Smith complained that the highwayman John Randal left off attending chapel on the 'frivolous Excuse, that his Linnen was put to washing and when it was brought Home, he would appear again' (he did not, Smith believed, because 'he was not willing to give an Account of his evil Life'). Some prisoners were indeed too wretchedly sick and poor to attend chapel: the burglar Sarah Griffiths who, 'by Reason of extreme Poverty ... dispos'd of all her Cloaths', and languished 'naked in the Hold' (wrapped in 'an old clouted Matte'), was necessarily 'kept ... from publick Worship' until some of her clothes were returned to her several days before her execution. The Ordinaries sometimes suspected that malefactors merely 'pretended to be sick' in order to avoid attending service or, like the murderer Matthias Brinsden, claimed to be Catholic 'only to prevent him being forced to the Chapel, that he might indulge himself in Sloath and Idleness'. Other recalcitrant Catholics were told, as was the Irish robber Andrew Macmanus (a 'rigid Papist') in 1741, that they 'must either come [to chapel] or be closely confined' – presumably for fear that they would otherwise create disturbances or attempt to escape.[37]

Nonetheless, as we shall see, numerous Catholics (and Dissenters and even Jews) were willing to conform to Anglican services, while many of those who were ill seemed so genuinely penitent that they either requested private instructions from the Ordinary in their cells, or managed to attend chapel, as did three condemned men in June 1748, despite being so ill with typhus 'as scarce to be able to crawl'. The Catholic burglar Edward Ward, hanged in 1751, at first attended services but refused to return to chapel after recognizing a surgeon amongst the spectators who, he suspected, was eyeing him as a prospective medical specimen. (In 1732, the condemned robber Daniel Tipping was so annoyed at the sight of spectators 'looking through the Grate' at the prisoners in the chapel that 'he ran furiously, and snatched a Pail of Water which he threw upon them'.) The condemned prisoners in Newgate in the late summer of 1725 expressed their 'great Satisfaction that ... they had no very remarkable criminal amongst them, to occasion stairing and whispering when they came to Chappel ... as it would have hindered their Devotions, and discomposed the frame of their Minds'. Several months earlier, the coiner Robert Harpham, condemned alongside the notorious Jonathan Wild, complained of being 'expos'd as a gazing-stock' to the 'crowd and Tumult of People who flock'd to see the Malefactors' in chapel. On this and several other occasions, Thomas Purney acceded to the request of the malefactors 'to administer the Sacrament to them in a Place near to the Chapel, to avoid the crowd'.[38]

Nowhere was the religiosity of the condemned more apparent than in their almost universal desire to receive the sacrament. The Ordinary complained of the ignorance of a few malefactors, such as Jane Worsely, condemned in 1721 for robbery, who 'refus'd to receive the Sacrament; or indeed to learn what the Sacrament was', and marvelled at what was presumed to be 'diffidence' on the part of Hannah Dagoe, hanged in 1763 for theft, who 'would never be prevailed on to be a communicant'. However, Worsely probably and Dagoe (an Irishwoman) almost certainly were Catholics who had, like the Irish highwayman James Carrick, already 'received the Sacrament according to [their] Way' at the hands of one of the many priests who visited Newgate discreetly in the late seventeenth and early eighteenth century, and more openly thereafter. By all accounts, most condemned were anxious to receive the Lord's Supper – many clearly viewing it, in the disapproving words of one mid-eighteenth-century minister, 'as a *Charm*, or a *Passport*' to the next world. Moreover, for the vast majority of late seventeenth- and early eighteenth-century Protestant prisoners – apart from those few who were attended by their parish ministers or other visiting divines (generally speaking, the most eminent or notorious malefactors) – the Ordinary was the only means of obtaining this 'necessary passport'.[39]

Mid-eighteenth-century Ordinaries of Newgate appeared to feel increasingly obliged to defend decisions to withhold communion to those who refused to deliver a confession of their guilt. In his *Account* of May 1763, Stephen Roe appealed to 'every reasonable and impartial person' to acknowledge that it was 'an indispensable duty annexed to the office of Ordinary' to bring 'notorious offenders' to a full confession of their crimes and accomplices, 'without being exposed to be accused and abused by an obdurate criminal, as being impertinently curious and officious to collect materials only to fill up his account'. In May 1763, the self-styled Macheath, Paul Lewis, attempted to 'force himself to the Lord's Table', swearing at Roe, accusing him of being a drunkard, a 'scoundrel' and a 'Jacobite parson', and threatening to 'lick' him 'if he don't give me the sacrament'. In the end Roe, evidently subjected to some pressure by two visiting ministers, admitted Lewis to the sacrament; although the latter, while making 'proper answers in general', refused to betray the oaths he had sworn to his former accomplices by disclosing their names (he had, he claimed, 'wrote and sent to them all, to quit their wicked courses'). It is probably not insignificant that Lewis had given his account to a competing publication, as did another convict 'of the M'Heath order' whom several months later Roe also admitted – with some misgivings – to the sacrament, Charles Speckman, alias Brown (who, Roe complained, had strung him and several others along with promises of a full confession).[40]

Roe's defensiveness may have reflected his awareness of a growing discomfort on the part of his audience with the confessional genre generally. But he also may well have been uncomfortably conscious of the scrutiny of his brother clergymen;

in particular, the ministers who had visited Lewis, and who seem to have brokered a détente between the irascible Ordinary and the recalcitrant malefactor. Lewis, as both a famous highwayman and a clergyman's son, was of course a special case. But mid-eighteenth-century Ordinaries were also generally defensive, and frustrated, because their effective monopoly over even working-class criminals was eroding under the encroaches of other clerical and lay visitors, including Catholic priests and Methodists.

TOLERATION AND DIVERSITY

There was a surprising degree of religious toleration in Newgate and Tyburn even in the late seventeenth and early eighteenth centuries. The assistance of various visiting Protestant divines, often including moderate Nonconformists or continental Lutheran or Calvinist ministers, was usually accepted in good part by Newgate chaplains; and, despite the harsh legal penalties still on the books – if seldom enforced – against Catholics and Protestant Dissenters, even Catholic priests and more radical sectarians, such as Quakers, were generally tolerated in practice.[41] Newgate chaplains complained vociferously about priests and non-juring ministers, who not only attended the condemned at Tyburn, but forbade their co-religionists to join the Ordinary and the rest of the malefactors in prayer. (Praying with someone of another confession was anathema both to early modern Protestants and Catholics, as it was tantamount to recognizing the legitimacy of the other's religion, and thus suggested there could be more than one true church.) Paul Lorrain indignantly reported that, at their 1716 execution, the Jacobites William Paul and John Hall were permitted to have 'a Minister of their own Communion (as they call'd it)' join them in the cart, grumbling that they would not pray with him, or 'kneel at my Prayers, as they did at their Nonjuring Minister's' (although, the Ordinary claimed, William Paul was so 'affected' by his discourse that he 'would have knelt' if he had not been prevented by 'a Person standing near him'). As for John Hall, he 'all the while turn'd his Back upon me; a Thing which no Protestant ever did before on such an Occasion'. At the printer William Anderton's execution for treason in 1693, Samuel Smith tried to order a non-juring minister out of the cart, giving 'him very ill words' and insisting to the attending officers that 'He ought not be there, nor should he be suffered'. The Ordinary was overruled by the sheriff, who told him to 'hold his Peace', for 'it was a thing never deny'd to a dying man'.[42]

Even during periods of intensified religious persecution, such as in the wake of various real or imagined treason plots or Jacobite rebellions, most officials seemed willing to uphold the principle that condemned men and women were, at the place of execution, entitled to be attended by a minister, or even a priest, of their own communion. In 1718, Lorrain objected in his *Account* to the 'free

Admittance' granted a Catholic priest (despite his known 'Opposition to the Government', not to mention his 'insults' to the Ordinary) both at Newgate and the gallows, where he 'had the Presumption to give [the Jacobite James Sheppard] Publick Absolution, tho' he visibly dy'd without Repentance'. In 1730 the condemned Irish Catholic highwayman, James O'Brian, prayed audibly at Tyburn to the saints and 'read in a Book of his own so loud, that I [Guthrie] was oblig'd to desire him to read lower and not to interrupt our Worship'. Guthrie was equally irate when, during the execution of Jepthah Big the previous year, 'two Men in the Cart' (probably Catholic priests) 'forbid me to Pray, because they said, he was of another Communion'; the chaplain persevered, however, despite the fact that for the 'most part of the time, I was Praying, one of them was officiously Speaking something to him'.[43]

Even viewed through the lens of the *Account*, it would seem that most of the Ordinary's attempts to illustrate to Catholic malefactors that the 'Popish Belief' was a 'false religion' fell on deaf ears. Robert Green, one of the first of the innocent victims of the Popish Plot, told Samuel Smith that 'he did not believe some of the grossest points of Popery' but 'was resolved to live and die in the Roman Catholick Religion (as he called it) because he was born and bred in it'. When the Ordinary 'most appositely' riposted that 'he might likewise resolve to live and die in sin, because born in, and too much accustomed to that also', Green remained steadfast: 'he would venture his Eternal State in cleaving to the Religion he had been bred in, and would hear no Arguments to the contrary'. Many such malefactors seemed anxious to avoid a heated dispute which might prevent them from maintaining an appropriately calm and charitable penitential state of mind. When Samuel Smith and several other ministers 'took great pains with Walter Mooney to persuade him to believe in Jesus Christ (he being a Roman Catholic)' – the assumption being that Catholics, who recognized the efficacy of prayers to the saints and of good works, did not rely on Christ alone for salvation – the latter would only reply, 'that he would rather take an Affront from any Man, than give one'. The Catholic Thomas Smith, hanged in 1722, told the Ordinary that 'there was one God, one Faith, one Baptism, &c. that he was born and would die in that Communion' and, cutting the debate short, 'went abruptly away'. In 1698 John Johnson, alias Denny, another Catholic, refused to be dissuaded of 'his false Opinions in Religion', saying 'That every Tub must stand upon its own Bottom'.[44]

Some Catholics attended chapel but, like Luke Nunny in 1723, refused to 'joyn in Prayer, or Communion with the other Criminals'. Others were apparently more liberal (or, as the Ordinary would say, 'not bigotted') in terms of their willingness to passively conform to Anglican ritual. Bryan Macguire 'always attended in Chappel' and 'comply'd with the Devotion, and made regular Responses', yet declared himself 'firmly addicted to the Church of Rome'. Thomas Payne, an

'Irish-man' of the 'Romish religion ... seemed however to take [Lorrain's] Admonitions in good Part'; in 1704, Lorrain described the Catholic Sebastian Reis as 'very devout in his own Way' but 'also very willing to hear me, and to receive Instructions from me'. Guthrie similarly conceded in 1740 that John Lineham 'was a Roman and very ignorant, but behav'd decently, and was easy about Principles'. Many Dissenters were similarly amenable: in 1723 John Tyrrel attended chapel and even agreed to 'receive the Sacrament ... either kneeling or sitting, as he should be directed'. The Ordinary suspected many, like the Catholic pirate Philip Roche in 1723, of attending chapel simply 'for the Benefit of the Air'. In 1740 Guthrie complained that Rachel Isaacs, 'a bigotted Jewess', only 'came to Chapel ... for the sake of a little Air, and a short Relief from her Cell'. Yet the temptation of thus gaining converts was too strong to be denied: in 1747, another Jewish malefactor, Hosea Youell, was 'indulged' in his request to attend chapel, the Ordinary adding piously, 'if his Attendance there has ... any ways tended to the Furtherance of his Hopes of God's receiving his Soul, I should have Cause exceedingly to rejoice at it'.[45]

The Ordinary often complained that Catholics who initially passed themselves off as Anglicans only did so in the hopes of improving their chances of a reprieve: in 1740, the Irish robber John Sawney 'pretended to be a Protestant, till the Day before the execution'; in 1730, the Irish highwayman John Doyle 'profess'd himself of this Church, until the Report [Dead Warrant] was made, and then when all hopes of Life were over, he declar'd himself a Roman Catholick, and would come no more to Chapel'. In this way the embittered Ordinary lost some of his best penitents: in 1721 Thomas Cane 'diligently frequented the Chappel, and appear'd to be very Devout, using always his Common Prayer-Book, and reading earnestly the Psalms, and the Responses ... Till the Thursday before he was executed', when he told Thomas Purney that 'he could not any more frequent our Place of Worship, being a Roman Catholic'. Still more malefactors delayed such declarations until they were at the place of execution, presumably not only because there the stakes were higher, but also because access to Catholic priests was then less problematic. A few avowed Catholics continued to be relatively amenable: John Goffe, hanged in 1702, when asked if he was willing to join in prayer with his fellow condemned at Tyburn and 'have the Prayers of the Standers-by', replied diplomatically, 'I desire the Prayers of all Protestants while I am alive, and of all Roman Catholicks, when I am dead'. Other Catholics, often prompted by priests and other co-religionists, were more scrupulous: in May 1690, three of the condemned, who 'appear'd at the time of their Execution to be Papists, tho' visited often by the Ordinary', prayed only among themselves, turning their heads away from the Ordinary and the other malefactors (although Smith was careful to note that one of them 'seem'd to attend devoutly' to his own ministrations, which his two fellows 'check'd him for').[46]

Various Ordinaries complained that many such malefactors would have chosen to die in the Church of England, if not threatened or cajoled by priests and other co-religionists. In 1730 Guthrie claimed that James O'Brian had attended chapel regularly until 'they sent some-body to him in Disguise, who indoctrinated him otherways', and 'would have died in our Communion, if some of his Friends had not importun'd and press'd upon him to adhere to their Faith; although one may think', he added bitterly, that 'he had not so much Religion as that it was worth the contending for'. In 1722, Purney claimed that two of the condemned 'durst not appear' in chapel because a Catholic priest had 'threatn'd, that in Case they did, he would deny them Absolution'. Needless to say, much of the Ordinaries' ire stemmed from their being denied confessions: in 1710, Lorrain was convinced that a Catholic housebreaker had been instructed by several priests that withholding his confession 'was a Duty which his Religion, or at least his Teachers, requir'd of him'. In 1722, one of the condemned supposedly informed Purney that 'a certain Nonjuror had assur'd him, that 'twas not necessary to confess any thing'.[47]

Complaints about other ministers and priests poaching the confessions of the condemned mounted over the course of the eighteenth century, especially after a 1728 ruling, renewed in 1735, by the Court of Aldermen that 'any Clergyman of Reputation' would henceforth 'have Liberty to visit the Prisoners in their Cells, without paying any Thing [i.e., entrance fees] for it'. There is evidence to suggest that, in practice, officials often comprehended within this definition not only Protestant Nonconformists but even Catholic priests. This policy of religious toleration at Newgate was by the 1740s referred to as a custom of long standing, an Ordinary's *Account* from 1743 reporting that the Jewish Abraham Pass 'was allowed, as is usual in those cases ... Clergy of [his] own Communion'. (Pass was visited by several rabbis who expressed their approval when Guthrie read from the Psalms, but balked at his reading the New Testament.) From at least the early 1740s, one or more Catholic priests seemed to have been regularly installed at Newgate and in almost every *Account* there is some mention of Catholic prisoners being 'permitted to have a proper Person, whom they made choice of to attend them', or simply to their being 'visited as usual'; by the 1760s, there are casual references to 'the visitor of that persuasion'. By mid-century, the Ordinary clearly no longer had authority to oblige Catholic malefactors to attend chapel or be confined to their cells, periodically complaining of those malefactors who 'were not suffered to attend, from pretended Reasons of a Faith' which was 'at the Bottom very uncharitable'. Although Jews formed a much smaller proportion of the condemned than Catholics, it seems that they, too, were increasingly well informed of their rights: in 1743 Guthrie complained that several Jewish convicts 'were more scrupulous than others of that Nation use to be', when they insisted that 'it was only lawful to hear the Scriptures read, and to pray with their Heads covered'. Upon Guthrie's asking the rabbis who visited them 'why they did not believe in Christ, who had all the Marks of the true messia', he was told, 'it was none of my Business to attack them on these Heads'. (The Ordinary, or perhaps his editor Applebee, evinced some ethnographic interest in the fact that the four Jewish malefactors were buried fully clothed, 'the Jews never stripping any Person, who does not die a natural Death').[48]

Mid-century Ordinaries complained more and more frequently of the 'invasion of our province' on the part of both priests and opportunistic convicts who, it was implied, preferred the easier terms of salvation supposedly offered by the Catholic Church. In more and more *Accounts*, Newgate chaplains bitterly enumerated first the Catholic malefactors and then those who 'became Roman Catholicks some how or other' – often leaving those who 'remained Protestants' in the minority. All three of the malefactors hanged at Tyburn in May 1753 were Catholic, and had been 'taught their Lesson before Conviction'; that is, that they need give the Ordinary, John Taylor, no account of their lives. One of them, Thomas Jones, 'took it into his Head, that he would be a Roman Catholick, because his Father was so', although Taylor claimed that he 'quarrelled with Protestantism, and would needs die a Catholick' only 'because he could not have the Liberty of the Press-Yard'. Another, Thomas Morriss, 'too must be a roman Catholic', claiming to have 'been bred' in that religion, but Taylor doubted this: 'scarce any Thing he said to me having proved true'. Some malefactors shopped, or threatened to shop, for the best spiritual terms: in 1756, Alexander Thomson initially told the Ordinary 'that tho' he was bred a protestant, yet having been so ill used … by persons of that church, he should chose to die a Roman catholic', but later asked 'to be excused for what he had said in a hurry and confusion of mind'. The Ordinary was not the only victim of the opportunism of prisoners: Mary Green, hanged in 1746 for robbery, was 'attended by a popish priest' who 'supported her with money, in order to persuade her to be his religion', only to discover that she and several of her fellow inmates had 'combined together to rob [him] of his money, and then very honestly returned him his religion back again'. Others seemed to object to the Ordinary personally: in February 1753, Taylor pressed the robber William Morriss to admit his guilt so vociferously that the latter 'resolved to go up to Chapel no more, and determined to die a Roman Catholick.'[49]

After mid-century, the Ordinary complained more and more frequently that he was unable to give any further report of criminals because they were 'under the Care of one, from whom I could expect no Particulars' and, 'after the Priest had seen [them], I could expect to have little to do with [them]'. The resentment of Newgate chaplains such as John Taylor was palpable: he often prefaced his accounts of condemned Catholics with sarcastic remarks such as, 'Being a Papist, it was prejudicial to his Salvation to own the Truth for the publick Good'. This became one of Taylor's standard introductions, subject to some variations, as in the account of the Irish street robber Edward Dempsey, hanged in 1750, 'Being a Papist I could have no Account of his past Life and Behaviour in the World from himself, not being used, nor expected to keep the Secrets of Auricular Confession'. (Fortunately, however, Dempsey had 'not been so private in his Wickedness' that the Ordinary was obliged to pass him over in complete silence.) With the number of not only avowed Irish Catholics on the increase, but more English Catholics also coming out of the woodwork, many later Ordinary's *Accounts* are conspicuously bare of even the most basic biographical details of the condemned. In May 1753, John Taylor concluded his *Account* by informing the reader that he could 'give no Account' of the execution itself, 'because as they all three died Roman Catholics, I did not choose to attend, to give them the Opportunity of turning their Backs upon me, as a Protestant Minister'.[50]

It was rare for an Ordinary (even the evidently sensitive John Taylor) to carry a fit of pique so far as to boycott the execution itself; or, indeed, for his civic employers to have permitted him to do so. However, in the climate of effective religious toleration which prevailed at the mid- and late eighteenth-century gallows the Ordinaries were increasingly liable to be upstaged. Sometimes those of a different faith distinguished themselves merely by abstaining from all or part of the observances, like the Quaker Jonathan Thomas in 1738, who at Tyburn 'did not sing Psalms as the rest did, in not being agreeable to the Custom used by his Friends'. Others were more obtrusive: at one 1743 execution, Guthrie complained that the Jewish malefactors sang Hebrew prayers so loudly 'that I was obliged to desire them to sing, or speak, more quietly'; they were 'somewhat displeased' at the reproof, pointing out 'they ought to pray in their own Way; this I allowed, but not in such a noisy way, as to disturb the Christians in their Devotion'. In one 1741 execution, Guthrie claimed that, although his own flock 'seemed very devout, and joined heartily in the Prayers and the singing of Psalms', they were distracted and interrupted 'on both Sides by different Persuasions': one a 'Papist, praying loudly to the Saints', whom the Ordinary 'was obliged to rebuke, by telling him he acted contrary to the Laws of our Land, and might be complain'd on'. Perhaps more significantly, as it was a sign of things to come, Guthrie also felt obliged to quell 'On the other Side ... a Methodist, who by his Behaviour seemed rather crazy than devout'.[51]

Guthrie's successors were not so successful in silencing Methodists at Tyburn – who, indeed, proved to be louder and more obnoxious than Catholic priests or even Jewish rabbis, especially after Silas Told's effective Newgate ministry began in the late 1740s. Told's attendance at Newgate was at first violently resisted by the then Ordinary John Taylor, who 'stationed himself a few doors from Newgate' for hours at a time to prevent Told's admittance, creating a 'tumult' when such 're-pulses' were foiled; or, in Told's view, when 'the God of all compassion frequently made an entrance for me'. Although Wesley and his followers were still nominally comprehended within the Church of England, Methodism, like 'enthusiasm' generally, was viewed with suspicion and distrust by mid-eighteenth-century clergymen, and perhaps Newgate Ordinaries in particular. James Guthrie, and later Samuel Rossell, John Taylor and John Wood, complained vehemently of the interference, 'officiousness' and indecorous behaviour of Methodist preachers and visitors, referring to them as 'intruding, busy and unqualified zealot[s]' and 'ignorant busy people'.[52]

For many contemporaries, the Methodists' emphasis on extempore prayer and emotional spiritualism on the one hand, and confession on the other, united the twin bogeys of the previous century – opposite on the politico-religious spectrum but equally pernicious in their effects: 'enthusiasm' (drawing inspiration and guidance from the inner light of the spirit rather than from scriptural and clerical instruction) and 'bigotry' (i.e., 'popery', and its supposed association with superstition and tyranny). Individual Methodists not only challenged the Ordinary's pastoral authority over convicts, but Methodism generally threatened to cast the *Account* into disrepute, throwing into sharp relief the increasingly problematic issue of free grace in regard to those of known ill life – for, after 1740, John Wesley openly preached a radical and peculiarly optimistic brand of free grace, divorced from its older Calvinist predestination moorings; that is, free not only for the elect, but for any that truly repented, the greatest of sinners not excepted. (Wesley, although backward-looking in many respects, had his foot firmly in the eighteenth century in that he repudiated the notion of reprobation as abhorrent to a loving God.) Thus Methodists' visitors offered – and converts trumpeted – assurances of the forgiveness of sins and the promise of salvation in terms that no orthodox mid-eighteenth-century Anglican clergyman could easily countenance.

METHODISM AND THE DECLINE OF THE *ACCOUNT*

As we have seen, over the course of the eighteenth century, the various Ordinaries of Newgate gradually retreated from the older identification of the condemned as an Everyman: a 'glass' or mirror held up to the sins of his reader, a 'sea mark' raised to warn all men and women of the inherent depravity of human nature and the rocks upon which they might all (but for the grace of God) be dashed. From the late seventeenth century, 'rational religion' – in which man was the rational creature of a reasonable, benevolent, and increasingly distant creator – gradually came to replace the older, pessimistic Calvinist conception of mankind as frail and degenerate, and God as a vengeful and frequently interventionist judge. Increasingly, morality was internalized in the 'Conscience, that Natural Magistrate in every Man's Heart'. There was a corresponding shift, in both confessional literature and in religious discourse generally, away from an emphasis on free grace and eleventh-hour conversions towards that of 'Holiness' in 'Heart and Life' as the indispensable condition of salvation.[53]

In their sermons to the condemned, early and mid-eighteenth century Ordinaries repeatedly stressed that 'Faith without Works is dead being alone': that saving faith was 'not consisting in empty speculative Notions, as some are too apt to explain it, but affecting the Heart with heavenly divine Thoughts', so that the true penitent became 'wholly a new Creature'. By the early eighteenth century, Anglican clergymen had more and more difficulty with the traditional notion that one's final moments were of critical spiritual significance, and that a 'good death' could outweigh a less than exemplary life. This notion that 'the tree lies as it falls' – that, essentially, spectators could read in the peaceful and cheerful countenance of the individual who died easily, and without apparent pain or struggle, evidence of his or her salvation – while already under attack in the seventeenth century, long persisted in popular culture; indeed, the fact that such noted preachers as John Donne and John Bunyan inveighed against this 'opinion of the ignorant' only testifies to its currency and prevalence. But by the late eighteenth century, even the determinedly perverse Samuel Johnson was in step with most of his (educated) contemporaries when he maintained that 'if a man has led a good life for seven years, and then is hurried by passion to do what is wrong, and is suddenly carried off', he would, nonetheless, 'have the reward of his seven years' good life'. Johnson interpreted the scriptural reference to the tree lying as it fell as referring 'to the general state of the tree, not what is the effect of a sudden blast' – as Boswell explained, 'to condition, not to position'.[54]

Late seventeenth- and eighteenth-century latitudinarian Anglicanism reflected what was an inherently optimistic assessment of human nature, advocating a view of the holy life in which persecution and suffering were not only not indispensable ingredients or requirements (and even, insofar as they smacked of 'enthusiasm', vaguely indecorous), but in which the emulation of Christ was not beyond reasonable aspiration. Indeed, as the gap between human spiritual potentiality and divine perfection was apparently closing, Jesus himself was frequently characterized as a reasonable and tolerant Anglican gentleman: Edward Fowler was only partly tongue-in-cheek when he wrote that, if Christ 'were now upon the Earth, and conversant here among us', he 'would ... narrowly escape the reproach of the Long Name' – that is, that of a latitudinarian. While optimistic and at least nominally inclusive, however, such discourse served to erode the traditional notion of the criminal as Everyman, and an associated investment in his or her exemplary penitence and translation to a 'monument of grace'. In 1757 the Ordinary of Newgate, Stephen Roe, argued, after complaining at some length of the rigours of his 'station' (it was no 'light task', after all, 'to revive the worse than senseless mass, to a moral sense and spiritual life'), that 'however some empirics in theology may boast of instantaneous conversions, and sudden changes in moral characters', the 'seeds of virtue' required 'time' before they could truly bear '*fruit*'.[55]

From the late seventeenth century, and with increasing frequency thereafter, many Anglican divines began to qualify or to reinterpret (i.e., as analogy rather than literal truth) scriptural precedents of eleventh-hour conversions. John Evelyn recorded hearing various sermons on the dangers of 'defering a thing so momentous' as repentance, including one in which it was suggested that the penitent thief in Luke 'might have ben converted ... while in prison' (although Evelyn privately disagreed, thinking 'it was by an immediate & extraordinary Faith & Grace'). As the latitudinarian William Whiston speculated in regard to the parable of the labourers who had received the same reward for one hour's work in the vineyard as those who had toiled the entire day, one day could be read as the 'Space corresponding to the time of their Whole Life'; an hour as a period of years. As for the penitent thief, there was nothing in Scripture to prevent the interpretation that, 'altho' he once had been a very Wicked Malefactor, yet for some (perhaps a long) time before this, he had changed his Course, and was become a very Penitent and a very Religious Person'.[56]

But in the mid-eighteenth century, this older Calvinist emphasis on free grace was given a new lease of life in Methodist publications preaching God's 'wonderful method of saving sinners, the worst of sinners ... the vilest of the vile, the foulest of the foul not excepted'. Many of these works drew explicit parallels between the reader and the common felon, the gentleman and the highwayman, all of whom alike were 'under sentence of death' for sin; if anything, the 'advantage' was 'on the malefactor's side' as he knew he must 'make the best of his short time'. Anticipating that some respectable 'Readers' would be offended by the claim that they were 'by nature in a corrupt and lost estate', and 'blame' them 'for supposing, that a penitential Office, proper for a dying malefactor' would 'suit any other true penitent', such authors invoked both older and newer arguments in their defence, citing universal human depravity on the one hand and the claims of humanity on the other. After all, it was neither 'humane nor reasonable' to '*drive the cart* of our compassion from under poor dying criminals ... as if we were creatures of a far more excellent species than they'.[57]

Methodist visitors to Newgate and other prisons, most notably John Wesley and Silas Told, published narratives of the miraculous conversions of the most hardened malefactors in terms strongly reminiscent of the accounts of sixteenth- and seventeenth-century martyrs. Wesley describes the rapturous speeches and comportment of a group of the condemned visited by Sarah Peters and Silas Told in the autumn of 1748: the six malefactors spent the night before their execution 'wrestling with god in prayer', finally achieving 'a transport not to be expressed'.

When the Bellman had come at midnight to say his verses over the condemned, reminding them that they were soon to die, they shouted out in unison: 'Welcome news! Welcome news!' The highwayman John Lancaster was represented, and indeed characterized himself, as 'a Christian triumphing over death', joyously testifying as his irons were struck off and he and his fellow-condemned – in Lancaster's words, 'our little flock' – were put on carts to be taken to Tyburn. When one of the officers looking on remarked sourly that 'I think it is too great a flock upon such an occasion', Lancaster hastened to assure him that 'it is not too great a flock for such a Shepherd as Jesus; there is room enough in Heaven for us all'. Lancaster and the others were described as dying with all the marks of grace, Silas Told reporting that not 'the least alteration in his visage or features, or any appearance of violence' could be discerned on Lancaster's corpse – only 'a pleasant smile ... and he lay as in a sweet sleep'. Told noted the 'singular' fact that, after the execution, the group of sailors who had carried off Lancaster's body, tiring of the burden, agreed 'to lay it on the step of the first door they came to' – which, by a remarkable (and clearly providential) coincidence, happened to be the doorstep of Lancaster's own mother.[58]

The characterization by Wesley and his followers of their prison penitents as glorious monuments of grace conformed in many respects to the conventions of seventeenth-century confessional literature, while the underlying Methodist emphasis on universal human frailty and depravity recalled the language of Puritans and Dissenters (for instance, Bunyan, who characterized himself as 'the chief of sinners' in his 1666 spiritual autobiography, *Grace Abounding*). But the Wesleyan notion of free grace was in one respect alarmingly different from that of its earlier Calvinist incarnation; that is, it was seen not only as a free gift of God but something that men and women were themselves free to choose, thus putting the emphasis on human rather than divine agency. Such an approach struck many contemporaries not only as blasphemous and presumptuous but dangerously radical (or 'levelling', to use the contemporary phrase), rekindling traumatic Civil War memories of popular enthusiasm ('Enthusiastick Rant') and personal revelation (the dangerous delusion of mistaking what was 'mere darkness' for 'a light within'). Not only did Whitefield and Wesley's open-air sermons to the 'Vulgar' 'detain' the latter 'from their daily Labour', but gave them notions above their station – to the point where 'low mechanics, ignorant women, and even children' felt qualified 'to preach the gospel'. Horace Walpole, mindful of the events of 'an hundred years ago', saw in the Evangelical Revival the threat of a new 'reign of fanatics'. The provocation was, significantly, a funeral sermon for a condemned forger preached by George Whitefield, in which auditors were assured that the deceased 'was now in heaven' – a dangerous encouragement for 'people to forge, murder, etc., in order to have the benefit of being converted at the gallows'.[59]

Newspaper attacks on both Whitefield and Wesley reflected the mid-eighteenth-century polite distaste for enthusiastic public displays. Not only were such 'outward Signs of Sanctity' evidentially dubious (after all, 'Man cannot enter into the heart of Man') but inherently suspect as to motive – unlike true private piety, which 'flow'd' from benevolence rather than 'insolent Affectation'. Ironically, or perhaps inevitably, critics of Methodism identified it not only with enthusiasm but with popery, thus conflating the two opposite extremes of the politico-religious spectrum. Increasingly, good works were denuded of their older 'papist' connotations and reconstituted as a solidly Protestant counterweight to the kind of 'spiritual tyranny' exercised by 'the church of Rome ... for temporal purposes'. Increasingly, the unseemly paroxysms of the 'new birth' were conflated with Catholicism and the confessional; deathbed repentances and prison conversions, with popish absolution – an absolution given, it was implied, on scandalously easy terms.[60]

And indeed, Told writes of one of his Newgate converts, Mary Piner, as raising the spirits of one of her despairing fellow prisoners by asking him, first, if he believed 'that Jesus Christ died for you?'; and, upon his replying that he did, assuring him that there was then 'no room to doubt of your salvation' (the consequent 'revival' of this man's 'spirit', we are told, 'continued till his last breath'). As Silas Told reassured the notorious murderess Elizabeth Brownrigg, Christ had 'made a full, sufficient sacrifice ... for the sins of the whole world, for hers and mine in particular: that we were not damned so much for certain crimes committed, as for not believing in the great truths of the Gospel'; that is, that 'God sent his Son into the world not to condemn the world, but that the world through Him might be saved'. One 1767 newspaper report of Brownrigg's execution remarked in disgust: 'How happy are they who are true Methodists! for let them be never such atrocious Criminals they are sure of Salvation when they die'. (Brownrigg, who had so cruelly mistreated a young parish apprentice that the girl had died, was an object of particular public loathing.)[61]

No one, of course, entered into such sentiments quite as bitterly as did the various mid-eighteenth-century Ordinaries of Newgate. Stephen Roe warned that no 'surviving criminal' should delay his repentance on hopes raised from the report of 'a dying criminal making a decent exit at the place of execution', as 'there is no judging, by present superficial outwards appearances, of their true spiritual state at present, nor of [their ultimate] judgment'. It was a 'dangerous delusion', Roe had written several years earlier, 'to teach [malefactors] their sins are forgiven, without fulfilling' the 'conditions' of true repentance – which included a full confession and 'an open acknowledgement of the justice of their sentence'. Not the least of the grievances of both Roe and his predecessors was the fact that 'the lips of the new convert' were 'effectually sealed'; the public – and the Ordinary himself – thus 'deprived of any discoveries that might afterwards be useful'. But most offensive of all, not only to the Ordinary, but to other criminal biographers, was the 'confidence' of 'new modelled' Methodist converts, 'unbecoming the humility and modesty of a condemn'd malefactor'. This 'Faith of Assurance' (an 'odd and strange Doctrine' for a 'Vile Criminal') reeked to most eighteenth-century Anglicans of antinomianism – the belief that salvation could be obtained without adherence to 'the moral law as delivered in the Ten Commandments, and the gentle but steady and safe conduct of our church'. According to James Guthrie, the terms offered by Methodists for salvation (i.e., merely having faith in the efficacy of Christ's sacrifice) were such as 'a man might be under no dread of what he does, since he stands clean before the eyes of God from that day, that Christ suffered upon the Cross'.[62]

Newgate chaplains had long viewed themselves as entrusted with steering their flock through the Scylla and Charybdis of despair on the one hand and presumption on the other. In their opinion, such 'modern *Sectarists*' disrupted 'the happy composure of mind' of repenting criminals, exploiting the vulnerability of 'weak minds' weakened further by their 'deplorable circumstances'. Numerous prisoners, like the robber John Wilkes, hanged in 1752, were reported to have complained to the Ordinary that they had 'deferred seeking of God too long' because 'some evil-minded People' (i.e., Methodists) 'deceived him' into thinking that 'there was not that Occasion for Sorrow and Repentance, that he was inclined to think there was'. Roe was particularly incensed when, in 1758, his strenuous efforts to 'soften and prepare' the burglar William Stevens 'by a true sorrow and contrition' were suddenly jeopardized by the encroachment of 'a smart methodist exhorter' who, meeting with Stevens on the chapel steps, asked the latter if he was sure he was saved. Stevens, after answering 'with a becoming humility, that he had strove and applied with all the care he could of it, but dare not say more than that *he earnestly hoped he should be saved*: to which the other replied, *can I be sure I have this hat in my hand?* intimating, so sure may you now be of your salvation'. 'Such crude assertions', fumed the indignant Ordinary, from someone 'utterly ignorant' of his 'crimes, repentance, faith and whole spiritual state' came 'well nigh' to spiritually shipwrecking the unfortunate Stevens. For, Roe lamented, after all his efforts to 'steer [Stevens] clear of those two dangerous rocks called presumption and despair', he 'is met by a forward ignorant pilot, who if he cannot push him on the former, will run him on the latter'.[63]

Thus, both the rise of effective religious toleration at Newgate and the effective end of the Ordinary's monopoly over the confessions of poorer prisoners, as well as renewed anxieties over enthusiasm and its potential for moral and social disorder, clearly played a significant role in the end of the *Account*. So too did the gradual relegation of the notion of the criminal as Everyman – a view increasingly identified as Methodist – to the intellectual periphery. What appeared to be the increasingly liberal religious views of the Ordinaries themselves may have also had a role to play in the decline of the confessional genre. This shift is perhaps best illustrated by one 1763 Tyburn exchange, in which Stephen Roe appealed to a group of Catholic malefactors 'to join with us in prayer, as being all christians on one foundation', and was answered in kind: 'There is but one God, but many ways to worship him'. Later Ordinaries also seemed increasingly philosophical about resigning Catholic malefactors' confessions to the jurisdiction of their own priests: in 1770, John Wood reported that several of the condemned persisted in their innocence, but that he was not privy to their 'real inward thought' as they were not 'obliged, nor [was it] indeed consistent with their religion [i.e., 'the Church of Rome'], to make confession to any but a pastor of their own profession', who, Wood charitably added, 'would I believe divulge any thing material, or necessary to be made public for the common good'.[64]

Similarly, by the 1760s, Methodist visitors seem to have been tolerated as, at worst, a necessary evil, while Silas Told's relationship with Stephen Roe and Joseph Moore (Ordinary from 1764 to 1769), judging both by the evidence of the *Account* and Told's autobiography, came to resemble that of an assistant or deputy rather than that of an interloper; indeed, by the late 1760s, Told makes casual reference to his travelling with Roe in his coach to Tyburn. It is significant that Told officiated as Newgate chaplain after John Wood stepped down from the post due to ill health in 1772, and was even proposed by the Lord Mayor (the Wilkite James Townsend) as Wood's successor as Ordinary. In the end, however, it was John Villette and not Told who was appointed Ordinary after Wood's formal resignation in 1774, either because dissenting voices prevailed ('some Aldermen thought Mr Toll [sic] an enthusiastic Methodist, who had done more harm than good'), or because there were problems ordaining Told into the Church of England.[65]

Clearly, Newgate chaplains continued to find Methodists a source of irritation: the year after his appointment, Villette complained to the City of Told's continuing attendance on, and interference with the prisoners. But if many late eighteenth-century clerics and lay people retained their prejudices against Methodists as vulgar and officious, for others, these same qualities made them seem all the more appropriate for the cure of common criminals. Samuel Johnson's views on the 'discipline proper for unhappy convicts', as on any subject, can be hardly seen as typical, but are nonetheless suggestive; that is, that 'one of our regular clergy will probably not impress their minds sufficiently: they should be attended by a Methodist preacher, or a Popish priest'. Certainly the late eighteenth- and early nineteenth-century Ordinaries John Villette and Brownlow Forde viewed their dignity as Anglican clergymen better served at some remove from the Newgate hoi polloi.[66] But the decline and fall of the Ordinary's *Account* was not due solely to the personalities of the Ordinaries or to their publishers, but to a general confluence of religious and cultural factors which affected the sensibilities of the audience for the *Account* as well as that of the Ordinaries themselves. Not least of these was the decline of the notion of the gallows as a sacralized space in which the words and actions of the condemned were invested with metaphysical and political consequence, a theme which we will pursue at further length in the following chapters.

7

Dying Game: Bridegrooms and Highwaymen

Die game: 'to die courageously, uncomplainingly, and without impeaching one's accomplices'.

Eric Partridge, Dictionary of the Underworld (1950)

As clever Tom Clinch, while the rabble was bawling,
Rode stately through Holborn, to die in his calling;
He stopped at the George for a bottle of sack,
And promised to pay for it when he came back.
His waistcoat and stockings, and breeches were white,
His cap had a new cherry ribbon to tie't.
The maids to the doors and the balconies ran.
And said, lackaday, he's a proper young man.
But, as from the windows the ladies he spied,
Like a beau in his box, he bowed low on each side;
And when his last speech the hawkers did cry,
He swore from his cart, it was all a damned lie.
The hangman for pardon fell down on his knee;
Tom gave him a kick in the guts for his fee.
Then said, 'I must speak to the people a little,
But I'll see you all damned before I will whittle.
My honest friend Wild, may he long hold his place,
He lengthened my life with a whole year of grace.
Take courage, dear comrades, and be not afraid,
Nor slip this occasion to follow your trade.
My conscience is clear, and my spirits are calm.
And thus I go off without prayer-book or psalm'.
Then follow the practice of clever Tom Clinch,
Who hung like a hero, and never would flinch.

Jonathan Swift, Clever Tom Clinch Going to be Hanged (1726/7)

One of the most famous, and certainly the most colourful, of all eighteenth-century figures is the 'game' criminal: the bold and dashing highwayman or street robber who dressed like a beau, drank like a lord, and went without tears or trembling to the gallows. The stereotype is perhaps most vividly expressed in Jonathan Swift's 1727 satirical poem 'Clever Tom Clinch going to be hanged'. During his triumphal procession from Newgate to Tyburn, Tom bows jauntily to his female admirers and stops at an alehouse for a bottle of sack, promising (with true gallows humour) 'to pay for it when he'd come back'. At the place of execution, instead of forgiving the hangman, let alone tipping him (both were customary), 'Tom gave him a Kick in the Guts for his Fee', assuring spectators that he would 'see [them] all damn'd' before he would 'whittle' (turn informer). And so it was that with his 'Conscience … clear' and his 'Spirits … calm' – but, notably, 'without Pray'r Book or Psalm' – Clever Tom Clinch 'hung like a Hero, and never would flinch'.[1] This, at any rate, was the caricature. But the game criminal was much more than a caricature: he represented an ideal to which many real-life criminals aspired, with varying degrees of success – and an ideal which (as we shall see) differed considerably from the caricature. The game criminal was at once the darling of Augustan satirists and the bugbear of contemporary moralists who appropriated him, variously, as a vehicle to expose the corruption and hypocrisy of the age on the one hand, and its worldliness and impiety on the other. For nineteenth- and early twentieth-century commentators, he came to epitomize the brutality and 'grossness' of the eighteenth century, and the noisome excesses of the Tyburn procession in particular.

Much of the stereotype of the game criminal owes its origins to the attacks of critical pamphleteers such as Mandeville and Fielding, who almost invariably portrayed such men (for the game criminal was by definition male) as vainglorious, drunken and impious. There were indeed some very badly behaved criminals at Newgate. There were men as apparently unconcerned about an imminent reckoning as the robber Isaac Aslien, alias 'Black Isaac', who brazenly stole half a dozen handkerchiefs during Sunday services in the Newgate chapel a little more than a week before his May 1728 execution, casually explaining that 'he must have something to subsist on'. There were a few of the condemned, like the street robbers Featherby, Vaux, Barnham and Levee (hanged the same year as 'Black Isaac') who were so disruptive and 'outragious' that they had to be chained 'down in the old Condemn'd Hold'. The behaviour of the leader of the gang, John Featherby, was especially 'rude, boisterous and shocking': while in chapel, 'he threw sticks at a Gentleman, laughing and talking to his Companions, sometimes insulting and beating those who were near him'. He 'put on this Ferocity in his Manner', according to the author of a 1735 collection of criminal lives, 'in order to support his Authority, and preserve that Respect and Superiority of which these Wretches are observed to be inexpressibly fond'.[2]

Such prisoners were however in the minority, if only judging from the fact that their bad behaviour tended to elicit indignation and complaints from other condemned. In 1721, William Spiggot, himself a particularly obstinate case – standing 'mute' at his trial and being subjected to the horrific ordeal of *peine forte et dure*, or being 'pressed' by heavy weights, until he agreed to plead – joined with his fellow sufferers in requesting that his former accomplice, Thomas Cross, whose bad behaviour distracted them from prayers, be confined elsewhere. And even those men who, like Spiggot, refused to enter a plea, and whose resolution to submit to the press was typically attributed by the Ordinary and other commentators to a vainglorious 'Foolhardiness', or a kind of macho posturing, were not, it would seem, entirely impious by their own lights. Spiggot, while undergoing the torture of the press, responded to the Ordinary's exhortations to yield by crying out 'Pray for me; Pray for me!' After his trial and condemnation Spiggot 'constantly attended the Prayers in the Chappel, twice a-day' and, although not as sorrowful as the Ordinary would have liked, insisted that he was 'truly penitent, and as sincerely so, as he who show'd his Sorrow by his Tears'. Nathaniel Hawes, another defiant young highwayman who the same year also braved the *peine forte et dure*, was nonetheless described as 'Grave and Serious in his Deportment' as his execution drew near, receiving the sacrament 'with all the outward marks of Devotion', and going 'to his Death very Composedly'.[3]

To be sure, some of the condemned seemed, as Fielding complained, to view 'the Day appointed by Law for the Thief's Shame' as their own 'Day of Glory'. Mandeville wrote of 'young Villains' following the Tyburn procession, so eager to claim acquaintance with the condemned that they would tear their clothes squeezing through the crowd in order to shake hands with malefactors in the cart. In 1726, when Edward Burnworth (who, incidentally, had also been 'pressed' before submitting to enter a plea) and five of his gang of street robbers were transported from Newgate to be tried at the Kingston assizes, 'they endeavoured to shew themselves very merry and pleasant by their facetious Discourse to the Spectators, and frequently threw Money amongst the people who followed them'. One of these scattered halfpennies was retrieved by 'a little Boy', who called out to one of the robbers, William Blewitt, 'that as sure as he the said Blewit, would be condemned at Kingston, so sure would he have his Name engraved thereon'. Blewitt responded by giving the lad a shilling, 'telling him, "there was something towards defraying the Charge of engraving, and bid him be as good as his Word", which the Boy promised he would'. A few malefactors not only revelled in their notoriety, but advertised their defiance: on the night before his 1739 execution, the robber John Albin 'cry'd out of his Cell' at the Bellman as he recited his verses over the condemned, 'God bless my fellow Prisoners, and hang the Cryer'. At his 1728 execution, the robber Stephen Barnham 'laugh'd twice after he was ty'd up to the Gallows' and, after the Ordinary had finished praying with the group, 'took his Prayer-book and threw it up against the gallows with all the Passion and Folly imaginable'. It was also noted that Barnham 'had the Figure of a Man hanging in Chains, done with Gunpowder upon his left Arm' – essentially, a tattoo, as though he were daring authorities to do their worst.[4]

However, many even of these bravoes were seemingly eager to pursue repentance and to die well, if on their own terms. It is interesting that Barnham himself had 'declar'd, that he repented of his Sins, and died in Peace with all the World', asking the Ordinary 'to publish, that his Brother had been in no ways instrumental to his Misfortunes, but that he always endeavour'd to reclaim him, altho' his perverse Disposition was such, that all Advices were ineffectual'. Many of the most famous dashing robbers of the eighteenth century were described as dying, like Jack Sheppard, decently and 'very gravely'. However, it is clear that the Ordinary and other clergymen and authorities differed from the condemned (and some pamphleteers, not to mention spectators) in their idea of what constituted appropriate penitential behaviour. The robber Russel Parnel, hanged in 1752, was described by the Ordinary as having 'scarce Sense enough' to properly 'repent; notwithstanding it was always uppermost, and ready at his tongue's End, "I hope I shall make Peace with God"'. The chaplain took pains to point out that 'he died, to all Appearance, as hardened as scarce ever in the least to change Countenance' – a physical sign that a sympathetic observer might have interpreted as evidence of innocence or grace. Even the Ordinary would have conceded that most of the condemned became more amenable to instruction as their execution drew nearer: in 1722, the highwayman James Shaw was at first 'little sensible of his sad and distress'd Condition, having a kind of undaunted expectation and wild assurance of future Happiness', yet 'when Death approached him', became more serious in his devotions.[5]

To a large degree, dying game functioned quite simply, as V. A. C. Gatrell and others have pointed out, as a strategy 'to cope with the pain and shame of scaffold death'.[6] But dying game was also bound up with and measured against contemporary ideals of dying well, and thus cannot be divorced from larger questions regarding the spiritual fitness of the condemned. Indeed, it was the game criminal's conformity to most of the conventions of the good death that made his ultimate statement of impenitence – his inappropriately high spirits – so subversive in the eyes of contemporaries. For as we shall see, few even of the boldest highwaymen seemed willing to die, like Clever Tom Clinch, 'without prayer-book or psalm', let alone with a parting kick at the hangman. Rather, the game criminal who went to the gallows betraying neither dread of pain in this world nor judgement in the next, typically advertised not only his willingness but his fitness to die: like the penitent, he forgave his enemies, assumed responsibility for his actions, and declared his willingness to die for them. But both in his cheerful demeanour and his refusal to succumb to tears – the traditional signs not just of penitence, but of an acknowledgement of guilt – the game criminal resembled not so much the penitent as the martyr.

The game criminal's courage was problematic, not least because it communicated a potentially subversive message: that is, that the condemned was ready and willing to refer his cause to a higher court. The brave scaffold death has continued well into the modern era to have resonance and political implications. It is interesting to note the degree to which one Holocaust survivor's eye-witness account of the execution of a Jew in a Lithuanian ghetto during the Second World War conforms, in all important essentials, to that of the quintessential eighteenth-century game death. The young man, one Mazavetski, condemned for trying to smuggle a piece of bread in his pocket back to his family, was hanged not only in front of all the Jews of the ghetto (ordered to attend the execution), but also in view of hundreds of Lithuanian Catholics returning from church, carrying their Bibles. 'Mazavetski told the two Jews who were assigned to hang him, "I know that you are forced to do it. I forgive you"' His last words were, "In one minute from now I will be in heaven. I will pray to God for you". When Mazavetski saw his wife and child being brought to watch his execution, he suddenly 'kicked away the stool from under him and was dead' – thus 'depriv[ing]' the furious German commandant of the 'long show' he had intended. Thus, 'although the Jews were being killed by the thousands [i.e., in that area], the hanging of Mazavetski had an impact on the people of the ghetto' – indeed, even the Lithuanian (Gentile) community was apparently shocked and moved by the spectacle. 'He became a symbol, a martyr, because he died with dignity'.[7]

DYING LIKE A MAN

Although I have used the expression 'game' to refer to the criminal who died advertising his courage, his cheerful indifference to death and his refusal to implicate comrades, the term itself is anachronistic, as it did not come into common use until the early nineteenth century. The *Oxford English Dictionary* attributes its first entry for 'dying game' to *The Beggar's Opera* (1728) – a plausible etymology, given the fact that the 1720s (the age of Macheath, Clinch, and many colourful real-life criminals, such as Jack Sheppard) seems to have marked the apogee of the highwayman or robber as a criminal celebrity. I have, however, found no trace of the term in any authorized edition of the play (although it is possible the attribution originated from an extemporization on the part of one of the actors at some point during the eighteenth century).[8] The first printed use of the word may well date from a 1752 Ordinary's *Account*, in which the young William Signal and 'his profligate companions' told the disapproving John Taylor that 'by G-d, they were resolved to die game'. Although it is not unlikely that such expressions were deliberately omitted from the record, I have not found another instance of the term in the criminal annals until 1805, when another young robber, Richard Haywood, whose 'constant boast' was that he would 'surpass the notorious Abershaw' in his 'contempt of death', also broadcast his determination to '*die game*'. 'Dying game' was, all authorities agree, originally a cant term and seems to have made its first formal appearance as such in Grose's 1785 canting dictionary. In the 1811 edition it is given as a synonym for dying 'hard' – that is, 'to shew no signs of fear or contrition at the gallows; not to whiddle or squeak'.[9]

While it is important to bear in mind that 'dying game' may have some connotations peculiar to a later period, I have nonetheless chosen to retain the term, in part because it is familiar and evocative, and in part because it seems to have derived largely from earlier terms of roughly equivalent meaning – that is, to die 'hard' or 'brave' or 'like a hero' or 'like a man'. Almost fifty years before Clever Tom Clinch 'hung like a hero', a condemned highwayman in the late seventeenth-century Newgate comedy *The Revenge: Or, a Match in Newgate* (reprised in 1715, with some modifications, as *A Woman's Revenge*) exhorted his comrades to lay all their money out 'in Drink', and 'when the Hour comes, dye like Hero's [sic], sing the Psalm merrily, and then – we'll be hang'd till we're sober'. The most famous fictional highwayman of them all, Macheath, consistently entertained audiences from the play's first performance in early 1728 with his resolve that, 'since I must swing – I scorn, I scorn to wince or whine'. Nor, would it seem, was there any dearth of real-life Macheaths who, like the highwayman Abraham Stacey, vowed 'that since he must die, he would as he phras'd it, *Die like a Man*'. Isaac Darkin, another highwayman who, while in prison 'frequently diverted himself with reading *The Beggar's Opera*', supposedly announced that 'it was always his Determination, whenever he should have the ill Fortune to be taken, 'to suffer without discovering the least Dread of death; never to betray his Connections, but to die like a Hero'. And Darkin would complete the game formula by, at the place of execution, stepping off the ladder before it was 'turned': thus effectively communicating to his audience that, while he was not afraid to die, he would do so at the moment of his own choosing.[10]

The term 'game' itself derives from 'game-cock'; thus, to 'die game' meant simply to die with the spirit and the 'pluck' of the cockfight rooster, although the double entendre was as obvious in the eighteenth century as it is today. In the 1715 play, *A Woman's Revenge*, one condemned robber bids farewell to a comrade: 'Pray remember my kind Love to my Brother Sam, and be sure [to] tell him I dy'd like a Cock, damn'd hard'. This memorable image resurfaces in a 1728 pamphlet in which the narrator claims to have overheard 'one rogue' saying 'to another … G-d D-mn … Jack Such-a-one made a clever figure when he went to Tyburn [the] other Day, and died bravely, hard, like a cock'.[11] Clearly, dying game was a masculine cult. While there were some women who died resolutely, without naming accomplices, on the whole female courage at the gallows tended to be denigrated as a species of hardihood and 'masculine boldness'. The coiner Barbara Spencer, who broadcast her refusal to implicate others even to save her own life, and who was reprimanded by the Ordinary for her unbecoming levity, was at her 1721 execution pelted so violently with stones by disapproving spectators that she was 'beat quite down'. The vast majority of women criminals are described as dying penitently and, for the most part, tearfully, including even such picaresque heroines as the Irish pickpocket Mary Young, hanged in 1741 (nicknamed 'Jenny Diver' and immortalized in eighteenth- and nineteenth-century criminal literature).[12]

Dying 'game' or 'hard' or 'like a man' could have less profane associations and applications. In the second volume of *The Pilgrim's Progress*, where Christian's wife follows him on pilgrimage to the Celestial City, the champion Great-Heart (whose task it was to guide the more frail Christiana on her journey) asks his fellow traveller, Honest, what he would do if along the road they were beset by robbers. After the latter assures him that he 'would have fought as long as breath had been in me ... for a Christian can never be overcome, unless he shall yield himself', Great-Heart responds approvingly: 'Well said, father Honest ... for by this I know that you are a cock of the right kind'. Dying 'like a man' – that is, bold and unyielding even in the face of the so-called 'King of Terrors', or death, had obvious soteriological connotations, particularly in the seventeenth century. This was, after all, a period in which the image of the godly man was primarily that of 'the martial hero' 'manfully' waging 'continual warfare' against the 'crafts and assaults of the Devil'. And while I am not implying that condemned highwaymen and robbers who died bravely were saints – far from it – nonetheless we should not overlook the extent to which early modern discourses of manly valour were bound up with religious tropes and imagery, with 'fighting the good fight' (as it were). Moreover, self-denial and an indifference to pain or suffering were viewed by late seventeenth-century divines as peculiarly 'masculine' virtues, best exemplified by the martyr who – in the words of the future Ordinary of Newgate, Samuel Smith – 'having attained to a more Masculine State in Christianity' (as opposed to more 'effeminate' worldlings) 'chearfully submits' to the worst of deaths, if such was God's will.[13]

It is hardly surprising, then, that attacks on criminals who died bravely consistently emphasized their total want of religious feeling. Henry Fielding complained vociferously of the 'Mock-Heroism' of the 'miserable Wretches' at Tyburn, who 'seemed to vie with each other in displaying a Contempt of their shameful Death, and a total Indifference as to what might befall them after it'. Mandeville expressed a similar disgust at the proceedings at Tyburn where, he claimed, 'the further a Man is removed from Repentance, nay, the more void he seems to be of all Religion, and the less Concern he discovers for Futurity, the more he is admired by our sprightly People'. This stereotype of the cheerfully impenitent highwayman received much reinforcement from the picaresque and semi-fictionalized collections of highwaymen lives so popular in the early eighteenth century. When Captain Alexander Smith's highwaymen, Zachary Clare and James Lawrence, were asked at their 1715 execution if they had anything to say, 'quoth Lawrence to the sheriff, "I wish I was safe in Bed with your Wife now". And quoth Clare, "I wish, Sir, that I had the — of that young Woman there": at the same Time pointing to her'. The highwayman Sawney Douglas, hanged in 1662, was supposed to have carried the Ballad of Chevy Chase (rather than a prayer book) to Tyburn, 'where he bid the hangman to be speedy, and not make a great deal of Work about … a meer Trifle'. According to Captain Charles Johnson, Tom Cox, executed in 1690, not only refused to join with the Ordinary in prayer, but (like Clever Tom Clinch) swore at him and kicked both chaplain and executioner out of the cart.[14]

This charge of kicking the hangman (and the Ordinary) out of the cart was almost certainly untrue, as the Ordinary's own account of the execution mentions only that Cox and another criminal 'were very Impertinent' and had to be 'Check[ed]' for having 'reflected on the Government'. Surprisingly few such incidents were in fact recorded: Narcissus Luttrell reported that, in 1694, the condemned murderer Paynes 'kicked the Ordinary out of the cart at Tyburn, and pulled off his shoes, saying he'd contradict the old proverb and not die in them'; in 1771 the *Gentleman's Magazine* claimed that the highwayman John Hogan 'struck the Executioner when he was put into the cart'.[15] It would indeed be difficult to think of an accusation more damning, literally: for, in the context of a culture that placed a tremendous importance on charity – forgiving others as one hoped to be forgiven – kicking or striking the hangman instead of pardoning him (it was customary for the executioner to beg forgiveness before carrying out his office) was nothing short of a renunciation of God.[16] But, outside of fiction, there seem to have been few game criminals willing to renounce God or, at least, to appear as though they had done so. Fielding himself acknowledged as much with his complaint that, on the way to Tyburn, any criminal who had 'Sense enough to temper his Boldness with any Degree of Decency' was regarded by spectators with 'Approbation'.[17]

Indeed, sometimes the most notorious characters made the greatest show of piety. The street robber James Dalton, who scarcely did himself justice when he described himself as 'one of the most impudent, irreclaimable Thieves, that ever was in England', nonetheless 'behaved always civilly in Chappel' and 'professed himself a penitent'. At the place of execution, Dalton joined heartily in prayers and hymns, requesting they sing the 'Humble Suit of a Sinner'. The notorious street robber William Blewitt was reported as praying 'with great earnestness' at his execution, where he 'not only named the Penitential Psalm … but repeated the words of it to the other Criminals, as set the tune to it', all 'with a loud Voice'. Similarly, the 'very bold, hardy and daring' robber William ('Cockey') Wager, often 'reproved' by the Ordinary for smiling and laughing during service, not only 'profess'd himself a Penitent', but at the place of execution 'with an audible voice read to all of them [the condemned]'. Indeed, many of these 'undaunted and bold' malefactors seemed, like the street robber John Levee, to be activated by a desire to cut as sharp a figure as penitents as they had distinguished themselves as 'Bravoes' before. Levee received the sacrament 'with a great deal of Devotion', was 'earnest' in his prayers, and declared that 'he hop'd he *had fought the good fight*, as formerly against innocent Man, so now against *Satan*, and evil Spirits'. Perhaps significantly, at the place of execution, Levee 'evinced a strange Anger and Passion that his Hands must be tyed like the others, and that his Cap must be pulled over his Face'; however, 'Passion signifying nothing there, he was obliged to submit as the others did'.[18]

Levee's 'Passion' may well have reflected the fact that he had resolved to approach his penitence in an active and arguably masculine manner – that is, to fight 'the good fight' – only to have thrust on him, at the most critical moment, a passive role. The conflict here was not so much that of piety versus impiety, but rather between two competing versions of what constituted appropriate penitential behaviour. The Ordinary and other clergymen exhorted 'Sinners and Criminals' to strive for 'that happy mean between presumption and despair'; in other words, a humble and 'lowly Hope in Gods free Mercy', rather than the active and bold approach exhibited by 'Bravoes' like John Levee. True penitence was distinguished by 'self-condemnation' – a full confession accompanied with expressions of unworthiness – and a 'broken and contrite heart' (Psalm 51:17). Conversely, the 'kind of Courage' or 'Resolution' that consisted in 'neither shedding Tears or appearing much dejected' was castigated by the Ordinary and other clergymen as both 'untoward' and 'unchristian'.[19]

Even those criminals who otherwise behaved 'decently' and 'gravely' were often faulted for not having a nice enough sense of their condition. In February 1721 the Ordinary of Newgate noted that 'no exceptions could be taken ... against [the] Behaviour' of four of the six condemned, 'unless they were perhaps entered too in the Notion, that they ought to bear their Misfortunes like Men, without Grief and Sorrow, and without any manner of Fear or Concern at their being so soon to dye'. Typically, clergymen ascribed the refusal to succumb to tears to misplaced masculine pride, the Ordinary reminding the condemned that weeping 'for sin' was 'no dishonourable imputation of Effeminacy' (frequently invoking as a model the warrior-king David who, 'tho a Man of War from his Youth, yet greatly Humbled himself before the Lord'). Interestingly, dry-eyed men often responded, as did the robber William Spiggot, that he 'thought himself ... as sincerely [penitent] as he who show'd his Sorrow by his Tears, but that it was not easily in his Power to weep'. (Spiggot added that he could remember weeping on one occasion only: at his 'final parting with his little Son'.) Underlying such exchanges was the desire on the part of the Ordinary and other clergymen to dismiss such stoicism as a species of pride, rather than a calm resignation to death. Tears were not simply evidence of penitence, but also of a grief for sin, and hence, an acknowledgement of guilt and the incompleteness of one's repentance. It is perhaps not insignificant that Cranmer, the only one of Foxe's martyrs described as shedding tears of sorrow (rather than joy) at the stake, was also alone in having recanted his faith.[20]

Various Ordinaries of Newgate also stressed, however, that tears of true penitence stemmed from grief from offending God, rather than from a selfish and cowardly fear of punishment. According to the Ordinary Thomas Purney, Joseph ('Blueskin') Blake, despite having 'acquired amongst the Mob the Character of a brave Fellow ... was in himself but a mean spirited timorous Wretch', whose 'Cowardice appeared manifestly in his Behaviour at his death': both in chapel on the morning of his execution and at the gallows 'he wept much ... tho' he drank deeply to drive away Fear'. James Guthrie observed that the condemned wife-killer 'Mr Hallam, was very decent in his Carriage, though at first he sometimes wept; yet he came to be of a more composed, manly temper' (women, needless to say, were unlikely to be reproved for weeping). It may well be that such commentary reflected a growing early eighteenth-century suspicion of, and distaste for, emotional ('enthusiastic') displays, and a concomitant shift in emphasis from the countenance and bearing of the condemned in their final moments ('grace') to a more generalized assessment of past deeds and character ('works'). Yet tears were in the mid and late eighteenth century a hallmark of sensibility and gentility, if shed for the right reasons – and, perhaps, by the right person. At his 1777 execution for forgery, the disgraced, but widely pitied, Dr William Dodd 'wept', saying 'probably his tears would seem to be the effect of cowardice, but it was a weakness he could not well help; and added, he hoped he was going to a better home'. Few of Dodd's contemporaries would have thought such a hope presumptuous or misplaced.[21]

And unlike the tearful penitent, the game criminal was typically 'obstinate' in that, while willing enough to own up to a general catalogue of sins – from Sabbath-breaking on – he balked at delivering the detailed, or 'particular' confession that was considered necessary for salvation. For, as far as most churchmen were concerned, a general confession was worse than none at all, as its focus on the 'private sins' to which all men and women were prone and, by extension, on universal human depravity, tended to extenuate rather than to aggravate the guilt of the individual transgressor. Needless to say, game criminals, whose refusal to 'whittle', or to betray accomplices was proverbial (if often disingenuous: many who were loudest in proclaiming this resolve had in the past implicated comrades to save their own lives), frequently came into conflict with the Ordinary on this point. The game robber William Russell, hanged in 1728, freely acknowledged his guilt and that 'there was no Pretence of Necessity for his betaking himself to

such a Course; the only Cause having been his own Wickedness', declaring at the
gallows that the evidence against him, James Dalton, 'had proposed to him to
join in that Information he gave against their Companions, but that he scorned
to save his life by so mean a Practice as betraying those who had received him
into their Friendship'. In 1764 the Ordinary expressed his disapproval when the
otherwise 'humble and attentive' condemned forger John Prince claimed 'that
he might have saved his own life had he put others in his place, but this he did
not chuse to do'.[22]

The Ordinary frequently complained of malefactors who, like the burglar
Richard Clay, hanged in 1747, confessed to and expressed remorse for their
robberies, but 'did not chuse to particularize them; having, as is too often
the Case with these unhappy Wretches, more Regard for their surviving
Companions than for their own precious Souls'. It would seem that many such
men genuinely regarded their refusal to name confederates as a species of charity.
The highwayman James Wright, for example, refused 'to declare his Associates,
or how they might be found, saying that perhaps they might Repent ... and he
would not bring them to the same ignominious Death with himself'. We are told
that in 1707 Charles Moor's and William Elby's 'wicked Obstinacy' prevented
them from divulging the names of any of their accomplices. According to Moor,
'What good would it do me to hang three or four men, and ruine their Families
as well as mine?' As for Elby, 'he intended to die in Charity with all the World;
which he could not do, if he brought any into trouble'. It would seem that many
who were described by the Ordinary as 'hardened' or 'obstinate' were in other
respects conventionally quite penitent, leaving aside their refusal 'to make
particular Confessions'. In 1753, the housebreaker John Higgins, who admitted
he had accomplices, 'but would tell us no names', was simultaneously described
as behaving 'with ... apparent Undauntedness' and 'very quietly', joining 'very
heartily' in prayers.[23]

It was characteristic of the game criminal to maintain his innocence of the
crime for which he had been condemned but at the same time to accept sole
responsibility for his fate – exonerating relatives, spouses, etc. Like the robber
John Mackrady, the game criminal often seemed to take a perverse pride in
declaring himself 'the most wicked, flagitious, disobedient, undutiful young
Wretch upon Earth' who 'suffer'd most justly, for the innumerable Villainies of
his Life'. James Dalton 'absolutely deny'd ... the Crime for which he suffer'd'
– and, perhaps to symbolize his innocence, 'illuminated his Cell with six Candles'
when the Bellman came to read the verses over the condemned on the eve of their
execution. Yet Dalton nonetheless freely 'own'd ... that for twenty Years past he
never rose out of his Bed, but he deserv'd the Gallows'. This was a frequent refrain:
in 1711, the housebreaker William Maw refused to deliver any confession other
than that 'he knew he had been a very great Sinner, and God was just, in bringing

him to this Death'. Similarly, James Shaw 'spake much as to the asserting his own innocency, as to the present crime', but acknowledged that 'former sins' had aroused God's anger, 'or he would not have suffered him now to be condemned'. The notion that a persistence in a course of venial sin caused God to remove his 'preventing grace' (without which all men and women were capable of the worst enormities) was a popular one, particularly in the seventeenth century, and had the advantage of implying that the condemned was in fact no worse than many others whose sins went undetected and unpunished.[24]

Moreover, the admission of being guilty of all crimes (murder excepted), save that for which they were to suffer, somehow conveyed the impression that the condemned actually *chose* to die. John Gulliford, a self-confessed 'Old Offender', claimed that he went 'as easy to Execution, as if I was going to suck at my Mother's breast; and I think it is doing a great deal of Good to hang me out of the Way'. As for Thomas Reeves, hanged in 1722, 'he was so far from fearing Death' (he said) 'that he rather chose to die than live' and 'constantly affirmed, that he was in no doubt of his going to Heaven … for he believed he might as well find the Way to Happiness from the Gallows, as from the Bed'. Not that such sentiments were necessarily credited. The highwayman Jeffrey Everett, who spent most of his time in Newgate in attempts to procure a pardon, convinced few people with his claim (delivered after he had been detected trying to escape) that 'were Death, where he pointed with his Right-hand, and were my Pardon, where he pointed with his Left, and I was told to go to my Pardon upon Condition of being a Villain, I would fly into the Arms of Death'. But the game criminal who claimed, like the robber James Walker, that 'he forfeited his Life willingly' reflected the popular belief that one could 'answer with the loss of his Life for all his Faults'. Indeed, when the Ordinary attempted to convince the highwayman John Bennet, alias Freeman (the 'Golden Farmer') that 'his Repentance could not be syncere' until he made a full 'Restitution' of all the money he had stolen, the latter replied that 'he thought this to be a strange Doctrine, when as, he said, he dyed for Robbing'. Nor was the idea of dying to expiate one's sins unique to criminals: death was commonly characterized as the 'debt … that every man owes to Nature' – that is, the sentence laid on all men and women as a result of original sin.[25]

This notion that dying for one's sins wiped the slate clean long pre-dated Macheath's famous line, 'Death is a debt … so take what I owe'. But certainly after *The Beggar's Opera*, if not before, it is not difficult to read into such sentiments the suggestion that, in the context of a world in which most men and women were sinners, the condemned was no worse than most, and better than many, in that he was willing to own up to his sins and to pay for them with his life. This may have been what John Macnaghton meant to convey when, at his execution in 1762, he 'told some of his prosecutors … that he forgave them, but he did not ask forgiveness of any'. More pointedly still, the condemned Jacobite printer

William Anderton 'told the Spectators, that his Sentence was very hard and severe' but 'that he forgave his judges' (the Ordinary retorting that 'they needed not his Forgiveness; for they were satisfied in their Consciences, that they had acted justly'). Some were even less subtle: the would-be Macheath and self-professed 'true christian' Paul Lewis shocked the Ordinary not only by his insistence that he 'only robbed from the rich to give to the poor', but by merrily singing 'if gold from the law can take out the sting' – an air from *The Beggar's Opera* (set to the tune of 'Greensleeves'), containing what was arguably the play's most overt social critique.[26]

The game criminal was also famous for his high spirits and (literally) his gallows humour. The highwayman Walter Conolly informed spectators at his 1738 execution that he was guilty of the robbery for which he died, 'forgave all the world, and hoped he should enter the Kingdom of Heaven'. When the hangman proceeded to put the noose around his neck, and drawing 'it somewhat straight', Conolly quipped: 'there is no Occasion to choak me before my Time' (he added, too, his wonderment that authorities would hang seven such 'Fellows that would face the Devil' while the 'Spaniards are taking the English every Day'). When at their sentencing, the Jacobite Charles Ratcliffe and his fellow prisoners were asked if they had anything 'to offer in arrest of Judgment', Ratcliffe facetiously (and loudly) advised another defendant 'with a very Prominent Belly' to 'plead your Belly, many have got off that had not so large an Excuse'. The robber John Rogers, hanged in 1749, far from being 'in the least concern'd at his approaching Fate … rather made a Joke of it'. When a woman who had handed him a glass of wine found a fly in it, and offered to fish it out, Rogers cheerfully quaffed the glass, saying 'Pho, Pho … 'tis no Matter, the blind eat many a Fly, and drink 'em too'. While getting into the cart, he bade farewell to one of the turnkeys, Abraham Mendez, a former servant of Jonathan Wild, saying ''tis a fine Day, and I am going the same Way your Master went, but 'tis a Matter of Indifference to me which Way, or When I go'.[27]

The game criminal also sang 'the Psalm merrily' – typically the fifty-first (a penitential psalm, doubly familiar as its opening lines constituted the so-called 'Neck Verse', the reading test to qualify for benefit of clergy). As William Blanchar, hanged in 1689, exhorted his more timorous fellows: 'Ne're fear, God will have Mercy upon us; but however, let us have some Prayers, and a merry Psalm; I don't fear Death at all. Gentlemen, I have been a great Highway man, but I hope God will have Mercy upon me'. And perhaps the most subversive of all the messages communicated by the game criminal was that his cheerfulness and courage stemmed not from bravado, impiety or brutish insensibility, but from his 'great Assurance of God's mercy to him' – an assurance that was, in the words of the 'undaunted' Captain Vratz, hanged in 1682, 'not hope but certainty'. When the visiting minister Gilbert Burnet 'warned him of the danger of affecting to be a

Counterfeit bravo', Vratz replied, 'That I should see it was not a false bravery, but that he was fearless to the last'. Burnet then 'wished him to consider well upon what he grounded his confidence: he said, he was sure he was now to be received into Heaven; and that his sins were forgiven him'. The Ordinary frequently warned of the dangers of such ill-advised presumption in his sermons to the condemned: 'a Wicked Man', he thundered, 'may sometimes desire to be like the Godly in a happy Death, yet such his Desire will always prove fruitless to him' who does not 'live an Upright, Righteous, and Holy Life here in Earth'.[28]

Such discourse reflected the longstanding tension within English Protestantism between an emphasis on faith and grace on the one hand, and 'holiness of heart and life' on the other.[29] By the end of the seventeenth century, as we have seen, most Anglican divines were increasingly uncomfortable with the notion of free grace and its concomitant emphasis on divine omnipotence and excellence and human inadequacy and depravity. Criminal literature reflected this shift, with late seventeenth-century accounts portraying criminals as 'monuments of grace' testifying to the awesome power of God to save even the worst of sinners, gradually superseded by biographies retracing the criminal's progress down the slippery slope of sin.[30]

This, of course, is not to suggest that game criminals were doctrinal Calvinists or radical sectarians: to the extent that they practised any religion, most were Anglicans or Irish Catholics. Nonetheless, their cheerful confidence that they could, like 'the Thief on the Cross [be] accepted at the Moment of ... Death' raised troubling, even antinomian implications, especially after 1740, when the Wesleyan doctrine of free grace divorced from reprobation began to be preached in prisons throughout Britain. While the penitent thief was often invoked by malefactors as an example of effectual last-minute repentance, most Anglican ministers took pains to demonstrate that, as a conversion before the dissemination of the gospel – and probably a miraculous one at that – this was strictly a one-off.[31] John Purdy, who claimed to have 'never robb'd any poor Person' but only those who 'had too much' ('and Master', he said, 'there's no great Sin in that') was no Methodist, but his claim 'he could repent himself as clean from all his sins in half an Hour as well as in 7 Years', was surely troubling enough. So too was the notion expressed by the street robber Robert Wilkinson, denied the sacrament after refusing to deliver a full confession: namely, that 'he was under no great Concern on that Account; for he said, if he might not go to Heaven as the rest did, he hop'd to find the Way by himself'. As he 'had heard that Fasting was a good Expedient for that Purpose' he 'neither eat or drank for three Days and three Nights before his Execution'.[32]

FALSE COURAGE AND CHRISTIAN COURAGE: CHANGING SENSIBILITIES

It was at the gallows that the game criminal made his most dramatic statement; namely, that he was neither unwilling nor afraid to die. To be sure, a few meditated or attempted escape on the way to the gallows (or even, like Jack Sheppard, hoped to be resuscitated afterwards), but resistance to the act of execution was almost unheard of, doubtless because such resistance would have implied cowardice. One of the rare exceptions was the highwayman James Cook, hanged in 1739. Although conforming in most important respects to the stereotype of the game criminal – affecting, at least in prison, a cheerful unconcern for his fate – at the gallows Cook declared 'That he would not be accessary to his own Death', and struggled so violently that three men had to hold him up to put the halter around his neck. Yet, in his rejection of the passive role at least, Cook was characteristic of other game criminals who flaunted their willingness to die. The housebreaker James Turner, at his 1664 execution, first 'directed the Executioner to take off his Halter from his shoulders, and afterwards taking it in his hand, [kissed] it, and put it on his neck himself'. When the hangman 'tyed him up', Turner rallied him ('What, dost thou mean to choak me?') and facetiously instructed him on how to 'put the knot'. He was 'undaunted … to the last breath of life', speaking calmly, raising his hands in prayer, and kissing his hand to a female acquaintance seconds before being turned off.[33]

Adjusting, or removing and replacing, both the blindfold or cap and the halter itself were common game gestures. In 1722 the Irish highwayman James Carrick 'laughed and smiled upon those he knew' at the place of execution and 'gave himself genteel airs in fixing the Rope aright about his Neck'. Another 'undaunted' malefactor hanged the same year, the 'notorious Foot-Pad' Thomas Wilson, refused to allow 'the Rope' to be 'fastned' around his neck until he 'shew'd himself several times by standing up to the Spectators'; he then made a speech endorsing his authentic 'Paper' and declared, on the oath of a 'dying Man', that one Phelps, whom he heard had been committed for a robbery, was innocent of the crime, which Wilson had himself committed alone. Only then did Wilson 'put the Rope about his [own] Neck, and submitted to his Death with great Resolution'.[34]

Perhaps the most distinctive feature of the game death was the attempt on the part of the condemned to impose on the event his own active presence: most famously, by jumping off the ladder before it was 'turned', or leaping from the cart before the signal was given for the horses to drive away. This was the signature of self-styled 'Heroes' such as Richard (Dick) Turpin, Isaac Darkin and Paul Lewis – the latter throwing himself 'off the cart so violently' that he broke his neck. At his 1777 execution the highwayman James Frankling (apprehended after returning to kiss the ladies in a coach he had just robbed) 'behaved in a most undaunted manner at the gallows, placed the rope about his neck, and threw himself off the ladder with a force as if to pull his head off'. While at the gallows, Thomas Crookhall was reported to have thrown his hat into the crowd, and 'several times looked undaunted around ... as if he bid defiance to grim death and all its terrors'; the Ordinary noted that, 'with what intent or view I cannot pretend to say', Crookhall 'also raised his feet from the cart, when tied up to the gallows, laying his intire weight upon the rope' before being turned off. Nor were extempore feats of courage less impressive. At the execution of the street robber Thomas Reeves in 1722, the crush of spectators knocked down one of the horses before the cart could be drawn away, leaving him in 'a half-hanging Posture; but that not pleasing him, and being impatient to wait 'till the Horse got up again, he threw himself over the Side of the Cart, and swung in good Order'.[35]

While such men may have been exercising their preference for a quick death over a slow one by strangulation (the drop was not introduced in London until 1783) they also communicated two strong messages. One was that they were willing to die; the other, that they were not physically afraid. The two were not exactly the same thing: the first expressed one's confidence in receiving pardon at the 'Judgment-Seat of Christ'. The second suggested that one died in a good cause – in other words, that one's courage and composure proceeded from the same source as the 'constancy' of martyrs; that is, not from any 'natural Power of their own, but unto the power of God's holy Spirit'. According to Richard Baxter, 'the Spirit of Christ' was the 'Comforter of the Saints ... If a draught of Wine, or some spiritful reviving liqour [sic] can take off fears, and make men bold; what then may the Spirit of Christ do by his powerful encouragements and comforts on the soul?'[36]

That the scaffold performances of common criminals borrowed the shorthand of Protestant hagiographic tradition does not seem altogether far-fetched in the light of the enduring appeal of the works of Foxe and other martyrologists on the one hand, and the popular equation 'of persecution with tyranny and error, and martyrdom with truth and virtue', on the other. Added evidence of the popular connection between the game and the good death may be inferred from the vehemence with which the Ordinary and other ministers maintained that 'it was a False-Courage, for Malefactors sentenced to dye, to appear wholly Careless and Unconcern'd ... which rather shows Obdurateness and Insensibility, than a Manly and becoming Resolution'. Such behaviour was rooted in pride – valuing the 'good Opinion of Men, more than the Praise of God and Angels' – rather than true 'Christian Courage', which flowed from God, and was not afraid to confess to sin. As the contrite Dr Dodd noted before his own execution, 'he did not think that heroism was a proper state of mind for [malefactors]; humble hope was the highest they could aspire to: heroism and triumph belonged to martyrs'.[37]

'False Courage', as the Ordinary and other clergymen argued, was a compound of 'Dissembl[ance]' and 'the Effort and vigor of natural courage'; not only was the courage of such 'False Martyrs' likely to abandon them at the gallows, but their 'anticke' attempts to assume a 'jocund Countenance' were clearly forced. '*Real* Martyrs, having the *secret* Consolations of *God's* Spirit, are not Transported with *Aiery* joys, neither are they *Theatrical* in their Carriage', claimed the Ordinary of Newgate in 1679 (in reference to the five Jesuits who died far too well for the comfort of most Protestants); rather, God-given courage was 'constant' and 'uniform': it '*becalm*[ed]', not aroused, 'the Passions'. According to Gilbert Burnet, it was 'not in the swellings of a Hero, or the affectations of a vain Man, but in the well-grounded expectations of a greater glory to follow it' that 'a Man may conclude he is under the Divine Conduct'. Burnet warned that sometimes 'Ill Men' might manifest the cheerful 'springing of the Heart' that normally denoted grace, merely from 'a head of Blood, and a flush of Spirits' that 'Good Men that are more steady and composed, may be without'. A 1720 condemned sermon preached by the Ordinary, Thomas Purney, illustrated the 'difference between the Righteous and the Sinners, at the Hour of Death' in simple terms: the 'wicked Man ... is in Tremblings and Agonies, while the Good Man is compos'd and serene'.[38]

Indeed, many people in the seventeenth and early eighteenth century appeared to apply a sort of primitive polygraph test to determine whether someone was guilty or innocent, saved or damned. During his trial for treason, Algernon Sidney responded to Judge Jeffreys' suggestion that he was not 'fit' to die by challenging him to check his 'Pulse' to see whether he was 'disordered'. Many game criminals seemed similarly anxious to demonstrate that they were free from any physiological symptoms of fear, passion, or agitation. While the game criminal adjusted his halter or blindfold, joked with the hangman, sang psalms, or bowed or even kissed his hand to the ladies, he provided opportunities for spectators to judge whether or not his hands, his legs, or his voice shook. It was no accident that one of the central dramatic details of the account of Dick Turpin's 1739 execution was that, despite the latter's 'amazing Assurance ... as he mounted the Ladder, his Right Leg trembled, on which he stamp'd it down with an Air, and with undaunted Courage look'd round about him'.[39]

Clearly, many malefactors believed that they could demonstrate their innocence by dying boldly and in a way that implied their consent – that is, by leaping from the ladder or cart. At his execution in 1709, Christopher Slaughterford, who solemnly attested to his innocence of the murder of his sweetheart, requested only that 'he might throw himself off'. Sometimes unforeseen (or, as contemporaries may have believed, providential) accidents provided additional evidence. At the execution of the genteel malefactor John Macnaghton in 1762, the latter took the halter from the executioner 'and put it round his neck himself: he then went up to the very top of the ladder and threw himself off with great force'. When the rope broke and Macnaghton fell to the ground, he 'did not appear to be in the least disconcerted', but 're-ascended the ladder with great calmness and composure'. The author of the pamphlet clearly suggests that 'false courage' alone could not have withstood such an ordeal. Many ordinary malefactors seemed equally anxious to use such accidents as opportunities to prove their undauntedness: when John Carr's rope broke during his 1741 hanging for robbery, he was at first 'somewhat stunn'd' by the fall, but made a point of asking the executioner 'to let him see the Light of this World once more'; upon which his cap was drawn down, and 'he looked stedfastly around him and upon [his fellow condemned] that was hanging, for the Space of two Minutes', before being turned off himself.[40]

Needless to say, those 'Counterfeit bravos' and 'Pseudo-Martyrs' who (in the view of chroniclers) died more cheerfully than their case should have warranted, were frequently accused of having had recourse to 'Artificial Courage' – that is, 'Cordial-Spirits'. Alcohol blunted the fear of death because it impaired the rational faculties; in the words of Macheath, 'valour the stronger grows/ The stronger liquor we're drinking/ And how can we feel our woes,/ When we've lost the trouble of thinking?' Mandeville complained of malefactors drinking copiously to 'stifle their Fear' before setting off for Tyburn, only to stop 'a half a dozen times, or more' along the way to refortify their 'Courage'. While the degree to which condemned criminals drank was doubtless exaggerated by those keen to dismiss their courage as 'Artificial', there is little doubt that many did drink on their way to Tyburn, especially before stricter regulations were imposed in the 1730s – in part simply because they were afraid, but also at least in part because drinking was a traditional ritual of reconciliation. Some malefactors certainly drank too much, both on the way to Tyburn and in Newgate: the former hangman John Price, hanged in 1718 for murder, was described as being 'drunk for several Days successively' after his condemnation, committing 'most horrid Outrages'.[41]

It is also clear, however, that many of the condemned made a point of refusing alcohol, at least publicly. The author of a sympathetic account of the attorney Thomas Carr makes much of the fact that the latter, while on his way to Tyburn, not only 'constantly persever'd in his Innocence', but remained unmoved when heckled by a spectator, and 'refus'd' a proffered glass of wine 'with the calmest Submission'. In short, he 'behaved like a Man, and like a Christian'. Similarly, Christopher Layer, executed for treason in 1723, cheerfully declined the 'Liquors' offered to him 'to revive and sustain his Spirits'. (Nor did he betray the slightest 'uneasiness' as he was dragged to Tyburn on a low sledge, despite the fact that 'the Dust and extreme Heat were ready to stifle and suffocate others in Coaches and on horseback'.) Conversely, of course, hostile authors were quick to attribute the high 'Spirits' of traitors to 'strong Cordials'. Accounts of the regicides' deaths were particularly partisan, as was that of Lord Stafford – one sympathetic pamphlet claimed that Stafford's scaffold 'Courage' was 'Divinely elevated, a constancy more then [sic] humane'; others, that he had taken 'some Liquors that had intoxicated his brain ... to bear up his Spirits'. In 1697 Samuel Smith warned ordinary malefactors against 'Drinking excessively strong Liquors' in the misguided belief that 'this will animate you against the Terrours of Death': such 'stupefying Bravado', he maintained, only 'strengthens Agonies in dying' and rendered the condemned unfit 'to appear at Christ's Tribunal'.[42]

Critics also explained away the apparent dauntlessness of dying malefactors either as a function of their being so hardened in a continual course of sin that they despaired of salvation, or as a manifestation of atheism, or 'Roman Courage', which 'outfaces Death with a stupid ignorance of a future Judgement'. Bishop Morely, who attended Lord Capel before his 1649 execution, suspected that he was not allowed to pray with him at the scaffold so 'that they would have the people believe, that the lord Capel died indeed resolutely like an old roman' – that is, that he chose to have no minister with him ('which was most false') – and that his 'constancy and courage ... was but an effect of his natural temper and constitution, and not of a christian faith and hope'. Certainly, the courage of ordinary condemned burglars and robbers was typically attributed to an atheistic disregard for the eternal consequences of their actions. Before his 1726 execution the notorious street robber Edward Burnworth supposedly told several visiting clergymen 'that the Apprehension of Death were no ways terrible to him'; he had, he said, 'no Notion' of a 'future State', claiming to view 'Death to a Thief to be no more than Bankruptcy to a Shopkeeper'. Burnworth was like Shakespeare's Barnadine: 'a man that apprehends death no more dreadfully but as a drunken sleep; careless, reckless, and fearless of what's past, present, or to come'; his was a 'brutal, not manly courage', resting on foundations as demonstrably precarious as his hopes of immortality.[43]

Game criminals, supported by alcohol, worshipped at the feet of that 'Idol' of 'Honour and bravery': worldly pride. Needless to say, the 'daring temper' mistaken by 'the Vulgar' for courage arose 'only from a wicked ambition of being thought brave' rather than true 'heroic Constancy of Mind', the product of 'Integrity and Innocence'. The Ordinary of Newgate regularly attributed the game criminal's refusal to 'shew any Fear or Terror at the Approach of Death' to his 'Desire of appearing brave, and making the Figure of a Hero in low Life'. The Ordinary was, however, quick to point out those criminals who, like the street robber James Hacket, hanged in 1707, thought it 'a gallant and honourable thing' to 'shew a bold and undejected Countenance' in 'publick', but showed 'another Disposition' – one 'more humble and more contrite' – in 'private'. The Ordinary and other chroniclers typically characterized the 'pretended Bravery' of game criminals as 'false courage', noting such telltale signs as changes in 'Countenance', flushing or sudden pallor ('sure Marks of Disturbance within'); or, simply falling back on claims that 'fearfulness and trembling were, notwithstanding, in [the] hearts' of those robbers who 'endeavoured to put on the appearance of undauntedness, and indeed but an appearance'.[44]

The game criminal had always been, and would continue to be, characterized as drunk, impious, and vainglorious. However, after the first third of the eighteenth century, critics focused less on the game criminal's failings as a Christian than on his social pretensions. And increasingly, the highwayman who, like Isaac Darkin, 'studied more to appear like a Gentleman than a Christian' shifted from being a vehicle for social commentary to being himself the butt of satire; or at best, an object of pity or scorn. Several would-be penal reformers suggested imposing sentences of hard labour on highwaymen, rather than death, as the former would more effectually mortify the pride of 'this infatuated race of men', whose sole aspiration was 'to enjoy the ease and dissipation of Gentlemen' before making 'an heroic exit'. The courage of the game criminal was increasingly attributed to a desire to imitate his betters. In one 1737 fictive newspaper description of an execution, we are told that those malefactors who 'affected ... Intrepidity' did so 'Because they would have the Glory of dying like Gentlemen'. Thus, they left 'the World either like Brutes or Ideots, having nothing in their Thoughts but how to obtain a few idle Praises!'[45]

While criminals who died boldly had always been characterized as 'hardened' or 'ignorant' by the Ordinary and other commentators – and this would continue through the eighteenth century and beyond – this suggestion that all game criminals were by definition 'Brutes or Ideots' reflects a subtly changing discourse about the nature of scaffold courage. While any man or woman who persisted in a course of sin could become hardened, and anyone could be ignorant for want of religious instruction, brutes and idiots were by definition incapable of true religious feeling. In the context of early and mid-eighteenth-century rational religion – in which both Creator and creature were rational beings – reason was the measure of all things. According to the author of a 1735 collection of criminal lives, 'there is no courage so reasonable as that which is founded in Christian Principles ... neither constitutional Bravery, nor that Resolution which arises either from Custom [or] from Vanity ... preserves that steady firmness at the Approach of Death'. Far from having the secular connotations it has today, reason clearly demonstrated to the rational being the existence of God and the inevitability of death and judgement. Thus, the attorney Thomas Carr's 'want of Concern' at his fate is defended by a sympathetic chronicler as 'a rational contempt of death' – that is, a reasonable conviction of his salvation.[46]

Conversely, the game criminal's courage was increasingly attributed to his inability to reason, to foresee the eternal consequences of his behaviour. In the words of one 1747 Ordinary's *Account*: 'Let such abandoned Wretches remember, that there is an HEREAFTER, when they must appear before the Judgement Seat of a justly offended God, to give an Account of all their actions'. As one contributor to the *Gentleman's Magazine* explained, 'a *love of fame* may raise a brutal hardiness above all sense of ignominy, or future distress', especially as 'these wretches' had 'little or no apprehension' of an afterlife: 'The soul, – they know nothing of it … as they have scarce any ideas of a future existence so they as little comprehend the miseries that await a life of impiety, and abandoned debauchery'.[47]

Rational religion not only elevated man from the abject position he occupied in Calvinist thought to that of a reasonable being, created in the image of a reasonable God, but held that this 'wise Creator … has implanted a Principle within us' that distinguished right from wrong; that is, 'Conscience, that Natural Magistrate in every Man's Heart'. This internalization of 'Vertue' and vice tended to undermine the notion that divine truths were manifested by the external signs (cheerfulness, composure, courage) traditionally associated with the good death. By mid century, most writers agreed that reason was the criterion by which a cause should be measured, not the behaviour of the person who suffered in it. The author of the life of the Jacobite Charles Ratcliffe, executed in 1746, argued that there was no 'Honour' in 'a Man's dying for his Principles, which he cannot defend by the least Arguments drawn from Reason, or the Principles of sound Policy'; rather, this was 'Enthusiasm … the Effect only of a warm Heart and weak Head'.[48]

The divorce of the dying behaviour of the condemned from the justice or iniquity of the cause for which he or she suffered unravelled the very seams of the confessional genre. The debate over the execution of the Jacobite lords Balmerino and Kilmarnock in 1746 marks a watershed in this regard: both were described as dying well, despite the fact that Balmerino went to the block with 'uncommon firmness and intrepidity'. Indeed, Balmerino was not only extolled 'as a hero and a martyr' by Jacobites, but 'many of the friends to the [Glorious] revolution and the present government', while lamenting Balmerino's 'erroneous political principles' nonetheless 'admir'd his fearlessness, and say he shew'd much *greatness of soul*, and died like a brave soldier'. Balmerino's critics responded by arguing that 'we can in no case, from the mere boldness and intrepidity of the sufferer, infer the goodness of his principle': indeed, 'the *presumptions of enthusiasm* are always more forward and assuming than the confidence inspired by rational religion'. And while I do not want to overstate the suddenness and completeness of such a shift – the notion that 'no Man without Virtue can be Courageous' was, after all, persistent – the suggestion by both Balmerino's admirers and detractors that it was possible to die well in a bad cause marked a dramatic turning point in the history of execution. Adam Smith's confident pronouncement in 1759 that 'the most heroic valour may be employed indifferently in the cause either of justice or injustice' would have been unthinkable sixty years earlier.[49]

In all the newspaper debate over the executions of Balmerino and Kilmarnock, there was however a consensus on the issue of those, less eminent, felons who died bravely. The 'contumnacious Contempt of Death, which some haughty Malefactors affect to assume at their Executions … is properly nothing else, but the Fear or Inability of calmly considering and looking it in the Face; and all their pretended Bravery or Defiance may be said to do the same Office only to their Minds, that the Headband, or Night-Cap does to their Eyes'. The apparent courage of the game criminal may have been only bravado, deployed as it was 'without one grain of reason, the foundation of a good conscience'; nonetheless, judging from mere externals, 'Great Men and the Vulgar, or the Good and the bad … often meet Death with the same Face'. There was, however, the 'inward and invisible Distinction, that Faith, Conscience, or a true Sense of Honour, preserves the Decorum in one, which, in the other, proceeds from an harden'd Boldness, from Ignorance and Stupidity impenetrable'.[50]

Real courage could, however, be distinguished from false by virtue of the fact that only a rational being was capable of true (rational) Christian courage. Rational courage consisted both in following the dictates of the conscience and mastering one's passions. Indeed, self-restraint was increasingly promoted to an 'active' rather than a 'Passive Courage'. According to an essay 'on HONOUR' reprinted in the London Magazine, featuring a gentleman who refused to partici-pate in a duel, 'there was more true Courage and Generosity' in restraining one's passions than in giving vent to them, as the former 'was much more difficult: That Bulls and Bears had Courage enough, but it was a brutish Courage, whereas ours should be such as should become reasonable Creatures and Christians'. The true gentleman, wrote Clement Ellis, 'conquer[ed] himself' rather than others, looking 'upon it as the basest degree of Cowardice, to yeild [sic] unto those feeble passions, which did not both Reason and Religion step into their succour, would certainly become the prey of every light and empty toy'. According to one 1762 execution pamphlet: 'in mere natural courage there is no merit, for it is little more than insensibility of danger'; real 'Courage', however, 'as the virtue of a rational being, is that strength of mind by which a sense of danger is surmounted; and fear, as a principle of action, over-ruled'. Significantly, if many contemporaries were impressed by Balmerino's scaffold courage, others pointed out that he died not just with 'the intrepidity of the hero, but with the insensibility of one too'. In contrast, his fellow-sufferer Lord Kilmarnock was admired for manifesting an appropriate sensibility and appreciation of the horrors of death, but without succumbing to despair: upon first viewing the scaffold, he remarked to a witness 'this is terrible' ('pronounced', however, 'in such a Manner as shewed no Signs of a broken or disconcerted mind'). Boswell saw Dr Johnson's 'aweful dread of death, or rather "of something after death"' as both rational and laudable, not at all at odds with his conviction that 'no man was ever more remarkable for personal courage' than Johnson.[51]

Recent scholarship on the subject of masculinity has demonstrated that, although some defining masculine attributes ('sexual mastery' and 'household authority', for instance) remained historically constant, ideals of manliness underwent a distinct shift towards the end of the early modern period. While the traditional masculine ideals of 'independence, moderation, courage and self-command' remained central, from the late seventeenth century, increasing emphasis was placed on civility, as the ideal of 'the polite man of the eighteenth century replaced the martial hero of earlier periods'. And with the emergence of the 'culture of sensibility' in the middle of the eighteenth century, sensibility came to be viewed as both a touchstone of true civility and gentlemanliness and a corrective to artificial politeness and over-refinement. Nor was there any inherent contradiction between sensibility and manliness, as Adam Smith maintained: 'Our sensibility to the feelings of others, so far from being inconsistent with the manhood of self-command, is the very principle upon which that manhood is founded', as 'the man who feels the most for the joys and sorrows of others, is best fitted for acquiring the most complete control of his own joys and sorrows'.[52]

In contrast, the courage of the game criminal was, by mid-century, increasingly dismissed not merely as a function of 'natural' (animal) or 'artificial' (alcoholic) courage but, because of his presumed incapacity for reason and want of sensibility, as an inability to manifest or even to comprehend true, 'rational' Christian courage. The game criminal's courage, or hardiness rather, was the product of mere brutish insensibility, as empty as his pretensions to being a gentleman. True manly courage consisted not in bravado or ostentatious gestures, but in a heroic (yet composed) mastery of one's own passions and, not least, all the terrors of remorse and keen awareness of metaphysical consequences to which a delicate mind was susceptible. Indeed, the relegation of the game criminal to a kind of *gentilhomme manqué* served to diffuse or even silence what had once been a potentially subversive discourse. Increasingly, the language of righteousness and courage alike were denied the game criminal. The right to express such home truths had become, it seemed, the monopoly of the reasonable – and 'sensible' – Christian who was, by definition, a gentleman.[53]

Mid and late eighteenth-century Ordinary *Accounts* and other criminal publications reflected this emphasis on, and preoccupation with sensibility, shifting their primary focus from the scaffold words and gestures of the condemned to their behaviour in prison in the days and weeks before their execution, and paying particular attention to moving letters from, and affecting interviews with, bereaved family members. To be sure, late seventeenth- and early eighteenth-century confessional literature often touched on grieving parents and spouses, and soon to be orphaned children, but the sheer volume and detail of such descriptions increased dramatically after the 1720s. Many young burglars and robbers were cast as prodigal sons of poor but honest and tender parents. The 23-year-old street robber Thomas Past, hanged in 1732, had thwarted all attempts on the part of his father, a brickmaker, to keep him on the straight and narrow. After being apprehended for robbery and released upon turning evidence against some of his confederates, his parents and other relatives attempted to reclaim him by sending him to sea. While the family were at a public house, 'intending immediately to put him on board', Past, 'pretending to [go] make Water', gave them the slip, 'and they never saw him again 'till after he was taken up and capitally convicted'. Past's mother was described as 'almost crazy' with 'Grief', his father and aunt visiting him in Newgate and crying 'out bitterly in a Flood of Tears, whilst he stood obdurate' (as the Ordinary thought; Past himself explained that 'he had unspeakable Grief and Vexation upon his Mind, though he could not express it outwardly'). The condemned thief Thomas Williams (later reprieved on condition of transportation) was openly distraught upon hearing that his 'Father, having been to see him under Condemnation, at four of the Clock, dyed with the vast concern of it at six', and that 'his Mother was like to be Distracted and to meet with the same sad Fate'.[54]

Early eighteenth-century criminal speeches and lives occasionally recorded moving and affecting scenes between working-class husbands and wives, parents and children. In 1736 the smuggler George Watson and his wife were described as 'embrac[ing] each other very tenderly, and with so feeling a Sympathy, that all the By-standers were sensibly affected at such a melancholy Sight'; we are told that Watson was particularly 'disturb'd' upon hearing that his 14-year-old son had been told of his condemnation, and that 'both cried most bitterly'. The horse-thief William Tyler is similarly portrayed as having 'burst immediately into a Flood of Tears' and having 'cryed bitterly over' his two sons, when he visited with them the day before his 1750 execution. Yet it goes without saying that genteel offenders tugged most effectually at the heartstrings of readers. When the so-called 'gentleman highwayman' James Maclaine, the black sheep of a reputable family, was asked if had children, he replied 'yes; he had a Girl of Five years old: And added, in a very pathetic Tone of Voice, lifting up his Hands, O my dear innocent Babe! – I have brought Infamy and Shame upon thee!' The author of a book on the execution of a number of Jacobites who had fought in the 'Forty-Five included a 'Story' which 'very much affected me, as I doubt not but it will you, and all who hear it', about the betrothed of one of the young men executed, a young lady of such exquisite sensibility that she 'expired' from 'Excess of Grief' only seconds after 'she found he was no more'.[55]

Such accounts emphasized the degree to which the sensibility of more genteel offenders could move even the hardest of hearts, including even the gaolers of Newgate. We are told that in 1738, 'the moving Scene' in which the forger William Newington knelt at his grieving widowed mother's feet, begging for forgiveness, 'drew Tears from the Eyes of those who were accustom'd to Scenes of Black Distress and Death'. An account of three Highland deserters executed in 1743 claimed that the 'courteous Behaviour' and 'Christian Composure' of the condemned 'gained so much upon the Affections of their Warders' that the 'melancholy Scene' of their execution 'raised Compassion from all, and drew Tears from many of the Spectators', even of 'the harden'd Sort'. One Newgate visitor was surprised to find that the condemned Irish pickpocket, Mary Young ('Jenny Diver') was a 'comely Woman, cleanly dress'd' and in whose 'Air and Countenance', moreover, could be discerned 'a Distress infinitely superior to any of the rest'. The narrator then recounted a moving scene in which Young wept over her child, 'a pretty Infant about two Years old', pathetically lamenting the fact that she would never kiss its daughter's lips again, and fainting with her child clasped to her arms – a sight which apparently moved even the gaolers to compassion, and one even to tears. Another newswriter, commenting on this story, was led to remark: 'so far does Affliction with a genteel Behaviour and Dress move Compassion beyond what is shewn to the Generality of Objects seen there [Newgate]'. After all, 'we are more nearly concerned for [condemned] Persons ... when they are at last sensible of their Crimes and wish they had acted a more rational and honest Part'. On the other hand, one could 'pity' – but not 'sympathise' with (an important distinction) – 'those abandoned Wretches, who do not pity themselves'.[56]

Such scenes were compelling and moving to contemporaries, not merely because they were sentimental (to a degree which may seem mawkish or cloying to the modern reader), but because they had as their subject the sympathetic faculties: the ability to feel deeply and to sympathize with the sorrows of others, a capacity all the more laudable and sublime when the individual in question was on the brink of death, but still able to forget or to surmount his or her own misfortunes in the contemplation of the pain he or she had inflicted on loved ones. Thus tears of true sensibility for others recalled the tears of true repentance; that is, expressing grief for offending God, rather than self-pity or sorrow for the punishment. However, this shift in emphasis – from the sinner's relationship with an offended God, to his or her relationship with others – may be seen as part of a larger reconfiguration, beginning in the late seventeenth century, of moral and religious sensibilities; that is, from 'First Table' values (i.e., the first four commandments concerning offences against God), to those of the 'Second Table' (the last six commandments concerning offences against one's fellow man).[57]

Mid- and late eighteenth-century criminal accounts also seem to reflect a more optimistic view of human moral and intellectual capacity, and a concomitant reconfiguration of God as a loving father, at once less vengeful and interventionist and more familiar and less remote. It is tempting, at any rate, to view the shift from dramatic, and awful, gallows confessions and conversions to affecting prison interviews with longsuffering and grieving parents as working on some level as religious analogy. Certainly, the central relationship of many mid- and late eighteenth-century criminal lives and confessions is no longer between the condemned and God (or the Ordinary or other clergyman), but between the condemned and family members – most often, a loving and compassionate father whose attempts to save his feckless child have been strenuous, if unavailing. While the 15-year-old condemned robber John Swift and his fellow sufferers were being drawn to the place of execution in 1763, Swift 'saw his afflicted father close to the [cart], weeping and wringing his hands, the poor boy returned tear for tear; the multitude were greatly affected at the sight, many turned away and dropt a tear, unable to bear the sight with a dry unconcern'. Most such fathers – especially genteel ones – are depicted as too overcome by grief to witness their children's execution, saying their farewells in prison, as did the fathers of several condemned Jacobites in July 1746. One fell on his son's 'Neck' and 'was just able to say, "Oh my dear Child, what would I give were it in my Power to save thee!" – with other melting Expressions, which brought Tears from the Eyes of all that beheld them'; in short, 'Words cannot describe this moving Scene'. Another sufferer who had up until then maintained 'an undaunted Resolution … could not forbear being affected with [the] Tenderness' and 'deep Affliction' of his father 'for the unhappy Fate of his Son'.[58]

Joseph Powis, hanged in 1732 for burglary, was the son of 'reputable Parents', and 'a good, kind, indulgent Father' whose 'Lenity', Powis tearfully confessed, he had done nothing but 'abuse'. In one account of Powis's life, he is reported as having had a vivid dream while sleeping out of doors, a fugitive on the run, in which his father appeared to him and, 'looking very stedfastly on me, said, "Oh Son! will you never take Warning, till justice overtakes you? the Time will come when you will wish, but too late, that you had been ruled by me"'. Powis then awoke 'under an inexpressible Horror of Mind', and resolved to return home to his father – a resolve which soon evaporated upon meeting up with an acquaintance who invited him to drink with him at an alehouse, where 'I washed away all those good Thoughts I had entertained'. The Ordinary's *Account* of the 17-year-old highwayman John Stockdale, who had been 'bred up in a genteel Manner with great Tenderness', similarly exploits the sentimentally charged (and metaphorically suggestive) theme of the prodigal son and the longsuffering and forgiving father. When the latter visited his son in prison, 'a Flood of Tears gush'd from' young Stockdale's eyes, and he 'burst out into' such extravagant 'Exclamations' of grief and repentance that 'his Father rightly judging, from the Agony he saw him in, that instead of reproaching him … he stood rather in need of spiritual Comfort and Assistance', consoled him with pious 'Exhortations' on the mercy of God. The elder Stockdale attended his son's trial, but left town immediately afterwards – his grief and sensibility being such that he was not 'able to see the Sentence of Death executed upon his Son'.[59]

Sensibility and sympathy were among the cardinal virtues of mid- and late eighteenth-century English polite society. Sympathy, as Randall McGowen reminds us, 'spoke more of a capacity to feel than of particular emotions', and many eighteenth-century gentlemen (and even ladies) were eager to demonstrate and to 'test' their sympathetic faculties by visiting Newgate or Bedlam, or witnessing executions. James Boswell congratulated himself on the depth of his emotional response to the hanging of his former client, the sheep-stealer John Reid, clearly believing that his 'acute sensibility ... enabled him not only to sympathize with, but ... even outstrip Reid's [own] feelings'. Indeed, according to McGowen, such attempts to measure 'sympathetic feelings became one more way of describing the gulf and valorizing the difference between classes'; in other words, the capacity for sensibility and sympathy could serve as cultural shibboleths demarcating, and reinforcing, the boundaries between plebeian and polite society. As Johnson's friend Mr Thrale remarked, in regard to Selwyn's taste for viewing executions, 'the sole Source of Pleasure in such perverse Appetite must be the consciousness of one's own Security'. Moreover, as V. A. C. Gatrell has argued, sympathy or sensibility could serve as 'alibis' for more prurient or voyeuristic impulses and, as open expressions of curiosity became socially unacceptable in the later eighteenth century, degenerated into 'squeamishness' or other mechanisms of denial.[60]

If not squeamishness, then something like it certainly extended to mid-eighteenth-century Ordinaries such as John Taylor, who routinely signed off the *Account* with such phrases as 'All was done with such Decency, as the Nature of the Thing admits'. Gallows attendance on the part of upper-class men such as Selwyn and Boswell was increasingly viewed as a kind of eccentricity (a 'perverse Appetite'). In his 1741 *Letters Written to and for Particular Friends on the Most Important Occasions*, Samuel Richardson includes a letter supposedly written by a 'Country Gentleman in Town, to his Brother in the Country, describing a Publick Execution in London'. Here the sympathetic faculties of the normative polite letter writer are put to a stern test, the author professing to be in the grip not only of 'the affecting Concern which is unavoidable in a thinking Person, at a Spectacle so awful, and so interesting, to all who consider themselves of the same Species as with the unhappy Sufferers', but still more shocked at the 'unexpected Oddness of the Scene' – that is, the reactions of the execution crowd. The spectators are characterized as the 'most abandon'd and profligate of Mankind ... so stupid' to 'any Sense of Decency' that 'all the Preparation of the unhappy Wretches seems to serve only for Subject of a barbarous kind of Mirth, altogether inconsistent with Humanity'. This is evidently less a description of a real execution (the details do not match with any near-contemporary Tyburn hanging, for one thing), than a composite moral sketch, both of the dismal 'Scene' and the appropriate response to it. The author concludes the letter by communicating his unwillingness to repeat such an experiment.[61]

As Richardson's description suggests, mid- and late eighteenth-century polite observers regarded the crowd as inherently incapable of genuine sympathy; far from engaging their pity or horror, the execution spectacle could only further harden and brutalize them. While attending the notorious murderess Elizabeth Brownrigg to her execution at Tyburn in 1767 for the cruel murder of a poor parish apprentice, the Ordinary of Newgate Joseph Moore was 'greatly shocked' at 'the unchristian' behaviour and 'horrid imprecations' of spectators, who shouted out to the chaplain to 'pray for her damnation, and not for her salvation', and that they 'hoped she would go to hell, and was sure the devil would fetch her soul'. The Methodist preacher accompanying them was equally horrified at the behaviour of the 'wicked multitude' whom he compared to demons (the 'powers of darkness' and 'spirits let loose from the infernal pit').[62]

Disgust for and criticisms of the bacchanalian excesses of 'Tyburn Fair' were of course nothing new, having been voiced by Bernard Mandeville in the 1720s and Henry Fielding and Samuel Richardson in the 1740s and 1750s. Mid- and late eighteenth-century newspapers frequently complained that 'the frequency of executions of late years, instead of creating terror and compassion in those that attend them, only hardens their hearts, and makes them strangers to pity'; the insensate mob viewed hangings not as dreadful examples, but as 'holidays'. But mounting attacks on the deleterious effects of the Tyburn procession in the 1770s were predicated not so much on the corrupting and demoralizing potential of the execution ritual as on the mental insensibility of the crowd: such 'awful solemnities' could make no lasting 'impressions ... on the minds of vulgar spectators', who were unable to draw the rational inference between cause and effect: they had, one author reflected, 'no abstract ideas'.[63]

By the second half of the eighteenth century, it had become more common for the Ordinary and other commentators to conflate the condemned felon and the execution crowd as equally bestial and insensible. Many polite observers similarly concluded that the Ordinary, by association, must also be hardened and insensible: as Anthony Morris Storer wrote to his correspondent George Selwyn in regard to Dodd's execution, 'There were two clergymen attending him, one of whom seemed very much affected. The other, I suppose, was the Ordinary of Newgate, as he was perfectly indifferent and unfeeling in everything that he said and did'. But the most insensible, not to mention obnoxious, of all gallows figures was the game criminal, whose apparently wilful disregard for the eternal consequences of his behaviour was not only applauded but imitated by hardened and demoralized spectators – or so, at least, moralists claimed. In 1750, the Ordinary of Newgate, John Taylor, complained of the 'intolerably indecent' behaviour of the 17-year-old street robber Benjamin Campbell Hamilton, who 'talked to the Mob, and to his Fellow-Sufferers in the Cart, with as much Ease and Unconcern as a Man would do that was going to a Jubilee, and continued so till within a few Minutes of his

Death'. At Tyburn, Hamilton continued 'talking and laughing almost all the while the Executioner was tying them up, and using such expressions as are better stifled than reported'. And it would not be long before the expressions and speeches of such would-be 'heroes in low life' were indeed almost uniformly stifled, not only by the Ordinary, but by other journalists and pamphleteers as well.[64]

WEDDINGS AND HANGINGS

In a scene from the 1715 play *A Woman's Revenge*, the condemned vintner Mixum is accosted in Newgate by his wife, asking if 'we are to find the Halter, or they?' Despite her husband's exasperated denial ('why do'st thou ask such a Question – they, they, to be sure'), she is nonetheless so solicitous as to bring him a sturdy length of cord. The running gag of the play, a retread of the earlier Newgate comedy *The Revenge* (1680), is the similitude of hanging and marriage – not only do both 'go by destiny', but it was difficult to choose between them: both plays end with the condemned characters reprieved from the gallows but yoked in matrimony. This association between hangings and weddings was not only a common literary trope (figuring most famously in *The Beggar's Opera*) but seemed to have informed popular beliefs about gallows pardons. It may be recalled that before the 1722 execution described in detail in the introductory chapter, six (or seven, depending on the account) young women dressed in white, 'and carrying white Wands in their Hands', carried a petition to St James's, promising one of them would marry the condemned robber John Hartly if his life were spared; the petition, needless to say, was not successful.[65]

The late seventeenth-century Swiss traveller Henri Misson noted the similarities between wedding and gallows rituals, with the condemned taking great 'Care to get himself shav'd, and handsomely drest, either in Mourning or in the Dress of a Bridegroom', with those choosing the latter attire obtaining gloves, nosegays and often accompanied by girls dressed in white and carrying 'Baskets full of Flowers and Oranges, scattering these Favours all the Way they go'. Another early eighteenth-century pamphlet describes condemned malefactors wearing white gloves and carrying prayer books in one hand, and nosegays or oranges in the other. White gloves, ribbons, scarves, oranges, flowers, rings and other favours were commonly associated with wedding celebrations, although there was often considerable overlap between marriage and funereal rituals – a distinction easily blurred, for obvious reasons, in the case of condemned malefactors.[66]

A 1728 pamphlet claimed that 'one Thing that increases our number of Town Thieves, is to see the Criminals go to Execution as neat and trim, as if they were going to a Wedding'. The famous highwayman Dick Turpin, hanged in 1739 at York, was reported to have, in preparation for his execution, 'bought himself a new Fustian Frock and a Pair of Pumps', and given £3 10s. 'to 5 Men who were to follow the Cart as Mourners, with Hatbands and Gloves to them and several others' (again, however, the distinction between mourners and groomsmen could be ambiguous). The highwayman Henry Simms (or 'Gentleman Harry') went to his 1747 execution 'cleanly dress'd in a White Fustian Frock, White Stockings, and White Drawers; and just as he got into the Cart at Newgate, threw off his Shoes'. By the middle of the eighteenth century this distinction between bridegrooms and mourners had become an integral part of the iconography of Tyburn. As befitted an aspiring Macheath, the game highwayman Paul Lewis wore a smart white, silver and blue suit to his 1763 execution, in marked contrast with his more appropriately clad fellow sufferer, the forger John Rice, who 'was very decently dressed in a new suit of Mourning'.[67]

Moreover, the sartorial conventions of dying game became, if anything, visually more elaborate and pronounced as verbatim accounts of execution speeches and behaviour declined after 1760, and gallows reportage was increasingly confined to brief newspaper notices focusing primarily on whether or not the condemned were 'decently dressed' – that is, 'in Mourning'. Gallows gestures may have become both more frequent and more self-consciously theatrical: for instance, kicking off one's shoes, either at the place of execution or (more commonly) before being put in the cart. While an old practice – many seventeenth-century malefactors were reported as claiming that they would thus defeat the predictions of relatives and acquaintances that they would die with their shoes on (i.e., suffer a violent and untimely death) – the kicking off of shoes seemed to have become de rigeur for mid- and late eighteenth-century game criminals. It is interesting to note that, like the oranges often carried or eaten, or thrown to the crowd by game criminals (or vice versa), and the wearing and distributions of rings, gloves and ribbons, shoe tossing may have also had associations with wedding rituals. There is no doubt, however, that this practice was meant in large part as a gesture of defiance, of thumbing one's nose at authorities. In 1753 the robber George Robertson, 'just as the Cart began to move ... kick'd off his Shoes from among the Mob, with the utmost Disdain, and as if he despised any Thing that could be done to him'. The previous year the Ordinary reported that the 17-year-old Irish robber John Macnamar 'slipped his Shoes in the Press-Yard, but they were ordered to be pulled up again at the Heels'; once in the cart, however, 'he kicked off one Shoe immediately' but, 'the other not coming off so easily', he cried out 'with Anger'. (Evidently proof, in the Ordinary's opinion, that he was unfit to die.) It may also have sometimes been intended as a declaration of innocence, a rejection of the felon's death. At his 1733 execution John Beach 'denied the Fact, for which he suffer'd, to the last; and when he went into the Cart at Newgate, said, "It shall not be said I died in my Shoes", and then kicked them both off amongst the Populace'.[68]

As Peter Linebaugh has argued, the game criminal's 'flash clothes' could symbolize, above and beyond the popular association between weddings and hangings, both 'a flaunting, ostentatious display of opposition to the severities of the law' and the 'anticipation of divine union or a proclamation of innocence before God and the Sheriffs'. Some simply articulated the connection: Thomas Reynolds, hanged in 1750, claimed that 'he went to be hanged with as much Satisfaction as if he was going to be married; for that he was innocent of the Crime for which he suffer'd and freely forgave the Prosecutor'. Others, like Thomas Randal, hanged for robbery and murder in 1696, made much the same point by dressing 'all in white'. As Linebaugh, Gatrell, and others have noted, white (or sometimes blue) cockades or ribbons were often worn by the condemned as a symbol of innocence. But such sartorial statements should be seen not so much as a defiance of as a self-conscious engagement with contemporary moral discourse. In 1764 the condemned robber Joseph Redmond ('innocent of the crime, but willing to die for his other sins') claimed to have been following 'his clergyman's advice' when he wrote to his family requesting *white cloaths* to appear in on the morning he was to suffer'. In 1774 the highwayman Jack Rann scandalized many observers by going to Tyburn wearing 'white Ribbands ... intended as a declaration of his Innocence'; however, he was reported as saying that he would not have worn them 'if he had not been told it was decent'.[69]

As I have suggested, the innocence claimed by the condemned was often relative rather than literal. The highwayman Thomas Jackson 'owned he was guilty of the Facts he stood condemn'd for', but 'pretended his Condition not to be altogether so bad as theirs whom he look'd upon to be greater Offenders than himself'. Henry St John, in a letter to the noted execution-goer George Selwyn, simply assumed that John Weskett (or Waiscott), a porter executed for the burglary of Lord Harrington's house, 'went to the gallows with a white cockade in his hat, as an emblem of his innocence'. However, according to the Ordinary of Newgate, Weskett had in fact confessed the crime, but 'gave this Reason' for putting the 'white Ribbond into his Hat': 'I believe I am come to an untimely End, in order that my Soul might be saved; and I look upon this as my Wedding-Day.' Edward Barcock, although tacitly confessing the robbery for which he was hanged in 1738, 'would not acknowledge it, in all its Circumstances'; nonetheless he 'blessed God, that the dismal Cells of Newgate had brought him to a Sense of his Sins ... and that his Afflictions would be the means of drawing him to God'. At Tyburn, where he 'appear'd very penitent and exprest his assurance of heaven', Barcock and his accomplice, Henry Fluellin, wore 'white Cockades in their Hats, in token of their Triumph over the World'.[70]

Men such as Barcock and Weskett were invoking the popular belief that suffering was both providential and purgative. This providential discourse was adopted not only by those of the condemned who claimed to be innocent, but also by those who acknowledged their guilt, but whose sufferings (they believed) exceeded their crimes. The highwayman James Brown, condemned (but later reprieved) in 1763, who clearly thought his poverty mitigated his offence, claimed to be 'easy and resigned in his mind, willing to die, and persuaded he should be a *rich man* and *very happy* on Wednesday next'. When the Ordinary and other visiting divines expressed their scepticism, he remained adamant: 'the more he suffered and the worse he was treated, the better he hoped to fare hereafter'. And indeed, many game highwaymen were reported as mortifying themselves in various ways, fasting (like Robert Wilkinson), or abstaining from sleep, or deliberately exposing themselves to cold and other discomforts. The notorious robber James Shaw was reported to have, upon being confined to the condemned hold, 'stripp'd himself to his Shirt, and put on his Night Cap, designing to continue so till his Execution, he having no hopes of Mercy'. The gallant highwayman James Wright went to Tyburn 'in a Shroud, and would not admit of any other Garment' (despite the fact it was late December).[71]

Such beliefs persisted well beyond the period under consideration here. In 1827 the prison reformer Elizabeth Fry would complain that many condemned criminals not only clung to 'their evil habits ... until the very hour of their execution', but that they 'pacif[ied] their conscience with the dangerous and most fallacious notion that the violent death which awaits them will serve as a full atonement for all their sins'. Moreover, such beliefs continued to fuse with a discourse of relative guilt that recalls the social commentary of early modern rogue literature and Augustan satirists such as Butler, Garth and Gay. Samuel Romilly was much struck by a conversation with Fry in which the latter told him that:

> it is frequently said [by the condemned] that the crimes of which they have been guilty are nothing, when compared to the crimes of Government towards themselves: that they have only been thieves, but that their governors are murderers. There is an opinion, too, very prevalent among them, that those who suffer under such unjust and cruel sentences are sure of their salvation ... All the crimes they have committed, they say, are more than expiated by the cruel wrongs they are made to endure.[72]

Such popular beliefs proved resilient, persisting long after the late eighteenth-century disappearance of the Ordinary's *Account* (and, in one form or another, into the present day). And even if last dying confessions and criminal lives died out as mainstream genres, ephemeral execution literature and highwayman ballads continued to be hawked or sung in the streets well into the nineteenth century, long after the age of highway robbery itself was distant memory. Not only did the game criminal continue to have resonance and vitality in popular culture, but so too did the discourse of the relativity of guilt he typically invoked – and sealed with his willingness to die. In the words one early twentieth-century penny dreadful put in the mouth of the highwayman Dick Turpin, on trial for his life:

> If the pillage done by an army is glorious conquest, the wealth wrested by a man from wholesale thieves and tyrants is something yet more brave. There are men now in this very court who are sordid sycophants, preaching, but not practising what they preach … I shall not shrink in fear from my fate. I go to it undismayed. My life is in your hands; take it for what it is worth.

Or, in the words of Macheath: 'death is a debt,/ A debt on demand. So take what I owe'.[73]

8

God's Tribunal: Providential Discoveries and Ordeals

The words of dying persons have been always esteemed as of greatest authority; because uttered then, when shortly after they are to be cited before the high tribunal of Almighty God.

William Harcourt (one of the five Jesuits executed in June 1679)

What the Devil are you Afraid of? We shan't be Tried by a Cumberland Jury in the other World.

Thomas Coppach (Jacobite hanged in 1746, to a fellow sufferer)

On 13 June 1679, Thomas Whitebread, William Harcourt, John Fenwick, Anthony Turner and John Gavan were tried at the Old Bailey courthouse for high treason; they were subsequently convicted and condemned to death and, a week later, hanged at Tyburn. These men, known to contemporaries simply as 'the five Jesuits', were among dozens of innocent people executed for their alleged part in the 'Popish Plot': purportedly, a conspiracy to assassinate Charles II, to overthrow the government and to reinstate Catholicism in England. The legal proceedings had all the hallmarks of the modern show trial. The five accused men and their Catholic witnesses were mercilessly cross-examined, even heckled, by the unsympathetic and frequently sarcastic presiding judges, Sir Francis North and Sir William Scroggs. The defendants' attempts to establish alibis, to point out inconsistencies in the evidence, and to question the credibility of the prosecution witnesses – the turncoat and informer 'Dr' Titus Oates, 'Captain' Bedlow, a convicted thief, and Stephen Dugdale, a former steward who had embezzled vast sums of money to pay his gambling debts – were consistently drowned out by derisive laughter and anti-papist cheering. According to one Catholic witness, 'never was Bear-bayting more rude and boyterous then [sic] this Tryal'.[1]

The verdict (reached in fifteen or thirty minutes, depending on the account)[2] was a foregone conclusion, and the defendants seemed composed, even resigned, to their fate. John Gavan, at about forty the youngest of the five, had put up the most spirited defence, at several points in the trial becoming evidently frustrated as his objections to the prosecution's testimony were interrupted or ignored, and his own witnesses first asked if they were Catholics, and then laughed or shouted down. Finally, exasperated at his inability to prove his innocence in terms his auditors could accept, Gavan made a remarkable petition: could he 'put himself upon the trial by ordeal, to evidence his own innocency?' This strange request elicited an equally interesting response on the part of Lord Chief Justice Scroggs:

> You are very fanciful, Mr Gavan; you believe that your cunning in asking such a thing, will take much with the auditory: but this is only an artificial varnish. You may do this with hopes of having it take with those that are Roman Catholics, who are so superstitious as to believe innocency upon such desires; but we have a plain way of understanding here in England and that helped very much by the Protestant religion: So that there is scarce any artifice big enough to impose upon us. *You ask a thing that sounds much of a pretence to innocency, and that it would be mighty suffering, if you should miscarry, because you ask that you know you cannot have* (my emphasis).[3]

In other words, Scroggs not only accused Gavan of making such an offer simply in order to impress the jury, but implied that the latter would not have dared to subject himself to such a trial if he had not been confident that his bluff would not be called. We are left with the impression that the Protestant chief justice was not as far removed from the mentality of the Catholic defendants as he would have liked to suggest. And indeed, this notion that the words and behaviour of men and women under duress provided uniquely compelling testimony was, in the beginning of our period at least, shared by both Protestants and Catholics, learned and unlettered, rich and poor. It was moreover only one of a constellation of beliefs and practices relating to the 'sacramentality' of suffering – some suggesting vestigial memories of purgatory and the ordeal – which were surprisingly tenacious, persisting well into the eighteenth century.

I have returned to this story of the five Jesuits because it provides a particularly vivid, and useful, entry point into the early modern English belief system, one that is in many respects very different from that of the present day – and nowhere more so, perhaps, than in its sacralized conception of right and wrong, justice and injustice, as evidenced by men and women *in extremis*.[4] As we have seen in the preface to this book, the five Jesuits were at their execution finally accorded the hearing (and Gavan the ordeal) which they had been denied at their trial. At Tyburn these five men died so bravely and so well, 'pardoning their Accusers' and 'hartily praying for them', and with such solemn avowals of their innocence as to 'stagger' the most hostile of spectators and even to sow the seeds of doubt that the Popish Plot might in fact be what the defendants had all the time maintained: a tissue of lies.[5]

MAN'S JUSTICE AND GOD'S JUSTICE

While scholars have long viewed public execution as a ritual of social reintegration, my focus here is on the extent to which the gallows was perceived as a portal to the other world, in which the body of the condemned provided, literally, a conduit to divine truth. While contemporaries often differed in their interpretation of what the dying words and behaviour of the condemned actually meant, it was in the late seventeenth and early eighteenth century nonetheless widely agreed that the gallows provided, as it were, a liminal or sacralized space in which truth could be sifted from untruth. Interested parties routinely gathered around the scaffold on hanging days, questioning the condemned about his or her guilt, previous crimes or testimony. But the 'truth' that most spectators sought was the preview of God's judgement that a careful scrutiny of gallows speeches and performances could provide. On rare occasions, even the principals themselves could return to testify as to their future state: in November 1740 William Duell, condemned for taking part in a horrific gang-rape and murder, survived being hanged at Tyburn, and was later granted a transportation pardon. Despite the fact that Duell was supposed to have declared that he remembered nothing of his botched execution, reports of what we would now call his 'near-death experience' later surfaced in a newspaper which claimed that Duell had 'imagined himself in Paradice, and saw an Angel who told him his Sins were forgiven'. The notion that such a hardened and apparently impenitent criminal could escape so lightly was peremptorily dismissed by one pamphlet as 'improbable and incongruous'; significantly, the same writer went on to describe Duell's *actual* 'glimpse of Eternity' as a 'Scene of 'Horror' featuring both 'the Image of the unfortunate Woman whom he had Robb'd, Ravish'd, and Murdered, standing ready to appear against him, at the Tribunal of Divine Justice', and 'the Spectre' of one of his accomplices who had died in prison, 'howling in Hell's devouring Flames, claiming [Duell] as his Companion'.[6]

The afterlife constituted the obvious frame of reference for contemporaries pondering issues of guilt or innocence, justice and injustice. 'Ghosts' of traitors and other malefactors occasionally acted as mouthpieces through which metaphysical, if invariably partisan, truths could be expressed. In one of the many anti-Catholic pamphlets published after the execution of the five Jesuits, it was claimed that the latter's ghosts had appeared 'to Two Gentlemen of Eminent Credit'; this 'Strange Apparition' being 'a wonderful Token of their [spiritual] Disquiet, and some Things considerable referring to their Guilt'. Apparently, the five Jesuits had been turned out of hell because they were too unruly, and (here the pamphleteer cannot resist an obvious joke) such inveterate plotters that the Devil was afraid 'to let them have any Gunpowder, lest they blow the whole place up'. In a similar vein, a 1718 pamphlet printed after the execution of the Jacobite

James Sheppard features a dialogue between Sheppard's ghost and one of his former companions, the latter questioning the shade as to his 'State': 'were you justly hang'd, or did you die a Martyr?' Sheppard's ghost, whose object was to 'strike … out' his signature from the 'Paper' asserting his innocence, admitted that his speech was a lie: thus he had died 'in a wicked condition' which left no doubt as to his present (and eternal) 'State'.[7]

Though such 'ghost stories' are obviously literary tropes (and often jokes, too), they nonetheless reflect both a very real preoccupation with the spiritual state of those who died well for crimes of which they claimed to be innocent, and the political implications of whether such individuals were 'justly hang'd' or died 'Martyrs'. Even 'real' ghosts could act as propagandists, judging by the paper war generated by the 'ghost' of Lord Russell, who had been executed in July 1683 for his part in the Rye House (the so-called 'Protestant') Plot. According to a Whig publication, *The Night-Walker of Bloomsbury*, some 'Politick Heads' of 'both Sexes … hatch'd' a 'barbarous and papistical' conspiracy aimed at demonstrating that the solemn avowals of innocence contained in Russell's last dying speech were penned not by Russell himself, but by his friend and spiritual advisor, Gilbert Burnet. According to this paper, a vintner (in collaboration with 'a Brace of fishmongers' and other mean characters) draped himself in a white sheet and, walking near Russell's house in Bloomsbury Square, 'groan'd' and issued a series of 'Lamentations', culminating in 'Oh – I have no rest because of the Speech that I never made, but Dr Burnet'. The 'faigned Goblin' was then confronted with a night watchman who, after giving him a few well-deserved buffets, exposed him as a fraud and extracted a full confession. This account was immediately counted in a Tory newspaper, *The Observator*, which claimed there had never been a ghost – only a vintner who, to win a wager of a bottle of wine, walked around Bloomsbury Square with an apron on his head. Apparently clinching the matter, we are told that Langley Curtis, the printer of this 'Libell' (as well as the Ordinary's paper), had the week before been soundly thrashed in a coffee-house in Fleet Street by a 'Loyall' citizen after refusing to pledge the health of the Duke of York.[8]

The invocation (literary or otherwise) of ghosts illustrates the contemporary obsession with knowing the truth about the 'State' of the dead; in comparison, the desire to do justice to the living seemed to take a poor second place. Even if, in theory at least, human justice was patterned on a divine ideal, it was widely acknowledged that the secular courts were eminently fallible. Late seventeenth- and early eighteenth-century men and women were seemingly comfortable with, or at least ostensibly resigned to, this disparity between man's justice and God's. It is all too easy for the modern reader to conclude from this that early modern providentialist discourse was exclusively normative, and to equate it, for instance, with the socially conservative prescriptive evangelical literature of the late eighteenth and early nineteenth century. In a classic example of this genre, Hannah More's anti-Jacobin tract 'Turn the Carpet' features two weavers sitting at work, arguing about politics. One cites the great injustices on Earth: the fact that he has to work hard and go hungry while the rich are idle and well-fed; moreover, it seems to him that everywhere the good are oppressed, while the wicked prosper. The second (and wiser) weaver reminds his fellow that mortals can only know *part* of God's plan. To illustrate his point, he refers to the carpet they are working on, which, unfinished, 'had no middle, where's the border? The carpet now is all disorder'. However, he adds, when finished and turned over, 'then shall we see the whole design' and realize that the carpet, like God's plan, was perfect. This parable none too subtly promotes a reliance upon a kind of 'compensatory justice' which legitimated socio-economic inequity in this world by promising redress in the next. But providential beliefs could function in subversive as well as in normative ways, for if the gallows provided the platform, providentialism provided the language in which ordinary men and women could speak not only to their own individual guilt or innocence, but raise larger questions of relative guilt and social justice by invoking the disparity between man's justice and God's.[9]

The early modern English criminal trial should not be seen as a quest for the truth, or even a contest between two different versions of what passed for it. Seventeenth- and eighteenth-century trials were less about determining a defendant's guilt or innocence of a specific crime than a kind of 'sentencing hearing', aimed at weighing the character of the accused, and his or her likelihood of offending again. In the absence of plea bargaining, guilty pleas were actively discouraged by the bench on the grounds that, even in cases where the defendant had confessed to the crime, a trial would allow for the introduction of mitigating circumstances or information about the offender's character which were critical in determining whether he or she would be pardoned, reprieved, or convicted of a lesser (non-capital) offence. Indeed, a larger proportion of eighteenth-century trials – at least those for property offences – was taken up with calling character witnesses than it was in examining evidence relating to the crime.[10]

Character was paradoxically all the more important in a world in which all human beings were believed to be tainted with original sin. Guilt tended to be expressed as a relative property: all people were guilty; the question was merely whether an individual were so hardened as to be incapable of rehabilitation. Criminality was invariably expressed in popular discourse as well as in the court-room, not as the function of one particular act, but as a point on a continuum, the part of the slippery slope from which one could not return.[11] Moreover, if an innocent man or woman was condemned, this was because 'God, for wise ends, is pleased to permit the innocent sometimes to suffer in this world, and the guilty to go unpunished'. After all, 'All Tryals in Human Courts, are of uncertain Issue

... For there Men stand or fall, by Understanding and Dispositions of Judges and Juries' whose 'Hearts and Minds are in no Hand but Gods, who Turns and Governs them as he pleases'. Even those that suffered for crimes they did not commit should 'regard the justice of God ... and say, *That God has punished you less than your iniquities have deserved*', consoling themselves with the thought that 'all things will be set straight at the great judgement day'. In his sermons, the Ordinary of Newgate frequently exhorted the condemned not to brood over perceived injustices, but to prepare themselves for that 'universal Assize' at which 'all Accounts' would be 'ballanced'.[12]

Such pious platitudes were typically expressed by prison chaplains or in the prayer books issued to prisoners, and reflect the all too familiar invocation of providence as a mechanism of 'compensatory justice'. But providential discourse could challenge as well as legitimate the status quo. Richard Evans has identified the 'only real sign of dissent' in early modern German trials and executions as the 'ritual cursing of the judges at the passing of the verdict', in which felons 'issued a formal invitation to those who had condemned them to join them at the Last Judgement in the Valley of Jehosaphat, where God would judge those who had judged unjustly'.[13] The nineteenth-century Australian bushranger and game criminal, Ned Kelly, famously told Redmond Barry, the judge who sentenced him to death, that he would see him again where he was going – presumably, in hell; needless to say, many contemporaries (and subsequent mythologisers) read significance into the fact that Barry died only twelve days after Kelly's execution. But such defiant speeches were relatively rare; even in England, where judicial torture (at least after the late seventeenth century) was not applied to those who refused to confess, malefactors tended to choose their words carefully – not through a fear of physical punishment, but because threats and passion denoted a dangerous deficiency of Christian charity. Instead, those who wished to communicate that they had been condemned unjustly tended to emphasize, in the words of the printer William Anderton, executed in 1693 for treason, their eager anticipation of 'a joyful Resurrection, and the coming of the righteous Judge, before whom [King] William and [Queen] Mary and Anderton ... shall appear without any other difference or respect, than what their Sins or their Virtues shall make'. On his way to chapel, the burglar Christopher Freeman was supposed to have 'said in a jocular way to his Fellow-Sufferers, "This is a fine Act indeed, you thought there would be an Act of Indemnity, which I believe will be at the Place of Execution on Monday next"'. And after he had received sentence of death, the Jacobite Thomas Coppach rallied a tearful fellow prisoner with a hearty, 'What the Devil are you Afraid of? We shan't be Tried by a Cumberland Jury in the other World'.[14]

Those who wished to deliver an effective critique of their sentence were generally careful to buttress such complaints with evidence that they were otherwise 'in peace with all the world'. After being publicly whipped at the cart's tail in 1715, George Musson, the so-called 'High Church Cobler', issued a short speech decrying the 'Malice' of those 'Whigs and Phanaticks' who had prosecuted him, and then 'treated' the officers who had administered the punishment with a bottle of wine 'to shew he was in Charity with them'. Even if many expressions of charity were grudging or disingenuous, they nonetheless reflect the notion that the words of people who died in a passion – either of anger or of fear – were essentially invalidated, as this indicated that the dying person was both spiritually unfit and afraid to die and to make his or her appearance before 'God's Tribunal'. Lack of charity was seen not only as a mark of reprobation but even as a species of irrationality or even insanity, as in the case of John Hewlet, a watchman executed in 1725 for murdering a man in a brawl. Hewlet stubbornly maintained his innocence, and 'instead of shewing any marks of Penitence or Contrition, he raved against the witnesses … call'd them all Perjured, and Pray'd God to inflict some dreadful Judgement on them'; going so 'far as to desire that … after his Death his Apparition might come and terrify them to their Graves'. Hewlet's inability to compose himself – even after 'it was represented to him how odd this Behaviour was, and how far distant from the Calmness and Tranquility of Mind, with which it became him to Cloath himself before he went into the Presence of his Master' – could be explained by the fact that, after receiving a head injury several years previously, he had undergone a 'Trepan': an operation which involved the removal of part of his skull. After this dubious 'Cure' Hewlet 'never had his Senses in the same manner he had before, but upon the least drinking he fell into Passions which were but very little remov'd from Madness'.[15]

The most explicit criticisms of justice tended to be voiced in regard to what historians have termed 'social crimes' – offences which could be classified as capital felonies, but which a large proportion of society viewed as relatively minor infractions. Social crimes included smuggling, poaching, rioting and returning from transportation before the expiration of one's term. John Whalebone, hanged for the latter crime in 1725, 'pretended [claimed] that he thought it no Crime for a Man to return into his own Country', and many of 'the Vulgar … [who] take Occasion to harrangue against the Severity of a Law that they do not understand', evidently concurred. The 'Waltham Blacks', a group of poachers executed in December 1723, were similarly 'hard to be persuaded that the Things they had committed were any Crimes in the Eyes of God', as 'Deer were wild Beasts, and they did not see why the Poor had not as good a Right to them as the Rich'. Nonetheless, 'as the Law condemned them to suffer they were bound to submit' and 'behaved themselves very orderly, decently, and quietly, while under Sentence'. Indeed, most 'social criminals', including those who complained of the severity of their sentences, seemed to have died well enough. John Catt, hanged in 1741, 'thought Smuggling an Offence, but no great Sin'; however, 'he behaved exceeding well, came always to Chappel, and was very devout and attentive, often weeping at the Thoughts of dying as a Criminal'. Charles Towers, executed in 1725 for participating in a riot with his face blackened, 'professed his Innocence in being in Disguise' (the point that, under the infamous 'Black Act', made his offence capital), complaining that 'the sentence of the Law was too severe', but 'own'd that the Judgement of God was exceeding just, for the many Offences he committed'. Many malefactors were seemingly eager to communicate that, as they accepted God's judgement, but not man's, they would make their peace with the former on their own terms, and as 'private' rather than 'public' sinners (i.e., criminals). According to three smugglers executed in 1749, refusing to make confessions, 'they knew best what they had done, and for what was amiss they would seek God's Forgiveness'.[16]

Many of the condemned who most loudly proclaimed their innocence were as ostentatious in 'forgiving' prosecution witnesses, judges and juries. Richard William Vaughan, executed in 1758 for counterfeiting, delivered a paper claiming that 'the Verdict against me was not just', but insisting that 'I freely forgive the Jury, and all the World, and die in Charity with all Mankind'. John Johnston, hanged in 1690 for kidnapping an heiress, spoke at length of his innocence and his many 'Hardships' and 'Tryals', but nonetheless reiterated that he did not 'find any Fault, or any ways arraign the Constitution of the Laws of Justice of the Nation, no I would not do that by any means'. Many of the condemned would claim (however disingenuously) to be resigned to their punishment because it was God's will, and thus providential. Henry Harrison, hanged in 1692 for murder, claimed to 'bless the day wherein I was falsely Accused: for by that means I was brought to a sense of my former sins'. Needless to say, he 'most heartily' forgave those 'who are the occasion of my Death', quoting various 'comfortable sayings' from the Bible – namely, Psalm 71:3, Matthew 11:28 & 17:11, 1 Timothy 1:15. Only the last makes any reference to repentance for sins; the others are all prayers for those persecuted unjustly. Harrison placed particular emphasis on Isaiah 3, the point at which the Bible opened after his condemnation: a chapter dealing with the oppression of the righteous by the unjust, and the eventual revenge of the former over the latter.[17]

In the context of a society in which everyone was guilty and deserving of death, but in which some 'public' sinners discharged their 'debt to nature' with more apparent alacrity than many seemingly respectable 'private' sinners, the relativity of guilt could easily translate into social critique. As we have seen, it was a commonplace of early modern rogue literature that while all men and women were rogues (and whores), great – or 'State' – villains not only committed with impunity the same kind of offences for which little rogues routinely hanged, but on a far greater scale. Little rogues were moreover 'honester' than their betters, not merely because their crimes were 'enterprized upon a Justifiable Score, the

Maintenance of Life', but because they (again, unlike their betters) were neither hypocrites nor cowards.[18] This critical discourse of relative culpability was rendered all the more powerful when coupled with an apparent willingness to die, the essential ingredient of the 'good death'. For although guilt and innocence were relative, God's judgement was absolute: you were either saved or damned. And it was widely believed that salvation or damnation could be demonstrated by both gallows speeches and performances and by sacred oaths and signs: literally, by calling God to witness.

CALLING GOD TO WITNESS: SACRED OATHS AND SIGNS

The central theme of seventeenth-century murder sheets was the providential discovery – whether through information passed on by the ghost of the deceased victim to his or her relatives or by other supernatural means – of those who had shed 'Mans Blood', a crime so heinous that God seldom or never 'suffer[ed]' it 'to go Unpunished even in this World'.[19] This discourse of providential discovery could be appropriated by those who believed that the execution of the innocent was tantamount to murder. At his trial, the Fifth Monarchist John James, executed in November 1661 for delivering a treasonable sermon, quoted Jeremiah 26:14–15: 'I am in your hands: do with me as seemeth good and meet unto you ... But know ye for certain, that if ye put me to death, ye shall surely bring innocent blood upon yourselves'. A partisan account of James's trial and execution concludes by enumerating the subsequent sudden deaths of several of his persecutors – including a woman who had been heard to say 'That Hanging was too good for them [Fifth Monarchists]', and a man who 'much rejoyced to hear that [James's] Head should be set up in the Street near his house', but did not live to see it put there.[20]

One popular belief that persisted even in educated circles into the late seventeenth century was that of 'cruentation', the notion that the corpse of a murdered person would bleed, or sometimes shed tears, if touched by the murderer. As Keith Thomas has suggested, this ordeal could prove a valuable tool of detection as the (guilty) suspect's own belief in this practice could result in a confession, or simply a reluctance to touch the body, in itself evidence of guilt – much like refusing to take a polygraph, or a 'lie detector' test today. John Palmer, one of two Worcester gentlemen executed for murder in 1708, refused to touch the body of the murder victim (his own mother) reputedly because when the other, Thomas Symonds, went 'near the Body', his 'Nose fell a bleeding, and which could not be stopp'd till he went from the Body; and upon his Return, fell bleeding afresh, and did not leave off till he left the Body again'. In 1726 the murderess Catherine Hayes attempted to demonstrate her innocence by ardently kissing the glass in which the decapitated head of her husband was preserved, even persevering in her attentions when the head was removed from the jar. (In this case, however, the very 'Assidu[ity]' of Mrs Hayes's behaviour was viewed as evidence of duplicity arising out of 'the Consciousness of her own Guilt' – thus demonstrating that the best methods of detection confirm what we already suspect.)[21]

This popular belief in cruentation – or some other revelatory symptom triggered by physical contact between murderer and victim – may have also been transposed to what were considered cases of judicial murder. In 1760 William Odell was convicted and hanged for beating his wife to death and, despite the fact that there was little doubt of his guilt, he died vehemently asserting his innocence. The main prosecution witness, Mary Middleton, a neighbour and friend of the deceased, claimed not only that Odell frequently abused his wife, but that shortly after the latter's death he had effectively admitted to having killed her. Afterwards, Middleton testified at the trial, Odell 'desired me never to tell any body, for if I told any body he said he should be hang'd; and if he was hang'd, he said he should walk to me again [i.e., haunt her]. I told him he never could'. Middleton's denial of Odell's ability to 'walk to her' probably reflected less rationalist scepticism than it did a popular belief that only those hanged unjustly could return to haunt their judges or prosecutors. Unlike the medieval ghost, who only wanted masses said for his soul, the early modern English ghost typically 'came to denounce some specific injustice', acting as a means of 'supernatural detection' of those crimes that would in the regular course of things go unpunished.[22]

It seems that Odell sincerely believed in his own innocence; he may well have told himself that as he had intended only to 'correct' his wife, not kill her, he was guilty only of manslaughter. In any case he repeatedly and solemnly swore to his innocence (although he was careful to say that 'he forgave the witnesses, and prayed to God to forgive them and turn their hearts'). On his way to Tyburn to be hanged, Odell 'made an odd request to the Sheriff', asking the latter, on his way back from the place of execution, 'to stop at the house of M[ar]y M[id]d[leto]n … with his body, and get her to touch it, or shake hands with him'. Presumably Odell hoped that Middleton's reaction to touching or viewing his corpse would demonstrate his own innocence, and thus literally lay his blood at her door. Despite the fact that by the middle of the eighteenth century few educated people subscribed to a belief in cruentation, 'Mr Sheriff with great humanity promised to perform his request'. When the officers carrying Odell's body to be hung in chains paid a visit to Middleton's house along the way, 'desir[ing] she would view it, and afterwards touch it', her husband denied them entrance, claiming that 'his Wife was sick in Bed', and assuring them that 'she persisted in her old Story, and that what she swore on the Trial was true'. One contemporary newspaper suspended judgement, but noted that 'the Case is dreadful either Way: an innocent Man's Life taken away, or he has died with a Lie in his Mouth'.[23]

Eighteenth-century execution crowds were known to deposit bodies of the condemned on the doorsteps of prosecutors and witnesses. In 1764, in compliance with the last request of a man hanged for returning from transportation before expiry of his sentence (a 'social crime'), the mob secured the man's corpse after execution and laid it at the door of the principal prosecution witness, where they 'behaved so riotously ... that it was no easy matter to disperse them'. In 1763, the body of Cornelius Saunders, a blind man executed for the theft of a large sum of money from a house, 'was carried and laid before the prosecutrix's door', where 'great numbers of people assembled', plundered the house, and set fire to a heap of assorted furniture and 'all the salmon tubs' (Saunders had claimed that he had not stolen but found the money in a 'salmon kit' he had bought from the prosecutor).[24]

Although belief in semi-miraculous providential discoveries was clearly on the wane in the eighteenth century, belief in the sacramentality of oaths had a much longer life. It is a testament both to the seriousness with which contemporaries viewed oaths and to the tenacity of the view that even the guilty should be subjected to a formal trial that defendants were barred from testifying on oath until 1898.[25] Similarly, defence witnesses could not be sworn until 1691, when this privilege was granted to witnesses in trials for treason; in 1707, this was extended to all felonies. Prior to these dates, defence witnesses 'spoke upon their Credits' only. In theory, of course, denying the oath to defendants and their witnesses was supposed to protect them from jeopardizing their immortal souls; in practice, it tended to privilege the evidence brought by the prosecution over that of the defence. Several of the peers who had bowed under those 'impetuous ... Oatesian storms' which 'noised [men] out of their lives' (i.e., the perjured evidence of Titus Oates), condemning the Earl of Stafford for the Popish Plot, were later to claim that although they had had serious doubts as to Stafford's guilt, they had felt 'bound to judge according to the proof of the facts; [for] the witnesses swore the facts'; in other words, that they had been obliged to credit prosecution testimony simply because it was sworn on oath.[26] Jurors during such periods of hysteria were of course subject to other pressures, particularly from the bench. At the trial of the five Jesuits, one judge told a (Catholic) defence witness not to worry as 'your provincial there [Whitebread] can give you a dispensation for what you say'. Not to be outdone in sarcasm, Scroggs instructed the jury that, although the defendants had been denied the 'favour' of having their witnesses sworn, the unsworn testimony of Catholics should nonetheless be regarded as of equal weight as that given under oath, for 'as they are of a religion that can dispense with oaths, though false, for the sake of a good cause', they were 'really to be believed much alike without an oath, as with one'.[27]

Defendants could attempt to overcome this handicap by using expressions which amounted to oaths affirming the truth of their words. John Gavan, for instance, continually provoked his judges by peppering his testimony with 'upon my salvation', 'upon my soul', 'upon my conscience', 'I call God to witness' or 'as I hope to see the face of God, I am innocent of what is charged upon me'.[28] While, in comparison, the trials of common criminals tended to be perfunctory affairs that did not allow for grandstanding, there were other ways in which accused men and women could sanctify their claims of innocence. As what made oaths binding was the presence of God as a witness, in theory He could be summoned merely by invoking His name (hence the prohibition against doing so in vain). In practice, however, contemporaries seemed to believe that a more powerful invocation was necessary – for instance, one performed within a sacred space.

Although the Ordinary and other clergy tried, largely in vain, to discourage this practice, many criminals clearly believed that oaths taken during the administration of the Lord's supper were particularly binding. Palmer and Symonds, executed in 1708 for murder, pressed so earnestly for the sacrament that they aroused the suspicions of attending ministers, and were forced to admit 'That the end for which they had desir'd the Sacrament, was, That protesting their Innocence upon receiving it, People might be induced to believe them innocent'. In 1738 Gill Smith 'earnestly desired' the sacrament 'because he wanted to clear his Conscience in relation for which he was then going to die'; when his request was granted, 'he declared in the most solemn Manner, that he was entirely innocent of the Murder of his Wife'. Some, like the robber Edward Burnworth, may have viewed themselves as serving a higher, rather than a literal truth: Burnworth would later admit that his 'averring to the Ordinary of Newgate, and offering to take the Sacrament upon the Truth' of his committing a crime for which another prisoner had been condemned, had been 'only a Contrivance between Jones and him, in order to save the other's Life'. When Burnworth saw 'the Skit would not Bear', he retracted the story, claiming 'that as he had liv'd with a Pistol in his Hand, so would he scorn to die with a Lye in his Mouth'.[29]

As I have suggested, oaths taken at the gallows carried particular weight, especially if accompanied by a calm, cheerful, charitable demeanour. At Tyburn, the convicted murderer and would-be revenant William Odell 'solemnly returned thanks to God, that he was as innocent as a babe'; and, despite being reminded by the Ordinary of the dire consequences attending such an oath if it were false, persisted in declaring 'his innocence, in the strongest terms, so as really to stagger [the Ordinary's] opinion of the veracity of the witnesses against him'. At his execution the ('trepanned') watchman John Hewlet 'was not satisfied with protesting his Innocence to the People, but designing to have one of the Prayer Books which was made use of in the Cart, he kissed it as People do when they take Oaths, and then again turning to the Mob, declared as he was a dying Man, he never gave Candy [the victim] a blow in his Life'. In 1720, when the highwayman John Trippuck was at the gallows, he rejected 'as an utter Falsity' the report that he had murdered a man, 'pointing to the Rope about him, said, "as you see this Instrument of Death about me, what I say is the real Truth"'.[30]

Many of those who prayed aloud at the place of execution also testified to their innocence, presumably relying on a popular assumption that the guilty would falter over the sacred words. In 1679, the convicted murderer Robert Freeman read 'all the way' to Tyburn, where he 'persisted in denying the Fact, with several solemn expressions, too tedious to be here related: he repeated the Lords-Prayer with much appearance of zeal, as likewise the Creed'. Thomas Carr, an attorney hanged in 1737 for robbery, convinced many contemporaries of his innocence by taking a solemn oath to that effect during communion; at the place of execution, he 'set the Psalm, reading every Line, with great Composedness'. At his 1730 execution, the street robber James Dalton requested that the penitential hymn 'the Humble Suit of a Sinner' be sung, after which he 'once more denied in the most Solemn manner, the Fact for which he was to suffer', before being turned off. Sometimes the choice of material was more pointed. Captain Joseph Halsey, hanged for murder in 1759, stubbornly maintained his innocence, although advertising 'his entire and humble resignation to the will of God'. He prayed 'repeatedly' for 'God to forgive his enemies, persecutors, and slanderers, and to turn their hearts', particularly 'those who had borne false witness against him'. Halsey requested that Psalm 35 (also expounding on the themes of 'false witnesses' and persecutors) be read out, both when he received the sacrament on the morning of his execution, and at the gallows. The Ordinary complied with the first request, but not the second, at which venue he saw fit to recommend 'a more evangelic temper'. The same year, the convicted murderess Mary Edmondson, who also insisted on her innocence, was reported to have relayed 'her last kind Love to the Rev. Mr King', asking 'that he will read in the Church the 139th Psalm' – another notably unforgiving psalm.[31]

And as we have seen, many game criminals who admitted the 'Fact' for which they were to suffer could nonetheless make powerful statements about their assurance of salvation. In 1733 the highwayman Richard Cass freely 'confessed that he had been guilty of all vices but doubted not but that there might be mercy for him'; slipped his own head in the noose, saying 'he had no occasion for a hangman'; recited the 'lord's prayer, without any trembling or change of countenance'; and then 'gently turned himself off the ladder, as if he were turning himself in bed'. Despite Cass's admission of guilt and his appearance of 'unconcern', the conclusion of the account leaves little doubt as to Cass's final destination.[32]

THE MEANING OF SUFFERING

While today we tend to view physical suffering as an evil in itself, both inhumane to the sufferer and demoralizing to the perpetrator, in a pre-Enlightenment context suffering was often seen as constructive, as a means to an end. Suffering could be redemptive in that it was, according to one historian of torture in early modern France, 'a positive technique for the destruction of selfishness, of ego, so as to make room in the heart for God', and diagnostic, in that it tapped 'the spontaneous truth of the body' which, unlike the mind, 'could not dissimulate'. Laura Gowing has written about the way in which midwives and other neighbourhood matrons would interrogate women in labour about the paternity of illegitimate children, and the weight accorded to solemn oaths sworn during this 'time of extremity'.[33] Execution specifically, although often referred to as an 'ignominious' end, had less shameful associations: the ultimate exemplar of the good death was of course Christ, who to redeem mankind also, in the words of a 1768 Methodist execution account, 'suffered the death of the Tree'. Moreover, in what is almost a complete reversal of modern popular perceptions, a lingering and painful death was considered preferable to a quick and painless one, as – in contrast to the dreaded *mors improvisa*, or sudden, unforeseen death – it granted the sufferer time to repent and to prepare to meet his or her maker. Condemned malefactors were in one sense ideal candidates for the good death, in that 'being humbled under the mighty Hand of God, they have become more eminent Objects of his Mercy, and fitly moulded for his saving Grace to work on'. Moreover, such 'monuments of free-grace' served to glorify God all the more because they were sculpted from common clay, reinforcing the Calvinist emphasis on the contrast between human depravity and unworthiness and divine omnipotence and magnanimity.[34] Scholars have argued that, after the Reformation, 'the criminal on the scaffold took over in Protestant folk culture the role which continued to be played by the statue of Christ on the cross'. In Catholic areas, in contrast, 'the doctrine of purgatory made it difficult to regard the holiness of executed criminals untainted' as 'the route [to heaven] was by no means direct or instantaneous for them'.[35]

Not merely torture, but any kind of suffering or proximity to death was believed to lay bare one's relationship to God and, by extension, one's guilt or innocence, at least in spiritual terms. One modern biographer of Oliver Cromwell recounts with some disapproval the fact that Cromwell reported 'without emotion' to Parliament the horrible spectacle of several priests and friars being burnt alive in a church during the siege of Drogheda in 1649, in which 'the voice of a miserable human torch was heard crying out: "God damn me, God confound me; I burn, I burn"'. However, for Cromwell this episode was significant, not because a human being suffered dreadfully, but in that it served as a vindication of the slaughter:

such blasphemous dying words would have been seen as conclusive evidence of the monk's reprobation – not to mention the falsity of his religion. For the elect, the prospect of death was supposed to inspire not curses, but elation. Thomas More, while imprisoned in the Tower of London awaiting trial, comforted his daughter Margaret in terms suggestive of nothing so much as sexual ecstasy: 'I finde no cause, I thanke God, Megge, to recken my selfe in woorse case [here] then in mine owne house; for me thinketh God maketh me a wonton, and setteth me vpon his lappe, and dandleth me'. Similarly, the Jacobite Colonel Oxburgh, while in Newgate awaiting execution, 'seem'd to put on the Wanton, like an Old Man that has Married a young Wife, on whom he Doats, so perfectly was he persuaded of the J[ustic]e of his Cause'.[36]

In an early modern context, suffering was popularly viewed as redemptive: after all, God was a strict but loving father who chastised His children in order to correct them and to bring them back to the straight and narrow. While post-Restoration orthodox churchmen (i.e., Anglicans) were distinctly uneasy about the older Calvinist investment in the idea of suffering as a sign of election, such notions persisted among Dissenters such as John Bunyan and Richard Baxter, the former 'rejoyc[ing]' at being the target of 'slanders, foolish or knavish lies', as Christ had ordained that victims of worldly persecution would be rewarded in heaven. The condemned murderer John Marketman believed that God had 'suffered me to fall into this last [sin; i.e., murder] as a means to draw me to himself' when lesser sufferings – 'Sickness, Poverty and the like' – 'would not awaken me'. Other criminals thanked God both for the 'mercy in the foresight of Death' He so generously bestowed and the time 'to prepare for it'.[37]

A related, and still more popular, belief was that 'pre-mortem' suffering was somehow purgative. Despite the fact that 'preachers repeatedly warned their audiences that God was not as merciful as people liked to believe' and that the popular notion that one's 'temporal sufferings' could make 'satisfaction to God's Justice for your sins' was a dangerously misplaced hope, many persisted in viewing salvation in terms of a balance sheet: their sufferings and sins, as credits and debits.[38] In the words of the penitential hymn 'the Humble Suit of a Sinner' (the same requested by James Dalton at his 1730 execution): 'Let me have, with Job, this Consolation, That afflicting me, thou would'st not spare me here, to punish me hereafter … let my punishment be here in this Life, that I may find thee to be a God of Mercy in the Life to come'. In February 1724, a group of condemned malefactors in Newgate 'abstain[ed] from eating and drinking, to humble themselves before God, and punish their bodies' for several days before their execution; the most zealous, a burglar named Stephen Gardiner, insisted on going to Tyburn dressed only in a thin burial shroud, 'tho' the Weather was very cold … for he was of Opinion, that he could not too much punish and afflict his Body for the Crimes he had committed': 'there must be an Attonement and

Compensation for vice, either in this Life, or in the next'. Several days before her 1720 execution for murdering a servant maid, Jane Griffin could 'not be perswaded to sit on a Chair, but would sit on the Floor saying that she ought to humble herself in Dust and Ashes ... to attone for her Crime', asking the Ordinary 'if it was proper' to accept visits from her husband, and 'if she might go to Bed any more?' The street robber Robert Wilkinson, no model penitent, was denied the sacrament after refusing to 'unburthen his Conscience' to the Ordinary; nonetheless, he declared that 'if he might not go to Heaven as the rest did, he hop'd to find the Way by himself'. As he 'had heard that Fasting was a good Expedient for that Purpose' he 'neither eat nor drank for three Days and three Nights before his Execution'. William Faulkner, another robber turned unconventional penitent, 'acknowledg'd that he had been a notorious criminal' for 'which God had justly afflicted him', and insisted on sleeping in his coffin for the three nights preceding his 1735 execution.[39]

William Odell, like many who claimed to be unjustly condemned, also professed to take 'great comfort, that he was to suffer innocently ... and hoped that he should be forgiven his other sins, on account of his present suffering patiently, and without cause'. Here the Ordinary reminded him that his sins could only be forgiven through 'the merits of Christ's sufferings, and not his own'. Odell, seemingly willing to 'correct his wrong opinion', settled on a compromise position: he 'might have gone on in his other sins, to the end of his life if God had not brought him to repentance ... to save him ... by this dreadful and awakening punishment'. As we have seen, this providential discourse was adopted by many other criminals who acknowledged their guilt, but whose sufferings (they believed) exceeded their crimes. Charles Weaver, hanged for murder in 1723, 'hop'd that his Misfortunes, like those of the prodigal Son, had reclaim'd him; and that he should attain to the Portion of the Righteous, by dying the Death of the Wicked'. William Bond, hanged for returning from transportation, 'hoped he should find, for his suffering here, the less Punishment hereafter'; similarly, the robber Thomas Burden 'comfort[ed] himself with the Hopes that his temporal Punishment here, might preserve him from feeling everlasting Misery'. The highwayman John Trippuck even removed his shirt and showed the Ordinary of Newgate 'a great Number of Scars' including several old bullet wounds, asking, 'will not these good Doctor ... and the vast Pains I have endured in their Cure, in some sort lessen the Heniousness [sic] of the Facts I may have committed?' (He was assured they would not.)[40]

If purgatorial beliefs survived in slightly transposed form in popular culture, so too it seems did even older notions relating to the ordeal. Certainly, there was a persistent conviction that those who died well – embracing their punishment willingly and without signs of resentment or fear – were assured of salvation. There had always been some dissenting voices, to be sure: in a 1631 sermon,

John Donne questioned the notion that those who died without 'reluctation' were saved, rather than simply being in the grip of 'a dangerous damp and stupefaction'; for 'the Tree lies as it falls; 'Tis true; but yet it is not the last stroke that fells the Tree; nor the last word, nor last gaspe that qualifies the Soul ... Our Criticall day is not the very day of our death, but the whole course of our life'. Yet the argument itself is testament to the prevalence and tenacity of such beliefs.[41]

The practice of *peine forte et dure*, the punishment meted out to prisoners who 'stood mute', or refused to plead at their trials, provides a vivid illustration of how popular convictions about suffering, justice and true manly courage intersected in seventeenth- and eighteenth-century England.[42] By the sixteenth century, the unfortunate person sentenced to the *peine forte et dure*, or to be 'pressed', was tied or chained spreadeagled and face up on the floor, naked 'except for something to hide his Privy Members', while 'as much Iron or Stone, as he can bear, and more' was 'laid upon his Body' until, in theory, he expired. *Peine forte et dure* had its origins in the replacement of trial by ordeal by trial by jury after 1215, and is thought to have been a corruption of *prisone forte et dure*, a term of 'hard and severe imprisonment' imposed on those who refused jury trial, rather than execution proper; 'pressing' to death was a late medieval refinement. However, by the late seventeenth century *peine forte et dure* seems to have been viewed (by the court, at least) as a means to induce a plea rather than as a slow form of execution, an intention demonstrated by the preliminary punishment of tying the 'mute' prisoner's thumbs together tightly with whipcord, 'that the pain of that might compel him to plead' which, after the Restoration, became 'the constant practice at Newgate'.[43]

There were always some recalcitrant prisoners, like the pickpocket Mary Andrews, who, 'notwithstanding the Admonition of the Court, was so obstinate as to suffer three Whipcords to be broke in tying her Thumbs', or the robbers William White and Thomas Thurland, who remained 'contumnacious' even after their thumbs 'were tied together with Whipcord and drawn by the whole Force of two Men ... above a Quarter of an Hour'. Most, including Andrews, White and Thurland, eventually backed down, cowed perhaps less by the whipcord than by hearing the dreadful sentence of being pressed to death pronounced in court. But there still remained a handful of men like the robber James Parker, who 'forced' the court 'to commit him to the press', and was 'very much bruised ... before he would recant his obstinacy'.[44] Why, then, would individuals subject themselves to what was by all accounts a dreadful and excruciatingly painful death? The conventional explanation has been that they wished to escape both the 'corruption of blood' and the forfeiture of estate that a felony conviction would entail. However, even if prisoners who were pressed to death could bequeath their estates to their heirs (and some judges seemed to believe that death by *peine forte et dure* constituted a felon's death and hence *did* entail 'corruption of blood'), not only were moveable goods forfeit, but the bulk of the condemned were in any case property offenders with no estates or property worth confiscating. Moreover, by the late seventeenth century, juries seem to have routinely returned the judgement that convicted felons had 'no goods'; even in the case of more wealthy offenders, according to the Swiss commentator Cesare de Saussure, the crown only 'very rarely' exercised its privilege of confiscating estates, 'almost always giv[ing] up these possessions in favour of the families of the criminals'.[45] So, while concern for securing titles and property for one's heirs may have been uppermost during the late medieval period, by the late seventeenth century the most likely motivations for undergoing the press seem to have been the desire to preserve one's reputation or to express one's rejection of the tribunal – or, as we shall see, both.

Some prisoners who refused to enter a plea were simply obstructionist, like John Durant, who at his 1734 arraignment claimed to be deaf – and unable to read – although several court officers claimed that he could hear 'when they baul'd to him in Newgate'. (After some thumb-tying and threats of pressing, Durant's hearing improved enough for him to plead not guilty.) Others were animated by spite: in 1727 Thomas Johnson, alias 'Handy', refused to plead to his indictment for theft, 'saying, the Prosecutors thought to hang him for the sake of the 40 Pounds allowed by the Government [as a reward], but he would baulk their Expectations, for he would be hanged for returning from Transportation ...' 'Handy' (so called because he had the use of only one hand, the other having atrophied after a childhood accident) had been transported for theft but, 'as he alleg'd, he was forc'd to come Home' before serving out his sentence, because 'No Body would buy him, because he wanted a Hand'. Johnson finally consented to take his trial, and the jury found him guilty of a single (i.e., non-capital) felony. But 'upon his Confession', the luckless Handy was indicted for returning from transportation, a capital offence. He was hanged a little over two weeks later.[46]

Most prisoners who 'stood mute' were attempting (however unsuccessfully) to strike some sort of bargain with the court. At the Old Bailey in 1673, David Pearce and William Stoaks refused to hold up their hands, claiming they were being tried in the wrong jurisdiction, the robberies with which they were charged being committed in Rutlandshire. When their hands were forcibly raised, 'they replied, although their hands were forced up, their tongues should not be forc'd to speak'. (Holding up one's hand at the bar both identified the defendant and indicated that he or she was willing to put him or herself on 'the country', or jury; refusal to do so was a form of 'standing mute'.) They were given a day in which to decide whether they would take their trial or be 'prest', eventually opting for the former. Similarly, in 1728, the highwayman James Harris refused to plead on the grounds that he had cooperated with authorities and thus should be admitted as an evidence (i.e., be granted immunity from prosecution). He, too, thought better of it after being threatened with the press and being given a day to reconsider, although not before a show of bravado in which he claimed 'he could but die, and the Manner in which he died was indifferent to him'. In 1770 George Powditch, indicted for breaking out of prison while he was under sentence of transportation for stealing a sack of peas, 'refused to plead, unless the Judge should promise, that in case he should be convicted, his sentence should not be transportation again'. The judge 'remonstrated' sternly with him, and read out the sentence of *peine forte et dure*. Powditch, too, eventually backed down, but not before cursing the judge ('You may die and be d — d yourself'); on his way out of the court, he knocked down the hangman for good measure. In this way Powditch succeeded in ensuring that he was not transported, but rather hanged.[47]

Others demanded the return of money, clothes, and other items taken from them upon arrest. According to a 1692 'Act for encouraging the apprehending of Highwaymen', the 'Horse, Furniture, and Arms, Money or other Goods' of suspected robbers could be divided amongst those who had brought them to justice, even before the accused had been brought to trial (although such items were supposed to be returned in the case of acquittal). Once again, most who, like the highwayman Henry Cooke in 1741, refused to plead until their goods or money were returned to them, thought better of their 'resolution' after it became clear that the court was serious in its threats to subject them to the press. Upon their arraignment in 1726, the street robbers William Blewitt and Emanuel Dickenson 'refused to plead till their Irons were taken off'; they were accordingly 'freed of their Hand-Cuffs' and then 'said they would be content to stand in their Fetters, and give the Court no farther Trouble'. But Edward Burnworth, the leader of their gang – a macho type and an amateur boxer, nicknamed 'Frasier', after a famous prize fighter – remained adamant, 'absolutely refusing to plead, till his Hat and Periwig, and a Gold Watch, that the Constables and others took away … were return'd again'. 'Continuing contumnacious' even after the usual preliminaries, Burnworth was at last subjected to the press, where for a little over an an hour he endured a weight of over three hundred pounds on his chest, 'endeavouring to beat out his Brains against the Floor' while 'the High Sheriff … frequently exhorted him to plead to the Indictment; which at last he consented to do'.[48]

In a similar episode in 1721, the robbers Thomas Cross and William Spiggot announced that unless their property was returned, 'they would not Plead notwithstanding all the Admonitions that could be given them', and were accordingly sentenced 'to be prest to death'. While Cross quailed at the sight of the Press Room, Spiggot, 'continuing still Resolute', withstood a weight of 350 pounds for a half an hour; upon another fifty pounds being added, however, he 'beg'd that he might be carried back to plead, which Favour was granted'. Later that same year, yet another young robber ('not 20 Years old'), Nathaniel Hawes, 'affecting to appear unconcerned', refused to plead until a 'handsome Suit of Cloaths' was returned to him. After several 'Cords' were broken on his thumbs to no avail, Hawes was put under the press, where he lay for 'about seven Minutes … under a Weight of 250 lb.' until at last 'he desired to be carried back'. At his trial, he 'said nothing in his Defence, and only insisted on having his Cloaths returned'.[49]

Even more so than those of the condemned who refused to acknowledge their guilt, prisoners who refused to plead posed an implicit challenge to the legitimacy of the court. Indeed, at least one contemporary acknowledged that the press was applied to those prisoners who 'refused to plead *or contest the authority of the tribunal over [them]*' (my emphasis). As the late eighteenth-century jurist Daines Barrington noted, 'the common reason given [is] that the prisoner must acknowledge the jurisdiction of the court'. After reading out the sentence of *peine forte et dure* to Nathaniel Hawes, the judge went on to lecture him on the 'equity of the law of England', its '[tenderness] of the Lives of its Subjects', and the 'Humanity of our Constitution' in framing 'so fair, so equal a Trial' presided over by a court which acted as 'Council' to the accused, and 'twelve honest Men ready to enquire impartially into the Evidence that shall be given against You'. The exertions of early modern courts to grant even avowedly guilty defendants a trial were often invoked as evidence of the particular mercy of the English criminal law. But many property offenders clearly resented the nature of early modern English trial, in that it functioned like a modern sentencing hearing – placing more emphasis on assessing the character of the accused and the likelihood of his or her rehabilitation than on examining the facts of the case. Far from being impartial and objective, early modern jurors, like the judges themselves, would have recognized repeat, or 'old Offenders' such as Burnworth, Spiggot and Hawes. Moreover, the same men who served on Old Bailey juries (many of them, repeatedly) often had first- or second-hand knowledge of the accused in their capacity as masters, employers, constables, poor law officials or other parish officers. Thus, refusal to plead may well have reflected a more generalized resistance to a form of trial that tended to deny the accused an active voice, placing more emphasis on the discretion of social superiors – prosecutors, judges, juries and character witnesses – than the (unsworn) testimony of the defendant.[50]

There is no doubt that those who administered the seventeenth- and eighteenth-century criminal law were in a position to exercise 'naked power', and perhaps nowhere more so than in the courtroom, where impressions were all important, and gestures of penitence and deference could make the difference between life and death.[51] Men like William Spiggot, Nathaniel Hawes and Edward Burnworth, repeat offenders whose robberies were compounded with violence, had scant hopes of acquittal or pardon to begin with. Nonetheless, those of the accused who, like George Powditch, 'insulted the Court' – or even those who, like Thomas Johnson alias 'Handy', displayed an unbecoming disregard for the seriousness of their predicament – in effect signed their own death warrants. When, in 1728, the highwayman James Harris attempted to withhold his plea as a bargaining tactic, 'the Court informed him, that they would enter into no Altercutions with a Prisoner at the Bar'; when Harris 'persisted obstinately' in his refusal to plead, 'he was told from the Bench, that such a Behaviour was not a Method proper to excite the Mercy of the Court ...' Men and women who refused to plead or who attempted to impose conditions on the court violated a culture of deference that, nominally at least, made mercy conditional upon the observance of certain forms. Not least of these was the ritual by which those whose sentences of death were commuted or who received full pardons were obliged to beg such pardon on their knees; even those who were acquitted were also made to bless both the monarch 'and all the honourable Court' while kneeling. We can only imagine how much it would have rankled Edward Burnworth's pride to be forced to make, on his knees, a 'Humble Application to the Judge that his Sentence of being press'd to Death might be remitted' – all so that he could be tried on capital charges, convicted and hanged.[52]

Overt violations of courtroom deference seem to have been fairly rare, although difficult to quantify: while sometimes mentioned in the Ordinary's *Account* (in the context of the chaplain upbraiding the condemned for previous misbehaviour), such incidents tended to be omitted in the Old Bailey *Proceedings*. In 1734 Guthrie 'reprov'd' the young burglar George Peters 'for Cursing at the Bar, when he was convicted'; the Irish highwayman Patrick Dempsey, hanged in 1750, was supposed to have been drunk at his sentencing, where 'as if in Defiance of all Law and Justice, he wore his Hat in the Court', and loudly insisted on the innocence of his co-defendant (who, it was believed, was his younger brother), 'taking the whole Villainy on himself'. The robber Robert Lake 'insolently turned about, and put on his Hat, uttering some taunting and opprobrious words' when the jury brought in the verdict of guilty at his 1752 trial. At his 1770 conviction, Charles Stevens also put on his hat, 'with an air of great contempt', and stalked out of the courtroom saying, "Tis well you can do no worse.' Newspapers sometimes reported on the courtroom antics of more famous criminals: in 1724, Jack Sheppard was told by the court that he could only hope for 'his Majesty's Clemency' if he made 'an ingenuous Discovery of those who abetted and assisted him in his last Escape'. Sheppard replied that he 'had not the least Assistance from any Person, but God Almighty', and was duly 'reprimanded for prophaning the Name of God'. Seemingly piqued at the imputation that he had needed an accomplice to effect his famous, second, escape from Newgate, Sheppard then 'told the Court, that if they would let his Handcuffs be put on, he, by his Art, would take them off before their Faces, but it was not agreeable to the Solemnity of the Court to let him play his Tricks there'.[53]

However rare – or infrequently reported – violations of this culture of courtroom deference could, briefly at least, tear the veil from what one scholar has termed the 'public transcript': the normative, but inherently unstable discourse purporting to legitimate and to normalize power differentials between dominant and subordinate groups.[54] In May 1679, during the height of public belief in the Popish Plot, one John Morgan was tried and condemned as a Catholic priest, an offence made capital under a 1585 Act, but rarely enforced to its fullest rigour. Morgan was offered a pardon but created a stir when he 'could very hardly be brought to accept of this Pardon, or to Kneel whilst it was read, alledging that he had committed no Crime, needed no Pardon, had not sued for this, &c.' Court officers were left with several undesirable alternatives, both of which would provide Morgan with a platform upon which he could testify to the righteousness of his cause: they could force him to his knees or let him hang. Luckily, a third alternative presented itself: citing the currently credible 'Testimony of Doctor Oates and others that he was somewhat maddish', the court 'excused his extravagancy' and thus 'got him into the Pardon' despite his refusal to beg for it. Thus Morgan's challenge to the justice and mercy of the court was dismissed as a species of irrationality, even insanity. Interestingly, similar arguments would be deployed against those early eighteenth-century game highwaymen and robbers who refused to submit to jury trial. The Ordinary of Newgate attempted to impress upon Nathaniel Hawes that 'Fool-hardiness was not Courage', and 'that to be Unconcern'd at his Disasters, was not a laudable Bravery, but a stupid Insensibility'. This equation of plebeian 'Boldness' with wilful irrationality was echoed in the judge's final appeal to Hawes after the latter had been sentenced to the *peine forte et dure*: 'what hinders then, that you should submit to so fair, so equal a Trial, and wherefore will you by a Brutish obstinacy, draw upon You, that heavy Judgement which the Law has appointed for those who seem to have lost the rational Faculties of Men?'[55]

It is, in our secular age, difficult to appreciate the early modern valorization of courage as a kind of sacramental article, and the degree to which even a professed willingness to embrace suffering and death lent legitimacy and force to the implicit challenge to the court that standing mute represented. Significantly, *peine forte et dure* could theoretically extend not only to those who refused to plead, but to anyone who in general rejected the tribunal. After a defendant in 1664 challenged thirty-six prospective jurors, so that he could not be tried, the panel of judges decided 'that he should be hanged and not pressed to death', despite the fact that precedent suggested 'that he should be pressed as a Person that refused the Law'. As John Langbein has pointed out, even after trial by jury had become 'the regular mode of proof in cases of serious crime', it still 'retained', at least in popular memory, 'its consensual element'. According to one late eighteenth-century legal commentator, 'the common question asked the criminal, viz. Culprit, *how wilt thou be tried*? is improperly answered, *By God and my country*. It originally must have been, *By God* or *my country*, i.e. either by *ordeal* or by *jury*; for the question asked, supposes an option.' And clearly, many prisoners who refused to plead did so, under the pretext at least, that they chose to be tried 'by God' rather than the jury. At the 1615 trial of Richard Weston for poisoning Sir Thomas Overbury, Weston being 'demanded how he would be tried, he answered, he referred himself to God, and would be tried by God; refusing to put himself and his cause upon the jury or country'. Weston – who, it seems likely, was not technically guilty of the murder, although almost certainly involved in the poisoning – persisted in this refusal for some time, despite all the remonstrations of Sir Edward Coke, the Lord Chief Justice, who, after reading out the awful sentence of *peine forte et dure*, allowed him until the following Monday to reconsider. (Weston did in the end take his trial, pleading not guilty; he was convicted and hanged.)[56]

Some late medieval examples of *peine forte et dure* suggest that the punishment was originally viewed as an ordeal which could be 'passed'. In 1384 one John atte Puttes 'was pardoned after enduring peine forte et dure for so long it seemed a miracle he remained alive'; in 1359, Cecilia Rygeway, accused of murdering her husband, received a full pardon after she survived without food or drink for forty days 'after the manner of a miracle and contrary to human nature'. Moreover, cultural memories of the press as a trial 'by God' rather than a jury of one's peers seem to have persisted. In 1586 the Catholic martyr Margaret Clitherow died under the press after refusing to plead to charges of harbouring Jesuits and priests, claiming that if 'I must be tried, I will be tried by none but by God and your own consciences'. Clitherow denied that 'she sought her own death' (a mortal sin); rather, she refused to take her trial out of 'a marvellous charity' both to her neighbours and family, so that they would not be called to testify against her, and to her prosecutors, so that they would not be made 'accessory to [her] death'. She endured all the indignities and privations of her imprisonment with a 'joyful countenance' that detractors attributed to a 'merry devil', and supporters to her having 'received comfort from the Holy Ghost'; finally going 'cheerfully to her marriage, as she called it'. A sharp stone was placed under Clitherow's back, presumably to hasten her death; she expired after bearing 'seven or eight hundred-weight at least' for fifteen minutes.[57]

There are several seventeenth-century accounts of criminals suffering under the *peine forte et dure*. In perhaps the most famous case of all, that of Giles Corey, pressed to death during the Salem witch hunt, Corey reportedly refused to subject himself to what he clearly believed to be an unjust tribunal, 'knowing there would be the same Witnesses against him' and the same jury that had 'cleared none [of the others accused of witchcraft] upon Tryal'. In 1672, Henry Jones, who confessed to having murdered his own mother, refused to take his trial, apparently believing that, since his crimes were so 'odious both in the sight of God and man', being pressed to death was a fitter punishment than hanging. We are told that Jones suffered under the press for almost two days before expiring, 'yet endured it with that courage and patience, as become one that was sensible that his sins were washed away in the blood of Iesus'.[58] Most instances of individuals undergoing the *peine forte et dure*, however, emphasized not so much a desire to purge sins as to demonstrate a manly courage that was its own proof, if not of innocence, then of a kind of righteousness. (Margaret Clitherow constitutes a special exception: her courage, like that of Foxe's female martyrs, would have been classified as masculine; the ability to transcend feminine weakness with a 'manful' or 'christian constancy' or 'manly stomach', evidence of divine assistance.)[59]

This equation of an appropriate manly courage – a 'stout, but Christian-like manner of dying' – with relative (if not strictly legal) innocence is illustrated by the case of George Strangwayes, pressed to death in 1658 for refusing to plead to the charge of murdering his brother-in-law. Strangwayes, a former Cavalier officer whose life had been hitherto characterized 'by a constant course of worthy and manly actions', tacitly admitted involvement in the crime, but denied having intended or committed murder (and seemed to demonstrate his innocence by taking his 'dead Brother-in-law by the hand, and [touching] his wounds'). With what was evidently considered a proper mix of 'courage and contrition', Strangwayes justified his decision to undergo the *peine* by the fact that 'each man oweth a death, I two by this untimely fact: The one to my maker, the other to the Law'; moreover, he claimed he would 'pay the one the more willingly, being confident that the other is cancelled by the all-seeing eye of divine Mercy and justice'. Strangwayes wore all white to his execution, advertising the eagerness of his soul 'to meet her Celestial Bridegroom', and dying with a 'Christian confidence' and 'Passive Valour (high as ever was his Active)' that left no doubt as to his ability to discharge all metaphysical debts.[60]

And although commentators were quick to dismiss the posturing of eighteenth-century game criminals as mere bravado or 'false courage' – 'that silly contempt of death, which with the Vulgar Passes for Resolution' – the equation of true manly courage with righteousness continued to resonate in popular culture. In 1721 Nathaniel Hawes 'refus'd to plead, saying, that as he had liv'd like a Man, he was resolv'd to die so, and not be hang'd in such a shabby coat as he then appear'd in'. Yet Hawes ('with a great deal of warmth') denied that 'he chose pressing because the Court would not let him a good suit of Cloaths to be hanged in'; rather, he claimed, 'as he had lived with the Character of the boldest Fellow of his profession he was resolved to die with it'. Hawes exemplified what one chronicler described as perhaps the most 'dangerous' of all the 'many odd notions which are pick'd up by the common People' – the 'Idea they got of Courage, which with them consists either in a furious Madness, or an obstinate Perseverance, even in the worst Cause'. Needless to say, that 'great Affectation of Intrepidity and Resolution' which Hawes 'always put on' was rooted entirely in 'Vanity' and a lamentable concern for 'Reputation'. Pride and concern for reputation indeed figured largely in the 'Reasons' William Spiggot gave for 'enduring the Press' (probably in ascending order): 'that he might preserve his Effects for the Use of his Family, that it might not be urged to his Children that their Father was hang'd, and that Lindsey the Evidence, should not tryumph over him by saying he had sent him to Tyburn'. Certainly he would, as the 'Spiggot that bore 350 lb. wt. on his Breast', earn a berth among the most 'eminent Convicts' cited in advertisements for an edition of the *Select Trials* published twenty years after his death.[61]

But the attempts of these men to bargain with and to challenge the court cannot be explained solely in terms of ignorance or misguided vainglory; rather, they opened up a space in which they could for a time both seize the initiative (or, as historians would now say, exercise 'agency') and demonstrate their resolution and courage – attributes which were always at a premium, but whose worth could be tested, theoretically, against divine truths: for as a portal to death, the press, no less than the gallows, was imbued with a kind of sacramentality. At the heart of such displays of bravura was the rejection of a tribunal apparently calculated to undermine or suppress such performances. When Edward Burnworth was asked why he had subjected himself to the press, he said 'it was because they design'd to make Fools of him and his Comrades, by appointing their Trial for an April-Day' (they were tried on April Fool's Day). As Nathaniel Hawes proclaimed at his arraignment: 'the Court was formerly a place of Justice, but now it was become a place of Injustice; that he doubted not, but that they would receive a severer Sentence than that which they had pronounced upon him [pressing]'. But 'for his part', he declared, 'he made no question of dying with the same Resolution with which he had often beheld Death, and leave the World with the same Courage with which he had lived in it'.[62]

Conclusion: The Adjournment of God's Tribunal?

> The broadsides disappeared [in the late eighteenth century, along with] the glory of the rustic malefactor and his sombre transformation into a hero by the process of torture and execution ... The man of the people was now too simple to be the protagonist of subtle truths. In this new genre [detective novels] there were no more popular heroes or great executions; the criminal was wicked, of course, but he was also intelligent; and although he was punished, he did not have to suffer ... The split was complete; the people was robbed of its old pride in its crimes; the great murders had become the quiet game of the well behaved.
>
> Michel Foucault, *Discipline and Punish*

In an essay published in the *Annual Register* in 1770, two years before *peine forte et dure* was abolished by statute, several gentlemen in a coffee-house expressed their 'astonishment' at the 'folly' of 'the shocking wretch who refused to plead to his indictment at Kingston' – that is, the same recalcitrant George Powditch discussed in the previous chapter.[1] Their conversation, while fictional, nonetheless reflects the degree to which, by the second half of the eighteenth century, educated people viewed the *peine forte et dure* as irrational and benighted – one of an increasingly discomfiting constellation of legal practices that enlightened thinkers castigated as barbaric, such as the drawing and quartering of men, and the burning of women for treason. Still more significantly for our purposes, it also reveals the general lack of first-hand knowledge of, or familiarity with, capital or aggravated punishments on the part of late eighteenth-century polite gentlemen (not to mention ladies). One gentleman reflected that the 'best defence' of this otherwise 'ridiculous regulation or institution' was 'the infrequency of its application', going on to claim that he believed that there was 'but one instance of a person's having gone through with it since the last century, who was a master of a ship, charged with piratical practices'. He seemed to be referring to John Smith alias Gow, who was threatened (but not in fact subjected) to the press in 1725. Interestingly, there is no mention of the rash of game criminals pressed in the 1720s, nor of John Weekes, a man executed under the *peine forte et dure* at the Sussex assizes in 1735.[2]

A similar selective amnesia extended to the aggravated death sentence of burning women for treason. By the 1780s newspapers routinely assumed that women executed for treason were burnt alive, despite details of such executions often found in the same papers demonstrating that the women in question were, in fact, first strangled to death. While such assertions served to publicize and to condemn a practice viewed with increasing horror and repugnance by readers (and, indeed, by the City officials who were obliged to oversee the sentence), they also seemed to suggest that, by the later eighteenth century, few genteel or middling people – aside from a few cranks like George Selwyn – actually attended executions. In 1786, Lord Chief Justice Loughborough claimed that there was no need to abolish this provision, as 'this sentence ... was rarely inflicted ... so that the burning for coining was not inflicted above once in half a century'. The implication is that Loughborough did not think this punishment excessive in the case of petty treason; that is, the murder by a woman of a husband or master. Moreover, Loughborough was mistaken even about female coiners, at least three of whom had been burnt in London since 1750.[3]

In contrast, various newspaper accounts of the 1726 execution of Catherine Hayes for the murder of her husband took note of the fact that there had been a 'special Order ... sent to the Sheriff' for Hayes to be 'burnt alive, without the Indulgence of being first strangled as is customary in such cases'. Apparently Hayes was singled out to suffer the full 'Rigour of her Judgement' both because the crime had been 'aggravated by such Circumstances of Wickedness & Barbarity' and 'to deter others from Offences of so heynous a Nature'. Several accounts of Hayes' execution reported that, when the wretched woman 'begg'd for the Sake of Jesus, to be strangled first', the executioner relented, tightening the noose around her neck, but almost immediately dropped it again when his hand was singed by the flames. But by the 1770s, when the issue of the burning of women began to be revisited in the press, newspaper readers evidently lacked a familiarity with execution ritual that reporters in their parents' and grandparents' day seem to have taken for granted.[4]

As we have seen, by the later eighteenth century, public interest in the printed accounts of the lives and the last dying words of those ordinary property offenders who, presumably, lacked the requisite sensibility to fully engage the sympathy of respectable readers, was sharply on the decline. By 1775 the Ordinary of Newgate's *Account* was defunct; newspapers reported briefly on only the most remarkable crimes and provided minimal details of the behaviour of the condemned; pamphlets tended to concern themselves only with the crimes and indiscretions of the aristocratic bigamist or adulteress, the occasional eminent murderer or gentleman highwayman or genteel forger, such as Dr William Dodd or the Perreau brothers.[5] While the street-robbers, housebreakers and pickpockets who had dominated the pages of earlier accounts continued to live on in various late eighteenth- and early nineteenth-century 'Newgate Calendars', their lives were repackaged and effectively refurbished for a class of readers who viewed them as exotic relics of a 'gross and brutal' and 'bloodthirsty' age, long since thankfully consigned to the proverbial dustbin of history. Francis Place, shocked at the lewd advertisements and 'ignorant gross ungrammatical' style of the Ordinary's *Account* (although, almost invariably, the objectionable material singled out was in fact penned not by the Ordinary, but inserted by Applebee in the Appendix), contrasted the depravity of the eighteenth-century reading public with the comparative respectability of that of the early nineteenth century. Many subsequent nineteenth- and early twentieth-century commentators found such publications so morally reprehensible that they simply assumed that the audience for eighteenth-century criminal literature was primarily if not exclusively 'vulgar', and 'that the largest proportion of these papers and books circulated among the criminal population'.[6]

Interestingly, the Old Bailey *Proceedings* (or Sessions Paper), briefly continued to flourish after the mid-eighteenth-century editorial crisis and the subsequent decline of its former sister publication, the Ordinary's *Account*. Although the Sessions Paper provided only brief, third-person summaries of trials in the late seventeenth century, after about 1715 reportage became more extensive, often taking the form of verbatim, first-person accounts. The *Proceedings* tended to devote most copy not to the common property offenders who made up the bulk of defendants (and whose trials often continued to be briefly summarized), but to those cases which either involved eminent or notorious offenders or crimes – murder, for instance – or were particularly salacious, such as rape, sodomy and 'stealing from the person' – generally, prostitutes picking the pockets of their clients. The decline of the *Proceedings* as a commercial publication after the 1770s reflects not so much a decreasing interest in trial accounts per se, but the degree to which increasing pressures on the part of the City for the Sessions Paper to offer a more official and comprehensive account of trial interfered with its profitability. By the later eighteenth century the longer and comparatively expensive *Proceedings* could no longer compete with newspaper accounts, which were not only published more frequently (and were thus able to 'scoop' headlining sessions news) but also had the advantage of being able to report only on the most interesting or notorious trials.[7]

But the early eighteenth-century rise of verbatim trial reportage of common criminals (transcripts of trials of traitors and other notable political prisoners had, of course, been widely published since the seventeenth century) is significant not least because it reflected, and perhaps reinforced, a generic distinction between defendants and other courtroom actors and the audience for the Sessions Paper. If last dying speeches traditionally presented the criminal as a 'Seamark' to warn readers, or a glass through which they could see their own frailties – in effect, an 'Everyman' with whom they were intended to identify – verbatim trial reportage invited the audience to adopt the perspective of judge and jury. Shorthand trial reporting mercilessly, and sometimes comically, recorded the blunders, inanities, and verbal idiosyncrasies of working-class English and immigrant deponents. In one 1725 trial an Irish prosecutor, whose accent the *Proceedings* attempted to recreate by rendering his 's's' into 'sh's', described how the accused, a prostitute, attempted to 'shit' in his lap. After a 1727 trial in which the prosecutor's stutter (or hiccoughs – he may have been drunk) punctuated his particularly ineffectual testimony, the editors inserted a less than convincing disclaimer insisting that the trial was reported 'directly as it was spoken' only to emphasize the importance of 'proper Terms of Speech' in the courtroom, 'and not to please the vulgar part of the Town with Buffoonery, this not being a Paper of Entertainment'. On rare occasions, defendants themselves appropriated the role of buffoon, presumably as an expression of their contempt for the proceedings. In their 1722 trial the Irish highwaymen James Carrick and John Molony 'made a very frivolous Defence', 'attempting to rally the Evidence that was produced against them, and to make the People smile at their Premeditated Bulls'. In his cross-questioning of a prosecution witness, for instance, Carrick insisted that he had been holding *two* pistols during the robbery, not one, as the witness had testified. For the most part, however, the courtroom was an arena in which defendants could exercise little agency, and where 'Premeditated Bulls' originated from the other side of the bar.[8]

To some degree the decline of the investment in the criminal as a kind of an 'Everyman' reflected a changing discourse of guilt, as Enlightenment notions undercut traditional assumptions about universal human depravity. It was only after the early eighteenth century that the much-vaunted 'presumption of innocence' believed to ensure 'the peculiar excellence' of the English criminal law began to make significant inroads. In the 1720s Saussure reported that 'Englishmen say that it is better that twelve culprits should escape human justice rather than one innocent man should perish'. The 'very just Maxim' – that is, 'that it is better that ninety-nine guilty Persons should escape, than one innocent Person should suffer' – was, by the second half of the eighteenth century, one 'generally admitted by all moralists', and enshrined in Blackstone's *Commentaries* (although there scaled down to ten to one). In 1767 the Ordinary of Newgate rhapsodized about the 'peculiar excellence of our laws', in which 'every person accused is presumed to be innocent' and 'treated with every degree of tenderness and humanity'. It is significant that by 1775 one newspaper, claiming it was 'impossible … for a Man of humane Feelings to view a procession to the public Place of Execution, without being inspired with a Wish to prevent the Necessity of exhibiting such horrid Spectacles', implicitly invoked the presumption of legal innocence in defence of moral reform. 'There is surely more Merit in saving one Member of Society from destruction, than in punishing a hundred' – a 'Duty' incumbent on those 'Parish Officers, to whom are entrusted … the Morals of the lower Ranks of People'.[9]

This concern for the sanctity of human life (not to mention the overtly class-specific definition of criminality) was a radical departure from earlier notions emphasizing not only original sin, but also the relative insignificance of this world compared to the next. The space between sentencing and execution was, in the late seventeenth and early eighteenth century, commonly invoked as evidence of the 'particular Clemency' of the English criminal law, affording the condemned time to 'make their Peace with God, and by their sufferings under the Hands of Men, prevent eternal Condemnation'. Respites were typically granted not so much to those whose guilt was in doubt, but rather so that the guilty 'may the better prepare themselves for their latter end'. Indeed, the worse the crime, the more likely the chances of a respite. Jack Blewit, condemned in 1714 for rape and murder, successfully requested a fortnight's respite 'as his Crime was Heinous'; in 1657, the murderer Nathaniel Butler, through the efforts of the Mayor of London and 'other judicious Persons', was granted 'a longer time than usual to prepare for another world'. In 1679 the Bishop of London obtained a respite for the disgraced minister Robert Foulks, who had murdered his own bastard child; the previous year, the murderer Thomas Short, 'his Crime being of the deepest Die ... had more time than usual allowed him to repent'.[10]

By the mid-eighteenth century, however, priorities had visibly shifted. The 1767 pamphlet *The Cries of Blood, or the Juryman's Monitor*, enumerated various 'extraordinary' miscarriages of justice, and warned that 'judges and magistrates cannot be too tender and diffident in inflicting capital punishments upon their fellow creatures'. Newspapers which paid scant attention to the execution of common criminals invoked those 'melancholly' cases in which innocent people were hanged as warnings to 'Mankind' to be 'more cautious in Swearing, where Life is concerned', and expressing the conviction that the King would, if informed, surely intervene to put an end to incidents which 'must fill every breast with grief, indignation, and horror'. The late eighteenth-century Ordinary John Villette added his voice to the chorus, warning 'Prosecutors and Witnesses' that they could not 'be too tender and scrupulous in giving Evidence ... where the Life of a Person ... is concerned'.[11]

City officials, too, seemed increasingly prone to such scruples. In 1769 the sheriffs of London and Middlesex delayed the execution of Moses Alexander for over three hours because they thought that a reprieve might be forthcoming; although Alexander was hanged after none materialized, such a delay was itself unprecedented. In 1773 Francis Talbot was granted a respite of a week after one of his fellow sufferers declared his (Talbot's) innocence at the place of execution. The following year Patrick Madan obtained a reprieve after a spectator in the execution crowd announced that he had committed the crime for which Madan was (literally) about to be hanged. In another dramatic incident in 1777, the Ordinary of Newgate and the deputy sheriff abruptly halted an execution when, at the last minute, one of the condemned confessed that he had falsely impeached his fellow prisoner John Whitaker, also about to be hanged. An urgent message was sent to the Secretary of State but, upon learning that both the latter and the King were unavailable, the deputy sheriff took it upon himself to stay Whitaker's execution – or, as the reporter, quoting Shakespeare, described it, 'To do a *great* right', he 'did a *little* wrong'. Not only was Whitaker subsequently pardoned but, according to a foreign observer, 'the King also pardoned the under Sheriff who had assumed a power he was not invested in by right, and the approbation of the whole kingdom was the reward of his firmness'.[12]

Older beliefs locating the site of divine justice at the gallows gradually gave way to the conviction that the secular courts could, and should, act as the ultimate arbiters of guilt and innocence. In a literal sense, the pre-eminent tribunal of justice shifted from the place of execution to the criminal courts with the passage of the Murder Act in 1752. This statute was intended to underscore the connection between cause (crime) and effect (judgement) by stipulating that convicted murderers be sentenced immediately after their trials and hanged within two days of sentencing – or three, if one of the intervening days was a Sunday. Thus, those very criminals who would in the late seventeenth century have been able to make a strong case for a respite (in the interests of preventing their eternal perdition), were now executed immediately 'in order to impress a just Horror' of the crime and its (temporal) punishment – following much the same advice as that given by Henry Fielding the previous year in his *Enquiry into the Causes of the Late Increase of Robbers.*[13] The causal connection between crime and human retribution arguably received further reinforcement in London after 1783, when the site of execution shifted from Tyburn, located on the outskirts of the city (and at a crossroads, traditionally seen as a liminal space), to the Debtor's Door outside Newgate, a stone's throw from the Old Bailey courthouse, as well as from Surgeon's Hall where, under the provisions of the 1752 Murder Act, the bodies of condemned murderers were publicly anatomized. Not only the abolition of the Tyburn procession, but the mechanics of the new execution ritual itself – in which all of the condemned fell simultaneously through a drop or trap door under their feet, dying (theoretically) almost immediately from having their necks broken – served to detract attention away from individualized gallows gestures and behaviour, the signs traditionally so carefully scrutinized by execution-goers.[14]

Increasingly, too, the gallows lost its centrality in moral discourse. Once individuals could express seditious politics by 'hanging Tyburn with mourning' (draping the gallows in black cloth), as Charles Newey was accused of doing after the death of Queen Mary in 1694. In 1739 glovemakers reacted to competition from stocking weavers by hanging Tyburn 'with women's Thread and Cotton Gloves, to disgrace the wearing of them'. And while such gestures were made impracticable by the removal of the permanent gallows in 1759, the old associa-tion between the gallows and justice and injustice (or 'gallows symbolism') lived on in the popular imagination, as V. A. C. Gatrell has argued: as late as the 1830s, radical sheets inverted conventional morality by depicting judges' wigs hanging on the gallows. As I have suggested, such beliefs and practices had a much longer purchase in popular than in elite culture. Ephemeral gallows publications were printed or sung in the streets well into the nineteenth century, and the highwayman in particular continued to have cultural resonance and vitality in popular culture long after he had been adapted for the consumption of middling and upper-class children by being both bowdlerized and safely consigned to a mythical past.[15]

The notion that cultural practices and beliefs persist longest in popular culture is both disappointingly commonsensical and suspiciously nostalgic. Just as the middle class is always rising, the notion that the gulf between popular and elite culture is always widening has become something of a historical cliché. Yet few historians would deny the basic assertion that the world-view of the average educated gentleman or woman changed fundamentally between 1675 and 1775, a shift particularly apparent in the decline of gallows confessions and last dying speeches. This was not only a matter of elites distancing themselves from outmoded or superstitious practices but, as I have suggested, ordinary criminals themselves clinging tenaciously to an older moral explanatory paradigm and the notion of the gallows as a sacralized space. Much in the same way that scholars of popular culture have written about 'chase and flight' – in which fashion is not simply a function of 'trickledown' from above, but generated and even initiated by pressures from below – this process may reflect not only the degree to which people with power are more quick to adapt and to shape new discourses in order to maintain cultural hegemony, but also the ability of the socially and economically disadvantaged to appropriate older discourses to question social and legal inequities.[16]

It is perhaps more helpful to view this cultural transformation not in terms of secularization – a hard claim to substantiate, especially given the mid- and late-eighteenth-century Evangelical Revival – but desacralization; that is, the abandonment of older beliefs and practices predicated on the conviction that 'the sacred, non-material world could be present in, and experienced through, the profane and the material'.[17] What we see is less a decline than a redefinition of religiosity: over the course of the eighteenth century, educated Englishmen and women eschewed 'enthusiasm' and providentialist beliefs for a 'rational religion' in which rationality was both a human and divine attribute, and a means of perceiving and demonstrating the perfection – and benevolent reasonableness – of God's immutable laws.[18] 'Laicization' is perhaps a better term still: the optimistic conviction that laymen and women could live a holy life, and pursue a programme of moral and social reform in this world.[19] This apparently narrowing gulf between human potentiality and divine perfection entailed both a reconfiguration of God as a tolerant and loving father, and the eighteenth-century 'decline of hell'. Daniel Defoe complained of those of his contemporaries who 'will acknowledge a God', but only 'such a one as they please to make him; a fine, well-bred, good-natured, gentleman-like deity, that cannot have the heart to damn any of his creatures to an eternal punishment, nor could be so weak as to let the Jews crucify his own son'.[20] Rationalism had, of course, its reaction, both in the form of Methodism and early Romanticism. John Wesley – who saw the latitudinarian and rationalistic tendencies of mid-eighteenth-century Anglicanism as fatal first steps down a slippery slope towards natural religion or 'Materialism', deism and, inevitably, atheism – lamented the desacralization of the world, believing that the repudiation of a belief in witches and apparitions 'is, in effect, giving up the Bible'.[21]

But even if the belief in a sacralized universe remained deeply embedded in popular culture well into the nineteenth century,[22] from the middle of the eighteenth century most educated people, at any rate, agreed that God no longer intervened directly in human affairs.[23] In Old Testament times, as the evangelical Hannah More explained in regard to Joseph's gift of prophecy, 'signs and wonders were … used, in order to prove that the God of Joseph was the true God. But now we no longer need signs and wonders, for the Holy Scriptures plainly declare him to us'. God's judgement no longer manifested itself in the workaday world through sacred signs; rather, His dictates were best obeyed by heeding that monitor or 'principle' that 'the wise Creator of our Beings has implanted [within] us' – namely, one's conscience. Criminal literature similarly reflected a shift from an older emphasis on the soul, often characterized as feminine and described as external to the individual, to an internalized 'Conscience, that Natural Magistrate of every Man's Heart', the seat of one's (rational, and thus presumably masculine) moral faculties.[24]

By the middle of the eighteenth century, most educated Englishmen and women had abandoned the conviction that dying well or bravely had metaphysical correlations. Increasingly, the discourse of courage, like that of God's judgement, became internalized as it was gradually disentangled from divine truths and increasingly seen as a function of education and character. Historians of the duel have noted that, by the second half of the eighteenth century, the outcome of the contest was less important than the demonstrable courage of the participants; moreover, this courage was evidenced not by an 'active assertion of bravery' but rather by 'more passive demonstrations of 'courage', of standing firm in the face of fire'.[25] As Samuel Richardson's eponymous hero Sir Charles Grandison would demonstrate, the calm refusal to engage in a duel was itself the strongest proof of courage. Grandison, who exemplified the perfect mid-eighteenth-century gentleman much in the same way that his female counterparts, Pamela and Clarissa, embodied ideals of feminine virtue and sensibility, is a model of civility and humanity. He treats the Italian lady with whom he was romantically entangled and her Catholic relatives with courtesy, forbearance and charity; he even refuses to conform to fashion by docking his horses' tails (although otherwise anxious to avoid the appearance of 'singularity'), on the grounds that this would interfere with their ability to protect themselves from insects. Most importantly, Grandison's courage (fortunately never in doubt, thanks to his early rescue of the English heroine from the clutches of an abductor) is of the 'charmingly-cool, because truly brave' variety: that is, he is master of his passions.[26]

Grandison refuses a challenge from the villainous Pollexfen not because he lacked spirit – 'I am naturally passionate. You know not the pains it has cost me, to keep my passion under' – but because he refused on principle to draw sword 'but in my own defence'. If this was interpreted as cowardice, so be it: 'I live not to the world: I live to myself, to the monitor within me'. Nonetheless, Grandison sees fit to demonstrate to his 'challenger … that he has better motives than fear, for his refusal', going alone to visit Pollexfen and a number of his dissipated companions. Many pages are devoted to describing the steadiness of Grandison's voice, hand, and principles, as he calmly remonstrates with Pollexfen and his associates, finally vanquishing even them with the ocular demonstration that 'the man, who can subdue his passion, and forgive a *real* injury, is an hero'. Grandison concludes by explaining that 'it is perhaps as happy for you as for myself, that I have a fear of a higher nature' and would 'not dare to risque the rushing into my maker's presence from the consequences of [such] an act'; nonetheless, he stresses, '*Be the event what it will, the test you would provoke me to, can decide nothing as to the justice of the cause on either side*' (my emphasis).[27]

Less than one hundred years separate John Gavan, the Catholic martyr, and Sir Charles Grandison, that Anglican paragon of manly civility, yet they stand on either side of a vast cultural divide. The secret springs, or inner workings, of those men and women who rejoiced at the prospect of a traitor's death, or who willingly subjected themselves to the *peine forte et dure*, are hardly less opaque to us than they would be to the average educated late-eighteenth-century gentleman. There is an immense gulf between the world of John Gavan, who died because he was a Jesuit, but who embraced his death so cheerfully and so bravely that he effectively trumped the rulings of the secular courts, and that of Charles Grandison, who was willing to marry a Catholic and to respect her religion (although without abandoning his own), and who refused to fight duels because it was morally wrong to endanger his own life or someone else's. It is a gulf so wide that, from the vantage point of the twenty-first century, we can hardly see our way across it.

Appendix A: The Ordinary's Account

Origins: Samuel Smith was the first Ordinary to publish regular accounts of the confessions, behaviour and last dying speeches of the malefactors executed at Tyburn, beginning about 1676 (one of his early seventeenth-century predecessors, Henry Goodcole, had published a few execution sheets, but on an occasional basis only). The earliest accounts refer to the Ordinary in the third person and are not regularly signed – a signed January 1678/9 account of the execution of several men implicated in the Popish Plot is probably exceptional. After 1684 Smith assumes a first-person authorial voice and begins to conclude his paper with his name, title and the date. Although the wording varies, such signed attestations thereafter become standard; for example, 'This is all the Account I can give of this Sessions. Dated January 29. Sam. Smith, Ordinary'. It is probably not coincidental that this same year, 1684, the *Account* became semi-official (published by authority of the City of London).

Title: Like the earliest *Old Bailey Proceedings* (OBP), or Sessions Paper, the Ordinary's paper was published under different titles in the seventeenth century; for example, *The Confession and Execution of the Prisoners Suffering at Tyburn* …; *The Behaviour, Confession, and Execution* …; *The Execution, last Speeches & Confessions* …; *A True Narrative of the Confession and Execution* …; *Fair Warning from Tyburn* …; *The Last Dying Speeches and Confessions* …; *A True Account of the Prisoners Executed at Tyburn* … After 1701, it assumed its standard title: *The Ordinary of Newgate His Account of the Behaviour, Confessions and Dying Speeches of the Condemned Criminals that were Executed at Tyburn*, followed by the date. (This title was subject to minor variations, for instance in the number of malefactors executed; in cases where only one or two were hanged, their names might be included in the title.)

Forgeries: Forgeries of the Ordinary's *Account* or competing publications (such definitions were relative; the Ordinary viewed all other last dying confessions as 'Sham-Papers') were very common in the late seventeenth century, a time when the *Account* had not yet assumed a standard title. Sometimes forgeries can be identified by comparing the name of the printer to that of the authentic *Account*, although this can be difficult in the seventeenth century when it was common

for the same printers to alternate between publishing the Ordinary's paper
and those of competitors. Genuine accounts contain the text of the Ordinary's
sermon and, after 1684, his subscription. Even after the standardization of the
title of the *Account* after 1700, some forgeries persisted, often published under
the Ordinary's name, slightly misspelled; for example, 'Paul Lorrane', 'Lorain'
or 'Larrain' instead of Paul Lorrain; 'T. Pureny' instead of Thomas Purney (the
misspelling of Purney's name as Puyney in a 24 September 1722 *Account* is
probably a typographical error, however; the *Account* seems genuine otherwise,
and is published by the regular printer, John Applebee). Sometimes a misspelled
version of the name of the printer of the genuine *Account* indicates a forgery; for
example, an imprint reading 'John Appleybee' instead of John Applebee.

Format (organization): From the late 1670s to the middle of the eighteenth
century, the *Account* retained the same core format: a brief summary of the
sessions at which the criminals were condemned, often including a list of those
subsequently reprieved (occasionally substituted in early *Accounts* for various
moral discourses); a recapitulation of the Ordinary's sermons and a report on
the behaviour of the condemned in chapel and in their cells, followed by short
biographies of all the condemned and finally a section (titled, after about 1720,
'At the Place of Execution') detailing the dying behaviour of the malefactors.
The earlier *Accounts*, especially those published under Paul Lorrain (1700–1719)
ran various advertisements after the Ordinary's subscription; after the 1720s,
the number of advertisements decline sharply. From about 1732 to 1744, an
'Appendix' containing additional material relating to the condemned (accounts,
correspondence, etc.), is often added to the *Account*; from 1740–44, the paper is
often issued in two Parts. From 1745, the Appendix is abandoned and sermons
generally omitted or replaced with essays or editorials on moral and social issues.
There is in later accounts more discussion of the malefactors' crimes and trials,
rather than their 'confessions' per se, although the final section (now called 'On
the Morning of Execution'), is retained.

Format (appearance): The earliest Ordinary's *Accounts*, in the late 1670s, were
generally from six to eight octavo pages; they were published in the early 1680s on
folio broadsides (i.e., one large sheet folded to make up four pages), and from the
late 1680s on single double-sided broadsides, reverting to longer octavo pamphlets
after 1712 to evade the Stamp Act (10 Anne, c. 19), a tax aimed at single sheets,
but exempting pamphlets (generally defined as publications longer than five or
six pages). The *Account* returned to double-sided broadside (four-page) format in
May 1725 after this loophole closed (11 George, c. 8). The *Account* would remain
at four pages until late 1730, occasionally including more text with the addition of
a third column. After about 1732, the *Account* is numbered and, from mid-1745

to the late 1760s, paginated consecutively according to the mayoral year. After December 1730, and particularly under the period of John Applebee's editorial control (late 1735 to late 1744), the *Account* lengthens dramatically: about 15–20 pages and often over 20 pages after 1733; after 1732, the *Account* often includes an 'Appendix' or (from 1740 to 1744) additional parts, frequently running to about 40 pages. After Guthrie sacks Applebee in late 1744, the Appendix is discontinued and the *Account* decreases in length (usually between 12 and 20 pages).

Printers (initials are given when full names are unknown): Seventeenth-century Ordinary's *Accounts* alternated between a wide variety of printers, many of whom would also publish competing papers at different times.

1670s: The principal printers of the Ordinary's *Account* from 1676 to 1680 are David Mallet; Langley Curtiss, with a few (probably competing) accounts published by R. G. and Thomas Pankhurst, T. Davies; others (certainly competing accounts) do not bear a publisher's imprint.

1680s: The principal printers in the early 1680s are Langley Curtiss and Elizabeth Mallet; George Croom publishes official account from 1684 to 1685 (with Elizabeth Mallet, Langley Curtiss, E. R. and Randal Taylor publishing competing papers); from 1686 to 1689 Elizabeth, and later David, Mallet publish the official account (George Croom, and J. C. publish competing papers); from 1689 to 1693 Langley Curtiss takes over as the Ordinary's printer (competing papers printed by J. C., Richard Baldwin, W. Brown, Randal Taylor); from 1693 to 1703 Elizabeth Mallet prints official account (J. Johnson, J. Williams publish competing accounts).

1700s: Elizabeth Mallet continues as the regular printer of the official *Account* until 1703–4; from 1704–5 Joseph Downing is printer; Dryden Leach prints the *Account* from 1706 to 1707; in October 1707 T. Bradyll (with Benjamin Bragg as bookseller) publishes the *Account*; from December 1707–1709/10 Benjamin Bragg is publisher (B. Briggs and H. Hills publish competing accounts).

1710s: John Morphew is the printer of the *Account* from 1710 to 1718 (James Blow publishes a competing account); S. Briscoe becomes printer in 1719; J. Jefferies (with J. Morphew as bookseller) publish the *Account* briefly in 1719, reverting again to Samuel Briscoe in June 1719.

1720s, 1730s, 1740, 1750s: John Applebee prints the *Account* from January 1719/20 to December 1744; J. Watson prints the March 1744/5 *Account*; Mary Cooper is printer from June 1745 to at least June 1746 (there is a competing account written by an anonymous clergyman printed by J. Thompson on 4 April 1746); Thomas Parker and C. Corbett publish the *Account* from August 1746 to

February 1754 (Parker sometimes listed alone); Thomas Parker and R. Griffiths from April 1754 to 1758; from May 1758 to March 1759, T. Parker is listed as printer and Mary Cooper as bookseller (a June–July 1758 execution account published under a different title is printed by Stephen Roe, the Ordinary, and sold by Cooper); from November 1759 to at least September 1760, Mary Cooper is listed as the bookseller.

1760s, 1770s: There are unfortunately insufficient data for this period to attempt an exhaustive or exact list of printers/booksellers. *Accounts* are sometimes described as being printed for the author – i.e., the Ordinary – after about 1760. Mary Cooper often acts as bookseller in the early 1760s; J. Dixwell and J. Hinxmen are also listed as booksellers in this period. M. Lewis is listed as bookseller in 1763; in early 1764 J. Cook is printer, and the *Account* is billed as 'sold by all Booksellers and News Carriers'; M. Lewis resumes publication of the *Account* from June 1764 until early 1765; the April–May 1765 *Account* is sold by J. Meres; M. Lewis ('and Son') resumes publication of the *Account* in September 1767; J. Kingsbury *et al.* are listed as booksellers in a 22 November 1769/14 February 1770 *Account*; M. Lewis prints and sells what may be the last two regular *Accounts* (27 May 1772 & 8 July 1772).

Price: between about 1¼ to 2 pence in the seventeenth and early eighteenth century; generally between 2 and 3 pence in the 1720s and early 1730s; and after about 1733 ranging from 4 to 6 pence, but generally 6 pence; price is almost invariably 6 pence after 1739.

Time/Frequency of publication: The Ordinary's *Account* was published up to eight times a year in the late seventeenth and early eighteenth century, and sold the late morning or afternoon of the day of execution. In the seventeenth century, it would seem that most of the copy was prepared in advance, with a brief concluding section concerned with the behaviour of the condemned at Tyburn added later. Rival seventeenth-century publications claimed that the Ordinary's paper was published *before* the execution had actually taken place in order to get a leg up on the competition (see, for instance, *A True Account of the Behaviour, Confessions and Last Dying Words of Captain James Watts [et al.] … who were Executed at Tyburn* [18 December 1684], p. 5); such complaints persisted into the early eighteenth century, with the disgruntled former printer of the *Account*, Dryden Leach, claiming that he had 'not only been with Mr Lorrain in Newgate, with the last dying Speech (as it was call'd) in my Pocket, but have had the Copy for Mr Lorrain 2 Days before the execution very frequently' (*A True Account of the Behaviour, Confession and Last Dying Speech of John Herman Bryan … [24 October 1707], p. 2). After the 1730s – and particularly after the 1752 Murder

Act, which ruled that condemned murderers should be executed within two days of sentencing (three, if one of the intervening days was a Sunday) – when two sessions are often combined in one, there are sometimes as few as five or even four numbers. The *Account* seems to die out as a regular serial after the late 1760s, although it is briefly revived in the early 1770s under John Wood.

Appendix B: Ordinaries of Newgate, 1676–1799

Earlier ministers of Newgate include Henry Goodcole, who described himself as a 'Minister' and 'Visiter' of Newgate and who published several accounts of notable confessions and executions from 1618 to 1635; John Weldan (or Welden), appointed Ordinary on 28 July 1663; Henry Gerrard, identified as Ordinary in July 1669; and Edmond Cressy, Samuel Smith's immediate predecessor, who died in the late spring of 1676.

Samuel Smith: 15 June 1676 until his death on 24 August 1698. (Smith's eldest son was reported as officiating as Ordinary between his father's death and the appointment of John Allen.)

John Allen: 10 October 1698 until his dismissal for corruption on 30 May 1699.

Roger Wykes: from about June 1700 until his death in October 1700.

Paul Lorrain: 7 November 1700 until his death on 10 October 1719. Thomas Browne acts as a temporary replacement between Lorrain's death and Thomas Purney taking up the office.

Thomas Purney: 17 November 1719 until he ceases to act as Ordinary due to ill health in September 1725 (Purney dies on 14 November 1727). During Purney's leaves of absence due to illness in the summer of 1724 and the winter of 1724–5, James Wagstaff officiates in his stead; after September 1725, James Guthrie becomes acting Newgate chaplain.

James Guthrie: Newgate chaplain after Purney becomes ill from 29 September 1725 and after Purney's death, but only officially instated as Ordinary on 19 February 1733/4 (winning out over competitor Samuel Rossell). Guthrie serves until he is dismissed, ostensibly because of ill health and old age, on 14 May 1746.

Samuel Rossell: 17 June 1746 until his death on 12 March 1747. (Between Rossell's death and Taylor's appointment, James Paterson officiates as Ordinary, although he does not publish any *Accounts*.)

John Taylor: 12 May 1747 until his resignation on 28 June 1757, pleading his great debts.

Stephen Roe: 12 July 1757 until his death on 22 October 1764.

Joseph Moore: 20 November 1764 until his death on 20 June 1769. Few of Moore's *Accounts* survive after 1765, perhaps suggesting that the paper was briefly discontinued in this period.

John Wood: 18 July 1769 until he first takes leave of absence in May 1772 and formally resigns in January 1774 due to ill health. The *Account* seems to have been published only sporadically under Wood's tenure. The Methodist minister Silas Told officiates as acting Ordinary in Wood's absence and before Villette's appointment.

John Villette: 8 February 1774 until his death on 25 April 1799. Villette compiles *The Annals of Newgate* (1776); publishes a few pamphlets on the execution of prominent malefactors, and early in his tenure (1774–5) provides accounts of the confessions and speeches of malefactors to several newspapers (e.g., *Morning Chronicle; and Evening Advertiser; The Gazetteer and New Daily Advertiser*), but does not resume the regular publication of the *Account*.

SOURCES

1. CLRO, Court of Aldermen Repertories, 69 f. 172, 80 f. 154b seq; 81 f. 216b; 82 f. 214b; 104 f. 340; 105 ff. 6–7; 124 ff. 23–4; 137 f. 438; 137 f. 438; 138 f. 115; 138 f. 210; 150 ff. 240–1; 150 ff. 284–6; 151 f. 251; 161 ff. 321–3; 161 f. 357; 168 f. 357; 169 ff. 13–15; 173 f. 427; 173 ff. 451–3; 176 ff. 269–70; 178 f. 65; 178 ff. 103–5; 203 f. 257

2. *Notes and Queries*: 10th series, volume viii (6 July 1907), entry by William McMurray, 10; 11th series, volume iii (4 February 1911), entry by Horace Bleackley, 86; 11th series, volume iii (4 March 1911), entry by Bleackley, 173.

3. Horace Bleackley, *The Hangmen of England* (1929; repr. in *State Executions Viewed Historically and Sociologically*. Montclair, New Jersey: Patterson Smith, 1977. Patterson Smith Series in Criminology, Law Enforcement and Social Problems. Publication No. 170).

4. Newspapers: *The Post Boy* 3–6 September 1698; *The Flying Post* 13–15 September 1698; *Weekly Journal; or, British Gazetteer* 10 October 1719; *London Journal* 23 February 1733/4.

Notes

Notes to Preface

1 J. P. Kenyon, *The Popish Plot* (Harmondsworth, 1972), ch. 5; *Lying allowable with Papists to Deceive Protestants* ... (1679), long title.

2 See, for instance, *An Impartial Consideration of Those Speeches ... of the Five Jesuits*, long title; Samuel Smith (Ordinary of Newgate), *An Account of the Behaviour of the Fourteen Late Popish Malefactors*, long title. See also *The Speeches of the Five Jesuits; The Behaviour, Last Words, and Executions of the Five Grand Jesuits ... Who all justly Suffered ...; The Last Speeches of the Five Notorious Traitors and Jesuits; An Answer to the Reflections on the Five Jesuits Speeches*; Israel Tongue, *The New Design of the Papists Detected; An Answer to Blundell the Jesuit's Letter; The Justification; Proving* [the five Jesuits] *Died as Innocent as the Child Unborn* (all published in 1679); see also trial and pamphlet accounts reprinted in *State Trials*, 7:311–418.

3 *State Trials*, 7:492; Burnet, *History of his own Time*, 2:223.

4 Michel Foucault, *Discipline and Punish: The Birth of the Prison*, trans. Alan Sheridan (London, 1977), p. 46.

5 Arlette Farge, *Fragile Lives: Violence, Power and Solidarity in Eighteenth-Century Paris*, trans. Carol Shelton (Cambridge, MA, 1993), p. 199; Pieter Spierenburg, *The Spectacle of Suffering: Executions and the Evolution of Repression* (Cambridge, 1984), p. 43.

6 Sharpe, 'Last Dying Speeches', p. 159.

7 Linebaugh, 'Tyburn Riot' and *London Hanged*; Gatrell, *Hanging Tree*, esp. ch. 4; Thomas W. Laqueur, 'Crowds, Carnival and the State in English Executions, 1604–1868', in A. L. Beier, David Cannadine and James M. Rosenheim, ed., *The First Modern Society* (Cambridge, 1989).

8 Peter Lake with Michael Questier, *The Antichrist's Lewd Hat: Papists, Protestants and Players in Post-Reformation England* (New Haven, 2002), p. 228; see also Andrea McKenzie, 'Martyrs in Low Life? Dying "Game" in Augustan England', *Journal of British Studies* 42 (April 2003), 167–205; Peter Lake and Michael Questier, 'Agency, Appropriation and Rhetoric under the Gallows: Puritans, Romanists and the State in Early Modern England', in *Past & Present* 153 (1996), 64–107; and Hal Gladfelder, *Criminality and Narrative in Eighteenth-Century England: Beyond the Law* (Baltimore and London, 2001), pp. 55–7.

9 J. A. Sharpe, 'Civility, Civilizing Processes, and the End of Public Punishment in England', in Peter Burke, Brian Harrison and Paul Slack, eds., *Civil Histories* (Oxford, 2000), pp. 221–22.

10 Michael J. Braddick and John Walter, eds., *Negotiating Power in Early Modern Society: Order, Hierarchy, and Subordination in Britain and Ireland* (Cambridge, 2001), pp. 35–6, 9.

11 D. R. Woolf, 'The Rhetoric of Martyrdom: Generic Contradiction and Narrative Strategy in John Foxe's Acts and Monuments', in Thomas F. Mayer and D. R. Woolf, eds., *The Rhetorics of Life-Writing in Early Modern Europe* (Ann Arbor, 1995), p. 252; Lake and Questier, 'Agency, Appropriation and Rhetoric', 69; Alexandra Walsham, *Providence in Early Modern England* (Oxford, 1999), p. 5.

12 John Langbein, 'The Criminal Trial before the Lawyers', *University of Chicago Law Review*, 45 (1978), esp. 272, 315, and 'Shaping the Eighteenth-Century Criminal Trial', *University of Chicago Law Review*, 50 (1983), 4–166; Linebaugh, 'Ordinary of Newgate'; Harris, 'Trials and Criminal Biographies'.

13 Peter Lake, 'Popular Form, Puritan Content? Two Puritan Appropriations of the Murder Pamphlet for Mid-Seventeenth-Century London', in Anthony Fletcher and Peter Roberts, eds., *Religion, Culture*

and Society in Early Modern Britain (Cambridge, 1994), and 'Deeds Against Nature: Cheap Print, Protestantism and Murder in Early Seventeenth-Century England', in Kevin Sharpe and Peter Lake, eds., *Culture and Politics in Early Stuart England* (London, 1994).

14 Francis Place Papers, BL Add Ms 27825, Vol. 1: Manners, Morals.

Notes to Chapter 1: From Newgate to Tyburn: Setting the Stage

1 *Hell upon Earth: or the most Pleasant and Delectable History of Whittington's Colledge, Otherwise (vulgarly) called Newgate* (1703), p. 11; see alternate versions in *The Whole Life and Conversation, Birth, Parentage, and Educations of Thomas Browning [&c]* (1712), p. 6, Francis Place Papers, BL Add Mss 27826, ff. 25–6, and W. Eden Hooper, *History of Newgate and the Old Bailey* (London, 1935), pp. 112n–113n. The Bellman or sexton of St Sepulchre's was paid a stipend in accordance with the bequest of a charitable Jacobean citizen; see John Stow, *A Survey of the Cities of London and Westminster*, revised ed. (1720), pp. 17, 270.

2 OA 4 May 1722, pp. 3, 5–6.

3 *LMRC*, 1:143, 1:148. The fate of the soul between death and resurrection was a controversial and divisive issue among Protestants: while orthodox Anglicans viewed the theory that the soul 'slept' until the Day of Judgement as heretical, many were also uncomfortable with the notion that the saved rested in 'the Bosom of Abraham' in that it suggested the possibility of an intermediate place between heaven and hell and thus smacked uncomfortably of the Catholic doctrine of purgatory. See Peter Marshall, '"The Map of God's Word": Geographies of the Afterlife in Tudor and Early Stuart England', in Bruce Gordon and Peter Marshall, eds., *The Place of the Dead: Death and Remembrance in Late Medieval and Early Modern Europe* (Cambridge, 2000), p. 117.

4 OA 4 May 1722, p. 5.

5 *LMRC*, 1:147; OA 4 May 1722, p. 6.

6 King, *Crime, Justice, and Discretion*, esp. ch. 9.

7 OA 4 May 1722, pp. 4, 6.

8 See, for instance, Walter Besant, *London in the Eighteenth Century* (1902; repr. London, 1925), p. 549.

9 Douglas Hay, 'Property, Authority and the Criminal Law', in Hay *et al.*, *Albion's Fatal Tree*; see also King, *Crime, Justice, and Discretion*.

10 Beattie, *Crime and the Courts*, p. 431. The courts were not so lenient before the Restoration; see K. J. Kesselring, *Mercy and Authority in the Tudor State* (Cambridge, U.K., 2003), p. 78.

11 OBP 4–6 April 1722.

12 Roger Finlay, *Population and Metropolis: the Demography of London, 1580–1650* (Cambridge, 1981), p. 51; E. A. Wrigley and R. S. Schofield, *The Population History of England 1541–1871: A Reconstruction* (London, 1981), pp. 531–4.

13 *The Journals of Two Travellers in Elizabethan and Early Stuart England: Thomas Platter and Horatio Busino* (London, 1995), pp. 36, 148 (The journals date from 1599 and 1617–8, respectively); William Harrison, *The Description of England*, ed. Georges Edelen (Ithaca, 1968), p. 193; Narcissus Luttrell, *A Brief Historical Relation of State Affairs from September 1678 to April 1714*, 6 vols. (Oxford, 1857); OA 31 October 1718, p. 6. In a letter written in February 1726, the Swiss visitor Cesare de Saussure claimed that 'five, ten, or fifteen criminals are hanged [every six weeks]' in London; see Mme. Van Muyden, trans. and ed., *A Foreign View of England in the Reigns of George I & George II* (London, 1902), p. 127.

14 These figures are provided by Simon Devereaux in his forthcoming work, *Capital Punishment in Hanoverian London, 1689–1837*; I am assuming there were eight execution days in a year, which was usually the case in the early eighteenth century. There were, in this twenty-year period, 962 condemned (830 men; 132 women) or 86% men and 14% women; 91% of the total (92% of men, 88% of women) for property crimes. Of the condemned, 65% were executed; 35% received conditional or full pardons. Compared to only 34% of women, 69% of condemned men were executed. Women were not only less likely than men to be hanged, but much less likely to be hanged for property offences: 70% of female property offenders were reprieved, compared to only 32% of their male counterparts.

15   J.M. Beattie, *Policing and Punishment in London, 1660–1750* (Oxford, 2001), pp. 366–7; p. 20.

16   John Bellamy, *Crime and Public Order in England in the Later Middle Ages* (London, 1973), p. 187; *A declaration of the lyfe and Death of Iohn Story* (1571), xvi; see also Alfred Marks, *Tyburn Tree: Its History and Annals* (London, 1908), p. 142; CLRO, Rep 84, f. 233; *The Confession and Execution of the Five Prisoners that suffered on the New Gallows at Tyburn on Friday the 6th of September, 1678* (1678); *Whitehall Evening Post* 16–19 June 1759; 2–4 October 1759.

17   Horace Bleackley, *The Hangmen of England* (1929); repr. in John Lofland, ed., *State Executions Viewed Historically and Sociologically* (Montclair, N.J., 1977), p. 143–4; OA 18 June 1708, p. 2; *The Post Man*, 19–21 November 1696.

18   OA 22 September 1704, p. 2; *The True Narrative of the Confession and Execution of Elizabeth Hare which is burnt for High-Treason, in Bun-Hill Fields* (30 October 1683); *The True Narrative of the Execution of John Marketman, Chyrurgian, of Westham in Essex* [1680], p. 3; Mather, *Wonders of Free-Grace*, p. 82.

19   Frederick Kielmansegge, *Diary of a Journey to England in the Years 1761–1762*, trans. Countess Kielmansegge (London, 1902), p. 159.

20   OA 3 August 1709, p. 1; OA 21 July 1703, p. 1

21   Earlier in the seventeenth century the Dead Warrant appeared to come down as late as the day before the execution; see *The Manner of the Execution of Eleven Notorious Offenders … on the 8th of this Instant December* [1682], p. 4; the Dead Warrant for Reeves and the others came on the Tuesday before the Friday they were hanged; see *The Daily Journal* 2 May 1722.

22   *The Execution, last Speeches & Confessions of the Thirteen Persons that suffered on Friday the 24th of October* (1679), p. 3; OA 5 March 1732/3, p. 25.

23   In 1684, when Captain Richardson, the keeper of Newgate 'was asked what days were usual for Execution', he 'replyed Wednesdays and Frydays'; see *An Impartial Account of the Material Circumstances Relating to Sir Thomas Armestrong, Kt. Who was Executed at Tyburn for High-Treason* (20 June 1684), 6; *Journals of Two Travellers*, p. 149; Johnson, *General History of the Pyrates*, p. 286; *A True Account of the Behaviour and Confession of the Eighteen Criminals that were Executed at Tyburn* (15 July 1689), p. 2; *Read's Weekly Journal*, 16 February 1751; OA 23 March 1752, p. 51; *Authentic Memoirs of the Life and Surprising Adventures of John Sheppard* (1724), pp. 67–8.

24   OA 28 May 1733, pp. 18–19; *Post Man*, 14–16 August 1697; LMRC, 1:458–9; OA 9 May 1726, p. 4; *Parker's Penny Post*, 11 May 1726.

25   *London Evening Post* 25–27 September 1750; *London Evening Post* 13–15 January 1767; OA 4 May 1763, p. 40; OA 24 May & 15 September 1760, p. 15; John Taylor (Ordinary of Newgate), *The Only Genuine and Authentic Narrative of the Proceedings of the Late Capt. James Lowrey* (1752), p. 50; *An Account of the Execution of the Late Laurence Earl Ferrers* (1760), pp. 5, 7; 'An Act for better preventing the horrid crime of Murder', 25 George II, c. 37.

26   OA 29 January 1719/20, p. 6; *Hogarth Moralized. Being a Complete edition of Hogarth's Works* (1768), p. 94. The Methodist in the cart with Idle is unlikely to be Silas Told. Told himself dates the beginning of his Newgate ministry as 1744, when he first visited a group of the condemned, including the robber-cum-penitent John Lancaster, and later attended them in their execution at Tyburn. However, Told is often inaccurate about dates, and the malefactors in question were actually hanged on 28 October 1748 (*Life of Silas Told*, pp. 70–71); earlier editions of his autobiography also identify the Ordinary with whom he initially clashed as Taylor (Ordinary from 1747–57), rather than Guthrie (Ordinary until 1746).

27   Samuel Richardson, *Letters Written to and for Particular Friends on the Most Important Occasions* (1741), pp. 241, 239–40; see alternate versions of the Bellman's verses in *The Whole Life And Conversation, Birth, Parentage, and Education of John Sutton* (1711), p. 8, and *The Whole Life and Conversation, Birth, Parentage, and Educations of Thomas Browning* (1711), p. 6.

28   *Post Man* 21–23 June 1698; *Morning Chronicle* 22 July 1775; OA 8 March 1730/1, p. 17; *Public Advertiser* 17 August 1775; *Public Advertiser* 20 October 1778; *A True Account of the Confession and Behaviour of the Three Late Notorious Traytors* [Thomas Walcot, William Hone and John Rouse] (1683), p. 2.

29   *Public Advertiser* 17 August 1775; *Hell upon Earth*, p. 12; *The Behaviour of the Condemned Criminals in Newgate … Executed at Tyburn on Friday the 17th of October* (1684), p. 4; *Parker's London News* 13

November 1724; Charles G. Harper, *Half Hours with the Highwaymen* (London, 1908), 1:178.

30 Saussure, p. 124; Bernard de Mandeville, *An Enquiry into the Causes of the Frequent Executions at Tyburn* (1725), p. 23; *Select Trials* (1742), 4:45; OA 11 November 1724, p. 6; *LMRC*, 3:87–8; OA 21 May 1722, p. 6.

31 *LM* July 1735, p. 389–90; Richardson, *Letters*, p. 241; *LM* February 1750, p. 91; *GM* July 1750, p. 328; *Some Observations on the Trial of Mr Thomas Carr* (1737), p. 10; *Morning Chronicle* 16 January 1776; OA 15 June 1763, p. 51; *Public Advertiser* 17 August 1775.

32 OA 2 November 1736, p. 5; OA 18 March 1740/1, p. 17; Charles Hitchen, *The Regulator: Or, a Discovery of the Thieves, Thief-Takers, and Locks, alias Receivers of Stolen Goods in and about the City of London* (1718), p. 16; *The True and Genuine Account of the Life and Actions of the Late Jonathan Wild* (1725), p. 252; Joseph Hunter, ed., *The Life of Mr Thomas Gent, Printer, of York, Written by Himself* (London, 1832), p. 162; *Parker's Penny Post* 26 May 1725; *The Daily Journal* 25 May 1725. Jonathan Wild was condemned for accepting money in exchange for arranging the return of stolen goods without apprehending the thieves, an offence made capital under a clause in the 1718 Transportation Act, supposedly drafted with Wild in mind.

33 Saussure, p. 126; *An Exact Narrative of the Bloody Murder, and Robbery committed by Stephen Eaton [et al.]* (1669), p. 8; OA 18 March 1740/1, p. 17; *The Behaviour, Confession, and Execution of the Twelve Prisoners that Suffered on Wednesday, the 22d of Jan.* (1678/9), p. 6; *True Copies of the Papers wrote by Arthur Lord Balmerino [et al.]* (1746), 2:36; *Public Advertiser* 1 December 1774; *GM* July 1769; *GM* July 1762; *London Evening Post* 15–17 January 1767.

34 *Post Man* 24–26 November 1696; OA 14 March 1759, p. 14; Charles John Fox, ed., *The Official Diary of Lieutenant-General Adam Williamson, Deputy-Lieutenant of the Tower of London 1722–1747*, Camden 3rd series, Vol XXII (London, 1912), p. 131; *Applebee's Original Weekly Journal* 14 November 1719, quoted in *Notes and Queries*, 10th series, Volume viii (9 November 1907; entry by Alfred F. Robbins), p. 365; *Penny London Post* 5–8 October 1750; OA 23 March 1752, pp. 46–7; *Select Trials* (1764), 2:137–9; *Whitehall Evening-Post* 11–13 July 1758; Saussure, p. 126; *Daily Post* 14 March 1741; Henry Angelo, *The Reminiscences of Henry Angelo* (New York, 1969), 1:363; *Daily Journal* 10 May 1726; OA 24 August 1763, p. 64; *Lloyd's Evening Post* 3–5 December 1770; *LM* January 1776; *Morning Chronicle* 30 January 1777.

35 OA 6 November 1723, p. 6; *LMRC*, 1:472–3; *An Acconut [sic] of the Deportment and Last Words of Mr Richard Langhorne* (1679), iv [n.p.]; OA 23 December 1713, p. 5.

36 OA 17 April 1730, p. 4; OA 7 February, 1728/9, pp. 2, 4; *Daily Journal* 8 February 1728/9.

37 OA 22 August 1729, p. 4; *The True Account of the Behaviour and Confession of the Criminals Executed* (21 October 1687), p. 4; OA 8 August 1750, p. 80; OA 22 December 1729, p. 4.

38 *LMRC*, 1:349; OA 13 February 1739/40, p. 19; OA 23 March 1752, p. 45; OA 7 & 28 March 1764, p. 35; OA 16 September 1741, pp. 7–8.

39 William Smythies (curate of St Giles Cripplegate), *A True Account of the Several Passages relating to the Execution of Sir John Johnston* (1690), p. 1; *LMRC*, 1:320.

40 *Execution of the Late Laurence Earl Ferrers*, p. 10; *The Old Whig* 15 March 1735, quoted in Bleackley, *Hangmen*, p. 72; *The Diary of John Evelyn*, ed. E. S. de Beer, 6 vols. (Oxford, 1955), 4:456; *A True Account of the last Speeches, Confessions and Execution of Christopher Vrats, George Boriksie, and John Sterne* (1682), pp. 6–7.

41 John Heneage Jesse, ed., *George Selwyn and his Contemporaries* (London, 1882), 1:11; *The Dying Speeches and Behaviour of the several State Prisoners that have been Executed the last 300 Years* (1720), p. 86; OA 5 March 1732/3, p. 15; *An Account of what passed at the Execution of Sir Will. Parkyns, and Sir Joh. Friend* (1686), p. 2; *A True Account of all Passages at the Execution of John Ashton, Gent* (1690), p. 2; *A True Account of the Dying Behaviour of Ambrose Rookwood, Charles Cranburne, and Major Lowick*, p. 1; *Diary of John Evelyn*, 4:332; *The Apologie of John Ketch, Esq ... In Vindication of himself as to the Execution of the Late Lord Russel* (1683), p. 2.

42 *The Speech and Deportment of Col. Iames Turner at his Execution in Leaden-hall-street* (1664), p. 3; *Weekly Journal; or Saturday's Post* 22 March 1717/8; OA 14 May 1731, p. 17; OA 26 October 1720, p. 5; *LM* July 1750, p. 331; *A Narrative of the ... Execution of John James Who Suffered at Tiburne* (26 November 1661), pp. 26, 46.

43 William Blackstone, *Commentaries on the Laws of England* (1767–9), 4:195; *The Last Dying Speeches, Confession, and Execution of John Stokes, Isaac Davis, and Mary Williamson* (5 March 1684/5), p. 4; *The Journal of William Schellinks' Travels in England 1661–1663*, trans. and ed. Maurice Exwood and H. L. Lehmann (London, Camden Society, 1993), p. 86; *A True Relation of Four most Barbarous and Cruel Murders Committed in Leicester-shire by Elizabeth Ridgeway* (1684). I will discuss the case of Catherine Hayes in more detail in Chapters 3 and 9.

44 OA 29 April 1724, p. 6; OA 8 August 1750, p. 80; John Villette, *Annals of Newgate; or, Malefactor's Register* (1776), 4:377; Henri Misson, *M. Misson's Memoirs and Observations in his Travels over England*, trans. M. Ozell (1719; French edition 1698), p. 123; *A True Account of the Behaviour, Confession, and Last Dying Speeches of the Criminals that were Executed at Tyburn* (17 April 1695), p. 2; OA 9 July 1734; *LMRC*, 3:209; *The Flying Post* 22–24 September 1698; OA 25 March 1751, p. 76; OA 21 May 1722, p. 6; *Weekly Journal; or British Gazetteer* 21 November 1724; *LM* December 1752, p. 575.

45 *Select Trials* (1742), 2:139; *Authentic Memoirs*, p. 68; *British Journal* 21 November 1724; *Newes from the Dead; or a True and Exact Narration of the miraculous deliverance of Anne Greene* (1651), pp. 2–3; *LM* November 1740, p. 560–1; *God's Justice Against Murther, Or the Bloody Apprentice Executed* (1668), p. 11; *LM* July 1736, p. 399; OA 26 July and 11 August 1736, p. 12; *LM* September 1736, p. 519; Luttrell, *Historical Relation* 5:623; *The Bloody Register* (1764), 1:93; *Daily Journal* 14 February 1722.

46 *Whitehall Evening-Post* 1–4 April 1758; *Public Advertiser* 20 October 1778; *Dawks's News-Letter* 26 January 1698/9; *Hell upon Earth*, p. 12; *Daily Post* 9 February 1720/1; *Weekly Journal; or British Gazetteer* 8 February 1728/9; *Daily Post* 8 February 1728/9; *LMRC*, 1:453.

47 See Linebaugh, 'Tyburn Riot'; for popular views about dissection, see also Ruth Richardson, *Death, Dissection and the Destitute* (London, 1988); *London Evening Post* 13–15 March 1738/9; *Weekly Journal; or Saturday's Post* 21 November 1724; *GM* April 1739, p. 21; *A Full, True and Genuine Account of the Uncommon Behaviour of Mr Gill Smith* (Southwark, 1738), p. 16; *London Evening Post* 2–4 October 1750; *Weekly Journal; or British Gazetteer* 16 November 1728; *London Evening Post* 7–10 April 1739; *LM* August 1763, pp. 446; *Annual Register* 5 May 1764.

48 Angelo, *Reminiscences*, 1:369; Michel Foucault, *Discipline and Punish: the Birth of the Prison*, trans. Alan Sheridan (New York, 1978), p. 66; Pieter Spierenburg, *The Spectacle of Suffering* (Cambridge, 1984), pp. 59, 60; Sharpe, 'Last Dying Speeches', pp. 158–9. For a discussion of the 'carnivalesque', see Thomas W. Laqueur, 'Crowds, Carnival and the State in English Executions, 1604–1868', in A. L. Beier, David Cannadine and James M. Rosenheim, eds., *The First Modern Society* (Cambridge, 1989); for resistance generally, see Linebaugh, 'Tyburn Riot', and his *London Hanged*, as well as Gatrell, *Hanging Tree*, especially ch. 4. The notion that the gallows formed a 'contested' and 'unstable' space has recently become more fashionable; see for instance, Peter Lake and Michael Questier, 'Agency, Appropriation and Rhetoric under the Gallows: Puritans, Romanists and the State in Early Modern England', in *Past & Present* 153 (1996), 64–107; and Hal Gladfelder, *Criminality and Narrative in Eighteenth-Century England: Beyond the Law* (Baltimore and London, 2001), pp. 55–7.

49 Linebaugh, *London Hanged*, p. xx.

50 Sharpe, 'Last Dying Speeches', p. 159.

51 *A Trip Through the Town: Containing Observations on the Customs and Manners of Age* (1735), pp. 28–9; this pamphlet is quoted extensively by Walter Besant in his description of executions in *London in the Eighteenth Century* (1902).

52 Misson, pp. 123–4; Francois Lacombe, *Observations sur Londre [sic] et ses Environs* (Paris and London, 1777), pp. 186–7 (my translation); Misson, p. 125.

53 Misson, pp. 124–5; *An Exact Narrative of the Bloody Murder, and Robbery Committed by Stephen Eaton [et al.]* (14 July 1669), p. 1; *Compleat Collection of Remarkable Tryals*, 1:58–9.

54 Francis Place Papers, BL Add Ms 27826, ff. 97, 48, 58, 107; James Boswell, *Boswell's Life of Johnson*, ed. R. W. Chapman (Oxford, 1980), p. 1238; for 'touching' hanged corpses, see Lacombe, *Observations*, p. 186; *GM* October 1759, p. 493 and May 1767, p. 276.

55 *Dawks's News-Letter* 25 May 1699; *Flying Post* 20–22 July 1699; Saussure, *Foreign View*, p. 93; *The Diary of Sylas Neville, 1767–1788*, ed. Basil Cozens-Hardy (London, 1950), p. 25; *Walpole's Correspondence*, 9:46; Francis Place Papers, BL Add Ms 27826, f. 226.

56 *The Diurnal of Thomas Rugg, 1659–1661*, ed. William L. Sachse (London: Camden Society, Vol. 91,

1961), pp. 142–3; *A Sad and Dreadful Account of a most Unusual and Barbarous Murther Committed upon the Body of the Wife of one William Langstaff* (1689), p. 2; *Weekly Journal; or British Gazetteer* 16 November 1728; *The Affecting Case of the Unfortunate Thomas Daniels* (1761), p. 20; *Applebee's Original Weekly Journal* 2–9 August 1718; *Applebee's Original Weekly Journal* 6 June 1719; *LMRC*, 2:206, 2:212; *Select Trials* (1742), 3:2.

57   *Diary of John Evelyn*, 3:492; 5:549; *Journals of Two Travellers*, p. 149; Luttrell, *Historical Relation*, 4:669; *Diary of Samuel Pepys*, ed. Robert Latham and William Matthews, 11 vols. (London, 1995), 1:309.

58   Angelo, *Reminiscences*, 1:367.

59   John Knott, *Discourses of Martyrdom in English Literature, 1563–1694* (Cambridge, 1993), p. 154; John Bunyan, *Grace Abounding: With Other Spiritual Autobiographies*, ed. John Stachniewski with Anita Pacheco (Oxford, 1998), pp. 91, 92; *State Trials*, 4:1132; *The Speeches and Prayers of Major General Harrison* [*et al.*] (1660), p. 12.

60   Richard Baxter, *A Treatise of Death, the Last Enemy to be Destroyed* (1672), p. 35; John H. Langbein, *Origins of Adversary Criminal Trial* (Oxford, 2003), pp. 62–3; J.M. Beattie, 'Scales of Justice: Defense Counsel and the English Criminal Trial in the Eighteenth and Nineteenth Centuries', *Law and History Review*, Fall (1991), p. 223; *The Narrative of the Persecution of Agnes Beaumont*, repr. in Bunyan, *Grace Abounding*, p. 222.

61   *LMRC*, 3:150–2; OA 25 July 1729, p. 4.

62   *Trial at Large, Behaviour, and Dying Declaration of Mary Edmondson* (1759), pp. 14, 16; *A Genuine Narrative of the Trial and Condemnation of Mary Edmundson* (1759), p. 19; *Life of Silas Told*, pp. 87–88.

63   Burnet, *History of His Own Time*, 1:228, 295–5.

64   *An Account of what passed at the Execution of the late Duke of Monmouth* (1685), pp. 2–3; John Donne, *Death's Duell*, ed. Geoffrey Keynes (1631; repr. Boston, 1973), pp. 15–17; John Bunyan, *The Life and Death of Mr Badman*, ed. James F. Forrest and Roger Sharrock (1680; repr. Oxford, 1988), pp. 157–8, 167–8; *LM* April 1738, p. 203; *Life of Silas Told*, p. 88; *The Dying Speeches and Behaviour of the Several State Prisoners* (1720), pp. 302–3.

Notes to Chapter 2: From the Gallows to Grub Street: Last Dying Speeches and Criminal 'Lives'

1   *A Collection of Dying Speeches of all those People call'd Traytors* (1718), pp. 11–12.

2   OA 29 January 1732/3, p. 22.

3   Daniel Defoe, *Colonel Jack*, ed. Samuel Holt Monk (Oxford, 1989), p. 307.

4   For earlier murder sheets and crime pamphlets, see Malcolm Gaskill, *Crime and Mentalities in Early Modern England* (Cambridge, 2000); Peter Lake with Michael Questier, *The Antichrist's Lewd Hat: Protestants, Papists and Players in Post-Reformation England* (New Haven and London, 2002); Frances E. Dolan, *Dangerous Familiars: Representation of Domestic Crime in England, 1550–1700* (Ithaca, 1994).

5   Lincoln B. Faller, *Crime and Defoe: a New Kind of Writing* (Cambridge, 1993), p. 6; Faller, *Turned to Account*, p. 171.

6   See Ian Watt's seminal work, *The Rise of the Novel* (London, 1957); see also John J. Richetti, *Popular Fiction before Richardson* (Oxford, 1969); Lennard J. Davis, *Factual Fictions: the Origins of the English Novel* (New York, 1983); Michael McKeon, *The Origins of the English Novel 1600–1740* (Baltimore, 1987); Faller, *Crime and Defoe*; Michael Mascuch, *Origins of the Individualist Self: Autobiography and Self-Identity in England 1591–1791* (Cambridge, 1997); Hal Gladfelder, *Criminality and Narrative in Eighteenth-Century England: Beyond the Law* (Baltimore, 2001).

7   F. W. Chandler, *The Literature of Roguery* (Boston, 1907), 1:181. For more recent studies, see Linebaugh, 'Ordinary of Newgate', Michael Harris, 'Trials and Criminal Biographies'; Sharpe, 'Last Dying Speeches'; Faller, *Turned to Account*; Gatrell, *Hanging Tree*, esp. ch. 4.

8   See, for instance, Roger Chartier, ed., *The Culture of Print: Power and the Uses of Print in Early Modern Europe*, trans. Lydia G. Cochrane (Princeton, 1989), p. 4; Tessa Watt, *Cheap Print and Popular Piety 1550–1640* (Cambridge, 1991), p. 3.

9   Charles Tibbits, *Trials from the Newgate Calendar* (London, 1908), iii. The notion that middling sorts formed the primary audience for criminal literature is now generally accepted; see Philip Rawlings, *Drunks, Whores and Idle Apprentices: Criminal Biographies of the Eighteenth Century* (Cambridge, 1992), p. 4; see also Jonathan Barry, 'Literacy and Literature in Popular Culture: Reading and Writing in Historical Perspective', in Tim Harris, ed., *Popular Culture in England, c. 1500–1850* (Basingstoke, 1995), p. 7.

10 *The Life and Penitent Death of John Mausgridge ... Penn'd from his own Accont* [sic] *of himself, and approv'd of by him, before his Death* (1708), p. 2.

11 *The Diary of John Evelyn*, ed. E. S. de Beer, 6 vols. (Oxford, 1955), 4:361–2, 4:362n.

12 See Harris, 'Trials and Criminal Biographies', pp. 16–19. In his *Checklist of the Writings of Daniel Defoe* (Bloomington, 1960), J. R. Moore attributed to Defoe numerous criminal biographies and pamphlets, many of them published by Applebee; most of these titles have been subsequently de-attributed by P. N. Furbank and W. R. Owens, *Defoe De-Attributions: a Critique of J. R. Moore's Checklist* (London, 1994); see also their *A Critical Bibliography of Daniel Defoe* (London, 1998). I have attributed only undisputed works to Defoe.

13 *A True Relation of the Execution of Mr Edward Coleman* (1678), p. 3; L. B. Smith, 'English Treason Trials and Confessions in the Sixteenth Century', *Journal of the History of Ideas*, xv (1954), 471–98; J. A. Sharpe, *Judicial Punishment in England* (London, 1990), pp. 31–33; *Observations on the late famous Tryal of Sir G. W. Father Corker, &c. Together with the Behaviour, Confession, and Execution of the six Prisoners that suffered at Tyburn on Wednesday the 23th of this instant July* (1679), p. 1.

14 *The Speeches and Prayers of Major General Harrison* [*et al.*] (1660), pp. 60–1, 63; p. 33; John Foxe, *Acts and Monuments*, ed. George Townsend (New York, 1965), 6:698.

15 Burnet, *History of his own Time*, 1:296 (Burnet mentions drums at Vane's execution, while Ludlow and subsequent collections specify trumpets); *The Speeches, Discourses, and Prayers, of Col. John Barkstead, Col. John Okey, and Mr Miles Corbet* (1662), p. 24; *The Proceedings against Sir Thomas Armstrong ... As also an Account of what passed at his Execution* (1684), p. 3; *Schellinks' Travels*, p. 82; Burnet, *History of his own Time*, 1:295; *The Dying Speeches and Behaviour of the several State Prisoners That have been executed the last 300 Years* (1720), pp. 294–8.

16 *The Dying Speeches and Behaviour of the several State Prisoners*, p. 297.

17 Burnet, *History of his own Time*, 1:296; Edmund Ludlow, *A Voyce from the Watch Tower, Part Five: 1660–1662*, Camden Fourth Series, Vol. 21, ed. A. B. Worden (London, 1978), p. 313.

18 OA 24 September 1731, p. 17; OA 23 December 1713, p. 5; OA 17 February 1743/4, p. 12; *The Dying Speeches and Behaviour of the several State Prisoners That have been executed the last 300 Years* (1720), p. 267.

19 *The Speech of Richard Langhorn Esq* (1679), p. 1; *Mr Langhorn's Memoirs*, repr. *State Trials*, 7:501–2; *A Genuine Account of the Behaviour, Confession and Dying Words of [those] Who were Executed the 30th Day of July, 1746, at Kennington Common, for High Treason* (1746), pp. 43–4; *The Proceedings to Execution ... against Captain Thomas Walcot, William Hone, and John Rouse, for High Treason* (1683), p. 3.

20 *The Speech of the Late Lord Russel, to the Sheriffs* (1683), p. 1; *LMRC*, 2:359; OA 13 February 1726/7, p. 4; OA 9 July 1734, p. 21; *An Account of what passed at the Execution of Sir Will Parkyns, and Sir Joh. Friend, At Tyburn* (1696), p. 1; *A Full and Genuine Account of the Lives, Characters, Behaviour, last Dying Words and Confessions, of the Four Malefactors ... at Kennington-Common* (6 April 1739), p. 4.

21 *The Observator* 25 July 1683; *A True Account of the Dying Behaviour of Ambrose Rookwood, Charles Cranburne, and Major Lowick* (1696), p. 1; OA 4 & 5 January 1724/5, p. 6. See also E. P. Thompson, *Whigs and Hunters: the Origin of the Black Act* (London, 1975). 'Social crimes' are loosely defined as those offences (e.g., smuggling, poaching, rioting) which, although proscribed by law, were viewed with some degree of tolerance by a large segment of the population. See John Rule, 'Social Crime in the Rural South in the Eighteenth and Early Nineteenth Centuries', in John Rule and Roger Wells, eds., *Crime, Protest and Popular Politics in Southern England, 1740–1850* (London, 1997), ch. 8.

22 Burnet, *History of his own Time*, 2:282–3; *The Condemnation, Behaviour, Last Dying Words and Execution of Algernon Sidney* (1683), p. 1; *A True and Exact Copy of the Paper Delivered by Christopher Layer* (1723); *A True Account of the Behaviour, Confession, and Last Dying Speeches of the Criminals*

that were Executed at Tyburn (26 January 1697/8), p. 2; *A Narrative, Being a True Relation of what Discourse passed between Dr Hawkins and Edward Fitz-Harys* (1681), p. 8.

23 OA 18 May 1709, p. 2; Kielmansegge, *Journey to England*, p. 158; *Portledge Papers*, pp. 95–6; Mather, *Wonders of Free-Grace*, long title, viii; *CSPD*, vol. 25, p. 432.

24 *An Appeal of Murther from certain unjust Judges, lately sitting at the Old Baily, to the righteous Judge of Heaven and Earth; and to all sensible English-men, containing a Relation of the Tryal, Behaviour, and Death of Mr William Anderton, Executed June 16 1693 at Tyburn, for pretended High-Treason* (1693); *A True Copy of the Paper delivered to the Sheriffs of London and Middlesex, by Mr William Anderton* (1693), long title. Not surprisingly, neither publication bore an imprint.

25 *LMRC*, 1:90–1; *A Candid and Impartial Account of the Behaviour of Simon Lord Lovat* (Dublin, 1747); OA 24 May 1736, p. 19 (Wreathcocke's death sentence was commuted to one of transportation for life); *The Genuine History of the Life of Gill Smith ... Executed at Kennington-Common, April 10* (1738), p. 45; OA 29 April 1724, p. 6; OA 23 February 1718/9, pp. 4–5; *[A True] Copy of the Paper Written by Lieutenant Bird: And Delivered to his Friends in Newgate the night before his Execution; which he desired should be Printed ...* 'Published by Order of his Parents' (1719).

26 Brad S. Gregory, *Salvation at State: Christian Martyrology in Early Modern Europe* (Cambridge, Mass., 1999), p. 21; see also pp. 9–21. See also Lake, *Antichrist's Lewd Hat*, pp. 227–8.

27 Richard Sherlock, *The Practical Christian: Or, the Devout Penitent* (1699), p. 54; Burnet, *History of his own Time*, 2:282–3.

28 *Collection of Dying Speeches Of all those People call'd Traytors*, p. 4; *Diary of John Evelyn*, 4:332; *CSPD* (1660–1685), p. 215.

29 Henry Fielding, *The History of Tom Jones*, ed. R. P. C. Mutter (London, 1985), p. 226.

30 The former group include Victor Neuberg, *Popular Education in Eighteenth-Century England* (London, 1971), Margaret Spufford, 'First Steps in Literacy: the Reading and Writing Experiences of the Humblest Seventeenth-Century Spiritual Autobiographers' in *Social History*, 4 (1979) and Keith Thomas, 'The Meaning of Literacy in Early Modern England', in Gerd Baumann, ed., *The Written Word: Literacy in Transition* (Oxford, 1986); the latter, Roger Schofield, 'Dimensions of Illiteracy, 1750–1850', in *Explorations in Economic History*, 10 (1972–3), and 'The Measurement of Literacy in Pre-Industrial England', in Jack Goody, ed., *Literacy in Traditional Societies* (Cambridge, 1968), and David Cressy, *Literacy and the Social Order: Reading and Writing in Tudor and Stuart England* (Cambridge, 1980).

31 Adam Fox, *Oral and Literate Culture in England, 1500–1700* (Oxford, 2000), p. 19; see also John Feather, *A History of British Publishing* (London, 1988), p. 95.

32 *LM* April 1735, p. 218.

33 *Misson's Memoirs and Observations*, pp. 17–18.

34 Elizabeth Fry, *Observations on the Visiting, Superintendence, and Government of Female Prisoners* (London, 1827), p. 4.

35 OA 21 June 1704, p. 1; OA 12 May 1721, p. 3.

36 Samuel Rossell, *The Prisoner's Director* (1742), pp. 81, 77 (Rossell was himself Ordinary of Newgate from 1746 to 1747); OA 18 July 1707, p. 2; OA 19 September 1720, p. 6; *LMRC*, 2:79–80; *The Autobiography of Francis Place*, ed. Mary Thale (London, 1972), p. 45; OA 4 August 1740, p. 10.

37 OA 19 December 1733, p. 10; OA 1 August 1746, p. 48; OA 14 March 1725/6, p. 3; OA 27 June 1726, p. 2; OA 23 October 1751, p. 119; OA 30 April 1725, p. 3; OA 7 June 1745, p. 8.

38 *Select Trials* (1764), 4:246; *Walpole's Correspondence*, 13:23n; 40:65; *The World* 19 December 1754, p. 317 (such incidents seemed to have been fairly customary by the 1720s; see, for instance, *LMRC*, 3:77); OA 16 September 1741, pp. 12–13, 17.

39 Fox, *Oral and Literate Culture*, pp. 5–6; see also R. A. Houston, *Literacy in Early Modern Europe: Culture and Education 1500–1800* (London, 1988), p. 223; Harris, ed., *Popular Culture in England*, pp. 4–5; James Raven, Helen Small and Naomi Tadmor, eds., *The Practice and Representation of Reading in England* (Cambridge, UK., 1996), p. 21; Roger Chartier, *The Cultural Uses of Print in Early Modern France*, trans. Lydia G. Cochrane (Princeton, 1987), esp. pp. 3–7.

40 *The Behaviour, Confession and Execution of the Twelve Prisoners that Suffered ... at Tyburn* (22 January 1678/9), p. 1.

41 *The Life of Martin Bellamy … Dictated by himself in Newgate, and Publish'd at his Request, for the Benefit of the Publick* (1727/8), pp. 8–10, 6–8, 34; *LMRC*, 3:26–7; OA 27 February 1728, pp. 3–4; see also J.M. Beattie, *Policing and Punishment in London, 1660–1750* (Oxford, 2001), p. 383.

42 *The Bloody Register* (1764), 1:iii–iv; Tobias Smollett, *Roderick Random*, ed. David Blewett (London, 1995; originally published 1748), p. 383; *The Last Words of a Dying Penitent … written with his own Hand after Condemnation* (1692), p. 26; *The Faithful Narrative … of the Trial of Bartholomew Greenwood, Gent* (1740), iii. For more on Grub Street, see Pat Rogers, *Grub Street: Studies in a Subculture* (London, 1972).

43 *A True and Faithful Narrative of the Life and Actions of John Oneby* (1726), pp. 20, 24–5.

44 OA 14 March 1759, p. 10; *The Only Genuine and Authentic Narrative of the Late Capt. James Lowrey … delivered by Himself, in Manuscript, into the Hands of the Revd Mr Taylor, Ordinary of Newgate, some short Time before his Execution* (1752), pp. 2, 50; OA 7 and 28 March 1764, pp. 26–7.

45 *The True Account of the Behaviour and the Confession of the Condemned Criminals in Newgate,* (10 June 1685), p. 1; *The Behaviour, Confession & Execution of the several Prisoners that suffered at Tyburn,* (9 May 1679), p. 1; *A True Account of the Prisoners Executed at Tyburn,* (23 May 1684), p. 2; 'The Case of Paul Lorrain, Ordinary of Newgate, humbly offered to the Honourable House of Commons', in London Goldsmith's Library (1712), *Hanson 1688 Br 232* (devotional literature was exempt under a statute passed the previous year; Lorrain's petition was denied, and the *Account* was subsequently published in pamphlet form to evade the tax); *The Behaviour and Execution of Robert Green and Lawrence Hill,* (21 February 1678/9), p. 5. I will discuss the Ordinary and his *Account* at more length in Chapter 5; see also Linebaugh, 'Ordinary of Newgate', and Harris, 'Trials and Criminal Biographies'.

46 *A True Account of the Behaviour, Confession and Last Dying Speech of John Herman Bryan* (1707), p. 2; *A True and Genuine Account of the Confession … of Thomas Jones and James Welch, for the Barbarous Rape and Murder of Sarah Green* (1751), p. 3; the authorized account was published under Howard's name as *A True and Impartial Account of the Behaviour, Confession and Dying Words of the Four Malefactors … Executed at Kennington-Common* (6 September 1751); see also Harris, 'Trials and Criminal Biographies', p. 23.

47 *The Life, Travels, Exploits, Frauds and Robberies of Charles Speckman* (1763), p. 53; *The History of the Remarkable Life of John Sheppard* (1724); repr. in Horace Bleackley and S. M. Ellis, *Jack Sheppard* (London, 1933), p. 155 ('Ginger-bread' probably means 'something showy and unsubstantial' [OED]); Gilbert Burnet and Anthony Horneck, *The Last Confession, Prayers and Meditations of Lieuten. John Stern [et al.]* (1681/2), p. 11; *Life and Penitent Death of John Mausgridge*, p. 2; *A Compleat and True Account of all the Robberies Committed by James Carrick, John Molhoni, and their Accomplices* (1722), pp. 1, 23–4.

48 *Select Trials* (1742), 1:78; *LMRC*, 1:455; *Select Trials* (1742), 1:305, 1:311, 1:236; see also 1:129, 1:139; *Last Dying Speech of John Herman Bryan*, p. 2; OA 23 November 1763, p. 16.

49 See also Harris, 'Trials and Criminal Biographies', pp. 23–4.

50 *The Arraignment, Tryal, Conviction and Condemnation of Henry Harrison, Gent.* (1692), ii; *Memoirs of the Life and Remarkable Exploits of the Noted Dennis Neale, alias John Clark* (1754), ii; *The Authentick Tryals of John Swan, and Elizabeth Jeffryes* (1752), iii; *Genuine Narrative of the Memorable Life and Actions of John Dyer* (1729), ii; *The Life and Actions of James Dalton … As Taken from his own Mouth in his Cell in Newgate* (1730), iv.

51 *Grub-Street Journal* 15 March 1732/3; *Daily Journal* 17 November 1724; OA 21 November 1729, p. 4; OA 7 October 1733, p. 18.

52 *A True Narrative of the Proceedings at the Hertford Assizes, this Instant July* (1676), p. 2; *The Confession of the Four High-Way-Men; As it was Written by one of them, and allowed by the Rest* (1673), long title; OA 9 August 1732, p. 15; *The Tyburn Chronicle; or, Villainy Display'd in all its Branches* (1768), 2:333; OA 1 May 1758, p. 36; OA 29 January 1732/3, p. 22.

53 OA 12 May 1730, p. 1; OA 14 September 1741, p. 8; William Hawkins, *A Full, True and Impartial Account of all the Robberies Committed … by William Hawkins, in Company with Wilson, Wright, Butler, Fox and others not yet Taken* (1722), iv, vi.

54 For Newgate fees, customs and conditions, see *A Companion for Debtors and Prisoners* (1699), pp. 10–17; *Hell upon Earth* (1703); *The History of the Press-Yard* (1717); B. L., *An Accurate Description*

of Newgate (1724), pp. 41–2, 47; *The Memoirs of Capt. Peter Drake* (Dublin, 1755), p. 144–7; W. J.
Sheehan, 'Finding Solace in Eighteenth-Century Newgate', in J. S. Cockburn, ed., *Crime in England
1550–1800* (London, 1977); R. B. Pugh, 'Newgate Between Two Fires', *Guildhall Studies in London
History* 3, in 2 parts (October 1978 and April 1979).

55 *Life … of Charles Speckman*, p. 49; [Fifield] Allen, *An Account of the Behaviour of Mr James Maclaine*
4th ed. (1750), p. 31; OA 4 May 1763, pp. 34, 39.

56 *A Narrative of the Robberies, Escapes, &c. of John Sheppard*, 8th ed. (1724), p. 3; OA 2 October 1734,
p. 9.

57 *LMRC*, 3:71–2; OA 18 January 1737/8, pp. 15–16.

58 OA 20 February 1748/9, p. 17; *LMRC*, 1:184–6.

59 Defoe, *Colonel Jack*, p. 2.

Notes to Chapter 3: Everyman and the Gallows: Contemporary Explanations for Criminality

1 OBP 16–19 January 1739/40, p. 46. The defendant, Thomas Hawkins, was subsequently reprieved, but
died in Newgate; see *LM* February 1740, p. 101.

2 *LMRC*, 2:274.

3 Aubrey Townsend, ed., *The Writings of John Bradford* (Cambridge, 1848), 2:xliii.

4 1 Corinthians 10:12; Psalm 14:3; *The Penitent Murderer: An Exact and True Relation Taken from the
Mouth of Mr William Ivy* (1673), p. 7; *A True Account of the Behaviour, Confession and Last Dying
Speeches …* (16 June 1693), p. 1; *A True Account of the Behaviour of Thomas Randal* (29 January
1695/6), p. 1.

5 *The Behaviour, Confession & Execution of the Several Prisoners* (9 May 1679), p. 1; Mather, *The Wonders
of Free-Grace*, p. 21; *The Vain Prodigal Life, and Tragical Penitent Death of Thomas Hellier* (1680), title
page; John Reynolds, *The Triumph of God's Revenge against … Murther*, 5th ed. (1670), p. 153; *Fair
Warning to Murderers of Infants* (1692), iii, v; *The Behaviour, Confession & Execution of the Several
Prisoners …* (9 May 1679), p. 1; OA 18 May 1709, p. 1; *The Works of that Eminent Servant of Christ, Mr
John Bunyan*, 2nd ed. (1736), xiii; *The Exceeding Abundant Grace of God, Displayed in the Conversion
of William Gymer a Penitent Malefactor and Murderer* (1696), p. 16.

6 OA 13 February 1739/40, p. 4; *GM* April 1777, p. 187; for both the decline of free grace narratives
and the rise of environmental explanations for crime in American criminal literature, see Daniel
A. Cohen, *Pillars of Salt, Monuments of Grace: New England Crime Literature and the Origins of
American Popular Culture, 1674–1860* (Oxford, 1993); for the eighteenth-century Anglican shift from
predestinarian Calvinism to an emphasis on 'action rather than conviction', see Michael Mascuch,
Origins of the Individualist Self: Autobiography and Self-Identity in England, 1591–1791 (Cambridge,
1997), pp. 155–6.

7 Joel Peter Eigen, *Witnessing Insanity: Madness and Mad-Doctors in the English Court* (New Haven and
London, 1995), p. 29; Mascuch, *Origins of the Individualist Self*; Dana Y. Rabin, *Identity, Crime, and
Legal Responsibility in Eighteenth-Century England* (Houndmills, 2004).

8 Eigen, *Witnessing Insanity*, p. 21; Nigel Walker, 'The Insanity Defense before 1800', *Annals of the
American Academy of Political and Social Science*, Vol. 477, *The Insanity Defense* (January 1985),
pp. 29–30; for the Tudor period, see K. J. Kesselring, *Mercy and Authority in the Tudor State*
(Cambridge, Cambridge University Press, 2003), p. 95.

9 For a discussion of the ambiguity in Hogarth's 'Industry and Idleness', see Ronald Paulson, *Hogarth,
Volume II: High Art and Low, 1732–1750* (New Brunswick, NJ, 1992), pp. 289–322.

10 *An Account of the Lives of the Most Notorious Murderers and Robbers*, 2nd ed. (1726), p. 43; *The
Behaviour of the Condemned Criminals in Newgate* (19 December 1684), p. 4.

11 *A True Account of the Behaviour, Confession and Last Dying Speeches of the Six Criminals* (12 September
1690), p. 1; *A True Account of the Behaviour, Confession and Execution of Samuel Alderton* (7 August
1685), p. 2; *The Confession and Execution of the Seven Prisoners suffering at Tyburn* (6 March 1677/8),
p. 6; *A True Account of the Behaviour, Confession and Last Dying speeches of the Criminals that were
Executed at Tyburn* (24 January 1693/4), p. 2; *The Behaviour of the Condemned Criminals in Newgate*

(17 October 1684), p. 2; *A True Account of the Behaviour, Confession, and Last Dying Speeches of the Criminals that were Executed at Tyburn* (13 December 1695), p. 2.

12 *A True and Wonderful Relation of a Murther Committed in the Parish of Newington* (1681), p. 1; *The Confession of Francis Nicholson* (1680), p. 2; *The Sufferers Legacy to Surviving Sinners* (1684); *The Wicked Husband and Unnatural Father* (1705), p. 7; *A True Account of the Behaviour, Confession and Last Dying Speeches of the 4 Criminals that were Executed at Tyburn* (23 October 1691), p. 2; *A True Account of the Behaviour, Confession and Last Dying Speeches of the Criminals that were Executed at Tyburn* (23 October 1693), p. 2.

13 *LMRC*, 3:423; OA 26 July 1743, pp. 44–5; OA 27 April 1752, p. 67.

14 *The Truth of the Case: Or a Full and True Account of the Horrid Murders, Robberies and Burnings* (1708; repr. Worcester, 1758), p. 8; George Lillo, *The London Merchant; or, the History of George Barnwell* (1731; repr. London, 1906), p. 49; *Select and Impartial Account of the Most Remarkable Convicts* (1745), 1:105; OA 15 December 1710, p. 1.

15 OA 28 July 1721, p. 3; *LMRC*, 3:55; OA 23 December 1713, p. 4; *LMRC*, 1:122, 1:114, 1:141, 1:188, 1:436; *A True Account of the Behaviour, Confession, Last Dying Speeches of the Seven Criminals that were Executed at Tyburn* (9 May 1690), p. 2.

16 *Select and Impartial Account of the Most Remarkable Convicts* (1745), 1:105; OA 21 December 1739, p. 9; *LMRC*, 2:137; *The Confession, Behaviour and Dying Speeches of the Pirates at Execution Dock* (12 July 1700), p. 2.

17 *A True Account of the Behaviour, Confession, and Last Dying Speeches of the Criminals that were Executed at Tyburn* (18 September 1695), p. 1; *Select Trials* (1742), 3:56; *LMRC*, 2:114; *Select and Impartial Account of the Most Remarkable Convicts* (1745), 1:v; OA 25 April 1746, pp. 22, 25.

18 *The British Journal* 5 March 1724/5.

19 *A True Narrative of the Proceedings at the Sessions-house in the Old Bayly* (12–15 December 1677), p. 8; *Weekly Journal; or Saturday's Post* 2 December 1721; OA 20 December 1704, p. 1; OA 31 October 1712, p. 4; OA 2 February 1714/5, p. 4; *The Post Man* 6–8 May 1697.

20 *The Execution, Last Speeches & Confessions of the Thirteen Prisoners* (24 October 1679), p. 1; *The Confession and Execution of the Nine Prisoners that Suffered at Tyburn* (28 April 1680), p. 1; *A True Copy of the Paper deliver'd by John Smith* (1704), p. 1; *A Brief Historical Account of the Lives of the Six Notorious Street Robbers* (1726); repr. in G. H. Maynadier, ed., *Freebooters and Buccaneers* (New York, 1935), p. 353; *LMRC*, 1:293–4; OA 3 October 1750, p. 105; OA 11 November 1724, p. 5.

21 OA 2 November 1742, pp. 8–9; OA 12 June 1741, pp. 7–8; OA 7 February 1749/50, p. 7.

22 *LMRC*, 1:150–1; OA 24 December 1744, p. 6; OA 26 July 1731, p. 11.

23 OA 2 October 1758, iii–iv; OA 11 October 1752, p. 131; OA 11 February 1750/1, p. 45; see also Peter King and Joan Noel, 'The Origin of "The Problem of Juvenile Delinquency": The Growth of Juvenile Prosecutions in London in the Late Eighteenth and Early Nineteenth Centuries', *Criminal Justice History*, 14 (1993), 32.

24 *LMRC*, 1:411–21; 2:318–335; 2:371–393; on the subject of determining the reformability of malefactors, see Beattie, *Crime and the Courts*, p. 613; Peter King, 'Decision-Makers and Decision-Making in the English Criminal Law, 1750–1800', *Historical Journal* 27 (1984), 34–43; Cynthia Herrup, *The Common Peace: Participation and the Criminal Law in Seventeenth-Century England* (Cambridge, 1987), pp. 165–192; these calculations are derived from figures from Simon Devereax's forthcoming work, *Capital Punishment in Hanoverian London, 1689–1837*.

25 Daniel Defoe, *The Family Instructor*, ed. Paula Backsheider (1715; repr. New York, 1989), p. 68; *The History of the Remarkable Life of John Sheppard* (1724); repr. in Horace Bleackley and S. M. Ellis, *Jack Sheppard* (London, 1933), pp. 138–9; Paula Backscheider, *Daniel Defoe* (Lexington, 1986), p. 152; OA 17 June 1723, p. 6.

26 OA 5 March 1732/3, p. 26; *Memoirs of the Life of William Henry Cranstoun, Esq.* (1752), p. 4; *Murder Will Out: An Impartial Narrative of the Notorious Wicked Life of Capt. Harrison* (1692), pp. 3–4; *Weighley, alias Wild: A Poem in Imitation of Hudibras* (1725), p. 3; *LMRC*, 2:335.

27 OA 23 December 1730, p. 10; OA 7 April 1742, p. 7; OA 31 December 1750, p. 34; *LMRC*, 1:112.

28 *LMRC*, 1:112; *Memoirs of the Right Villanous John Hall* (1708), pp. 17–18; Hannah More, *The Execution of Wild Robert: Being a Warning to all Parents* [1796]; *Fair Warning from Tyburn: Or, the Several*

Confessions and Execution of the Fifteen Notorious Malefactors that Suffered There (8 March 1679/80), p. 4; *LMRC*, 2:75–6; *A Genuine Account of Anne Whale and Sarah Pledge* (1752), p. 9.

29   *LMRC*, 1:94, 1:273, 1:225; OA 15 June 1763, p. 49; *Select Trials* (1742), 4:113.

30   *Select Trials* (1742), 2:26; *Inhumanity and Barbarity Not to be Equal'd* (1740), p. 31; quoted in G. J. Barker-Benfield, *The Culture of Sensibility: Sex and Society in Eighteenth-Century Britain* (Chicago, 1992), p. 106.

31   *LMRC*, 1:21–2; OA 12 May 1730, p. 3.

32   *Some Reasons Humbly offer'd why the Castration of Persons found Guilty of Robbery and Theft, May be the best Method of Punishment for those Crimes* (Dublin, 1725), p. 2; *A True Account of the Behaviour, Confession and Last Dying Speeches of the 8 Criminals that were Executed at Tyburn* (26 January 1689/90), p. 2; *LMRC*, 1:38.

33   Thomas Fuller, *Gnomologia: Adages and Proverbs* (1732).

34   *LMRC*, 1:14; OA 23 December 1730, p. 6; OA 8 November 1738, p. 10; OA 11 February 1733/4, p. 8.

35   *Select Trials* (1742), 1:208–9; OA 22 December 1721, p. 4; OA 15 March 1744/5, pp. 6, 7, 10.

36   *The Genuine Lives of Christopher Johnson, John Stockdale and William Peers* (1753), pp. 9–10, 6; *Select Trials* (1742), 1:274; *A Genuine Narrative of the Life and Surprising Robberies and Adventures of William Page* (1758), p. 44; *Select Trials* (1742), 1:212–13.

37   OA 17 February 1743/4, p. 33; *A True Account of the Behaviour and Confession of the Nine Criminals that were Executed at Tyburn* (31 May 1689), p. 2; OA 30 April 1724, p. 5; *Some Considerations upon Street-Walkers* (1726), p. 18; OA 18 May 1743, p. 19; OA 15 March 1744/5, p. 5; OA 16 May 1750, p. 41; OA 6 August 1740, pp. 6–7; see also M. Dorothy George's classic study, *London Life in the Eighteenth Century* (London, 1925), esp. ch. 1.

38   OA 17 February 1743/4, p. 4; OBP 19–21 April 1721, p. 3; OA 18 July 1722, p. 4; OA 24 September 1722, p. 2; OA 13 February 1765, p. 27.

39   William Blackstone, *Commentaries on the Laws of England* (1767–9), 4:15; *Colonel Jack*, ed. Samuel Holt Monk (Oxford, 1989), p. 163; Henry Fielding, *An Enquiry into the Causes of the Late Increase of Robbers*, ed. Malvin R. Zirker (1751; repr. Oxford, 1988), pp. 77, 157; Bernard de Mandeville, *An Enquiry into the Causes of the Frequent Executions at Tyburn* (1725), preface; OA 7 June 1740, p. 5; *Select and Impartial Account of the Most Remarkable Convicts* (1745), 2:45.

40   OA 14 March 1721/2, p. 3; OA 7 November 1744, pp. 5–6.

41   OA 5 July 1721, p. 3; OA 24 November 1740, p. 5.

42   OA 31 October 1718, p. 5; OA 22 September 1715, p. 5; *LMRC*, 2:350–1; OA 13 February 1727/8, p. 2; OA 22 November 1742, pp. 6–7.

43   OA 20 February 1748/9, p. 10; OA 29 January 1732/3, pp. 13–14; OA 18 March 1740/1, p. 5.

44   OA 6 June 1707, p. 1; *The True Account of the Behaviour and Confession of the Convicted Criminals* (25 May 1687), pp. 3–4; OA 16 July 1714, p. 5; OA 27 January 1715/6, p. 3; *A True Account of the Five Criminals Executed at Tyburn* (17 July 1691), p. 2; OA 11 May 1715, p. 4.

45   OA 21 April 1711, p. 2; OA 28 August 1724, p. 2; *The True Account of the Behaviour and Confession of the Criminals* (21 April 1686), p. 4.

46   *LMRC* 1:17–18; OA 29 January 1719/20, p. 4.

47   OA 8 March 1733/4, p. 13; OA 16 June 1731, p. 6; OA 14 March 1725/6, p. 4; OA 15 December 1710, p. 2; OA 18 March 1740/1, p. 18; OA 18 January 1737/8, p. 8; OA 9 August 1732, p. 8; OA 17 February 1743/4, p. 10.

48   *The Confessions, Behaviour and Dying Speeches of the Criminals that were Executed at Tyburn* (5 September 1700), p. 1; OA 4 June 1770, p. 41; OA 3 April 1721, p. 3; OA 8 February 1720/1, p. 4; OA 12 May 1721, pp. 4–5; OA 24 May 1725, p. 2; OA 5 October 1744, p. 6.

49   OA 12 May 1721, p. 6; OA 18 March 1740/1, p. 6; OA 4 April 1746, p. 10; OA 22 November 1742, pp. 6, 10.

50   OA 31 October 1712, pp. 4, 5; *A Genuine Account of the Behaviour, Confessions and Dying Words of the Malefactors … Executed at Kennington-Common* (25 August 1743), p. 14; OA 2 October 1735, p. 20; *A True Account of the Behaviour, Confession and Last Dying Speeches of the Criminals that were Executed at Tyburn* (8 March 1693/4), p. 2; OA 27 January 1715/16, p. 2.

51   OA 31 October 1712, p. 5; OA 31 January 1712/3, p. 6; OA 22 September 1715, p. 6; John Beattie, 'Crime and Inequality in Eighteenth-Century London', *Crime and Inequality*, eds. John Hagan and

Ruth D. Peterson (Stanford, 1995), pp. 137–8; see also Lynn MacKay, 'Why They Stole: Women in the Old Bailey, 1779–1789', *Journal of Social History* (Spring 1999).

52   John Bunyan, *The Life and Death of Mr Badman* (1680), ed. James F. Forrest and Roger Sharrock (Oxford, 1988), p. 55; *Weekly Journal; or Saturday's Post* 17 September 1720, p. 562; OA 23 March 1752, p. 48.

53   *A Genuine Narrative of the Trial and Condemnation of Mary Edmundson*, 2nd ed. (1759), pp. 3–4; OA 12 June 1741, p. 4; OA 18 October 1749, p. 84; *Post Man* 26–29 December 1696; OA 19 September 1716, p. 5; for changes in perceptions of women after about 1740, see Barker-Benfield, *Culture of Sensibility*.

54   *Select Trials* (1742), 4:33; *A Hellish Murder Committed by a French Midwife, on the Body of her Husband* (1687/8), pp. 30–1, 33–4.

55   OA 9 May 1726, pp. 2–3, 4; *LMRC*, 2:231; *Parker's Penny Post* 11 May 1726; *Select Trials* (1742), 3:20–23; *Weekly Journal; or British Gazetteer* 23 April 1726.

56   *The Authentic Tryals of John Swan and Elizabeth Jeffryes for the Murder of Mr Joseph Jeffryes of Walthamstow in Essex* (1752), pp. 56–7; *The Tryal of Thomas Colley at the Assizes at Hertford … Likewise a Narrative of the Cruel Murder of Mr Joseph Jeffryes* (1751), p. 11; *Authentic Memoirs of the Wicked Life and Transactions of Elizabeth Jeffryes, Spinster* (1752), pp. 6–7, 8; 2–3.

57   *The Case of Miss Blandy Consider'd as a Daughter, as a Gentlewoman and as a Christian* (1752), pp. 16, 19; *Miss Mary Blandy's Own Account of the Affair between Her and Mr Cranstoun* (1752), p. 63; *GM* April 1752, p. 189; for less sympathetic accounts of Blandy, see *Walpole's Correspondence*, 20:312, 317, as well as *A Genuine Account of the most Horrid Parricide Committed by Mary Blandy, Spinster* (1751).

58   This, however, seems to have been a relatively new development in the Anglo-American law; see Holly Brewer, *By Birth or Consent: Children, Law, and the Anglo-American Revolution in Authority* (Chapel Hill and London, 2005), pp. 181–2.

59   OA 1 February 1724/5, pp. 5–6; *Read's Weekly Journal; or British Gazetteer* 5 August 1732; OA 24 December 1744, p. 10; OA 28 June 1756, p. 46; *Annual Register* 21 May 1763 (1764), p. 77.

60   OA 6 & 11 June 1764, p. 39; OA 7 & 28 March 1764, p. 34; OA 9 December 1754, p. 9; OA 23 October 1751, p. 120; *Select Trials* (1764), 3:166.

61   OA 22 September 1752, p. 122; *The True Narrative of the Confessions and Execution of the Seven Prisoners at Tyburn* (24 October 1683), p. 3; OA 11 February 1733/4, p. 10; OA 22 September 1752, p. 116; OA 17 June 1751, p. 93; OA 9 October 1732, p. 15; OA 5 March 1732/3, p. 13; OA 28 May 1714, pp. 6, 4.

62   Fielding, *Enquiry into the Causes of the Late Increase of Robbers*, p. 164; *LMRC*, 3:7; see also 1:304 and 1:432.

63   *Select and Impartial Account of the Most Remarkable Convicts* (1745), v; OA 7 June 1745, pp. 3, 11; CLRO, Court of Alderman Papers, 'The Humble Complaint of James Guthrie Ordinary of Newgate. Read 19 February 1744/5'.

64   OA 1 August 1746, pp. 50–1, 44; OA 17 June 1747, p. 4; OA 17 March 1748/9, p. 30.

65   OA 28 April 1760, pp. 16, 9; OA 5 October 1757, ii; *The Reward for Murder: a Faithful Narrative of … Daniel Looney, and Robert Greenstreet … Executed for Murder at Tyburn* (14 December 1751), p. 5.

66   OA 5 October 1757, p. 5; OA 19 December 1759 & 11 February 1760, p. 21; John Villette, *A Genuine Account of the Behaviour, Confession, and Dying-Words of William Hawke and William Jones* (1774), pp. 5–6; OA 27 May 1772, p. 2; OA 2 October 1758, iv; OA 19 April 1770, p. 31.

67   OA 1 August 1746, p. 44; OA 26 July 1745, p. 36; OA 20 June 1746, pp. 37–8.

68   *Select Trials* (1764), iii; Randall McGowen, 'The Changing Face of God's Justice: the Debates over Divine and Human Punishment in Eighteenth-Century England', *Criminal Justice History* 9 (1988), 63–98; OA 26 July 1731, p. 4.

69   OA 29 January 1713/4, p. 2; OA 29 June 1737, p. 3; OA 6 August 1740, p. 4; *LMRC*, 1:323; *A Genuine Account of the Life, Robberies, Trial and Execution of William Cox* (27 October 1773), pp. 29–30; OA 5 October 1757, p. 38; OA 1 May 1758, p. 21; OA 4 April 1746, p. 9.

70   See for instance, Barker-Benfield, *Culture of Sensibility*.

71   OA 4 April 1746, p. 5; OA 1 May 1758, p. 31.

Notes to Chapter 4: Highwaymen Lives: Social Critique and the Criminal

1   *GM* May 1763, p. 211; OA 4 May 1763, pp. 32, 36, 35. See John Gay, *The Beggar's Opera*, ed. Bryan
    Loughrey and T. O. Treadwell, p. 118 (Act III, Scene XIII, Air LXVII).

2   *Letters from the Late Most Reverend Dr Thomas Herring ... to William Duncombe* (1777), 3n;
    John Ireland and John Nichols, *Hogarth's Works* (London, 1883), 2:295; *Boswell's London Journal,
    1762–1763*, ed. Frederick A. Pottle (New York, 1950), p. 264; see also Michael D. Friedman, '"He was
    just a Macheath": Boswell and *The Beggar's Opera*', in Paul J. Korshin, ed., *The Age of Johnson*, Vol. 4
    (New York, 1991), pp. 97–114; and Philip Carter, 'James Boswell's Manliness', in Tim Hitchcock and
    Michèle Cohen, eds. *English Masculinities 1660–1800* (London, 1999), pp. 111–130.

3   Michael Mascuch, *Origins of the Individualist Self: Autobiography and Self-Identity in England
    1591–1791* (Cambridge, 1997), p. 180.

4   For a recent synthesis and overview of rogue literature, see Craig Dionne and Steve Mentz, eds., *Rogues
    and Early Modern Culture* (Ann Arbor, 2004); for the highwayman as a 'social critic', see Faller, *Turned
    to Account*, ch. 8.

5   Gillian Spraggs, *Outlaws and Highwaymen: the Cult of the Robber in England from the Middle Ages to
    the Nineteenth Century* (London, 2001), p. 211; Linebaugh, *London Hanged*, pp. 189, 218; Faller, *Turned
    to Account*, pp. 3–4, 171.

6   For a larger historical overview of the heroic English robber, see Spraggs, *Outlaws and Highwaymen*.

7   Peter Haining, *The English Highwayman: A Legend Unmasked* (London, 1991), p. 14; Beattie, *Crime
    and the Courts*, pp. 152–3.

8   Attributed to Defoe by J. R. Moore in his *Checklist of the Writings of Daniel Defoe* (Bloomington, 1960);
    de-attributed by P. N. Furbank and W. R. Owens, *Defoe De-Attributions: a Critique of J. R. Moore's
    Checklist* (London, 1994).

9   *No Jest Like a True Jest* (1657), pp. 18–19 [n.p.]

10 George Fidge, *The English Gusman* (1652), p. 40; George Fidge, *Hind's Ramble* (1651), pp. 16–17;
    Smith, *Lives of the Highwaymen*, 2:148, 1:285–6.

11 Daniel Defoe, *The True Born Englishman*, 9th ed. (1701), p. 25; Smith, *Lives of the Highwaymen*, 2:90;
    Johnson, *General History of the Highwaymen*, p. 315; *Grub-Street Journal* 28 August 1735.

12 Johnson, *A General History of the Pyrates*, pp. 587, 222; Johnson, *General History of the Highwaymen*,
    p. 153.

13 Johnson, *General History of the Highwaymen*, p. 1, i.

14 Smith, *Lives of the Highwaymen*, 1:279, 1:275–6; Captain Alexander Smith, *Memoirs of the Life and
    Times of the Famous Jonathan Wild* (1726; repr. Malcolm J. Bosse, ed., New York, 1973), p. 152–3;
    Johnson, *General History of the Highwaymen*, p. 152.

15 Samuel Garth, *The Dispensary* (1699), Canto I, pt. 1.

16 Quoted from a letter dated 30 March 1728 reprinted in *GM* 1773, Supplement, p. 653; *GM* September
    1773, p. 464; OBP 1 May 1728, 4 December 1728; *Lloyd's Evening Post* 29 October–1 November 1773;
    A Genuine Account of the Life, Robberies, Trial and Execution of William Cox (1773), p. 10; *The Life and
    Actions of James Dalton* (1730), p. 46.

17 Michael Denning, 'Beggars and Thieves'.

18 *The History of the Remarkable Life and Death of John Sheppard* (1724), reprinted in G. H. Maynadier,
    ed., *The Works of Daniel Defoe*, Vol 16 (New York, 1905), p. 187; *A Narrative of the Robberies, Escapes,
    &c. of John Sheppard*, 8th ed (1724), p. 27; *Select Trials* (1742), 2:140; *Parker's London News* 4 November
    1724; *Select Trials* (1742), 2:141–2.

19 *British Journal* 4 December 1725; *Authentic Memoirs of the Life and Surprising Adventures of John
    Sheppard*, 2nd ed. (1724), viii, 64, ix.

20 *Authentic Memoirs*, iii; *The Prison-Breaker; or, the Adventures of John Sheppard* (1725), pp. 22–3. This
    play was published, but never performed, although much of its content was later incorporated into
    another play with Sheppard as hero, *The Quaker's Opera*, first performed at Bartholomew Fair in
    1728.

21 *The Quaker's Opera* (1728), p. 19; *Authentic Memoirs*, pp. 26, 52.

22 *Memoirs of the Right Villanous John Hall, the Late Famous and Notorious Robber, penn'd from his own
    Mouth some time before his Death*, 4th edn. (1708), p. 21.

23 *John Ketch, esq: His Letter to the Directors of the South-Sea* (Dublin, 1721), p. 8; Johnson, *General History of the Pyrates*, p. 134.

24 Charles Hitchen, *The Regulator: Or, a Discovery of the Thieves, Thief-Takers, and Locks, alias Receivers of Stolen Goods in and about the City of London* (1718); *The Last Dying Speech and Confession of the Late Parliament; Made on Saturday the 10th of March, Before their Execution* (1722), pp. 4, 9.

25 [Philip Wharton], *An Epistle from Jack Sheppard to the Late L[or]d C[hance]ll[o]r of E[nglan]d* (1725); [Daniel Defoe], *The True and Genuine Account of the Life and Actions of the Late Jonathan Wild* (1725), repr. Henry Fielding, *Jonathan Wild* (Harmondsworth, 1982), p. 252; *History of the Remarkable Life and Death of John Sheppard*, p. 195; OBP 14–21 October 1724; *Newgate's Garland* (1725). This song was later adapted for use in the play *Harlequin Sheppard* (1724).

26 *The Craftsman* 19 August 1732; *The Craftsman* 30 July 1737; *LM* January 1739, pp. 33–4; *The Craftsman* 26 April 1735; *The Craftsman* 19 August 1732.

27 *Hanging No Dishonour. Being a Modest Attempt to Prove that such Persons as have the Honour to make their Exit at the Triple Tree are not always the great Villains of the Nation* (1747), pp. 4, 6, 9, 16; *Quaker's Opera*, p. 48; *Beggar's Opera*, pp. 115–16 (Act III, Scene XI, Air LVII).

28 *Public Advertiser* 7 June 1774; *Morning Chronicle; and Evening Advertiser* 28 March 1775; *Morning Chronicle; and Evening Advertiser* 12 October 1774. The *Public Advertiser* explained that Rann was called Sixteen-String Jack 'on account of 16 Strings being affixed to each Knee of his Breeches to answer the purpose of Buttons' (2 June 1774). According to Francis Place, 'before *he* changed the fashion knee buckles were worn'(Francis Place Papers, BL Add Mss 27826, f. 85).

29 *Daily Journal* 4 July 1722; *Select Trials* (1742), 1:205; OA 18 July 1722, p. 6.

30 *Walpole's Correspondence* 20:88, 20:169; John Villette, *Annals of Newgate; or, Malefactor's Register* (1776), 4:377.

31 OA 14 March 1721/2, p. 3; *LM* July 1746; for the connection between 'crime waves' and war, see Douglas Hay, 'War, Dearth and Theft: the Records of the English Courts', *Past and Present* 95 (May 1982), 117–60; Beattie, *Crime and the Courts*, ch. 5.

32 *Diary of John Evelyn*, ed. E. S. de Beer, 6 vols. (Oxford, 1955), 5:366; *Dawks's News-Letter* 24 January 1698/9; *LMRC*, 3:30; *An Account of the Lives Of the most Notorious Murderers and Robbers, Edward Burnworth alias Frazier [et al.]*(1726), p. 11; *LMRC*, 2:158, 2:160–1; *LM* December 1748.

33 *Remarks on the Importance of the Study of Political Pamphlets, Weekly Papers, Daily Papers, Political Music &c* (1765), quoted in R. C. Alston, 'The Eighteenth-Century Non-Book: Observations on Printed Ephemera', in Giles Barber and Bernhard Fabian, eds., *Buch und Buchhandel in Europa im Achetzehnten Jahrhundert* (Hamburg, 1981), p. 352; *The Flying Post: Or, Weekly Medley* 1 March 1728/9.

34 OA 12 July 1742, p. 18; Ralph Wilson, *A Full and Impartial Account of all the Robberies Committed by John Hawkins etc.* (1722), p. 7; *LMRC*, 2:273–4;*The Confessions, Behaviour, and Dying Speeches of the Criminals Executed at Tyburn*, 20 July 1700, p. 1.

35 OA 8 February 1720/1, p. 5; OBP 13–15 January 1720/1; OA 16 September 1741, p. 5; *Lives of the Most Notorious Murderers and Robbers*, p. 67.

36 Andrea McKenzie, '"This Death Some Strong and Stout Hearted Man Doth Choose": The Practice of Peine Forte et Dure in Seventeenth- and Eighteenth-Century England', *Law and History Review* 23 (Summer 2005).

37 OA 8 February 1720/1, p. 5; OBP 13–15 January 1720/1; OA 16 September 1741, p. 5; *Lives Of the most Notorious Murderers and Robbers*, p. 67; *LMRC*, 3:71–2, 3:74; 1:108; OA 22 December 1721, p. 5.

38 *Mist's Weekly Journal* 26 March 1726; *Weekly Journal; or British Gazetteer* 9 April 1726; OA 11 November 1728, p. 3; *LMRC*, 2:179; *LMRC*, 2:179, 3:82.

39 See Harris, 'Trials and Criminal Biographies', pp. 15–19.

40 William Hawkins, *A Full, True, and Impartial Account of all the Robberies Committed ... by William Hawkins [et al.]* (1722), vi.

41 OA 18 January 1737/8, p. 15; OA 7 April 1742, p. 13. See also Linebaugh, *London Hanged*, p. 187.

42 OA 5 October 1737, p. 11; OA 13 December 1706, p. 1; *Select Trials* (1742), 2:124; *The Genuine Lives of Christopher Johnson, John Stockdale, and William Peers, Executed for Murder* (1753), p. 14; OA 4 September 1724, p. 5.

43 *The Behaviour, Confession & Execution of the several Prisoners that suffered at Tyburn* (9 May 1679), p. 6; *A True Account of the Behaviour and Confession of the Nine Criminals that were Executed at Tyburn* (31 May 1689), p. 2; OA 8 February 1720/1, p. 6; *LMRC*, 3:4; OA 22 December 1721, p. 2.

44 OA 16 September 1741, p. 15; OA 28 July 1721, p. 5; OA 8 February 1722/3, p. 5; OA 7 May 1742, p. 13; OA 4 February 1735/6, p. 15.

45 *A True Account of the Behaviour, Confession and Last Dying Speeches of the Criminals that were Executed at Tyburn* (27 January 1692/3), pp. 1–2; OA 7 February 1704/5, p. 2; OA 26 July & 11 August 1736, p. 17; OA 9 September 1723, p. 3; OA 17 December 1707, p. 2.

46 OA 26 July 1731, p. 14; *The Whitehall Evening-Post* 14–17 January 1758; *Read's Weekly Journal* 7 April 1750; *The Life of Henry Simms, alias Young Gentleman Harry* (1747), p. 30.

47 *Lives of the most Notorious Murderers and Robbers*, p. 6; *Select Trials* (1764), 4:116.

48 *A True Account of the Behaviour, Confession and Dying Speeches of the 12 Criminals that were Executed* (1–2 May 1691), p. 2; OA 24 May 1736, p. 13; OA 5 October 1737; OA 12 April 1743, p. 35; *A True Copy of the Paper of Thomas Bean* (1716).

49 Nicholas Rogers, *Crowds, Culture and Politics in Georgian Britain* (Oxford,1998), pp. 50–1.

50 Ralph Wilson, *A Full and Impartial Account of all the Robberies Committed by John Hawkins etc.* (1722), pp. 10, 28; *Lives of the most Notorious Murderers and Robbers*, pp. 7, 19.

51 See 'Clever Tom Clinch Going to be Hanged' (1728), in *The Poems of Jonathan Swift*, ed. Harold Williams, 2nd edn. (Oxford, 1958), pp. 399–400.

52 OBP 14–16 May 1741, p. 10. See *Beggar's Opera*, p. 79 (Act II, Scene V, Air XXV); Johnson, *General History of the Pyrates*, p. 244; Andrew Knapp and William Baldwin, *The Newgate Calendar*, 3 vols. (1824), 2:287; *The Authentic Trial, and Memoirs of Isaac Darkin, alias Dumas* (Oxford, 1761), p. 27; *Beggar's Opera*, p. 117 (Act III, Scene XII); *The London Chronicle* (3–5 May 1763), p. 429.

53 Faller, *Turned to Account*, p. 193. Robert Shoemaker has seen this development as occurring later, after about 1770, viewing mid-century representations of 'the polite gentleman highwayman' such as James Maclaine as primarily sympathetic, in marked contrast to the image of the 'violent urban street robber' (Shoemaker, 'The Footpad, the Street Robber and the Gentleman Highwayman: Representations and Perceptions of Robbery in London, 1690–1800'), *Cultural and Social History* 3 (2006), 381–405.

54 *LMRC*, 3:2-3, 3:5; OA 17 February 1743/4, pp. 10, 33.

55 *The Daily Advertiser* 10 November 1749; *Walpole's Correspondence*, 20:88; *A Genuine Account of the Life and Actions of James Maclean, Highwayman* (1750), pp. 13, 15, 23.

56 *A Complete History of James Maclean, the Gentleman Highwayman* (1750), p. 54; *Genuine Account of the Life … of James Maclean*, pp. 22, 10; OA 3 October 1750, p. 85.

57 *An Account of the Behaviour of Mr James Maclaine … by the Reverend Dr Allen*, 4th edn. (1750), pp. 25, 26; *London Penny Post; or the Morning Advertiser* 1–3 April 1751; Paula Backsheider and Douglas Howard, eds., *The Plays of Samuel Foote*, Vol. 1 (New York, 1983), p. 39.

58 Adam Fitz-Adam, *The World*, No. 103, 19 December 1754, pp. 315–16, 317–18. Charles 'Flemming', alias Johnson, was convicted at the Old Bailey for highway robbery on 23 October 1754, and executed at Tyburn on 9 December 1754.

59 *The History of the Robinhood Society* (1764), pp. 97–8, 101.

60 *Beggar's Opera*, p. 117 (Act III, Scene XII); *The Whitehall Evening-Post* No. 1, 30 March 1728, p. 3, repr. *GM* Supplement (1773), p. 653.

61 OA 28 July 1755, p. 69; *Genuine Account of the Life … of William Cox*, p. 31; *A Genuine Narrative of the Life and Surprising Robberies and Adventures of William Page* (1758), pp. 46, 41; *GM* May 1763, p. 210.

62 William Augustus Miles, *A Letter to Sir John Fielding, Knt. Occasioned by His extraordinary Request to Mr Garrick for the Suppression of the Beggar's Opera* (1773), p. 42; OA 13 July 1752, p. 110.

63 'The Highwayman' (1790), repr. in Eric Partridge, *Pirates, Highwaymen and Adventurers* (London, 1927), p. 160.

64 For later execution literature see Gatrell, *Hanging Tree*, chs. 4 & 5.

65 NA (formerly PRO) Home Office Papers (HO) 42/82 ff. 430–3.

Notes to Chapter 5: The Ordinary's Account: Confession and the Criminal

1   Daniel Defoe, *Moll Flanders* (Harmondsworth, 1989), p. 353; *The Newgate Calendar, or Malefactors Bloody Register* (1773), 3:10. While Defoe wrote *Moll Flanders* in 1722, the novel was supposed to have been penned by the heroine herself in 1683; Sarah Malcolm was hanged in March of 1732/3.

2   *Newgate Calendar* (1773), 3:10.

3   *The Memoirs of Capt. Peter Drake* (Dublin, 1755), pp. 156–7.

4   *The Life, Travels, Exploits, Frauds and Robberies, of Charles Speckman, alias Brown* (1763), p. 56; *Historical Manuscripts Commission*, 63rd series, *Egmont Diary*, Vol 1:11, 28 January 1729/30.

5   *Some Observations on the Trial of Mr Thomas Carr* (1737), pp. 1–2; *The Life, Travels, Exploits ... of Charles Speckman*, p. 53; BL Add Mss 27825, Francis Place Papers, Vol. I, Manners. Morals, ff. 79, 111; Charles G. Harper, *Half hours with the Highwaymen* (1908), 1:125; Arthur Griffiths, *The Chronicles of Newgate* (1884), 1:322, 1:354.

6   Lincoln Faller, 'In Contrast to Defoe: the Rev. Paul Lorrain, Historian of Crime', *Huntington Library Quarterly* 60 (1976), pp. 60, 62–3; Linebaugh, 'Ordinary of Newgate', p. 252. See also Robert R. Singleton, 'Defoe, Moll Flanders and the Ordinary of Newgate', *Harvard Library Bulletin* 24 (1976), 407–13.

7   A significant – if surprising – exception is Peter Linebaugh, who has viewed the biographies contained in the *Account* as 'records of the truth', despite the Ordinary's own 'moralistic blindness'(*London Hanged*, xx; 'Ordinary of Newgate', p. 264).

8   Ordinaries such as Paul Lorrain were occasionally reported as having 'furnished Materials' for collections of trials (*Weekly Journal; or British Gazetteer* 8 March 1717/8).

9   OBP 25–30 June 1752; for the early evolution of both the Ordinary's *Account* and the *Proceedings*, see Harris, 'Trials and Criminal Biographies'; John Langbein, 'The Criminal Trial before the Lawyers', *University of Chicago Law Review* 45 (Summer 1978), and also his 'Shaping the Eighteenth-Century Criminal Trial: a View from the Ryder Sources', *University of Chicago Law Review* 50 (Winter, 1983). See Appendices for more on the Ordinaries and the *Account* generally.

10   *The Last Words and Sayings of the True Protestant Elm-Board* (1682); Gilbert Burnet, *Some Sermons Preach'd on Several Occasions* (1713); *The Truth of the Case: Or, a Full and True Account of the Horrid Murders, Robberies and Burnings* (1708).

11   *History of the Press-Yard* (1717), pp. 51, 53.

12   Defoe, *Moll Flanders*, pp. 366–7.

13   One late seventeenth-century newspaper suggested that the office of Ordinary of Newgate was in fact in the Bishop of London's 'disposal' (*Dawks's News-Letter* 3 September 1698), and certainly the opinion of senior churchmen, particularly the Bishop of London, would have carried considerable weight. Not surprisingly, Thomas Purney, whose name was put forward for Ordinary in 1719 by the Bishop of Peterborough, Justice Eyre and Dr Laughton of Clare Hall, Cambridge, received more votes from the Court of Aldermen than his competitor, Randolph Ford, recommended only by several (unnamed) 'Principal Inhabitants' of his former parish; see CLRO Rep. 124, ff. 4–5 (10 November 1719).

14   CLRO Rep. 82 f. 214b (5 July 1674); Rep. 150 ff. 284–6 (17 June 1746); Rep. 80 f. 154 seq. (8 April 1675) and Rep. 95 f. 251 (31 March 1690/1); *The Confession and Execution of the Five Prisoners that suffered at Tyburn* (19 December 1677), p. 4.

15   CLRO Rep. 69 f. 172 (28 July 1663); Rep. 138 f. 17 (13 November 1733); Andrew Knapp and William Baldwin, *Criminal Chronology; or, the New Newgate Calendar* (1809), 1: vi; *Mist's Weekly Journal* 10 October 1719; *GM* June 1746, p. 329; CLRO Rep. 203 f. 321 (18 June 1799). See also Linebaugh, 'Ordinary of Newgate', p. 250.

16   Three Ordinaries – Samuel Smith, Paul Lorrain and Thomas Purney – have entries in the *Oxford Dictionary of National Biography*; see also the Appendix for a full list and brief biographical sketches.

17   BL Add MS 40778, f. 10, Vernon Papers; *The Post Boy* 8–10 September 1698; see also similar 'Elegy' published in *The Post Boy* 3–6 September 1698.

18   CLRO Rep. 104, f. 340 (30 May 1699); John Allen's *A Full and True Account of the Behaviours, Confessions and Last Dying Speeches of the Condemn'd Criminals* (19 April 1700) contains a purported confession by John Larkin alias Young implicating Charles Newey for libel (p. 2). Allen and the former

Margaret Dewey's convoluted feud with Captain Charles Newey can be traced in *Captain Charles Newey's Wonderful Discovery … to which is added his Case and Vindication* (1700); *Captain Charles Newy's Case, Impartially Laid Open* (1700); and *Mr Allen's Vindication* (1700). The various charges and a copy of a petition against Allen presented by a number of Newgate prisoners to the Lord Mayor are contained in *An Account of a New and Strange Discovery That was made by John Sheirly, alias Davis, & Joseph Fisher, the same Day of their Execution, Relating to the Ordinary of Newgate* (1700).

19   *Oxford Dictionary of National Biography*, entry on Paul Lorrain (by Tim Wales); *A True Account of the Behaviour, Confession and Last Dying Speech of John Herman Bryan* (1707), p. 2; OA 21 April 1714, p. 6; OA 4 May 1705, p. 2; OA 19 September 1712, p. 1; see also OA 28 December 1763 & 15 February 1764, p. 9, and Alexander Cruden, *The History of Richard Potter, a Sailor, and Prisoner in Newgate* (1763), p. 13; OA 24 January 1706/7, p. 2.

20   *History of the Press-Yard*, pp. 50–2.

21   Bernard de Mandeville, *An Enquiry into the Causes of the Frequent Executions at Tyburn* (1725), p. 19; *The Post Boy* 8–10 September 1698. Purney was, however, frequently absent because of ill health, especially near the end of his tenure; his deputy James Wagstaff officiated in his place at Jack Sheppard's execution, for instance.

22   *News from the Dead: or a Dialogue between Blueskin, Sheppard and Jonathan Wild* (1725), p. 5.

23   *Some Observations on the Trial of Mr Thomas Carr*, p. 10; Henry Fielding, *Jonathan Wild*, ed. David Nokes (Harmondsworth, 1982), pp. 205–10; for the Ordinary's reputation as a gourmand, see John Heneage Jesse, ed., *George Selwyn and his Contemporaries*, 4 vols. (London, 1882), Gilly Williams to George Selwyn, 29 June 1763, 1:245.

24   OA 25 May 1719, p. 6; B.E., *A New Canting Dictionary of the Terms Ancient and Modern of the Canting Crew* (1699).

25   OA 9 October 1732, p. 19; *Daily Journal* 7 September 1732.

26   *The Confession and Execution of the Seven Prisoners suffering at Tyburn* (6 March 1677/8), p. 7; *News from Tyburn* (16 September 1674), p. 3; *A True Account of the Behaviour and Confession of the Eighteen Criminals that were Executed at Tyburn* (15 July 1689), pp. 1–2; *An Account of the Confessions, Behaviour, and Dying Speeches of the Criminals that were executed at Tyburn* (20 December 1700), p. 1; OA 15 December 1710, p. 2; OA 24 September 1708, p. 1; OA 19 September 1712, p. 6; OA 29 January 1713/4, p. 6.

27   Linebaugh, 'Ordinary of Newgate', p. 269; Faller, 'In Contrast to Defoe', p. 60; Singleton, 'Defoe, Moll Flanders and the Ordinary of Newgate', pp. 410–11; *Select Trials* (1742), 1:244.

28   *The Execution, Last Speeches & Confessions, of the Thirteen Persons that Suffered on Friday* (24 October 1679), p. 2; OA 22 June 1715, p. 1; OA 17 December 1707, p. 2; OA 19 April 1770, p. 31; OA 2 July 1739, p. 5; for the 'Black Assizes', see Beattie, *Crime and the Courts*, pp. 304, 306; R. B. Pugh, 'Newgate Between Two Fires', *Guildhall Studies in London History* 3 (October 1978), p. 151 and (April 1979), p. 201; W. J. Sheehan, 'Finding Solace in Eighteenth-Century Newgate', in J. S. Cockburn, ed., *Crime in England 1550–1800* (London, 1977), pp. 229–230.

29   OA 23 December 1730, p. 4; OA 9 October 1732, pp. 2–3; OA 7 April 1742, p. 6.

30   OA 29 January 1700/1, p. 2; OA 13 January 1741/2, p. 12; OA 8 March 1733/4, p. 6; OA 18 September 1727, p. 1; OA 12 July 1742, p. 4; OA 28 April 1708, p. 2; OA 26 April 1749, p. 50.

31   *The Post Man* 2–4 April 1696; *An Answer to Mr Collier's Defence of his Absolution of Sir William Parkins, at the Place of Execution* (1696), p. 5; Paul Lorrain, *Walking with God: Shewn in a Sermon Preach'd at the Funeral of Mr Thomas Cook* (1703), p. 16; [Daniel Defoe], *A Hymn to the Funeral Sermon* (1703), p. 1; [Paul Lorrain], *Remarks on the Author of the Hymn to the Pillory. With an Answer to the Hymn to the Funeral Sermon* (1703), p. 4; OA 24 October 1707, p. 1.

32   *The True Account of the Behaviour and Confession of the Criminals Condemned on Thursday the 15th day of April … At Justice-Hall in the Old-Bayly* (1686), p. 1; OA 8 August 1711, p. 1; Samuel Rossell, *The Prisoner's Director* (1742), p. 32; OA 24 May 1736, p. 9; OA 16 November 1730, p. 1; OA 27 March 1728, p. 3.

33   Daniel Defoe, *Roxana: the Fortunate Mistress*, ed. John Mullan (Oxford, 1996), p. 129; *A True Account of the Behaviour, Confeesion [sic], Last Dying Speeches of the seven Criminals that were Executed at Tyburn* (9 May 1690), p. 1; *A True Account of the Behaviour, Confession, and Last Dying Speeches of the Criminals that were Executed at Tyburn* (8 May 1693), p. 1; Rossell, *Prisoner's Director*, p. 28.

34   George Swinnock, *The Christian-man's Calling* (1662), p. 502; Jeremy Taylor, *The Rule and Exercises of Holy Dying*, 13th edn. (1682), pp. 199–200; OA 20 May 1715, p. 3; OA 23 February 1718/9, pp. 4–5; *The Confession and Execution as well of the several Prisoners that suffered at Tyburn* (17 April 1678), p. 6; OA 28 May 1733, p. 19; CLRO Rep. 112, ff. 332–3 (6 July 1708); H. O. White, ed., *The Works of Thomas Purney* (Oxford, 1933), xx.

35   Paul Lorrain, *The Dying Man's Assistant* (1702), p. 5; Rossell, *Prisoner's Director*, vii; OA 24 October 1711, p. 2; OA 7 December 1715, p. 5.

36   OA 17 December 1707, p. 2; OA 10 March 1713/4, pp. 3, 5, 6.

37   OA 5 December 1715, pp. 4–5.

38   OA 22 May 1732, pp. 11–12; OA 16 November 1730, pp. 2–3; OA 7 May 1740, p. 7; OA 27 March 1728, p. 2; OA 14 March 1738/9, p. 7; OA 3 March 1736/7, pp. 3, 5. For a different interpretation of such episodes, see Linebaugh, 'Ordinary of Newgate'.

39   Rossell, *Prisoner's Director*, pp. 239; 238; 239–40.

40   James Foster, *An Account of the Behaviour of the Late Earl of Kilmarnock* (1746), pp. 3–4; *Natures Cruell Step-Dames* (1637), pp. 13, 12. While this anonymous account has been attributed to Henry Goodcole, he was no longer officiating as minister at Newgate after 1636 (see entry by Christopher Chapman in *ODNB*).

41   Ralph Houlbrooke, 'The age of decency, 1600–1760', in Peter C. Jupp and Clare Gittings, eds., *Death in England* (New Brunswick, NJ, 2000), p. 180; William Perkins, *A Salve for a Sicke Man* (1625), pp. 107–8; *The Book of Common Prayer* (1662; repr. London, 1999), 'Visitation of the Sick', p. 312; Taylor, *Holy Dying*, p. 192.

42   *The Behaviour and Execution of Robert Green and Lawrence Hill who Suffered at Tyburn* (21 February 1678/9), p. 5; *A True Account of the Behaviour, Confession and Last Dying Speeches of the Criminals that were Executed at Tyburn* (8 March 1692/3), p. 1; OA 28 January 1701/2, p. 1; *The Confessions, Behaviour, and Dying Speeches of the Criminals that were Executed at Tyburn* (6 September 1700), p. 1; Rossell, *Prisoner's Director*, p. 65.

43   OA 19 July 1738, p. 3; OA 11 August 1703, p. 1; *A True Account of the Behaviour, Confession, and Last Dying Speeches of the Criminals that were Executed at Tyburn* (26 July 1693), p. 1; *A True Account of the Behaviour, Confession, and Last Dying Speeches of the Criminals that were Executed at Tyburn* (8 May 1693), p. 2; Lorrain, *Dying Man's Assistant*, pp. 111–12.

44   *A True Account of the Behaviour, Confession and Last Dying Speeches of the Criminals that were Executed at Tyburn* (24 October 1690), p. 3; *A True Account of the Prisoners Executed at Tyburn* (23 May 1684), p. 4; *A True Account of the Behaviour, Confession, and Last Dying Speeches of the Criminals that were Executed at Tyburn* (12 July 1695), p. 2.

45   OA 23 May 1701, p. 2; see especially Faller, 'In Contrast to Defoe', pp. 60–1.

46   Mike Hepworth and Bryan S. Turner, *Confession: Studies in Deviance and Religion* (London, 1982), p. 14 (see also Sharpe, 'Last Dying Confessions'); OA 2 November 1715, pp. 3–4.

47   OA 29 April 1713, p. 5; OA 24 September 1708, p. 2; *The Confessions, Behaviour, and Dying Speeches of the Criminals that were Executed at Tyburn* (6 September 1700), p. 1; OA 5 August 1723, p. 3; OA 4 April 1746, p. 7; *The Confession and Execution of the Two Prisoners that suffered at Tyburn* (16 December 1678), p. 7; OA 12 May 1730, p. 3; OA 9 September 1723, p. 2.

48   Gilbert Burnet and Anthony Horneck, *The Last Confession, Prayers and Meditations of Lieuten. John Stern [et al.]* (1681/2), p. 7; OA 6 & 11 June 1764, p. 43; *Select Trials* (1764), 4:233, 4:155; OA 4 May 1763, p. 35.

49   *A True Account of the Behaviour, Confession, and Last Dying Speeches of the 15 Criminals* (22 December 1690), p. 2; *A True Account of the Prisoners Executed at Tyburn* (23 May 1684), p. 3; *A True Account of the Behaviour, Confssion [sic] and Last Dying Speeches of the Criminals that were Executed at Tyburn* (27 January 1692/3), p. 2; *A True Account of the Behaviour, Confession, and Last Dying Speeches of the Criminals that were Executed at Tyburn* (9 March 1697/8), p. 2; *The Life and Penitent Death of John Mausgridge, Gent.* (1708), p. 2.

50   *LMRC*, 3:86; OA 19 September 1712, p. 5; *A True Account of the Behaviour, Confession and Last Dying Speeches of the 13 Criminals* (26 & 27 February 1690/1), p. 1; *LMRC*, 1:73; OA 12 September 1707, p. 1.

51   *A True Account of the Behaviour, Confession and Last Dying Speeches of the Criminals that were Executed at Tyburn* (23 July 1690), p. 2; OA 28 May 1714, p. 4; OA 24 September 1722, p. 6; *A True Account of the Behaviour, Confession, and Last Dying Speeches of the Criminals that were Executed at Tyburn* (22 December 1697), p. 1; OA 8 June 1719, p. 5; OA 26 April 1749, p. 38.

52   *A True Account of the Behaviour and Confession of the Eighteen Criminals that were Executed at Tyburn* (15 July 1689), p. 1; Samuel Smith (1588–1665), *David's Repentance*, 25th ed. (1694), pp. 93, 133; Rossell, *Prisoner's Director*, p. 242; Jeremy Taylor, *Holy Dying*, pp. 20–23.

53   OA 5 July 1721, p. 4; OA 4 May 1763, p. 37; OA 18 July 1722, p. 6; [Fifield] Allen, *An Account of the Behaviour of Mr. James Maclaine*, 4th edn. (1750), p. 15; Jeremy Taylor, *Rule and Exercises of Holy Dying*, p. 212; OA 4 February 1735/6, p. 4; OA 8 April 1723, p. 6; OA 27 October 1708, p. 2.

54   OA 6 November 1723, p. 6; *LMRC*, 1:472; OA 27 January 1717/8, p. 5; *The Life, Travels, Exploits, Frauds and Robberies, of Charles Speckman, alias Brown* (1763), p. 49; Taylor, *Holy Dying*, pp. 212–13. The practice of withholding communion from those malefactors who refused to confess to their crimes was by no means unique to Newgate: in 1708, the Ordinary of Worcester Castle refused to administer the sacrament to the condemned murderers and arsonists John Palmer and Thomas Symonds after they recanted their earlier confession of guilt (inveigled from them, they claimed, by the promise of a reprieve). The clergyman salved his conscience, however, by assuring Palmer that if he were 'really innocent, my denying him the Sacrament could be no Disadvantage to him; for that God, in such case, would accept the Desire for the Performance'; see *The Truth of the Case: Or, a Full and True Account of the Horrid Murders, Robberies and Burnings* (1708), p. 49.

55   OA 28 April 1760, p. 9; OA 13 October 1762, pp. 55–6; OA 11 July & 15 August 1764, p. 67.

56   *A True Account of the Five Criminals Executed at Tyburn* (17 July 1691), p. 2; OA 21 April 1711, p. 2.

57   *A True Account of the Behaviour and Confession of the Nine Criminals that were Executed at Tyburn* (31 May 1689), p. 1; *The True Account of the Behaviour and Confession of the Condemned Criminals in Newgate* (24 July 1685), p. 3; OA 22 December 1725, p. 3; *The True Account of the Behaviour and Confession of the Criminals to be Executed upon Hounslow-Heath* (15 July 1687), p. 4; OA 24 March 1728/9, p. 3.

58   OA 25 September 1713, p. 6; OA 3 November 1703, p. 2; *LMRC*, 1:303; OA 29 April 1724, p. 6.

59   *The Account of the Behaviour, Confession and Last Dying Speech of Sir John Johnson* [sic] (23 December 1690), p. 2; *A True Relation of the Execution of John Smith, alias Ashburnham (for Murder) [and] … of Edward Jackson, Executed the same Day at Tyburn, for High-Treason* (26 May 1684), pp. 3–4.

60   *A True Account of the Behaviour and Confession of the Eighteen Criminals that were Executed at Tyburn* (15 July 1689), p. 1; *A True Account of the Behaviour, Last Dying Words, and Execution of John Hutchins* (17 December 1684), pp. 2–3; *A True Account of the Behaviour, Confession, and Last Dying Speeches of the Criminals that were Executed at Tyburn* (12 July 1695), p. 1; *Daily Post* 8 September 1741; Taylor, *Holy Dying*, p. 194.

61   *Select Trials* (1742), 1:102; *Select Trials* (1764), 1:239; OA 22 March 1726/7, p. 3; OA 31 May 1718, pp. 3–4.

62   *The Confessions, Behaviour, and Dying Speeches of the Criminals Executed at Tyburn* (20 July 1700), p. 2; OA 11 October 1752, pp. 133–4; OA 22 August 1729, p. 4; OA 4–5 January 1724/5, pp. 6, 4–5; OA 7 December 1715, p. 3.

63   CLRO, Court of Aldermen Papers, 'The Humble Complaint of James Guthrie Ordinary of Newgate Read 19 February 1744/5'; *The Grub-Street Journal* 30 October 1732; *Achilles Dissected … To which is added, The First Satire of the Second Book of Horace, Imitated in a Dialogue between Mr Pope and the Ordinary of Newgate* (1733), p. 30.

64   CLRO Rep. 150, ff. 240–1 (14 May 1746); CLRO, Court of Aldermen Papers, 'The Humble Petition of James Guthrie, AM' (1733/4); CLRO Rep. 137, f. 438 (16 October 1733); *GM* September 1733, p. 493; CLRO Rep. 138, f. 210 (19 February 1733/4); CLRO Rep. 144, f. 265 (3 June 1740).

65   *The Ordinary of Newgate's Account of the Behaviour, Dying Words and Confession; Birth, Parentage, and Education, of the Several Malefactors That were Executed at Westminster on Friday last, for the horrid Crimes of B[riber]y and C[orruptio]n. To which is annexed, Mr P[elha]m's Speech immediately before his execution* (1747); *A Genuine Copy of the Tryal of Thomas Grimes, Esq. Alias Lord S—, for a*

barbarous and inhuman Rape [1748], p. 39; Oliver Goldsmith, *Essays by Mr Goldsmith* (1765), Essay XXV, pp. 176–9.

66 CLRO Rep. 167, f. 436 (4 October 1763), Rep. 169, ff. 13–15 (29 November 1764), Rep. 173, ff. 451–3 (18 July 1769); Rep. 178, ff. 103–5 (8 February 1774); OA 14 February 1770, p. 9; CLRO Rep. 203, f. 321 (18 June 1799).

67 *The British Magazine* 2 July 1772.

68 In the 1730s Applebee had frequently published some of the dying speeches in his *Weekly Journal*; in the mid-1740s *The Penny London Post* reprinted selected excerpts from the Ordinary's *Account*, and in 1775, *The Morning Chronicle* briefly reported gallows speeches in their entirety.

Notes to Chapter 6: Dying Well: Martyrs and Penitents

1 John Kettlewell, *An Office for Prisoners for Crimes, Together with Another for Prisoners for Debt* (1697), pp. 22–3, 25.

2 J. Sears McGee, *The Godly Man in Stuart England: Anglicans, Puritans and the Two Tables, 1620–1670* (New Haven, 1976), p. 70.

3 *A True Account of the Behaviour and Confession of the Nine Criminals that were Executed at Tyburn* (31 May 1689), p 1; OA 17 February 1743/4, Part II, p. 35.

4 OA 4 May 1763, p. 37; George Lillo, *The London Merchant; or the History of George Barnwell* (1731; ed. Adolphus William Ward, Boston, 1906), pp. 95–6; OA 1 June 1730, p. 3; *The Confession and Execution of the Five Prisoners who Suffered at Tyburn* (16 March 1676/7), p. 5; *A True Account of the Behaviour, Confession, and Last Dying Speeches of the 15 Criminals that were Executed on Monday* (22 December 1690), p. 1.

5 OA 12 May 1721, p. 6; Paul Lorrain, *The Dying Man's Assistant* (1702), pp. 112–13; Francis Kirkman, *The Counterfeit Lady Unveiled* (1673), p. 208; *LM* July 1738, p. 361; William Wilson and Dr Comber, *The Account of the Behaviour, Confessions, and Dying Words, of the Malefactors ... Executed at Kennington Common ... and Likewise ... in the Market-Place at Kingston* (10 & 11 April 1735), p. 5.

6 OA 27 April 1752, p. 61; *The Confession and Execution of the Five Prisoners suffering at Tyburn* (16 March 1676/7), p. 23; OA 3 February 1723/4, pp. 5–6; OA 8 February 1722/3, pp. 3, 6; OA 16 June 1731, pp. 7, 8.

7 *The Sufferers Legacy to Surviving Sinners: Edmund Kirk's Dying Advice to Young Men* (11 June 1684), p. 1; Sharpe, 'Last Dying Speeches', p. 165; Mather, *Wonders of Free-Grace*, pp. 66, 124.

8 *Life of Silas Told*, p. 73; Mitchell B. Merbeck, *The Thief, the Cross and the Wheel: Pain and the Spectacle of Punishment in Medieval and Renaissance Europe* (London, 1999), p. 156; see also Phillipe Ariès, *The Hour of Our Death*, trans. Helen Weaver (New York and Oxford, 1981), pp. 10–13, 108, 118.

9 *The Execution of the 11 Prisoners that Suffer'd at Tyburn* (22 January 1678/9), p. 4; John Wesley, *Free Grace: A Sermon Preach'd at Bristol* (1740), p. 5.

10 OA 22 November 1742, p. 13; OA 23 October 1721, p. 5; *LMRC*, 1:61; OA 7 February 1749/50, p. 7.

11 *The Penitent Thief* (1773), p. 12; OA 14 February 1731/2, pp. 3–4; Mather, *Wonders of Free-Grace*, p. 152; *A True Account of the Behaviour, Confession and Last Dying Speeches of the Criminals that were Executed at Tyburn* (8 March 1692/3), p. 2.

12 OA 7 November 1750, p. 18; OA 21 November 1729, p. 4; OA 1 August 1746, p. 56; OA 26 June 1728, p. 4; OA 23 November 1763, p. 16.

13 David E. Stannard, *The Puritan Way of Death: a Study in Religion, Culture and Social Change* (New York, 1977), pp. 73–5, 83; Bankes Crooke, *Mr Crooke's Two Sermons Preached before the Condemn'd Criminals at Newgate* [1695], vi; Brad S. Gregory, *Salvation at State: Christian Martyrology in Early Modern Europe* (Cambridge, Mass., 1999), pp. 16–21; D. R. Woolf, 'The Rhetoric of Martyrdom: Generic Contradiction and Narrative Strategy in John Foxe's *Acts and Monuments*', in Thomas S. Mayer and D. R. Woolf, eds., *The Rhetorics of Life-Writing in Early Modern Europe* (Ann Arbor, 1995), p. 252; Murray Roston, *Biblical Drama in England* (London, 1968), p. 71; see also John Knott, *Discourses of Martyrdom in English Literature*, 1563–1694 (Cambridge, 1993).

14 *The Dying Speeches and Behaviour of the several State Prisoners That have been executed the last 300 Years* (1720), p. 171; John Bunyan, *Grace Abounding: With Other Spiritual Autobiographies*, ed. John

Stachniewski with Anita Pacheco (Oxford, 1998), pp. 91–2; *The Speeches and Prayers of Major General Harrison* [*et al.*] (1660), p. 70; *Dying Speeches and Behaviour of the several State Prisoners*, p. 200.

15 *King Lear*, Act IV, Scene vi; *Blundel the Jesuit's Letter of Intelligence* (1679), p. 1; *Speeches and Prayers of Major General Harrison*, p. 1; *A Narrative of the Apprehending, Commitment, Arraignment, Condemnation and Execution of John James* (1662), p. 38; *The Acts and Monuments of John Foxe*, ed. George Townsend (New York, 1965), 7:547.

16 *Stafford's Memoires* (1681), p. 62; William Roper, *The Life of Sir Thomas More*, repr. in George Cavendish ed., *Two Early Tudor Lives* (New Haven and London, 1962), p. 254; *The Speeches, Discourses, and Prayers, of Col. John Barkstead, Col. John Okey, and Mr Miles Corbet* (1662), p. 22; *State Trials*, 11:881; 8 October 1685, no. 1709, p. 344; *The Dying Speeches of several Excellent Persons, who Suffered for their Zeal against Popery, and Arbitrary Government* (1689), p. 28; *Speeches and Prayers of Major General Harrison*, p. 10.

17 *A True Copy of Sir Henry Hide's Speech on the Scaffold* (4 March 1650/1), p. 15; *Short Memorandum's upon the Deaths of M. Philip Evans and M. John Lloyd both Priests, who were Executed at Cardiff in Glamorganshire* (22 July 1679), p. 1; *State Trials*, 7:501; *The Chiefe Heads of Mr John Sares Speech, and other passages at the time of his execution at West-Chester* (20 October 1652), p. 1; *The Mirror of Martyrs*, 6th edn. (1685), vi; *Dying Speeches and Behaviour of the several State Prisoners*, p. 195.

18 *Compleat Collection of Remarkable Tryals*, 2:82–3; OA 22 March 1703/4, p. 2; OA 7 February 1704/5, p. 2.

19 *True Copy of the Paper at Large, left by Mrs. Deborah Churchill* (1703), p. 1; OA 4 May 1705, p. 1; OA 18 February 1725/6, p. 4.

20 OA 29 April 1713, p. 5; OA 5 March 1732/3, p. 12; OA 22 September 1715, p. 4.

21 OA 9 October 1732, pp. 11–12; OA 21 September 1716, p. 5.

22 OA 19 December 1733, p. 20; OA 12 September 1726, p. 2; OA 12 May 1721, pp. 4–5; *Select Trials* (1742), 2:35–6.

23 OA 8 February 1721/2, p. 3; OA 18 February 1725/6, pp. 3–4; OA 3 August 1726, p. 4.

24 OA 2 October 1734, pp. 23, 25; William Wilson and Dr Comber, *The Account of the Behaviour, Confessions, and Dying Words, of the Malefactors … Executed at Kennington Common … and Likewise … in the Market-Place at Kingston* (10 & 11 April 1735), pp. 5–6.

25 OA 24 September 1722, p. 5.

26 *A Compassionate Address to Prisoners for Crimes* (1742), p. 80; *Remarkable Trials* (1765), 1:29; OA 11 May 1748, p. 54; *The Confession and Execution of the Nine Prisoners that Suffered at Tyburn* (28 April 1680), p. 4; OA 9 November 1722, p. 4.

27 OA 24 May 1736, p. 17; OA 30 April 1725, p. 3; OA 17 June 1747, p. 12; OA 17 June 1751, pp. 91–2.

28 OA 3 August 1739, p. 9; OA 1 June 1730, p. 3; OA 7 April 1742, p. 10; *LM* October 1750, p. 474; OA 17 June 1747, p. 16.

29 OA 7 April 1742, p. 7; OA 26 July 1731, p. 18; OA 15 May 1706, p. 1; OA 14 March 1725/6, p. 4.

30 Gilbert Burnet, *Some Passages of the Life and Death of … John Earl of Rochester*, 6th edn. (1724), p. 27; Albert C. Outler, ed., *The Works of John Wesley: Sermons* (Nashville, 1984–1987), 3: 499; Isabel Rivers, *Reason, Grace and Sentiment: A Study of the Language of Religion and Ethics in England, 1660–1780*, Vol. I: *Whichcote to Wesley* (Cambridge, 1991), pp. 44, 230; R. W. Chapman, ed., *Boswell's Life of Johnson* (Oxford, 1980), p. 623; OA 24 October 1713, p. 4; OA 24 September 1722, pp. 1, 3.

31 OA 9 May 1726, p. 1; OA 20 May 1715, p. 2; Gilbert Burnet and Anthony Horneck, *Last Confession, Prayers and Meditations of Lieuten. John Stern* (1682), p. 10; *Mrs. Elizabeth Torshell's Letter to the Ordinary of Newgate* (1705), p. 1; D. P. Walker, *The Decline of Hell: Seventeenth-Century Discussions of Eternal Torment* (London, 1964).

32 OA 3 April 1721, p. 3; OA 19 September 1712, p. 2; OA 17 February 1743/4, Part II, p. 36; OA 4 May 1763, p. 35.

33 Ralph Houlbrooke, *Death, Religion, and the Family in England, 1480–1750* (Oxford, 1998), pp. 54–5; OA 4 May 1722, pp. 5–6; OA 15 June 1724, p. 5; Burnet and Horneck, *Last Confession, Prayers and Meditations of Lieuten. John Stern* (1682), p. 2.

34 *An Account of the Behaviour of the Fourteen Late Popish Malefactors, whil'st in Newgate* (1679), p. 7; OA 19 September 1720, p. 5; OA 11 August 1727, p. 1; Burnet and Horneck, *Last Confession, Prayers and Meditations of Lieuten. John Stern*, pp. 1, 6.

35 *A True Account of the Behaviour and Confession of the Nine Criminals that were Executed at Tyburn* (31 May 1689), p. 2; OA 14 March 1725/6, p. 4; *Weekly Journal; or, British Gazetteer* 19 March 1725/6; *LMRC*, 2:141.

36 OA 3 April 1721, p. 6 (this James Dalton is probably the famous street robber, hanged in 1730); OA 8 February 1720/1, pp. 5, 6; OA 6 November 1723, p. 1; *LMRC*, 1:472. Newgate prisoners were segregated by sex, but during the day both visitors who had paid the requisite fees and inmates not confined to their cells – debtors, or felons not considered a security risk – moved with relative freedom between the different sections of the prison.

37 OA 22 November 1742, p. 7; *A True Account of the Behaviour, Confession and Last Dying Speeches of the Criminals that were Executed at Tyburn* (16 June 1693), p. 2; OA 20 November 1727, pp. 1, 4; OA 3 August 1738, p. 9; OA 24 September 1722, p. 2; OA 4 May 1741, p. 4.

38 OA 22 June 1748, p. 60; OA 17 June 1751, p. 84; OA 9 August 1732, p. 12; *LMRC*, 2:80; OA 24 May 1725, p. 3.

39 OA 5 July 1721, p. 4; OA 4 May 1763, p. 37; OA 18 July 1722, p. 6; [Fifield] Allen, *An Account of the Behaviour of Mr James Maclaine*, 4th edn. (1750), p. 15.

40 OA 4 May 1763, p. 30; OA 10 November 1762, pp. 73–4; OA 11 July & 15 August 1764, p. 67; OA 4 May 1763, pp. 35, 36, 39; OA 23 November 1763, p. 10.

41 However there is evidence to suggest that during the height of the persecution of English Catholics during the Popish Plot (1678–81), some gaolers exercised cruelty towards Catholic prisoners; the Catholic midwife Elizabeth Cellier would claim that some of those detained were mistreated and even tortured in an attempt to extort confessions; see *Malice Defeated and the Matchless Rogue* (1680; repr. Los Angeles, 1988), pp. 5–7.

42 OA 23 July 1716, pp. 5–6; *An Appeal of Murther from Certain Unjust Judges … Containing a Relation of the Tryal, Behaviour, and Death of Mr William Anderton* (1693), pp. 33–4.

43 *A Narrative; or, the Ordinary of Newgate's Account of what passed between him and James Sheppard* (17 March 1717/8), p. 6; OA 16 November 1730, p. 4; OA 16 & 19 May 1729, p. 4.

44 *A True Account of the Behaviour, Confession and Last Dying Speeches of the Criminals that were Executed at Tyburn* (23 July 1690), p. 1; *The Behaviour and Execution of Robert Green and Lawrence Hill … Who Suffered at Tyburn* (21 February 1678/9), p. 7; *A True Account of the Behaviour, Confession and Last Dying Speeches of the Prisoners that were Executed* (21 December 1689), p. 2; OA 21 May 1722, p. 3; *A True Account of the Behaviour, Confession and Last Dying Speeches of the Criminals that were executed at Tyburn* (26 January 1697/8), p. 2.

45 OA 25 May 1723, p. 6; OA 22 November 1742, p. 5; OA 26 June 1728, p. 2; *The Confessions, Behaviour and Dying Speeches of the Criminals that were Executed at Tyburn* (6 November 1700), p. 2; OA 13 February 1739/40, p. 5; OA 21 June 1704, p. 2; OA 17 June 1723, p. 5; *A True Account of the Behaviour, Confession and Dying Words of Capt. John Massey* (1723), p. 1 (Roche, however, discontinued his visits when a family member began sending a priest to visit him in his cell); OA 6 August 1740, p. 4; OA 16 November 1747, p. 4.

46 OA 7 May 1740, p. 10; OA 1 June 1730, p. 2; OA 5 July 1721, p. 4; OA 30 December 1702, p. 2; *A True Account of the Behaviour, Confession [sic], Last Dying Speeches of the Seven Criminals that were Executed at Tyburn* (9 May 1690), p. 2.

47 OA 16 November 1730, pp. 1, 3; OA 5 August 1723, p. 1; OA 15 September 1710, p. 2; OA 21 May 1722, p. 6.

48 CLRO Rep. 132, f. 362; *LM* July 1735, p. 389; OA 21 November 1743, pp. 10–11; OA 20 February 1748/9, p. 4; OA 26 March 1750, p. 19; OA 24 August 1763, p. 59; OA 7 February 1749/50, p. 3; OA 17 February 1743/4, pp. 3, 12.

49 OA 24 August 1763, p. 59; OA 17 June 1751, p. 80; OA 28 May 1753, pp. 62, 52, 60; OA 8 December 1755 & 21 February 1756, p. 27; OA 4 April 1746, pp. 8–9; OA 11 December 1752 & 12 February 1753, p. 24.

50 OA 16 April 1753, p. 36; OA 23 March 1752, p. 47; OA 26 March 1750, p. 33; OA 7 February 1749/50, p. 13; OA 28 May 1753, p. 63.

51 OA 8 November 1738, p. 7; OA 17 February 1743/4, p. 12. According to a 1585 statute, it was a treasonable offence for Catholic priests to proselytize in England, although the effective punishment

had been downgraded from death to life imprisonment by an Act of 11 William III and was, in any case, after the Glorious Revolution seldom, if ever, enforced to its full rigour. Although the Act prescribing life imprisonment for priests was repealed in 1775, the bulk of discriminatory legislation against Catholics was not repealed until 1829; see Gordon Rupp, *Religion in England, 1688–1791* (Oxford, 1986), p. 185.

52   *Life of Silas Told*, pp. 77–8; OA 25 April 1746, p. 25; OA 19 April 1770, p. 24; OA 28 April 1760, p. 18.

53   *A True Account of the Behaviour, Confessions and Last Dying Speeches of the 8 Criminals that were executed at Tyburn* (26 January 1689/90), p. 1; OA 18 September 1727, p. 1.

54   OA 18 September 1727, p. 1; OA 20 November 1727, p. 1; OA 16 June 1731, p. 4; John Donne, *Death's Duell*, ed. Geoffrey Keynes (1631; repr. Boston, 1973), pp. 15–17; John Bunyan, *The Life and Death of Mr Badman*, ed. James F. Forrest and Roger Sharrock (1680; repr. Oxford, 1988), pp. 157–8, 167–8; Boswell, *Life of Johnson*, p. 1238.

55   J. Sears McGee, 'Conversion and the Imitation of Christ in Anglican and Puritan Writing', *Journal of British Studies* 15 (Spring 1976), 21–39; Isabel Rivers, *Reason, Grace and Sentiment: A Study of the Language of Religion and Ethics in England, 1660–1780* (Cambridge, 1991); Edward Fowler quoted in Rivers, p. 83; OA 5 October 1757, p. 36.

56   *Diary of John Evelyn*, ed. E. S. de Beer (Oxford, 1955), 5:146–7, 5:162; William Whiston, *Sermons and Essays upon Several Subjects* (1709), pp. 7–8, 12.

57   John Fletcher, *An Appeal to Matter of Fact and Common Sense* (Bristol, 1772), pp. 25, 38, 66, 67, 70, 72; *The Penitent Thief: Or a Narrative of two Women fearing God, who visited in prison a highway-man* (1773), p. 36.

58   *The Works of the Rev. John Wesley*, ed. John Emory (New York, 1856), 3:442–3; *Life of Silas Told*, pp. 72, 73–4.

59   GM May 1739, pp. 241, 257; Stephen Roe, *A Remarkable Narrative of ... Jacob Romert* (1 July 1758), p. 53; *A Letter to the Rev. Mr M-re B-k-r, Concerning the Methodists* (Dublin, 1752), p. 48; *Walpole's Correspondence*, 1:134–5.

60   LM August 1739, pp. 452–3; *Letter ... Concerning the Methodists*, p. 33.

61   *Life of Silas Told*, pp. 104, 113; *London Evening Post* 12–15 September 1767.

62   OA 7 & 28 March 1764, p. 19; OA 1 May 1758, p. 41; OA 7 June 1754, p. 76; OA 24 May & 15 September 1760, p. 20; OA 28 April 1760, p. 15; *The Behaviour, Confession and Dying Words of Thomas Homan* (18 November 1742), p. 15; OA 10 November 1762, p. 66; OA 25 April 1746, p. 25.

63   OA 7 June 1754, p. 76; OA 11 October 1752, p. 135; OA 1 May 1758, pp. 34–5.

64   OA 15 June 1763, p. 52; OA 19 April 1770, p. 30.

65   *Life of Mr Silas Told*, p. 99; *Lloyd's Evening Post and British Chronicle* 18–20 October 1773.

66   CLRO Rep. 179, ff. 108–9 (17 January 1775); *Boswell's Life of Johnson*, p. 1319. Forde, who opposed capital punishment and clearly saw his attendance upon the condemned as degrading, was dismissed after an 1814 inquiry into Newgate conditions; see Basil Montagu, *An Inquiry into the Aspersions upon the late Ordinary of Newgate* (1815); Arthur Griffiths, *The Chronicles of Newgate* (1883; repr. New York, 1987), pp. 374–5.

Notes to Chapter 7: Dying Game: Bridegrooms and Highwaymen

1   Harold Williams, ed., *The Poems of Jonathan Swift*, 2nd edn. (Oxford, 1958), pp. 399–400. Williams dates the poem to 1726, but the alternate date of 1727 is often given, suggesting that it was originally written in early 1727 (New Style).

2   OA 20 May 1728, p. 4; *Weekly Journal; or British Gazetteer* 9 November 1728; *LMRC*, 3:81, 3:74.

3   OA 8 February 1720/1, p. 5; *LMRC*, 1:110; OA 22 December 1721, p. 5; *LMRC*, 1:112.

4   Henry Fielding, *An Enquiry into the Causes of the Late Increase of Robbers and Related Writings* (1751), ed. Melvin R. Zirker (Oxford, 1988), p. 167; Bernard de Mandeville, *An Enquiry into the Causes of the Frequent Executions at Tyburn* (1725), pp. 23–4; *LMRC*, 2:176-7; OA 21 December 1739, p. 10; *Fog's Weekly Journal* 16 November 1728.

5   OA 11 November 1728, p. 5; *LMRC*, 1:388; OA 13 January 1751/2, p. 29; OA 8 February 1721/2, p. 3.

6   Gatrell, *Hanging Tree*, p. 111.
7   Leon Brett, 'The Law in Lithuania', in Anita Brostoff and Sheila Chamovitz, eds., *Flares of Memory: Stories of Childhood during the Holocaust* (Oxford and New York, 2001), p. 68.
8   The *OED* lists as its first entry for 'dying game': '1727 [i.e., 1727/8] GAY *Beggar's Opera*. "Good bye captain ... die game, captain"'. The reference to the play (but not the quotation) can be traced to Eric Partridge, *Dictionary of the Underworld* (London, 1950), s.v. 'die game'. The most likely source for this passage may be John Baldwin Buckston, *Jack Sheppard* [1840] Act 4, Scene 3, in which John Gay is supposedly inspired to write *The Beggar's Opera* after witnessing Jack Sheppard's execution and overhearing his comrades bid him farewell; i.e., 'good bye! good bye, Jack ... Die game, Jack' (I am indebted to Beppe Sabatini for this last reference).
9   OA 13 July 1752, p. 110; Andrew Knapp and William Baldwin, *Criminal Chronology; or, the New Newgate Calendar* (1809), 3:287; Francis Grose, *A Classical Dictionary of the Vulgar Tongue* (1785), s.v. 'game'; *A Dictionary of Buckish Slang, University Wit, and Pickpocket Eloquence* (1811), s.v. 'die hard or game'.
10   Thomas Betterton, *The Revenge: Or, a Match in Newgate* (1680), p. 58; John Gay, *The Beggar's Opera*, ed. Bryan Loughrey and T. O. Treadwell (London, 1986), p. 117; *Compleat Collection of Remarkable Tryals*, 1: 160; Andrew Knapp and William Baldwin, *The Newgate Calendar* (1824), 2:287; *The Authentic Trial, and Memoirs of Isaac Darkin, alias Dumas* (Oxford, 1761), p. 27.
11   Christopher Bullock, *A Woman's Revenge: Or, a Match in Newgate* (1715), p. 55; *Street-Robberies, Considered* (1728), p. 52 (this pamphlet was attributed by Moore to Defoe; de-attributed by Furbank and Owen). The expression 'to die like a cock' seems to have become common by the late eighteenth century; see *General Evening Post* 26–28 October 1773.
12   OA 4 May 1763, p. 40; OA 5 July 1721, pp. 5–6; OA 18 March 1740/1, p. 17.
13   John Bunyan, *The Pilgrim's Progress* (1678; repr. Ware, Hertfordshire, 1996), p. 202; J. Sears McGee, *The Godly Man in Stuart England: Anglicans, Puritans, and the Two Tables, 1620–1670* (New Haven, 1976), p. 43; Jeremy Gregory, 'Homo Religiosus: Masculinity and Religion in the Long Eighteenth Century', in Tim Hitchcock and Michèle Cohen, eds, *English Masculinities, 1660–1800* (London and New York, 1999), pp. 90–1, 99; Richard Sherlock, *The Practical Christian: Or, the Devout Penitent* (1699), p.12; [Samuel Smith], *The Character of a Weaned Christian: Or the Evangelical Art of Promoting Self-denial* (1675), pp. 14, 21; see also Alan Bray, 'To Be a Man in Early Modern Society: the Curious Case of Michael Wigglesworth', *History Workshop Journal* 41 (Spring 1996), 155–65.
14   *Covent-Garden Journal* 28 March 1752, repr. Bertrand A. Goldgar, ed., *The Covent-Garden Journal and a Plan of the Universal Register-Office* (Middletown, 1988), p. 416, see also entry for 28 April 1752, p. 428; Mandeville, *Enquiry into the Causes of the Frequent Executions at Tyburn*, p. 32; Captain Alexander Smith, *Memoirs of the Life and Times of the Famous Jonathan Wild* (1726), p. 203; Johnson, *General History of the Highwaymen*, pp. 314, 342. In his version of the execution of Clare and Lawrence, Johnson renders the deleted word as 'Maidenhead' (Johnson, *General History of the Highwaymen*, p. 442).
15   *A True Account of the Behaviour, Confession, and Last Dying Speeches of the Six Criminals that were Executed at Tyburn* (12 September 1690), p. 2; Narcissus Luttrell, *A Brief Historical Relation of State Affairs from September 1678 to April 1714* (Oxford, 1857), 3:274; GM October 1771, p. 471.
16   The custom of forgiving the hangman dated at least from the Middle Ages; see J. Huizinga, *The Waning of the Middle Ages* (New York, 1949), pp. 11–12; and Pieter Spierenburg, *The Spectacle of Suffering* (Cambridge, 1984), p. 33, and Richard Evans, *Rituals of Retribution: Capital Punishment in Germany, 1600–1987* (Oxford, 1996), p. 67.
17   Fielding, *Enquiry into the Causes of the Late Increase of Robbers*, p. 167.
18   OA 13 May 1730, pp. 3–4; *The Tyburn Chronicle; or, Villainy Display'd in all its Branches* (1768), 2:250–51; OA 3 March 1736/7, pp. 5, 12; OA 8 February 1722/3, pp. 5–6; LMRC, 1:220–21. The scriptural reference is to 2 Timothy 4:7: 'I have fought a good fight, I have finished my course, I have kept the faith'.
19   OA 4 May 1763, p. 37; John Kettlewell, *An Office for Prisoners for Crimes, Together with Another for Prisoners for Debt* (1697), p. 24; Richard Sherlock, *The Practical Christian; or, the Devout Penitent* (1699), p. 5; *A True Account of the Prisoners Executed at Tyburn* (23 May 1684), p. 3; *The Execution and Confessions of the Seven Prisoners Executed at Tyburn* (19 December 1679), p. 2.

20 OA 8 February 1720/1, p. 3; *The Behaviour, Confession & Execution of the Several Prisoners that Suffered at Tyburn* (9 May 1679), p. 7; *The Behaviour of the Condemned Criminals in Newgate* (19 December 1684), p. 2; OA 8 February 1720/1, p. 5; *The Acts and Monuments of John Foxe*, ed. George Townsend (New York, 1965), 8:86. For more on men and tears, see Philip Carter, *Men and the Emergence of Polite Society, Britain 1660–1800* (Harlow, 2001), pp. 94–6.

21 *LMRC*, 1:370–71; OA 16 June 1731, p. 7; John Villette, *A Genuine Account of the Behaviour and Dying Words of William Dodd* (27 June 1777), p. 21.

22 Samuel Smith, *David's Repentance*, 25th ed. (1694), pp. 94–6, 133, 157–8; OA 20 May 1728, p. 2; *LMRC*, 3:381; OA 7 & 28 March 1764, p. 28.

23 OA 21 January 1746/7, p. 8; *LMRC*, 1:101, OA 12 September 1707, p. 1; OA 20 November 1727, p. 2; OA 16 April 1753, p. 48.

24 OA 9 October 1732, p. 17; OA 12 May 1730, p. 4; *LMRC*, 3:251; OA 24 October 1711, p. 2; *The Behaviour of the Condemned Criminals in Newgate … who [were] Executed at Tyburn* (17 October 1684), p. 3.

25 OA 13 January 1741/2, p. 16; OA 4 May 1722, pp. 5–6; OA 7 November 1750, p. 15; OA 21 & 23 December 1747, pp. 25, 27; OA 12 September 1707, p. 2; *A True Account of the Behaviour, Confession, and Last Dying Speeches of the 15 Criminals that were Executed* (22 December 1690), p. 1; *The Speech and Deportment of Col. James Turner at his Execution* (21 January 1663/4), p. 3.

26 *Beggar's Opera*, pp. 115–16; *Some Authentic Particulars of the Life of the Late John Macnaghton, Esq.* (1762), p. 54; *A True Account of the Behaviour, Confession and Last Dying Speeches of the Criminals that were Executed at Tyburn* (16 June 1693), p. 2; OA 4 May 1763, p. 35.

27 *A Full, True and Genuine Account of the Uncommon Behaviour of Mr Gill Smith [et al.]* (Southwark, 1738), p. 15; *The Life and Character of Charles Ratcliffe, Esq.* [1747], p. 18; OA 26 April 1749, p. 55.

28 Betterton, *The Revenge*, p. 58; *Compleat Collection of Remarkable Tryals*, 1:58; Gilbert Burnet and Anthony Horneck, *Last Confession, Prayers and Meditations of Lieuten. John Stern* (1682), pp. 6, 7; OA 21 April 1714, p. 1.

29 John Greene, *Salvation by Grace, But not without Holiness in Heart and Life* (1761).

30 See for instance Daniel A. Cohen, *Pillars of Salt, Monuments of Grace: New England Crime Literature and the Origins of American Popular Culture, 1674–1860* (Oxford, 1993), and Michael Mascuch, *Origins of the Individualist Self: Autobiography and Self-Identity in England, 1591–1791* (Cambridge, 1997), pp. 155–6.

31 OA 15 June 1724, p. 5; see for instance, T. B., *The General Inefficacy and Insincerity of a Late, or Death-bed Repentance* (1670), pp. 2–4; William Sherlock, *A Practical Discourse Concerning Death*, 36th edn. (1810), pp. 277–84; Paul Lorrain, *The Dying Man's Assistant* (1702), p. 96; John Stevens, *Christ made Sin for his People, and they made the Righteousness of God in Him* (1760), pp. 23–5.

32 OA 5 October 1737, p. 11; *Select Trials* (1742), 1:255.

33 *Full and Genuine Account of the Lives, Characters, Behaviour, Last Dying Words and Confessions of the Four Malefactors … Executed … at Kennington-Common* (6 April 1739), p. 15; *Speech and Deportment of Col. James Turner*, pp. 20–1.

34 OA 18 July 1722, p. 6; *LMRC*, 1:185–6.

35 *The London Chronicle; or Universal Evening Post* 3–4 May 1763, p. 429; *GM* April 1777, p. 191; OA 19 April & 16 May 1770, p. 30; *Select Trials* (1742), 1:151.

36 *An Impartial Account of the Behaviour of Sir Thomas Armstrong* (1684), p. 2; *The Mirror of Martyrs*, 6th edn. (1685), vi; Richard Baxter, *A Treatise of Death, the Last Enemy to be Destroyed* (1672), pp. 33, 35.

37 Peter Lake and Michael Questier, 'Agency, Appropriation and Rhetoric under the Gallows: Puritans, Romanists and the State in Early Modern England', *Past & Present* 153 (1996), 69; OA 8 February 1720/1, pp. 2–3; *A Relation of Dr Dodd's Behaviour in Newgate* (1777), p. 7.

38 Samuel Smith, *An Account of the Behaviour of the Fourteen Late Popish Malefactors, whil'st in Newgate* (1679), p. 37; Gilbert Burnet, *Some Sermons Preach'd on Several Occasions* (1713), pp. 166–7, 163; OA 13 April 1720, p. 2.

39 *The Arraignment, Tryal & Condemnation of Algernon Sidney, Esq; for High Treason* (1684), p. 67; *The Genuine History of the Life of Richard Turpin* (1739), p. 33.

40 *An Account of the Dying Behaviour of Christopher Slaterford [sic] Executed at Guilford* (9 July 1709), p. 2; *Some Authentic Particulars of the Life of the late John Macnaghton, Esq.* (1762), p. 55; OA 4 May 1741, p. 8.

41 Burnet and Horneck, *Last Confession, Prayers and Meditations*, p, 7; *An Account of the Behaviour of the Fourteen Late Popish Malefactors*, p. 8; *Beggar's Opera*, p. 117; Mandeville, *Enquiry into the Causes of the Frequent Executions at Tyburn*, p. 23; Evans, *Rituals of Retribution*, p. 74; *Weekly Journal; or Saturday's Post* 31 May 1718.

42 *Observations on the Trial of Mr Thomas Carr*, p. 10; *A Supplement to the London Journal, of February 2, 1722–3. Being a Large and Impartial Abstract of the Tryal of Christopher Layer* (1723), p. 5; *The Indictment, Arraignment, Tryal, and Judgements at Large, of Twenty-nine Regicides* (1724), xx–xxi; *Stafford's Memoires* (1681), pp. 68–9; *The English Gazette* 29 December 1680 – 1 January 1680/1; *A True Account of the Behaviour, Confession, and Last Dying Speeches of the Condemned that were Executed at Tyburn* (28 May 1697), p. 1.

43 *The Behaviour, Confession & Execution of the several Prisoners that suffered at Tyburn* (9 May 1679), p. 7; *State Trials*, 4:124; *An Account of the Lives of the Most Notorious Murderers and Robbers, Edward Burnworth alias Frasier [et al.]*, 2nd edn. (1726), p. 65; *Measure for Measure*, Act IV, Scene iii; *A Brief Historical Account of the Lives of the six notorious Street Robbers executed at Kingston* (1726), repr. G. H. Maynadier, ed., *Freebooters and Buccaneers* (New York, 1935), p. 379.

44 *Last Confession, Prayers and Meditations of Lieuten. John Stern*, p. 12; *LM* June 1733, pp. 273–4; *LMRC*, 3:74; *Select and Impartial Account of the Most Remarkable Convicts* (1745), 2:155; OA 6 June 1707, p. 2; OA 22 September 1752, pp. 118, 127; OA 30 April 1725, p. 6; OA 8 December 1755 & 21 February 1756, p. 32.

45 *Authentic Trial, and Memoirs of Isaac Darkin*, p. 2; *GM* June 1776, p. 255 (see also *The Malefactor's Register* [1779], 1:vii); *Fog's Journal* 19 March 1737.

46 *Observations on the Trial of Mr Thomas Carr*, p. 9; *LMRC*, 3:140–1.

47 OA 21 January 1746/7, p. 11; *GM* December 1750, p. 533.

48 OA 29 June 1737, p. 3; *A True Account of the Behaviour, Confession and Last Dying Speeches of the 8 Criminals that were Executed at Tyburn* (26 January 1690/1), p. 1; *The Life and Character of Charles Ratcliffe, Esq.* (1747), p. 5.

49 *GM* June 1746, p. 394; *Westminster Journal* 13 September 1746; *Westminster Journal* 13 September 1746; *GM* May 1738, p. 275; Adam Smith, *The Theory of Moral Sentiments* (1759; repr. New York, 1966), p. 351.

50 *LM* September 1746, p. 433; *GM* August 1746, p. 412; the analogy of the 'Nightcap' comes from one of la Rochefoucauld's *Maxims* (i.e., XXII).

51 *LM* September 1732, p. 278; *LM* February 1741, p. 82; Clement Ellis, *The Gentile Sinner, Or England's Brave Gentleman Character'd in a Letter to a Friend* (Oxford, 1672), p. 144; *Some Authentic Particulars of the Life of the late John Macnaghton*, p. 51; John Heneage Jesse, ed., *George Selwyn and his Contemporaries* (London, 1882), 1:109; *LM* September 1746, p. 431; R. W. Chapman, ed., *Boswell's Life of Johnson* (Oxford, 1980), p. 580.

52 John Tosh, 'The Old Adam and the New Man: Emerging Themes in the History of English Masculinities, 1750–1850', in Hitchcock and Cohen, eds., *English Masculinities*, p. 225; Carter, *Men and the Emergence of Polite Society*, p. 70; Gregory, 'Homo Religiosus, p. 99; G. J. Barker-Benfield, *The Culture of Sensibility: Sex and Society in Eighteenth-Century Britain* (Chicago, 1992); Smith, *Theory of Moral Sentiments*, pp. 213–14.

53 See, for instance, Steven Shapin, *A Cultural History of Truth: Civility and Science in Seventeenth-Century England* (Chicago and London, 1994), p. 69.

54 OA 6 March 1731/2, p. 10; OA 9 November 1722, p. 1.

55 OA 5 July 1736, pp. 9, 10; OA 3 October 1750, p. 103; [Fifield] Allen, *An Account of the Behaviour of Mr James Maclaine*, 4th edn. (1750), p. 17; *True Copies of the Papers wrote by Arthur Lord Balmerino [et al.]* (1746), 2:33.

56 OA 19 July 1738, p. 16; *The Behaviour and Character of … the Three Highland Deserters who were Shot at the Tower* (18 July 1743), p. 14; *LM* March 1740/1, p. 136; *GM* March 1740/1, p. 162.

57 J. Sears McGee, *The Godly Man in Stuart England: Anglicans, Puritans and the Two Tables, 1620–1670* (New Haven, 1976).

58   OA 15 June 1763, p. 52; *A Genuine Account of the Trials, Behaviour after Sentence of Death, and Execution of Francis Townley* [*et al.*] (1746), p. 1.

59   OA 16 October 1732, pp. 5, 7; *Penny London Post* 16–19 November 1750; OA 23 June 1753, pp. 25–6.

60   Randall McGowen, 'A Powerful Sympathy: Terror, the Prison, and Humanitarian Reform in Early Nineteenth-Century Britain', *Journal of British Studies* 25 (July 1986), 322; Carter, *Men and the Emergence of Polite Society*, p. 192; Katharine C. Balderson, ed., *Thraliana: The Diary of Mrs. Hester Lynch Thrale* (Oxford, 1942), 1:253; Gatrell, *Hanging Tree*, p. 239.

61   OA 5 August 1753, p. 97; Samuel Richardson, *Letters Written to and for Particular Friends on the Most Important Occasions* (1741), pp. 238, 241.

62   OA 14 September 1767, p. 16; *Life of Silas Told*, pp. 115–16;

63   *Morning Chronicle; and Evening Advertiser* 14 July 1775; *Morning Chronicle; and Evening Advertiser* 17 August 1775; William Augustus Miles, *A Letter to Sir John Fielding, Knt. Occasioned by His extraordinary Request to Mr Garrick for the Suppression of the Beggar's Opera* (1773), pp. 39–40, 42.

64   *George Selwyn and his Contemporaries*, 3:198; OA 16 May 1750, p. 52.

65   Christopher Bullock, *A Woman's Revenge: Or, a Match in Newgate* (1715), pp. 54, 57; Thomas Betterton, *The Revenge: Or, a Match in Newgate* (1680); *Weekly Journal; or Saturday's Post* 5 May 1722; *LMRC*, 1:146. The origins of the tradition of matrimonial gallows pardons are lost in the mists of time, but seem to have been common to other European countries; see Arlette Farge, *Fragile Lives: Violence, Power and Solidarity in Eighteenth-Century Paris*, trans. Carol Shelton (Cambridge, MA, 1993), p. 186.

66   Henri Misson, *M. Misson's Memoirs and Observations in his Travels over England*, trans. M. Ozell (1719; French edition 1698), p. 124; *Hell upon Earth: or the most Pleasant and Delectable History of Whittington's Colledge, Otherwise (vulgarly) called Newgate* (1703), p. 11.

67   *Street-Robberies, Considered*, p. 52; *The Genuine History of the Life of Richard Turpin* (1739), p. 32; *GM* April 1739, p. 213; OA 17 June 1747, pp. 16–17; *A True, Genuine, and Authentic Account of the Behaviour, Conduct, and Transactions of John Rice* [*et al.*] (1763), pp. 24, 21; Frederick A. Pottle, ed., *Boswell's London Journal, 1762–1763* (New York, 1950), pp. 252–6.

68   *Public Advertiser* 26 October 1775; OA 23 October 1753, p. 126; OA 13 January 1752, p. 29; *LM* December 1733, p. 641.

69   Linebaugh, 'Tyburn Riot', p. 115; OA 7 November 1750, p. 18; *Post Man* 21–23 January 1695/6; Gatrell, *Hanging Tree*, p. 276; OA 6 & 11 June 1764, p. 40; *Public Advertiser* 1 December 1774; *Morning Chronicle* 9 December 1774.

70   OA 19 September 1716, pp. 3–4; *George Selwyn and his Contemporaries*, 1:345; OA 17 December 1764 & 9 January 1765, p. 14; Linebaugh, 'Tyburn Riot', p. 112; OA 8 November 1738, pp. 5, 7.

71   OA 1 September & 12 & 22 October 1763, p. 76; *Daily Journal* 18 January 1721/2; *Weekly Journal; or Saturday's Post* 30 December 1721.

72   Elizabeth Fry, *Observations on the Visiting, Superintendence and Government of Female Prisoners* (1827), p. 73; Samuel Romilly, *Memoirs*, 3rd edn. (1860), 3:332–3.

73   'Tom King to the Rescue', *The Dick Turpin Library*, no. 11 (London, 1904–5); Osborne Collection of Early Children's Books, Toronto Public Library, p. 14; *Beggar's Opera*, pp. 115–16.

Notes to Chapter 8: God's Tribunal: Providential Discoveries and Ordeals

1   *Blundel the Jesuit's Letter of Intelligence* (1679), p. 1.

2   *Blundel the Jesuit's Letter* gives half an hour; *State Trials*, fifteen minutes (7:417). However, even fifteen minutes was a fairly long time for a seventeenth- or eighteenth-century jury to deliberate. Most verdicts were returned within minutes without the jury retiring at all; see John Langbein, 'The Criminal Trial before the Lawyers', in *University of Chicago Law Review*, 45 (1978), p. 284; Beattie, *Crime and the Courts*, pp. 379–389. In the case of the five Jesuits – and trials of the period generally – jurors were strongly influenced by instructions from the bench (Langbein, 'Criminal Trial', pp. 284–7; Beattie, *Crime and the Courts*, pp. 425–7).

3   *State Trials*, 7:383.

4   'Sacramentalism', or the belief that the sacred could overlap with and manifest itself within the secular, has been identified by the cultural historian Robert Scribner as one of the 'two characteristic features of the pre-modern mentality' (the other being magic); see his 'Elements of Popular Belief' in Thomas A. Brady, Heiko A. Oberman and James D. Tracy, ed., *Handbook of European History, 1400–1600: Late Middle Ages, Renaissance and Reformation* (Leiden, 1994), Vol.1, p. 235.

5   *Blundel the Jesuit's Letter*, p. 1; *Lying allowable with Papists to Deceive Protestants* … (1679), long title.

6   OA 24 November 1740, p. 18; *News from the Dead, Or a faithful and Genuine Narrative of … the Case of William Duell* (1740), pp. 7, 14, 12.

7   *A Relation of the Strange Apparition of the Five Jesuits Lately Executed at Tyburn* (1679), p. 4; *J[ames] S[hepar]d's Ghost: Being News from t'other Side of the World* (1718), pp. 14, 19.

8   *The Night-Walker of Bloomsbury* (1683), p. 1; *The Observator* 11 October 1683.

9   *The Works of Hannah More* (London, 1818), 18 vols., 1:282–3; Bob Scribner, 'Reformation, Carnival and the World Turned Upside-Down', *Social History* 3 (October 1978), 327.

10 For trials as 'sentencing hearings', see Beattie, *Crime and the Courts*, pp. 337–8, and 'Administering Justice Without Police: Criminal Trial Procedure in Eighteenth-Century England' in R. Donelan, ed., *The Maintenance of Order in Society* (Ottawa, 1982), pp. 12–22; as well as John Langbein, *The Origins of Adversary Criminal Trial* (Oxford, 2003), pp. 18–19. For plea bargaining, see John Langbein, 'Understanding the Short History of Plea Bargaining', in *Law & Society*, (Winter 1979), 262–279.

11 See for instance, the discussion in Cynthia Herrup, *The Common Peace: Participation and the Criminal Law in Seventeenth-Century England* (Cambridge, 1987), pp. 165–192.

12 Kettlewell, *Office for Prisoners*, pp. 12, 20, 50; OA 28 August 1724, p. 2; OA 5 August 1723, p. 2.

13 Richard J. Evans, *Rituals of Retribution: Capital Punishment in Germany 1600–1987* (Oxford, 1996), p. 84.

14 *An Appeal of Murther from certain unjust Judges, lately sitting at the Old Baily, to the righteous Judge of Heaven and Earth* [1693], p. 41; OA 24 May 1736, p. 15; *True Copies of the Papers wrote by Arthur Lord Balmerino [et al]* (1746), 2:40.

15 *The Weekly Journal* 6 August 1715; *LMRC*, 1:439–41.

16 *LMRC*, 2:95–6, 1:347–8; OA 18 March 1740/1, p. 11; *LMRC*, 1:409; *Select Trials* (1764), 1:258–9. For more examples of popular attitudes towards 'social crimes', see OA 14 March 1725/6, p. 3; OA 29 July 1747, p. 23; OA 16 November 1747, pp. 6, 11; OA 31 December 1750, p. 32. See also E. P. Thompson, *Whigs and Hunters: the Origin of the Black Act* (1975; repr. Harmondsworth, 1990), pp. 225–9.

17 *Select Trials* (1764), 4:43; *The Account of the Behaviour, Confession and Last Dying Speech of Sir John Johnson* (1690), p. 2; *The Last Words of a Dying Penitent* (1692), pp. 27, 31.

18 *The British Journal* 4 December 1725.

19 *A Full Relation of the Barbarous Murder, Committed upon the Body of Esq; Beddingfield* (1684), p. 1. For murder sheets in general, see Malcolm Gaskill, *Crime and Mentalities in Early Modern England* (Cambridge, 2000), ch. 6; see also his 'Reporting Murder: Fiction in the Archives in Early Modern England', *Social History* 23 (1998), 1–30.

20 *A Narrative of the Apprehending, Commitment, Arraignment, Condemnation, and Execution of John James* (1662), pp. 6, 40.

21 Keith Thomas, *Religion and the Decline of Magic* (London, 1971), pp. 261–2; *The Truth of the Case: Or, a Full and True Account of the Horrid Murders, Robberies and Burnings* (1708), p. 12; *LMRC*, 2:219–20. For more on cruentation, see Malcolm Gaskill 'Reporting Murder', pp. 1–13.

22 OBP 10 September 1760; Thomas, *Religion and the Decline of Magic*, pp. 713–15; Gaskill, 'Reporting Murder', pp. 14–16.

23 OA 24 May & 15 September 1760, p. 20; *Whitehall Evening-Post* 16–18 September 1760.

24 *Annual Register* (1764) 5 May; *LM* August 1763, p. 446; OBP 6 July 1763.

25 Criminal Evidence Act, 61 & 62 Victoria, c. 6. See discussion in Langbein, *Origins of Adversary Criminal Trial*, p. 14.

26 Barbara J. Shapiro, *Probability and Certainty in Seventeenth-Century England: A Study of the Relationships between Natural Science, Religion, History, Law, and Literature* (Princeton, 1983), pp. 183–7; Langbein, *Origins of Adversary Criminal Trial*, pp. 51–3; Roger North, *The Lives of the Right*

Hon. Francis North, Baron Guildford; the Hon. Sir Dudley North; and the Hon. and Rev. Dr John North, ed. Augustus Jessop (London, 1890), 1:202, 1:204. See also *Captain Newy's Case, Impartially Laid Open* (1700), p. 12.

27 *State Trials*, 7:360–1, 7:412.

28 *State Trials*, 7:326, 7:333, 7:417, 7:408.

29 *The Truth of the Case*, pp. 26–7; *A Full, True, and Genuine Account of the Uncommon Behaviour of Mr Gill Smith* (1738), p. 6; *An Account of the Lives of the Most Notorious Murderers and Robbers*, 2nd edn. (1726), p. 24. See also OA 10 March 1713/4, p. 4.

30 OA 24 May & 15 September 1760, p. 19; *LMRC*, 1:441, 1:13.

31 *The Behaviour, Confession, and Execution of the Twelve Prisoners that Suffered on Wednesday* (22 January 1678/9), p. 4; *Some Observations on the Trial of Mr Thomas Carr* (1737), pp. 9, 10; *LMRC*, 3:252; OA 12 May 1730, p. 4; OA 14 March 1759, pp. 13–14; *The Trial at Large, Behaviour, and Dying Declaration of Mary Edmondson* (1759), p. 17.

32 *Grub-Street Journal* 9 August 1733.

33 Lisa Silverman, *Tortured Subjects: Pain, Truth and the Body in Early Modern France* (Chicago and London, 2001), pp. 8–9; Laura Gowing, 'Ordering the body: illegitimacy and female authority in seventeenth-century England', in Michael J. Braddick and John Walter, eds., *Negotiating Power in Early Modern Society: Order, Hierarchy and Subordination in Britain and Ireland* (Cambridge, 2001), p. 54.

34 *An Account of the Conversion of Edward Lee, a Malefactor, Who was Executed at Haverford-West, in Wales, for a Robbery* (1756), p. 3; Michael Merbeck, *The Thief, the Cross and the Wheel: Pain and the Spectacle of Punishment in Medieval and Renaissance Europe* (London, 1999), p. 156; Phillipe Ariès, *The Hour of Our Death*, trans. Helen Weaver (New York and Oxford, 1981), pp. 10–13, 108, 118; Mather, *Wonders of Free-Grace*, vii–viii.

35 Evans, *Rituals of Retribution*, pp. 96–7.

36 Antonia Fraser, *Cromwell: Our Chief of Men* (London, 1973), p. 338; Nicholas Harpsfield, *The Life and Death of Sir Thomas Moore, Knight, sometymes Lord High Chancellor of England*, in *The Early English Text Society*, no. 186, ed. Elise Vaughan Hitchcock (London, 1932), p. 171; *History of the Press-Yard*, p. 90.

37 John Bunyan, *Grace Abounding: With Other Spiritual Autobiographies*, ed. John Stachniewski with Anita Pacheco (Oxford, 1998), p. 85; Mather, *Wonders of Free-Grace*, p. 84; OA 16 November 1730, p. 4.

38 Ralph Houlbrooke, *Death, Religion and the Family in England, 1480–1750* (Oxford, 1998), pp. 65, 54–5; *A Compassionate Address to Prisoners for Crimes* (1742), p. 74; see also J. Sears McGee, *The Godly Man in Stuart England: Anglicans, Puritans, and the Two Tables, 1620–1670* (New Haven and London, 1976), p. 31.

39 Thomas Gibbs, *Practical Discourses* (1700), pp. 139, 141; OA 3 February 1723/4, pp. 1, 6; OA 29 January 1719/20, p. 6; *Select Trials* (1742), 1:255; *Penny London Post* 17–19 December 1750.

40 OA 24 May & 15 September 1760, p. 20; OA 19 September & 12 & 22 October 1763, p. 76; OA 8 February 1722/3, p. 3; OA 8 February 1720/1, p. 4; *LMRC*, 1:303, 1:13.

41 John Donne, *Deaths Duell*, ed. Geoffrey Keynes (1631; repr. Boston, 1973), pp. 15, 17.

42 I discuss this practice at more length in 'This Death Some Strong and Stout Hearted Man Doth Choose': The Practice of Peine Forte et Dure in Seventeenth- and Eighteenth-Century England', *Law and History Review*, Vol. 23, 2 (Summer 2005), pp. 279–313.

43 Sir John Kelyng, *A Report of Divers Cases in Pleas of the Crown* (1708), pp. 27–8.

44 OBP 25–27 May 1721; OBP 17–19 May 1716; *The Confession and Execution of the Eight Prisoners suffering at Tyburn* (30 August 1676), p. 4. Andrews was acquitted; Thurlow, White and Parker were hanged.

45 Sir Thomas Smith, *De Republica Anglorum* (1583), ed. Mary Dewar (Cambridge, 1982), p. 112; John Langbein, *Torture and the Law of Proof: Europe and England in the Ancien Régime* (Chicago, 1977), pp. 75–6, 184 n. 20; Alfred Marks, *Tyburn Tree: Its History and Annals* (London, 1908), pp. 40–1; *Select Trials* (1742), 1:116; Beattie, *Crime and the Courts*, p. 338; Cesare de Saussure, *A Foreign View of England in the Reigns of George I and George II*, trans. Mme. Van Muyden (London, 1902), p. 120. See also *The Suffolk Parricide. Being the Trial, Life, Transactions, and Last Dying Words, of Charles Drew* (1740), p. 42.

46   OBP 27 February–1 March 1733/4 (Durant was convicted of a non-capital felony); OBP 30 August
      – 1 September 1727; OA 18 September 1727, p. 3.

47   *News from Newgate: A Gaol-Delivery for the City of London and County of Middlesex* (3–10 September
      1673), p. 6; *LMRC*, 3:62–3; *An Authentic Account of the Trials, Behaviour, and Dying Declaration, of
      the Five Malefactors, who were Executed at Kennington-Common* (23 April 1770), p. 5.

48   4 & 5 William and Mary, c. 8; OBP 28 August–1 September 1741; *Lives of the Most Notorious Murderers*,
      p. 58; Johnson, *General History of the Highwaymen*, p. 476.

49   OBP 13–15 January 1720/1; *Select Trials* (1742), 1:16; *Applebee's Weekly Journal* 14 January 1720/1;
      The Daily Post 4–16 January 1720/1; *Select Trials* (1742), 1:111.

50   Saussure, *Foreign View of England*, p. 120; Daines Barrington, *Observations on the More Ancient Statutes
      from Magna Charta to the Twenty-First of James I. Cap XXVII*, 4th edn. (1775), p. 87; *LMRC*, 1:109;
      J. M. Beattie, 'London Juries in the 1690s', in *Twelve Good Men and True: the Criminal Trial Jury in
      England, 1200–1800*, ed. J. S. Cockburn and Thomas A. Green (Princeton, 1988), pp. 266–9.

51   King, *Crime, Justice and Discretion*, p. 346.

52   *LMRC*, 3:62 (Harris was hanged on 11 September 1728); *Hell upon Earth: or the Most Pleasant and
      Delectable History of Whittington's Colledge* (1703), p. 10; William Eden, *Principles of Penal Law* (1771),
      p. 67; *Proceedings … held for the County of Surry, at Kingston* (30 March–4 April 1726), p. 2.

53   OA 11 February 1733/4, p. 11; OA 7 February 1749/50, p. 14; OA 4 June 1770, p. 36; *Weekly Journal;
      or Saturday's Post* 14 November 1724.

54   James C. Scott, *Domination and the Arts of Resistance: Hidden Transcripts* (New Haven and London,
      1990).

55   *The Proceedings at the Sessions at the Old-Baily* (27–28 August 1679), p. 4; OA 22 December 1721, p. 5;
      LMRC, 1:109.

56   Kelyng, *Pleas of the Crown*, p. 36; Langbein, *Torture and the Law of Proof*, p. 75; Barrington,
      Observations on the More Ancient Statutes, 84n; *State Trials*, 3:913–14, 3:929–30n; see also Alastair
      Bellany, *The Politics of Court Scandal in Early Modern England: News culture and the Overbury affair,
      1603–1660* (Cambridge, 2002), p. 72.

57   John Mush, 'A True Report of the Life and Martyrdom of Mrs. Margaret Clitherow', in John Morris,
      ed., *The Troubles of Our Catholic Forefathers Related by Themselves*, 3rd series (London, 1877), pp. 413,
      418, 431–2; see also Peter Lake and Michael Questier, 'Margaret Clitherow, Catholic Nonconformity,
      Martyrology and the Politics of Religious Change in Elizabethan England', *Past & Present*, 185
      (November 2004), 43–90.

58   Robert Calef, *More Wonders of the Invisible World* (1700), p. 106; *The Bloody Murtherer, of the
      Unnatural Son His Just Condemnation* (1672), p. 54; *A Most Barbarous Murther, being a True Relation
      of the Tryal and Condemnation of Henry Jones and Mary Jones … for Murthering of their own Mother*
      (1672), p. 8.

59   *The Acts and Monuments of John Foxe*, ed. George Townsend (New York, 1965), 5:550, 8:102; 8:326.

60   *The Unhappy Marksman. Or a Perfect and Impartial Discovery of that late Barbarous and Unparallel'd
      Murther Committed by Mr George Strangwayes* (1659), pp. 14, 21, 22, 26–7.

61   *LMRC*, 2:179; OBP 6–13 December 1721; *LMRC*, 1:110, 1:104, 1:108; OA 8 February 1720/1, p. 5; OA
      12 July 1742, p. 20.

62   *Lives of the Most Notorious Murderers and Robbers*, p. 63; *LMRC*, 1:110.

Notes to Chapter 9: Conclusion: The Adjournment of God's Tribunal?

1   The 1772 Act (12 George III, c. 20) ruled that standing mute should be taken as a plea of guilty; this
     was amended by an Act of 1827 (7 & 8 George IV, c. 28), which ruled that refusal to plead should be
     taken as a plea of not guilty.

2   *Annual Register* 1770, pp. 163–4. Interestingly, this essay mistakenly claimed that the accused pirate
     was 'pressed to death in Newgate, in the press-yard there'. Mute defendants were subjected to the
     peine forte et dure in the 'Press Room' inside the prison, not in the adjacent Press Yard, which housed
     better-off prisoners.

3   Simon Devereaux, 'The Abolition of the Burning of Women Reconsidered', *Crime, History, Societies*,

Vol. 9, 2 (2005), esp. pp. 82, 90; quote from Loughborough on p. 90; see also Shelley Gavigan, 'Petit Treason in Eighteenth Century England: Women's Inequality Before the Law', *Canadian Journal of Women and the Law* 3 (2, 1989–1990), 335–74.

4   *British Journal* 14 May 1726; *Mist's Weekly Journal* 14 May 1726; NA., SP 44/124, p. 284; *Parker's Penny Post* 11 May 1726. Some later accounts assumed that Hayes was burnt alive because of the incompetence of the hangman; see *LMRC*, 2:236–7.

5   See, for instance, Gerald Howson, *The Macaroni Parson: A Life of the Unfortunate Dr Dodd* (London, 1973); Donna T. Andrew and Randall McGowen, *The Perreaus and Mrs. Rudd: Forgery and Betrayal in Eighteenth-Century London* (Berkeley, 2001).

6   *The Autobiography of Francis Place 1771–1854*, ed. Mary Thale (London, 1972), p. 82; Arthur Griffiths, *The Chronicles of Newgate* (London, 1884), 1:354; Francis Place Papers, BL Add Ms 27825, Vol. 1. 'Manners. Morals', f. 79; F. W. Chandler, *The Literature of Roguery* (Cambridge, 1907), 1:181; William Lee, *Daniel Defoe, his Life and Recently Discovered Writings* (1869; repr. New York, 1969), 1:343.

7   Simon Devereaux, 'The City and the Sessions Paper: 'Public Justice' in London, 1770–1800', *Journal of British Studies* 4 (1996), 466–503; see also his 'The Fall of the Sessions Paper: The Criminal Trial and the Popular Press in Late Eighteenth-Century London', *Criminal Justice History*, 18 (2003), pp. 57–88, and 'From Sessions Paper to Newspaper? Criminal Trial Reporting, the Nature of Crime, and the London Press', *The London Journal*, 32, 1 (2007), 1–27.

8   OBP 5 April 1725; OBP 5 July 1727 (see also Harris, 'Trials and Criminal Biographies', pp. 10–11); OBP 4 July 1722.

9   ˌOA 14 September 1767, p. 6; Saussure, *Foreign View of England*, p. 120; *Read's Weekly Journal* 26 May 1750; *The Cries of Blood, or Juryman's Monitor* (1767), ii; William Blackstone, *Commentaries on the Laws of England* (1767–9), 4:27; OA 14 September 1767, p. 6; *Public Advertiser* 11 January 1775.

10 *LMRC*, 2:80; *CSPD*, 19 May 1687, p. 428; Captain Alexander Smith, *Memoirs of the Life and Times of the Famous Jonathan Wild* (1726; repr. Malcolm J. Bosse ed., New York, 1973), pp. 232–3; Mather, *Wonders of Free-Grace*, pp. 8, 43, 57.

11 *Cries of Blood*, ii; *Read's Weekly Journal* 26 May 1750; *GM* May 1765, p. 236; John Villette, *A Genuine Account of the Behaviour, Confession, and Dying-Words of William Hawke and William Jones* (1 July 1774), pp. 12–13.

12 *Public Advertiser* 10 August 1769; *General Evening Post* 28–30 October 1773; *The Life of Patrick Madan* (1781), pp. 24, 28; *Annual Register* (1774), pp. 141–2, 146; *Morning Chronicle* 7 August 1777; Johann Wilhelm D'Archenholz, *A Picture of England* (1797), p. 257. The latter account is much more severe upon the Ordinary of Newgate, John Villette, who, in contrast to the newspaper report, is portrayed as attempting to carry out the execution regardless of the new evidence.

13 25 George II, c. 37; Henry Fielding, *An Enquiry into the Causes of the Late Increase of Robbers and Related Writings* (1751), ed. Melvin R. Zirker (Oxford, 1988), p. 169.

14 For the abolition of the Tyburn procession, see Steven Wilf, 'Imagining Justice: Aesthetics and Public Executions in Late Eighteenth-Century England', *Yale Journal of Law and the Humanities* 5, 1 (Winter, 1993), 51–78, and Simon Devereaux, 'Recasting the Theatre of Execution in London: the End of Tyburn', *Past & Present*, forthcoming.

15 *Captain Charles Newey's … Case and Vindication* (1700), p. 1; *The Flying Post* 16–18 January 1699/1700; *LM* August 1739, p. 411; Gatrell, *Hanging Tree*, pp. 192–5. For later execution sheets and street-ballads, see Francis Place Papers, BL Add Mss 27825–6, Vols. I & II, 'Manners. Morals. Grossness'; Leslie Shepard, *The History of Street Literature* (Newton Abbot, 1973), and also his *The Broadside Ballad* (London, 1962); Robert Collison, *The Story of Street Literature: Forerunner of the Popular Press* (London, 1973). For a more recent study of 'plebeian texts' (street-ballads and late eighteenth- and early nineteenth-century broadsides), see Gatrell, *Hanging Tree*, esp. chs. 4 & 5.

16 Grant McCracken, *Culture and Consumption: New Approaches to the Symbolic Character of Consumer Goods and Activities* (Bloomington and Indianapolis, 1988), pp. 93–103; see also Michel de Certeau, *The Practice of Everyday Life*, trans. Steven Rendall (Berkeley, 1984).

17 Robert W. Scribner, 'Elements of Popular Belief' in Thomas A. Brady, Heiko A. Oberman and James D. Tracy, eds., *Handbook of European History, 1400–1600: Late Middle Ages, Renaissance and Reformation* (Leiden, 1994), Vol.1, p. 235.

18   Alexandra Walsham, *Providence in Early Modern England* (Oxford, 1999), pp. 333–4; Malcolm Gaskill, *Crime and Mentalities in Early Modern England* (Cambridge, 2000), pp. 296–7.

19   Norman Sykes, *Church and State in England in the Eighteenth Century* (Cambridge, 1934), p. 379; see also Jeremy Gregory, 'Homo Religiosus: Masculinity and Religion in the Long Eighteenth Century', in Tim Hitchcock and Michèle Cohen, eds., *English Masculinities, 1660–1800* (London and New York, 1999), p. 91; W. M. Jacob, *Lay People and Religion in the Early Eighteenth Century* (Cambridge, 1996).

20   Daniel Defoe, *Serious Reflections during the Life and Surprising Adventures of Robinson Crusoe With his Vision of the Angelic World* (1720), p. 101; see also Houlbrooke, *Death, Religion and the Family*, p. 56; D. P. Walker, *The Decline of Hell: Seventeenth-Century Discussions of Eternal Torment* (London, 1964).

21   *The Works of the Rev. John Wesley*, ed. John Emory (New York, 1856), 25 May 1768, 4:279; see also Owen Davies, 'Methodism, the Clergy, and the Popular Belief in Witchcraft and Magic', *History* 82 (April 1997), 252–65.

22   See, for instance, Ruth Richardson, *Death, Dissection and the Destitute*, 2nd edn. (London, 1988), p. 11.

23   Houlbrooke, *Death, Religion and the Family*, p. 211.

24   Hannah More, *Cheap Repository Tracts. Sunday Reading: Joseph in Prison*, part 2 [1800], p. 12; OA 29 June 1737, p. 3; *A True Account of the Behaviour, Confession and Last Dying Speeches of the 8 Criminals that were Executed at Tyburn* (26 January 1690/91), p. 1. As Alexandra Walsham has noted, however, the early modern idea of 'conscience' differed from our own: far from being 'an autonomous inner moral voice', conscience was viewed as 'an invisible witness to give sentence against sin', or 'God's Spy and Deputy' (*A True Account of the Behaviour, Confession and Last Dying Speeches of the 8 Criminals that were Executed at Tyburn* [26 January 1690/1], p. 1); see Alexandra Walsham, 'Ordeals of Conscience: Casuistry, Conformity and Confessional Identity in Post-Reformation England', in Harald E. Braun and Edward Vallance, eds., *Contexts of Conscience in Early Modern Europe, 1500–1700* (Houndmills, 2004), pp. 32–3.

25   Robert B. Shoemaker, 'The Taming of the Duel: Masculinity, Honour and Ritual Violence in London, 1660–1800', *The Historical Journal*, 45, 3 (2002), 536.

26   Samuel Richardson, *The History of Sir Charles Grandison*, ed. Jocelyn Harris (1754; repr. London, 1972), 1:183, 3:184.

27   *Sir Charles Grandison*, 1:206, 1:242, 1:248, 1:256, 1:265.

Index

ON = Ordinary of Newgate, followed by date of tenure; ex = executed, followed by date and crime; re = reprieved; ex & re = reprieved after surviving hanging; aq = acquitted; d = died in prison before execution; s = committed suicide before execution; sp = sentenced to punishment less than death; pr = pressed to death (followed by charge to which defendant refused to plead).

Abbot, Henry (ex 1718 burglary) 76

Abershaw, Lewis Jeremiah (ex 1795 murder) 195

advertisements 63, 128, 253, 262

Afflack, Alexander (ex 1742 burglary) 169

Albin, John (ex 1739 robbery) 193

alcohol *see* drinking, drunkenness, gin

Alexander, Moses (ex 1769 forgery) 255

Allen, Edmund (ex 1695 murder) 142

Allen, John (ON 1698–9) 127–8, 267

Allen, Mary (ex 1747 theft) 169

Anderton, William (ex 1693 treason) 39, 176, 202–3, 230

Andrews, Jasper (re 1721 returning from transportation) 173

Andrews, Mary (aq 1721 theft) 241

Angier, Humphrey (ex 1723 robbery) 111

Applebee, John (printer) 33, 36, 37–8, 46, 49, 50, 88, 91, 101, 108–10, 152, 180, 253, 262–3

Applebee's 'Appendix' 49, 88, 109–10, 152, 253, 262–3

Appleton, James (ex 1722 burglary) 75, 105–6

Armstrong, Thomas (ex 1684 treason) 34

Arnold, Richard (ex 1742 robbery) 81

Aslien, Isaac ('Black Isaac'; ex 1728 robbery) 192

atheism 84, 142, 146, 170–1, 209, 258

Attaway, James (ex 1770 robbery) 80

Austin, John (ex 1725 robbery) 62, 149

Awdry, Roderick (ex 1714 burglary) 87

Backscheider, Paula 67

Badham, Samuel (ex 1740 murder) 43, 74

Bailey, Jeremiah (ex 1758 robbery) 20

Baker, Anne (ex 1764 theft) 16

Baker, James ('Stick in the Mud'; ex 1733 robbery) 43

Baker, William (ex 1750 forgery) 9

ballad singers 39, 44, 45, 57, 100–1, 154 *see also* street ballads

Balmerino, (Lord) Arthur (ex 1746 treason) 13, 211–12

baptism 132–3

Barcock, Edward (ex 1738 robbery) 221

Barkstead, John (ex 1662 treason) 34, 164

Barnet, John (ex 1730 robbery) 68–9

Barnham (alias Barnet), Stephen (ex 1728 robbery) 107–8, 192, 193–4

Barnwell, George (*The London Merchant*) 61, 89, 158

Barrington, Daines 244

Barry, Redmond 230

Barton, John (ex 1726 burglary) 79, 169–70

Barton, William (ex 1721 robbery) 71, 80, 166

Baxter, Richard 206, 239

Beach, John (ex 1733 robbery) 220

Bean, Thomas (ex 1716 rioting) 113

Beaumont, Agnes 27

Beck, Thomas (ex 1731 robbery) 138–9

Beckwith, William (ex 1760 burglary) 147–8

Bedford, (Dr) Arthur 122

Bedlam (Bethlem, or Bethlehem Hospital) 24, 217

Bedlow, William 225

Beggar's Opera (1728) 12, 93–4, 99–100, 103, 105, 115, 118, 195–6, 203, 219

Bellamy, Martin (ex 1728 robbery) 45–6, 135

Bellman of St Sepulchre's 1, 7–8, 10, 23, 64, 184, 193, 201, 270n invoked as warning 64

benefit of clergy 42, 63, 127–8

Bennet, Elizabeth (re 1741 infanticide) 83

Bennet (alias Freeman), John ('Golden Farmer'; ex 1690 murder & robbery) 144, 202

Benson, Elenor (ex 1728 robbery) 162

Benson, Thomas (ex 1684 rape) 60

Betts, Thomas (ex 1706 burglary) 169

Bewley, Michael (ex 1743 burglary) 113

Big, Jepthah (ex 1729 extortion) 177

Billings, Thomas (ex 1726 murder) 84, 170

Bird, Edward (ex 1719 murder) 40, 136

Bishop, William (aq attempted sodomy 1732) 131

Black Assizes (1750) 133 see also typhus

Black, Francis (ex 1691 theft) 60

Blackstone, William 18, 75, 254

Blake, Daniel (ex 1763 murder) 44

Blake, Joseph ('Blueskin'; ex 1724 robbery) 11, 13, 64, 103, 105, 111, 130, 200

Blake, William 123

Blanchar, William (ex 1689 robbery) 203

Blandy, Mary (ex 1752 murder) 68, 85

Blewit, John ('Jack'; ex 1714 rape & murder) 255

Blewitt, William (ex 1726 robbery) 64, 193, 198, 243

bloodsports 24, 25 see also cockfights

'Bloody Code' xv, 3–4, 62

Blueskin see Blake, Joseph

Bond, William (ex 1721 returning from transportation) 80, 240

Boronsky, George (ex 1682 murder) 173

Boswell, James 24, 26, 94, 183, 212, 217

Bourn, William (ex 1726 theft) 44

Bow Street 104, 119

boxing, boxers 52, 61, 134, 243

Bradford, John (ex 1555 heresy) 56

Bradshaw, John 24

Branch, Benjamin (ex 1728 robbery) 139

Branch, Elizabeth (ex 1740 murder) 71

Branch, Randolph (ex 1752 robbery) 86

branding 4, 42, 63
    see benefit of clergy

Brinsden, Matthias (ex 1722 murder) 167–8, 174

Bristol 7, 20

Bristow, William (ex 1690 burglary) 61–2

Brocklesby, (Dr) Richard 170

Brown, James (re 1763 robbery) 222

Brown, William (ex 1733 burglary) 166

Brownrigg, Elizabeth (ex 1767 murder) 186, 218

Bunhill Fields 7

Bunyan, John 27, 28, 57, 82, 162, 163, 183, 185, 239

Burden, Thomas (ex 1724 robbery) 150, 240

Burnet, Gilbert xvii, 28, 34, 40–41, 48, 125, 144, 172, 203–4, 207, 228

burning women 13, 18, 24, 84, 251–2
    for high treason 6, 18, 252
    for petty treason 6, 18, 84, 252

Burnworth, Edward (ex 1726 robbery & murder) 105–8, 112, 114, 193, 209, 236, 243–5, 249

Butledge, Thomas (ex 1721 robbery) 73, 110

Butler, James (ex 1723 robbery) 111

Butler, Nathaniel (ex 1657 murder) 255

Butler, Samuel 222

Calvinism 56–7, 90, 155, 161, 176, 182, 184, 185, 204, 211, 238, 239

Campbell, James (ex 1725 robbery) 44, 168

Cane, Charles (ex 1756 theft) 86

Cane, Thomas (ex 1721 theft & returning from transportation) 178

Cannon, Elizabeth (ex 1743 burglary) 74

cant (criminal slang) 100, 114, 131, 196

Capel, (Lord) Arthur (ex 1649 treason) 209

capital punishment, opposition to 25–6

Carleton, Mary ('German Princess'; ex 1673, theft) 159

Carr, John (ex 1741 robbery) 208

Carr, Thomas (ex 1737 robbery) 12, 130, 208, 210, 237

Carrick, James (ex 1722 robbery) 48, 105, 175, 205, 254

Cass, Richard (ex 1733 robbery) 237

Catholics and Catholicism 122, 125, 130–1, 140–1, 144, 164, 172, 174–82, 186, 188, 195, 225–6, 235, 238–9, 259

Catt, John (ex 1741 returning from transportation) 231

Cecil, Richard (ex 1720 burglary) 169

censorship xvii, 31, 34–40

Chamberlain, Benjamin (ex 1750 robbery) 15, 19

charity 14, 35, 36–7, 58, 145, 165–70, 198, 201–3, 230–2, 237, 247 see also dying well

charity schools 42–4

Charles I 27, 33

Charles II 99, 225

'chase and flight' 257

Chesterfield, Earl of see Stanhope, Philip Dormer

Chickley, Henry (ex 1718 robbery) 147

children of condemned 51, 79–83, 166–8, 199, 213–15

Churchill, Deborah (ex 1703 murder) 165

Churchill, Elizabeth (re 1686 theft) 79

Cibber, Theophilus 153

civility 213, 259

Clare, Zachary (ex 1715 robbery) 198

Clarissa (1747–8) 258–9

Clark, Ann (ex 1738 theft) 80

Clark, Margaret (ex 1679 arson) 160

Clark, Matthew (ex 1721 murder) 61

Clark, William (ex 1744 theft) 74

Clay, Richard (ex 1747 burglary) 201

Clerkenwell New Prison 45, 63

Clever Tom Clinch (1727) 114, 191–2, 194, 195, 196

Clitherow, Margaret (pr 1586 treason) 247, 248

Cluff, James (ex 1729 murder) 27–8

'Cockey Wager' *see* Wager, William

cockfights 24, 196

coffee houses 33, 48, 228

Coke, (Sir) Edward 247

Cole, Joseph (ex 1736 burglary) 111

Collet (alias Cole), John (ex 1691 burglary) 148

Collier, Jeremy 134

Colonel Jack (1722) 29, 53, 66, 107

Compton, Katherine (re 1720 theft) 82–3

Compton, Mary (ex 1693 murder) 60

condemned sermons 7, 124–5, 126, 231, 137, 139, 162–3, 204, 207, 230, 262

condemned hold (or 'Hole') 7, 43, 136, 138, 173, 192

confession(s) 16, 45, 47, 51–2, 121–55, 179–81, 182, 186–8, 200–2, 211
  criminals' resistance to 48, 107, 129, 132, 137, 144–8, 174–5, 200–2
  necessity for 47, 140–4, 146
  scriptural arguments for 140–2
  see also criminal accounts

Congden, Robert (ex 1691 robbery & murder) 145

Conolly, Walter (ex 1738 robbery) 203

Cook, James (ex 1739 robbery) 205

Cook, Ralph (ex 1680 coining) 168

Cook, Thomas (ex 1703 murder) 134–5

Cooke, Duke (ex 1695 clipping) 62

Cooke, Henry (ex 1741 robbery) 44, 107, 243

Cooke, John (ex 1660 treason) 34

Cooper, Anthony Ashley (Earl of Shaftesbury) 71

Cooper, John (ex 1742 robbery) 76, 174

Cooper, Mary (printer) 88, 263

Coppach, Thomas (ex 1746 treason) 225, 230

Corey, Giles (pr 1692 witchcraft) 247

Cornish, Henry (ex 1685 treason) 164

corpses 10, 17–18, 19, 20–1, 23, 24–5, 71, 81, 84, 185, 233–4, 248, 256
  laid at door of prosecutors, witnesses 185, 234–5
  riots over 14, 19, 20–1, 23, 185, 235
  stripped at gallows 18
  see also cruentation, dissection, surgeons, dress, gibbets

courage
  'artificial' or 'cordial courage', 118–19, 206, 208–9, 213 *see also* drinking
  'Christian' (rational) 119, 210–13, 258–9
  'divinely assisted' xvi, 28, 164–5, 203, 206–7, 248
  'false' 108, 119, 193, 197–99, 203–4, 206–13, 246, 248–9
  'Roman' 209 *see also* atheism

Court of Aldermen 6, 7, 12, 39, 126, 127, 152–4, 179

Cox, Thomas (ex 1690 robbery) 198

Cox, William (ex 1773 robbery) 91, 100, 105, 118

Cranburne, Charles (ex 1696 treason) 37

Cranmer, Thomas (ex 1556 heresy) 200

Cranstoun, William (accomplice) 68, 85

Crawford, Thomas (ex 1750 robbery) 15

crime, causes of
  environmental 57–8, 89–90
  moral 55–9, 82, 89–90, 257
  nurture 70–1

'crime waves' 5, 105–6

criminal accounts or 'lives'
  appropriation by criminals 52–3, 107–8, 113, 120, 135, 193, 257
  audience for 26, 32–3, 38, 45, 91–2, 106–7, 120, 125, 154–5, 175, 188–9, 252–3, 257
  authenticating 37–41, 48, 49–50, 53
  competition over 45–53, 106, 128
  forgeries 38, 40, 48, 124, 127, 153, 261–2
  justifying utility of 47, 50
  see also confession

'criminal class' 88–90

Cromwell, Oliver 24, 25, 99, 238–9

Crookhall, Thomas (ex 1770 burglary) 206

Croom, George (printer) 33

Cross, Thomas (ex 1721 robbery) 107, 173, 193, 243

cruentation 233–4, 248

Curll, Edmund (bookseller) 152

Curtis, Langley (printer) 228, 263

Dagoe, Hannah (ex 1763 theft) 175

Dalton, Edward (ex 1732 murder) 71

Dalton, James (ex 1730 robbery) 49, 50, 71, 100, 173, 198, 201, 237, 239

Darkin, Isaac (ex 1761 robbery) 115, 196, 205, 210

Davis, John (ex 1731 robbery) 169

Davis, John (ex 1733 robbery) 8–9, 136

Davis, Lumley (ex 1724 robbery) 16

Davis, Vincent (ex 1725 murder) 20

Dead Warrant 1, 7, 51, 86, 135, 148, 173, 178

deathbed repentance 135–6, 184, 186

Debtor's Door 6, 16, 256 *see also* Newgate

Defoe, Daniel 31, 33, 53, 55, 66, 67, 75, 96, 97, 122, 126, 134, 135, 258

deism 2, 84, 90, 170, 258

Dempsey, Edward (ex 1750 robbery) 181, 245

Dempsey, Patrick (ex 1750 robbery) 245

desacralization 257–8

devil 56, 59–61, 65, 199, 227, 247

Dickenson, Emanuel (ex 1726 robbery) 243

discretion 4, 7, 67, 82–3, 244

dissection 20–1, 24, 256

Dissenters 126–7, 144, 148, 174, 176, 178, 179, 185, 239

Dodd, (Dr) William (ex 1777 forgery) 57, 154, 200, 206, 218, 252

Dolzell, Alexander (ex 1715 piracy) 138

Donne, John 28, 183, 241

Douglas, Sawney (ex 1662 robbery) 198

Doyle, John (ex 1730 robbery) 178

Drake, Peter 122

drawing and quartering 18, 24, 164, 251

dress of condemned
 'flash' dress ('bridegroom') 22, 114, 118, 191–2, 219–20, 248 *see also* weddings
 mourning 219–20
 perquisite of hangman 17–18
 poorest reduced to rags, charity 16, 174
 ribbons or cockades 219–21
 shrouds 9, 159, 222, 239–40

Drew, Charles (ex 1740 murder) 168

drinking and drunkenness 3, 11–12, 16, 58, 61, 62–3, 73–4,

75, 76, 118, 121, 123, 137, 149, 150, 161, 200, 206, 208–9, 245

Drogheda 238

Drummond, James (ex 1729 robbery) 15

Drummond, Robert (ex 1730 robbery) 15

Duce, William (ex 1723 robbery) 144

Duell, William (ex & re 1740 rape & murder) 20, 227

duels 46, 116, 212, 258–9

Duffus, George (sp 1721 sodomy) 151

Dugdale, Stephen 225

Dunciad (1728) 129, 152

Duncombe, Charles 118

Durant, John (1734 theft) 242

Duval, Claude (ex robbery 1670) 110–11

Dyer (alias Brown), Jane (ex 1705 theft) 165

Dyer, John (ex 1729 robbery) 50

dying game 114–15, 192–223, 298n *see also* game criminals

dying ill 14, 65–6, 93–4, 138–9, 147, 168–9, 173–4, 192

dying well 23, 52, 58, 75, 92, 165–70, 194, 198–9, 248 *see also* penitence, charity

Dymar, Mary (ex 1749 robbery) 83

Easter, Thomas (accomplice) 109

Edmondson, Mary (ex 1759 murder) 28, 29, 83, 237

Elby, William (ex 1707 robbery) 145, 201

Ellard, Samuel (ex 1744 returning from transportation) 76

Ellis, Clement 218

Emerton, John Alexander (ex 1733 forgery) 31, 50

evangelicalism 57, 161–2, 185, 228–9, 257–8

Evans, Richard 230

Evelyn, John 25, 106, 184

Everett (alias Anderson, George), Jeffrey (ex 1750 theft) 202

Everett, John (ex 1730 robbery) 19, 50

'Everyman', criminal as xix, xx, 32, 56–7, 87–92, 149, 155, 182–3, 187, 253–4

evidence, turning (informing against accomplices) 12, 14, 15, 45–6, 51, 52, 63, 65, 71, 79, 85, 103, 106, 113, 145, 151, 168, 191–2, 200–1, 214, 242, 249

execution
 as 'God's Tribunal' xvi–xvii, 26–9, 57, 188–9, 209, 211, 227, 231, 249, 258 *see also* sacramentality
 by beheading 6, 17, 29, 164
 by burning *see* burning women
 by hanging *see* hanging(s)
 by pressing *see peine forte et dure*

Execution Dock (Wapping) 6–7, 9, 142

executioner *see* hangman

Exelby, John (ex 1747 burglary) 168–9

Eyre, (Lord Chief Justice) Robert 114

Faller, Lincoln 32, 67, 115, 132

Falstaff (Sir) John, 120

Farr, James (ex 1762 forgery) 148

Faulkner, William (ex 1735 theft) 240

Featherby, John (ex 1728 robbery) 192

Feild, Greenway (ex 1689 murder) 37

female offenders 5–6, 63–4, 67, 81–5, 196–7
 proportion of accused 82
 proportion of executed 5–6

Fenwick, John (ex 1679 treason) 225 *see also* five Jesuits

Ferrers, (Earl) Lawrence (ex 1760 murder) 9–10, 16

Fielding, Henry 23, 41, 75, 87, 130, 192, 193, 197, 198, 218, 256

Fielding, (Sir) John 44, 119

Fifth Monarchists 18, 163–4, 233

Fink, Bernard (ex 1731 robbery) 65–6, 112

Fitz-Harys, Edward (ex 1681 treason) 38

Fitzpatrick (alias Green, Boswell), Katherine (ex 1726 theft) 166

five Jesuits xvi–xvii, 26, 34, 163, 207, 225–6, 227

Fleming, Charles (ex 1754 robbery) 86, 117

Fluellin, Henry (ex 1738 robbery) 221

Foote, Samuel 117

Ford, Isaac (ex 1689 robbery) 150

Forde, Brownlow (ON 1799–1814) 154, 188

forfeiture 241–2

'Forty–Five (Jacobite Rebellion) 214

Foster, John (ex 1740 murder) 74

Foucault, Michel xvii, 21, 251

Foulks, Robert (ex 1679 murder) 255

Fowler, Edward 183

Fox, John (ex 1727 theft) 151

Foxe, John xviii, 27, 43, 161, 163, 200, 206, 248

Frankling, James (ex 1777 robbery) 205–6

free grace 57, 134–5, 155, 161–3, 172, 182–7, 200, 204, 238

Freeman, Christopher (ex 1736 burglary) 230

Freeman, Robert (ex 1679 murder) 237

Fretwell, Joseph (ex 1733 robbery) 165–6

Friend, (Sir) John (ex 1686 treason) 17, 37

Fry, Elizabeth 42, 222

Gadd, Henry (ex 1744 robbery) 65, 85

Gahagan, Usher (ex 1749 coining) 53, 151

game criminals 2, 14, 16, 17, 22, 27, 53, 114–15, 165, 191–2, 198–211, 213, 218–23, 246, 248–9, 251, 254 see also dying game

gaming and gaming halls 116–117

gangs 2, 64–5, 85, 105, 112, 114, 192, 193, 243

'gaol fever' see typhus

Gardiner, Stephen (ex 1724 burglary) 64, 159, 239

Gardner, James (ex 1706 burglary) 110

Garth, Samuel 93, 99, 222

Gates, William (ex 1726 Black Act) 43–4

Gatrell, V.A.C. 194, 217, 221, 257

Gavan, John (ex 1679 treason) 163, 225–6, 235–6, 259 see also five Jesuits

Gavenor, Elenor (ex 1712 theft) 82

Gay, John 93, 100, 222

genteel offenders 9, 13, 44, 136, 170–1, 200, 207, 214–16, 252

George I 101

ghosts 138, 146, 227–8, 231, 234, 258

gibbets 10, 24

Gilbert, William (ex 1705 murder) 60

Gillfoy, Mary (ex 1751 theft) 83

gin 21, 74, 130

Girdler, William (ex 1752 robbery) 15–16

Goffe, John (ex 1702 robbery) 178

Goldsmith, Oliver 153

Goodcole, Henry 261, 267

Gosse, George (ex 1700 burglary) 151

Gower, John (ex 1684 murder) 142

Gowing, Laura 258

grace see free grace

Green, Mary (ex 1712 burglary) 145

Green, Mary (ex 1746 robbery) 180

Green, Robert (ex 1679 murder) 177

Greene, Anne (ex & re 1650 infanticide) 19–20

Gregg, William (ex 1708 treason) 134

Grey, Thomas (ex 1714 robbery) 138

Griffin, Jane (ex 1720 murder) 240

Griffiths, Sarah (ex 1727 burglary) 174

Grose, Francis 196

Grub Street 46, 50, 51, 53, 101, 124, 129, 152, 154

guilt, relativity of 56, 150–1, 221–3, 229, 232–3, 248

Gulliford, John (ex 1742 robbery) 202

Gunpowder Plot (1605) 227

Guthrie, James (ON 1725–46) 50, 65–6, 81, 85, 88, 90, 131, 133–4, 136–9, 144, 152–3, 158, 160, 167, 171–3, 177–82, 187, 200, 245, 263, 267, 272n

Gwynn, Nell 99

Hacket, James (ex 1707 burglary) 78, 209

Hadley, William (ex 1757 burglary) 89

Hall, James (ex 1741 murder) 50–1

Hall, John (ex 1708 robbery) 69, 102

Hall, John (ex 1716 treason) 176

Hallam, Robert (ex 1732 murder) 200

Halsey, (Captain) Joseph (ex 1759 murder) 237

Hamilton, Benjamin Campbell (ex 1750 robbery) 218–19

Hancock, William (ex 1695 robbery) 19

hanging(s)
  accidents at 2–3, 14, 16–17, 206, 207–8
  audience at 13, 26, 217–18
  by the 'drop' 16, 120, 206, 256
  condemned malefactors
    adjusting halter, rope 17, 105, 205, 207, 237
    drawn by carts 9, 220; sledges 9, 208; coaches 9–10
    handkerchiefs, caps, blindfolds worn by 16–17, 199, 205, 207, 212
    kicking off shoes 220
    leaping from cart, ladder before being 'turned off' 3, 19, 115, 206, 207–8, 237
    numbers of 5–6
    pulling legs of 19
    signals given by 17, 119, 205
    tying hands of 8, 199

hanging(s) (*continued*)
  escape attempts at 8–9,
    136–7, 205
  pickpockets active during
    13, 64
  riots over cadavers 19, 20–1,
    235
  seating at 13–14
  special locations of 7
  survival of or resuscitation
    after 19–20
  usual days of 8
  see also Tyburn
hangman 7, 18–19, 63, 102, 151,
  159, 191–2, 198, 203, 205, 208,
  219, 252
  tipping the 17, 192
  expediting death of
    condemned 19, 252
Harcourt, William (ex 1679
  treason) 225 *see also* five
  Jesuits
Hardcastle, Deborah (ex 1713
  theft) 82
Harding, Stephen (ex 1757
  burglary) 51
Hare, Elizabeth (ex 1683
  coining) 7
Harold, John (ex 1700 burglary)
  80, 141
Harper, Andrew (ex 1714
  robbery) 145
Harpham, Robert (ex 1725
  coining) 174
Harris (alias How), James (ex
  1728 theft) 242–3, 245
Harris, Mary (ex 1741 robbery)
  16
Harrison, Henry (ex 1692
  murder) 49, 232
Harrison, James (evidence) 52
Harrison, Robert (defence
  witness) 55
Harrison, Thomas (ex 1660
  treason) 27, 163–64
Harrison, William 5
Hartly, John ('Pokey'; ex 1722
  robbery) 1–4, 5, 7, 16, 219
hats
  doffed or carried by
    condemned 10–11
  held out by highwaymen
    110, 112

thrown into crowd by
    condemned 206
  worn in court as statement of
    defiance 245
Hatton, William (ex 1751
  burglary) 86
Hawes, Nathaniel (ex 1721
  robbery) 63, 108, 193, 243–4,
  246, 248–9
Hawke, William (ex 1774
  robbery) 118
Hawkins, John (ex 1722 robbery)
  12, 107
Hawkins, William (evidence)
  109
Haycock, Mary (ex 1735
  coining) 81
Hayes, Catherine (ex 1726
  murder) 14, 18, 25, 84, 85, 170,
  233–4, 252
Hayes, John 25, 84, 170
Haynes, Robert (ex 1727
  murder) 36
Haywood, Richard (ex 1805
  robbery) 195
Hazzard, Anne (ex 1743 murder)
  81
Head, Richard 109
hell 2, 69, 130, 170–1, 218, 227,
  228, 230, 258
Henderson, Matthew (ex 1746
  murder) 62–3
heredity as cause of criminality
  71–2
Herring, Elizabeth (ex 1773
  murder) 13
Hewlet, John (ex 1725 murder)
  231, 236
Hicks' Hall 131
Hickson, Robert (ex 1750
  robbery) 65, 161
Higgins, John (ex 1753 burglary)
  201
highwaymen
  'Act for encouraging the
    apprehending of' 4&5
    William and Mary, c. 8
    (1692) 243
  reputation for civility,
    chivalry 95–6, 109–13,
    222–3, 257
  social ambiguity and
    pretensions 95, 97–8, 100,

115–19, 210 *see also* 'social
    critic'
highwaymen 'lives' 93–120,
  197–8
Hind, (Captain) James (ex 1652
  treason) 95–7, 99, 110
Hobry, Mary (ex 1688 murder)
  83–4
Hogan, John (ex 1771 robbery)
  198
Hogarth, William 10, 21, 23,
  58–9, 101, 125
'holiness in heart and life' 158,
  182–4, 200, 204
Holliday, John (ex 1720 returning
  from transportation) 172
Holloway, William (ex 1712
  murder) 171
Holocaust 195
Hopgood, Peter (ex 1760 theft)
  89
Horn, John (ex 1724 robbery) 78
Horneck, Anthony 48, 125,
  170–1
Houlbrooke, Ralph 171
Housden, Jane (ex 1712 murder)
  171
Howard, Leonard (rector of St
  George the Martyr) 48
Howard, William (Lord Stafford;
  ex 1680 treason) 164, 208–9, 235
Howard, William (ex 1734
  burglary) 52
Howard, Zachary (ex 1652
  murder & robbery) 99
Hunter, Thomas (ex 1704
  burglary) 42
Hutchins, John (ex 1684
  murder) 150
Hyde, (Sir) Henry (ex 1651
  treason) 164

'idle apprentice' ('Thomas Idle)
  58, 61, 89, 106 *see also* Industry
  and Idleness
idleness 59, 72–3, 75–9,
  as social emulation 73,
  115–19, 210
Industry and Idleness (1747) 10,
  58–9, 125
informing, informers *see*
  evidence, turning
insanity 58, 61, 171, 246

Ireton, Henry 24
irons (fetters, shackles) 100, 102, 104, 245
    struck off before embarking for gallows 8, 29, 159, 162, 185
    worn by defendants in court 243, 245
    worn by security risks on way to Tyburn 8
    worn in Newgate 93, 102, 173
irreclaimability of offenders 64–5
Isaacs, Rachel (re 1740 theft) 178
Ives, John (ex 1764 burglary) 144

'Jack Ketch' see hangman
Jackson, Daniel (s 1740 murder) 80
Jackson, Edward (ex 1684 coining) 150
Jackson, Nathaniel (ex 1722 robbery) 72–3
Jackson, Robert (ex 1720 robbery) 43
Jackson (alias Purchase), Thomas (ex 1716 robbery) 221
Jacobites 13, 23, 24, 36, 37, 38, 77, 113, 134, 137, 140, 152, 175, 176–7, 202–3, 214–16, 225, 227–8
James II 110, 228
James, John (ex 1661 sedition) 18, 163–4, 233
James, Richard (ex 1721 robbery) 161
Jefferis, Edward (ex 1705 murder) 171
Jeffreys, (Sir) George ('Hanging Judge') 98, 207
Jeffryes, Elizabeth (ex 1752 murder) 84–5
Jenkinson, Charles (Lord Liverpool) 120
Jennings, John (ex 1742 robbery) 64
Jervas, Thomas (ex 1687 burglary) 78
Jews 11, 127, 174, 179–80, 181, 195, 258
Johnson, ('Captain') Charles 33, 96–9, 102, 107, 111, 119–20, 198

Johnson, (alias Denny) John (ex 1698 burglary) 38, 177
Johnson, John (ex 1741 robbery) 65
Johnson, Joseph (ex 1705 robbery) 111, 165
Johnson, (Dr) Samuel 24, 170, 183, 188, 212, 217
Johnson, Thomas ('Handy'; ex 1727 returning from transportation) 242, 245
Johnson, William (ex 1677 robbery) 159
Johnston, (Sir) John (ex 1690 kidnapping) 16, 38, 150, 232
Jones, Henry (pr 1672 murder) 247–8
Jones, (Colonel) John (ex 1660 treason) 163
Jones, John (ex 1721 robbery) 73
Jones, Thomas ('Toothless Tom'; ex 1704 theft) 165
Jones, Thomas (ex 1749 forgery) 77
Jones, Thomas (ex 1753 forgery) 180
Jordan, Christopher (ex 1742 robbery) 133, 169

Kello, John (ex 1762 forgery) 144, 148
Kelly, Ned 230
Kemp, Joseph (ex 1729 burglary) 15
Kerney, Paul (sp 1728 forgery) 100
Kérouaille, Louise de (Duchess of Portsmouth) 99
Kidd, (Captain) William (ex 1701 piracy) 142–3
Kilmarnock, (Earl) William (ex 1746 treason) 13, 140, 211–12
King Lear 163
Kirk, Edmund (ex 1684 murder) 60, 160
Kirkman, Francis 109
Knight, Mary (ex 1716 theft) 81–2

laicization 257–8
Lake, Robert (ex 1752 robbery) 159, 245

Lamb, James (accomplice) 113
Lancaster, John (ex 1748 burglary) 185
Langbein, John 246
Langhorn, Richard (ex 1679 treason) 36, 164
Langley, George (re 1756 theft) 86
last dying speeches xviii, 15–16, 26, 32, 33–41 46, 169–70, 198, 200–1, 202–3, 205, 213, 220, 226, 230, 232, 236–7, 252, 253
    attempts to silence 31, 34–7, 39 see also censorship
    audibility of 38
    origins of 33–4
    see also criminal accounts
latitudinarianism 57, 90, 183–4
Lawrence, James (ex 1715 robbery) 198
Layer, Christopher (ex 1723 treason) 38, 208
Leach, Dryden (printer) 39, 47, 128, 263-4
Leath, Joseph (ex 1731 robbery) 35, 80, 115
Lee, Charles (ex 1689 robbery) 110
Legrose, Robert (ex 1741 burglary) 77
L'Estrange, Roger 113
Levee, John (ex 1723 robbery) 111, 199
Levee, Peter (ex 1728 robbery) 192
Lewis, Paul (ex 1763 robbery) 51, 93–4, 99, 115, 119, 144, 171, 175–6, 203, 205, 220
Lilburne, John 163
Lillo, George 59, 61, 82, 158
Lincoln's Inn Fields 6
Lindsey, Joseph (evidence) 249
Linebaugh, Peter 21, 123–4, 132, 221
Lineham, John (ex 1740 robbery) 178
literacy 41–5, 172 see also reading aloud
Liverpool, Lord see Jenkinson, Charles
Locke, John 71
London Bridge 24
London earthquake (1750) 115

London Merchant (1731) 59, 61, 82

Lorrain, Paul (ON 1700–1719) 5, 47, 63–4, 78, 87, 90, 122, 127–38, 142–4, 147, 159, 171, 176–9, 262, 264, 267

Loughborough, (Lord Chief Justice) *see* Wedderburn, Alexander

Lovat, (Lord) Simon Fraser (ex 1747 treason) 39

Love, Christopher (ex 1651 treason) 165

Lovewell, John (ex 1687 robbery) 15

Lowrey, (Captain) James (ex 1752 murder) 9, 47

Luttrell, Narcissus 5, 25, 198

Maccay, Morgan 121–2

Macclesfield (Earl of) *see* Parker, Thomas

McGowen, Randall 217

Macguire, Bryan (ex 1728 robbery) 177

Macheath, 'Captain' (*The Beggar's Opera*) 93–4, 100, 103–5, 114–15, 118–19, 175, 195–6, 202–3, 208, 220, 223

Mackrady, John (ex 1732 robbery) 201

Maclaine, James ('gentleman highwayman'; ex 1750 robbery) 44, 51, 105, 115–17, 169, 214

Macnaghton, John (ex 1762 murder) 202, 207–8

Macnamar, John (ex 1752 burglary) 220

Madan, Patrick (re 1774 robbery) 255

'maiden sessions' 5

Malcolm, Sarah (ex 1733 murder) 8, 49–50, 68, 70, 83, 121

malicious prosecutions 56, 131, 151

Mandeville, Bernard de 11, 23, 75, 129, 192, 193, 197, 208, 218

Mansfield (Lord Chief Justice) James Murray 119

Map, John (ex 1725 robbery) 9

March, James (Mayor of Norwich) 120

Marian martyrs xviii, 34, 56, 164, 200

Marketman, John (ex 1680 murder) 7, 239

Marsden, William (court clerk) 44

Marslin, William (ex 1698 robbery) 145

martyrs and martyrology xviii, 27, 161, 163–5, 206–7, 228, 247, 248, 259

Mary II 256

masculinity, manliness 138–9, 197, 212–13, 248 *see also* dying game, game criminals

masquerades 116–17

masters, cruel or abusive 58, 72, 75–7

Mather, Increase 38, 160

Matilda (Maude), queen of Henry I 11

Mattocks, John (ex 1726 robbery) 167

Mausgridge, John (ex 1708 murder) 33, 48, 145

Maw, William (ex 1711 burglary) 137, 201–2

Mayhew, Henry 90

Mead, John (accomplice) 111

Meers, William (ex 1740 robbery) 76

Mendez, Abraham (gaoler) 203

mental incapacity 63, 74, 231 *see also* insanity

Methodists 10, 57, 89, 125, 127, 155, 161–2, 176, 181–2, 184–8, 204, 238, 258

Metyard, Sarah (ex 1762 murder) 13

Middlesex 6, 7

Middleton, Mary (witness) 234

Milksop, Thomas (ex 1722 robbery) 145–6

Miller, Andrew (ex 1744 murder) 171

Miller, William (ex 1727 robbery) 76

Minor (1760) 117

Misson, Henri 42, 219

'mob' 2, 9, 10, 21, 23–4, 26, 36, 38, 85, 200, 218, 220, 235, 236

Moll Flanders (1722) 66, 73, 107, 121–2, 126

Molony, John (ex 1722 robbery) 254

Monmouth, Duke of *see* Scott, James

Montagu, John (Earl of Sandwich) 44

Mooney, Matthew (ex 1742 robbery) 161

Mooney, Walter (ex 1689 murder) 177

Moor, Anne 145

Moor, Charles (ex 1707 robbery) 145, 201

Moore, John (ex 1695 coining) 150

Moore, John (ex 1746 robbery) 81

Moore, Joseph (ON 1764–69) 154, 188, 218, 268

More, Hannah 69, 229, 258

More, (Sir) Thomas (ex 1535 treason) 164, 239

Morely, George (Bishop of Winchester) 209

Morgan, David (re 1761 robbery) 112–13

Morgan, John (re 1679 treason) 246

Morris, Hugh (ex 1730 robbery) 139

Morriss, Thomas (ex 1753 theft) 180

Morriss, William (ex 1753 robbery) 180

mors improvisa 160, 238

Motte, Thomas (ex 1740 burglary) 15

murder 12, 110–13, 146, 151, 171

Murder Act 25 George II, c. 37 (1752) 10, 21, 256, 265

murder indictments 61

Musson, George (sp 1715 sedition) 231

Nashe, Thomas 55

naval service 3, 61, 75–6, 105–6, 214

Neal, Henry (ex 1733 burglary) 77

necessity 58, 75–83

'Neck Verse' (Ps. 51:1) 42, 128, 203 *see also* benefit of clergy

Neeves, Thomas (ex 1729 robbery) 11, 15, 20, 145
Nelson, Archibald (ex 1764 fraud) 148
Newey, (Captain) Charles (sp 1699–1700 bigamy) 127, 256
Newgate Calendar 124, 154, 252
Newgate
  (attempted) escapes 8, 50, 172, 173, 202, 245
  chapel 7, 43, 51, 66, 125, 131–2, 137–9, 146, 162–3, 167, 169, 173–4, 177–80, 192, 193, 230, 232
  site of execution 256
  spectators and visitors 7, 93–4, 105, 114, 122, 131–2, 137, 162, 169, 157, 173, 213–17
  visiting ministers 125, 126–7, 162–3, 172, 175–82, 184–8, 222
Newington, William (ex 1738 forgery) 214
Newman, William (ex 1751 robbery) 44
newspapers 13, 21, 24, 25, 32, 33, 44, 45–6, 103–4, 124, 152–3, 185, 186, 211, 218, 245, 252, 253, 255
Nichols, Mary ('Trolly Lolly'; ex 1715 burglary) 82
Nichols, Richard (ex 1728 robbery) 15, 20
Nicholson, Francis (ex 1680 murder) 60
Nicholson, John (printer) 48
Nonconformists *see* Dissenters
non-jurors 126–7, 134, 176
Norridge, John (ex 1720 burglary) 146
Norris, Henry (ex 1710 theft) 79–80
North, (Sir) Francis 225
North, Mary (re 1721 returning from transportation) 171
Nunny, Luke (ex 1723 murder) 177

Oates, Titus 225, 235, 246
oaths, 51, 169–70, 235–7
O'Brian, James (ex 1730 robbery) 177, 179

Odell, William (ex 1760 murder) 234, 236, 240
Oglesbay, Charles (ex 1731 robbery) 79, 160
Old Bailey courthouse 3, 4, 55, 64, 82, 93, 103, 106, 112, 128, 130, 133, 145, 225, 242, 244, 256
Old Bailey Proceedings xviii, 32, 55–6, 124–5, 154, 245, 253–4, 262
'Old Offenders' 3, 42, 62–4, 67, 79, 82, 86–7, 143, 160, 202, 244
Oneby, (Major) John (s 1726 murder) 46–7
ordeal *see* trial by ordeal
Ordinary (chaplain) of Newgate
  criticisms of 47–8, 51, 121–3, 127–39, 175, 218
  description and duties 126, 131–2, 267–8
  salary and perquisites 47, 122, 127, 153
  see also entries for Smith, Lorrain, Purney, Guthrie, Taylor, *etc.*
Ordinary's *Account*
  criticisms of 48–9, 121–3, 253
  decline 152–5, 179–89, 252–3, 265
  description xviii, 124–5, 149, 153, 261–5
  value as source xviii–xix, 47–9, 78 123–6, 245
  see also criminal accounts
original sin 59, 114, 202, 229 *see also* guilt, universal human depravity
Orton, Samuel (ex 1767 forgery) 9
Overbury, (Sir) Thomas 247
Oxburgh, (Colonel) Henry (ex 1716 treason) 239
Oxford 19
Oxford, Bishop of *see* Talbot, William

Page, William (ex 1758 robbery) 73, 118, 119
Paine, Edward (ex 1711 theft) 78, 148
Pallioti, (Marquess) Ferdinando (ex 1718 murder) 17

Palmer, John (ex 1708 arson & murder) 233, 236
Palmer, Margaret (ex 1694 burglary) 60
Pamela (1740) 33, 258–9
pardons 4–5, 83, 245, 246
pardon petitions 80–1
parents of condemned 68–71, 76, 78, 81, 86, 145, 165–6, 213–16
Parker, James (ex 1676 robbery) 241
Parker, Joseph (ex 1740, returning from transportation) 139
Parker, Thomas (Earl of Macclesfield) 101, 103
Parkhurst, Nathanael (ex 1715 murder) 136, 170
Parkin, John (ex 1756 forgery) 86
Parkins, (Sir) William (ex 1686 treason) 17
Parkinson, William (ex 1724 burglary) 172
Parnel, Russel (ex 1752 robbery) 194
partial verdicts 4, 74
Pass, Abraham (ex 1743 burglary) 179
Past, Thomas (ex 1732 robbery) 158, 213–14
Patrick, Charles (ex 1732 robbery) 166
Pattison, Alice (ex 1684 coining) 18
Paul, William (ex 1716 treason) 176
Payne, Thomas (ex 1700 robbery) 177–8
Pearce, David (ex 1673 robbery) 242
Pearson, Anne (prosecutor) 100
peine forte et dure 107–8, 192–3, 241–4, 246–9, 251, 259
Pelham, Henry 153
penitence 157–60, 161–2, 198–201, 222 *see also* dying well, charity
penny dreadfuls 222–3
Penny Post 98
Penruddock, (Colonel) John (ex 1655 treason) 163
Pepys, Samuel 25, 128

Perkin, Robert (ex 1721 returning from transportation) 76

Perkins, Edward (ex 1732 robbery) 86

Perreau, Daniel (ex 1776 forgery) 252

Perreau, Robert (ex 1776 forgery) 252

Perrot, John (ex 1761 fraud) 144

Peters, George (ex 1734 burglary) 86, 245

Peters, Sarah (Methodist visitor) 184

Phillips, James (ex 1693 robbery) 145

Phillips, Stephen (ex 1736 theft) 111

Pickard, Thomas (ex 1713 theft) 170

Piggot, Francis (ex 1741 robbery) 114–15

Pilgrim's Progress (1678) 197

pillory 4, 71

Piner, Mary 186

Pinks, Thomas (ex 1742 robbery) 111

'pious perjury' 4, 74 *see also* partial verdicts

pirates 6, 8, 33, 96, 98, 102, 114–15, 138, 142–3

Place, Francis xix, 23–4, 121, 122–3, 253

'pleading the belly' 4–5, 83, 203 *see also* reprieves, pardons

Plunket, William (accomplice) 115–16

Pope, Alexander 129, 152

Popish Plot xvi, 33–4, 36, 225–6, 235, 261

population of England, London 5

Portsmouth, Duchess of *see* Kérouaille, Louise de

poverty *see* necessity

Powditch (alias Allen), George (ex 1770 theft) 243, 244, 251

Powell, Elizabeth (re 1742 theft) 134

Powis, Joseph (ex 1732 burglary) 216

Press Room 243

Press Yard 8, 9, 137, 162, 220

pressing *see peine forte et dure*

presumption of innocence 254

Price, Elizabeth (ex 1712 burglary) 63

Price, John (ex 1718 murder) 151, 208

Price, John (ex 1725 burglary) 43

Price, William (ex 1716 rioting) 166

Prince, John (ex 1764 forgery) 47, 201

printers and publishers 33, 37–8, 39–40, 45–53, 125, 128, 154, 188, 262–4

prostitution, prostitutes ('lewd women') 4–5, 55–6, 61, 74, 81–3, 91, 94, 167, 253, 254

providential beliefs
 as normative 228–30
 as subversive 229–30
 discoveries and signs 60, 162, 185, 207–8, 233–5
 dispensations and warnings 64, 78–9, 150–1, 161, 221–2, 239–40
 see also sacramentality

'public sphere' 32

Purdy, John (ex 1737 robbery) 109–10, 204

purgatory 171, 226, 238, 240

Purney, Thomas (ON 1719–1725) 43, 129–30, 137, 144, 152, 159, 160, 166–7, 174, 178–9, 200, 207, 262, 267, 289n

Putris, James (ex 1715 burglary) 76

Puttes, John atte 247

Quail, Richard (ex 1740 theft) 77

Quakers 25, 176, 181

Raby, Mary (ex 1703 robbery) 149

Randal, John (ex 1693 robbery) 174

Randal, Thomas (ex 1696 murder) 221

Rann, John (Jack; ex 1774 robbery) 13, 19, 104–5, 118, 221

Rantzau, Lewis (ex 1690 murder) 72

rape 12, 20, 46, 48, 60, 111, 145–6, 151, 253

Ratcliffe, Charles (ex 1747 treason) 203, 211

rational religion 90–2, 182–4, 210–13, 257–9

Rawlins, George (ex 1679 robbery) 110

reading aloud 43, 45 *see also* literacy

recidivism *see* 'Old Offenders'

Redmond, Joseph (ex 1764 robbery) 86, 221

Reeves, Thomas (ex 1695 robbery) 60

Reeves, Thomas (ex 1722 robbery) 2–4, 5, 7, 14, 16, 19, 23, 171–2, 202, 206

regicides 23, 33, 34, 163, 208

rehabilitation 64–5, 66–7, 79

Reid, John (ex 1774 theft) 217

Reis, Sebastian (ex 1704 burglary) 178

religious beliefs of condemned 2, 22–3, 145–52, 161–2, 170–5, 239–40 *see also* providential beliefs

reprieves, respites 4–5, 83, 135, 159, 214, 255–6
 at gallows 11, 115, 219, 255–6
 see also pardons, 'pleading the belly', transportation

rewards
 for the apprehension of criminals 15, 45, 103, 242
 for return of stolen goods 44
 see also evidence, turning

Reynolds, Edward (ex 1726 robbery) 107, 167

Reynolds, Thomas (ex 1736 Black Act) 20

Reynolds, Thomas (ex 1750 treason) 162, 221

Rhodes, Robert (ex 1742 forgery) 107

Rice, John (ex 1763 forgery) 9, 220

Rice, Thomas (ex 1722 theft) 74–5

Richardson, George (ex 1733 robbery) 50

Richardson, Samuel 10, 12, 33, 55, 217–18, 258–9

Ridley, Nicholas (ex 1555 heresy) 164

Riggleton, John (ex 1743 murder) 61

Rivington, Charles (printer) 33

Roberts, David (ex 1739 coining) 169

Robertson, George (ex 1753 robbery) 220

Robin Hood 95, 97, 109, 120

Robin Hood debating society 117–18

'Robinocracy' 99 see also Walpole, Robert

Robinson, Francis (ex 1684 robbery) 144–5

Roche, Philip (ex 1723 piracy) 178

Rochester, Earl of see Wilmot, John

Rockett, James (ex 1764 robbery) 86

Roe, Stephen (ON 1757–64) 47, 66, 144, 147–8, 153, 154, 171, 175, 183–4, 186–8, 264, 268

Rogers, John (ex 1749 robbery) 134, 203

rogue literature 94–5, 153, 232–3

Romilly, Samuel 222

Rossell, Samuel (ON 1746–7) 88, 90, 135–7, 139, 141–2, 146, 153, 182, 267

Rowland, William (ex 1748 smuggling) 168

Roxana (1724) 135–6

Rumbold, Richard (ex 1685 treason) 31, 164

Russell, Nathaniel (ex 1678 murder) 59

Russell, William (ex 1728 robbery) 200

Russell, (Lord) William (ex 1683 treason) 6, 17, 36, 37, 38, 40–1, 125, 228

Rye House Plot, 31, 38, 41, 228

Rygeway, Cecilia 247

Sabbath-breaking 3, 23, 58, 60–1, 62, 89, 129, 148–9, 150, 200

sacrament (Lord's Supper) 48, 51, 128, 138, 147–8, 172, 174–6, 199, 236, 237

sacramentality 226–8, 233, 246, 249, 257–9

St Augustine (of Hippo) 59

St John, Henry 221

St Sepulchre's 7, 10, 64

Salem witch hunt 247

Salisbury, John (ex 1752 robbery) 61

Salmon, John (ex 1739 robbery) 37

salvation
    criminals' assurance of 2, 23, 60, 161–5, 171–2, 203–4, 221–2, 237
    evidenced by 'good death' 28–9, 183, 207, 240–1
    promised to convicts 186–7 see also free grace, Methodists

Sandwich, Earl of, see Montagu, John

Sares, John (ex 1652 treason) 164

Satan see devil

Saunders, Cornelius (ex 1763 theft) 235

Saussure, Cesare de 11, 13, 242, 254

Savage, Thomas (ex 1668 murder) 20

Sawney, John (ex 1740 robbery) 178

Schellinks, William 18

Scot, Thomas (ex 1660 treason) 34, 35–6

Scott, James (Duke of Monmouth; ex 1685 treason) 17, 28

Scroggs, (Sir) William 225–6, 235

secularization 257 see also laicization, desacralization

Select Trials 124, 154, 166, 249

Sells, Samuel (ex 1726 robbery) 165

Selwood (alias Jenkins), William (ex 1691 robbery) 113

Selwyn, George 17, 26, 217, 218, 221, 252

Senior, Anne (re 1727 theft) 172

sensibility 83, 213–18, 258–9 see also sympathy

Sessions Paper see Old Bailey Proceedings

Shaftesbury, Earl of see Cooper, Anthony Ashley

Shakespeare, William 163, 209

Sharpe, J.A. xvii

Shaw, Edward (ex 1715 burglary) 143

Shaw, James (ex 1722 robbery) 166, 194, 202, 222

Shaw, Joseph (ex 1738 robbery) 52–3, 109

Shaw, William 74 (sp 1721 theft)

Sheppard, James (ex 1718 treason) 177, 228

Sheppard, John (Jack; ex 1724 burglary) 8, 11, 19, 21, 48, 50, 51–2, 67, 100–105, 110, 130, 154, 194, 195, 205, 245

Sheppard, Richard (ex 1720 robbery) 79

sheriffs (of London and Middlesex) 7, 9, 12, 18, 36, 38, 50, 142, 153, 176, 221, 234, 243, 252, 255–6

Short, Thomas (ex 1678 murder) 255

Shorter, John (ex 1697 robbery) 146

Shrewsbury (alias Smith), Joseph (ex 1726 robbery) 62, 68

Shrimpton, Ferdinando (ex 1730 robbery) 15

Sidney, Algernon (ex 1683 treason) 38, 207

Signal, William (ex 1752 robbery) 119, 195

Simms, Henry ('Gentleman Harry'; ex 1747 robbery) 104, 111, 112, 169, 220

Simpson, George (ex 1722 robbery) 12

Simpson, John (ex 1700 robbery) 107

Simpson, William (ex 1729 theft) 162

Singleton, Robert 132

Sir Charles Grandison (1753–4) 258–9

Skip, Mary (ex 1715 robbery) 78

Slaughterford, Christopher (ex 1709 murder) 207

'slippery slope' xx, 58, 59–67, 200

Smith, Adam 211, 213

Smith, ('Captain') Alexander 93,
    96–9, 107, 111, 109, 119–20,
    128, 198
Smith, Bryan (ex 1725 robbery)
    9
Smith, Ely (ex 1750 robbery) 15
Smith, George (ex 1713 robbery)
    143
Smith, Gill (ex 1738 murder) 29,
    39, 236
Smith, John ('Half-Hanged'; ex
    & re 1704 burglary) 20, 64
Smith (alias Mackintosh), John
    (ex 1715 burglary) 166
Smith (alias Gow), John (ex 1725
    piracy) 251
Smith, Samuel 146
Smith, Samuel (ON 1676–98)
    60, 74, 78, 79, 125, 127, 129,
    131, 132, 134, 136, 142, 144–6,
    149, 158, 159, 162, 172, 174,
    176–8, 197, 209, 261, 267
Smith, Sarah (ex 1704 theft) 63
Smith, Thomas (re 1707
    robbery) 135
Smith, Thomas (ex 1722
    burglary) 177
Smithfield 6, 29
Smollett, Tobias 46
social control xvii, 4, 22, 123, 143
'social crimes' 37, 231–2, 235
'social critic', robber as 94–9,
    101–5, 109–10, 113–15, 117,
    119, 232–3
Society for Promoting Christian
    Knowledge (SPCK) 42
sodomy 56, 84, 131, 146, 151,
    253
soul 90, 211, 235, 241, 248, 258
South Sea Bubble 99, 102–3,
    113
Speckman (alias Brown), Charles
    (ex 1763 robbery) 48, 49, 51,
    122, 147, 162, 175
Spencer, Barbara (ex 1721
    coining) 196–7
Sperry, William (ex 1725
    robbery) 80
Spiggot, William (ex 1721
    robbery) 107–8, 173, 192–3,
    199, 243, 244, 249
spouses of condemned 78–83,
    166–9, 213–14

Squire, John (ex 1742 robbery)
    174
Stacey, Abraham (ex 1693
    robbery) 196
Stacey, George (ex 1741 robbery)
    81
Stafford (Lord) see Howard,
    William
Stamp Tax 47, 262
Stanhope, Philip Dormer (Earl
    of Chesterfield) 153
Stanley, ('Captain') John (ex
    1723 murder) 71
Stansbury, James (ex 1746
    burglary) 73
state criminals see traitors
step-parents 58, 76, 166
Stern, (Lieutenant) John (ex
    1682 murder) 160, 172
Stevens, Charles (ex 1770
    murder) 245
Stevens, William (ex 1758 theft)
    187
Stillingfleet, Edward 125
Stirn, David Francis (ex 1760
    murder) 9
Stoaks, William (ex 1673
    robbery) 242
Stockdale, John (ex 1753 murder
    & robbery) 216
Stone, John (ex 1718 coining)
    147
Storer, Anthony Morris 218
Strangwayes, George (pr 1658
    murder) 248
street ballads and ephemeral
    gallows sheets 39, 44, 48, 57,
    95, 119–20, 145, 222, 257
suffering
    as mark of election 183, 239
    as diagnostic 238, 240–2
    as purgative 159, 204, 222,
        239–40
suicide 47, 133, 247
surgeons 20–1, 81, 174 see also
    dissection
Surgeon's Hall 20, 24, 256
Swan, John (ex 1752 murder)
    84–5
Sweet, William (ex 1735 theft)
    167
Swift, John (ex 1763 robbery)
    70, 216

Swift, Jonathan 114, 191–2
Swift, William (ex 1726 robbery)
    169–70
Symonds, Thomas (ex 1708
    arson & murder) 233, 236
sympathy 214–18

Talbot, Francis (re 1773
    burglary) 255
Talbot, Thomas (ex 1751
    robbery) 169
Talbot, William (Bishop of
    Oxford) 125
Tarlton, John (ex 1736 theft)
    113
Taverner, Thomas (ex 1734
    robbery) 36
Taylor, Jeremy 136, 141, 146–7,
    150–1
Taylor, John (ON 1747–57) 47,
    66, 88, 134, 153, 159, 180–2,
    195, 217, 218, 267, 272n
tears (of condemned)
    of joy 160, 200
    of repentance 2, 10, 15, 139,
        141, 142, 158–9, 167–9,
        200, 214–16, 232
    refusal or inability to shed
        114, 193, 194, 199–200, 214
    sign of cowardice, despair 66,
        116, 133, 134, 200
tears (of spectators) 86, 150,
    214–16
Thomas, George (ex 1746
    robbery) 162
Thomas, Jonathan (ex 1738
    coining) 181
Thomas, Keith 233
Thompson, John (ex 1721
    receiving) 80–1, 159
Thompson, John (ex 1722
    robbery) 1–4, 5, 7
Thomson, Alexander (ex 1756
    bankruptcy fraud) 180
Thornhill, (Sir) James 101
Thrale, Henry 217
thumb-tying see peine forte et
    dure
Thurland, Thomas (ex 1716
    robbery & murder) 241
Tilley, Judith (ex 1746 theft) 91
Tims, James (ex 1722 robbery)
    1–4, 5, 7

Tipping, Daniel (ex 1732 robbery) 50, 80, 174
Told, Silas 10, 28, 29, 160, 181–2, 184–6, 188, 218, 268
Tom Jones (1749) 41
Tower Hill 6, 10, 29
Tower of London 13, 24, 34, 239
Towers, Charles (ex 1725 rioting & theft) 37–8, 151–2, 232
Townsend, (Lord Mayor) James 188
Tracey, Elizabeth (ex 1734 coining) 167
Tracey, Katherine (ex 1734 coining) 167
Tracey (alias Stracey), Martha (ex 1745 robbery) 74
traitors 9, 11, 14, 18, 33–5, 38, 41, 164–6, 208 *see also* Jacobites, martyrs, Popish Plot, Rye House Plot
transportation 4, 63, 66–7, 74, 114, 121, 166, 243
    pardon on condition of 4–5, 20, 134, 168, 214
    returning from before expiry of sentence 14, 76, 80, 166, 231, 242
Tremane, Christopher (ex 1690 burglary) 145
trial
    as 'sentencing hearing' 229–30, 244
    countenance of defendant at 27, 28
    culture of deference 82–3, 244–6
        violations of 108, 241–6, 254
    defences 55–6, 58, 74, 83, 86
    kneeling to plead pardon at 245–6
    oaths and testimony 235–6
    questioning justice of 39, 67, 93, 98, 113, 114, 150, 151, 168, 245, 249
    reporting 253–4 *see also Old Bailey Proceedings*
    spectators at 64, 84–5
    standing mute at *see peine forte et dure*
    verdicts and sentencing 4–5

trial by ordeal 226, 240, 246–7
Triple Tree 6 *see also* Tyburn
Trippuck, John (ex 1720 robbery) 236–7, 240
Tudor, Edward (ex 1734 burglary) 79
Turner, Anthony (ex 1679 treason) 225 *see also* five Jesuits
Turner, (Colonel) James (ex 1664 robbery) 17, 205
Turner, ('Civil') John (ex 1727 robbery) 110, 115
Turpin, Richard (Dick; ex 1739 robbery) 21, 98, 104, 205, 207, 219–20, 223
Tyburn
    location 6
    named as meeting place 44
    procession 7–21, 23–4, 208, 218
        abolition of 6, 256
    removal of permanent gallows 6, 256–7
    sight of as warning 64
    vandalism of 6
        as political commentary, 256–7
    see also execution
Tyler, William (ex 1750 robbery) 214
typhus ('gaol fever') 15, 133, 174
Tyrrel, John (ex 1723 theft) 178

Udal, William (ex 1739 robbery) 139
universal human depravity 56, 115, 151, 200, 254

Vane, (Sir) Henry (ex 1662 treason) 28, 29, 34–5
Vaughan, Richard William (ex 1758 forgery) 50, 232
Vaux, Thomas (ex 1728 robbery) 192
venereal disease 63, 130–1
Vernon, James (Secretary of State) 127
victims' rights movements 58
Villette, John (ON 1774–99) 89, 154, 188, 255, 268
Vratz, (Captain) Christopher (ex 1682 murder) 17, 48, 144, 170–1, 203–4

Wager, William ('Cockey'; ex 1737 robbery) 139, 198–9
Wagstaff, James (deputy ON 1724) 78, 267, 290n
Waldon, Jesse (ex 1742 burglary) 109
Walker, James (ex 1747 robbery) 202
Walpole, Horace 24, 44, 85, 105, 115, 117, 185
Walpole, Robert 45, 94, 102, 103–4, 105, 108–9
Waltham Black Act (1723) 37, 232
Waltham Blacks 231 *see also* social crimes
Wann, Elizabeth (ex 1694 theft) 81
Ward, Abraham (ex 1752 murder) 19
Ward, Edward (ex 1751 burglary) 174
Ward, George (ex 1736 burglary) 168
Ward, John (ex 1765 robbery) 75
Watson, George (ex 1736 murder) 214
Weaver, Charles (ex 1723 murder) 160, 240
Wedderburn, Alexander (Lord Chief Justice Loughborough) 252
weddings
    association with executions 163–4, 219–21, 247, 248
    popular belief in matrimonial pardons 2, 219
    wedding favours (gloves, rings, nosegays, oranges, etc) worn, distributed by condemned 219–21
    see also dress of the condemned
Weekes, John (pr 1735 robbery & murder) 251
weeping *see* tears
Wells (alias White, Dyer), Jane (ex 1713 theft) 149
Weskett, John (ex 1765 theft) 221
Wesley, John 155, 161, 170, 182, 184–5, 204, 258 *see also* Methodism

West, William (ex 1733 burglary) 86–7

Westley, Anthony (ex 1751 burglary) 66

Weston, Richard (ex 1615 murder) 247

Weymouth, Charles (ex 1714 robbery) 138

Whalebone, John (ex 1725 returning from transportation) 231

Whiston, William 184

Whitaker, John (re 1777 burglary) 256

White, James (ex 1723 returning from transportation) 14, 147, 173

White, Mary ('Mary Cut and Come Again'; ex 1745 robbery) 44, 45

White, William (ex 1716 robbery & murder) 241

Whitebread, Thomas (ex 1679 treason) 225, 235 see also five Jesuits

Whitefield, George 185

Whitney, James (ex 1693 robbery) 111

Whittington, Richard ('Dick') 91

'whittle', 'whittling' see evidence, turning

Wild, Jonathan ('Thief-taker General'; ex 1725 receiving) 12–13, 64, 68, 96, 103, 113–14, 130, 174, 191, 203

Wileman, Benjamin (ex robbery 1729) 15, 151

Wilkes, John (ex 1752 robbery) 151, 187

Wilkes, John (Lord Mayor) 104–5

Wilkinson, Philip (ex 1735 theft) 159, 167

Wilkinson, Robert (ex 1722 murder & robbery) 204, 222, 240

Williams, Jane (ex 1691 theft) 78

Williams (alias Spencer), Mary (ex 1716 theft) 83

Williams, Richard (ex 1719 robbery) 146

Williams, Thomas (re 1722 theft) 168, 214

Williamson, John (ex 1767 murder) 13

Wilmot, John (Earl of Rochester) 170

Wilson, Ralph (evidence) 51, 113

Wilson, Thomas (ex 1722 robbery) 53, 75, 170, 205

Winship, John (ex 1721 robbery) 111–12, 145

Winstanley, Gerrard 110

Wise, John (ex 1684 murder) 11

witchcraft 247, 258

women see female offenders

Wood, John (ex 1719 robbery) 146

Wood, John (ON 1769–74) 133, 154, 182, 188, 265, 268

Wood, Thomas (d 1726 murder) 84

Woodford, Henry (ex 1721 returning from transportation) 80

Woodmarsh, Francis (ex 1731 murder) 18

Woolridge, Thomas (ex 1725 burglary) 43

Worsely, Jane (ex 1721 robbery) 175

Wreathcocke, William (re 1736 robbery) 39, 277n

Wright, Ann (ex 1715 burglary) 63–4

Wright, James (ex 1721 robbery) 110, 201, 222

Wykes, Roger (ON 1700) 62, 141, 144, 267

York 7, 11, 21, 220

York, Duke of see James II

Youell, Hosea (ex 1747 murder & robbery) 178

Young, John (ex 1730 robbery) 158, 169

Young, Mary ('Jenny Diver'; ex 1741 theft) 197, 215

young offenders 64–6, 67, 85–7, 166